The Quest for Utopia

An Anthology of Imaginary Societies

Glenn Negley, Professor of Philosophy, Duke University

J. Max Patrick, Associate Professor of English, Queens College

The Quest

An Anthology of Imaginary Societies

Henry Schuman, New York

for Utopia

Preface

Utopists are not nearly so disdainful of the problems of practical construction as general opinion seems to assume. They would have demanded, we are sure, an explanation of the mechanics of our construction in assembling this anthology of their works. What we intend to present here is a representative sample of utopian thought in Western civilization. Very few utopias could be packed whole into our available space, and we agreed at the outset on three criteria to determine selection from the great abundance of material in this field. The first of these criteria would clearly have to be a definition of what could properly be accepted as utopian literature, although it was manifest that such discrimination would be both difficult and arbitrary. In the second place, it seemed rather fruitless to offer readers utopian works which are at present available in reprint editions or likely to be found in any adequate library. Finally, our appreciation of the utopists dictated that we allow them, as nearly as possible, to speak in their own words.

The third criterion, for example, necessitated a resistance of the temptation to crowd more material into our space by digesting the thought of the utopists or presenting the bare bones of numerous utopian frameworks in bloodless outline. This kind of emasculation deprives utopian literature of the very interest and vigor which distinguish utopia from all the other forms which man's speculation and planning have assumed. Hardly less important than the ideas and ideals which these writers strive to communicate are the tone and temper, the sincerity or amusement, the literary skill or naïveté with which they portray their visions of utopian society. The decision to deviate from chronological order in presenting the works of the modern period first was determined mainly by this principle of retaining as much as possible of the literary genre of the utopists. With this relatively recent material, it was possible to achieve completely our purpose of letting the utopists speak for themselves.

In the selections from this period, there have been no additions of words or even punctuation to the original text; the material has been selectively edited and shortened, but in every case the language is that of the original. Such a procedure was obviously impossible with the utopias of earlier periods, but every effort was made to preserve the literary form and style of these works. It appeared reasonable to change antiquated spellings to contemporary usage, and in the case of translations to render obsolete terms in meaningful English. Wherever some paraphrasing or synopsis of the texts prior to 1850 seemed necessary, care has been exercised to indicate clearly this procedure. It should be remarked that the reason for selecting 1850 as a dividing point in the classification of utopias is not, however, merely a literary device, nor is it arbitrary; the critical commentary of the text indicates the grounds for this distinction.

There are two exceptions to the principle of restricting the selection to out-of-print and unavailable utopias. It seemed improper to present an anthology of utopian literature without a gesture of some sort to Sir Thomas More who, in coining the word itself, propagated the pun which can be interpreted to mean *good place* or *no place*. Another classic, Campanella's *City of the Sun*, while available in reprint form, is not accessible in anything approaching a satisfactory translation. We are indebted to William J. Gilstrap for the new translation presented here; readers who compare this with the traditional Halliday version may well discover a new appreciation of *Civitas Solis*. Other translations in the period prior to 1850 have been done by J. Max Patrick, except that, where possible, existing translations have been used. With the exception of the two works noted above, the remainder of the utopias represented in these selections are, to our knowledge, not available in print; many of the items are indeed inaccessible except in a very few library sources.

The selection of "representative" specimens from such a great breadth and range of material as that which comprises utopian literature is an extremely difficult task, and the decision must to some extent be an arbitrary one. Happily, the present editors had no trouble in agreeing upon what seemed to be an appropriate and representative list of works; our only dissatisfaction arose from the unavoidable limitations of space, which meant that many favorite and choice utopias simply could not be included. It was especially difficult to adhere to the policy of using space only for unavailable works when we came to Edward Bellamy; as in the case of More, Bellamy's name has become almost synonymous with utopia. However, Bellamy's work is quite accessible, and it is in modern English which needs no translation or correction; our hope is that these samples of utopian literature will encourage the reading of *Looking Backward* and other available utopias. Our agreement on the works to be included implies a basic similarity in our ideas of what constitutes utopian literature. The introductory chapter to the selections will discuss briefly this definition of utopian literature, and hence attempt to explain the principle of our first criterion: What is a utopia?

The critical chapters included in the text are intended to serve the purpose of historical continuity; their brief commentary is as selective and representative as the entire anthology had necessarily to be. The work as a whole is the product of complete collaboration and agreement; as for the division of labor, Glenn Negley has been primarily responsible for Chapters 1-13, 32, and 33, J. Max Patrick for Chapters 14-31.

Contents

1

Introduction

The land of utopia has never been properly or completely charted. There are indeed some rather famous landmarks along the flat plains of the shore: The Republic, the City of the Sun, New Atlantis, Oceana. These and a few others are familiar sights to the traveler on literary excursions, and occasionally even a philosopher or a political scientist finds himself forced in close to the shore of utopia by shifting currents.

The hinterland of utopia, however, is almost unknown; only a few venturesome souls have any idea of the vast unexplored territory, of the incredible diversity of peoples and societies which exist in the central and rougher terrain of the country. Every conceivable kind of community has existed in this area, and though many of these are no longer known even to the literary observer, their remains have in most cases been marvelously preserved by the salubrious climate of utopia. The exploration of this mysterious land of light and shadow is an arduous undertaking, but not a dangerous one. The natives are, almost to a man, very friendly and generous; they almost never carry weapons of any kind; and, in fact, the explorer who does not keep his wits about him may very well find himself converted by the engaging and insistent missionary zeal of the inhabitants of every community he visits.

It is questionable whether there are in the English language two more ambiguous words than *utopia* and *utopian*. In both denotation and connotation, these words have acquired a latitude of usage which almost defies definition. The dictionary appropriately credits Sir Thomas More with the coinage of the word, and then makes its customary obeisance to the vagaries of usage by describing *utopia* as "an impracticable scheme of social regeneration," *utopian* as "ideal" and "chimerical," and a *utopian* as a "visionary," an "idealist," and even an "optimist." Only the foolhardy would enter the lists against common usage; *utopian* has become, and will probably remain, one of those verbal darts which the indiscriminate find useful to throw at random in the hope of perchance hitting a target.

Quite contrary to this debasement in the vernacular, utopia represents in fact one of the noblest aspirations of man. What could be of more significance in the history of civilization than that man, since he first began to think and write, has continued ever to dream of a better world, to speculate as to its possible nature, and to communicate his longings to other men in the hope that the ideal might, at least in part, become reality? True, there have been many utopias constructed by crackpots, as many religions and systems of philosophy have been. Some utopists have expressed as ideal what seems no ideal at all, but in fact a regression from the real to a backward state. Others of these dreamers have dreamed so vaguely or so ambitiously that what they envision appears more like a prospect of heavenly existence than any conceivable earthly state. Yet, in historical perspective it is clear that the vision of one century is often the reality of the next or the next after that; as the older ideal approaches closer to reality, the new ideal extends its vision still farther. Utopia is eternal, and who can calculate the inestimable influence which utopists have had in stimulating men to the dream of a better world, of prodding them to reshape reality closer to the ideal? In a few cases, we can point to rather clear instances of influence which particular utopists have had in shaping the events of history, as in the cases of Harrington and Bellamy, to name but two. Generally, however, the influence of utopia is more subtle; sometimes the utopist accomplishes his end by indirection, portraying through his ideal the imperfection and inadequacy of the existing real.

The utopist, on the other hand, is not merely a reformer or satirist, not just a dreamer, nor yet only a theorist. Utopia is a distinct vehicle of expression, and it would be as meaningful to call "poet" anyone who scribbled a rhyme as to designate "utopist" any proponent of a scheme of social reform or change. Utopia is distinguishable from the other forms in which men have expressed their ideals, as philosophy is from poetry, or legal codes from political tracts. Just as one could hardly expect to appreciate the quality of poetry without realizing what distinguishes poetry from other forms of expression, so it is impossible to understand utopian literature if all manner of speculations, idealizations, vagaries, plans, political platforms and programs are to be considered utopias.

There are three characteristics which distinguish the utopia from other forms of literature or speculation:
1. It is fictional.
2. It describes a particular state or community.
3. Its theme is the political structure of that fictional state or community.

Any such definition may, of course, be considered highly arbitrary; but there are good and satisfactory reasons, both historical and analytical, for stating these three qualifications as necessary to constitute what can properly be called a *utopia*.

In the first place, utopia literally means "no place," and the use of the fiction of an imagined or mythical state is indeed a characteristic mark of utopian writing. This primary and necessary discrimination eliminates from utopian literature all speculation the form of which indicates that it should properly be designated political philosophy or political theory. Utopias are expressions of political philosophy and theory, to be sure, but they are descriptions of fictional states in which the philosophy and theory are already implemented in the institutions and procedures of the social structure. Contrary to the general opinion of utopian construction, this description of a state as if it were real ought to impose on the utopist a severe restriction to which the theorist and philosopher are not directly subject, for the utopist must beware the possible absurdity of ideals described as real. The effort to foment revolution against an existing state of affairs, the interpretation of the historical process, the elaboration of a generalized theory of the principles of government, the statement of a system of values or ideals which ought to be realized— none of these are utopian. The *Declaration of Independence* is a historic and compelling statement of political ideals; it is not a utopia. The *Sermon on the Mount* is a moral prescription for the relations of men, but it does not describe a utopia. The *Communist Manifesto* is a political tract of high emotive significance, but Marx and Engels were not utopists.

The fictional nature of utopia does not, however, give complete license to the imagination; there is a point at which sheer fantasy ceases to be utopian in any definable sense. The feet of the utopist rest solidly on the soil of a real state and an actual community, and it is to be expected, therefore, that utopia will usually bear some resemblance to the existing society of the utopist. It is well that the fictional state of utopia should be an idealized vision of the existing state, for only thus could men gain from the utopian vision a hint of the direction of progress beyond their own present society. In short, this is saying little more than that utopias are appropriate to their own historic period, and that one would naturally expect a utopia written in the twentieth century to differ essentially from one written in the seventeenth century, if for no other reason than the intervening three hundred years of historical development. Yet, utopia represents a real effort to escape any restraints of historical time and place, and it is for this reason that utopia is necessarily fictional in form. It is commonplace that men escape the language and usage of their own age rarely and with the greatest difficulty; but the utopist must to some extent escape, and this he does through the romantic fiction of the imaginary society. Utopia is not simply a planned society in the sense of contemplated changes in the existing social structure. Utopia is society planned without restraint or handicap of existing institutions and individuals. The utopist may populate his fictional state with a race of men wiser, healthier, and more generous than any society has ever seen. The utopist may take advantage of his fictional license, and often does, to construct a configuration of institutions the like of which the world has never known. The fiction of utopia therefore allows the utopist to reach as far toward the ideal as he can stretch the limitations of his language and his environment. Utopia is not merely a society reconstructed according to specifically planned changes, nor is it prediction of what changes may or must come about in an existing social structure. These are often close on the periphery of utopian speculation, but they are not essentially of it. Utopia is fiction in the classic sense of "as if"; utopia is a world of *as if*.

The use of an imaginary state or society is characteristic of other forms of literary construction, so the final qualification of utopian writing must immediately be noted. The utopist is concerned with the social and political structure of his fictional state, and this is really his only concern. True, he quite often elaborates the fiction of his constructed state by adding a touch of romance or adventure to his descriptive narrative, but romance and adventure are not his true concern. In fact, these ingredients which are basic to other forms of literary expression are likely in utopias to appear as a kind of obvious cosmetic designed to make the offering more attractive; and because the utopist is so often quite unskilled in the writing of romance and adventure, his efforts in this direction are occasionally amusing, sometimes ridiculous. Mere tales of adventure or of romance are not utopias, even though their settings be in a mythical state, an imagined community, or an idealized environment. Supermen and super-scientists may ride space-rockets to other worlds or into the future, but if it is mere adventure and fantasy that they seek, they will not find utopia. The true utopist seeks and finds a better society, and what makes that society better is the subject of his attention and exposition. All else is incidental to his quest.

The description of these essential characteristics of utopia removes to the periphery of utopian literature, if not indeed to entirely different fields of exposition, those works which should be designated predictions, fantasies, and planning administration. In quite another category is the extensive and fascinating material on experimental ventures in utopian communities. Many of these experiments were inspired by utopian writing, and indeed some utopists, such as Cabet and Hertzka, wrote their utopias with an eye to the possibility of an experimental test of the ideal hypothesis. Experiments in the actualization of the utopian ideal have some analogy to the wishful thinking that hopes to realize the romantic ideal of fiction. Romantic novels ought not to be judged according to criteria appropriate for evaluating the success of marriage relationships, nor can utopias be properly analyzed by reference to experiments in ideal community organization.

There are two main classifications of utopias in respect to the literary form they assume: the speculative or constructive utopia and the satire. The distinction is more or less self-evident; the speculative utopist takes a positive view of the ideal of society, and his purpose is to portray the better society which the realization of those ideals would promise. He may be compelled to present the picture of this ideal society even though he is quite pessimistic about the possibility of its realization. Irony or pathos may tinge his speculative construction, and sometimes therefore the clear distinction between constructive and satirical may break down in a single work. The perspective of the satirist is negative. More often than not his fictional society is an "idealization" or extrapolation of the existing state, wherein he seeks to show by contrast how far existing conditions and their development are from satisfactory ideals and values. In one respect, successful satires are much more difficult to accomplish than positive speculative constructions, for the satirist must make clear by indirection what his positive construction would have been if he had chosen to write positively. In short, satiric utopias which are merely negative are not likely to be very interesting or very effective as utopias. The basic distinction, therefore, between the speculative and the satiric utopia is essentially one of literary form, and it is significant that the more difficult form of satire has been successfully accomplished almost entirely by utopists with considerable literary skill.

The fantasy cannot be entirely eliminated as a possible vehicle for utopian expression. The sheer fantasy, which simply elaborates the esoteric or exotic vagaries of imagination, is of no utopian interest; but occasionally the form of fantasy is used for true utopian expression. The utopian fantasy, like the satire, requires consummate literary skill for successful presentation. Like the satire in another respect, the fantasy lends itself more readily to the negative portrayal of ideals which appear lost or abridged in existing society. Thus, both the satire and the fantasy are likely to concentrate on one particular value of the social texture, and to portray, for example, a society in which all values derive from the integrity of the family unit, or a society in which mechanization has destroyed the values of individual enterprise.

Satire and fantasy suggest another distinction in the form which utopias can assume: namely, the progressive or retrogressive perspective. Because they are essentially negative in form, the fantasy and satire often take the retrogressive form: that is, they look backward to a former condition of society which was more nearly ideal in character than the existing form which is the subject of attack. Of course, this "former" social order turns out to be as fictional in nature as the most imaginative constructions of the speculative utopists. The fundamental distinction which is involved between the progressive and retrogressive utopists—and it is a rather important distinction—seems to rest on a basic disagreement as to the essential value of centralization or decentralization in the social framework of institutions. It is relatively unimportant whether the utopist chooses to place his imaginary society backward in time or forward into the future, but it is of primary importance to note whether the values which he proposes as ideal are supposed to result from an increased centralization of the political structure or whether he is advocating a process of decentralization. Progressive utopias generally emphasize centralization, and retrogressive forms usually decry centralizing tendencies as destructive of values. It is ambiguous, however, to put too much weight on the distinction in literary form between the progressive and retrogressive. The problem of centralization *vs.* decentralization is not only the important basic issue, but it is perhaps the most significant principle of analysis and classification of utopian speculation in respect to its political or philosophical implications.

The distinguishable conflict between reliance upon a centralized social structure to realize ideal values and the opposite argument that centralization involves the degradation of values is a reflection of the perplexing, and apparently perpetual, problem of individual *vs.* institution. Utopists, for example, were in the vanguard of the great march of individualism in the seventeenth, eighteenth, and nineteenth centuries. This was the era of the communitarian ideal, with emphasis upon the individual as the only source of value; the better society of utopia was better because individual men and women were better. In this wave of decentralization, almost all institutions were banned from utopias, for was it not true that the imperfect institutions of existing society had prevented men from realizing the perfection of which they were capable? Therefore, urged the utopists, the ideal society will not tolerate the impedimenta of institutional religion, politics, law, and economics; decentralization of society will allow men of intelligence and good will to achieve the greatest possible values.

In the latter half of the nineteenth century, utopists began to return to an emphasis on the ordering of institutional structures in society, convinced now that men could not realize ideal values unless the social environment provided satisfactory conditions of existence, however good their wills might be. New utopias of highly centralized structure began to emerge, and it is significant to note what the utopists generally thought to be the necessary principle of that centralized organization. It was not religion, as was the case in the older theocracies, nor was it education, as in some of the pre-individualistic utopias which looked to science to provide a sufficient principle for the centralization of the social structure. In the modern period, the centralization of the social structure of utopia was to be accomplished by the organization and centralization of economic activity within society. This development has in the modern period brought to sharp focus in utopian thought what is probably the most important general problem of political philosophy and practice in our day.

Can the highly centralized institutional organization which seems necessary to provide adequate conditions of existence in society today be maintained without sacrificing the individual values which utopists have always considered of primary importance? Of course, the utopist proclaims the freedom and happiness of the individual in his ideal society, but the reader must ponder the questionable status of the individual in the completely centralized and institutionalized economic or political or religious society. It was fear of the institutionalization of men that alarmed such satirists as Huxley and Orwell. The historic development and the contemporary nature of this social problem are nowhere more plainly and strikingly evident than in the history of utopian speculation.

There is, therefore, an observable historical sequence in the development of the general pattern of utopian speculation. In this respect, the history of utopias is a history of social, intellectual, and political development. Here we have time to mention the reflection in utopian thought of only one facet of the intellectual development which was to presage historical changes of the greatest magnitude. Let the reader of the following selections note carefully the dates of the utopias presented; even in the relatively few utopias of this anthology there will be evident a clear picture of the changing focus of opinion as it appears dramatically in these descriptions of ideal societies planned to exemplify ideals. Note, too, the professions and vocations of these utopists; they could certainly not be called a group of irresponsible or witless dreamers. The ideals of such men in the past are the realities of the present; their ideals today will be the realities of the future. Utopia *is* the society of the future.

SELECTED LIST OF GENERAL COMMENTARIES

Much commentary on utopian literature is both inadequate and incorrect; the following are generally reliable and correct. Here, and in other bibliographies to follow, listing is by short title.

BERNERI, MARY LOUISE *Journey Through Utopia,* 1950.

BLOCK, ERNST *Freiheit und Ordnung,* 1946.

BLÜHER, RUDOLF *Moderne Utopien,* 1920.

CAULLET, PAUL *Éléments de Sociologie . . . systèmes et Utopies,* 1913.

COSTE, F. H. P. *Towards Utopia,* 1894.

DUPONT, V. *L'Utopie et le Roman Utopique dans la Littérature Anglaise*, 1941.

LE FLAMANC, A. *Les Utopies Prérévolutionnaires et la Philosophie du 18 siècle*, 1934.

GEHRKE, ALBERT *Communistische Idealstaaten*, 1874.

HERTZLER, JOYCE O. *History of Utopian Thought*, 1923.

HEVESI, LUDWIG *Katalog einer merkwürdigen Sammlung von Werken utopistischen Inhalts*, 1911.

KAUFMANN, MORITZ *Utopias*, 1879.

KIRCHENHEIM, ARTHUR VON *L'Éternelle Utopie*, 1897.

" " " *Schlaraffia Politika; Geschichte der Dichtungen vom besten Staate*, 1892.

REINER, JULIUS *Berühmte Utopisten*, 1906.

RENOUVIER, CHARLES *Uchronie*, 1901.

RUSSELL, FRANCES T. *Touring Utopia*, 1932.

SCHMITT, E. H. *Der Idealstaat*, 1904.

2

Modern Utopias 1850-1950

The selection of a specific date to differentiate historic periods is always a somewhat arbitrary decision; so it is with the chronology of utopian works. On the other hand, there are very good reasons for making the middle of the nineteenth century a dividing point in the history of utopias in the Western world. Perhaps it would be an exaggeration to say that the utopian novel came of age during the latter half of the century; certainly it is true that this orphan of literary, philosophical, and political society grew in size and became so comely in form that the utopia was to be seen with increasing frequency in the best literary circles. During this period, the utopian novel became more than a method of making palatable or of tastefully disguising the substance of the hard strictures of the reformer. The utopia as a literary vehicle was dignified and exploited by the attention of Edward Bulwer Lytton, William Morris, Samuel Butler, Anatole France, William Dean Howells, and W. H. Hudson, to name a few in addition to the ubiquitous H. G. Wells. In the temper of the time, the popular Victorian satirists, Gilbert and Sullivan, used the vehicle for their playful operetta, *Utopia, Ltd.*

It is not our concern here, however, to examine the literary influence and development of the utopian novel. The remarkable increase in the use of utopia as a literary vehicle during the modern and contemporary period is one facet of a developing intellectual ferment during the nineteenth century, in which utopian works played a significant and vital role. It would be strange indeed if men of literature were not influenced by the winds of social reform which swept the Western world. Many factors were responsible for the spectacular development of political thought in the nineteenth century, a development which produced a veritable flood of utopian works during the latter part of the century, ranging from the fantastic and exotic to the deadly serious and bitterly satiric. In order to understand the nature and influence of utopias in modern thought, it is necessary to consider them as fruitions of the philosophical and political speculations of the eighteenth and early nineteenth centuries. Here we can indicate only very briefly the general pattern of this speculation as it was interpreted by utopian writers; indeed, the change of focus will be amply apparent in the selections from works of this period.

The most obvious and widespread change in the construction of utopia was the arrogation of the economic to a position of primary and determining importance. That this was, in fact, a change of emphasis indicative of a profound intellectual and philosophical influence cannot be emphasized too strongly. Whatever may be one's opinion of the economic interpretation of history and institutional structure, there is certainly no question of the impact of this interpretation on modern and contemporary thought. The influence has been so profound in terminology and analysis that it is extremely difficult to assume a proper historical perspective toward the utopian thought of an earlier period which did not presuppose the dominating role of the economic in social organization. Thus, we are inclined to interpret the utopias of the eighteenth and early nineteenth centuries as indicative of the same economic determination that is common to those of the more modern writers. To be sure, few utopists were so disdainful or cavalier toward the economic as Plato, and during the seventeenth and eighteenth centuries there was evident an increasing attention to the problem of organizing work and distribution within the utopia. Men like Harrington and Winstanley, for example, appear primarily interested in some particular aspect of economic reform. These instances, however, indicate either a use of the utopian form to convey a suggestion of change in the existing economic structure, or, more commonly, the recognition forced upon any but the most fanatical that the growing complexities of commerce and trade and industry necessitated some attention to the economic within the framework of any society. It seems rather generally to be assumed that the numerous communal or communitarian experiments of the eighteenth and early nineteenth centuries were primarily, if not exclusively, experiments in economic planning. Nothing could be farther from the truth, as even a superficial examination of the writings and records of these groups will indicate. Many of these experimental communities, especially the earlier ones, were sectarian and were motivated primarily by deep and sometimes fanatical religious beliefs and emotions. The nonsectarian communities (in the few instances in which they lasted for more than a year or two) were likewise held together by common emotions and beliefs—belief in the communitarian ideal. In this ideal, economic activity was generally assigned a minor role, the common assumption being that if men were united in common purpose and communal brotherhood, economic maladjustments and inequalities would—indeed *could*—no longer prevail within the structure of the community. The unsympathetic critic of the utopian ventures of the eighteenth and nineteenth centuries might suggest that it was precisely this unrealistic attitude in respect to economic production and distribution that spelled quick dissolution for almost all these noble experiments. In the long run, only those communities which maintained an almost fanatical religious belief and fervor managed to survive. Perhaps the most paradoxical instance of this neglect of the economic in the passion for communitarian idealism was that of Robert Owen and the New Harmony community. Here was an industrial manager who had made a fortune in the turbulent textile industry, so impassioned by the communitarian ideal that he spent his fortune in propagandizing the ideal and underwriting the generous but abortive experiment at New Harmony. It is not necessary to make a profound study of the career of Robert Owen or of the history of the New Harmony colony to realize that Owen was completely vague about economic policy in the community and actually uninterested in the problems of economic organization which beset the group. The experiment was a debacle of production and distribution from its very beginning.[1]

Surely Edward Bellamy was as idealistic and as humanitarian as Robert Owen, but the two men represent the fundamental and significant change of attention in utopian speculation which occurred in a relatively short period. New Harmony began its disintegration in 1827 and Owen died in 1858 still enamored of the communitarian ideal. Yet, when Bellamy drafted his plan for an ideal society in 1888, the entire structure of the organization was built on a fundamental and primary system of economic relationships. All aspects of life and all institutions in Bellamy's society were ordered according to their relation to the basic economic policy. Adjustment to the organization of the "Industrial Army" included even religion, which the pious Bellamy could not free from the economic strait jacket in which he had encased his utopia.

The communitarian ideal of the sixteenth, seventeenth, and eighteenth centuries was foredoomed by the rapid industrialization and urbanization of Western culture. The ideal of a self-sufficient community of simple and uncomplicated economic structure, happy in the enjoyment of simple values of artisanship, family, and natural piety became in the latter nineteenth century the vehicle of satire or nostalgia, as in Morris's *News From Nowhere* and Howells's *Through the Eye of the Needle*, or a picture of fantasy as in Hudson's *A Crystal Age*. For one thing, the simple geographical isolation necessary to preserve the utopian community had become so unrealistic by the middle of the nineteenth century that it could be conceived only as a somewhat fantastic literary device. Atlantis had indeed been engulfed by the waves of history. This rapid shift from the accepted values of the communitarian ideal to a new pattern of social activity which necessitated new and as yet uncognized value patterns was a source of profound disturbance to many men who saw only futility and disaster in the prospect of a mechanized future. Thus, there is in the modern period an understandable increase in the

---

[1] For a scholarly and definitive treatment of Owen and New Harmony, see *Backwoods Utopias: The Sectarian and Owenite Phases of Communitarian Socialism in America: 1663–1829*, by Arthur Eugene Bestor, Jr., University of Pennsylvania Press, 1950.

number of satiric works of utopian significance. From the standpoint of value connotation, these may be classified as *regressive* utopias, as compared with the *progressive* utopists who accepted the changed order of relationships in modern society and based their speculative construction of the ideal state on a new and different system of values. While perhaps deprecating the values of the progressive utopist, those who held steadfastly to individualistic values found it increasingly difficult to advocate realistically the return to the communitarian ideal. Many turned to the negative method of satire, but cherished value-systems die, if they succumb at all, a lingering death. The communitarian ideal has suffered a relapse in the modern period, but with the advent of the atomic bomb and other methods of mass destruction, it may well be that the immediate future of utopian speculation will be rich in suggestions that the self-destruction of the scientific-industrial age will in its collapse force men back to communitarian organization. Such speculations, however, remain largely in the periphery of satire and fantasy.[2]

Constructive utopian works of the latter nineteenth and early twentieth centuries are, therefore, characterized by an acceptance of the consequences of industrialization and urbanization.[3] Such acceptance involves the abandonment, for other than purely literary purposes, of any such notion of geographical isolationism as would make possible a city-state or community utopia. Long before the concept of One World became a part of our political jargon, in an era when practical politics and common opinion were still operating at a level of extreme nationalistic fervor, utopists were recognizing that not even national entities could serve as self-sufficient units of the ideal social structure. In other words, the dominant characteristic of utopias of this period was an emphasis upon the establishment and maintenance of proper *institutional* relationships as the *sine qua non* of a good or ideal society. Such emphasis represents, as has already been suggested, a radical change from the general utopian philosophy of the preceding period which assumed that the achievement of

[2] A modernized version of the communitarian ideal, most stimulating in its suggestion, is the theme of *Architecture and Modern Life*, by Baker Brownell and Frank Lloyd Wright (1938). This is not a utopia, but a philosophy of planning-administration. The argument is that science and industry have now advanced to a stage in which decentralization would in many instances increase efficiency. The emphasis is on the reestablishment of individual values of artisanship, family cooperation, and living on the land. The idea is rich in suggestiveness for utopists; indeed, it had already been anticipated by several utopists, as in *Sybaris and Other Homes*, by Edward Everett Hale (1869).

[3] This is true even though the "principle" of organization may not be economic, but a higher development of individualism, as in Cirkel's *Looking Forward*, or the changing of human nature, as in Coste's *Towards Utopia*, or a fanatical religious dogmatism, as in Benson's *The Dawn of All*.

good and proper *individual* relations among men would automatically produce a happy and harmonious social and political and economic organization. In a period of almost unrestrained individualism, free enterprise, and "the less government the better" politics, utopists were anticipating the "welfare state," the nationalization of industries, "socialized" medicine and health programs, unemployment insurance, old-age pensions, and numerous other such proposals which were fantastically "radical," "dangerous," or "preposterous" in the latter nineteenth century, but which in 1950 have become a part of every man's political vocabulary.[4] Our historical analysis is not a matter of evaluating the proposals and plans of the utopists in terms of "good" or "bad"; one may disagree with the ideas of a specific utopia or even look with grave suspicion on the general trend evident in utopias of the modern period; the important consideration is that the utopists of this period were discussing at the speculative level the problems of social organization which were, in two or three generations, to become the questions of practical political debate and action. That these utopian thinkers constituted one of the most important single sources of influence in molding public opinion seems unquestionable, and this is true even though some of the specific schemes they proposed may appear "crackpot" and some of the utopists themselves close to the lunatic fringe.

The utopias of this period were, then, fertile and influential methods for the transmission to general or public opinion of a philosophy of social structure, change, and progress which was to result in radical and revolutionary political movements and events. From this point of view, the utopias of the latter half of the nineteenth century are one of the most fruitful sources from which to gain that historical perspective which enables one to understand how such tremendous changes in political beliefs and actions could have come about so rapidly. Without this understanding, there is an element of the ridiculous and unbelievable in the observable shift of belief and action in the United States, for example, in the few years between 1900 and 1930. To be sure, it would be an exaggeration to claim a determining role for the utopists, but the impact of utopian speculation on practical affairs has been greatly underestimated. The influence is intangible in most cases and difficult to assess, but it is a very questionable kind of historical analysis of social and political change in the United States, for instance, which does not include a consideration of Bellamy's *Looking Backward*, which sold a half-million copies within a few years of publication, and, sixty years later, has still a substantial annual sale.

[4] William Morris, in *News From Nowhere* (1890), was not only anticipating the failure of capitalism but the subsequent failure of state socialism.

Another kind of superficiality is involved if it is not recognized that these utopists were, on the whole, propagating a social philosophy distinctly contrary to the Anglo-American philosophy of the seventeenth and eighteenth centuries. However, to assume that the utopists of the period were but the unwitting tools of the "socialist" propaganda of the nineteenth century is a vital error which precludes a proper consideration of certain basic problems which their works portray with a dramatic impact lacking in more pedantic speculations. Most of these utopists were sincere proponents of individual freedom and rights, but they believed with equal conviction that the exercise of individual freedom and rights depended in modern society upon the maintenance of an institutional structure which would allow man access to the instruments through which alone he could be properly free and good. It is natural, then, that these utopists should assume that the primary task of social organization was the creation of a proper institutional order of society as the prerequisite for the betterment of men as individuals. It has been noted that the prevailing thought of this period was that a proper ordering of institutions was dependent upon, and followed from, the establishment of order in economic production and distribution. It might be suggested that this uncritical reliance on economic order as the ground and source of all order in institutional and individual relationships was naïve. The utopists of this period manifested a naïvete of a different order, but of about the same degree, as that evidenced by those of the previous period who based their confidence in the possibility of an ideal social order on ideal personal relations between men. For it is precisely here that the utopists of the modern period illustrate so clearly the most vital problem of contemporary political philosophy: namely, how can we avoid doing violence to individual values in achieving a successful institutional ordering of society? However sincerely and loudly individual values of freedom and right are proclaimed, social analysis and experiment both attest the abridgement, if not the elimination, of individual values which is necessary in order to achieve the degree of order in economic production and distribution which the utopists present as the prerequisite of the ideal society. Will not education and religion, family relations and intellectual endeavor, art and poetry, freedom of work and movement—will these not have to be adjusted to the maintenance of the prescribed economic order, by force if necessary? It is this concern which inspired the satirical utopists of the period to decry the increasing realization in contemporary society of the speculative demands of the utopists for institutional order. Morris, Brown, Donnelly, Howells, Huxley—these are but a few who have seen in the industrialized, institutionalized economic order of the future utter catastrophe in the loss of individual rights, freedom, goodness, and value.

The following selections will, it is hoped, adequately illustrate the argument of this brief analysis. Two main factors have governed the selection of these particular works. In the first place, consistent with the policy stated in the Preface, attention has been concentrated on those utopias which are not now available in print. In the modern period in particular, this has necessitated the omission of many of the most historically important works, but such authors as Bellamy, Morris, Butler, Howells, Bulwer-Lytton, and Huxley are readily available, many in inexpensive reprint editions. On the other hand, many of the important and significant utopias of the period, while written in the recent past, are now almost unavailable outside major library sources. It is natural that works of intrinsic literary merit and entertainment value are precisely those which are most likely to be reprinted. In this respect, therefore, the following selections are not truly representative, but rather are typical of the unknown or less popular productions. These, too, had their influence, large or small, on opinion and belief, and in many instances probably exerted a stronger impact on men than more amusing or diverting literary classics. In other words, literary merit has not served at all as a criterion in the selection of the following examples. Utopian rhetoric, especially in the modern period, runs the gamut from substantial literary construction to instances in which the romantic tale which provides the vehicle of exposition is itself almost a collector's item of asininity and literary ineptness. On the other hand, no deliberate negative use of the literary criterion has been employed; if the reader suspects that one or two of the following selections must surely be the nadir of grace in literary exposition, he is invited to explore further among the works cited in the bibliography of utopias. An endeavor has been made to select works which represent types of utopian speculation in the modern period, both in regard to the principles of organization proposed by the utopist and the method by means of which he suggests achieving this ideal. There is an example of the purely speculative utopia (Wells) as well as an illustration of utopian optimism so strong that it brings the work close to the field of planning (Hertzka). The use of utopia to convey subtle satire (Tarde) is placed alongside a much grosser satirization of the socialist ideal (Pallen).

It should be remarked that the style and language of the utopias of the modern period made possible a method of presentation which cannot be employed with the works of the seventeenth, sixteenth, and earlier centuries. The selections which follow are entirely in the words of the authors. There has been no paraphrasing nor other alteration of the original works except condensation. No effort has been made to make awkward rhetoric more graceful nor to reduce the glare of the purple prose which characterizes much of the utopian writing of the period. An occasional obvious typographical error in the original has been corrected in the condensation, but no words have been added to the original. Our sin is that of omission, not commission. It is hoped that this process of extraction will prove less painful than one of complete disfigurement, that enough of the tone and spirit, as well as the content, of the utopist will survive the operation to preserve him as a figure. The development of utopias in the modern period into substantial and comprehensive surveys of the entire complex social structure involved an increase in length from the generally shorter works of earlier periods, indeed in many cases to multivolume productions, as with Bellamy, Brown, Wells, and others. Even the best of literary constructions is violated in such condensation; if time has not disfigured the works of the utopists, the demands of space most certainly have. For the violence done in dwarfing their giants to midgets, we apologize to these respected utopists.

SELECTED LIST OF UTOPIAN WORKS 1850–1950

The following are the better known and/or more important utopian works of the period, confined almost entirely to those in English or available in translation. Dates represent as nearly as ascertainable original date of publication. Pseudonyms are indicated where known.

1854 PEMBERTON, ROBERT *The Happy Colony*
1869 HALE, EDWARD EVERETT *Sybaris and Other Homes*
1871 LYTTON, EDWARD BULWER *The Coming Race*
1872 BUTLER, SAMUEL *Erewhon. (Erewhon Revisited,* 1901*)*
1875 CLEMENS, SAMUEL L. (*Pseud.* MARK TWAIN) *The Curious Republic of Gondour*
1877 MALLOCK, W. H. *The New Republic*
1883 HELLENBACH, L. B. *Die Insel Mellonta*
1883 MACNIE, JOHN (*Pseud.* ISMAR THIUSEN) *The Diothas*
1883 SCHELLHOUS, E. J. *The New Republic*
1885 GRONLUND, LAURENCE *The Co-operative Commonwealth*
1887 DODD, ANNA B. *The Republic of the Future*
1887 HUDSON, W. H. *A Crystal Age*
1888 BELLAMY, EDWARD *Looking Backward*
1888 BESANT, SIR WALTER *The Inner House*
1890 BACHELDER, JOHN *A.D. 2050*
1890 DONNELLY, IGNATIUS (*Pseud.* EDMUND BOISGILBERT, M.D.) *Caesar's Column*

1890   HERTZKA, THEODOR   *Freiland.* (*Freeland Revisited*, 1894).
         (*Tr.* Arthur Ransom)
1890   MICHAELIS, RICHARD C.   *Looking Further Forward*
1890   MORRIS, WILLIAM   *News From Nowhere*
1890   SALISBURY, H. B.   *The Birth of Freedom*
1890   VINTON, ARTHUR D.   *Looking Further Backward*
1891   GEISSLER, LUDWIG   *Looking Beyond*
1891   MUELLER, ERNST   *Ein Rückblick*
1891   SIMPSON, WILLIAM (*Pseud.* THOMAS BLOT)   *The Man From
         Mars*
1891   THOMAS, CHAUNCEY   *The Crystal Button*
1891   WASSERBURG, PHILIPP (*Pseud.* PHILIPP LAICUS   *Etwas Später*
1891   WILBRANDT, CONRAD   *Mr. East's Experiences in Mr. Bellamy's
         World.* (*Tr.* Mary J. Safford)
1892   CHAVANNES, ALBERT   *The Future Commonwealth*
1892   DONNELLY, IGNATIUS   *The Golden Bottle*
1892   EVERETT, HENRY L.   *The People's Program*
1893   GILBERT, W. S. AND SULLIVAN, ARTHUR   *Utopia, Ltd.* (Date
         of first performance)
1893   OLERICH, HENRY   *A Cityless and Countryless World*
1893   ROBERTS, J. W.   *Looking Within*
1893   RUSSELL, A. P.   *Sub-Coelum; A Sky-Built Human World*
1894   ASTOR, JOHN JACOB   *A Journey in Other Worlds*
1894   BOUVÉ, EDWARD T.   *Centuries Apart*
1894   GILES, FAYETTE S.   *Shadows Before*
1894   HOWELLS, WILLIAM D.   *A Traveler from Altruria*
1894   ROSEWATER, FRANK   *'96: A Romance of Utopia*
1894   SCHINDLER, SOLOMON   *Young West*
1894   WELCOME, S. B.   *From Earth's Centre*
1895   CHAVANNES, ALBERT   *In Brighter Climes, or Life in Socioland*
1895   HOLFORD, CASTELLO   *Aristopia*
1895   WELLS, H. G.   *The Time Machine*
1897   ADAMS, FREDERICK U.   *President John Smith*
1897   BELLAMY, EDWARD   *Equality*
1897   BROWN, JOHN M. (*Pseud.* GODFREY SWEVEN)   *Riallaro, the
         Archipelago of Exiles*
1897   CARYL, CHARLES W.   *New Era*
1897   MANTEGAZZA, PAOLO   *L'Anno 3000*
1898   ADAM, PAUL   *Lettres de Malaise*
1898   CRAIG, ALEXANDER   *Ionia*
1899   MERRILL, ALBERT A.   *The Great Awakening*
1900   EDSON, MILAN C.   *Solaris Farm*
1900   GRIGSBY, ALCANOAN O. (*Pseud.* JACK ADAMS)   *Nequa*
1900   PECK, BRADFORD   *The World a Department Store*

1901 TAYLOR, WILLIAM A. *Intermere*
1901 THIRION, EMILE *Neustria*
1903 BROWN, JOHN M. (*Pseud.* GODFREY SWEVEN) *Limanora, the Island of Progress*
1903 HALEVY, DANIEL *Histoire des Quatre Ans, 1997–2001*
1903 MERESCHKOWSKI, D. S. *Das Iridische Paradies.* (*Tr.* by H. Mordaunt)
1903 NOTO, COSIMO *The Ideal City*
1903 STANLEY, WILLIAM *The Case of The. Fox*
1904 TARDE, GABRIEL *Underground Man.* (*Tr.* C. Brereton)
1905 FRANCE, ANATOLE *The White Stone.* (*Tr.* C. E. Roche)
1905 MAGNUS, LEONARD A. *A Japanese Utopia*
1905 WELLS, H. G. *A Modern Utopia*
1906 CIRKEL, AUGUST *Looking Forward*
1906 PARRY, DAVID *The Scarlet Empire*
1907 BENSON, ROBERT H. *Lord of the World*
1907 BLATCHFORD, ROBERT *The Sorcery Shop*
1907 HOWELLS, WILLIAM D. *Through the Eye of the Needle*
1907 LONDON, JACK *The Iron Heel*
1908 FRANCE, ANATOLE *Penguin Island.* (*Tr.* A. W. Evans)
1908 HATFIELD, RICHARD *Geyserland*
1909 CLEMENS, SAMUEL L. (*Pseud.* MARK TWAIN) *Extract from Capt. Stormfield's Visit to Heaven*
1910 HERBERT, EDWARD G. *Newaera*
1910 SCHUETTE, H. GEORGE *Athonia*
1911 BENSON, ROBERT H. *The Dawn of All*
1911 SAUNDERS, W. J. *Kalomera*
1911 SWIFT, MORRISON *The Horroboos*
1912 HOUSE, E. M. *Phillip Dru: Administrator*
1913 PAIN, BARRY *The New Gulliver*
1914 WELLS, H. G. *The World Set Free*
1917 MARSHALL, ARCHIBALD *Upsidonia*
1918 GREGORY, OWEN *Meccania*
1919 PALLEN, CONDÉ B. *Crucible Island*
1919 PEZET, A. W. *Aristokia*
1920 ROSEWATER, FRANK *Doomed*
1921 MASSON, EMILE *Utopie des Iles Bienheureuses*
1923 KNOX, RONALD *Memories of the Future*
1923 OLERICH, HENRY *The Story of the World a Thousand Years Hence*
1923 WELLS, H. G. *Men Like Gods*
1924 HAUPTMANN, G. J. R. *The Island of the Great Mother.* (*Tr.* W. and E. Muir)

1924 MOSZKOWSKI, ALEXANDER *The Isles of Wisdom. (Tr. H. J. Stenning)*

1924 ZAMIATIN, EUGENE *We. (Tr. G. Zilboorg)*

1925 FIALKO, NATHAN *The New City. (Tr. author)*

1925 MADARIAGA, SALVADOR DE *The Sacred Giraffe*

1926 JAEGER, MURIEL *The Question Mark*

1927 MARQUIS, DON *The Almost Perfect State*

1927 OLLIVANT, ALFRED *Tomorrow*

1928 MAUROIS, ANDRÉ *A Voyage to the Island of the Articoles. (Tr. D. Garnett)*

1928 WELLS, H. G. *The Open Conspiracy*

1932 HUXLEY, ALDOUS *Brave New World*

1932 LEACOCK, STEPHEN *Afternoons in Utopia*

1932 PALMER, FREDERICK *So A Leader Came*

1933 HILTON, JAMES *Lost Horizon*

1937 JAFFE, HYMAN (*Pseud.* ALTEREGO) *Abdera and the Revolt of the Asses*

1938 WATTS, NEWMAN *The Man Who Could Not Sin*

1940 HICKS, GRANVILLE AND BENNETT, RICHARD M. *The First to Awaken*

1942 WRIGHT, AUSTIN T. *Islandia*

1944 LEWIS, C. S. *Perelandra*

1946 WERFEL, FRANZ *Star of the Unborn. (Tr. G. O. Arlt)*

1948 COBLENTZ, STANTON A. *The Sunken World*

1948 SKINNER, B. F. *Walden Two*

1949 GRAVES, ROBERT *Watch the North Wind Rise*

1949 ORWELL, GEORGE *Nineteen Eighty-four*

3

Caesar's Column

A Story of the Twentieth Century

*"The true poet is only a
masked father confessor, whose
special function it is to exhibit
what is dangerous in sentiment*   *by* **Edmund Boisgilbert, M.D.**
and pernicious in action by a
vivid picture of their   *(Ignatius Donnelly)*
consequences."—GOETHE

M. A. Donohue & Company
Chicago
New York
(1892)

Ignatius Donnelly (1831–1901)

was never a man who shirked an appointed task because it was controversial. In the literary world, he gained a dubious kind of notoriety as the author of *The Great Cryptogram; or, Francis Bacon's Cipher in the Shakespeare Plays*. In politics, his career was meteoric and erratic. Born in Philadelphia, he entered the bar in that city, but soon emigrated to the pioneer region of Minnesota. At the age of twenty-eight, he was elected Lieutenant Governor of Minnesota, reelected for another term, and during the remainder of his life served many terms in Congress and in the state assembly. He was twice candidate for Vice-President, first as the nominee of the People's party, in 1898, and again on the ticket of the Middle-of-the-Road People's party.

Unsympathetic critics called him a political opportunist. Certainly, he did shift his political position from Republican to Liberal Republican to Granger to Greenbacker. He constantly inveighed against political parties which supported only the interests of the "few." He stood firmly as one of the early supporters of Lincoln and later distinguished himself in Congress by his strong advocacy of non-punitive, constructive action toward the defeated South. To his credit, also, is his initiation of measures for the reforestation of the western plains.

During and between his terms of office he was an active editor and writer. From 1874 to 1879 he edited a weekly newspaper, the *Anti-Monopolist,* and later edited the *Representative,* a journal. He had a curious and inquiring mind, not afraid to explore a hypothesis, as his book *Atlantis* well indicates. This work, which went through twenty-one editions in America, several in England, and translations abroad, was an effort to prove the real existence of this fabled island by marshalling of archaelogical artifacts and data. *Ragnarok* achieved only eleven editions, and *The Golden Bottle* was really a piece of campaign propaganda aimed at the Middle Western farmer, but it used a semi-utopian form of presentation.

Caesar's Column is Donnelly's best-known work; sixty thousand copies were sold in one year, it was republished three times in England, and it was translated into several languages, including Norwegian and Swedish. The book does not follow the classic form of utopian construction; in fact, it is a combination of almost all the variations on the utopian theme. Approaching closely at times to the fantastic, Donnelly indulges liberally in satire of a rather broad and obvious nature. Subtlety was not his forte, and occasionally he almost loses the utopian theme in the blood and thunder of his adventure tale. Yet, there is an ideal, speculative element which is really the focal point of his attention, although the constructive is accorded less space in his treatment than is usual in utopian works. Donnelly is one of the school of utopists, characteristic of the modern period, who apparently see no hope for the establishment of an ideal society until there has been a general clearing away of the institutions which are directly responsible for existing social evils. Whatever may have been his views in the political arena, in *Caesar's Column* he takes the position that only violence and revolution can rid society of the vicious machinations of oligarchy, and he is depressingly realistic about the results of violence as a method of social change. It is questionable what importance attaches to the fact, but it is of some interest to point out that Donnelly wrote *Caesar's Column* at the age of sixty-one, after thirty-three very active years in politics; it is not, in short, the outpouring of undisciplined youthful impatience.

The editors wish to call attention to the indications of anti-Semitism which crop out in Donnelly's work. A firm editorial policy dictated that these should not be eliminated, although they have been much abridged in length and vigor. Any survey of utopian thought would be distorted if it did not indicate clearly that utopias include the prejudices of utopists. In many cases, indeed, utopia is used as a vehicle for prejudice. There will be numerous instances in the following selections of the personal biases of the architects of utopia. Men who play god almost always want to make man over in their own image.

Caesar's Column

New York, Sept. 10, 19—

My Dear Brother:
Here I am, at last, in the great city. My eyes are weary with gazing, and my mouth speechless with admiration; but in my brain rings perpetually the thought: Wonderful!—wonderful! New York contains now ten million inhabitants; it is the largest city that is, or ever has been, in the world. As we approached it in our airship, we could see, a hundred miles before we reached the continent, the radiance of its millions of magnetic lights, not fed, as in the old time, from electric dynamos, but the magnetism of the planet itself is harnessed for the use of man. Night and day are all one, for the magnetic light increases automatically as the daylight wanes; and the business parts of the city swarm as much at midnight as at noon. The streets are covered with roofs of glass, which exclude the rain

and snow, but not the air. Below are subterranean streets, where vast trains are drawn. High above the housetops, built on steel pillars, there are other railroads.

The whole territory between Broadway and the Bowery is occupied by the depot of the inter-continental air-lines. The speed of these aerial vessels is very great—thirty-six hours suffices to pass from New York to London.

I could spend hours telling you of the splendor of this hotel. The ancient elevator has expanded until whole rooms are carried up from the first story to the roof. In the dining-room, as I took my seat, a few feet in front of me rose out of the table a large mirror, on its surface a bill of fare. The table contained hundreds of little knobs, connected by electric wires with the kitchen. My dinner would be ordered on a similar mirror in the kitchen. In a little while the table parted and up rose my dinner. The mirror now contained the names of all the nations of the world. If I would touch the corresponding button the news of the day, from that state or country, would appear in the mirror.

The air of the hotel was purer and cooler than outside. A great canvas pipe pumped down air from a higher region. The whole city was warmed with hot water from the depths of the earth, distributed in pipes.

Would you believe, my dear brother, in this city they actually facilitate suicide! In all the public parks they have handsome houses. If a man has decided to die, he goes there. A doctor explains to him the different poisons, and he selects the kind he prefers. The truth is, that, in this over-crowded city, man is a drug, and I think many men end their lives out of a sense of their own insignificance.

I must bring this letter to an end. With love to all, I remain, your affectionate brother,

Gabriel Weltstein

My Dear Heinrich,

I little supposed that twenty-four hours could so completely change my circumstances. Yesterday morning I took the elevated train to Central Park. I saw a sight which made my blood run cold. A beggar was crossing the street in front of a magnificent open carriage. The flunkey made no effort to check the speed of his horses. In an instant the beggar was under the hoofs. The flunkey laughed! Quick as thought, I had the horses by their heads. The beggar crawled out, and the driver struck him with his whip. I caught it, dragged it from the hand of the miscreant, and with all my power laid it over him. As I raised my hand to lash the brute again, I became aware that there were ladies in the barouche, both strikingly handsome, one with a bold, commonplace look. Her companion was younger; her long golden hair fell nearly to her waist; her eyes were blue, and there was in them a look of honesty and calm intelligence.

I felt someone tugging at my coat and was surprised to find that the beggar was drawing me away by main force.

"Come," he said, "come quickly, or you will be arrested."

"What for?" I asked.   •

"I will tell you hereafter."

We rushed along and took one of the railroads in the air, threading our way backward and forward over the city. At length, as if the beggar thought we had gone far enough to baffle pursuit, we descended in front of a plain but respectable house. We entered a a degree of splendor of which the external appearance gave no prophecy. The beggar left me. I was thinking over these matters when a handsome young gentleman entered. I began to apologize for my intrusion. The gentleman, extending his hand, said:

"I am the beggar, and I thank you for the life you saved. I see that you are surprised. I was disguised for a purpose, which I cannot explain to you. May I request the name of the gentleman to whom I am under so many obligations?"

I replied, "My name is Gabriel Weltstein; I live in the new state of Uganda in the mountains of Africa, and I am engaged in sheep-raising. I belong to a colony of Swiss, who settled there seventy years ago. I came to this city to see if I could sell my wool directly to the manufacturers, and thus avoid the extortions of the Wool Ring, but I find they do not dare to deal with me; and thus I shall have to dispose of my product at the old price. Will you be good enough to tell me something about yourself?"

"Certainly," he replied. "I am a native of this city; my name is Maximilian Petion; by profession I am an attorney; I live in this house with my mother. You were in great danger. I could not leave you to be arrested and punished with a long imprisonment. That was the carriage of Prince Cabano, the wealthiest man in the city. Our courts are the merest tools of the rich."

I realized for the first time the perils of my situation. I was a stranger and hunted like a felon.

"But are we not in great danger?"

"I belong to a society which has its ramifications all over the world. So have no uneasiness. We are as safe here as if a standing army surrounded the house."

"I thought your Republic eschewed all titles of nobility."

"So it does by law. The Prince, when he comes to sign his name to a legal document, writes it Jacob Isaacs. But his father purchased a princedom in Italy for a large sum. The aristocracy of the world is now almost altogether of Hebrew origin. It is the greatest of pities that so noble and beautiful a civilization should have become rotten at the core."

"Rotten at the core!" I exclaimed, in astonishment; "what do you mean?"

"That civilization is a gross and dreadful failure for seven-tenths of the human family. It is pitiful to think what society is, and then to think what it might have been if our ancestors had not cast away their magnificent opportunities."

"But," I replied, "the world does not look to me after that fashion. Why, this city preaches at every pore the splendor of civilization!"

"True, my friend," replied Maximilian; "but you see only the surface. Tomorrow we will go out together, and I shall show you the fruits of our modern civilization. We will visit the Under-World."

But I must close for tonight, and subscribe myself affectionately your brother,

Gabriel

My Dear Heinrich:

Since I wrote you last night I have looked with my very eyes on Hell. My soul sorrows for humanity.

Max woke me very early. Yesterday he had dyed my fair locks dark brown and cut off some superfluous length, then arrayed me in the latest fashion. A half hour's ride brought us into the domain of the poor.

An endless procession of men and women streamed along the streets on their way to work. I observed that both were undersized, and a more joyless, sullen crowd I never beheld. They were all poorly clad, and many of them in rags. There were multitudes of children, but their faces were prematurely aged.

What struck me most was their silence. They seemed to me merely automata, in the hands of some ruthless and unrelenting destiny. Toil, toil, toil, from early morn until late at night; then home they swarm; tumble into their wretched beds; snatch a few hours of disturbed sleep, battling with vermin, in a polluted atmosphere; and then up again and to work; and so on, and on, in endless, mirthless, hopeless round; until, in a few years, consumed by disease, mere rotten masses of painful wretchedness, they die, and are wheeled off to the great furnaces, and their bodies are eaten up by the flames, even as their lives have been eaten up by society.

From the shops and mills of honest industry, Maximilian led me into the criminal quarters. It seems to me that the great criminals of the world are not those who break through all laws, but those who, equally selfish, corrupt the fountains of government and create laws and conditions by which the millions suffer, and out of which these murderers and robbers naturally and unavoidably arise.

But I must bring this long letter to a conclusion, and subscribe myself, with love to all,

Your affectionate brother,

Gabriel

My Dear Heinrich:

One morning I asked Maximilian whether he had noticed the two young ladies in the Prince of Cabano's carriage.

"No," said he, indifferently; "probably a couple of the Prince's mistresses."

I half rose from my chair, my face suffused and my eyes indignant. "Oh, no; but I am sure you are wrong. If you had looked, for but a moment, at the younger, you would never have made such a remark."

"I meant no harm," he answered, "but the Prince has a perfect harem in his palace; he has agents everywhere buying up handsome women."

"My dear Maximilian," I said, "I feel very confident that the younger of those two women is pure. God never placed such a noble countenance over a corrupt soul."

"Why," said he, laughing, "the arrow of Master Cupid has penetrated through all the plates of your philosophy. I can find out for you all that is known about her. We have members of our society in the household of every rich man in New York."

He went to the wall, wrote a message, placed it in a cavity, which connected with a pneumatic tube, and in a few minutes withdrew from a similar cavity a written message. He read out to me the following:

Miss Estella Washington.—*Aged eighteen. A lineal descendant of brother of the first President of the Republic. Father died, leaving family poor; mother two years later. Adopted by widow of brother of father, who last month sold her to the Master of Servants of Prince of Cabano. Estella believes she is to serve as companion for Miss Frederika Bowers, the favorite of the Prince, whom Estella supposes to be his niece.*

I forgot every pretense of indifference and cried out: "She must be saved!"

Maximilian was also stirred to his depths. "I will help you, my friend. The Master of Servants belongs to our Brotherhood. He will give us access to the poor girl. Come!"

We were soon at the house of the Prince. Rudolph, as the Master of Servants was called, brought the beautiful girl I had seen in the carriage. It was evident she recognized me; and I fancied the recognition was not unpleasant to her. Maximilian delivered the paper into her hand. The eyebrows began to rise and the blue eyes to dilate with horror.

"This is a base falsehood! A cowardly trick to wound me! A shameful attempt to injure my dear aunt."

"Rudolph," said Maximilian, solemnly, "I call upon you, by the oath you have taken, to say to this lady whether the contents of that paper are true."

"It is true," replied Rudolph.

She became deadly pale, and would have fallen to the floor, but that I caught her in my arms—(oh, precious burden!)—and bore her to a sofa. At last she looked around upon us and cried out:

"Oh, my God! What shall I do? I am sold—sold—a helpless slave. Oh, it is horrible!"

"You will never be without friends while we live," I said.

"But I must fly," she cried, "and how—where?"

"My dear Miss Washington," said Maximilian, "I have a dear mother, who will be glad to welcome you as her own child, until you have time to think out your future."

"Then let us fly at once," said Estella.

"No," replied Rudolph, "that would not do; this house is full of spies. On Monday night the members of 'the government' have their meeting here. I will procure a gentleman's dress for Miss Estella and a permit for a carriage to enter the grounds with the rest of the equipages. But I must have someone who will accompany Miss Estella from this room to the carriage, for I must not show myself."

I stepped forward, and said, "I will be here."

"There is one other matter," said Rudolph to Max; "the meeting Monday night is to be a very important one. If you can send me a discreet man I can hide him."

"Why could I not serve the purpose?" I said. "I will be here anyhow."

．　．　．　．　．

I cannot give you, my dear brother, a detailed account of every day's occurrences. I shall, however, jot down my reflections on sheets, and send them to you as occasion serves.

The more I have conversed with Maximilian, the more clearly I perceive that the civilized world is in a desperate extremity. This Brotherhood of Destruction, with its terrible purposes and its vast numbers, is a reality. I learn from Maximilian that their organization is most perfect. Every one of their hundred millions is armed. If I believed that this wonderful Brotherhood was capable of anything beyond destruction, I should not look with terror as I do upon the prospect.

"But what would you do, my good Gabriel," said Maximilian, smiling, "if the reformation of the world were placed in your hands? Every man has a Utopia in his head. Give me some idea of yours."

"First," I said, "I should do away with all interest on money. Interest is the root and ground of the world's troubles. It puts one man in a position of safety, while another is in a condition of insecurity. The borrower assumes all the chances of life in his efforts to repay the loan; behind all risks stands the money-lender in perfect security. The necessity to borrow is one of the results of borrowing. Large fortunes are usually the accumulations of wreckage, and every dollar represents disaster."

"Well," said Maximilian, "having abolished usury in your Utopia, what would you do next?"

"I would set to work to list all laws or conditions which gave any man an advantage over any other man, or tended to concentrate the wealth in the hands of a few, and abolish them."

"Men differ; some have more industry, or more cunning, or more acquisitiveness than others. How are you to prevent these men from becoming richer than the rest?"

"I should not try to," I said. "These differences are fundamental. It is only in their excess that they become destructive. I should establish a maximum beyond which no man could own property; I should require him to invest the surplus, under the direction of a governmental board of management, in works for the benefit of the laboring classes, to secure immortality by affixing his name and by placing his statue in a national gallery. So should I limit the amount of land he could own. I should abolish all corporations, or turn them back into individual partnerships. For one hundred and fifty years the production of gold and silver has been shrinking, while the population of the world has been rapidly increasing. Every decrease in the quantity, actual or relative, of gold and silver increases the purchasing power of the dollars made out of them; and the dollar becomes the equivalent for a larger amount of the labor of man. I would call the civilized nations together in council, and devise an international paper money, to be issued by the different nations, but to be legal tender in all countries. It should hold a fixed ratio to population, never to be exceeded. There would be no financial panics, for there could be no contraction. Government is the key to the future of the human race. The city of the future must furnish doctors for all; lawyers for all; entertainments for all; business guidance for all. It will see to it that no man is plundered, and no man starved, who is willing to work."

"Come, come," said Maximilian. "Let us go to dinner before you abolish all the evils of the world, or I shall be disposed to quit New York and buy a corner lot in Utopia."

.   .   .   .   .

Precisely as Rudolph had forecast, things came to pass. I arrived at the palace of the Prince at half past six. Watching our opportunity, we drew aside a heavy box in which grew a noble specimen of the cactus grandiflorus. I crawled through the opening; he pushed the box into its place again. Half-stooping, I found an aperture in the blossoms. The members of the government were arriving. The Prince welcomed each newcomer; when all were seated he spoke:

"I have called you together, gentlemen, because the evidences multiply that we are on the eve of another outbreak of the canaille. I have two men whom I thought that you should hear face to face. The first is General Jacob Quincy, commander of our ten thousand air-ships, or Demons. In these and the deadly bombs of poisonous gas, we find our safety and power. Another here tonight is a member of our secret police. You are aware that we have had trouble to ascertain anything about this new organization. Many of our spies have disappeared; this man Andrews has so far escaped. The last task I gave him was to discover who are the leaders in this conspiracy. The organization is cunningly contrived, made up in groups of ten. No one of the rank and file knows more than nine other members. The leaders of these groups are again organized in groups of ten. The highest body of all is a group of one hundred selected out of the whole force by an executive committee. Andrews has at length been selected as one. He is to be initiated tomorrow night. He came to me for more money; for he feels he is placing himself in great danger. I thought you would like to question him."

In a few moments a tall personage, dressed like a woman, with a heavy veil, entered and removed the bonnet, disclosing the face of a workman.

"Andrews," said the Prince, "tell these gentlemen what you have found out."

"My lord," replied the man, "I can speak only by hearsay. After tomorrow night I hope to be able to tell you everything. One year ago there were fifteen engaged in this work; I am the only one left. 'The Brotherhood of Destruction' extends all over Europe and America, and numbers one hundred million members. Nearly every workman of good character in New York belongs to it. It is claimed that every one possesses a rifle, with an abundance of ammunition.

The leaders—there are three, I am told—constitute what is known as 'the Executive Committee.' The commander-in-chief, it is whispered, is called Caesar Lomellini, of Italian descent, but a native of South Carolina. He is of immense size, about forty-five years of age. He went to farming, a quiet, industrious man. One year lightning killed his horses. Forced to mortgage his land to buy another pair, it was the old story. Caesar worked like a slave, and his family with him. At last the crash came; he was driven out of his home, and his eldest daughter had been seduced by a lawyer—the agent of the money-lender. Caesar and his family fled. He gathered a band of men and waged war on society; while he spared the poor, no man who preyed on his fellow-men was safe. The government massed troops; Caesar and his men fled to the Pacific coast; nothing more was heard of him for years. Then the negro insurrection broke out in the Mississippi Valley, and a white man, of gigantic stature, appeared as their leader. When that rebellion had been suppressed, the white man disappeared. It is now claimed that he is at the head of this Brotherhood."

The spy paused. The Prince said:

"Well, who are the others?"

"It is reported that the 'brains of the organization' is a Russian Jew, who organized the Brotherhood in Europe."

"Who is the third?" asked the Prince.

"I heard once that he was an American, a young man of wealth and ability, and that he had furnished much of the money. Several years ago a lawyer by the name of Arthur Phillips had made a study of the socialist writers, and had become a convert to their theories. He spoke at the meetings of the workmen, and was very much beloved by them. Of course, all this was distasteful to the ruling class, and they began to persecute him. At this time he had a lawsuit with a member of the government. Phillips produced a writing signed by two men and witnessed. All of them swore that their alleged signatures were false. Phillips was indicted for forgery and perjury, and sentenced to twenty years in the state prison. His friends said that the witnesses had been suborned. His son—Jenkins told me—was really the man who, out of revenge, was now the third member of the Executive Committee."

The Prince said quietly, "I have had detectives shadow young Phillips, and they report that he is a dissipated, worthless fellow, who spends his time about saloons."

I was an intent listener and felt certain that Maximilian Petion and Arthur Phillips were one and the same. I could now understand why a gentleman so intelligent and kindly by nature could have engaged in so bloody a conspiracy.

The door opened and closed behind a man with the insignia of a brigadier-general of the United States army.

"General Quincy," said the Prince, "I need not introduce you to these gentlemen; they are ready to hear you."

"Gentlemen," said the General, "I am not here of my own volition, but as the mouthpiece of others. The officers and men openly declare that those they maintain in power are enjoying royal affluence, which they could not possess without their aid. I have here a schedule of their demands; it ranges from $5000 per year, for the common soldiers, up to $25000 for the commanding officer."

The Prince said: "The salaries asked for are high; but they will come out of taxes; if you can assure me that your command will work with increased zeal, I should be disposed to accede."

There was a general assent around the table. The commander of the Demons was bowed out. The Prince returned.

"Gentlemen, you can see the ticklish ground we stand on. These men will demand more as the consciousness of their power increases. I propose that after this outbreak we shall order the construction of ten thousand more of these air-vessels, an excuse for sending a large force of apprentices. We will select from our relatives some young, able man to command these new troops. We will then seize the magazine; the officers we will execute, and the men send to prison for life. After that we will keep the magazine in the custody of men of our caste."

These plans met with general approval.

"But what are we to do with the coming outbreak?"

"It is to our interest to make it the occasion of a tremendous massacre. There are too many people, anyhow. We will strike such terror into the canaille that they will remain submissive for centuries. Let them build their barricades; we have then got them in a rat-trap. Then let our flock of Demons drop their bombs of invisible poison. These plans will be sent out to all cities and to Europe."

Carried away, I crawled out; the next moment I stood before them in the full glare of the electric lamps.

"For God's sake," I cried, "save the world from such an awful calamity! Have pity on mankind. For the sake of Jesus Christ, who died on the cross for all men, I appeal to you."

The Prince rallied his faculties. "How did you come here?"

Fortunately the coldness with which the Council met my appeals had restored my reason. The thought flashed over me that I must not betray Rudolph.

"I climbed up the ivy vine."

"The man is a religious fanatic," said one of the Council, "probably one of the street preachers."

The Prince spoke to Rudolph. I caught a few words: "Not leave
—alive." Rudolph took me by the arm. I went with him like a child.
He opened the door of a room. "Wait," he whispered.

A young gentleman standing at a window turned around. It was
Estella! I fell upon my knees.

"Oh, Estella, pardon me! I would have sacrificed you for mankind. I forgot everything to save the world."

"If you had done less, I should have loved you less."

I presumed nothing upon the admission she had made. This was a
woman to be worshiped, rather than wooed.

Rudolph entered. "This cloak," he said, "will help disguise you.
Walk boldly down these stairs. The guard will lead you to the carriage. Maximilian is the footman. God bless you."

I followed his directions; the guard led me through a mass of
carriages to where one stood somewhat back. I gave my hand to
Estella; she sprang in. We had gone hardly two blocks when Maximilian leaned down and said:

"We are certainly pursued by two carriages. The third one I
recognize as our own. Now observe what takes place."

I leaned far out at the side. Our pursuers are close behind, but
now our friends forge slowly ahead. A man stands up on the seat.
I could see his arm describe an arc; the next instant the report of
a tremendous explosion rang in my ears. Through the smoke I could
see the horses of our pursuers kicking, plunging, dying.

"It is all right now," said Maximilian quietly.

After several changes of direction—to throw any other pursuers
off the track, we drove to Maximilian's house. I told him all that
had happened.

"Gabriel, would you go with me tomorrow night and tell this tale
to the council of our Brotherhood?"

"I shall go with you most willingly," I said.

It was pleasant, that night, to think that Estella loved me.

. . . . .

"Now, Gabriel," said Max, "I will have to blindfold you."

It was a long drive. At last we stopped and descended a flight
of steps. I imagined it to be the cellar of some abandoned warehouse. Then a stern, loud voice said:

"Gabriel Weltstein, you do solemnly swear, in the presence of
Almighty God, that the statements you are about to make are just
and true; and you willingly accept death if you utter anything that
is false?" I bowed my head.

I told, in the midst of a grave-like silence, what I had witnessed
and heard.

"Uncover his eyes!" exclaimed the stern voice. "Unmask."

It was an extraordinary assemblage that greeted my eyes. Last night I had beheld the council of the Plutocracy. Here was the council of the Proletariat. I turned to the president. Such a man I had never seen before. He was, I should think, not less than six feet six inches high, and broad in proportion. This, then, must be Caesar, the commander of the dreaded Brotherhood. A movement attracted me to the man who sat below him. He was old and withered. One hand seemed to be shrunken, and his head was permanently crooked to one side. I should have picked him out anywhere as a very able and a very dangerous man. He was evidently the vice-president—the nameless Russian Jew who was accounted "the brains of the Brotherhood."

"Gabriel Weltstein," said the giant, "each person in this room will now pass before you, and I call upon you to say whether the spy is among them."

Here there was a rush behind me. Two men were scuffling with a third, who seemed to be trying to break out; then the crowd came dragging a man to where I stood.

"Speak," said Caesar, "is that the man?"

"It is," I replied.

The huge man gave a leap forward; then there was the sound of a heavy blow. The spy fell stone dead.

"Thus die all the enemies of the Brotherhood!" cried the thin voice of the cripple.

And long and loud they shouted.

Then, resuming his seat, the giant said, "The Brotherhood thank you for the great service you have rendered them. One thing more we shall ask of you, that you repeat your story for another man. Resume your masks."

Then the secretary entered, leading a large man.

"General Jacob Quincy, I have here a witness who is about to reveal to you everything you said last night."

I did so.

"You believe him to be a truthful witness?" asked the cripple. "Now proceed to tell what took place after this gentleman left the room."

The face of the general darkened with rage when I had concluded. "Could I have a private conference with the president?"

Twenty minutes passed, and they came out. The commander of the Demons withdrew. The president with excitement cried out:

"Brothers, we have got the world in our hands at last. The Demons are with us!"

The wildest demonstrations of joy followed. That monstrous chorus was chanting the requiem of a world.

It had been my intention to return to Africa before the outbreak. I need not say how greatly I love Estella. I could not leave her alone to encounter all the dangers. Would it be mean and contemptible to take advantage of her solitude and the danger, and thus coerce her into a marriage which might be distasteful to her? I poured forth my love in rapturous words. She put her arms around my neck and said:

"What kind of a weak heart or weak head have you, not to know that a woman never shrinks from dependence upon the man she loves?"

I folded her in my arms and began to give her all the kisses I had been hoarding up for her since the day we met.

. . . . .

A few days after our wedding, Max came running in, and said: "It is to be tomorrow."

He gave each of us a red cross to sew upon our clothes, and hurried out again. I had said to him that I desired to return home before the outbreak. He had begged me to remain. He said that at the interview with General Quincy it had been made a condition of the contract that each of the executive committee should have one of the air-ships placed at his disposal, well-manned and equipped with bombs.

Max had always had a dream that after the Plutocracy was overthrown the insurgents would reconstruct a purer and better state of society; but of late my conversations with him, and his own observations, had begun to shake his faith in this particular. He said that if I remained he would guarantee the safety of myself and wife, and after I had seen the outbreak he would send me home in his air-ship; and, moreover, if he became satisfied that the revolution had passed beyond control, he would, after rescuing his father, accompany me with his family, and we would settle down together in my distant mountain home. He had, accordingly, turned all his estate into gold, and I had filled one large room full of books and all the inventions which the last hundred years had given us.

In the afternoon Max returned, with a dozen men, bearing great boxes. They were old and trusted servants, and the boxes contained ammunition and hand-grenades. We were all armed. The men again returned, bearing quantities of food, sufficient to last us during a siege, and also during our flight to my home. Water was collected in barrels. The lower windows and the front door were covered with sheathings of thick oak plank. The back door was left free, but powerful bars were arranged across it. One of the men painted red crosses on the doors.

Max told us all to come up to the roof and whispered to me that the blow would be struck at six o'clock in Europe, and at twelve o'clock at night in America. The fighting therefore had begun in the Old World. The Brotherhood at twelve would barricade all the principal banks. Two hundred thousand men would be assembled to guard these barricades. They would then burst open the moneyed institutions. At daybreak one of Quincy's air-ships would come and receive fifty millions of the spoils in gold, as their share of the plunder, and the price of their support. As soon as this was delivered, the whole fleet would attack the troops of the Oligarchy.

I thought it must be nearly twelve. A confused buzz arose from below me. I could hear the march of thousands of feet. And then hundreds of busy figures were to be seen at work. So far not a soldier or policeman had been visible. The Oligarchy were carrying out the plan of Prince Cabano. They were permitting the insurgents to construct their "rat-trap."

Suddenly there was a terrific explosion, and again came other explosions. The fateful day was dawning. And then I could hear splendid melody. It was the defenders of society advancing with the swinging step of assured triumph. Some of the troops advanced toward the barricade. Far away to the west comes on the vast array of the Demons. They are above the streets packed full of the troops of the government. The crash—the bang—the explosions; the uproar, the confusion; and, most horrible of all, the inevitable, invisible death by the poison.

"The Demons" moved slowly on. They had earned their money. The mob stood still for a few minutes. They could scarcely realize that they were at last masters of the city. But quickly a full sense of all that their tremendous victory signified dawned upon them. The city lay prostrate, chained, waiting to be seized upon. At first, they were under the control of some species of discipline and moved toward the houses of the condemned, of whom printed catalogues had been furnished the officers. Civilization is gone, and all the devils are loose! No more courts, nor judges, nor prisons! That which it took the world ten thousand years to create has gone in an hour.

The Prince of Cabano had early received word of the turn affairs had taken. He had hurriedly filled a large satchel with jewels and had called Frederika to him and fled to the riverside. His fine yacht lay off in the stream, but no one replied from the vessel. He ran back to hide in the shrubbery of his own garden; there he might find a faithful servant who would get him a boat. But then came on the awful mob, led by a gigantic and ferocious figure. The Prince rose as the yell told him he was discovered. The next instant there was a crack of a pistol. The ball struck the Prince in the back of the neck. With a shriek he fell down and moaned in the most exquisite torture, "Kill me! kill me!" But Caesar had seen a prize worth pursuing. Frederika had arisen, and when the Prince was shot she fled. Caesar pursued her. And still the Prince screamed in agony, and begged for death. The mob had swept off to new slaughter.

A thief, hunting for plunder, was approaching. The Prince asked, "If I tell you where you can find a hundred thousand dollars, will you drive my knife through my heart? Then take the knife. I tell you what you must do. Kneel down over me; put the lapel of your coat between my teeth. I will then tell you where the treasure is, but you will have to slay me to escape from me."

The thief did as he was directed; and, through his shut teeth, the Prince muttered: "It is in the satchel beneath me."

Without a word, the thief drove the knife through the Prince's heart. The last of the accumulations of generations of extortion had sufficed to purchase their heritor a miserable death—in the embrace of a thief!

That day Maximilian returned home with a stranger. I could not long doubt who he was. He was sobbing like a child in the arms of his wife. He seemed very weak in body and mind.

"I have avenged my father," said Maximilian to me. "The Count had ruined my father by bribery, so I bribed his confidential friend to deliver him up to me. On the river bank were a body of my men; they had the other prisoners—the corrupt judge, the jurymen, and the four lying witnesses. They signed and acknowledged their confessions. I ordered the prisoners to chain the Count to a post and bring lumber; they piled it in great walls around him.

" 'Here,' I said to the judge, 'put a match to the pile.'

"In a few minutes the Count was screaming in the center of a roaring furnace. I gave a signal to my men. Each of the prisoners was manacled, and high above the walls of fire they were thrown, and all perished howling together."

"Max, dear Max," I said, "for Heaven's sake never let your mother hear that story. It was a madman's act! Never think of it again. You have wiped out the crime in blood; there let it end. And leave these awful scenes, or you will become a maniac."

"Caesar," said Max, "has fallen upon a scheme of the most frenzied and extraordinary kind. After I had avenged my father I proceeded to find Caesar. I heard that he was at Prince Cabano's palace. You never saw such a sight. He was so black with dust and blood that he looked like a negro. He had been drinking. Behind him were a bevy of young women. The Sultan had been collecting his harem.

"Here one of his principal officers came up, and the following dialogue occurred:

" 'I came, General, to ask you what to do with the dead.'

" 'Kill 'em,' roared Caesar, 'kill 'em—d——n—'em.'

" 'But, General, they are dead already,' replied the officer. 'A number of the streets are impassable already with the dead. There must be a quarter of a million soldiers and citizens lying about, and the number is being added to every minute. The weather is warm, and they will soon breed a pestilence that will revenge them upon their slayers. Those killed by the poison are beginning to smell already. We would have to burn up the city to destroy them in that way; there are too many of them; and it would be an immense task to bury them.'

"Caesar was standing unsteadily, looking at us with lackluster eyes. Suddenly an idea seemed to dawn in his monstrous head—an idea as monstrous as the head itself.

" 'I have it!' he shouted. 'By G——d, I have it! Make a pyramid of them, and pour cement over them, and let it stand forever as a monument of this day's glorious work! Hoorah!"

" 'That's a pretty good idea,' said the officer, and the others, courtier-like—for King Caesar already had his courtiers—applauded the idea vociferously.

" 'We'll have a monument that shall last while the earth stands,' cried Caesar. 'I, say—we won't make a pyramid of it—it shall be a column—Caesar's Column—by G——d. It shall reach the skies! And if there aren't enough dead to build it of, why, we'll kill some more. Put a lot of dynamite—hic—in the middle it, and if they try to tear down my monument, it will blow them to the d——l! And, I say, Max, that friend of yours must write an inscription. By G——d, we will build a monument that will beat the pyramids of all the other Caesars. Caesar's Column! Hoorah!'

"Sixty thousand prisoners set to work on the construction of Caesar's Column, and they are now building the monument on Union Square."

It was a dreadful night. Cruel and bloodthirsty peasants invaded the houses of friend and foe alike, and murdered men, women and children. One of the men came to me at midnight and cried:

"They are attacking the house!"

"Throw over a hand-grenade," I said.

There was a loud crash, and the cowardly miscreants fled. All night long the streets swarmed. Three times we had to have recourse to the hand-grenades. Fires sprang up all over the city.

Early in the morning Caesar's officer sent for the inscription for the monument. I sat down, and after some thought, wrote these words:

THIS GREAT MONUMENT
IS
ERECTED BY
CAESAR LOMELLINI
COMMANDING GENERAL OF
THE BROTHERHOOD OF DESTRUCTION
IN
COMMEMORATION OF
THE DEATH AND BURIAL OF
MODERN CIVILIZATION

It is composed of the bodies of a quarter million human beings, who were once the rulers, or the instruments of the rulers, of this mighty, but alas; this ruined city.

They were dominated by leaders who were altogether evil.

They corrupted the courts, the juries, the newspapers, the legislatures, the congresses, the ballot-boxes and the hearts and souls of the people.

They formed gigantic combinations to plunder the poor; to make the miserable more miserable; to take from those who had least and give it to those who had most.

They used the machinery of free government to effect oppression; they made liberty a mockery, and its traditions a jest; they drove justice from the land and installed cruelty, ignorance, despair and vice in its place.

Their hearts were harder than the nether mill-stone; they degraded humanity and outraged God.

At length indignation stirred in the vasty courts of heaven; and over-burdened human nature rose in universal revolt on earth.

By the very instruments which their own wickedness had created they perished; and here they lie, sepulchred in stone, and heaped around explosives as destructive as their own lives. We execrate their vices, while we weep for their misfortunes. They were the culmination of centuries of misgovernment; and they paid an awful penalty for the sins of generations of short-sighted and selfish ancestors, as well as for their own cruelty and wickedness.

Let this monument, O man! stand forever.

Should civilization ever revive on earth, let the human race come hither and look upon this towering shaft, and learn to restrain selfishness and live righteously. From this ghastly pile let it derive the great lesson, that no earthly government can endure which is not built on mercy, truth and love.

At noon Max returned. His clothes were torn, and around his head he wore a white bandage, stained with blood.

"It is all in vain," he said despairingly; "I thought I would be able to create order out of chaos and reconstruct society. But that dream is past. Last night the vice-president—the Jew—fled, in one of the Demons, carrying away one hundred million dollars. It is rumored that he has gone to Judea to re-establish the splendors of the Jewish race. The mob are wild with suspicions and full of rumors. They are gathered around the palace to prevent Caesar leaving them, like the cripple. They believe that he has another hundred millions hidden in the palace. I rose to address them. I told them they must establish some kind of government. If they did not they would soon be starving. The mob had eaten up all the food in the shops, and tomorrow they would begin to feel the pangs of starvation.

" 'He wants to make himself a king,' growled one ruffian.

" 'Yes,' said another, 'and set us all at work again.'

" 'He's a d——d aristocrat, anyhow,' cried a third.

"But there were some who had sense enough to see that I was right, and the mob at once divided into two factions. Words led to blows. A number were killed. Three wretches rushed at me. I shot one dead, and wounded another; the third gave me a flesh wound on the head. I fled and reached here. All hope is gone; I can do nothing now but provide for our own safety."

"Yes," I replied, "we cannot remain here another night."

At half past seven, equipped for the journey, we were all upon the roof, looking for the coming of the Demon. Quincy was true to his pledge. The ladies and Mr. Phillips were first helped up to the deck of the vessel; and the men began to carry up the boxes we had collected.

Just at this moment a greater burst of tumult reached my ears. Up the street came a vast concourse of people. At their head marched a ragged fellow with a long pole.

"My God," said Max, "it is Caesar's head!"

Max and I were the last to leave the roof. We stood on the deck; the great bird swayed for an instant, and then began to rise. As the mob saw us ascend, the bullets hissed around us, but our metallic sides laughed them to scorn. The mighty city lay unrolled before us, starred here and there with burning houses. Above the trees of Union Square, my glass showed me a white line, where Caesar's column was towering to the skies, bearing the epitaph of the world.

I said to Max:

"What will those millions do to-morrow?"

"Starve," he said.

"What will they do next week?"

"Devour each other," he replied.

"Will not civil government rise again out of this ruin?"

"Not for a long time," he replied. "Then the history of the world will be slowly repeated. Mankind will re-enact the great human drama, which begins always with a tragedy, runs through a comedy, and terminates in a catastrophe."

The next day we came in sight of the shores of Europe, all in ruins. After a time the yellow sands of the desert stretch beneath us. Before us, at last, rise great blue masses, a mighty mountain range. In another hour the ship settles down from its long voyage. We are at home.

. . . . .

[These concluding lines are from the journal of Gabriel Weltstein.]

Since my return home I have not been idle. I collected and put together the letters I had written to my brother from New York, because I thought they were important, as a picture of the destruction of civilization.

I summoned a meeting of the inhabitants of our colony—about five thousand men, women and children. I need not say that they were inexpressibly shocked by the awful narrative.

The first question for us, I said, was to ascertain how to best protect ourselves from like dangers. We determined to build up a high wall that would completely cut off communication with the external world. We trained some of our young men in metal working, and they made a large supply of magazine rifles, so that every man might be well armed. We also cast a number of powerful cannon on very high wheels, which could be fired vertically in case we were attacked by airships. We housed the Demon under a shed, intending to make other air-ships like it, with which to communicate with the external world, should we desire to do so.

Having taken steps to protect ourselves from others, we then began to devise means by which we might protect ourselves from ourselves; for the worst enemies of a people are always found in their own midst, in their passions and vanities. When we had formulated our scheme of government we called our people together again; and after several days of debate it was substantially agreed upon.

In our constitution we first of all acknowledged our dependence on Almighty God; believing that no government can prosper which does not possess his blessing.

We decreed, secondly, a republican form of government. Every adult man and woman of sound mind is permitted to vote. We adopted a system of voting that we believed would insure perfect secrecy and prevent bribery—something like that which had been in vogue, in some countries, before the revolution of the Proletariat.

The highest offense known to our laws is treason against the state, and this consists not only in levying war against the government, but in corrupting the voter or the office-holder; or in the voter or office-holder selling his vote or his services. For these crimes the penalty is death.

We decreed, next, universal and compulsory education. No one can vote who cannot read and write. We abolish all private schools, except the higher institutions. We believe it to be essential to the safety of the commonwealth that the children of all the people, rich and poor, should, during the period of growth, associate together.

We mingle with abstract knowledge a cult of morality and religion, to be agreed upon by the different churches; for there are a hundred points wherein they agree to one wherein they differ. And, as to the points peculiar to each creed, we require the children to attend school only five days in the week, thus leaving one day for the parents or pastors to take charge of their religious training in addition to the care given them on Sundays.

We abolish all interest on money, and punish with imprisonment the man who receives it.

The state owns all roads, streets, telegraph or telephone lines, railroads and mines, and takes exclusive control of the mails and express matter.

As these departments will in time furnish employment for a great many officials, who might be massed together by the party in power, and wielded for political purposes, we decree that any man who accepts office relinquishes, for the time being, his right of suffrage.

Our governing body, called The People, is divided into three branches. The first is elected exclusively by the producers, to-wit: the workmen in the towns and the farmers and mechanics in the country; and those they elect must belong to their own class. As these constitute the great bulk of the people, the body that represents them stands for the House of Representatives in America. The second branch is elected exclusively by and from the merchants and manufacturers, and all who are engaged in trade, or as employers of labor. The third branch, which is the smallest, is selected by the authors, newspaper writers, artists, scientists, philosophers, and literary people generally. This branch is expected to hold the balance of power, where the other two bodies cannot agree.

No law can be passed unless it receives a majority vote in each of the three branches, or a two-thirds vote in two of them. As, however, the experience of the world has shown that there is more danger of the upper classes combining to oppress the producers, it is therefore decreed that if the Commons, by a three-fourths vote, pass any measure, it becomes a law, notwithstanding the veto of the other two branches.

The executive is elected by Congress for a period of four years, and is not eligible for re-election. He has no veto and no control of any patronage. In the election of president, a two-thirds vote of each branch is necessary.

Whenever it can be shown, in the future, that in any foreign country the wages of labor and the prosperity of the people are as high as in our own, then free trade with that people is decreed. We decree that our Congress shall have the right to fix the compensation for all forms of labor, so that wages shall never fall below a rate that will afford the laborer a comfortable living, with a margin that will enable him to provide for his old age.

We declare in the preamble of our constitution that "this government is intended to be merely a plain and simple instrument, to insure to every industrious citizen not only liberty, but an educated mind, a comfortable home, an abundant supply of food and clothing, and a pleasant, happy life."

We shall not seek to produce uniformity of recompense for all kinds of work; for we know that skilled labor is intrinsically worth more than unskilled; and there are some forms of intellectual toil that are more valuable to the world than any muscular exertion.

This government shall also regulate the number of apprentices who shall enter any given trade or pursuit.

We deny gold and silver any function as money, except for small amounts. We issue a legal-tender paper money, not to be increased beyond a certain per capita of population.

We decree a limitation upon the amount of land or money that any one man can possess. All above that must be used, either by the owner or the government, in works of public usefulness.

There is but one town in our colony, called Stanley. The republic has taken possession of the land in and contiguous to it, not already built on—paying the owners the present price; and hereafter no lots will be sold except to persons who buy to build homes for themselves; and these lots will be sold at the original cost price. Thus the opportunity of the poor to secure homes will never be diminished.

We further decree that when hereafter any towns are to be established, it shall only be by the nation itself. Whenever one hundred persons or more petition the government expressing their desire to build a town, the government shall then take possession of a sufficient tract of land, paying the intrinsic, not the artificial price therefor. It shall then give the petitioners and others the rights to take the lots at the original price, provided they make their homes on them. We shut out all speculators. No towns started in any other way shall have railroad or mail facilities.

When once a municipality is created in the way I have described, it shall provide parks for recreation; no lot shall contain less than half an acre; the streets shall be very wide and planted with fruit trees in double and treble rows. In the center of town shall be erected a town hall, with an assembly hall large enough to seat all the inhabitants. The building shall also contain free public baths, a library, a reading room, public offices, etc. The municipality shall divide the people into groups of five hundred families each, and for each group it shall furnish a physician, to be paid for out of the general taxes. It shall also provide, in the same way, concerts and dramatic representations and lectures, free of charge. The hours of labor are limited to eight each day; and there are to be two holidays in the week, Wednesday and Sunday.

We do not give any encouragement to labor-saving inventions, although we do not discard them. We think the end of government should be—not cheap goods or cheap men, but happy families. If any man makes a serviceable invention, the state purchases it, at a reasonable price, for the benefit of the people.

.   .   .   .   .

[An extract from Gabriel's journal—five years later.]

I have just left a very happy group upon the veranda—Estella and our two darling children, my mother, and Mr. and Mrs. Phillips. Max is away on his sheep farm. God has greatly blessed us and all our people. There were a few conservatives who strenuously objected at first to our reforms; but we mildly suggested that we would transfer them to the outside world. They are now the most vigorous supporters of the new order of things.

The Demon returned yesterday from a trip to the outside world. Max's forebodings have been terribly realized. Three-fourths of the human race, in the civilized lands, have been swept away. In France, and Italy, and Russia the slaughter has been most appalling. In many places the Demon sailed for hundreds of miles without seeing a human being. The wild beasts are reassuming possession of the country. In Scandinavia and northern America, where the severity of the climate somewhat mitigated the ferocity of man, some sort of government is springing up again; and the peasants have formed themselves into troops to defend their cattle and their homes against the marauders.

But civility and culture seem to have disappeared. There are no newspapers, no books, no schools, no teachers. The next generation will be simply barbarians, possessing only a few dim legends of the refinements and wonderful powers of their ancestors. Fortunate it is, indeed, that here we have preserved all the instrumentalities with which to restore, when the world is ready to receive it, the civilization of the former ages.

Our constitution has worked admirably. Not far from here has arisen the beautiful village of Lincoln. It is a joy to visit it, as I do very often.

The wide streets are planted with fruit trees, the abundance of which is free to all. Around each modest house there is a garden. There are no lordly palaces. The poor man is not worked to death; he sings while he works. No dread shadow of hunger hangs over him. We are breeding men, not millionaires.

And the good wife sings also, for she remembers that this is the night of the play; and yonder lies the dress which her daughter is to wear to the weekly ball. And her sons are greatly interested in the lectures on chemistry and history.

Let us look in upon them at their supper. The merry, rosy faces of young and old; the cheerful converse; the plain and abundant food. The father is telling how the municipality bought, some three years ago, a large number of female calves at a small cost; and now they are milch-cows; and the town authorities are about to give one to each poor family that is without one.

And they praise this work; they love mankind, and the good, kindly government—their own government—which so cares for humanity and strives to lift it up. And then the father explains that each person who now receives a cow is to bring the first female calf raised by that cow, and the city will care for that, too, and then bestow it upon some other poor family; and so, in endless rotation, the organized benevolence does its work.

But come; they have finished their supper and are preparing to go to the play. Let us follow them. How the streets swarm! Not with the dark and terrible throngs that dwell so vividly in my memory, but a joyous crowd. And here we are at the door of the playhouse.

There is no fumbling to find the coins that can perhaps be but poorly spared; but, free as the streets, the doors stand open. The actors are their own townspeople—young men and women who have shown an aptitude for the art; they have been trained at the cost of the town, and are paid a small stipend for their services once a week.

And how little it costs to make mankind happy!

And what do we miss in all this joyous scene? Why, where are the wolves that used to prowl through the towns and cities of the world that has passed away? The slinking, sullen, bloody-mouthed miscreants, who would spring upon, and tear, and destroy the poor, shrieking, innocent people—where are they?

Ah! this is the difference: The government, which formerly fed and housed these monsters, under cunning kennels of perverted law, and broke open holes in the palisades of society, that they might crawl through and devastate the community, now shuts up every crevice through which they could enter; stops every hole of opportunity; crushes down every uprising instinct of cruelty and selfishness. And the wolves have disappeared; and our little world is a garden of peace and beauty, musical with laughter.

And mankind moves with linked hands through happy lives to happy deaths; and God smiles down upon them from his throne beyond the stars.

4

The Diothas

or, A Far Look Ahead

by **Ismar Thiusen**

(John Macnie)

New York
G. P. Putnam's Sons
27 and 29 West 23d Street
1883

is of considerable interest in the history of utopian thought in the United States, quite apart from whatever intrinsic merit there may be in *The Diothas*. This book was not widely read and is now rare and little known, but the charge persists that it was from this work that Bellamy took the plot and substance of *Looking Backward*, published five years after Macnie's utopia.

Macnie was born in Glasgow, Scotland, and received his bachelor's degree from Glasgow University. He came to this country in 1867 and taught, first at Easton, Connecticut, and later at the Newburgh (N. Y.) Preparatory School, an institution of some renown. His reputation as a Greek and Latin scholar was such that Yale University awarded him an honorary master's degree in 1874. His major field of interest, however, was mathematics, and in 1876 he published *A Treatise on the Theory and Solution of Algebraic Equations*, and in 1895, *Elements of Geometry, Plane and Solid*. Macnie went to the newly established University of North Dakota in 1885 to teach mathematics, physics, ancient and modern languages, and literature. He remained there for 22 years, retiring in 1907. Macnie was unquestionably a man of wide learning and scholarly ability, and the respect of his colleagues at the University of North Dakota is attested by the perpetuation of his name on one of the campus dormitories. His contribution to the life of the university in its early development even included authorship of the words of its Alma Mater.

The question of Bellamy's plagiarism from *The Diothas* is a matter which seems likely to remain ambiguous, inasmuch as the available evidence, beyond intrinsic similarities in the two texts, is almost entirely circumstantial and hearsay. Arthur Morgan, as a strong proponent of Bellamy, has very ingeniously tried to absolve him from any taint of plagiarism from Macnie or others. His brief comments in the volume *Edward Bellamy* are expanded in a pamphlet, *Plagiarism in Utopia* (Yellow Springs, Ohio, 1944). There is no real evidence that Macnie and Bellamy were acquainted before the publication of *The Diothas*, but there is very good reason to believe that they had met while Macnie was in Connecticut and New York, and that they had talked or corresponded before either published his utopia. The authorship of *The Diothas* was so carefully guarded at the time of its publication that neither publisher nor reviewers were aware of the identity of Macnie. Morgan admits fairly strong hearsay evidence from former colleagues of Macnie at the University of North Dakota that he had indeed sent a copy of the manuscript to Bellamy, and that he was somewhat irritated at the unacknowledged use of his material by Bellamy. The identity of literary devices, even to the name of the heroines, stretches the bounds of coincidence, although little weight should be attached to the employment by both of the technique of hypnosis to get the hero out of this world and into utopia, for this was a fairly standard device of the period. There are numerous points of similarity and identity, but the most nearly conclusive evidence that Bellamy and Macnie were acquainted is the biographical sketch which Macnie appended to *The Diothas*, in which he suggests that an anonymous friend, "E——," was the source and stimulation of the ideas he embodied in his tale. The personal portrait which Macnie draws of this friend "E——" could hardly fit any other person of the period than Edward Bellamy. In this evidence of previous acquaintance, Morgan finds grounds for the inference that Macnie simply beat Bellamy to publication by five years, and that Bellamy was probably not the "chief borrower." In the absence of any actual evidence, such an inference indicates little except the warmth of Morgan's feeling for Bellamy.

Much more important than these undocumentable inferences, however, is an analysis of the intrinsic differences in both substance and principle of the utopian speculation presented in the two books. It seems relatively unimportant whether Bellamy did actually take over for his purposes the literary vehicle suggested by Macnie. Also of relative triviality is the fact that Macnie, for all his shrewdness, was ridiculously inept in his predictions of technological progress in the world of A.D. 9600, while Bellamy's sublime optimism enabled him to envision quite a few useful devices which closely approximate the technical achievements of 1950. The important part of these utopian speculations is the form of the social structure which each presents and the method by which they propose that the ideal can be achieved from existing circumstances. It is difficult to assess Macnie's speculation, for it is doubtful whether he himself took it very seriously, a point upon which there is certainly no question in regard to Edward Bellamy's appraisal of his own writings. For one thing, it is questionable how much of *The Diothas* was intended by Macnie as gentle satire of the ideas of his friend "E——." Certainly, the biographical sketch of "E——," while friendly, betrays amusement at his ideas rather than conviction. Of "E——'s" hostility to law, Macnie remarks that it is his "strangest crotchet."

The positive elements in Macnie's speculation are, therefore, suggestive rather than systematic. It is a pity that he did not further elaborate his ideas, for *The Diothas* contains in embryo what might have been the most modern and the most profound utopia of the nineteenth century. Macnie had no hope of an immediate transformation of men and institutions; instead he set the date for the realization of order in society over 7500 years in the future. He was discouragingly realistic about the slow and tortuous development of society through dictatorship, world wars, and the devastation of monopolies of power. The most significant aspect of Macnie's thought, however, is his conviction that social order can be achieved only through law; he evidences little confidence in the innate goodness of men. Law must operate to achieve order in the institutional structure of society before there will be any possibility that men can achieve that degree of self-control which gives promise of the ideal society.

These ideas are but suggestions in Macnie's work; even had they been elaborated, their reception and influence would probably have been negligible. Bellamy was the spokesman of the utopian ideas and anticipations of the period; if Macnie's ideas were what *The Diothas* suggests that they were, they were anachronistic and would have been ill-received by men in 1883. After the popular success of *Looking Backward*, Macnie republished his work in two editions (1890), the American edition titled *A Far Look Ahead, or, The Diothas,* and the English edition under the title *Looking Forward; or, The Diothas;* both retained the pseudonym Ismar Thiusen. The English edition was apparently more successful than the American, but neither had any appreciable audience.

Because the romantic tale of *The Diothas* had to be sacrificed in the following selection to the exposition of Macnie's ideas, it should be noted that Diotha is the name of the family who befriend the visitor to utopia, and Ismar Thiusen is the name of the visitor translated into the language of A.D. 9600.

The Diothas

"What you assert is as incomprehensible as it is strange."

My old friend, usually so earnestly matter-of-fact, now so mysteriously earnest, regarded me with a quiet smile, much as an elder listens to the objections of a child.

"You have it in your power to judge for yourself, subject to the conditions already mentioned."

As I gazed at my interlocutor, his serene confidence began to dispel my incredulity, and produce that condition of trusting belief in his power demanded as an indispensable prerequisite for the purpose in view. What we intensely desire to be true, we strongly, almost inevitably, tend to accept as true.

"I am willing to try the experiment," said I, after a long pause.

"Remember the conditions," was the response. "Your mind is

imaginative and poetical; mine logical, and fairly stored with science and history. It is necessary to the success of our experiment, that your mind submit entirely to the guidance of mine."

"I consent," was my reply. "Let us begin at once."

Rising without a word from his seat on the opposite side of the fireplace, he turned down the lamp, so as to leave only a subdued light. Then, standing on the rug before me, he began to make the peculiar passes employed by mesmerists,—to whose influence, I may remark in passing, I have always been highly susceptible. Gradually the objects before me grew indistinct: the multitudinous noises of the busy street below died away to a gentle murmur, like the sound of distant waves. That, too, ceased. I was wrapped in a profound and dreamless sleep.

Suddenly I awoke. My friend was standing in the same position as before, and was regarding me intently, not without some appearance of anxiety. The apartment presented its usual appearance, as I could well see, the lamp being now turned up. Full of disappointment, I supposed the experiment to have failed. For there I was, as wide awake, apparently, as ever I had been, with no sign of anything unusual in my surroundings.

Evidently reading my feelings in my countenance, he said, pointing toward the door,—

"Beyond that slight partition you will find that future society upon which you have so often curiously speculated. It is now in your power to see and judge for yourself."

While speaking he had approached the door. After a momentary hesitation, I followed, and passed through. Outside, instead of the familiar landing and the stairs up which I had so often wearily plodded, extended, far as I could see, a fairly lighted corridor of handsome proportions. In surprise I turned involuntarily toward the door through which I had just passed: but that, too, had vanished. The corridor extended, apparently, as far in that direction as in the other. For the moment, at least, we two seemed to be the only occupants of this seemingly endless gallery. Smiling at my look of amazement, my companion said,—

"You seem surprised; but are you quite certain of never having seen this place before?"

"Absolutely certain!" was my emphatic reply.

My companion regarded me with a look of keen inquiry, seemed to repress some observation that rose to his lips, but went on to say,—

"On passing at a step from the nineteenth to the ninety-sixth century, you must naturally expect to find many changes. The New York you knew and dwelt in crumbled into dust almost eighty centuries ago, in the ages that are now regarded as the twilight of history. Its fragments form only the lowermost layer of the five fathoms deep of detritus on which the present city stands, the accumulated remains of a succession of cities, each more magnificent than its predecessor."

Meanwhile we had reached and entered one of the recesses from which the corridor seemed to receive its light. This recess was closed toward the street by a single sheet of glass, presenting no visible outlet. It yielded, however, to a gentle push from my companion, and, turning on a central pivot, offered a means of exit by which we passed to the open air. I was struck with amazement at the spectacle before me. How different this from the Broadway up which I had sauntered but a few hours before!

Manhattan Island, as might have been expected, had, long ages before, become, so to say, one enormous warehouse,—the chief port of entry for a population of more than a thousand millions. Space was far too valuable to be occupied with dwelling-houses. Besides, with their wonderful facilities for locomotion, a distance of fifty miles from the center of business was of less consequence than five at present.

All this, of course, was not learned during the few minutes I devoted to gazing at the buildings. They so engrossed my attention for the moment, that I bestowed scarcely a glance on the busy traffic at my feet. I not only asked no questions, but forgot even the presence of my companion, who stood by in silence. Soon, however, my eyes wandered from the works of man to man himself. From where I stood, only imperfect glimpses could be obtained of the numerous throng passing along the arcades. I readily assented, therefore, to my companion's proposal to descend to the busiest arcade, that a story below.

On reaching the main arcade, I found ample occupation for eye and mind in noting the person and costume of the handsome race whose representatives, of both sexes, were passing along with an elastic step that gave token rather of repressed energy than of feverish haste. The feminine costume, the most simple as well as graceful that had ever met my eye, appeared to me, unversed in such matters, to consist, as regards the upper portion, of a loose tunic of some white or grayish material. This was confined round the waist by a silken sash or girdle, and, when thus girded up, reached to about midway between knee and ankle. The tunic was, however, of such a length as to reach the instep when not sustained by the girdle. The lower part of the costume consisted of a sort of Turkish trousers confined round the ankles.

The wearers of this costume displayed no other covering on their heads than their luxuriant masses of wavy hair, gathered into a graceful knot, with or without braids; or allowed to flow freely behind, confined, at most, by a ribbon. This fashion of allowing the hair to hang down was confined, as I afterwards learned, to maidens not betrothed. Matrons and betrothed maidens were, again, distinguished by other peculiarities in the arrangement of their hair. This was both prescribed by express law, and established by what is yet stronger,—custom of immemorial ages.

"How is it," I inquired at last, "that we meet but one class of the population? These, I suppose, belong to the aristocracy of your city,—a noble and handsome race indeed. But where are the working classes? For some time I have been looking around for a specimen, but in vain. All seem to belong to a superior class."

"We have no aristocracy," was the reply, "if by that you mean a class living in idleness by the toil of others. Nor have we any working-class, if you mean a class that spends its life in toil that leaves no leisure for their development as intellectual beings. Such as these you so greatly admire compose the only class among us. You may call them an aristocracy if by that you mean a cultivated and ruling class, for such they are. You may also call them the working-class, for all support themselves by their own exertions."

"What!" I exclaimed. "That must imply Communism, or something like it."

"No; Communism, in the sense you mean, does not exist among us. Each is the owner of whatever property he acquires, whether by gift or his own exertions. But public opinion stigmatizes idleness as the meanest of vices, the fruitful parent of other vices, and of crime also. Now, it has been ascertained, by careful computation and by experiment, that if every able-bodied person in a community works between three and four hours every day, at some productive employment, the result will supply all with every necessary and comfort of life, with something to spare. Allowing ten hours for sleep and refreshment, there remain still ten for mental improvement, and such unproductive pursuits as individual taste may prefer.

"If any live in idleness, it is evident that others must toil to support them. Time-honored custom, therefore, requires that all children, whether boys or girls, shall acquire some handicraft. For the present, I must defer a full account of our social arrangements to some other occasion. I shall merely remark, that we consider the body as well as the mind to stand in need of due exercise to preserve it in sound condition. It has been found, that no physical exercise is so beneficial and pleasing as labor skilfully directed toward some definite object. All, therefore, whether possessing much or little, men and women, young and old, spend a certain number of hours each day in some productive employment, and no more dream of having their work done by others than of having eating, sleeping, or digestion performed by a deputy. In universal industry has been found a panacea for the worst of the evils that for long ages were the curse of society and the despair of legislators. Our labor, however, is not drudgery. We merely guide: the real work is performed by forces once allowed to go to waste."

Following my guide, I entered a vehicle standing near the curbstone on a sort of siding. Just before the car started, another passenger entered,—a lovely girl. I chanced to turn my eyes that way, as she momentarily paused in the doorway,—the pause of a dove about to alight. Many beautiful faces had come under my observation during our progress along the arcades: none, indeed, but beautiful faces were to be seen. But none had for me such an inexplicable attraction as that of the fair girl now appearing at the entrance. She was introduced under the name of Reva Diotha; I, as Ismar Thiusen. This name, which I did not recognize at the time as having any similitude to that I had hitherto borne, was really its legitimate descendant, according to the same law of phonetic change that had transformed my friend's name to Utis Estai.

Scarcely had we entered the car when Reva perceived a bevy of girls of her own age. She forsook us at once, with a smile and a bow, and hastened over to her fair friends. Just then the train slackened its pace. Utis and I alighted amid a crowd of passengers, among whom I lost sight of Reva; and presently we two were left alone on the platform, giving a last glance to the train as it vanished round a distant curve.

"You may look about here for a few moments," said Utis, "but do not wander far. I will not be long absent."

We had left the train at what appeared to be a small village. My attention was specially drawn toward the housetops. On these could be seen masses of dense foliage, which, seeming to overflow, draped the battlement-shaped cornices. This, to me, novel architectural embellishment was, as I afterwards found, in general use, even in the city. I was in the midst of these observations when Utis reappeared. He was seated on a vehicle, which, under his guidance, glided noiselessly as a canoe over the smooth concrete. The vehicle was, in form and construction, not unlike a two-seated tricycle. The motive power, however, was not supplied by the muscles of the rider, but by a compact electric motor, placed beneath the seat.

First starting at a moderate speed, we crossed the open square, then proceeded at a rapidly increasing rate down the main street of the village. A clear note, like that from a silver horn, and emitted from an instrument governed by a key inserted in the tiller, served to give warning of our approach.

"How do you like this?" said Utis, when our speed rose first to fifteen, then to twenty, miles an hour. "But now brace yourself!" he exclaimed, as we reached the brow of a long declivity. A glance, to assure himself of a clear roadway, a warning blast from the sounder, and down we flew with a velocity that reminded me of my once-enough experience on the cow-catcher of a locomotive. Such was the momentum imparted to the vehicle, that it carried us far up the opposite acclivity.

"What speed can these machines attain?" I inquired, with a lively recollection of our recent spin down the slope.

"On a level they easily maintain a speed of twenty miles an hour: on a long descent, they are never allowed to attain the velocity they might reach, for obvious considerations."

At this moment the long, clear blast of the sounder was heard from behind. After a brief interval a single rider on his curricle dashed past us at a rapid rate that soon took him out of sight.

"You see the white line running along the centre of the road," resumed Utis. "The rule of the road requires that line to be kept on the left, except when passing a vehicle in front. Then the line may be crossed, provided the way on that side is clear."

Meanwhile we had turned into a by-road, narrower, indeed, than that by which we had travelled so far, but with quite as smooth a surface, and bordered by fine trees. Yet another turn, this time into a pathway little more than wide enough for the passage of our vehicle, and we came to a halt beneath a porch projecting from the spacious veranda that surrounded the house.

"This is my home," said Utis, as we alighted, "and yours, too, till you weary of it."

By the time we reached home it was time for the mid-day collation. After this informal repast, Utis carried me off to his indoor retreat, a combination of study and workshop. Here was a workbench of ingenious mechanical construction, a lathe, and various tools adapted for delicate operations on glass or metal. From these articles, of which I had but little knowledge, I soon turned my attention to the contents of the book-cases. The number of volumes was not great,—about a thousand, besides a cyclopaedia in one hundred volumes.

"You see before you," said Utis, noting the direction of my eyes, "the distilled quintessence of the learning and genius of twelve thousand years."

"It seems but a small space to contain so much," said I doubtfully, calling to mind the immense libraries of London and Paris.

"The first hundred volumes or so, on the upper shelves, represent the world-classics, down to the twentieth century, the best of each great name comprised in a single volume. Life is too short for becoming acquainted with any but the very best. The next four hundred volumes represent the classics that have appeared since the twentieth century. All the rest are standard works of reference.

"As for the works of reference, as soon as one is superseded by a later and better work, it is relegated to the shelves of the great depository. Besides this central library, each State possesses a more manageable collection, of a million volumes, or so. The central depository is consulted chiefly for very special researches. Your father spent many an hour there, examining a unique collection of documents bearing on the nineteenth century. Here are two volumes of his works, which it is difficult for me to imagine as not familiar to your eyes."

As may be supposed, the work referred to was viewed by me with feelings of lively interest. Numberless questions occurred to me.

"I should wish to obtain some insight into your social system," said I. "Some glimpses I have, but these serve merely to excite my curiosity to know more. I understand that all among you are equal, socially, politically, and, to a large extent, in wealth also. Now, granting that such a state of things could once be brought about, how is it made permanent? How, in fine, are you able to arrest the operation of that economic law, once considered inevitable as the law of gravitation,—the tendency of some to rise above the average, of others to sink below it?"

"You have there stated in a few words," replied Utis, "a question requiring volumes of history for a fair answer. In the first place, however, I would warn you to disabuse your mind of those crude generalizations once known as economic laws."

What I learned in regard to the origin of the social condition and government of his period was communicated to me by Utis in a series of conversations. I here give the substance of these conversations, adhering to the original form as closely as is permitted by the comparative inferiority of our language as a medium of expression.

"The more or less democratical forms of government," he began, "that rose on the ruins of the decayed monarchical and aristocratical systems of your time, soon showed symptoms of decay. Loudly claiming to be the embodiment of justice and natural right, they soon rivalled the worst of former despotisms in corruption, and highhanded disregard of individual rights. The better disposed of their citizens had time to take alarm, on seeing the downward course of their neighbors. They resolved no longer to be oppressed under the forms of liberty, and robbed in the name of law.

"In the excitement of the times, many things were done that a cooler posterity has not approved. Here, in the United States, for example, the eighth article of the Constitution was abrogated by an enormous majority, in order to attain the means of bringing to justice the worst of the monopolists and their legislative tools. Trial by jury, having fallen into utter contempt, was abolished, except in political trials. Offences against the person were punished according to the *lex talionis*. The murderer was put to death, as nearly as possible in the manner he had slain his victim. In atrocious cases he was handed over to the mercies of physiological experimentists, to endure what they saw fit in the interests of the humanity he had violated.

"An earnest attempt, finally successful, was made to stamp out the criminal classes. The thief found guilty for the third time was put to death as incorrigible, painlessly as might be, but inexorably. The lazy and shiftless were gathered into what they soon found were workhouses in more than name, means being taken that effectually put it out of their power to curse society with a progeny similar to themselves. These severe measures elicited, at first, loud shrieks from the maudlin sympathizers with crime,—the Hugos and Dickenses of the period. But, finding themselves treated with contemptuous disregard, they finally held their peace.

"The two sets of nations developing thus on such divergent lines became known, finally, as Absolutists and Liberals. The Absolutists believed, or pretended to believe, that the rule of an intelligent despot is the highest type of government. This theory found eloquent advocates, whose zeal was not allowed to go unrewarded. The Liberals held the opposite view, but never found it worth while arguing the matter. For centuries Absolutists and Liberals, in spite of occasional bickering, and a few trials of strength, continued to develop, each in their own way attaining a high degree of material prosperity. But at last arose a great military genius. By a series of successful campaigns, he reduced all the Absolutist monarchies under one huge empire. He next attacked and overwhelmed, in spite of a desperate resistance, the Liberal nations of the Old World.

"Fired with the hope of universal empire, he next resolved on the subjugation of America. Never was the cause of liberty in greater peril. For almost a full year he held the whole Atlantic region; but finally, at a cost still frightful to recall, the invader was first checked, then driven back toward the coast, and, at last, captured with what remained of his army. The vanquished monarch would fain have prated of generosity to a fallen foe; but the gray-haired farmer, whom the course of events had raised to the dictatorship, took no such view. He sternly replied,—

" 'This has been no childish game. Two millions of our people have perished. Your success meant death to us: ours means death to you, and the system you represent.'

"The dictator kept his word. Within six months he carried out his threat by hanging, in his own capital, the 'Last of the Despots,' in company with all his ministers and chief officers. There had been but slight resistance. The nations joyfully accepted the free institutions for which they had long secretly pined. Despotism had received its final blow. A sort of federal union of nations was then formed, by which all became pledged to preserve a republican form of government throughout the world, and to guarantee to each nation the integrity of its territory, even amicable arrangements for transfer or union being subject to the approval of all.

"Since then, the progress of mankind in good government has been peaceful and continuous. The stern temper generated by the long struggle between rival principles gradually softened away; though the maxims, 'Resist the beginnings of evil,' and 'Mercy to the bad is cruelty to the good,' have become settled principles of action.

"Our main reliance, after all, is upon education. The training of the young is regarded as the one great duty, both of the family and of the State. Having no army, no navy, no expensive hierarchy of public functionaries, we are able to devote a great part of our energies and resources to this most important of duties. The acquisition of the knowledge to be obtained from books, though by no means neglected, we regard as the least important branch of education. Regarding a sound, equally developed body as the foundation of all the rest, we impart to our youth of both sexes a twofold physical training. The aesthetic training includes such exercises as tend to impart activity and grace. The industrial training includes such training as shall make the hands the reliable servants of the brain. Morals, including politeness, self-government, the acquisition of lofty ideals of conduct, we regard as specially, though not exclusively, the province of family training. At special schools, when arrived at a suitable age, the young receive instruction in the handicraft they intend to practise during life.

"The acquaintance with the tools of knowledge is usually obtained by the age of fifteen. At this age the boy,—I say boy, as I shall speak of his further training; though up to this point boys and girls receive the same training,—the boy, I say, is expected to have a fair mastery of language as an instrument of expression, and a slight knowledge of literature. I say a slight knowledge, because he has hitherto been carefully kept from indiscriminate reading. He is expected also to possess all the mathematical knowledge required for his further studies. In addition to drawing, photography, and similar aids, he has acquired the management of the most important tools, and has had practice in the working of metals and other materials. His handicraft is chosen for him."

"Can he not choose for himself?" I inquired.

"The matter is arranged somewhat as follows: if my son, for example, wishes to follow my pursuit, he may do so; since there are many evident advantages in doing so. But if, as is often the case, he does not wish to do so, he adopts the line of work assigned to him. A certain number of each class of employments is assigned to each district every year, and divided among the boys of the proper age. Much latitude is permissible, however, in the carrying out of this law; and none is made to adopt a trade to which he has a decided objection. As a great part of every trade is performed by machinery, and the boys have already great manual skill, a year suffices for them to master their handicraft. Then begins the serious study of his professional, skilled, or artistic pursuit."

"Has everyone two occupations?" I inquired.

"Yes; each follows two employments; some like myself, three. My handicraft is, as you have seen, bolt-making,—that of my father before me. By profession I am a physician. But there is so little call for my advice in my speciality, that first as an amusement, now as a business, I make the finer parts of microscopes."

During an interval in the labor of the following morning, Utis informed me that business called him that day to Nuiorc. Under ordinary circumstances he would make the journey by rail. But he now proposed to go by curricle, in order to afford me an opportunity of seeing the country.

My attention was frequently called, as we sped along, to spots of high historic interest. But to me the names were without interest, awoke no associations. We entered the city by one of the avenues assigned to the use of curricles. This was called the Avenue of Sciences. The emblematic statues, at the cross-streets, represented the various sciences in the persons of the two, one of each sex, who had most highly contributed to the advancement of that science.

Some account has already been given of the earlier education of the youth of the period. The fundamental training imparted in the schools and academies within easy reach of every home was so thorough, that upon it any superstructure could be raised. Years of effort were not wasted upon the acquisition of the language of a dead and buried civilization, in gaining more or less insight—usually less—into a system of thought, that, upon most matters of vital interest, is soon found, notwithstanding its charm of expression, to be crude to the verge of childishness.

Here each study had a well-defined purpose, as part of a carefully devised system of mental culture, in which the balance was nicely adjusted between the desirable and the attainable. Education was not looked upon as merely the special business of a few years, a task to be hurried over during the period of immature mental development. It was rather regarded as the main business of life, to which all else was merely accessory.

Each district had, accordingly, an institution for higher education, resorted to by some five hundred young people, for about four hours, on six days in the week. In these institutions, whether by local teachers, or by lectures delivered by the highest accepted authorities on special subjects, the young continued their education, concurrently with other duties, till marriage. The earliest legal age for this was twenty-five for men, and twenty-three for women. The young couple usually started on a two months' wedding journey and, on their return, it was usual for both to spend six months, at least, at some great university, to receive the finishing touches to their education.

The advanced study of certain subjects, medicine for example, could not be entered upon till after marriage, a great majority of physicians being women. Those, of course, that intended to make medicine a specialty, went through a more extended course. But, whatever else might be studied during the six months' residence, every woman was expected to go through a prescribed course, adapted to render her, on ordinary occasions, the physician of her own household. This was more feasible, because, while medicine had really become a science, the simple, regular course of life led by all had long banished the complicated ailments that now tax the skill of the physician. In like manner every man was required to go through such a course of law as rendered him capable of holding the official positions that all, in rotation, were obliged to accept. For, strange to say, office was no longer sought after as a boon worthy the sacrifice of every vestige of truth, honor, and self-respect, but was merely accepted with resignation, yet without repugnance, as an unavoidable duty to the community.

Of all the social changes brought under my notice, none surprised me more than the stringency of the laws governing the family relation. For the first time in the history of our race, the influence of women made itself directly felt in legislation. This influence, purifying in every direction, was especially active in the repression of the twin evils from which their sex had been the severest, and, for too long, the helpless, sufferers.

Intemperance was made simply impossible by a total prohibition, under severe penalties, of the manufacture or possession of intoxicating beverages. The wonderful improvement effected in the condition of society by a few years of this *régime* reconciled to it even those who, on general principles, had been most violently opposed to prohibitory legislation. The cessation of the enormous amount of waste of various kinds, estimated to amount to fully one-fifth of the total productive capacity of the community, was found to make all the difference between the existence of an ever-increasing substratum of hopeless poverty and a general diffusion of comfort and independence.

The purifying influence of women was nowhere more conspicuously exerted than in the legislation that tended to the protection of the sex that too long had been the slave or victim, despised or petted or flattered, of the coarser sex. Seduction was treated as a serious crime,—as, in certain cases, the basest and most cruel of crimes. The seducer was not, indeed, compelled to marry his victim, but was given the option between such reparation and being rendered incapable of offending again in that way. If one, or both, of the guilty parties was already married, both were purged from the land, unless it could be proved that one had sinned in ignorance.

Nor were these laws allowed to remain inoperative. The woman was tried by a judge and a jury of her own sex, who generally proved inexorable in vindicating the outraged dignity of womanhood. The condemnation of the woman necessarily drew after it that of the man. The stronger sex thus learned to be extremely guarded in its intercourse with the sex so long regarded as the lawful prey of the stronger. The state of things in which such laws had been necessary had, however, at the period of which I am writing, become as remote as is to us the society of the palaeolithic period. Offences that society now easily condones had become practically impossible, if for no other reason, because the idea of them would have aroused as instinctive an abhorrence as among us would the idea of dining on a tender infant.

Marriage being regarded as the most important step in life, and practically irrevocable,—for divorce, though allowed by the law in certain specified cases, was almost unknown,—the intercourse of the young people of both sexes was surrounded by a number of restrictions. These had for object the prevention of hasty choice and too early union. Till the age of twelve, there was no difference in the training of boys or girls. They attended the same classes, joined in the same sports. At twelve a slight change was made in the style of dress, as also in the course of study. The girls henceforth wore the *selvan*, or long tunic, and attained to the dignity of a colored border to the same. The boys now had their long hair cut short, and began to wear the shorter male tunic.

From this time till the age of seventeen, though the young people mostly attended the same classes, they sat separately. Much freedom of intercourse was still allowed, though always under the supervision of watchful matrons, who each takes her turn in what is regarded as an important public duty. If, toward the end of this period, the buddings of a more tender feeling make themselves felt, forewarned on the subject by their mother, and so trained as not to consider such a feeling as any thing to be ashamed of, they do not hesitate to make of her a confidant. If on any account,—too near propinquity of blood, or for any similar reason,—the mother does not think the feeling ought to be encouraged, she truthfully explains to them her reasons, and advises with them as a tender friend, trying, if necessary, the effect of absence. The girls, indeed, she aids as far as may be done; but, knowing that they are always certain of a suitable match if they choose to marry, her chief anxiety is about her son, who runs the chance of being obliged to pass an unwedded life. For him she anxiously studies the maiden toward whom his thoughts turn, and imparts the results of this study in appropriate advice as to the best means of attracting her thoughts toward him, and the most fitting manner of indicating his regard.

If a young man is rejected, even when the disappointment is most severe, he is expected to take the matter quietly. He merely anticipates the usual term of expatriation, and departs at once on the course of public duty and education that intervenes between seventeen and twenty-five. Even if successful in inducing the object of his preference to bind up for him her locks, he is still only on probation. For two months he is allowed to enjoy as much of her society as is consistent with the entirely probationary nature of their relation. Within doors their interviews always take place in the presence, though not necessarily within earshot, of the mother, or else someone entitled to take her place. He may also take her out every day for a ride on the high-road in his curricle. At this stage of courtship, no familiarities whatever are permissible; for the maiden may at any time break off the matter by re-appearing with tresses free and unrestrained.

By the end of the two months, the maiden has had time to make up her mind as to whether she will enter the first betrothal. By this ceremony she passes from the ranks of the *vioran* (from *vio*, a bud, whence *viora*, a budding beauty) to the ranks of the *zeruan* (from *zer*, a hand, whence *zeru*, a clasped hand, and *zerua*, a plighted maiden). The ceremony takes place in the presence of all members of both families that can at all conveniently attend. Rings are exchanged; and, for the first time, he gives her a kiss. They part immediately, not to meet again for probably, a full year.

Although, as before stated, there was neither army nor navy to maintain, there was, nevertheless, a sort of conscription in force that exacted for public purposes the service of all young men between the ages of seventeen and twenty-five. By these conscripts, called *zerdars*, were performed those labors which, however useful or indispensable, are not attractive as life employments to those not compelled to follow them.

At seventeen each young man was expected to report for duty at a certain place. There, unless allowed to return home for another year, he was at once assigned to some duty, always at a distance from home. According as exigency required, any *zerdar* might become a sailor, a miner, a member of the sanitary police, and so on. The nature of the training they had received rendered them fully competent for the management of the machinery that had superseded muscular labor in every department of life. In order to give the *zerdars* the educational advantage of becoming familiar, in turn, with every great division of the world, its climate, and its productions, the various nations had established a sort of universal labor exchange, somewhat on the plan of the postal unions of the present. In this way, during his seven or eight years of service, each *zerdar* would visit every part of the world, and certainly gain an extensive knowledge of mankind; no impediment existing in the way of difference of language, or class feeling, to prevent free social or intellectual intercourse.

All this time, too, he was receiving good pay, and his education was carefully attended to. A certain portion of every day was assigned to advanced studies under teachers of the highest class. This, indeed, was the busiest and most hard-worked part of a man's life, the dangers of idleness being guarded against by almost constant occupation. This the young submitted to cheerfully, looking forward, as they did, to an assured life of comparative ease on the expiration of their period of service. Though subject to an organization and discipline, resembling, in some degree, that of our armies, the *zerdars* were not quartered in barracks, but were assigned to homes among the households of the place where duty detained them. With all the facility of youth, the young man soon felt at home amid his new surroundings, and really accorded to his temporary guardians the respect and duty he had been trained to show his parents. At the season when transferred from one post of duty to another, each *zerdar* was allowed a furlough of a month or six weeks, in which to transport himself to his new sphere of duty. The transfers took place for one-half the number in spring, for the other half in autumn. In this way was secured the most desirable season of the year for travelling. At the close of his term of service, the *zerdar*, now a *manra*, or full citizen, was generally in haste to return home to claim the long-promised bride.

While the young men, as *zerdars*, did service to the community and completed their education abroad, the girls, whether *viora* or *zerua*, went through a somewhat similar experience at home. It was by their fair hands that, under skilful guidance, all the cooking and baking for the community were performed at the cooking depots, or laboratories as they should rather be called. Their tasks were carefully adjusted to their years and strength. Besides, the muscular exertion required was but slight. Machines of ingenious construction, demanding little beyond the guidance of mind, performed equally the most laborious and the most complex operations. By the hands of the maidens of the community, also, or, rather, under their guidance, was performed the large amount of laundry-work rendered necessary by the frequent customary changes of clothing.

As scientific investigators, women had shown a special predilection for chemistry and biology, as was readily seen on referring to any of the standard works on those subjects. As inventors they had, since education gave them a grasp of the principles of mechanics, enriched the world with many notable inventions.

Of these I will mention only two, both in photography, or, rather, in the extensive field of applied science of which photography is merely the humble beginning. These remarkable inventions, called respectively the *varzeo* and the *lizeo*, were, indeed, characteristically feminine in their purpose and application, as were the great majority of woman's inventions. By means of the one she was enabled, as in a magic mirror, and almost as well as if there present, to behold those distant scenes to which she had less free access than man,— before marriage, at least. By means of the other was presented to her eyes, endowed with the movement of life, the loved form separated by distance or death.

I have no intention of entering into a detailed statement of the prevailing forms of belief. The heterodoxy of one age is the orthodoxy of another: the devout statement of one would be outraged by the current belief of a succeeding age. I need merely state, that all believed in God, and in a future existence. There were two great schools of thought on this subject, which, in their general characteristics, reminded me of the saying, that all men are born either Platonists or Aristotelians. To one or other of these, individuals gave their assent, in accordance, as far as I could judge, with an inborn mental bias.

This was the more perceptible, seeing that all were left perfectly free to follow this bias. Parents did not feel justified in prejudicing the case by impressing their own religious opinions upon the unformed and helpless minds of children. When the proper time came, the distinctive views of the divine nature were displayed before the youth or maiden, with a warning not to come to a hasty decision. At least a year of reflection was enjoined before they should definitely unite with one or the other communion. The children attended a sort of Sunday-school, where they received instruction in morals, and in the fundamental truths of natural theology. Their instructors were chiefly the young people not yet admitted to the assembly of those who had definitely adopted a doctrine and a communion.

It was justly considered, that the attempt to force difficult questions upon the notice of immature or unprepared minds will generally result in a permanent aversion to the entire subject of which they form a part. It was strictly prohibited to print any reading of a kind unsuitable for unripe minds. Short of this, there was complete liberty of printing.

On one occasion, when conversing with Utis on this matter of unsuitable literature, I heard him express himself with the utmost indignation in regard to our carelessness about a matter concerning the highest interests, both of state and family. He could not, indeed, find words strong enough to utter his amazement at the cynical indifference of our legislators in regard to what the prejudices of his education taught him to look upon as one of the most abominable of crimes,—the pollution of the mind of youth by means of printed filth.

"A little more than two thousand years before your time," he went on, "the people of a certain great city were accustomed to sacrifice their children to an idol. What was the opinion of your period regarding this?"

"It was regarded by all that ever heard of it as an abomination, a wickedness almost inconceivable," was my reply.

"Yet, in my opinion," said Utis, "their conduct was noble and humane in comparison with that of your contemporaries. In their blind way, these people whom you so abhorred, were doing their duty as they understood it, while yours shamefully neglected theirs.

"There is a certain tragic grandeur in the idea of a father giving up his best beloved, perhaps his only child, to perish in fiery torments, in order to insure the safety of the commonwealth. We pity, we almost admire, even while we condemn. The fathers of your times I cannot but despise when I think, that, whether from indifference or cowardice, they allowed devilish miscreants to earn a despicable livelihood by poisoning the mind of youth. To my mind, the fiery death of the young Carthaginian was preferable to the moral death to which the fathers of your period seemed willing to have their children exposed. In the name of common sense and decency, what strange influence was at work, that parents tolerated for a single day the existence of such an iniquity? What were your legislators about? Was property, in those days, of more importance than life, life than moral purity?"

"If you knew anything of the average character of the legislators then sent from our city," replied I, "you would not be surprised at anything they did, or left undone. They generally represented, and were themselves of, the lowest of the low. As for the parents, many saw and deplored the evils to which you refer, but could effect little against banded greed, ignorance, and vice. Even when, by great efforts, a useful piece of legislation could be carried through, its execution was intrusted to officials elected mainly through the influence of the vicious classes, with whom they, accordingly, more or less openly sympathized."

"What you say," said Utis musingly, "agrees, upon the whole, with the little we know of the state of things in that misty past. One thing, however, surprises me. All history enforces the truth, that, in general, a people enjoys about as good a government as it deserves; that the character and conduct of the rulers fairly reflect that of the ruled. Do you mean to say, that, in your time, the vicious classes formed a majority of your population?"

"That could hardly be maintained," replied I.

"How, then, could they control the more intelligent majority?" inquired Utis.

"It was the old story of union against disunion," said I. "The vicious classes, or, rather, the more intelligent, who acted as leaders, and whom the rest followed like sheep, knew what they wanted, and took the shortest way to obtain it. The intelligent majority, as you call it, did not, for the most part, know exactly what they wanted, or, when they did know, differed greatly as to the best way of obtaining it. In other words, they belonged to different political parties. The control of both political machines being, at the time, in the hands of men equally intent on selfish ends, the well-meaning citizen saw himself reduced to impotence between two gangs of corrupt schemers, who adroitly played into each other's hands.

"Besides these two sets of self-seekers, who were, perhaps, rather contemptuously indifferent to, than actively hostile to, morality, there existed a class, small, indeed, in numbers, but powerful for mischief from their loud shrieking and confident self-assertion. This was the new sect of the Phrasolators. The high-priests of this grotesque cult were usually tolerant of a whole pantheon of deified phrases, though naturally reserving their special homage for the pet platitude or catch-word of their own invention, in the worship of which they sometimes played strange antics. No devout Romanist ever believed more implicitly in the virtues of some favorite relic than did the followers of this new sect in the efficacy of high-sounding phrases for the regeneration of mankind.

"Their patronage was an injury, even to what was intrinsically valuable. Liberty of the Press, Trial by Jury, Popular Government, had the misfortune to be placed among the idols of the Phrasolators. All associated with these phrases, or asserted to be so, was too sacred for discussion: criticism was sacrilege. No matter though the press became a poisoned fountain, the jury system a mere convenience for facilitating the escape of criminals, the suffrage the cogged dice of political tricksters: no change was to be tolerated, except in the direction of further degradation.

"These phrasemongers were frequently themselves of pure life and character, though the more or less indirect abetters of vice, of much culture though little common sense. The mischief they effected was chiefly by the cloak of decency their advocacy would throw over a cause that would have fared but poorly if left in its naked deformity to the advocacy of its natural guardians."

No system of government works well beyond the extent to which it represents the average moral and intellectual status of the governed. Laws not originating in the wants, and corresponding to the intelligent conviction, of those legislated for, are generally worse than useless. Enforced not at all, or only in show, they serve only to grant a monopoly of certain acts to the unscrupulous. Now, the system of government prevailing among the contemporaries of Utis presupposed a general moral and intellectual status surpassing that now prevailing, to an even greater degree than their knowledge and control of the forces of nature surpassed ours. The great fault with many of our present institutions is, that they pre-suppose an average citizen much superior in intelligence and public spirit to the really existing average citizen. The machine is too fine for its work. Too many of our laws seem to be the work of well-meaning phrasolators, who waste much ingenuity in framing laws that will enforce themselves. These are the devices of perpetual-motion cranks. Others, again, are the work of knaves, who throw a sop to an indignant public in an enactment they are well aware will prove worthless before the ingenuity of quibbling lawyers and time-serving judges. These are the devices of traitors.

"The government of Nuiorc, as organized at the period, was most peculiar. Its utter want of sense, and knowledge of human nature as then existent, is so evident, that the intention of its originators becomes an enigma to succeeding generations. The most plausible explanation, however, is that they had no intentions, if by that we mean settled principles of action. A set of incompetent bunglers had drifted into a position in which they were able to do much mischief, and did it. The result may be summed up in a few words. The revenues of one of the wealthiest cities of the world were surrendered as a prey to the organized offscourings of Europe.

"The direct contributors to the revenues were made a powerless minority: the tax-spending majority were reckless in lavishing what seemed to cost them nothing. The *régime* of aldermen, as the representatives of the proletariat were called, became too onerous, at last, for even the revenues of Nuiorc to sustain. The city became bankrupt. The city rulers would fain have imitated the course of certain States of that period, whose only use of a fictitious sovereignty was to commit rascally actions with apparent immunity. The city fathers soon found, however, that the city they dishonored did not possess this doubtful privilege. The revenues passed under the control of receivers. The docks, and large slices of the public parks, were sold to the highest bidder. From being the worst, Nuiorc became the best-governed, city in Christendom; for the police no longer granted favors to ruffians on the ground of their being heelers of Mike This or Pat That."

The just-related episode in the history of New York contains nothing to surprise an observant mind accustomed to note the present tendency of things in that city. But that Boston, the liberal, the cultured, the nursing mother of American literature,—that Boston should become the focus of Romanism, not for America only, but for the world,—should, in fine, become associated in the minds of man with all now associated with the name of Rome, will, no doubt, overwhelm others with the same incredulous astonishment the story at first evoked in me. But so it was. Driven from Italy, the Papacy found a welcome and a refuge in New England. Boston became, and remained during long ages, the chosen seat of that church of which its founders had a special abhorrence. In accordance with the same economic law by which the baser coin drives out the better, a lower class of labor drives out a superior. Thus the free population of Italy disappeared before the horde of imported slaves, the superior population of New England before the crowds of imported laborers of an inferior class. In all probability, Papacy could not have developed amid the original population of free Italy: it certainly could never have gained a foot-hold amid the original white population of New England.

All this, and more, I learned during an excursion to Thiveat (corrupted from Civitas Beata), the later name of Boston. The journey there and back occupied, in all, about five hours. The city itself was as changed in appearance as in name. The old familiar landmarks had disappeared. The bay, the islands, the general outline of the shore, were still recognizable; but all else was strange.

We had taken our stand upon one of the remaining towers of the cathedral, a once magnificent structure, erected on the site now occupied by the State House. Planned to surpass St. Peter's, and requiring for its completion a whole century of energetic effort and unstinted outlay, it had been justly regarded as one of the architectural wonders of the world. Now it was mostly crumbled into ruin. From this lofty position my companion was able to point out to me the ruins of the dungeon-like walls of the Palace of the Inquisition on Governor's Island: the whole surface was so covered with ruined masonry, that it had never been thought worth while to clear it away. Restored to good-humor by these signal examples of "Time's revenges," I turned to where, embosomed amid secular groves that permitted but glimpses of the stately structure, stood the buildings of the University. This, however, was not the immediate successor, though it was the worthy representative, of the "Fair Harvard" of the nineteenth century. During the reign of the church, Harvard had been converted into a Jesuit college, the centre of the order, the chief training-school of its members. Owing to the appropriation of the education fund to other, especially building, purposes, by the church during this period, secular education fell to a very low ebb indeed.

On our way home, Utis recounted to me the steps in the political and intellectual decadence of New England. These were, the accession to supremacy of an ignorant and superstitious foreign element; the accelerated emigration of the original stock; the establishment of a State church, in fact though not in name; decisions by obsequious courts that placed the education fund practically under the control of the priesthood; the removal of the seat of the Papacy to Boston; attainment, by the Jesuits, of a controlling power in many States, by adroit manipulation of parties; rapid decline and ultimate extinction of the Papacy, after its alliance with the invaders during the "Great Invasion."

"You have really worked hard," said Utis a few days after our excursion to Boston. "Let us celebrate by a water-excursion."

Instead of our usual forenoon work, we accordingly set off soon after breakfast for Grand Isle. On one of those electric boats I had first seen in use on the Hudson, Utis and I sped up the river towards Grand Isle.

The rays of the westering August sun were already entangled amid the tops of the lofty trees, whose lengthened shadows they cast, now upon the swift current, now on the smooth lawns that extended before the ancient mansions thickly scattered along the banks of the stream. Beautified by the labors of the many generations whose homes these mansions had been, Grand Isle presented a scene of fairy-like beauty, far unlike the unkempt ruggedness that at present there meets the traveller's eye. So rare are the gleams of perfect sunshine on the pathway of life, that we are almost afraid to enjoy the unwonted splendor; as in certain climes a sunrise of unsullied brightness is regarded as the sure precursor of a stormy day.

This passing mood may have been partly influenced by the increasing volume of sound that betokened our approach toward the grandest spectacle on our continent. A change of wind, indeed, was now causing the muffled thunder of the falls to reach our ears in one continuous though distant roar, fit herald of our passage from the beautiful to the sublime.

As we approached the northern extremity of the island, the current became ever swifter. On the course I was now obliged to adopt, the rapidly descending sun shone full in our faces. It was probably for that reason that I did not observe what, observed sooner, might yet have afforded us a chance.

"Is the current too much for us? We seem to be making scarcely any headway."

I was not so much startled as surprised. The current must indeed be strong to nearly neutralize the speed of a boat able to make fifteen miles an hour in still water. I accordingly slightly altered our course, and was now for the first time really alarmed. Hastily I examined the gauge that served to indicate the amount of available electric force in the reservoir. With difficulty I repressed a groan. The gauge indicated almost zero.

I headed for the eastern shore, and we reached within little more than a quarter of a mile of the shore. But at the same moment our remnant of motive-power became exhausted; and, seized by a powerful eddy, we were swept out to near the middle of the river, this time more than a mile farther down. We were now utterly helpless. Even the power of steering had ceased with the exhaustion of the motive-power.

I looked around to see whence aid could come, and waved a scarf at the end of a rod. Its being so near the dinner-hour, made it a bad hour of the day for us. Had our plight been perceived in time, efficient aid might possibly have reached us. As it was, I saw more than one boat dart forth, in eager answer to my signals of distress. We watched them, helpless to further their efforts even by changing the course of our boat.

"I am afraid it is all of no use," said Utis calmly, after attentively watching them for some time. "They cannot reach us before we pass those rocks."

"And then?" said I.

"Then, Ismar, we are beyond human aid."

We sat for some time after this in silence. We passed the fatal rocks, beyond which the waters seemed to slope with a frightful declivity toward the abyss beyond. As we did so, the boat that had come so daringly to our rescue, now scarcely a quarter of a mile off, turned rapidly in its course, and none too soon. The steersman's companion, a young and beautiful girl, buried her face in her hands, and seemed to weep.

At this moment, the boat seemed to give a wild leap into the air: then followed a horrible sensation of falling from a great height, amid a deafening roar, as of a universe crashing into ruin; then oblivion.

It was with a sort of confused surprise, that, on recovering the consciousness of existence, I found myself alive at all. Instead, too, of battling for life amid a chaos of whirling waters, I found myself seated in a commodious arm-chair, in a dimly lighted apartment. With difficulty I rallied my scattered thoughts so far as to recognize the fact that I was in my own room.

The events and personages of that strange experience have still for me a reality not surpassed by that of this actual existence. At times, indeed, I find myself inclined to doubt whether this is not the phantasmal and that the real, wondering whether I may not awake to find myself lying in the swinging cot in the house of Utis.

5

Edward Bellamy   1850-1898

In America, the name Bellamy is almost synonymous with utopia. Bellamy has assumed a position as the modern representative in the sequence of classic utopists: Plato, More, Bacon, Campanella, Bellamy. This reputation is understandable, for it is doubtful that any single utopia, including the classics, has had so great an impact on the thoughts and actions of men as can be claimed for *Looking Backward*. The number of copies published in the sixty-two years since it first appeared is well over a million; the work has been translated into every important language, including Bulgarian, Russian, and Arabic; and it would be impossible to determine the number of utopian works, both critical and speculative, which were directly inspired by *Looking Backward*. There were perhaps at least a hundred such, ranging from the famous reaction of William Morris in *News from Nowhere* to the works of men unheard of before or since. A full scale of changes was rung on Bellamy's title and hero, including Schindler's *Young West* (1894), Michaelis's *Looking Further Forward* (1890), Vinton's *Looking Further Backward* (1890), Cirkel's *Looking Forward* (1906), Geissler's *Looking Beyond* (1891), Roberts' *Looking Within* (1893), Wilbrandt's *Mr. East's Experiences in Mr. Bellamy's World* (1891), Giles' *Shadows Before* (1894), and Mueller's *Ein Rückblick aus dem Jahre 2037 auf das Jahr 2000* (1891). In addition, Bellamy was responsible for the principles of the Nationalist Movement, which in turn became the platform of the People's Party, and although the political promise of this movement was short-lived, the influence of the spread of Bellamy's ideas in America alone on the future course of political opinion is incalculable. It was also his dubious distinction to have his ringing declaration in the final chapter of *Looking Backward*, "I have seen Humanity hanging on a cross," appropriated and distorted by William Jennings Bryan in his popular and influential "Cross of Gold" oration. These and more detailed facts of Bellamy's influence are, if not well-known, at least readily available. Here we shall confine ourselves to a brief comment on Bellamy's historic importance in the development of utopian thought. His two utopian works, *Looking Backward* (1888) and *Equality* (1897), are available in reprint editions, and *The Religion of Solidarity*, written in 1874 when Bellamy was twenty-four, was finally made available in 1940 by the contemporary authority on Bellamy, Arthur E. Morgan.[1] *The Religion of Solidarity*, while only a few pages in length, is of particular significance as an early

[1] Author of the best single work on Bellamy, titled *Edward Bellamy*; Columbia University Press, 1944.

statement of Bellamy's general social philosophy which was to be incorporated in *Looking Backward*.

There are two main considerations in assessing Bellamy's historic position as a utopist: his general philosophy of social structure and organization, and the method of changing social structure which he proposes. In our introductory remarks on modern utopias, we stressed the significant change of focus from reform of the individual to reform of institutions. No better illustration of this institutional philosophy could be found than Bellamy. He believed that men were essentially and fundamentally good, and that the inadequacies and evil observable in the actions of men were directly attributable to the inefficient and inequitable institutional structure of their society. Basic to all institutional order and efficiency are economic production and distribution. Hence, for Bellamy, the Industrial Army represented a necessary plan of organizing all the units of society, both individual and institutional, in terms of economic efficiency. Stripped of its romance and humanitarian language, Bellamy's social philosophy is plain economic materialism. To be sure, the asserted end is the happiness and well-being of men as individuals, but on the assumption that economic, material efficiency was the prerequisite of that well-being, all other criteria were subordinated to that of economic efficiency.

Bellamy's use of the term "Army" was not merely figurative. He admired and glamorized the military as the most efficient type of organization in society. He asserted that the "military systems of the great European States" were examples of the method and order which could be achieved in organizing the affairs of men. The virtuous Bellamy was horrified at the thought of war, but his admiration for the military type of organization was unreserved. In this selection of the military as the prototype for his organization of society, Bellamy was more consistent to his institutional philosophy than perhaps he himself realized. For him, the military represented the one pursuit of men in which "every sordid standard of merit and achievement" was rejected. Consistent with his single-minded evaluation, Bellamy means by "sordid," economic; he admires the military because they "throw away the purse." If one is not so determined to make all classifications in terms of the economic alone, a somewhat broader interpretation of the suitability of the military organization to a philosophy of institutionalism may be suggested. The military, of all our institutions, is the one which has consistently achieved the highest degree of institutionalization; that is, it has more effectively subordinated and eliminated all individual values to the purposes of the institution. Within a military organization, the individual becomes a unit of the institutional structure rather than an individual.

The assumption of the institutional philosophy is that such organization increases the efficiency of the institution, an assumption which the individualist philosophy of course denies. Be that as it may, there is no question but that this was Bellamy's philosophy and his reason for conscripting society into one vast Industrial Army. It entails, as is plainly evident from a careful reading of Bellamy, that all other institutions as well as all individual values must be subordinated to the efficient operation of the fundamental economic Army. Education, religion, art, and music—all are evaluated in terms of their adaptability or contribution to the efficiency of economic production and distribution. It is unquestionable that in his emotional exacerbation over the economic inequalities prevailing in the nineteenth century, Bellamy simply did not realize the potential viciousness of the philosophy he was proclaiming. In fact, Bellamy was not a philosopher, but a reformer with the characteristic myopia of the reformer who sees the goodness of his end but cannot see the vitiating self-defeat of the method by which he proposes to achieve that end. Bellamy ignored any potential use of force by his economic hierarchy; he proposed the Army as the only organization of society for economic efficiency. It should be noted that Bellamy's high regard for the military was reciprocated; as early as September, 1888, a Boston Bellamy Club was initiated by a reading club composed of retired Army officers. This was, in fact, the beginning of the Nationalist Movement.

It is in respect to his method of accomplishing change in the social structure that Bellamy appears most astute. There are two obvious ways to effect change in society, by revolution or by evolution. The main difference between the two rests on the use of force or violence, although it is generally assumed that the time element is a decisive differentiation. However, revolution may conceivably be a long and drawn-out process while evolution can under certain conditions proceed with amazing rapidity. It is understandable that during the nineteenth century there should be an increasing acceptance of the method of revolution as necessary to bring about desired social change. Thus, the utopias of the modern period evidence in unprecedented degree a recognition of the possibility, even the necessity, of force and violence in accomplishing change within the social structure. We have already seen how the simplest of the evolutionary techniques, the establishment of utopia as an isolated community, ceased to be a real alternative in the modern period. Individuals may be changed by exhortation, by education, even by transportation; but when a philosophy of social structure is accepted which involves changing established institutions, these peaceful, intellectual methods seem inappropriate. In this period when force and violence were so generally accepted as an unavoidable con-comitant of social change, Bellamy establishes his rightful position in the classic line of utopists. It is paradoxical that this most significant aspect of his work should be the least known; it is mainly expounded in the little-known *Equality*, sequel to *Looking Backward*. There is no space here to describe in detail the inventive devices by which Bellamy accomplishes the radical transition to his social organization from the existing capitalistic economic structure. Through a gradual process of nationalization of production and distribution, without expropriation or violence, the scrip issued to the "public" employees of Bellamy's nucleus of the Industrial Army becomes so much more valuable in purchasing-power that it forces money out of circula-tion. Again, Bellamy's single criterion of the economic is the touch-stone, not only to order and efficiency, but to peaceful change as well.

On the other hand, while Bellamy was typical of his age in accept-ing the determining role of the economic in social organization, he never doubted the ability of men to achieve that organization. He not only believed that men were essentially good and would respond morally to a proper material environment, but he also had complete confidence in the intellectual capacity of men to resolve their prac-tical problems, once the unnatural obstacle of economic inequality was removed. The ingenuity of the scheme for peaceful conversion from capitalism to the new social order was but an instance of this conviction that man would, in the new order, rise to the necessity of invention. Only on the basis of this assumption could it be sup-posed that radical social change might be accomplished by evolu-tionary means, thus avoiding war and violence. It is ironic that Bellamy should have been criticized by some of his contemporaries because he "invented inventions" to overcome difficult problems in the operation of his society. These critics obviously did not really understand Bellamy. For him, invention was not merely a literary trick nor yet simple prediction; it was an integral part of his concept of the ideal society. He did not consider the ordering of institutions according to his economic policy to imply a system of controls and restrictions on the individual, however naïve his belief may appear to us. Bellamy thought of his economic order only as affording op-portunity for the release of individual capacities, in the new order where individuals would be free to be moral and intelligent. As for his actual "inventions," Bellamy proved more astute in his simple reliance on the intelligence of men than did those of his contempo-raries who based their "predictions" on wider acquaintance with science and economics. Bellamy's confident assurance in 1888 that men would meet certain practical problems with the invention of radio and television, of paved roads and tractors for farming, of automobiles and air transportation, of air conditioning and methods for forcing growth in plants—in 1950, these have no appearance of escape mechanisms.

It is this sublime confidence in the ability of man to rise to a proper state of dignity—even nobility—once the economic shackles that now bind him are loosened and cast off that gives Bellamy his distinctive position in the history of utopian thought and his particular place of eminence among modern utopists. His is a true utopian conception, the incorporation into his ideal of the conviction that men need not resort to religious resignation or some other form of intellectual anaesthesia in order to resolve satisfactorily the practical problems of existence. In an age of increasing distrust of the motives of men, of growing suspicion of the corruption of power, Bellamy thrusts aside all such doubt and suspicion.

> All thoughtful men agree that the present aspect of society is portentous of great changes. The only question is, whether they will be for the better or the worse. Those who believe in man's essential nobleness lean to the former view, those who believe in his essential baseness to the latter. For my part, I hold to the former opinion. *Looking Backward* was written in the belief that the Golden Age lies before us and not behind us, and is not far away. Our children will surely see it, and we, too, who are already men and women, if we deserve it by our faith and by our works.[2]

Bellamy thus establishes a spiritual continuity with the earlier proponents of the communitarian ideal; his ideal, too, rested upon confidence in the essential goodness and potential nobility of man. Bellamy, however, presents his ideal in completely modern perspective. His utopian speculation is uniformly progressive, the while retaining that sincere belief in the perfectibility of man without which the vision of the utopist would be but an empty dream. Perhaps empty dream it will prove to be, but who can say that in Bellamy it is not a noble and inspiring vision?

[2] From a Postscript to *Looking Backward*, written in reply to a reviewer for the *Boston Transcript* who had suggested that Bellamy should have set the date for the realization of his ideal society seventy-five *centuries* in the future.

6

The Crystal Button

*or, Adventures of Paul Prognosis
in the Forty-Ninth Century*

Chauncey Thomas

Edited by George Houghton

*Boston and New York
Houghton, Mifflin and Company
The Riverside Press, Cambridge
1891*

Chauncey Thomas (1822–1898)

was born in Howland, Maine, and began the vocation of carriage-maker at Bangor. He established himself in the carriage business at West Amesbury, Mass., and after ten years moved to Boston, where for some forty years he maintained a reputation as a master in carriage design and construction. One of his competitors said of him: "There was only one man in the business whom we all acknowledged to be our superior in the matter of the designs in carriage-building, and that was Chauncey Thomas."

The author of *The Crystal Button* has been erroneously identified as another Chauncey Thomas of the same period, onetime editor of *Smart Set* and other magazines, and author of several western stories. With the clarification that *The Crystal Button* was indeed written by a carriage-maker and businessman, the introduction to the volume may be taken at its face value. A part of this introduction is included in the following selection, mainly to indicate the attention paid Bellamy's *Looking Backward*, and the apparent necessity of remarking that Thomas had worked out his ideas independently. *The Crystal Button* is another typical venture in the utopian speculation which flourished in the 1890's.

Of his own career, Thomas is said to have remarked: "My life has been one of very hard work and with very few play days. I have had a fair measure of success, considering the difficulties of making a fortune at carriage-making. I have made many improvements in my line of business, some twenty of which have been patented." Very little more is known about Thomas. It is said that he had some scholarly interest, and that he once published some interesting material on prehistoric races in America, but we have found no record of these publications. He also wrote some verse, the only instance of which we have seen was not particularly inspiring. Thomas was primarily a businessman, and it is from that point of view that he wrote. He was chosen by Chauncey Depew to write an article on the development of the carriage industry in this country when the latter was editor of a project "One Hundred Years of American Commerce." Thomas was also active in the National Carriage Builders' Association and served on the board of government of the Massachusetts Charitable Mechanic Association. Of primary importance in evaluating *The Crystal Button* is the fact that the author was, during a period of hectic commercial strife, an experienced and successful manufacturer, respected and honored by his business associates and competitors for his business ability and acumen.

EDITOR'S PREFACE.
OPEN LETTER TO THE PUBLISHERS.

Dear Sirs:

For three months past, the undersigned has been engaged in the pleasant task of editing, for a Boston gentleman, the manuscript of a novel which may perhaps commend itself as a fitting companion-piece to Mr. Edward Bellamy's "Looking Backward."

Of course, neither author nor editor has any idea that it will rival that remarkable production; but, in many ways, it helps to supplement with details the same general picture of future possibilities that Mr. Bellamy has so skillfully and attractively painted. Permit me to state briefly that the present work was written many years ago by the well-known coach-builder of Boston. The thought was to foreshadow the future possibilities of mechanical and material development.

The original manuscript, now before me, shows that it was begun in 1872, and that the author wrote the closing page on February 9, 1878. Its chief defect, if such it may be called, is the fact that its general scheme so closely resembles that of Mr. Bellamy's book that it would be difficult to convince the public of its priority,—a task I should shrink from undertaking, although I know it to be a fact.

It will give me pleasure to submit the manuscript to you as soon as it is completed.

Very respectfully yours,
George Houghton.

Yonkers, New York, February 10, 1890.

The Crystal Button

The door-bell gave a sudden sharp alarum that was like a scream. Mrs. Prognosis sprang from her chair. "I suppose," she said, "it's another telegram asking your father to hurry over to the broken drawbridge. But he must be there by this time." She went to the door, her daughter following.

"Your pardon, ma'am," spoke up a hoarse voice, "but I've bad news for you."

"Paul—my husband—what has happened to him? Is he in any trouble?—is he dead?"

"No, not dead, ma'am; but he's been hurt. He is coming to you.

They are bringing him to you. No, ma'am, you musn't go. Here they come."

Without another word the woman ran to meet the approaching file of men, bowed by the weight they bore between them on an improvised stretcher. For the next hour, Dr. Clarkson kept the wife busily employed in doing whatever small tasks he could think of. Just before midnight, when breathing had been fully restored, he left her, saying: "I find no injury of any kind. He no doubt received a severe blow on the head, though I do not find even a scalp-wound. What the result will be, I cannot now foretell. He seems to be perfectly comfortable for the present."

. . . . .

From the time of that accident, Paul Prognosis never spoke an intelligible word, and never showed a sign of recognition of those about him, for a period of ten years. His life was spared, and his general health continued good, but the current of his thought was broken. Was it broken, or merely diverted? It was quite clear that the windows of Paul's mental dwelling place were closely shuttered. But inside those darkened shutters—what was going on there? There was life still there. And why not? If nothing material can be utterly destroyed how much less should we expect to see the immaterial blotted out of existence. Might not the swift current of his mental activity, accidentally diverted from its normal confines, have made for itself an underground course, where no eye, however sympathetic, could follow its secret windings? Might not his *could be* of yesterday have become the *now is*? Might not the occasional mutterings of his lips, although unintelligible to his hearers, be vague hints from a world unseen and unknown to those around him, yet none the less real to him?

. . . . .

"Well, as my name's Paul Prognosis, this is a pretty predicament for a respectable citizen of Boston to find himself in, tramping about the streets at day-dawn, and with nothing but a nightgown on. I wonder where my house is!"

To his surprise, he found himself standing in a public square, that was wholly unfamiliar to him, surrounded by buildings vast and magnificent. A brazen gateway suddenly opened before him without effort on his part, and he darted through it, then up a broad winding staircase, through another open doorway, and found himself in the midst of a snug library, where the warmth of an open fire cheered his eyes, and where, face to face with him, sat an elderly man at a table littered with papers, occupied with inspecting what appeared to be a small coffee-mill.

"I beg pardon, sir, for this intrusion, which must appear to you wholly unwarrantable, but I have lost my clothes, and do not know where I am. Can you please direct me, sir?"

The old gentleman looked up without any visible surprise—certainly without any appearance of annoyance. "Why, this is odd," said the gentleman, using a strange accent and a language that was not quite familiar to Paul, although he found that he could understand it readily enough,—"you are talking in Old English. I thought I was the only living man who could do that." Then he added reflectively: "Poor fellow, he must have escaped from some madhouse. But he speaks Old English remarkably well—better, I admit—much better than I can."

There occurred to Paul the similar thought, that he must have entered a retreat of some kind, but any apprehensions he might have felt were relieved when the gentleman calmly continued:—

"You say you are lost. Tell me where your home is."

"I live on Cedar Avenue, number 201. And if you will be good enough to send for a hack, I can go home at once without troubling you further."

"Strange, very strange!" repeated the old gentleman—"such perfect command of Old English words. But, my dear sir, where is Cedar Avenue?"

Remembrance of the great city through which he had recently prowled flashed across Paul's mind. It had not seemed like his native city. "Is this not Boston, sir?"

The gentleman looked at him sharply. "Why, my dear sir, do you not know that you are in the good city of Tone? Is it possible that you do not realize that the ancient city of Boston, like the ancient language you speak, is merely an historical fact of the remote past? What year is this?"

"Why, eighteen hundred and seventy-two," answered Paul quickly. "You see I have not altogether lost my wits."

"And who is the chief officer of state?"

"Ulysses S. Grant."

"Let us see, a moment," commented the Professor. "The present year being Anno Pacis 1372, and adding this to Anno Domini 3500, the Year of Peace, we are now, according to the old style, in the year 4872. Stranger, your friend Grant was President just three thousand years ago. You've had a good long nap, if you've been asleep ever since then."

Paul was now so thoroughly confused that he did not try to make any response, beyond a piteous sigh: "What am I to do?"

"Simply make yourself perfectly comfortable, and consider my home yours until further notice. I will see that you are supplied with everything you need."

. . . . .

After an absence of an hour, Paul returned to the library, attired in new costume."

"Mr. Prognosis," said the Professor, "as you are our guest, it is only proper for you to know that you may find my mind a little pre-occupied by reason of the preparations it is my duty to make in view of the near approach of the great event. It is to occur just three days from now. It is a brief call that will be paid our planet by the huge comet Veda,—she never appeared in your Christian Era. And now, if you are ready, we will go and do our errands, and meanwhile view the city."

"Three thousand years!" said Professor Prosper absently, as they passed along the street.

"Three thousand years!" echoed Paul; "and yet, by some strange fortune,—whether good or evil I hardly yet know,—I find myself permitted still to live and breathe and to gaze at the pleasant face of the earth. Three thousand years! and yet the sun still shines the same, and the fleecy cloud-ships overhead sail just as calmly, and the wind gives me the same brusque greeting as in the Decembers of old."

"Yes," responded the Professor; "and, as you will learn later, happy childhood plays just the same in mimicry of maturer life; there still reigns the golden age of love-making, accompanied by buoyant hope and castle-building; still there come the soberer joys and responsibilities of middle life; and still each man and woman is followed step by step by the shadow of old age and death. So rolls the world forever through its contrasting seasons. But life's road now is unquestionably much smoother and more comfortable for all of us than it was in your turbulent age of experiment and unrest."

"That is what I am particularly interested to know about. In what respect are you now more at ease? And does this ease extend to all classes? And are all classes happier in consequence?"

"I can answer Yes to your last two questions. Details you must see for yourself. In a general way, however, you will no doubt find the following points suggestive of some of the conditions you may ex-pect to find. Money-getting is no longer the chief goal of effort, and hence many unworthy ambitions have been stifled. Places of power and trust are now filled by strong and trustworthy men; the path to all high places is such that none others can attain them. We no longer have taskmasters, for the simple reason that we no longer have slaves. There is abundance in the way of the world's goods for all, and not so much for any one class as to make them uncomfortable. We have abolished classes."

"You apparently have no beggars in your streets," Paul said, half questioningly.

"I should hope not. Oh no, beggary is one of the many things of the remote past. It was merely the result of certain unhealthy conditions, including waste, extravagance, avariciousness, crime, and disease, which flourished in your time, and fruited and dropped their natural seed."

"But you cannot have abolished crime by legal enactments."

"No; but we have so reduced, where we have not entirely removed, the chief inducements to crime, including poverty, excess of wealth, injustice, and ambition for undeserved power, inevitably leading to tyranny, that it is now infrequent. While I was recently engaged in consulting newspaper files dating from the nineteenth century, I was painfully struck by the fact that nearly all the news most prominently heralded related to crimes, accidents, and wars or rumors of wars. Although the world is now much more densely populated, and the means of communication nearly instantaneous, our daily newspapers seldom make mention of crimes or accidents— simply because they seldom occur; and of course we no longer have our nerves excited, pleasurably or otherwise, by news of war or rebellion, as those are conditions quite impossible under the present regime. In brief, Mr. Prognosis, the news of your day was mainly detective news, while ours nearly all relates to social life, science, arts and amusements."

While thus speaking, they had descended to a broad stone platform skirting the subway.

"The Government runs and operates all lines of transportation for either passengers or freight, as well as other means of communication. And all are free—perfectly free. In your time you had started in this direction by making many of your highways and bridges free to the public, and mail-matter nearly so. Please understand that the people and the Government are one—they are synonymous terms."

When, after a few minutes of rapid flight in the railway, they alighted at the riverside, the Professor explained that he had stopped at this point in order to give his visitor an opportunity to see one of the several hospitals scattered about the suburbs of the city.

"You seemed interested by references I made to beggary and crime, and it occurred to me that you would like this opportunity to glance at one of our hospitals, which will indicate certain provisions now made for the maintenance of health, and having an important influence on those questions."

"You are very kind. You will find me an interested spectator and listener. But first, please let me ask you a few questions. You alluded to disease as one of the exciting causes of poverty, and hence of crime, in my day. You surely cannot have banished disease!"

"Not entirely, yet very largely. Death still awaits us all, and, throughout life, we still suffer those ills to which flesh seems naturally and inevitably heir. But the records show that most of the diseases that brought distress to the ancients were unnecessary; they were mainly such as were directly attributable to poor or inappropriate food, poor drainage, lack of sunshine and fresh air, lack of exercise or too much of it, vice of many kinds, and ignorance of even the simplest laws of physical well-being. By removing those prolific sources of disease, the world first cured the majority of its patients, then prevented further accessions to the ranks, and gradually reduced the liability of recurrence of the same weaknesses in offspring. Indeed, large classes of disorders which you looked upon as incurable are now practically unknown, excepting as sporadic examples that are rather welcomed than otherwise by our physicians.

"Let me tell you that we deal with disease as a deadly enemy that deserves no quarter. We first adopt every possible means of prevention. For instance, we respect certain marriage rules that you would no doubt consider arbitrary and harsh, but which have resulted in so improving the world's health that all people now recognize their justice and propriety. No diseased or deformed person who is liable to communicate serious imperfection of any kind to offspring is ever allowed to marry."

"But how can you prevent marriages?"

"By the same means that we effect them—by law; and our laws mean more than mere written statutes. They are founded on justice and right. The public recognizes this fact, and every person feels it for his own interest, as well as for the public good, to see that they are enforced. You were not so blind but that you found it right to prevent a lunatic or a leper from marrying—and you even banished the latter forever as a hopeless outcast. But you nourished in your homes diseases that were even more readily communicable, and quite as dangerous to life and health and moral stamina."

"True—too true!"

"But now let us take a distant view of the hospital, which, as you see, consists of a number of small buildings arranged in a semicircle on the little island before us. There are eighteen buildings in the line, and you will notice that they are divided by walls into three distinct groups. Those to the left are devoted to patients suffering from ailments affecting the mind, including imbeciles and the insane; the centre group to those who are physically ill or injured; while the three to the right are occupied by those who are morally deranged."

"Morally deranged?"

"Yes, I believe you used to apply the term 'prison' to the institution used for the confinement of moral patients."

"They are convicts, then? But why are these associated with your hospitals?"

"Why not? They constitute a part, though happily a small part, of the patients that come under the same management and treatment. We simply treat them as persons who are morally deformed or ailing."

"But how do you punish them?"

"We know no such thing as punishment in their case. We confine them, partly for their own good, to prevent them from doing further injury to themselves, and partly with reference to public safety; but the idea of 'punishment,' in the sense in which it was known to your system of criminal jurisprudence, has no part in ours. Vice and crime are sufficient punishment in themselves."

Leaving the hospital, they walked along the paved embankment.

"What you have seen today is not the result of any one act of any one person or of any million of persons, but of the combined efforts of all individuals who have thus far lent their influence, by even the simplest word or act, to the cause of truth and justice. That's the only way public sentiment is created, and Public Sentiment rules this world as God rules heaven! Today, Public Sentiment says all men have equal rights, if not equal capacities—and it means and enforces what it says. Today, Public Sentiment pronounces vice degrading, and ignorance the mother of vice, and says that neither shall be tolerated. Today, Public Sentiment pronounces labor ennobling, and it ennobles the laborer. That's all there is about it."

For a time neither spoke; and Paul had a full opportunity to examine the faces that passed him. He looked in vain for any that suggested vice, hunger, poverty, or even care. The streets were crowded, but no one was in a hurry, though all seemed bound on some pleasurable quest.

After a time, he ventured to inquire whether it was not found difficult to supply the various needs of the present increased population of the world.

The Professor at first answered a little sharply: "No Sir! We save what you wasted! We work, while you played at work! We give Nature and her vast forces an opportunity to work for us! And we know how to wisely use what we have!"

"Several subjects occur to me," said Paul reflectively, "as leading ones in my day, such as ownership of property, real and personal, which of course includes farm-lands as well as city buildings. I should be extremely interested to know something of the methods of modern agriculture, for, without some radical changes in this department of human industry, resources must be severely taxed to meet the wants of the population that now, as I understand, covers nearly the entire continent."

"Very well; let us begin with the last of your inquiries—that about agriculture, which also involves the question of land ownership. In the first place, you must keep clearly in mind the fact you have already stated, that a population, vast beyond the imagination of the nineteenth century, now occupies not only the American continent, but nearly every other habitable portion of the globe; and also that such habitable portion has been greatly increased during the later centuries. River banks that the beaver once overflowed by his engineering feats are now populous with towns; every town of old has become a city; every city a metropolis; every metropolis a cosmopolis, with its every human dwelling and workshop a little city in itself, towering to the sky."

"And the fields, the pastures, the grain prairies, the woodlands— are they still here?"

"Yes; though they would probably be scarcely recognizable to you at first glance. To support a population, whereof every thousand of old represents a present million, and where every unit of this million now lives in comparative comfort and plenty—this means myriad changes in methods of production and distribution. Whatever is produced is preserved, for waste is recognized as a form of wickedness that must mean want to some, even if the waster himself is exempted from suffering the inevitable penalty. For instance, every berry, every fruit, however perishable, is promptly submitted to the improved processes that chemistry has taught, and so prepared that it shall be ready for future need. To a considerable extent, the waste of past ages constitutes the riches of the present era, and helps to fill to overflowing the vast storehouses of food products that now gird the globe and prevent all possibility of hunger."

"And how about transportation?"

"That problem has been satisfactorily solved. No one centre is allowed to become overstocked with the world's goods at the expense of less favored outskirting provinces. Where the need is, there fly the needfuls. Railways, and lines of road-vehicles propelled by power, net the land; while the seas are highways over which processions of buoyant ships, built of aluminium instead of iron and propelled by electric motors, bear their brimming food baskets. Thereby, the Grand Council of Nations is able to deal with the globe as the market gardener of old did with his garden plat: whatever corner is best suited to a certain product, that corner is devoted to that product and to that alone."

"And the farmers—do they not still own their farms, and have the right to do as they will with their own?"

"Within certain limits—yes; but they no longer have the right to buy or sell the lands they occupy, for the reason—which some of your far-sighted thinkers perceived, and which experience has proved to be founded on principles of justice—that the general public has a direct interest, and consequently a prior right, in the improvement and productiveness of all lands, and is consequently responsible for results. The breadth of land under cultivation must be proportionate to the needs of the public, with an ample margin of excess to meet contingencies. It was discovered that a question of such vital importance to the public at large could not be trusted with safety to the will of irresponsible individuals; but that the improvement of lands, to insure the best results, must of necessity be under the management of authorities appointed as the public's representatives to secure its highest good.

"From what I have explained, you will readily understand the necessity of government authority in controlling all lands and requiring of farmers that certain breadths be planted, and with certain plants best suited to the particular soil and also most needed to meet the annual requirements in the several lines."

"Such authority must sometimes be oppressive to the farmers."

"Not at all. It simply consists in indicating to the farmer what his farm is best calculated to produce, and what products are to be most in demand. By thus preventing over-production in any one line, it helps to keep prices stable, and prevents speculation in food products, which, in your day, was a tyrannous vice. The uncertainties that attended the lot of the farmer as you knew him made him a very different sort of person from the farmer of to-day. Agriculturists —or horticulturists, more properly—are now a very thrifty class, and they constitute a large proportion of our population. Farming is now a favorite industry, as affording healthful occupation, variety of interests, and generous rewards; and most of our young men are perpectly contented, if they are so fortunate as to secure good leases."

"You have pictured, Professor, what appears to me quite an ideal state of suburban society; and I begin to understand how successfully you have dealt with the question of land monopoly and landlordism, that once gave opportunities for so much tyranny in some parts of the world. I should now be glad to know how other kinds of property are held, and whether you have any legal provisions preventing the accumulation of vast wealth by individuals or companies, which might be detrimental to the public welfare by permitting selfish control of production and prices."

"We have no evils of that kind to contend against. If any such danger arose, there is law enough and righteous public opinion enough to root it out at short notice. The public has learned to have small patience with individual usurpation of any of its privileges and birthrights. The tyrant of individualism has forever been put down. His hoarded and sluggish millions are now the lively small coins of the populace, begetting a hundredfold in the hands of an intelligent and industrious people. Custom is still a leading force that governs men, but custom founded on probity is now the rule of life; and business ethics are so firmly grounded among us that any infraction of our well-established customs would subject the offender to a prompt and effectual reprimand from his fellows. This is generally sufficient to bring avarice to its senses; but in places where moral evolution is less complete than with us here,—and there are such places,—laws of limitation and restraint are brought into action. Such laws include provisions for a special tax on individual possessions judged unduly great, which are designed ultimately to re-absorb into the public purse any incomes that are excessive beyond all reason."

"Do the farmers own their home and other buildings, and have any legal tenure on the lands they occupy?"

"The lands are simply leased by the Government to the occupants, who hold them as long as they please by paying a certain stipulated rental."

"And pleasure—has that any part in the scheme of the forty-ninth century, so far as the farmer is concerned?"

"Ay! To an extent that the nineteenth century knew not of. Mr. Prognosis, we have learned that willing work, in fields fitted to the capacity of the worker, is of itself one of the highest forms of pleasure; and freedom from all fear of future want contributes to assure that contentment and peace of mind that alone can give to leisure any possibility of pleasurable recreation. In brief, Mr. Prognosis, and as a sort of parting salutation, I am glad to tell you that the experimental age in farming is past; the age of realization has come."

•   •   •   •   •

Paul awoke at daybreak thoroughly refreshed, and soon proceeded to the Professor's library, where, being of a decidedly bookish turn of mind, he longed to acquaint himself with the rows of volumes that literally walled the room. But to his regret and vexation, he found himself a stranger to the pages of printed stenography that constituted the bulk of the collection.

At this point the Professor entered, with a cheerful "Good morning, friend Prognosis. I see you are also an early bird. I heard you moving about, and guessed what you were doing. But I fear you find some difficulty in getting at the meaning of our most recently printed books. Let me help you. To begin with, the title of the book you hold in your hand is 'Natural History and Destiny of Man,'—here's what you called evolution, carried several strides further than you ever imagined; the next is 'The True Social State as it now exists, compared with that of Former Times,'—which may sound mysterious, but it's sufficiently suggestive; this is 'Best Method of Checking Population within Reasonable Limits.' That sounds startling to you, no doubt, but it's a proposition we have been forced to meet. In your time, war, pestilence, famine, and unchecked diseases of many kinds, were agencies that amply performed the task; but, such are the sanitary provisions of the present time, that the world would soon be overstocked were it not for wisely adjusted limitations. Life may now be regarded as a privilege. Here in this next alcove are sets of encyclopedias, in which the sum total of knowledge in certain important branches of study is presented in brief."

"As I understand you," said Paul, "this, then, is the expressed substance of all possible invention, filtered, refined, and concentrated, and finally bottled in this compact form for ready reference."

"Exactly."

"But how many occupations are thereby dispensed with! Where are the inventors now?"

"The age of mechanical discovery is now practically past. We have no cause for inventors now. The energies that your inventors too often wasted in profitless hide-and-seek with the powers of nature are now directed toward perfecting instruments of every kind for enriching human lives. Please try to understand, Mr. Prognosis, that the age you called 'Mechanical' we now refer to as 'Experimental.' Your most knowing scientist would find himself ill at ease in to-day's primary class in mechanics."

Paul said nothing more on this subject. What could he say?

"By the way," said the Professor, "this crystal ornament on the lapel of my coat must have often excited your curiosity, though you have modestly refrained from questioning me in regard to it. It symbolizes an object that appealed to the sympathies of all men and women, without reference to the particular religious beliefs held by them, or lacked by them, and thus afforded common ground for the adoption of an ideal and inspiration that should be universal. Until you understand the token of this white button, you cannot understand the secret springs that animate modern civilization."

"All this is new to me."

"Yes, I know; but it happened not long after your time. And you must have seen abundant handwriting on the wall. You must have known the natural and inevitable results of such an artificial state of society, such foolish sectional pride, and such a preposterous attitude of governmental forces, as then existed in Europe. In those days, the very pride and strength of a nation meant its weakness. The growing disease pointed its own cure. Pride's pocket-book was at last emptied. Military glory was at last attacked in the rear, and compelled to droop its banners. It then lost its hold on the public sentiment. Then, suddenly, public opinion took in hand its gorgeous regalia, gave it a single hearty shake,—and there came an end of it all."

"When do you say all this happened?"

"I do not now recall the precise date, but it was not long after the two Americas had proclaimed democracy."

"And England—did even England have to succumb?"

"The English monarchy did. The only wonder is that her wise men did not act sooner."

"And Russia?"

"She was the last and most stubborn. But no power on earth can withstand the assaults of public opinion when thoroughly aroused to action. Well, in the midst of the chaos, and confusion, and biting poverty that followed the monarchical downfall in Europe, and by reason of the resulting shock that electrified the world's conscience, there arose a new reformer, a new prophet, with the simplest of all doctrines on his lips, the most cheerful of gospels, and a manly earnestness of manner that made him brother to all men."

Partly reading, partly conversing, the Professor gave the following summary of the subject.

Unlike all previous prophets, nothing is unknown or in any way mysterious about the biography of John Costor. Little of interest occurred during his early life, but that little he freely told, and such were the news facilities of the twentieth century that all he told was faithfully recorded. We have no legendary lore about him. He married, moved into the new country of the northwest, and made a thrifty home for his wife and children.

One night, while he was absent from home, his wife and children and several near relatives were murdered by Indians, who were then in revolt against the Government of Washington and consequently against all its white people, on the ground that solemn pledges had been broken and treaties trampled upon whenever the wishes of the whites came in conflict with those of their humble wards. The shock was too much for even his powerful organization. When his neighbors found him, he sat beside the grave of his wife, that he had heaped with apple blossoms, holding a crystal ornament that he had taken from her neck, and saying: "Even as you have always been the soul of truth, so this bit of clear crystal is the image of your spirit." For many weeks he was like one distraught, wandering about the ashes of his former home as in a dream, muttering: "Truth, truth! All that was mine is sacrificed to the ogre of political deceit!"

To the astonishment of all who knew him, he joined the very band of Indians who had committed the crime, and became a trusted companion of the chieftain. So it was that, for five years, nothing was heard of John Costor; and such was the rapid succession of exciting events then attracting public attention that his life-tragedy was well-nigh forgotten. When Costor emerged from his obscurity, he was well prepared for the solemn duty to which he had dedicated himself. His mind was thoroughly imbued with a deep sense of the widespread evils resulting from falsehood, deceit, and all forms of injustice. He rightfully believed that, if every man could be induced by any means to lead a life of absolute truthfulness and simple honesty, all forms of injustice and wrong would in time be swept away. The many tangles of belief and theory that held men in bondage or antagonism, he sought not to unravel. "Time will cure these errors," he said, "if truth continues to be the constant watchword."

He never generalized, but addressed himself to every hearer as an individual, saying: "I speak the gospel of Truth, which means peace on earth and good-will toward men. Let every man be true to himself and to his fellow-men, and Eden will again blossom on the earth. I have no word to tell you of the life hereafter, for I do not know,— but this I do know, that untruth is the serpent whose poison now taints every fountain of private and public life. Scotch that snake in the grass, and law will then mean justice, power will mean ability, work will mean abundance, and duty well done will crown all with happiness." Such was the general current of his thoughts.

"To each of you, as an individual, I now appeal, and ask you to make this promise, not to me, but to yourself: 'I will try, from this moment henceforth, to be true and honest in my every act, word, and thought; and this crystal button I will wear while the spirit of truth abides with me.'"

On this basis, he proceeded to form, in each city he visited, a local society of his followers, who at the start isolated themselves to some extent from the rest of the world. These societies took strong root and flourished mightily. Their form of organization was extremely simple, and of a character that could challenge no man's prejudices. "I bring you no new doctrine," he often repeated. "Think what you will, believe what you must, but do only that which you know to be right, and all will be well!" Of course, no man could take exceptions to such a doctrine as this.

"The centuries rolled on," continued the Professor, "and the activities of the Crystal Button societies continued to enter into the warp and woof of political as well as social life, and give a brighter aspect to all. The well-disposed portions of society throughout the world finally accepted the new rule and lived up to its teachings with more or less fidelity.

"And now, Mr. Prognosis, we come down to the time when the crowning glory of the new order of things is at hand,—the accomplishment of permanent and universal peace among men. Naturally enough, the initial movement in this direction came from the Costorians, whose clear-sighted leader had long before predicted this as an outcome of the principles he taught, when they should be sufficiently developed. Indeed, he had constantly urged his followers, and especially his teachers, to work steadily toward this end.

"When, in the judgment of the leaders of the order, a suitable opportunity offered, they issued a call for a council of all nations to be held in the interests of peace. Such had become the influence of the allied societies, and such was their world-wide distribution, that this call met with a prompt and favorable response from every nation addressed, most of which were democracies, and having Costorians of high-standing in nearly all positions of trust. The council assembled at the great city of Carrefour, located on the isthmus midway between the two Americas, whither the fleets and railways found easy access from all parts of the globe. Perfect harmony attended the sessions of this remarkable congress; and, before the sittings were ended, a plan was adopted and signed by every representative present, which promised, and in fact accomplished, the total extinction of warfare between nations. This enactment was afterward approved by every government, and even some of the savage tribes gave their hands to the solemn compact. An international police was maintained for some years to check any lawless tribes that might fail to keep their pledges, but the event proved that even these were unnecessary, as the disturbances of the peace that occurred subsequent to the action of the congress were few, and easily quelled by local authorities. A Court of Arbitration for each of the grand divisions of the world was shortly afterward established, for the purpose of deciding any disputed questions presented at their annual sittings; while those of international character were referred by such courts to the Grand Council of All Nations, whose decisions were final. Ample opportunity for discussion was thus allowed, but none for controversy.

"Peace at last! The new era had dawned! Those who have experienced the cheer that follows reconciliation after long estrangement from former friends, when mutual trust and cordiality once more take the place of cold reserve and jealous watchfulness, will understand the outburst of unspeakable joy that resounded throughout the world as the glad tidings were flashed over the wires that the great act, so long hoped for, had finally been consummated. Through the successive ages of stone, iron, bronze, and silver, civilization had finally passed to the attainment of its crystal age of Truth.

"Thus it was that the Crystal Button conquered the world. Thus it was that, from the ashes of thrones and false altars which had been cast down, arose a single pillar of crystal, to which all nations looked with fresh hope. The hope was not disappointed. It rejuvenated the human race.

"But now, Mr. Prognosis, let us to breakfast."

The Professor led the way to the breakfast-room, where he introduced his guest. "I take pleasure in introducing Mr. Prognosis—my wife, Madam Prosper."

At the close of the meal Paul felt as much at ease with the delightful household as if he had been acquainted with them for years.

The dinner that night, served as customary, from a pneumatic tube, was a distinguished success; and the animated and cheerful conversation of those present speedily banished the mental weariness which Paul naturally felt. Of course, the chief subject of conversation was the near approach of the great comet. Before the coming of tomorrow's daylight, a spectacle surpassing all glories of the past would sweep into view. Before the dawn, the prophecy of centuries would become a recorded fact in history.

"Now, if you are ready," said the Professor, "we will take a smoke in the library."

"Well, sir," Paul said, "if my privilege still holds good, I will begin our evening's talk by asking you how it came about that such a city as this, and such marvelous public works, were constructed. A new kind of quality of public spirit must be behind all. The form of government inaugurated by the Costorian movement you have described would, I should think, involve considerations of economy; and it can hardly be possible that private means can effect such results."

"You are right," said the Professor, "as far as you go. But we must go back further.

"First you must understand that, at the time of the proclamation of universal peace, the various governments of the world possessed an enormous amount of property in the way of war-ships, armaments, forts, arsenals, and the like. These had been sustained and augmented by heavy taxes on the people. Moreover, great numbers of the people were maintained in compulsory idleness in the standing armies. With the inauguration of peace, one of the first questions that arose was, what to do with the war material, that was now useless, and what to do with the soldiers, whose education had hardly fitted them for the pursuits of peace,—indeed, had unfitted them to immediately wear the yoke of individual responsibility. It was finally determined to let the usual revenues accumulate for a time, and to sell all government property that was now useless; and with the vast fund thus supplied, the Government employed the armies about to be disbanded, without wholly relaxing the former military rules, in building a variety of works of public utility and monuments in commemoration of the beneficent peace enactment. But this did not begin to exhaust the fund. Universities of learning were established and richly endowed, extraordinary works of internal improvement were undertaken, art received an unprecedented stimulus, and all industrial pursuits were marked by healthful activity. And still, in spite of steady decrease in taxes, the fund has steadily increased. Then, as Government and people grew closer in their mutual relations, the interests of the two began slowly to be merged. Even in your day, it was one of the signs of the times that small interests were beginning to be absorbed by corporations, and those by giant monopolies. By slow and peaceful steps the same movement progressed, until the Government itself came into possession of such industries as were of peculiarly public interest, including all means of communication and transportation, and life and fire insurance; and the land question was settled in the same manner."

"Certainly, the fund must speedily have been exhausted in that process."

"Only temporarily, for the investment proved remunerative; and later on, the surplus still further increased. The Government simply assumed all responsibility, and guaranteed a certain rate of interest to former proprietors for a certain period. No capital at all was required, excepting sufficient to meet the interest account, and this was covered many times over by the returns."

"Did not this result in great injustice to individuals?"

"Not at all. If it had, the movement would not have succeeded, for the public conscience had been quickened by Costor to regard truth and justice as foundation-stones in erecting the new structure of society. Of course the process was a slow one, and it continued through several generations; but the first step was hardest. The others followed more or less naturally. Under Grant's presidency, it seemed perfectly proper and just that the Government should conduct the postal service. Was it any less proper and just that it should conduct the telegraph, telephone, railway, and express service? And wasn't it equally desirable that the Government should sufficiently control the supply and distribution of food products, that no man or clique of men should be able to put the hand on these and say, 'This wheat is mine, and no man shall eat of it until he has paid me my price?' That is not an exaggeration of what used to happen in the nineteenth century, if we correctly understand the records."

I fear they are only too clear. But how about the land?"

"That was absorbed by the Government in just the same manner, by guaranteeing interest to previous owners and re-letting on equitable terms. At this point, the best skill of the best jurists of the world was required; but long before the scheme of leasing was perfected, it was recognized as far more just than the former method of land-tenure laws, which permitted individuals and corporations to monopolize a large portion of the world's most desirable districts for their own benefit or amusement. As we now look upon it, air, water, sunshine, and land are peculiarly the people's own, and it is with great difficulty that we can understand a state of society in which individuals were permitted to exercise any control over them."

"And you say that all these changes were made peaceably?"

"Yes; they could hardly have been made otherwise. The work was a slow one; it had to be done one step at a time, and public opinion was required to time each step. Whenever public opinion halted in giving its approval to a proposed step, the movement halted. Any violence at any stage of the proceedings, or any attempt to make unhealthy haste, would have retarded the movement indefinitely.

"But let us now give our whole attention for a few moments to the general structure of our government.

"In the first place, please understand that the government of the continent of North America is merely an integral part of the great structure which composes the world's government, just as one of your States was of the United States of Washington. All are based on precisely the same laws and principles; all are based on truth, which includes honesty, simplicity, and efficiency. In our law courts, for instance, we no longer have to trust our interests to more or less accidental verdicts of irresponsible juries; we no longer blush at the special pleading of counsel and the desperate efforts of men of eminent ability profaning their position to defeat the ends of justice by their arts of persuasion. We no longer listen to impassioned appeals to the emotions in behalf of known criminals,—even criminals who have admitted their crimes,—or to the badgering and browbeating and character-blackening of innocent witnesses. You will easily understand that much has been accomplished since your day, when I tell you that we now have no lawyers, no pleadings, no juries, no appeals, no exceptions taken, no pardons, and no favors on account of wealth or social position. Justice to-day is indeed blind, as you used to portray her."

"But how, then, are your laws administered?—for you certainly must have laws, and very elaborate ones, that need frequent exposition."

"I will give you an example, to illustrate the mode of procedure in a civil suit. John Doe charges Richard Roe with conspiracy in a certain business transaction, by which, it is alleged, said Doe has been defrauded. He goes to the Board of Examiners, which consists of three, five, or seven men, according to the importance of the case. These examiners summon the parties in dispute, listen to the statements of both, take evidence, and very carefully gather all facts in the case, which are committed to phonograph—to three phonographs —and distributed to three independent boards of judges for decision. The names of the contestants are not known to the judges, and the latter are usually far removed from the locality of the interested parties.

"When the decisions of the three boards are returned to the proper office, the three packets are opened in the presence of the contestants, and two out of three concurring decide the case beyond appeal, unless new facts afterward come to light. The examiners have the power to dismiss trivial complaints as unworthy of notice, and they also perform a valuable service in correcting errors in preliminary papers, and oftentimes as arbitrators in effecting compromises between those who would otherwise invoke the court.

"The laws themselves," continued the Professor, "are as simple as their administration. No new ones have been enacted for several centuries past, but those pronounced just by the most learned judges were long ago codified, and the code now in use throughout the world may be called the 'Code of Common Sense, founded on Truth.' Moreover, the penalties for criminal acts are sure to fall upon the offender, if convicted. They are sometimes severe, but they are felt to be proper and necessary, and they can never be set aside at the caprice of anyone claiming powers superior to those of the judges. They are so clearly determined and executed on a basis of justice that they are even respected by those who suffer them."

"But," exclaimed Paul excitedly, "if you make no new laws, you have no law-makers, and no need of them; and if no law-makers, then no legislative bodies; and if no legislatures, then no elections, no voting, no parties, no politics, no politicians!"

"Your deductions are correct," said the Professor, smiling; "and you may extend your list of defunct officials by adding generals, admirals, custom-house inspectors, kings, emperors, or even presidents; for, in the ancient sense, there are now no well-defined boundaries for official domain other than municipal."

"You do not add," said Paul, "that you no longer have any governments, although I almost expected to hear you append that to your list of outlived institutions. Please tell me, have you a government or not?"

The Professor smiled, and then, after a short pause that lent emphasis to what followed, he added seriously: "Yes, Mr. Prognosis, we indeed have a government—the simplest, the strongest, the most effective, the most enduring government that the world has thus far known, which has been slowly evolved out of the needs of the people. Yet if you should seek for its head, in the person of a single man, you would find none, for there is none. This is a government of established forms. These forms time has fixed inflexibly in the minds and consciences of the people. All the methods of administration have been carefully considered, and gradually shorn of objectionable features; and, so far as human wisdom can provide, they are the best possible forms suitable to existing circumstances. To distinguish it from all predecessors, this is called 'The Government of Settled Forms.'

"The Government of Settled Forms is very simple, and needs no tinkering. It is universal, having been accepted by all nations. It knows nothing of the uncertainties of law-making, and I am glad to tell you that it knows very little of law-breaking, for law-breaking is no longer amusing or profitable—no longer honorable. There can be no general disturbance of the public in these days, for the simple reason that education of an advanced type is now universal, all men and women are usefully employed, and there is no school of poverty or vice for developing a discontented class. Moreover, the population has again become homogeneous, with common customs, needs, language, religion, aims, ambitions. If we were called upon now to trust the decision of momentous questions to the nod of majorities, we could safely do so; but there is no longer any such need. The initial questions have been determined in the stormy past. We are now enjoying the results, and peacefully developing details.

"I have explained the workings of the Department of Justice. The other elements of our government may be classed as the departments of Education, Public Health, Agriculture, Meteorology, and Public Works. These are general in character, and the sub-departments are local in their operation, but under the direction of Division Councils, who in turn are guided by the decisions of the Grand Council of the World.

"The duties of the Department of Education are obvious, and need no explanation. That of Public Health has absolute control of everything pertaining to the sanitary condition of the people, such as the purification of rivers, water supply, disposition of refuse and its useful employment, and the location and character of all places of habitation.

"The Department of Agriculture determines the amount of seed to be sown each year, and the number of animals to be raised, to meet the requirements of the world. This department maintains the food conservatories of which I have already spoken, which are always amply supplied with a surplus, to compensate for short crops. In short, its duty is to see that the world has plenty to eat.

"The Department of Meteorology determines the proportion of forest growth to tillage land, and indicates to the Department of Public Works means of improving the climate, and, to some extent, of equalizing the rainfall.

"One of the first important acts of the Congress of Nations was the adoption of a new and universal unit of valuation, based on the world's surplus of food products, as accurately reported each decade, proportionate to the world's population at the same date. The result of the computation sometimes shows a slight variation; but this is trifling, as reduction from any cause in any one item or in any one section of the globe is nearly always counter-balanced by increase in others. Moreover, the ten years' period for which each standard is fixed is sufficiently long to allow the conditions to become known to the public and to be fully discounted; and there is consequently no possible danger of sudden revulsions in valuation. Do you understand? Government certificates, based on such surplus food products and guaranteed by them, are the current medium of exchange throughout the world; and each such certificate yields quarterly interest to the holder. This is intended to encourage the habit of saving, which is no longer liable to unhealthy development, inasmuch as money has now been shorn of most of the powers and privileges that once made it a despot.

"With the establishment of our Government of Settled Forms came also settled values; and the speculator, and consequently the millionaire, is now merely a picturesque memory of the remote past. By the same means, we also abolished the great army of bankrupts and men and women without means of support, which the 'wheel of fortune'—mainly by accident of sudden variations in value—whirled helplessly, hopelessly, to dependence and wretchedness. Incomes are less unequal now, and all are richer, and better, and more hopeful in consequence.

"Government annuities form an essential element of modern life. By a process of development that now seems simple enough, but which was the slow growth of several generations, such annuities revolutionized the system of investment. You will understand that, during the process of absorption by the Government of all monopolies seeking control of staple and needful products, the opportunities for industrial investment gradually decreased, while the means of the general public has steadily increased. Government insurance, in the form of life annuities, gradually took the place of these. By judicious management, under the supervision of several of the world's ablest financiers, these annuities were reduced to a system perfect in every detail. They were made convenient and sure as an investment; and they naturally became popular. Indeed, they became so popular that public demand made them almost indispensable to the position of citizenship. Although there is no law to this effect, it is not customary for any man or woman to become a citizen until thus secured against future dependence. It is also customary, before marriage, for both the man and the prospective wife to be thus provided for; and every child, before it receives the usual birth certificate, is supposed to have at least the minimum annuity that guarantees freedom from physical want. Thus, you see, it is considered incumbent on every person to be protected against future dependence; and the requirement is so clearly for the best interests of individuals, as well as for society in general, that it has willing support from poor as well as rich, and is one of the chief civilizing agents of modern life."

"How does this affect the rich man?"

"As our laws and customs allow him to hoard comparatively little of his wealth, annuities have also become his favorite form of investment, and many an employer has been led to grant annuities to hundreds of his employees."

"In preference to great public benefactions after death?"

"Yes, because real public needs are no longer left to the accident of individual benefactors, but are promptly provided for out of the public funds. Nowadays, the local Government establishes a library or hospital just as it would a bridge—because it is needed; and we are not subjected to the uncertainties of waiting upon the caprice of individuals in the form of post-mortem benefactions."

"What proportion of your people are thus provided for?"

"Nearly all. The annuity system means independence and a certain freedom of action, without which citizenship would be open to many temptations and perversions. It is just at this point that a gulf divides the forty-ninth from the nineteenth century, not only in sentiment but in fact: no citizen in these days is absolutely dependent upon any other person so far as the necessities of life are concerned. The first ambition in life, for woman as well as man, is independent citizenship; and both law and custom encourage this ambition, and afford every practicable means for its accomplishment. What one of your workmen spent for beer and tobacco would now suffice in a few years to assure him a competency. To be poor without good excuse, and consequently to be dependent, is now to be in disrepute."

"Bless me! that sounds unjust."

"But I assure you it is not. Public opinion, educated to its present standard, is never unjust. It does not demand the impossible of its citizens. It simply lends its aid to make things possible that were not so in your day; and then very properly frowns upon those who fail to use the opportunities it affords."

"But I cannot help thinking that you must have lost a certain element of progress in thus making each man independent of all other men."

"Why? We simply make him a free man, as he formerly claimed to be, but was not. We now know what liberty—liberty of action—really means. We discover that it means true manhood and womanhood. It means happiness unclouded by care and fear. It means free and full development of one's best abilities. It means the banishment of an army of evils that previously blocked the progress of civilization: starvation, penury, theft, prostitution, compulsory marriage, child-labor, and a multitude of others that will readily occur to you, which too often had their rise in immediate want, or fear of it in the future, on the part of self or those dependent."

"Your report is so pleasing," said Paul, "that it blinds my judgment; but I still cannot help thinking that such independence must mean annihilation of ambition in a large class. 'In the sweat of thy brow shalt thou eat bread' was in my day a truth that did not need the authority of Holy Writ. We used to be taught and to believe that, except for the struggle for life and the ambitions that maintained that struggle, life would hardly be worth living."

"That was one of those half-truths that are worse than falsehoods, because more difficult to disprove. All I can say is that time and experience have utterly refuted its conclusions. We no longer have cause to struggle for the bare necessities of life; but, for that very reason, our ambitions of youth, our highest and best ambition, —now no longer liable to be strangled by petty cares of mere animal existence,—are given an opportunity for realization to a degree of which the nineteenth century had no conception. You have already looked about you with searching eyes. What are the tokens you have observed? Have you not seen evidences of exalted ambition everywhere apparent?"

Paul was about to answer with great decision, when Madam entered the room, exclaiming: "Come, come at once! I believe it is already in sight."

The Professor arose precipitately. "Impossible!" He glanced at his watch. "Perfectly impossible, my dear!"

"Come and see for yourself." And she put an arm about him, and drew the trembling man to the terrace, Paul closely following. The scene that met Paul's gaze, as he leaned on the railing at the edge of the terrace, was of indescribable brilliancy. Utter silence characterized the scene, which might otherwise have been one of ordinary merry-making. No music was heard; and those who spoke, did so in whispers. He felt a sudden chill. There was no further need of examining the approaching visitor through the telescope, which now stood idle, casting its dark line like a bar sinister across the sky. Dimmer and dimmer grew the lights in the streets and along the terraces, until they—and with them, all the people—paled into complete obscurity. Brighter and brighter grew the heavens, and nearer and nearer swept the glowing fire-sphere, till it became a sun—till its heat grew scorching—till the world's enveloping atmosphere burst into a crackling sheet of flame—till all things crashed about the trembling spectator—till all was blackness—till, till—

The very chamber, with the eye of its night-lamp shaded, yet alert, had a look of expectancy about it. It was in the small hours of the night. From the bed came the sound of regular breathing, then a sigh, a gentle movement; and the one who lay there awoke by slow degrees, and looked vaguely about him. At last his eyes fell on a square of moonlight that lit with pale flame the otherwise obscure pattern of the carpet. His attention became gradually fixed upon it.

"Why, what does that mean?" he murmured. "Tomorrow is Christmas, and the moon fulled on the first day of the month. She is now in the middle of her last quarter, and ought not to be in the southwest until tomorrow."

Apparently the thought came to him that he might be dreaming; and, as if to still the doubt, he turned in the bed and whispered: "Mary, are you asleep?"

The curtains closing the adjoining room were quickly parted, and the pale face of the watcher drew near to his. "What is it, Paul?" The voice trembled with excitement, as well it might, for ten years had passed since he last called her by name.

．　．　．　．　．

I, Paul Prognosis, recently restored to health, have committed to paper the substance of the chapters that form this book. Sometimes I cannot help whispering to myself that it may be a boon vouchsafed to me that, if entire mental rest should again become requisite, I may once more be permitted to spend some hours amid the placid scenes of beauty and harmony that constitute Tone, the City of Truth. What then? Life has many experiences that are less to be desired; and what city of the after-life Death holds in his sacred keeping, I know not. Perchance—who will say nay?—each one of us is now building his own, even as I have builded Tone.

7

Freeland

A Social Anticipation

Dr. Theodor Hertzka

Translated by Arthur Ransom

New York
D. Appleton and Company
1891

Theodor Hertzka (1845–1924)

would have resented being placed in the company of most of the utopists here represented. He did not consider himself a utopist, but a scientific and practical economist, as he makes perfectly clear throughout *Freeland*. He was, in fact, a distinguished Viennese economist of the liberal Manchester school. He was editor of the economic section of the Vienna *Neue Freie Presse* from 1872 to 1879; he established and edited the *Wiener Allgemeine Zeitung*, 1879–1886; and after 1889 he edited the *Zeitschrift für Staats- und Volkswirtschaft*. He also was instrumental in founding the Society of Austrian National Economists. His published works include *Währung und Handel, Die Gesetze der Handels- und Sozialpolitik, Das Wesen des Geldes, Die Gesetze der sozialen Entwickelung*, and *Die Probleme der menschlichen Wirtschaft*.

If any utopian work of the modern period excited more attention than *Looking Backward*, it was *Freeland*. It unquestionably produced a greater immediate reaction, especially on the Continent, but after the initial furor of excited enthusiasm, *Freeland* became another utopia in the historical sequence of lands that never were. It was Hertzka's evident conviction that Freeland could be, and would be, if a sufficient number of men would but act according to his economic plan. Indeed, a surprising number of men did respond to his call. *Freeland*, which appeared first in 1890, had by 1891 already been translated into several languages; ten editions had been printed by 1896. Local Freeland societies to the number of almost a thousand were organized with the intent of putting Hertzka's plan for the ideal society into immediate effect. A central committee took over the task outlined in *Freeland*, and arrangements were made for a tract of land in British East Africa, almost exactly as described by Hertzka. A volunteer expedition even set out for the future Eden Vale—but here the dream ended. As so many noble and hopeful communitarians of the past had discovered, the world of nature is hard and recalcitrant, and men are remarkably shortsighted and selfish in their resistance to the best-laid schemes for achievement of the ideal.

Hertzka's is indeed perhaps the "best-laid" plan of all utopian blueprints. His attention to the details of economic, political, and technical organization is fascinating. In fact, it was precisely this content of detailed planning which so rapidly "dated" Hertzka's utopia and relegated it to the historical shelf. Yet, that Hertzka, too, was possessed of the utopian ideal is evident in his story of Freeland, and whatever his assurance of the practicality of his plan, the reader who has observed other utopists in action will detect the same optimism toward the prospects of men's rational and cheerful cooperation, the same assumption that in the new order all force will work for the good and never be put to evil purposes, the same blithe conviction that the utopian community will convert the world. Engineers may smile at the economist who plans to convert a jungle tract into a productive and technically efficient community in four months with the labor of two hundred men; even if it were possible to utilize all the mechanical equipment available in 1890, this would be little short of miraculous. A Chief of Staff, distracted from study of his budget, may smile at the utopia which has no army and no tax for military expenditures, but which yet has more efficient weapons than even the most warlike nations, with every citizen an expert in the use of those weapons. Hertzka, for all his detail of economic planning, properly belongs in the company of the utopists. Yet, in one respect Hertzka illustrates the development of utopian thought in the modern period better than most: in his recognition that the utopia of the twentieth century will have to face the problem of armed aggression and prepare to defend itself against the warring intervention of its non-utopian neighbors.

Freeland

In July 18 . . . the following appeared in the leading journals of Europe and America:

'INTERNATIONAL FREE SOCIETY.
'*A number of men from all parts of the civilised world have united for the purpose of making a practical attempt to solve the social problem.*

'*They seek this solution in the establishment of a community on the basis of perfect liberty and economic justice—that is, of a community which, while it preserves the unqualified right of every individual to control his own actions, secures to every worker the full and uncurtailed enjoyment of the fruits of his labour.*

'*For the site of such a community a large tract of land shall be procured in a territory at present unappropriated, but fertile and well adapted for colonisation.*

'*The Free Society shall recognise no exclusive right of property in the land occupied by them, either on the part of an individual or of the collective community.*

'*For the cultivation of the land, as well as for productive purposes generally, self-governing associations shall be formed, each of which shall share its profits among its members in proportion to their several contributions to the common labour of the association. Any-one shall have the right to belong to any association and to leave it when he pleases.*

'*The capital for production shall be furnished to the producers without interest out of the revenue of the community, but it must be reimbursed by the producers.*

'*All persons who are incapable of labour, and women, shall have the right to a competent allowance for maintenance out of the revenue of the community.*

'*The public revenue necessary for the above purposes, as well as for other public expenses, shall be provided by a tax levied upon the net income of the total production.*

'*The International Free Society already possesses a number of members and an amount of capital sufficient for the commencement of its work upon a moderate scale. As, however, it is thought, on the one hand, that the Society's success will necessarily be in proportion to the amount of means at its disposal, and, on the other hand, that opportunity should be given to others who may sympathise with the movement to join in the undertaking, the Society hereby an-nounces that inquiries or communications of any kind may be ad-dressed to the office of the Society at the Hague. The International Free Society will hold a public meeting at the Hague, on the 20th of October next, at which the definitive resolutions prior to the be-ginning of the work will be passed.*

'FOR THE EXECUTIVE COMMITTEE OF THE
INTERNATIONAL FREE SOCIETY,
'KARL STRAHL

The Hague, July 18 . . .'

This announcement produced no little sensation throughout the world. Any suspicion of mystification or of fraud was averted by the name of the acting representative of the Executive Committee. Dr. Strahl was not merely a man of good social position, but was widely known as one of the first political economists of Germany. Long before the 20th of October there was not a journal on either side of the Atlantic which had not assumed a definite attitude to-wards the question whether the realisation of the plans of the Free Society belonged to the domain of the possible or to that of the Utopian.

On the morning of the 20th of October the place of assembly—capable of seating two thousand persons—was filled to the last cor-ner. Amid the breathless attention of the audience, the President—Dr. Strahl—rose to open the meeting. 'The conviction that the community to the establishment of which we are about to proceed'—thus began the speaker—'is destined to attack poverty and misery at the root finds expression not simply in the words, but also in the actions, of the greater part of our members, in the lofty self-denying enthusiasm with which they—each one according to his power—have contributed towards the realisation of the common aim. When we sent out our appeal we numbered but eighty-four, the funds at our disposal amounted to only 11,400 £; today the Society consists of 5,650 members, and its funds amount to 205,620 £. Well-to-do and rich persons have joined us not merely as helpers, but also as seekers of help; they wish to found the new community not merely for their suffering brethren, but also for themselves. In carrying out our programme, a hitherto unappropriated large tract of land will have to be acquired for the founding of an independent community. There remains only Africa, the oldest yet the last-explored part of the world. We therefore propose to you that we should fix our new home in the interior of Equatorial Africa. And we are thinking particularly of the mountain district of Kenia. The new home must first be found and acquired. It is necessary that a number of selected pioneers should precede the general company. When the pioneers have accomplished their task, the rest can follow. Hitherto the business of the Society has been in the hands of a committee of ten; we ask from you a confirmation of our authority for the period of two years. At the expiration of this period we shall—we are fully convinced—not only have fixed upon a new home, but have lived in it long enough to have learnt a great deal about it.'

The first act of the executive committee was to appoint two persons with full powers to organise and take command of the pioneer expedition to Central Africa, one of them to command the expedition until a suitable territory was selected and occupied, and the other to take in hand the organisation of the colony. For the former duty the committee chose the well-known African traveller, Thomas Johnston. To take charge of the expedition after its arrival at the locality chosen, the committee nominated a young engineer, Henry Ney, who, as the most intimate friend of Dr. Strahl, was held to be the most fitting person to represent him. Dr. Strahl because his health was delicate consented to wait and to follow the pioneers with the main body of members; and Henry Ney went with the expedition as his substitute.

The account of the African expedition is taken from the journal of Dr. Strahl's friend:

My appointment as provisional substitute for our revered leader at first filled me with alarm. But my despondency did not last long.

I felt an unshakable conviction of the success of the work. It was unanimously agreed to fix the number of pioneers at two hundred of the sturdiest members of the Society. Dr. Strahl brought forward the idea of mounting the pioneers. It would be necessary to provide for the introduction and acclimatisation of beasts of burden, and he thought that we could travel much faster if we were mounted. The baggage was to be borne by 100 sumpter-horses, 200 asses and mules, and 80 camels. All the necessary purchases were at once made.

A young American lady had determined to join the expedition. She was rich, beautiful, and eccentric, an enthusiastic admirer of our principles, and evidently not accustomed to consider it possible that her wishes should be seriously opposed. But nothing could be done; we had refused several women wishful to accompany their husbands, and we could make no exceptions. She was petted and treated like a spoilt child that longed for the impossible, until Miss Ellen Fox was fairly beside herself.

She suddenly calmed down; and this occurred in a striking manner immediately after she became acquainted with another lady who also wished to join our expedition, my sister Clara. I found Clara wonderfully comforted, and I blessed the charming American for it. I most heartily congratulated myself on having thus got rid of a double difficulty.

On the 3rd of December Johnston and I reached Alexandria, where we found most of our fellow-pioneers awaiting us. Johnston set to work at once with the organisation of the troop. When the time to go on to Zanzibar came, we were a completely trained picked body of men. The language of command, as well as that of our general intercourse, was English. As many as 35 per cent. of us were English and American. At last the work was accomplished, and the journey into the interior could be begun. On the 5th of May we left the coast hills behind us and began our march.

When we were a few miles from Taveta, the leader of our advance-guard galloped toward us and cried: 'Your sister and Miss Fox are in Taveta.' What was to be done under such circumstances? It followed as a matter of course that the two Amazons must henceforth form a part of our expedition; and, to tell the truth, I knew not how to be angry with either my sister or Miss Fox for their persistency. Therefore I gave myself up to the joy of the unexpected reunion.

It was eight weeks since we had left Mombasa, a shorter time than had ever been taken by any caravan in Equatorial Africa to cover a distance of more than 600 miles. On the evening of the last day of June we pitched our camp on the bank of a considerable stream, the largest we had yet seen, about three miles from an extensive open valley-basin. Our experts estimated this valley at nearly sixty square miles, and all agreed that it was very fertile. Following this gorge upwards, we found ourselves suddenly standing in the sought-for valley.

The view was perfectly indescribable. Speechless with delight, we gazed long at this unparalleled natural miracle. The woman who was with us—Ellen Fox—was the first to find words. Like a prophetess in an ecstasy, she cried, 'Behold, the flaming sword of the archangel, guarding the gate of Paradise, has vanished at our approach! Let us call this place Eden!'

The name Eden was unanimously adopted. That this valley must be our future place of abode was at once decided by all of us. By the end of October we were able to contemplate our four months' labours with a restful satisfaction. Six hundred neat block-houses awaited as many families; 50,000 cwt. of corn and flour, copious supplies of cattle for slaughter and draught, building material and tools, were ready for the food, shelter, and equipment of many thousands of members. Our colleagues were working not less successfully, upon the road from Mombasa. First, in the places where there was a deficiency of water, wells had to be dug. In the second place, there was the road-making itself. The third part of the work consisted in the erection of primitive houses of shelter, at suitable places, for both men and cattle.

The first new arrivals—among them our beloved master—entered Eden Valley on the 14th of October; they were followed by an uninterrupted series of fresh companies.

Ellen was my betrothed when Dr. Strahl arrived at Eden Vale. Whether the joy with which I for the first time pressed to my heart the woman of my love was greater than that with which I welcomed the friend of my soul, the idol of my intellect, to the earthly paradise to which he had shown us the way—this I cannot venture to decide.

Long, long stood the master on the heights above Eden Vale, eagerly taking in every detail of the charming picture. When I said that to him belonged the office of finding a word for the country, he cried out: 'Freedom will find its birthplace in this country; FREELAND we will name it.'

Of the executive committee twelve were now in Freeland. There still remained three at a distance as authorised agents. Their duty was to receive fresh members, to collect and provisionally to have charge of the funds, and to superintend the emigrations to Eden Vale.

Their instructions respecting applications for membership were to receive every applicant who was not a relapsed criminal, and who could read and write. We were satisfied that Freeland would produce no criminals, but wished, in the beginning, to avoid being swamped by bad elements. We could use only such workers as were raised above at least the lowest stage of brutality and ignorance. The ignorant man must be under authority.

On the 20th of October the committee held its first sitting in Eden Vale, for the purpose of drawing up such rules as were required to regulate the constitution of the free associations that were henceforth to be responsible for all production in Freeland.

The fundamental feature of the plan of organisation adopted was unlimited publicity in connection with equally unlimited freedom of movement. Everyone in Freeland must always know what products were for the time being in greater or less demand, and in what branch of production for the time being there was greater or less profit to be made. To the same extent must everyone in Freeland always have the right and the power to apply himself to those branches of production which for the time being yield the largest revenue, and to this end all the means of production and all the seats of production must be available to everyone.

In order that labour may be free and self-controlling, the workers must combine as such, and not as small capitalists; they must not have over them any employer of any land or any name, not even an employer consisting of an association of themselves. They must organise themselves as workers, for only as such have they a claim to the full produce of their labour.

Productive capital is, strictly speaking, as ownerless as the land; it belongs to everyone, and therefore to no one. The community of producers supplies it and employs it, in proportion to the amount of work contributed by each individual; and payment for the expenditure is made by the community of consumers—again by each one in exact proportion to the consumption of each individual.

It remains now to say something of the measures adopted to ensure the most extensive publicity of industrial proceedings. Everyone may act as he pleases, so far as he does not infringe upon the rights of others; but, however he acts, what he does must be open to everyone. Since he here has to do not with industrial opponents, but only with industrial rivals, who all have an interest in stimulating him as much as possible, this publicity is to his own advantage. In conformity with this principle, when a new member was admitted by the outside agents, his industrial specialty was stated, and the report sent as quickly as possible to the committee. The consequence was that, as a rule, the new members on their arrival at the Kenia found suitable work-places prepared for them, such as would enable them at once to utilise their working capacity to the best advantage. No one forced them to accommodate themselves to these arrangements made without their cooperation, but as these arrangements served their advantage in the best conceivable way, they—with a few isolated exceptions—accepted them with the greatest pleasure.

The second and most important subject of publication were the trade reports of the producers, of the associations as well as of the comparatively few isolated producers. Of the former, as being by far the more important and by their very nature compelled to adopt a careful system of bookkeeping, a great deal was required—in fact the full disclosure of all their proceedings. In the case of the isolated producers, it sufficed to publish such details as would be disclosed by the regulation about to be described.

The buying and selling of all conceivable products and articles of merchandise in Freeland was carried on in large halls and warehouses, which were under the management of the community. No one was forbidden to buy and sell where he pleased, but these public magazines offered such enormous advantages that everyone who did not wish to suffer loss made use of them.

The supreme authority in Freeland was at the same time the banker of the whole population. Not merely every association, but every individual, had his account in the books of the central bank, which undertook the receipts and the disbursements from the millions of pounds which at a later date many of the associations had to receive and pay, both at home and abroad, down to the individual's share of profits on labour and his outlay on clothes and food. No one paid cash, but gave cheques on his account at the central bank, which gave him credit for his earnings, debited his spendings to him, and gave him every month a statement of his account. In this way the bank was informed of the minutest detail of every business transaction throughout the whole country. It not only knew where and at what price the producers purchased their machinery and raw material and where they sold their productions, but it knew also the housekeeping account, the income and cost of living of every family. Even the retail trade could not escape the omniscience of this control. Even if anyone had wished to do so, it would have been simply impracticable to conceal or falsify anything.

This comprehensive and automatically secured transparency of the whole of the productive and business relations afforded to the tax assessed in Freeland a perfectly reliable basis. The apportionment of the tax was very simply made as soon as the income existed, and that through the medium of the bank; and this was done not merely in the case of the associations, but also of the few isolated producers. In fact, by means of its bank the community had every-one's income in hand sooner than the earners themselves; and it was merely necessary to debit the earners with the amount and the tax was paid. Hence in Freeland the tax was regarded not as a deduction from net income, but as an outlay deducted from the gross product, just like the trade expenses. It was therefore quite correct to recognise no difference whatever betwen productive outlay by the commonwealth and the more private outlay of the associations and individuals, and accordingly to designate the former not as 'taxes,' but as 'general expenditure.'

This general expenditure, however, was very high. In the first year it amounted to thirty-five per cent. of the net profits, and it never sank below thirty per cent., though the income on which the tax was levied increased enormously.

One of its objects was to create the capital required for the purposes of production. But it was only at first that the whole of this had to be met out of the current tax, as afterwards the repayment of the loans partly met the new demands.

A constantly increasing item of expenditure was the cost of edu-cation, which swallowed up a sum of which no one outside of Freeland can have any conception.

The means of communication also involved an expenditure that rose to enormous dimensions, and the same has to be said of public buildings.

But the chief item of expenditure in the Freeland budget was under the head of 'Maintenance,' which included the claims of those who, on account of incapacity for work or because they were by our principles released from the obligation of working, had a right to a competence from the public funds. To these belonged all women, all children, all men over sixty years of age, and of course all sick persons and invalids. The allowances to these different classes were so high that not merely urgent necessities, but also such higher daily needs as were commensurate with the general wealth in Free-land for the time being, could be met.

On the other hand, the departments of justice, police, military, and finance, which in other countries swallow up nine-tenths of the total budget, cost nothing in Freeland. We had no judges, no police organisation, our tax flowed in spontaneously, and soldiers we knew not. Yet there was no theft, no robbery, no murders among us; the payment of the tax was never in arrears; and we were by no means defenceless. As to the lack of a magistracy, we were such arrant barbarians that we did not even consider a civil or a criminal code necessary, nor did we at that time possess a written constitution. The committee, still in possession of the absolute authority committed to it at the Hague, contented itself with laying all its measures before public meetings and asking for the assent of the members, which was unanimously given. For the settlement of misunderstandings, arbitrators were chosen, and from them appeal was allowed to the Board of Arbitrators; but they as good as had nothing to do. Against vices we did not exercise any right of *punishment*, but only a right of *protection*; and we esteemed *reformation* the best and most effectual means of protection. We considered casual criminals as mentally or morally diseased persons, whose treatment it was the business of the community to provide for.

Each member of the committee was president of one of the twelve branches into which the whole of the public administration of Freeland was provisionally divided. These branches were: 1. The Presidency; 2. Maintenance; 3. Education; 4. Art and Science; 5. Statistics; 6. Roads and means of communication; 7. Post—including later the telegraph; 8. Foreign affairs; 9. Warehouses; 10. Central bank; 11. Public undertakings; 12. Sanitation and administration of justice.

These are, in general outlines, the principles upon which Freeland was organised and administered. They stood the test of experience in all respects most satisfactorily.

There was in Freeland a great disproportion in the number of the sexes, particularly of young men and marriageable women. Of the 460 pioneers who had reached the Kenia between June and September, very few had either wives or betrothed in the old home; and among the later arrivals there was a preponderance of young unmarried men. It was not to be expected that the immediate future would bring an adequate number of young unmarried women unless some special means were adopted; but this forced celibacy could not continue without danger of unpleasant social developments in a community that aimed at uniting absolute freedom with the strictest morality. We had merely to make the state of affairs known in Europe and America, and to announce that women who remained single were in Freeland supported by the State, and we should very soon have had no reason to complain of a lack of women. But whether we should have been pleased with those whom such an announcement might bring is another question. We preferred, therefore, to instruct our representatives in the old home to engage women-teachers for Freeland. The salary was attractive, and we had a choice of numberless candidates. It was therefore to no one's injury if these highly cultured women, most of whom were young, gave up their teaching vocation not long after they reached Freeland and consented to make some wooer happy. The vacated place was at once filled by a new teacher, who quite as quickly made room for a fresh successor.

With respect to the hours of labour, the system originally adopted was on the whole retained. The men worked for the most part between 5 and 10 A.M. and between 4 and 6 P.M.; the women, assisted by natives, took care of the home and of the children when they were not at school. Yet no one felt bound to observe these hours—everyone worked when and as long as he pleased; and several associations, the work of which would not well bear the interruption of meal-times, introduced a system of relays which insured the presence of a few hands at work during the hot hours. But as no one could be compelled to work during those hours, it became customary to pay for the more burdensome midday work a higher rate than for the ordinary work, and this had the effect of bringing the requisite number of volunteers. The same held good for the night work that was necessary in certain establishments.

. . . . .

The meeting at the Hague had conferred full executive power upon the committee for the period of two years. This period expired on the 20th of October. On the 15th of September, therefore, the committee called together a constituent assembly. As the proposed fundamental law and detailed regulations were extremely simple, the debate was not very long-winded; and, on the 2nd day of October, the laws and regulations were declared to be unanimously approved, and the new constitution was put in force.

The fundamental laws were thus expressed:

1. Every inhabitant of Freeland has an equal and inalienable claim upon the whole of the land, and upon the means of production accumulated by the community.

2. Women, children, old men, and men incapable of work, have a right to a competent maintenance.

3. No one can be hindered from the active exercise of his own free individual will, so long as he does not infringe upon the rights of others.

4. Public affairs are to be administered as shall be determined by all the adult (above twenty years of age) inhabitants of Freeland, without distinction of sex, who shall all possess an equal active and passive right of vote and of election in all matters that affect the commonwealth.

5. Both the legislative and the executive authority shall be divided into departments, and in such a manner that the whole of the electors shall choose special representatives for the principal public departments, who shall give their decisions apart and watch

over the action of the administrative boards of the respective departments.

In these five points is contained the whole substance of the public law in Freeland; everything else is merely the natural consequence or the more detailed expression of these points.

With reference to the right of maintenance it may be remarked that this was regarded as corollary from the truth that the wealth of civilised man is not the product of his own individual capabilities, but is the result of the intellectual labour of numberless previous generations, *whose bequest belongs as much to the weak and helpless as to the strong and capable.*

Happiness and dignity, as well as the future salvation of humanity, equally demanded that woman should be delivered from the dishonourable necessity of seeing in her husband a provider, in marriage the only refuge from material need. But neither should woman be consigned to common labour. She must be no wheel in the bread-earning machinery, she must be a jewel in the heart of humanity. Only one kind of 'work' is appropriate to woman—that of the education of children, and, at most, the care of the sick and infirm. At the same time, our principles secured perfect liberty to woman. She was not forbidden to engage in any occupation, and isolated instances have occurred of women doing so, particularly in intellectual callings, but public opinion in Freeland approved of this only in exceptional cases—that is, when special gifts justified such action; and it was our women chiefly who upheld this public action.

The extension of the franchise to adult women calls for no special comment. It need only be remarked that this law included the negroes residing in Freeland. This was conditioned by exclusion from the exercise of political rights of all who were unable to read and write—and exclusion was automatically secured by requiring all votes to be in the voter's handwriting. We took considerable pains not only to teach our negroes reading and writing, but also to give them other kinds of knowledge; and as our efforts were in general followed by good results, our black brethren gradually participated in all our rights.

The community exercised control over all public affairs not through *one*, but through several co-ordinated administrative boards, elected separately by the community. There were in Freeland, besides the twelve different executive boards, twelve different consultative, determining, and supervising assemblies, elected by the whole people, in place of the single parliament of the Western Nations. These twelve assemblies were elected by the whole of the electors, each elector having the right to give an equal vote in all the elections; but the distribution of the constituencies was different, and the election for each of the twelve representative bodies took place separately. Some of those elections—those, namely, for the affairs of the chief executive and finance, for maintenance, for education, for art and science, for sanitation and justice—took place according to residence; the elections in the other cases according to calling. Membership of the respective constituencies depended upon the will of the elector—that is, every elector could get his or her name entered in the list of any calling with which he or she preferred to vote, and thus exercise the right of voting for the representative body elected by the members of that calling.

The natural result of this organisation was that every inhabitant of Freeland confined his attention to those public affairs which he understood, or thought he understood. Every branch of the public administration was in the hands of the most expert specialists. Attempts to influence the electors by fallacious representations or by promises would prove resultless. There is no elector who would vote in the elections of the whole twelve representative bodies. The women, in particular, with very few exceptions, refrain from voting in the elections in which the separate callings are specially concerned; on the other hand, they take a lively interest in the elections in which the electors vote according to residence; and in the elections for the board of education their votes turn the scale. By way of completing this description, it may be mentioned that the elected deputies are paid for their work at the rate of an equivalent of labour-hours for each day that they sit.

The election of the twelve representative bodies was at once proceeded with. The committees were all re-elected as heads of the different branches of the administration, except four who declined. The government of Freeland was now definitely constituted.

The board of education made vigorous efforts. A public opinion had grown up that the youth of Freeland, without distinction of sex and without reference to future callings, ought to enjoy an education which, with the exception of the knowledge of Greek and Latin, should correspond to that obtainable, for example, in the first six classes of a German gymnasium. Accordingly, boys and girls were to attend school from the age of six to that of sixteen years, and after acquiring the elements, were to be taught grammar, the history of literature, general history, the history of civilisation, physics, natural history, geometry, and algebra.

Not less importance was attached to physical education than to intellectual and moral. A healthy, harmoniously developed mind presupposed a healthy harmonious developed body. Moreover, in the cultivation of the intellect less stress was laid upon the accumulation of knowledge than upon the stimulation of the young mind to independent thought. No child was to be engaged in mental work—home preparation included—longer than at most six hours a day; hence the hours of teaching of any subject were limited to three a day, whilst two other school hours were devoted daily to physical exercises. A further principle was that the children should not be *forced* into activity any more than the adults. Our mode of instruction had to be such as would make school exceedingly attractive; but, when this had been achieved, our boys and girls learnt in half the time as much, and that as thoroughly, as the physically and intellectually maltreated European boys and girls of the same age.

Naturally such a system of instruction demanded a very numerous and highly gifted staff of teachers. In Freeland there was on an average one teacher to every fifteen scholars, and the best intelligence in the land was secured for the teaching profession by the payment of high salaries. But even such a demand for high intelligence Freeland was determined to meet out of its own resources. In the third year, therefore, a high school was founded, in which all those branches of knowledge were taught which in Europe can be learnt at the universities, academies, and technical colleges. Our observatories, laboratories, and museums had command of almost unlimited means, and no stipend was too high to attract and retain a brilliant teacher. The instruction in all faculties was absolutely untrammeled. In the fifth year of the settlement the high school had 7,500 students, the number of its chairs was 215; its annual budget reached as high as 2,500,000 £ and was rapidly increasing.

. . . . .

Twenty years have passed away—twenty-five years since the arrival of our pioneers at the Kenia. The principles by which Freeland has been governed have remained the same, and their results have not changed, except that the intellectual and material culture, and the number and wealth of the inhabitants have grown in a continually increasing ratio. The immigration had reached in the twenty-fifth year the figure of 1,152,000 heads. In order to convey into the heart of the continent as quickly as possible this influx to the African coast from all parts of the world, the Freeland system of railways has been either carried to or connected with other lines that reach the ocean at four different points. Thus we possess two direct railway connections with the Indian Ocean, and one each with the Mediterranean Sea and the Atlantic Ocean.

The densest Freeland population is still to be found on the highlands between the Victoria Nyanza and the Indian Ocean, and the seat of the supreme government is now, as formerly, in Eden Vale; but Freeland has largely extended its boundaries on all sides, particularly on the west, to an area of about 580,000 square miles. The total population of the territory at this time under Freeland influences amounts to 42,000,000 souls, of whom 26,000,000 are whites and 16,000,00 black or brown natives.

The products of Freeland industry comprehend almost all the articles required by civilised men; but mechanical industry continues to be the chief branch of production. This production is principally to meet the home demand, though the productive capacity of Freeland has for years materially surpassed that of all the machine-factories in the rest of the world. But Freeland has employment for more machinery than the whole of the rest of the world, for the work of its machines takes the place of that of the slaves or the wage-labourers of other countries. Therefore comparatively few of our machines—except certain specialties—go over our frontiers. On the contrary, agriculture is pursued more largely for export than for home consumption; indeed, it can with truth be asserted that the whole of Freeland corn-produce is available for export, since the surplus of the corn-production of the negroes which reaches our markets is on an average quite sufficient to cover our home demand. The chief item of import goods was that of 'books and other printed matter'; and next to this followed works of art and objects of luxury. It must not be inferred that the demand for books in Freeland is entirely, or even mainly, covered by the import from without. The Freeland readers during the same year paid more than twice as much to their home publishers as to the foreign ones. In fact, the Freelanders read more than three times as much as the whole of the reading public outside of Freeland.

The total value of the productions of the 7,500,000 producers during the last year was nearly seven milliard pounds sterling (7,000,000,000 £). Deducting from that amount two milliards and a half to cover the tax for the purposes of the commonwealth, there remained four milliard and a half as profit to be shared among the producers, giving an average of 600 £ to each worker. And to produce this we worked only five hours a day on the average, or 1,500 hours in the year; so that the average net value of an hour's labour was 8s.—little less than the average weekly wage of the common labourer in many parts of Europe. Almost all articles of ordinary consumption are very much cheaper in Freeland than in any other part of the civilised world.

We now came more and more into immediate contact with colonies under European influence. Our intercourse was everywhere directed by the best and most accommodating intentions, but a number of questions sprang up which urgently demanded a definitive solution. For instance, the neighbouring colonies found it inconvenient to be in close proximity to Freeland settlements; their population was drawn away by us like iron filings by a magnet. We were also compelled to moot the question, what would happen if Freelanders were to settle in any district belonging to a Western nation? Ultimately it would be unavoidable. Should we, in possession of the stronger form of civilisation, yield to the weaker and more backward one? For the sake of keeping peace with our neighbours we were compelled to try to obtain legal recognition of our institutions, in the first place, in the neighbouring colonial districts. In other parts of the world also, there came into existence a number of questions between ourselves and various governments, which urgently needed settling. Our offices and our ships were gratuitously at the service of all who wished to flee to us out of the sorrow of the old system of society. We were not disposed to allow ourselves to be turned aside from the fulfilment of our mission by the protests of foreign Powers. But it became impossible not to perceive that the relations between us and several European and Asiatic governments were getting more and more strained. They wished to control the influx of Freeland money, and to check the emigration to Freeland. No one in Freeland doubted that we were strong enough in case of need to resist any attempts to limit our activity. But all were agreed that every conceivable pacific means must be tried before we appealed to arms. The difficulty in the way of a bloodless settlement of the quarrel lay in the fact that the foreigners looked upon us as powerless from a military point of view. We were therefore convinced that a definitive threat by our plenipotentiaries would not be taken seriously, and that any attempt to maintain our position could produce the requisite effect only by actual war. And a war it was that confirmed our position everywhere abroad, but with an African power—a war which, though it had a very indirect bearing upon the subject in question, yet brought this question to a decision.

. . . . .

These letters were written by Prince Carlo Falieri, a young Italian diplomatist, who has since settled in Freeland, but who at the time to which these letters refer was visiting Eden Vale in his country's service.

Eden Vale: July 12, ——

I am writing to you from the chief city in Freeland, where my father and I have already been for some days. What has brought us to the country of social liberty? My chiefs have for some time not known how to deal with the brown Napoleon of the East Coast of Africa, the Negus John V. of Abyssinia; and our good friends in London and Paris have experienced the same difficulty. So the cabinets of the three Western Powers have agreed to seek an African remedy for the common African malady. We are commissioned to represent to the Freelanders that it would be to their interest as well as to ours if they allowed their country to be the theatre of war against Abyssinia. We ask nothing but passive co-operation.

We came from Brindisi to Alexandria by the 'Uranus,' one of the enormous ships which Freeland keeps afloat upon all seas for mail and passenger service. My father, who at first hesitated to entrust himself to a Freeland steamer which carries all its passengers free of charge and makes no distinction in treatment, admitted that he did not regret having yielded to my entreaty. We took the first express-train to the Soudan—express in little more than name. At Assuan we entered a Freeland train; and we now went on with a punctuality and speed elsewhere to be met only in England or America. It was characteristic that no fare was charged above Assuan. The food and drink consumed in the dining-cars had to be paid for—on the 'Uranus' even the board was given for nothing—but traveling accommodation is provided gratuitously by the Freeland commonwealth.

I could scarcely trust my senses when, on awaking on the fifth day of our railway journey, I caught sight of endless cultivated fields pleasantly variegated by luxuriant gardens and smiling groves, among which elegant villas, here scattered and there collected into townships, were conspicuous. We saw for the first time some Freelanders in their peculiar dress, as simple as it is becoming, and thoroughly suitable to the climate. This costume is very similar to that of the ancient Greeks; even the sandals instead of shoes are not wanting, only they are worn over stockings. The impression which the Freelanders made upon me was quite a dazzling one. I thought at first that this was the best society of the place. Their culture fully corresponded to their appearance. Yet these were but ordinary country people. Not less astonishing was the respectability of the negroes scattered among and freely mingling with the whites.

Towards noon we reached the Albert Lake. Here a very agreeable surprise awaited me. You remember David Ney, that young Freeland sculptor with whom we trotted about Rome together last autumn. After David left Europe at the close of his art studies, we corresponded; and he was therefore informed of my intended visit. His father is, as you know, a member of the Freeland government. He brought to my father and me an invitation from his parents to be their guests while we remained in Eden Vale. To my great satisfaction, my father cordially accepted this invitation.

The family Ney received us in the most cordial manner; nevertheless their dignified bearing impressed even my proud father. The ladies in particular were like princesses in disguise. Father Ney must be at least fifty years old, but he looks to be scarcely forty. The younger of the sons, Emanuel, technician by calling, is a complete duplicate of David. The mother, Ellen by name, an American by birth, must be about forty-five, but her youthful freshness gives her the appearance of a sister of her children. Bertha, a young copy of the mother, at once embarassed me by the indescribable charm of her presence.

David took us into two bedrooms with a common anteroom. Then followed a short explanation of the many provisions for the comfort of the users of the room. 'This telephone is for use within the house and for communication with the nearest watch-room of the Association for Personal Service; in two minutes a messenger of the association will have hastened to wait on you. The household work is done on the basis of a common tariff. Early in the morning messengers come noiselessly, take the clothing that has to be cleaned, put the clean clothes in the proper place, get ready the baths, clean the outer spaces and some of the rooms, and disappear. It is almost all done by machinery. A little later the workers of the association reappear to clean the rest of the rooms, and prepare everything for breakfast. And so these people come and go several times during the day, as often as is agreed upon, in order to see that all is right. We are served by intelligent, courteous, zealous men of business who are compelled by competition—for we have six such associations in Eden Vale—to do their utmost to satisfy the families that employ them.' The Association for Rendering Personal Services satisfied even my father's very comprehensive demands. He declares that he never found better attendance at the Bristol Hotel in Paris.

Two other members of the Ney family are David's aunt Clara, his father's sister, and her husband, Professor Noria, both originals of a very special kind. Aunt Clara, at heart an ardent Freelander, married the professor, because in him she found an indefatigable antagonist in her attacks upon Freeland. He labours at his great work, which, if it is ever finished, is to prove to the world that all the ills it has hitherto suffered can be explained by the facts expressed in heraldry.

I must now conclude for to-day, for I am tired; but I have a great deal more to tell you of my experiences.

Eden Vale: July 18, ——

Today I take up again the report which I began a week ago. Mr. Ney invited us to join him and his son on a tour round Eden

Vale. The carriage was already waiting. It was a light and elegant vehicle with steel wheels like those of a velocipede, and with two seats each comfortably accommodating two persons. The motive power is neither steam nor electricity, but the elasticity of a spiral spring. The spring will carry the vehicle about twelve miles and a half. The maximum speed attained by these ordinary *draisines* is a little over eleven miles an hour. Racing carriages attain nearly twice that speed. One can take with him one or more springs ready wound up. Besides, the Transport Association has a number of station-houses; it is possible to travel through the whole of Freeland certain of finding everywhere a relay of springs.

We went to the heights around Eden Vale. Here we perceived at once, even at a distance of nearly two miles, a gigantic building, unparalleled in size as it is incomparable in harmonious perfection. This wonderful structure is the National Palace of Freeland. It is the seat of the twelve supreme Boards of Administration and the twelve Representative Bodies. I will spare you the catalogue of the numberless handsome buildings, the purposes of some of which I could scarcely understand, as our 'civilised' Europe possesses nothing like them. As I was curious to see how the world-renowned Freeland benevolence, which for years past has richly furnished half the hospitals of the world with means, dealt with the sick poor in its own country, I asked David to take me to at least one hospital. 'I can show you a hospital as little as I can a prison or a barracks, in Eden Vale, for the very simple reason that we do not possess one in all Freeland,' was his answer.

'The absence of prisons and barracks I can understand; we knew that you Freelanders can manage without criminal laws or a military administration; but—so I thought—sickness must exist here: that has nothing to do with your social institutions!'

'Your last sentence I cannot unconditionally assent to,' said Mr. Ney, joining in our conversation. 'Even diseases have decreased under the influence of our social institutions. It is true they have not disappeared—we have sick in Freeland—but no poor sick, for we have no poor at all, either sick or sound. Therefore we do not possess those reservoirs of the diseased poor which in other countries are called "hospitals." We certainly have institutions in which sick persons can, at good prices, procure special and careful treatment, and they are largely patronised, particularly in cases requiring surgical operations; but they are private institutions, and they resemble both in their constitution and their management your most respectable sanatoria for "distinguished patients." '

David further told me that in Freeland the physician is not paid by the patient, but is a public official, as is also the apothecary. The study of medicine is nevertheless as free in the universities here as any other study, and no one is prevented from practising as a physician because he may not have undergone an examination or passed through a university. This is the inevitable consequence of the principles of the commonwealth. On the other hand, however, the commonwealth exercises the right of entrusting the care of health and sanitation to certain paid officials, as in every other kind of public service. These appointments are made, according to the public needs, by the head of the Education Department, who, like all other heads of departments, is responsible to his own representative board—or parliament of experts, as we may call it. It is the practice for the professors to propose the candidates, who, of course, undergo many severe examinations before they are proposed. Anyone who fails to get proposed *may* practise medicine, but as the public knows that the most skilful are always chosen with the utmost conscientiousness conceivable, this liberty to practise is of no value. Anyone who thus fails to get proposed, and has neither the energy nor the patience to attempt to wipe off his disgrace at the next opportunity, simply hangs his medical vocation on a nail and turns to some other occupation. The elected physicians are not allowed to receive any payment whatever from their patients. At first their salary is moderate, scarcely more than the average earnings of a worker—that is, 1,800 hour-equivalents per annum; but it is increased gradually, as in the cases of the other officials, and the higher sanitary officials are taken from among the physicians. As the payments are controlled by the departmental parliament, and as this is elected by the persons who in one way or another are interested in this branch of the government, the best possible provision is made to prevent the physicians from assuming an unbecoming attitude toward their patients. No one is obliged to call in any one particular physician. The physicians live in different parts of each town, as conveniently distributed as possible; but everyone calls in the physician he likes best; and as physicians are naturally elected as far as possible upon the Representative Board for Sanitation— whose sittings, it may be remarked in passing, are generally very short—the number of votes which the representatives receive is the best evidence of their relative popularity. It goes without saying that foreign physicians also, if they are men of good repute and do not object, have the same right as the Freeland physicians to submit their qualifications to the proposing body of professors. It should be added that in the larger towns, besides the ordinary physicians and surgeons, specialists are also appointed for certain specific diseases.

But I see that I must conclude without having exhausted my matter. Promising to give next time what I have omitted here,

Thine,

——————

Eden Vale: July 28, ——

I could not keep my promise to write again soon, because last week was taken up with a number of excursions which I made with David on horseback, or by means of *draisines* into the environs of Eden Vale and to the neighbouring town of Dana, and by rail to the shores of the Victoria Nyanza. In this way I have got to know quite a number of Freeland towns, as well as several scattered industrial and agricultural colonies. One gets the impression everywhere that care is unknown in this country. That ingenuous cheerfulness, which among us in Europe is the enviable privilege of the early years of youth, here sits upon every brow and beams from every eye. I asked David, 'Are you not afraid that this absence of care will eventually put an end to that upon which you rely— that is, to progress? Hitherto at least want and care have been the strongest incentives to human activity.'

'As if want had ever been the sole, or even the principal, spring of human progress! During the whole history of civilisation we owe the best achievements of the human intellect not to want, but to those other impulses which are peculiar to our race. The great thinkers, inventors, and discoverers of all ages and all nations have not been spurred on by hunger. The civilised man who has once acquired higher tastes will the more zealously strive to gratify those tastes the less his mental and physical energy has been weakened by degrading want, and the less doubtful the result of his effort is.'

I recalled a conversation I had had with the elder Ney about savings and insurance in Freeland, and it occurred to me that these were both things that did not harmonise with the absence of care. So I asked David, 'Why do men save in a country in which even those incapable of work are protected not merely against material want, but even against the lack of higher enjoyments?'

'Almost all men save in Freeland,' answered David. 'The object of this saving is to provide for the future out of the superfluity of the present. The distinction between our saving and the anxious care of other peoples lies merely here, that our saving is intended not to guard us against want, but simply against the danger of a future diminution of the standard of our accustomed enjoyments.'

Here David ended his instructions for the time; and I will imitate him.

Eden Vale: Aug. 2, —

For some time I have been deeply interested in the education of the young here, and the day before yesterday was devoted to the study of this subject. The elementary schools have four classes, and girls and boys are taught together. The teaching is entirely in the hands of women; only gymnastics and swimming are taught by men to the boys. We next went to the middle schools, in which boys and girls from ten to sixteen years are taught apart, the former solely by men, the latter partly by women. I learnt that, up to this age, the instruction given to all children is the same, except that among the girls less time is given to bodily exercises and more to musical training. At sixteen begins the differentiation. The girls either remain at home, and there complete their education; or they are sent as pupil-daughters, with the same view, to the house of some highly cultured and intellectually gifted woman. Others may enter the pedagogic training institutions, or they may hear a course of lectures on nursing, or devote themselves to aesthetics, art, &c.

The boys, on the other hand, are distributed among the various higher educational institutions. Most of them attend the industrial and commercial technical institutions. Every worker passes through one of these, whether he intends to be agriculturist, spinner, or what not. There is a double object in this: first, to make every worker familiar with the whole circle of knowledge and practice connected with his occupation; and next to place him in the position of being able to employ himself profitably, if he chooses to do so, in several branches of production. Young persons who have given evidence of possessing superior intellectual ability attend the universities, in which Freeland's professors, the higher government officials, physicians, technicians, &c., are educated; or the richly endowed academies of art, which send forth the architects, sculptors, painters, and musicians of the country.

The institution of public local and national exercises prevents the students from relaxing in their zeal for bodily exercises. I expressed my astonishment that Freeland, the home of social equity, could exhibit such enthusiasm for performances which, where everything breathed inviolable peace, could have no value but as simple exercises.

'Quite right,' answered David, 'only it is this very superiority in bodily exercises which secures to us the inviolable peace which we enjoy. We have no military institutions; and if it were not for our superiority in all that pertains to bodily strength and skill we should be an easy prey to any military Power that coveted our wealth. Our harmoniously developed men and youths perfected in the use of every kind of arm would completely annihilate an equally numerous body of men within range.'

'But how would you defend yourselves against the artillery of European armies?' I asked.

'By our own artillery,' answered David. 'Even this practice is begun at school. In brief, we have no army; but our men and youths handle all the weapons which an army needs infinitely better than the soldiers of any army whatever.'

In your last letter you give expression to your astonishment that our host with only a salary of 1440 £ as a member of the government is able to keep such an establishment—to live as luxuriously as only the richest are able to do among us at home. Everything here is fabulously cheap—in fact, many things are furnished gratuitously by the comonwealth, free personal transport, telephones, the post, electric lighting, &c. I will take this opportunity of remarking that almost every Freelander takes a holiday of at least six, and sometimes as much as ten weeks, and seeks recreation, pleasure, and instruction, as a tourist. Every simple worker lives essentially as our hosts do. The villas merely have fewer rooms, the furniture is plainer; instead of keeping saddle-horses of their own, the simple workers hire those belonging to the Transport Association; less money is spent upon objects of art, books, and for benevolent purposes: these are the only differences.

As to the question whether the right of maintenance does not attract into this country all the bodily and mental incapables, the cripples and the old people, of the rest of the world, I can only answer that Freeland irresistibly attracts everyone who hears of the character of its institutions; and that therefore the proportion between the immigrants who are capable of working and those who are not is dependent simply upon whether such information reaches the one class more quickly and easily than it does the other. It lies in the nature of things that the ablest, the most vigorous, offer themselves in larger numbers than those who are weak in body or mind.

My father said that he could perfectly understand that the Freeland institutions were thoroughly capable of meeting every fair and resonable demand. He nevertheless expressed his astonishment at the perfect satisfaction which the people universally exhibited with themselves and their condition. Did not *unreasonable* party agitations create difficulties in Freeland? Particularly he wished to know if Communism and Nihilism, which were ever raising their heads threateningly in Europe, gave no trouble here. 'In the eyes of a genuine Communist,' he cried, 'you are nothing but arrant aristocrats! There is not a trace of absolute equality among you! '

'Nothing easier,' answered Mrs. Ney. 'Supply everyone to satiety, and no one will covet what others have. Absolute equality is an hallucination of the hunger-fever, nothing more. Men are not equal, either in their faculties or in their requirements. When it is perceived that nothing but perfect equality of rights is needed *in order to create more than enough for all,* Communism disappears of itself like an evil tormenting dream. Nihilism is the inference drawn by despair from the doctrine that culture and civilisation are incompatible with equality of rights. We have demonstrated that civilisation is necessarily implied in the economic equality of rights. Hence Nihilism also must be unknown amongst us. Inequality exists only so far as the difference of capacity justifies it. Every kind of capacity is better paid the rarer it is. The earnings of gifted authors and artists in this country have no definite limits; as their works are above competition, so the rewards they obtain bear no proportion to those obtainable in ordinary business. Economic equality of rights never produces absolute and universal equality; but it is really accompanied by a general levelling of the enjoyments of all, and leaves unaffected only such incongruities as the most fastidious sense of justice will recognise as having their basis in the nature of things.'

Here ended this conversation, which will ever be a memorable one to me, because it confirmed my decision to become a Free-lander.

Eden Vale: Aug. 20,——

Your logic is right, Louis: I am in love—indeed I was from the first sight I had of Bertha, David's splendid sister; as soon as I could summon courage to propose to her, Bertha confessed, with that undisguised candour which is charming in her—more correctly, in all the women of Freeland—that on the very first evening of our acquaintance she felt she should either marry me or marry no one. And yet, on my first wooing her, I had to listen to a 'No' of the most determined character. The fact was that Bertha could not make up her mind to become an Italian duchess. My desire to settle in Freeland was regarded by my father as a foolish whim. Against my loving Bertha he made no objection, and asked her parents for the hand of their daughter for his son, the Prince Carlo Falieri. With a proud and indignant mien Bertha cried, 'Leave Freeland—leave it as *princess!*—never, never! Better die a thousand times! I love Carlo so much that I should be ready by his side to exchange the land of happiness for that of misery, but only on condition that we ourselves earned by honest labour what we needed. But to become *princess;* to have thousands of curses of men tortured to death clinging to the food I eat and the raiment I wear! I cannot become a princess—I cannot!'

This appeal was more than my father could resist, and he asked the Neys forthwith to make all the necessary arrangements. Mrs. Ney, however, asked what further preliminaries were necessary? We had mutually confessed our love, the blessing of the parents on both sides was not lacking; we might start off somewhere that very day on our wedding-tour. In Freeland the reciprocal declaration by two lovers that they wished to become husband and wife was all that was required to the conclusion of a marriage-contract. The fact that in Freeland divorces were quite unknown did not at once suffice to convince my father. He was content that I should take my Bertha according to Freeland customs and without any formal ceremony. Only *one* condition he insisted upon: there should be a fortnight's interval between betrothal and wedding. On the 3rd of September, therefore, Bertha will become my wife; but from to-day you must look upon me as a citizen of Freeland.

Ungama: Aug. 24.

When I finished my letter four days ago, I had not the slightest presentiment that momentous events would come between me and the fulfilment of my ardent desires. The war in which we are engaged produces remarkably little excitement in my new fatherland. On the morning after my betrothal, a despatch came to my father. John of Abyssinia, contrary to existing treaty of peace, treacherously fell upon Massowah and took it. Our vessels, as well as the English and French, seventeen in number, were also surprised and taken. This was bad tidings also for Freeland, for it meant war with Abyssinia. It had been resolved from the first to secure for the European Powers, as presumptive allies, peace with Abyssinia. The Eden Vale government intended to carry on alone the war with Abyssinia which now seemed inevitable. Moreover, the allies were told that before the English, French, and Italians could have got ready so great an expedition, we should have recaptured or destroyed the stolen fleet of Abyssinia. The Education Department of the Freeland government possesses a large number of cannon of different calibre for the exercise of the young men. As soon as the first news of the attack had been received, eighty-four giant guns had been put in motion towards Ungama from the adjoining districts. I started for Ungama. On the 23rd of August five Abyssinian ironclads and four gunboats appeared; as the harbour was thought to be defenceless, they attempted to steam in for the purpose of destroying the disabled vessels of the allies which lay there. Our young gunners opened fire simultaneously with thirty-seven cannons. The first volley sank a gunboat, and damaged the whole fleet so much that the enemy was thrown into visible disorder. Two minutes later our second volley swept over the waves; it could be plainly seen that this time not one of the thirty-seven shots had missed its mark. A second gunboat and the largest of the ironclad frigates sank. Three other volleys did still further damage to the fleeing enemy. Our batteries had lost only two men.

With the account of this Freeland deed of arms—in which I was simply an astonished spectator—I close this letter. When, where, and whether I shall write you another is known only to the God of war.

Massowah; Sept. 25, ——

It is just a month and a day since I sent you my last letter. During this brief time I have gone through experiences which must have afforded you in old Europe many a surprise, and which will, in their immediate consequences, be of decisive importance to the whole of the habitable globe. It is the freedom of the world, I believe, that has been won on the battle-fields of the Red Sea and the Galla country; a victory has been gained, not merely over the unhappy John of Abyssinia, but also over many another tyranny which has held nations in bondage in your so-called civilised world. I took part from the beginning to the end.

To-morrow David and I return to Ungama, where Bertha awaits us. The fortnight my father bargained for has passed more than twice—I shall meet, not my betrothed, but my wife, on the Freeland seashore.

. . . . .

Here end the Freeland letters of our new countryman, Carlo Falieri, to his friend the architect Luigi Cavalotti. The two friends have exchanged residences; Cavalotti has migrated to Freeland, Falieri on the contrary, after spending a few delightful weeks on a paradisiacal island on Lake Victoria Nyanza, has been withdrawn from us for a time. He obeyed a call from his native land to assist in the carrying out of those reforms which had to be undertaken there, as elsewhere throughout the world, in consequence of the events described in his letters. His wife accompanies him on his mission, in the furtherance of which our central government has placed the resources of Freeland at his disposal.

The moral effect of our Abyssinian campaign was immense. The former opponents of economic justice were not merely silenced, but actually converted. England, France, and Italy, which before the Abyssinian war were prepared to introduce our institutions into their East African possessions, now resolved to co-operate with us in the conversion of their existing institutions into others analogous to ours—a course which they could take without involving themselves in any very revolutionary steps. Several other European Powers, as well as the whole of America and Australia, immediately followed their example. We determined at once to invite all the nations of the earth to a conference at Eden Vale. On the 3rd of March, in the twenty-sixth year after the founding of Freeland, the congress met in the Eden Vale National Palace.

We now hasten to open the doors to this future!

CONCLUSION

The history of 'Freeland' is ended. I could go on with the thread of the narrative, and depict the work of human emancipation as it appears to my mental eye, but of what use would it be? Those who have not been convinced, by what I have already written, that we are standing on the threshold of a new and happier age, and that it depends solely upon our discernment and resolve whether we pass over it, would not be convinced by a dozen volumes.

For this book is not the idle creation of an uncontrolled imagination, but the outcome of earnest, sober reflection, and of profound scientific investigation. All that I have described as really happening *might* happen if men were found who, convinced as I am of the untenability of existing conditions, determined to act instead of merely complaining. Thoughtlessness and inaction are, in truth, at present the only props of the existing economic and social order. What was formerly necessary, and therefore inevitable, has become injurious and superfluous; there is no longer anything to compel us to endure the misery of an obsolete system; there is nothing but our own folly to prevent us from enjoying that happiness and abundance which the existing means of civilisation are capable of providing for us.

It will perhaps be objected, 'Thus have numberless reformers spoken and written, since the days of Sir Thomas More; and what has been proposed to mankind as a panacea for all suffering has always proved to be Utopian.' And I am willing to admit that the dread of being classed with the legion of authors of Utopian romances at first filled my mind with not a few qualms as to the form which I had chosen for my book. But, upon mature deliberation, I decided to offer, not a number of dry abstractions, but as vivid a picture as possible, which should clearly represent in concrete conceptions what abstract ideas would have shown in merely shadowy outlines. The reader who does not for himself discover the difference between this book and the works of imagination above referred to, is lost to me; to him I should remain the 'unpractical enthusiast' even if I were to elaborate ever so dry a systematic treatise, for it is enough for him to know that I believe in a change of the existing system to condemn me as an enthusiast. It matters not, to this kind of readers, in what form I state my proofs; for such readers, like fanatics in the domain of religion, are simply disqualified to estimate aright the evidence which is pointed against what exists.

The impartial reader, on the other hand, will not be prevented by the narrative form of this book from soberly endeavouring to discover whether my propositions are essentially true or false. If he should find that I have started from false premises, that the system of freedom and justice which I have propounded is inconsistent in any way with the natural and universally recognised springs of human action—nay, if, after reading my book, he should not have attained to the firm conviction that the realisation of this new order —apart, of course, from unimportant details—is absolutely inevitable, then I must be content to be placed in the same category as More, Fourier, Cabet, and the rest who have mistaken their desires for sober reality.

I wish once more expressly to state that the intrinsic practicability of my book extends beyond the economic and ethical principles and motives underlying it, to the actual stage upon which its scenes are placed. The highlands of Equatorial Africa exactly correspond to the picture drawn in the book. In order that 'Freeland' may be realised as I have drawn it, nothing more is required, therefore, than a sufficient number of vigorous men. Shall I be privileged to live until these men are found?

8

The Future Commonwealth
or, What Samuel Balcom Saw in Socioland

by **Albert Chavannes**

New York
True Nationalist Publishing Company
1892

Albert Chavannes (1836–1903)

came to America from Switzerland with his parents at the age of twelve. The family settled in Tennessee, and after the death of the elder Chavannes, Albert and his brother invested their inheritance in a dairy farm, which was a complete financial failure. Chavannes then moved to Berkshire, N.Y., where he operated a small water-powered woodworking shop, manufacturing, among other things, a wooden, reversible, horse-drawn hay rake. In 1870, he returned to Tennessee and bought a farm near Knoxville. From this time on he seems to have prospered in business, acquiring considerable land, undertaking the construction of small homes, serving as president of the Knox County Bank and Trust Company, and in 1894 establishing a lumber company of which his grandson is now vice-president.

During this busy and varied career, rather typical of the period, Chavannes began his writing and publishing. In 1892 he was an unsuccessful candidate for Congress, and in the late nineties he moved into the town of Knoxville and devoted his remaining years to writing and printing pamphlets, books, and two journals, *The Sociologist* and *The Modern Philosopher*. Among his writings are two or three pamphlets on mind and magnetism, one on *Heredity, Cross-Breeding, and Prenatal Influences* (1885), and several tracts on economic questions. *The Future Commonwealth* (1892), from which the following selections were taken, was supplemented in 1897 by a longer utopian speculation, *In Brighter Climes, or Life in Socioland*.

Recognition of the means by which Chavannes achieved his own personal success and satisfaction adds weight to the convictions which he expresses in the following selection. He appears to have been strongly influenced by the prevailing Spencerian views on social evolution, and his emphasis on the development of spirit and character is reminiscent of Macnie, also an immigrant to America. Yet, consistent with the tenor of utopian speculation of the time, Chavannes clearly considered economic adjustment to be the panacea for all social ills. In this respect, he was no more naïve than Bellamy and the great majority of utopists of the period, and he had at least the advantage over most of them of a lifetime of experience in the economic world. The emphasis upon apprentice training as the final stage of the educative process, while it is not unique, is more carefully integrated into the pattern of the social structure than in other utopias. *The Future Commonwealth* is typical of a vast number of utopian works which mark the 1890's in the United States as the most productive single period in the history of utopian thought. Certain characteristics were rather generally common to this speculation: unquestioning belief in the efficacy of economic equality to bring about social solidarity and order; faith in the essential intelligence and goodness of men who have been circumvented by economic inequality; deprecation of the necessity and function of law and law enforcement; and the conviction that once a society such as that suggested by the utopist was established, all men would concede its superiority and hasten to reconstruct their own communities on this pattern.

The Future Commonwealth

Spencer, Socioland, Africa,
June 1, 1950.

My dear friend Harry:
I have at last reached this place after a long and interesting journey, and I will at once commence a journal, which, when complete, will enable me to fulfil my promise that I would try to faithfully report to you whatever I should see or hear which could throw any light upon the social problems in which we are both interested.

I have no doubt, from what I have seen of the people since I entered the Commonwealth of Socioland, that if I do not find here a complete solution of the problems which perplex us, I will find at least the results of interesting experiments in Sociology, and valuable hints as to the best course to be followed to secure a better distribution of wealth, and increase of general comfort.

But before I enter upon a detailed account of what I see and hear, I want to tell you of the causes which led to the settlement of Socioland, as well as of the aims of the first emigrants. I am enabled to do so from information I received from Mr. Walter, an old gentleman whom I found on the boat, a native of Ohio, who nearly fifty years ago emigrated to this country, and took an active part in shaping the policy of the Commonwealth.

You know that the latter end of the XIXth century was a time of great changes. Not only of a great development of the natural resources and of the producing power of mankind through the increased use of steam and of electricity, but also of changes in the religious, scientific and philosophical beliefs of the educated classes.

It was then that through the researches of Darwin, Spencer and others, commenced that period of religious doubt in which we still are in the United States. Before their time society was willing yet to be controlled by persons who either believed, or claimed to believe, that the ten commandments were the expression of the will of

God and the misery of the masses due to the innate depravity of human nature, and the poor were kept quiet by alternate doses of charity and of promises of eternal bliss in the world to come.

The doctrine of evolution, taught and accepted towards the end of the century, sapped this belief at its basis, and it was soon recognized by those who undertook to follow it to its logical conclusions that the whole philosophy of the past, built upon a belief in special creation, would have to be remodeled until an entire change had been effected in religious beliefs, and that eventually the social institutions themselves would be thereby influenced.

Out of this intellectual struggle soon emerged here and there practical men and women who studied the laws of conduct in a scientific spirit, and with the firm intention to profit by any new truths they might discover. These persons, scattered in every part of the United States, were soon drawn together by a common aim, and under the name of Sociologists, or students of Social Science, formed themselves into clubs for the pursuit of social knowledge, and to seek for means of practical application of such knowledge as could help them to a more satisfactory mode of life and a better form of government.

It is not strange that out of such conditions grew an earnest desire to seek by emigration a land where their new ideas could find free development in a virgin and unoccupied country. The opening of the Dark Continent furnished them with the desired opportunity. They made a treaty with the protecting power which guaranteed to the proposed settlement complete autonomy in their internal government, and they were assured of protection against foreign foes so long as they could not protect themselves. In the meantime the home clubs had made ready for the coming emigration, and a comparatively large and steady exodus took place to the land of promise which they baptized with the name of Socioland.

I found Mr. Walter a very pleasant companion, and I received from him much valuable information.

"Mr. Balcom," he said to me one evening, "it will help you very much to understand what you will see in our country if you know the object we had in view in coming here. We had no settled plan, but we had a very clear idea of the results we were going to strive for. We believed that, if rightly taught, all persons would recognize that whatever promoted the general welfare would also promote personal happiness. Our object being the attainment of happiness, we believe that a righteous end sanctifies the means, and not as is taught among you that righteous means sanctify the end. We consider the distribution of products the most important question, and that its correct solution offers the best prospect of increasing human happiness. The rich have more than they can enjoy, while the poor have less. We made our new Commonwealth the great Capitalist, and thus prevented the undue accumulation of wealth in private hands.

"There is the whole secret of it. Co-operation on a large scale, not practised by a few, for the advantage of a few, as it exists among you, but carried by the Commonwealth, for the advantage of the whole population, for the rich as well as for the poor, for the women as well as for the men."

I must confess I was somewhat disappointed, for it was nothing new for me to hear such doctrines, and I exclaimed: "Oh! then your Socioland is simply a Socialistic settlement, where the state controls everything. It may suit you, but I doubt if it would suit me or many of the free and independent citizens of America."

A malicious twinkle gleamed in Mr. Walter's eyes.

"Reassure yourself, we have not abridged personal liberty as much as you have, and are not Socialists as you understand the term. All governments are somewhat Socialist, some a little more, others a little less. We are a little more, and have entrusted the Commonwealth with the accumulation and use of a portion of our capital for the benefit of our people, while you only entrust your government with the spending of such capital as you raise by unequal taxation, or by borrowing from the wealthy class, thus increasing the burdens of the producers by compelling them to pay the interest on the money your government spends.

"Whatever costs money to maintain, as the streets and the parks, the police and the fire department, etc., is placed in the hands of the government, and the people are taxed for its support, while those enterprises which offer opportunities to make money, as the supply of light and water, the life and fire insurance companies, are allowed to fall into the hands of corporations and individuals. We are so far Socialists as to keep in the possession of the people many valuable privileges which you give away to men who use them for their private benefit."

"Now," said I, "let us come down to Socioland, and to what you have done to ameliorate its social conditions."

"Certainly, I will tell you with pleasure," he answered. "We have abolished all taxes."

"What!" I exclaimed, "abolished all taxes! That is indeed a practical step toward happiness. But how then does your government raise the money to meet its necessary expenses?"

"Our Commonwealth," rejoined Mr. Walter, "carries on all the most extensive and profitable enterprises of the country, with the avowed object of making money to be spent for the good of the whole people. For the present the Commonwealth controls the

Wholesale Trade, the Transportation of Letters, Parcels, Merchandise, and Persons, the Telegraph and Telephone, the Banks, the Life and Fire Insurances, the Street Railways, the Supply of Lights and Water, the Working of the Mines and a portion of the Manufactures.

"To insure the success of our scheme we have made some radical changes in the methods of educating our young people. The great difference is in the industrial training of the youths of both sexes. The numerous business enterprises carried on by the Commonwealth and the Townships offer splendid opportunities for practical training, and all our young people are compelled to serve a six years' term of apprenticeship to the state.

"By making our Commonwealth a co-operative business concern, we have made it rich and placed its citizens above want. Yet we have retained sufficient fields of activity for private enterprises. By our system of public apprenticeship we are training our youths to useful occupations. It brings all classes together, and is the measure that will have the most far-reaching effects."

We were nearing Spencer, and I thanked Mr. Walter for his kindness to me.

"You are welcome indeed," he rejoined. "It is a pleasure to give information where it is so thoroughly appreciated. I would advise you to stop at one of the hotels kept by the city. It will be interesting, for it will be your introduction to one of our public institutions."

Spencer is the commercial center of Socioland, and is the gateway of communication with the civilized world. Now a city of 50,000 inhabitants, it has a great future before it. The hotel proved to be a large brick building of plain appearance, with City Hotel No. 3 over the entrance. Its interior did not differ materially from our large hotels; probably as much comfort, but less luxury. That which struck me at once was the number of young people who seemed to be busy in the house, and who I concluded were some of the apprentices Mr. Walter had told me of.

After supper I made my way to the parlor, where I found, besides many of the guests, quite a number of the attendants of the house, engaged in social pastimes and treated on terms of social equality. I quietly watched the novel scene, wondering what our United States friends would say if the menials of an American hotel should invade the parlor. A lady entered the room and, noticing my lonely position, came toward me and opened conversation. I managed to turn the conversation toward their peculiar method of treating the employees of the house.

"Yes," said the lady. "Do you see that young girl talking to that bright-faced boy? She is the daughter of one of our best men. He would in your country have accumulated great wealth, and she would have led a useless life. Nor would she have been happier, for she is born for better things. Her life here has been entirely different. Her father has used his abilities as one of our Managers, and is in easy circumstances and no more. His daughter has had to do her share of the public work ever since she was fourteen. She has steadily advanced, and now fills a position of trust in this house. But come, let me introduce you to Miss Bell. You will enjoy her society, I believe."

I was easily persuaded, and joined in some games. I thoroughly appreciated the friendly spirit which had so quickly made me feel at home among my new surroundings.

The lady with whom I had the conversation proved to be Mrs. Wilton, wife of the Manager of the hotel. I made the acquaintance of Mr. Wilton the next day, and had some interesting talks with him upon their methods of managing public business.

"Mr. Balcom," said he, "I understand that you should be surprised at our ways, for they are quite different from those of the United States. We all take life easy here, and no one has to hurry out early in the morning or work till late at night. But understand me, I am speaking of productive labor. If we have short hours of labor, we make good use of them, and all have to follow some useful occupation part of their time. One of the most striking results of the policy has been to so reduce the supply of labor for domestic services that there are very few persons here who are not obliged to wait on themselves more or less. When our young people have finished their term of apprenticeship, they all have a complete knowledge of some lucrative trade, and but few are willing to do menial labor. This fact, added to the difficulty of accumulating fortunes, prevents the formation of a class who can command the services of others. Having no drones to support, we can accomplish much more, and still be able to reduce the hours of labor. But you wished me to explain to you the way in which we manage public business."

"Yes, it is precisely what I want to know," I answered. "With us the assertion is usually made that whatever the government undertakes costs more than what is done by private management."

"Well, my dear Sir," Mr. Wilton replied, "probably there is a foundation for the opinion you express, although it may be fostered by those who have a direct interest in preventing the government from extending its operations.

"But there is a fundamental difference between your government and ours. Yours is a Republic, established to maintain civil and political rights. Ours is a Commonwealth, organized to secure those rights, and besides, to manage public business for public benefit. Our welfare is intimately connected with the pecuniary success of the Commonwealth, and we are all interested in its proper management. On that account the people never surrender the law-making power to their delegates, but exercise a constant supervision over all their actions, and if they fail to properly conduct the business committed to their case, they are quickly called to account for their mismanagement."

"You do not then," I said, "surrender to your political officers the business interests of the country, and do not expect your President and Governors to manage them through agents of their own selection."

"Not at all. In the first place we have no Presidents or Governors, their functions being filled by the Chairmen of the executive committees, but if we had, we would not place our financial interests in their hands.

"We have added to our government a Business department, independent of the Political and the Judiciary, which has entire charge of the business enterprises of the Commonwealth, and is responsible to the people alone for the result of their labor. Through this department we co-ordinate the productive power of the whole people, and constitute ourselves into a co-operative association.

"We, the people, thus become a business firm, and hire a certain number of men to manage the work for us. We recognize that there must be stability, and on that account the Managers and Advisers are elected for indefinite terms, and are retained in place so long as the people are satisfied with their services. But should dissatisfaction arise, specific charges must be laid before the Advisers, and if they are sustained, a new election is ordered which is the final verdict pronounced by the people."

"These principles," I remarked, "seem sound enough in theory, but I should be afraid that the public supervision would prove inefficient and easily evaded."

"You are right," answered Mr. Wilton, "and it is partly on that account that we have established Advisory Boards. The functions of these Boards are three-fold. To advise, to supervise, to co-ordinate. They are clothed with no authority except such as they need to attain the needed information, and report to the people through publication. It is to them we look for that close supervision so necessary to success. Their duties are to overlook the whole business situation, reconcile the different interests, keep watch over the receipts and expenses, study the best means to promote the general welfare, and suggest them to the public and to the Managers.

"The Managers really manage the business placed in their charge. I am the Manager of this hotel, and have all the needed power to run it successfully, provided I use that power according to the recognized policy of the Commonwealth.

"Some of our Managers are elected by the Commonwealth, for they direct enterprises which must be under a central control, but all local business is controlled by Managers elected by the Townships, a division we have adopted in place of counties or incorporated cities, and which replaces them both. These Townships have each a business department of their own which looks after their local interests.

"We have, as I told you, formed ourselves into a business firm, and have tried to follow the same course that a practical businessman would take under the same circumstances.

"We have retained political and judicial organizations, but their importance is steadily diminishing, not because their functions are encroached upon by the business department, but from the results of our policy, which are constantly diminishing the causes which compel the enactment of laws. All wars, disputes, contentions, are the outcome of the competitive spirit, either in nations or individuals. Instead of trying to remedy the evils of society by law, we use our intelligence in devising means to diminish the need of laws by creating harmonious relations between man and man."

Several days passed, which I spent in viewing the city and in getting acquainted with the people. I find everywhere the same satisfaction with existing conditions.

In a retail store I entered, I found the owner to be a quiet old gentleman, who liked to talk.

"I am surprised," I said to him, "that some of your energetic men do not crowd to the wall their less ambitious neighbors."

"I believe," he answered, "that if you were to remain here some time, you would understand it better. It is natural that in your country you should strive for wealth, for wealth is not only comfort, it is power. Under your system everything is for sale. Suppose I should bestir myself to accumulate a fortune, what should I do with it? All our most valuable property is in the hands of the Commonwealth. We have little inducement to increase our wealth beyond what will secure us a comfortable existence."

I expressed my fear that this stifling of private ambition might result unfavorably to the general prosperity.

"We have found out here that there are other things worth living for besides the acquisition of money. Our men have as much brain, and are just as enterprising as yours, but, unable to concoct schemes by which they can exploit their weaker neighbors for their own benefit, they have to place their intelligence and their activity at the disposal of the Commonwealth to be used for the people's benefit. Yours is the freebooter system, ours is the organized army of labor."

Still it seemed to me that all this government control could not be maintained without a serious loss of personal freedom. I asked him whether he was not compelled to order his goods from certain stores, and give for them a price arbitrarily fixed by the Government.

"Not at all," he answered. "Our wholesale trade is perfectly free, and the prices are regulated by the law of supply and demand as in all countries. It is true that we have some regulations here that do not exist in other countries, but they are for the protection of the whole people. One is a regular scale of profits, without any admixture of speculation in it. Another rule is that we must pay cash. The Commonwealth furnishes an abundance of money for all transactions, and as it never speculates, we have no panic or stringency in the money market. Again there is one wholesale price for all. Our customers can buy at the same price we do if they buy in sufficiently large quantities. We are only distributors whom the people are willing to pay for their trouble, but there is no chance for exorbitant profits. Many articles, as fruits, vegetables, meats, milk and others of a perishable nature, never find their way to the wholesale stores, but are left to private hands. Our system enables us to better provide for the people, and to protect them from trusts and other speculative combinations. And the profits derived from the wholesale trade form one of the most available public revenues.

"Order is one of the conditions of society, and must be enforced either by private edicts or public laws. All that we ask is that they should tend to accomplish the desired end with the least infringement of individual freedom."

Much more did the old gentleman tell me, and I must acknowledge that the more I understand the spirit which controls their public organization, the more I believe that they are moving in the right direction.

The next day I had occasion to resume my conversation with Mr. Wilton. I asked him to tell me more about the management of public business, especially of that part connected with the apprentices.

"I can probably best explain what you want to know," said Mr. Wilton, "by giving you a short account of the management of this hotel. We have eliminated the profit on the land which would have gone to some speculator, the profit on the material, which was mostly furnished by the wholesale stores, and the profit of the contractor. That which has cost more money has been the labor which commands high prices here, yet the final result has been to reduce the cost one third. When the house was finished, I presented myself as candidate for Manager, and was elected without opposition. My salary is liberal, but not extravagant. I took charge of the house which was not yet furnished. That part was purchased under my care, conjointly with one of the Advisers. When the work was done, the full Board was invited to carefully examine the hotel, the accounts were submitted, and when all was recognized as correct, a notice to that effect, as well as a full statement of our expenses, was published.

"Once in charge, I proceeded to hire help, and besides, made an application to the Apprentice Bureau for as many of them as I thought I could employ. Those young people, who receive no wages, are a great help to reduce expenses, and there is always a great demand for them. When we put in a requisition, we must state the kind of occupation we have, for it is not only the apprentices just called out that are free to choose to work for us, but all those in the Commonwealth. Except that all are expected to keep at work, they have freedom of choice. I can also send back to the Bureau any of them who does not give me satisfaction. It is also the duty of the Bureau to investigate the complaints of the apprentices, and if, as sometimes happens with Managers newly elected, it is found that they cannot get along with the young people, it is considered a sufficient reason to secure a new election.

"I am left free to run this hotel as if I owned it myself. I am expected to charge moderate prices, to give satisfaction to my guests, to deal kindly with my help, and to clear a moderate profit. I must keep a strict account of my receipts and expenses. My accounts must always be open to the inspection of the Board of Advisers. The result of this union of responsibility and freedom is to create a body of men trained to the management of public enterprises. It is the process of the survival of the fittest applied to public affairs, and makes Socioland the best managed country in the world."

"But, Mr. Wilton," I remarked, "do you not have trouble with some of the apprentices? Are not several of them careless and unreliable, and more anxious to play than to work?"

"No," he answered. "We have very little trouble. Probably it is due to the spirit which reigns in Socioland. All kinds of work are honorable here. Our children are not taught that labor is a curse entailed upon the human family by the fall of Adam. On the contrary, they are taught that it is through labor that all that makes life worth living has been attained, and that further progress will only result from the combination of labor. There is really more incentive to well doing in our system than there is under private competition, for the best prizes are won by actual merit, and not by favor or privilege.

"I have tried to explain to you, Mr. Balcom, how we try to foster from the start the spirit which alone can make our public policy a success. That is the base, the foundation, which lacking would wreck all our efforts. Public institutions are built upon private character."

This opinion of Mr. Wilton is worthy of a careful study. If he is correct, then a change in public spirit must precede a change in public institutions. The lessons of history would show that he is right, for several times nations have tried to advance further than was warranted by the state of public knowledge, and after short trials the ground gained was lost.

I am staying longer in Spencer than I had at first intended, but I am enjoying myself. You remember that the day of my arrival I was presented to Miss Bell. We have become very good friends indeed. I have not fallen in love with her, so my dear Harry, do not weave a little romance at my expense. I had not realized until I conversed with Miss Bell, how great a difference there is between their education and ours, especially from a religious point of view. Not only this girl, but all these youths, live in a country where there is no church, no Bible, no preachers, and where right and wrong are judged entirely upon the desirable or undesirable results of their actions.

The day after the conversation was Sunday, and she said, "Mr. Balcom, this is a holiday with us. I have most of the day free, and I would be pleased if you will come home with me and get acquainted with my parents."

Of course I gladly assented. Mr. Bell impressed me as possessing great will power and a sound judgment. His wife is quick and impulsive. They have two sons, the oldest one a thriving young lawyer. I was received very pleasantly by the family. After dinner we adjourned to the garden, and Mr. Bell remarked that if I wished he would explain some things which he thought might interest me.

"The United States is a very rich country," he commenced, "but it cannot be called a Commonwealth. As wealth cannot be created by individual effort alone, it is but justice that the whole nation should profit by its increased production. As a result of your extreme individualism, you have no public wealth to be handed down, and the child of the poor man does not benefit by the labor of his ancestors. Such a condition of things is not just.

"Let me explain to you how we went to work to establish what we consider a true Commonwealth. The first thing to be done was to create a fund which would enable the Commonwealth to carry on its own business enterprises. They brought but little wealth with them, and what they did bring was private property. The Commonwealth could, of course, have taxed some of that property, or it could have borrowed it, but either course would have been opposed to the policy they wanted to inaugurate. The first settlers managed the business of the Commonwealth precisely as a wise young man starting in life would have managed his own. They husbanded their resources, and kept their expenses below their receipts. The first money which came into their hands was made by providing the people with a medium of exchange. Treasury notes were issued, and no other money was recognized as having a legal existence. Then the land was thrown open for settlement, and rights of occupancy sold which helped to fill the Treasury.

"With the funds thus secured, the Commonwealth started the wholesale trade and the business of common carrier. Of course it was slow work at first, but it was for the common interest to see the public fund increase and prosper, and by good management and economy the profits accumulated till ample means were provided for all public enterprises.

"Yet it took nearly twenty-five years before the Commonwealth felt rich enough to commence repaying to its citizens the returns secured by their abstinence, but now that we are receiving the full benefits accrued to us by the wise policy of our parents, we can bless them. If you will tell me what is the amount of taxation in the United States, I will try to show you the difference to the working people between our policy and yours."

"I cannot tell you positively," I answered, "for we have city, county, state and federal taxes, levied in so many different ways, but I suppose that each person must contribute at least twenty dollars a year to support our different governments."

"Here we have no taxes at all. Instead the Commonwealth has an income over and above all expenses of twenty-five dollars to each person. This income is spent for the common good. A large proportion is re-invested each year in improvements, and in developing natural resources. Besides, a large amount is spent for the direct comfort of the people—public laundries, Club houses, parks, schools. You may not know that the bread cart furnishes to all citizens, free of cost, all the bread they wish to consume, or that both gas and water are free in every house, or that we pension the aged and the needy, and have free hospitals and asylums. The great reduction in the price of all necessaries of life has not been effected by forcing down the wages of the working men, but by eliminating all methods through which one class of people can live at the expense of the other."

We spoke of many other things, and the ladies were not so entirely left out as my account would make it appear, for in this advanced state the women are interested in public affairs, and not only vote, but hold positions of trust. Toward the middle of the afternoon Miss Bell proposed that we take a ride to the park. A merry and noisy crowd was enjoying itself heartily.

I seemed to realize more and more the advantages enjoyed by the people of this favored Commonwealth, and turning to my companion, I said to her:

"Miss Mary, you must be very happy here. Please tell me a little about your early life and your school days."

"There is really very little to tell, Mr. Balcom. My parents helped me to learn how to read and write, and I was eager enough to get all the information within my reach. I never went to school until I was ten years of age, and by that time I had gone as far as I could without teachers. So I was glad to receive help from competent persons who had ample time to devote to me. In school I found myself among children of my age or older, who were also interested in their studies and needed no urging from their teachers.

"Of course, all studies did not have the same interest for us, but we never were requested to learn what we did not want to. For instance, if a scholar did not wish to study arithmetic, the teacher would explain to him its use, and how much he would need it in his work, but no effort would be made to compel him, and if he could not see that it would be for his advantage to study it, the teacher would simply tell him that he was the one to decide, for if a mistake was made he would be the one to suffer from it."

"I think I have been told, Miss Bell, that the time of apprenticeship for girls commences in their fourteenth year. If that is the case, your school days are soon over. You have but four years, if I count right?"

"Yes, you are right, and then we enter into an entirely different, but not unpleasant life. The first two years we are requested to do housework, so I entered the hotel in the housekeeping department. At the end of two years I was allowed to make my choice of the kind of occupation I wanted to perfect myself in, and as my taste led me more toward office work, I commenced to learn short-hand, typewriting and bookkeeping."

"But, Miss Bell," I said, "this will not last. I do not suppose that Mr. Wilton can afford to keep you when he will have to pay you a salary."

"I do not know what I shall do when that time comes. I may get married, or I can return home and help mother, or find employment in some public office."

After a very pleasant ride we returned to the city, and I was invited by the family to spend the evening with them. You know, my dear Harry, that among the many social questions which influence the welfare of humanity, there is none of more importance than the ownership of land. I was aware that they had a somewhat different land tenure in Socioland, and I was glad of the opportunity offered by an evening spent with Mr. Bell to get some information from him on the subject.

"This land question," he said, "is one of the most difficult we had to contend with, and we cannot claim to have settled it yet. But I believe we have made some advance. Our predecessors decided unanimously that the Commonwealth would retain for ever the control of the land, but that all persons who desired to settle and improve some of it, should be allowed to acquire a right of occupancy to a vacant tract, and that this right should hold good against all private interests, but should be forfeited to the Commonwealth upon the payment of actual damages, whenever the land was needed for public purposes.

"The land was divided into zones, commencing at the centre of the city. In the inner zone no one could occupy more than one acre, in the next zone the limit was placed at five acres, in the next at ten acres, while it was decided that thirty acres for one person, or sixty for a married couple, would be the largest tract granted, and taking in consideration the public need of money and that all should have the same chance to the land of their choice, it was decided to sell the tracts at auction. We have reduced the size of the lots to suit the needs of our increased population. We give plenty of time for the changes to take place easily and gradually. A vote is taken and two or three years given, after which the occupants lose their rights to the excess of their property which reverts back to the Commonwealth without compensation."

"And what about the titles to these rights?" I asked.

"The Townships alone can grant those rights of occupancy or transfer them. Whenever a change is made, the former occupant relinquishes his right, which is cancelled, and a new one is issued. Transfer by inheritance follows the same rule. And the change once made is final, for we hold that it is of the utmost importance that the men who labor on the soil should feel all possible security. On the whole there are probably less changes in the occupancy of the soil in Socioland, than there is to be found under the absolute ownership of other countries."

I walked back to the hotel with Miss Bell, well satisfied with the way in which the day had been spent.

I believe I told you before, my dear Harry, that I had found an agreeable friend in William Bell, the older brother of Miss Mary. He is a lawyer by profession, but the word has an entirely different meaning here. Instead of fomenting trouble and fostering lawsuits, their work consists in settling differences. They act more as counsellors and advisers than as advocates. I think it will interest you if I repeat some of our talks upon their ideas of law and government.

I was telling him a few days ago that, as far as I know, there had been only two forms of government tried. One was the autocratic, where the rulers had succeeded in obtaining control of the power and were using it to their own advantage, and the other the representative form, where the people try to govern themselves by delegating their powers to legislative bodies who make the laws and provide the means to enforce them. But I said that it seemed to me that here in Socioland they were experimenting on a third method, where the people tried to govern themselves with as little intervention of delegates as possible.

"Yes," he answered. "Our system is peculiar to ourselves, and is the result of the philosophical beliefs of those who founded our Commonwealth. I have read extensively about the laws and customs of other nations, and I find that the constant trend of the oppressed has been to have justice meted out to them, and to gain possession of what they consider their rights. In the pursuit of these aims they have elaborated constitutions and enacted numberless laws. For us who have eliminated all forms of oppression as inimical to happiness, and believe in the evolution of man from a lower organism, and in the struggle for existence and the survival of the fittest, such a view is unscientific."

"What!" I said. "Do you not believe in the need of justice or the enforcement of rights?"

"No, not in the sense in which you use these words," he answered. "With us they only mean a form of conduct which experience has shown to be beneficent to mankind. We do not believe that in the light of the evolution theory there can be such a thing in nature as abstract justice, or that it is possible to attain perfect rights. These were the views entertained by the first settlers, so they sought to promote a spirit of friendliness, and shaped their laws so as to discourage litigation, and to induce the people to settle their differences among themselves. They abandoned the jury system as too expensive and cumbrous, and abolished the right of appeal to higher courts. The decision of the judge is final.

"We look upon the men who cannot agree among themselves as undesirable citizens, and we only settle their disputes for them because it is the best way for the peace and happiness of the community. But it must be done quickly, and at the least possible expense. If the parties do not like the judge's decision, they will be more inclined to come to a mutual understanding next time, or to resort to arbitration, which we favor by all means in our power.

"We do not try to make the people religious or moral by law. Marriage and divorce are free, religious convictions are never interfered with, all days are equal before the law, and all personal actions are left as much as possible to be controlled by the intelligent judgment of individuals. Criminal cases are treated differently. They are rare with us, because we have done away with the incentives to crime, but when they do occur, we look upon the culprits as diseased.

"It is by thus diminishing the number of laws, and teaching the people the art of individual control, that we can govern ourselves by direct legislation, and take from our legislative bodies the power they so often abuse in representative countries, and I believe our people get along as well or better than those nations who look for the proper regulation of conduct to the increase of laws. Our system is not at all calculated to promote extensive legislation, and if we were a law-making and a law-loving people, we would not be satisfied with it. But we look upon law at best as a necessary evil, and replace it as far as possible by conciliation and kindly feelings."

And now, my dear Harry, while I might write much more that would interest you, I will not extend this account of my visit, but I will send it to you, that you may reflect on what I have described, and see how it applies to the solution of the problems we are studying.

For my part, I am well satisfied of the superiority of the institutions of Socioland over those of the United States, but I realize fully that the progress they have made is due to the development of their character which enables them to place in the hands of the Commonwealth many of its most important industries, while at the same time they have been able to safely withdraw government control from the departments of morals and religion. The material being better, its cohesive power is greater, and they have been able to erect a much better structure.

For the present, the example of Socioland can only serve us as a beacon to guide our steps, trusting that those who come after us will be able to realize the hope which sustains us in our labors.

Your friend,
Samuel Balcom.

9

Limanora

The Island of Progress

Godfrey Sweven

Author of
"Riallaro, The Archipelago of Exiles"
(J. M. Brown)

G. P. Putnam's Sons
New York and London
The Knickerbocker Press
1903

John Macmillan Brown   (1846–1935)

was born in Scotland and was the recipient of an honorary LL.D. degree from the University of Glasgow. He was Professor at Canterbury University College, and in 1923 became Chancellor of the University of New Zealand. His publications were numerous, including several lectures on English writers: Shelley, Milton, Shakespeare, Carlyle. Some of his other works are: *A Manual of English Literature; Modern Education, its Defects and Their Remedies; Maori and Polynesian; The Dutch East; The Riddle of the Pacific; Peoples and Problems of the Pacific.*

Brown wrote his two utopian works under the pseudonym of Godfrey Sweven. The first of these, *Riallaro, the Archipelago of Exiles* (1897), is a delightful expansion of a trick quite common in classical utopian writing: namely, getting the recalcitrant, stupid, and unhealthy people out of the way so that the remainder of the population can proceed to construct utopia. Thus, in *Riallaro*, Brown is preparing the way for a description of *Limanora, the Island of Progress* (1903). The elders of Limanora had long ago come to the conclusion that no progress could be made in curing minor vices and achieving an ideal social order until those people possessed of major vices were eliminated from the society. Thus, they began a "diplomatic" purgation of the population of Limanora, luring the vicious to leave the island by monetary inducement, by the promise of freedom to indulge their vice without restraint, and, if these failed, by forcible removal.

The bite of Brown's satire is, of course, in the designation of "major" vices. In order to make the purgation and exile complete and final, the Limanorans set aside a separate island in the archipelago of Riallaro for the practitioners of each particular vice, where they might associate with those of their own bent. One of the first islands visited is Tirralaria, to which have been exiled all socialists. Absolute equality reigns on this isle where the traveler encounters only crowds of "rather noble-featured beggars." Educational institutions, the medical profession, and all other symbols of inequality have been abolished. The visitor finds it "the scurviest sight seen for many a day." To the island of Meddla have been banished all those people who want to convert others to their way of thinking; propaganda is their passion. People who thought they could accomplish anything simply by passing a law comprised the population of Wotnekst, and the visitor found it hard to believe that "there existed outside of lunatic asylums a people so far gone in hallucination." Foolgar was populated with snobs; here the only way in which service or attention could be had was by assuming an insolent and pompous manner. Awdyoo was the isle of journalists, and our informant tells us that "it was the foulest place on earth, and no one ever landed there who could avoid it." All who became insufferable because of their loquacity were exiled to Jabberoo, practical jokesters to Witlingen, and nasty-minded censors to Meskeeta. The inhabitants of Kloriole delighted in the mystic deification of sensory pleasures, especially those of sex.

Thus do the Limanorans dispose of those in their population so ridden by major vices that they forestall the development of the ideal society. The tale of Riallaro and Limanora is trivial and inconsequential; in the interest of getting as much of the substance of Brown as space permitted, explanation of the usual *tour de force* of utopia has been omitted. In brief, three New Zealand gold prospectors, while on a hunting expedition, find a strange person who has apparently flown to the region by means of attached wings. The nostalgic reminiscence of the mysterious stranger is the description of Riallaro and Limanora, which lie far across the ocean, inaccessible behind a dense wall of mist and fog. Incidentally, this mystic visitor also helps the prospectors to discover gold, a useful application of utopian prowess in a non-utopian setting.

If the Limanoran's elevation of science to the devotion of religion sounds too extreme, let the reader remember the words of Thomas Paine, in *The Age of Reason*: "That which is now called natural philosophy, embracing the whole circle of science, of which Astronomy occupies the chief place, is the study of the works of God, and of the power and wisdom of God in his works, and is the true theology."

Note should be made of one editorial liberty which has been taken with the selected material: the order of treatment of ethics and polity has been reversed for the sake of continuity; no change in context or meaning is involved.

Limanora

Every tenth decennium there occurred the event of the century, the Imanora, or prospicient review. It was not meant merely as a review of the past and a rearrangement of positions; it was rather a revision of aims and destinies, a futuritive evaluation of the powers of the race. Not merely the elders but the whole people were led up to a mount of vision whence they could see their future for hundreds of years spread out before them, bounded by the lines their past had drawn. Though all phases of the civilisation were reviewed in relation to the future, generally one phase took prominence and gave character to each Imanora.

In the more recent centuries ethics had again come to the front, new points of view having been shown by the great discoveries and inventions of many centuries. The first Imanora after the series of purgations was complete had been predominantly ethical. To be purer, truer, more tolerant, more generous, more gentle and modest and loving was their one idea of progress. But they soon saw the limits of such progress. Most of them indulged too eagerly in intro- spection and some turned morbidly self-critical, finding defects where there were none. In short, the whole race fell into a chronic spiritual invalidism and many of them were afflicted with moral hypochondria.

The elders, and through them the people, were persuaded that this absorbing pursuit of ethical improvement must be abandoned. The development of the physical system was the first distraction that they thought of. It was during this athletic period that flight through the air was achieved. It was in this era, too, that they mastered the secret of prolonging life. It soon came to be noticed, however, that a new but analogous hypochondria began to seize the race. There was too much direct attention paid to the state and development of the body to be wholesome.

The conclusions drawn from these two experiences were that variety of occupation was one of the first essentials of mental and bodily health. To every family and individual was assigned an ex- ternal work that would draw the thoughts away from self for the greater part of the twenty-four hours. No part of the body or mind was left without daily or weekly exercise. One of the subordinate aims of the elders was to introduce as great a variety as possible into the talents, faculties, and tendencies of the race. Equality, and still more similarity, of members of a community, they well knew from the laws of nature meant stagnation, if not complete national death. Diversity in unity was the ideal of family life in Limanora. The elders of a family watched with eagerness for any modification of the special faculties or powers, and nursed it with the most anxious care, if they decided that it would assist the advance of the race, and the medical elders were ever suggesting the proper cross for producing a new variety of the old talents. Indeed, one of the most responsible duties of the council of elders was to decide as to the matings and parenthoods of the community. Thus and thus alone were they able to keep up that divergence of new species which would ensure an ever-quickening flow of life in the race. They greatly encouraged variation and inequality within their state, but were certain that this was not enough. There must be the knowledge, if not the immediate presence, of another type of being, similar to their own yet higher in some features, in order to stimulate advance. To get this was the object of their system of couriers into space, both mechanic and human. They were never weary of gathering in all possible indications of higher intelligences in extra-terrestrial elements and regions. For a long period they had been satisfied with the reports of their idrovamolans [instruments for at once seeing and hearing at great distances], and other recorders of events which occurred on the earth. But it gradually pressed itself home upon them that the comedy of terrestrial existence gave no stimulus to progress. Rare, indeed, was it to witness a deed or phase of civilisation that gave them a new model, or inspired them to higher life.

Thus it became necessary to open up other spheres of stimulus and inspiration. The thoughts of the race gravitated, first to other stars, then to the exuberant life they found in interstellar space. Infinite space, instead of being a desert strewn with the wrecks or embryos of stars, is as full of life, and of the elements and nuclei of life, as any world which spins through it. Beings as intricately organised as themselves left impressions on their supra-aerial lavolans [revealers of the inner tissues and mechanism]. Here were beings loftier than themselves at the very gates of their senses, possible sources of exalted, if not divine, influence. There was no conceivable end to the ethical elevation and development they might reach, now that they had pierced the prison walls of the earth.

As soon as a code is proclaimed or a philosophical system worked out, it begins to be antiquated; the best find a better ideal in front of them and, striving after it, reveal the flaws in the life they have hitherto lived, astonished at the narrow and primitive moral law their forefathers have handed down to them. I realised this more and more clearly as I continued to live amongst this wonderful people, and to see into their lives. They would have laughed if they had been enjoined not to kill, or steal, or lie, or commit adultery. It would be like telling the civilised Europeans not to eat each other, especially when uncooked, or telling the latter-day Englishman not to enslave his brothers. The Limanorans desired close proximity to the non-human animal as little as they did to underdeveloped or degenerate man; intercourse with a lower stage of life and intelligence, they had long ago proved, leads ultimately to adoption of some of its features and much of its standard, even where there is in it the aloofness of the master to his slave, or the tamer to his beast; they desired no masterdom over lower natures and so they exiled all animals and all degenerate or undeveloped men from their island.

Their magnetic sense was the greatest foe to all deception or concealment. They could read the feelings that stirred in the heart of a neighbour, and were even conscious of the definite thoughts passing in his brain. Jealousy, envy, hate, malice, anger, lust, had become obsolete in the race, and only the young were afflicted with them now. Great pains had been taken with these moral childish maladies in former periods with the result that their appearance was now seldom virulent or dangerous and never fatal, and every household knew by heart the simple rules and specifics for checking their development. The worst characteristic of them was that they were infectious; but the solitary system of education rendered this inoperative; in fact this epidemic nature of the moral disorders of children made the adoption of the one-child household and the one-pupil school seem an absolute necessity. Already the virulence of these childish ailments had almost disappeared, and they had grown so mild in their attacks that few but the guardians observed their approach.

One of the last refuges of insincerity was artificial self-abasement. Ridicule soon put this habit of poor and common natures to rout. The Limanorans were now proud of anything they had done nobly and were not ashamed to acknowledge it. A trivial, yet pathetic phase of the comedy was the excessive self-esteem that ran parallel with the torrent of detraction. In Limanora the fountains of both had dried up together. As they gained clear-sightedness in estimating human actions and character, they found that the cues of vanity had disappeared.

Another defect that seemed to have vanished without effort was immodesty. The lustful had been exiled and it was easy to eradicate from the natures of those that remained all trace of sexual passion, and with it all pruriency. The chief purpose of sex in nature, that of propagation of the family, became its sole purpose; and this, by the control which the elders exercised over posterity, grew as rare as death. Its other ends, the development of self-sacrifice and the growth of love and friendship, had been completely detached from it and rationalised. Procreation with the extension of the race into the future was counted so tremendous a responsibility that most preferred to postpone it as far in life as the instinct of the people would allow. The sexual passion thus died out of their minds as out of their natures, just as the mere appetites of eating and drinking had died out.

There was, therefore, nothing to be ashamed of and nothing to conceal. Immodesty vanished with the cue and motive for modesty. They wore irelium draperies more to temper the power of heat and cold and the rigours of the upper atmosphere and to aid them in flight, than to hide their bodies from the eyes of others. For the draperies were gossamer-like and semi-diaphanous and emphasised the beauty and grace of the body as an expression of soul. It was not the face alone that interpreted the mind. Magnetism rayed from every limb. But if the sex-problem had retained its old obtrusiveness, this seemingly superficial but really important reform in dress would have been impracticable.

Amongst the earliest questions that the Limanoran scientists faced was the place of sex in the universe. After minute and wide research they came to the conclusion that it was not an essential of the propagation of life. Some species, like bacteria, multiply by mere fission, and others alternate asexual with sexual reproduction. The species that remained faithful to parthenogenetic propagation fell behind in the evolutionary race. Asexual propagation, the easier and more primitive, gave the advantage in numbers of individuals to the vegetal and lowly animal species that clung to it, but left them almost incapable of evolution. On and upwards have passed the dominant species through the invertebrates and the mammals up to man, guided by that bi-sexual principle which has in it the stimulus of two types of life. Nor did it seem to them contrary to the analogy that some worlds should have in the life upon them a tri-sexual or even a quadri-sexual mode of propagation. It was out of sexuality, they acknowledged, that all the higher phases of existence upon earth had come, love, friendship, self-sacrifice. They considered none the less that sex had almost finished its task in many worlds, and would, in no very distant age, have accomplished all it could do for the Limanoran race.

The Limanoran ideal was to develop the creative power of the human system so far that they would be able to supersede the sexual mode of propagation. As it was, they had gone far towards the complete mastery of the sexual principle, and could mould and guide it to any purpose that the future of the race demanded. They knew the conditions that would govern any new human variety they needed in the state just as well as they could produce new modifications of trees and plants and flowers. They read the nature of each individual on the island as easily as they could read a book. But besides this they had in the pedigree-annals a complete account of all the possibilities of any family. By the aid of the physiological and biological experts they were able to fix the two out of which the individual parents would have to be chosen; and from their knowledge of the character and history of every member, the elders of these two families along with the medical elders were able to indicate the man and the woman who would exactly fulfil the purpose of the state. Years were spent on maturing the pair in the directions required and in entangling their imaginations and affections mutually. None were allowed to assume the responsibilities of parenthood till they were matured to their fullest possibility.

One of the most singular features of this moulding of posterity was that they did not always choose the most highly developed to become the parents of the commonweal. For it had often been found in the past that the individual who had brought his peculiar faculties or qualities to the highest state of refinement in his own life had exhausted the natural well-spring of them, and that he handed them on in most diminished degree to his children.

When the pair had bred the child that was required, if they were not conspicuous for wisdom or self-control, it was taken from them and given to a new pair who became its true parents and trained it in the direction it ought to take. These proparents were generally more successful than parents in educating and moulding a character; the parents, besides being swayed by the pride of parenthood and the vigour of their affection for it, were too closely akin to it in qualities and character to view it from an impartial and independent standpoint. If a pair had proved themselves exceptionally successful in the production and moulding of the two children they owed to the community, they were allowed to adopt for a lengthened period the profession of parent, by far the most important, if not really the only, profession in the island. But they must bring one child up to maturity before they undertook another. For, they held, to sculpture a new and noble nature was considered the greatest creative work that a Limanoran could achieve for the state. Another reason for the unitary basis of the household was the moral contagion imperfect natures bring to bear on each other. Children were never allowed together except under the strictest supervision; for they soon undid all the work of their guardians, and confirmed in each other the retrogressive savagery through which they were passing.

That the two sexes were both needed for the training of a young nature to maturity was one of the most unhesitating conclusions from their experience. In spite of the obliteration of all demarcating lines between the sexes as to privileges and duties in the state, there was nothing more clear to them than the permanence of the distinction in their natures. To women was assigned work which required slow continuous effort. It was generally the men who did the most striking work. The women gathered the material for the sciences; the men invented and applied the great hypotheses leading to new advances. Whatsoever needed artistic talent was theirs to do. The women were the conservative element. If they had wholly guided the community, it would have stood still or moved at a rate that would not have been noticeable in the generations of men. Happily the masculine imagination dominated the civilisation, and hence it was ever quickening its pace. But the women were no less useful in preventing revolutionary progress, and in making the men wait and meditate over the leaps they thought of taking.

A few of the women who were especially fitted to be mothers were assigned to the maternal profession. There were other women who because of their nervous vigour and inclination to exhaust their best energies in work were not the most suitable for the production of children, and yet by their sympathy and wisdom and love of the young seemed especially created to bring up children as citizens; these adopted the proparental profession. A third type of women were, on account of their quick, irritable vigour and their super-emotional temperament and lack of self-control, considered incapable of either function except on rare occasions; and they formed the largest class, the worker women, rarely generative and always uneducative; they were engaged in the sedentary, acquisitive, and continuous employments that demanded no great strain on the imagination or the creative powers or the muscular vigour. But none in the community were wholly freed from daily active work both of body and mind, not even those whose lives were given up to the profession of maternity. Amongst men all were eligible as fathers; for though there were always a special diet and training for prospective paternity, these might be enforced simultaneously with the usual work. Not all, however, were called on to exercise paternity; it was a rare and little-noticed duty, and left small impress on the community. But there were some who on account of their great wisdom and self-control and lofty character were specially fitted for the rearing of youth, and these formed the male proparental profession. These had their other duties to perform in the family and to the state as well.

Of the numbers in these different classes the elders had full control. They could fill the exact number of vacancies to be anticipated in any class. For instance, if one was needed for the profession of maternity, almost all the energy of both parents was spent for a time in nutrition; they were isolated from most activities, surrounded with what in other civilisations would be called luxuries, and encouraged to spend their time in resting. So, if a male worker were required, the man and woman selected for parenthood were active workers themselves; and during their generative period their nutrition was reduced to the minimum for sustaining their energies, whilst they were encouraged to put all the activity they were capable of into their daily work. Embryology had become almost an exact science; the medical elders could investigate the health of the embryo and guide its development as well as in the case of the full-grown child. Training and education in the truest sense of the words began long before birth.

The newest addition to their list of sciences, the physiology of ethics, put into their hands one of the most effective aids to this plasmic art of character, prenatal and postnatal. With their instruments of investigation into the human tissue ever advancing in refinement and power, they were able at last to localise the physical centre and equivalent of each emotion. Whenever a Limanoran child became afflicted with an evil or retrogressive passion, he was hurried off to the ethical laboratory, and the nerve-centres of his emotional and moral nature were microscopically photographed as they worked. Then experiments were made in finding remedies which would check the growth of the disease in the tissue. At last something not unlike a science of the art of moral healing seemed to emerge out of the empiricism and chaos.

This culminated in the establishment of an ethical sanatorium, which was in reality a children's hospital for obstinate moral diseases. The mild moral ailments lasting for only a few hours or days were easily managed by the parents or proparents. Should the moral defect still hold out obstinately against all remedies, the patient was removed to the hospital for treatment. There were collected together as moral physicians and nurses the wisest and noblest personalities of the race, who applied all their therapeutic power to the centre that was supposed to be the source of the disease. Within recent times the ethical investigators had made great advances in their science. After some years' toil they supplied the ethical sanatorium with a complete scientific pharmacopoeia, for at least all the grosser forms of vice, all the offences against the moral codes that had been atavised or thrown into the ancestral past.

The nerve-centres concerned with these offences were easy to find and localise. But it was a more difficult task for the new art of therapeutic ethics to trace out the physiology of the newer moral codes. The moral offences they now had to deal with were sluggishness of the higher faculties of man, acts that dragged the thoughts downwards, dominance of a physical need, concessions to mere nature as against the highest knowledge of nature, excesses of emotion or disturbances of the mental equilibrium by passion, devotion to the past, superstition, stagnancy of belief, efforts to base belief on unreason or ignorance, faith in a moral code as the terminus of human ethics, or in a state of human scientific knowledge that was omniscient. Step by step the ethical investigators found their way to the nerve-centre that was disturbed when any one of these faults appeared in a man; and after long years of research and

experiment they were able to add to their pharmacopoeia the an-
tidotes to these maladies or weaknesses.

They would have thought the basis of existence irrational, if
they had persuaded themselves that ethics was unprogressive, whilst
all other things in the universe were subject to the law of evolution.
To advance, to raise his system higher, to evolve its possibilities, was
the first duty of man as understood by the Limanorans of this later
age. To know clearly and definitely the possibilities that lay before
them, and to be able to choose the best of them was the primary
and fundamental maxim of their ethical code. All others were corol-
laries of it. One of the first aims and maxims of their polity was to
let their citizens on reaching maturity think all through their lives
for themselves. There was no repression, no prohibition; the prerogative and duty of every man was to make himself fit to be a law
to himself. All they wished to be sure of was that the action was to
lead forward. The test of its morality was this: did it make the
human system progress?

Among the things they most deeply abhorred was despotism. And
the worst despotism of all, they held, was the social, that which is
exercised daily and hourly, and from the vantage-ground of proximity. The constant inspections and examinations by the elders might
seem to conflict with this horror of espionage and spiritual despotism. But these were voluntary on the part of mature Limanorans;
it was one of their recurring pleasures to be able to submit their
tissues and faculties to the wise observation of the elders, and to
gain the advantage of their experience. Had it been felt as a despotism, it would have been abandoned at once. With the children
and the immature it was a matter of discipline; they were in the
pre-purgation stages of Limanoran history, and had to be in pupillage and under authority.

Nothing that was evil, they held firmly, could lead ultimately to
good; nothing that was retrograde could in the end be progress.
They had learned from the revolutions of their past how snaky
and tortuous are the ways of deceit; and the first sure sign of its
triumphant success is the bold adoption of the doctrine that good
men may do evil, provided their aim is good. Every new step antiquated some universally accepted belief or maxim. Not so many
ages ago a crudely philanthropic spirit was considered one of the
noblest of the virtues. Now it was considered distinctly immoral
to philanthropise without taking care to foresee the results. Limanorans used to go out into the archipelagos and try to convert the
barbarians. It soon came to be acknowledged that intercourse with
inferior civilisations, even for the purpose of raising them, lowered
the moral standard of the missionaries, whilst failing in its original

motive. Much of the philanthropy that began at home was found to be no less obstructive and immoral. It fed and clothed the poor and improvident, and thus helped to slay and bury the only habit that could save them out of their slough, the habit of measuring every step they took, and seeing whither it led; and it helped to perpetuate the evil; for the ready yet limited supplies combined with the improvidence to make them breed like the lower animals, and the race of paupers and unprogressive was inordinately multiplied.

Another immorality that had once been a virtue was the pursuit of beauty for its own sake. When the race had been purified, beautiful things became the commonest features and necessities of life, and beauty ceased to be noticed as anything remarkable. Then to spend energies on producing what was artistic and beautiful without serving any other purpose than pleasing was reckless extravagance, and by wasting what should have been expended upon the progress of the race was condemned as immoral.

Another instance of a former virtue having become a vice was statesmanship and political patriotism, streaked with loquacity, conceit, self-seeking, hypocrisy, corruption, and intrigue, long before it came to be recognised as a vice. The purgations swept out all occasions for politics and patriots in exiling all the subjects of statesmanship. Where there were no paupers or criminals, no masters or servants, no uneducated or savage except young children, and no chance of plague or famine, the occupation of the statesman and politician vanished. Where every man was taught to be a law to himself, legislation had no place. To propose and argue legislative schemes for the benefit of any section of the race would have been accounted immorality, if it had not been taken as a symptom of atavism or mental disease. A hospital was the certain fate of anyone who indulged in political projects or political eloquence; the old virtue had passed beyond the stage of obstructiveness and vice, and had become one of the tests for insanity.

My final instance of the old virtue grown vice is of a different kind. It was the common error of taking a verbal originality or advance for a real, a mere change of name for a change in essence. Some of the greatest heroes of philosophy and science in the pre-purgation ages of the island had owed their fame to the substitution of fresh phraseology for what had grown outworn and trite, and most of the great writers had done nothing more for their fellows than re-illumine a linguistic world fallen dull and dark. Men grow sick of ideas that have worn the same verbal dress for a generation or more, and hail as a discoverer and benefactor anyone who tricks them out anew. This was especially easy in the domain of ethics, and the

Limanorans were constantly on their guard against the delusion of accepting a change of nomenclature as a moral advance. To take verbal ingenuity for true pioneering was the most grievous offence against the future of the race.

The great standard and test of morality was progress. If they could have brought themselves to believe that they had attained the fullest and the final light upon morality, the thought would have struck their very hearts to stone. It was this that kept them from formulating their morality or ethics in any definite code. They knew that a code would soon petrify morality. Up through the scale of energy the whole cosmos is ever climbing, with occasional lapses and falls, time being the only differentiating quality. Nothing could be good that stopped their ascent; nothing could be bad that compelled them to rise more quickly. There was thus no feature of their lives but came within the range of morality. Their sciences and arts, their experiments and inventions, were as much a part of their moral life as their character and their conduct towards each other. Morality was the relationship to the ever-developing, ever-advancing, aim of the race, and nothing in the whole range of their life was indifferent to that.

. . . . .

I had now reached the age and stage of my training which gave me the entry as audience to the councils of the race. My magnetic power and faculties had not been developed enough to interpret the silences between the rare speeches. The magnetism of thought and feeling was flowing from mind to mind. Now and again, when the divergence of thoughts was dominant, one of the oldest and wisest would call them in from their different tracks to a common centre. The speaker would review all the mental discussion and concentrate its lines, so that everyone present might have a view of the whole field from a high point. It was marvelous how rapidly they went through the business in hand by means of these noble silences, broken by occasional reviews.

The discussion gave me an insight into what I had long been curious about, their polity and methods of guiding the course of their commonweal. I had almost come to the conclusion that there was no such thing in Limanora as sovereignty or state. Though everything moved with the harmony and smoothness of perfect organisation I could never find the organising hand. At last I discovered part, at least, of the machinery of government. There was one assembly or council to which reformers could appeal with their schemes. The whole community often assembled; but it seemed to me that it was more for training, for the reintegration of some faculty or feeling, or for the purification and elevation of life than for legislative purposes. The only trace of any approach to selection and decision in these national gatherings was to be found in Loomiefa [the theater of futurition] and in the linguistic assemblies; in the one they practically accepted or rejected some proposed revision of their ideals placed before them in a new book; in the other they decided whether a new word, or the adaptation or application of a word, was worthy to live or die. I could see that these were the two great functions of a national assembly, to accept or reject a new departure in life or in language. The language in investigation and research was the most natural ambush of fallacies and the scientific work of a generation might be rendered nugatory by an ambiguous word or phrase.

I had now been led to see that there was a council for the decision of foreign questions. I soon came to recognise its domestic functions as more important than its policy abroad. The latter occupied its attention only once or twice in a generation. Monthly, almost weekly, it met to agree on questions and schemes which had no connection with the world outside of Limanora. It never passed a law; and yet its decisions were as clear, as valid, and as universal in their effects as if they had been written out, proclaimed, and printed in a statute-book. All the parents, proparents, and guardians were members of it, and along with them were associated as silent, inactive members the young men and women who had matured and had shown sufficient of the wisdom and virtues of the race to warrant such a privilege. These latter were in training for full and active membership many years before their spirit and influence were felt to have bearing on any decision.

The scheme of every new book came before this assembly prior to its publication in Loomiefa. Every new departure on the part of any family was brought up by its heads to be tested by the feeling of the council. But it rarely happened that any scheme was rejected; it was, as a rule, only revised and modified. Another branch of its duties was the preparation of practical problems and difficulties which were likely to obstruct the national progress till they were solved.

In all the meetings and discussions I came gradually to feel that there was a dominating spirit that influenced from behind the scenes. After a time I began to trace the vigorous currents that swept us on with such force, to the oldest men and women in the council, those who in Europe would have been thrust aside as incapable of good advice. They did not claim superior authority, but the deference to their opinion and instincts was spontaneous. In this way I learned that there was an inner council or cabinet, consisting of all the elders who had proved themselves able and wise by centuries of discovery, or invention, or penetrative and far-reaching advice. I could discover no formal election to it, everything in the shape of definite constitution or government being manifestly avoided. Age did not form the qualification for this senate although all the senators were men and women who could count their years by hundreds. It was rather weight of experience, and the fulness of development resulting from it, that admitted. Sex made no distinction in the choice; sex was a mere accident in the realm of reason and wisdom.

In all differences of opinion their decision was final. But it was seldom that any division of view came as far as a controversy which needed the influence of the elders. Where two individuals or families began to feel their opinions on any common topic drawing apart, they made eager efforts to understand the other's point of view; and their neighbours, recognising a discord in the mental atmosphere, came in with reconciling magnetism and reason. Long after arriving in the island I still wondered where their courts of law were; and thought there must be some secret tribunal that dealt summarily with all disputes. I came at last to see that there was no need of courts of justice, for there was never any approach to jarring or litigation; and, most of all, there was no written law to appeal to. Every man was a law to himself, in that he knew and fully recognised the aim of the community and the part he had to fulfil in its advance.

Another striking feature of this inner council was that their meetings were open to all but the young and immature. They would have nothing to do with the secret conclave, which, they held, was the beginning and principle of despotism. Their senate-house was arranged so as to be a vast linasan [recorder and reproducer of sounds]. Nothing was needed at the end of a meeting but to touch a spring, and the moving irelium-strip [irelium—iridescent metal applicable to all manner of purposes by the Limanorans], on which the proceedings imprinted themselves, was securely fixed on its roll and transferred to the valley of memories, there to be laid past in the archives for future reference, and a fresh strip took its place ready for the next debate. Knowing this, each senator weighed his every word with the utmost care. At all important assemblies and gatherings they had an instrument called an idrolinasan which recorded in permanence not merely all that was said or done, but the electric currents which passed from man to man. Whenever they needed to verify a memory of the past, the irelium-strip of the particular occurrence was brought out of the historical archives and placed in the reversible idrolinasan, and the whole scene flashed vividly before the senses. These machines had had a wonderful effect even upon the advanced Limanoran polity. Not even a gesture was wasted in their assemblies. Everything done and said was relevant and weighty.

It was astonishing how rarely the councils had to meet, and how brief their meetings were. And this was the reason why I had been so long in discovering any trace of constitution or polity in their midst. The guidance of the great public institutions needed little counsel or interference, but was almost automatic; everyone concerned knew by instinct what he had to do and had its interests so completely at heart that he required no reminder of the details of his duties.

But there was one department for which the inner council or senate was wholly responsible. This was Rimla, or the centre of force. Mechanical power was the one thing, they had all along felt, that must belong to the state and be controlled by the state. Only the wisest and best and the most imbued with Limanoran ideals were ever allowed to control the concentrated force of the island. In fact no one but a member of the inner council could be the master of force, and his term of control was limited to a few hours at a time, for which period he was chosen from day to day. It was the greatest honour the race could bestow. It was the duty, therefore, of everyone who was elected to the office, however often he had held it, however noble he had proved himself, however trusted he might be by all, to submit himself the hour before he entered Rimla to the tests of the inner nature and thoughts that the race knew, and this in the presence of the oldest of the senate. The workings of his brain and heart were stringently investigated, and after that he was sent to sleep, in order to have his dreams read and interpreted. If any of the tests gave dubious answer, he resigned his office and another was chosen in his place. For almost a generation this had never occurred, yet the precautions were as rigidly enforced as if the tests had often revealed defects. For the master of force held in his hands the key of their civilisation and progress. All this safeguarding of the probity and the sanity of the masters of force was therefore counted rather as a tribute to the importance of the office than a slur upon the individual.

It was not that private motive or stimulus had been annihilated. On the contrary they considered that the chief spur to progress was the struggle of the individual in competition with his fellows. To be respected and at last reverenced by his neighbours was longed for by every man in the community. Private property had not been abolished, but only disgraded. There had never been for centuries anyone who needed his neighbour or the state to aid him with food or clothing or other of the vital necessaries. If there had, he would have been too deeply ashamed of his mismanagement of his life, or his improvidence, to allow anyone to know of it. The arrangements of the state and the carefully proportioned size of the population left no room for him to throw the blame on others.

The state demanded nothing that could be called taxation from the citizens; part of their time, ability, and work was all that it required. But it was one of the methods of showing patriotism to give freely to the state. It was indeed one of the chief reasons for the retention of private property that it allowed of an easy and ever available means of cultivating benevolence. If the state possessed all and demanded all, then the citizens were little better than slaves; their virtues had no freedom, no exercise, and were bound to disappear. This singular people retained the institution of private property, fearing the apathy and languor that fall upon the energies of a socialistic people. They saw the inherent futility of all efforts to do away with the occasions of envy and jealousy, instead of eradicating the passions themselves.

A long experience of all types of body politic, and a minute knowledge and study of the history of the world, had made this people antagonistic to every form of great empire. Huge empires, instead of being guaranties of peace, are direct incentives to war, or at least to a permanent warlike attitude. Back must the world recede from vast empires if it would attain to any nobleness of aim, or any development of the higher elements in man. Its sole salvation lies in small communities covering its surface and remaining free from the taint of imperial effort and militarism. Only when the nation has complete command of the numbers within it through the family, that is, when the nation is small, will patriotism become commensurate with humanity, and the true goal of the human race be the aim of the individual.

The family is the natural unit of administration in a community; and as long as the heads form the common council that watches the interests and aim of all, it can never come into conflict with national unity and progress. The house and its goods belonged to the household in Limanora; and, although the members of it had equal rights to the livelihood that was counted fullest and best by the community, the individual, if mature, had freedom of action that would surprise a Western freeman; he was the equal of all members of the state; his destiny, it is true, had been shaped for him during his pupillage, but the fulfilment of it was his own. He had to contribute to the family treasury what was needed to keep it level with Limanoran affluence, and he was generally eager to give more; but all the rest was at his own disposal. The family had many buildings in common; but each full-grown member, whether male or female, had a separate house to retire to.

All the families were equal in their relations to the state, whatever their occupation or wealth or origin might be. All work was alike honoured, and personal worth was the test of the man and of the respect paid him. All the physical forms of toil that might at one time or other be considered offensive, were gathered into the hands of the state, and all men and women had to take their share of them. Thus two or three hours of every citizen's twenty-four were impounded by the state, much to his bodily and spiritual advantage.

The only contribution in money or kind that the state made compulsory was that which each family exchequer gave for the support of the medical, architectural, and other public professional families. An amount was fixed, which each had to contribute to every family that had the care of a public institution, or the performance of a public duty. But over and above this amount the voluntary gifts to them were very large. If there was any rivalry amongst the families and individuals in Limanora, it was in the delight of giving.

So devotional did I think the magnetism which ran through the community, that I plucked up courage to ask about the religion. My question was dealt with in the calmest and most rational way possible amongst human beings. There was no immediate reply, but I was led to a part of Fialume that I had not yet visited. Here were stored the records that illustrated the evolution of religion, records made by light, sound, and magnetism. It was immensely interesting for me to see so complete a museum of the natural history of worship. Every faith in the world had its due place. Day after day I returned to the study of this absorbing phase of human nature, and seemed to get to the very heart of every faith and its influence.

My guide did not need to teach me the lesson. I knew it as well as if I had learned it from infancy. I knew why there were no temples, no ceremonies, no hierophantic families, no outward sign of faith, amongst this far-seeing people. At first I wondered how it had been possible to uproot an institution that had evidently grown out of the most intimate instincts of the race. The higher dignitaries were so lordly and influential they might easily control even by their private alliances and social dominance the powers of the state; and the poorer hierophants had ingratiated themselves with the middle classes and proletariat, from which they came.

When the exilings were over, it was found that there was not a member of the priestly profession left on the island; nor was there anything of the wealth of the church, except the solid walls of the temples. All the vestments and altars and ornaments of the temples had vanished before the last expedition left the shores of Limanora; even the huge bells that had rung to service, and the baser metals for making the roofs water-tight, had disappeared. Nothing but the stones and mortar were left to indicate where the great faith of the past had housed itself. One or two expeditions were seen to set out from Tirralaria to fetch the very temples away stone by stone. To prevent the cupidity of the exiles from wasting itself on futile attempts against the island, the edifices were tumbled into the sea, and helped to make the bastions which guarded the shores.

It was with a certain tremor that they demolished the ancient temples, and put their stones to new and seemingly secular uses. But once the transformation was accomplished and no great catastrophe followed, even the less bold gathered courage. As time went on and the old faith was forgotten and no definite new creed took its place, it began to be felt that the terror of religious change and the belief that religion alone gave the guaranty of all morality and civilisation were alike baseless. Formerly the most religious had been the least trustworthy in the ordinary business of life, and they had not been able to understand why; for the deity they worshipped was a compound of all the noblest virtues they could conceive. Now they perceived that almost all religions, after their early and enthusiastic stage, are royal roads that seem to lead to the heights of heaven, and are but descents to hell. They had seen so much of the degeneration and immorality of faiths, not only in their own history but in the history of the world, that nothing would persuade them to formulate or define in words what they meant by religion at any stage of their development. For, once they had defined, there was a platform of self-opinion and self-interest to fight for, a nucleus of petrification.

Nothing in fact could be nearer to what other men call religion than Limanoran science; it was never weary of listening to the voice of God in the cosmos. Every discovery was the truest act of devotion, a step nearer to the centre of being; and anything that would obstruct such discoveries or the advance they stimulated was retrogressive, a sin against the being who was drawing all things into the path of development. Fixity of belief was the surest obstruction to progress, and, along with all superstition, the grossest immorality.

10

The Case of The. Fox

*Being His Prophecies Under
Hypnotism of the Period Ending A.D. 1950,
A Political Utopia*

by **William Stanley**

*Author of "A New Reform Bill"
"Notes on the Nebular Theory"
"Properties and Motions of Fluids"
"Joe Smith and his Waxworks" etc.*

*London
Truslove & Hanson Ltd.
1903*

William Ford Robinson Stanley   (1829–1909)

was an inventor and scientific instrument maker. Born in Bunting-
ford, Hertfordshire, England, his early education was limited, but he
assiduously continued technical-school training while working in
engineering shops. His ingenuity and inventiveness soon became
manifest; he gained some fame as the first to use a steel-spider wheel
in place of wooden wheels and spokes. Inventions to his credit include improvements of cameras and lenses, surveying instruments,
the meteorometer, the integrating anemometer, the Spirometer, and
one of the first penny-in-the-slot machines, a height-measuring device.

Stanley's most widely known published work is probably *A Descriptive Treatise on Mathematical Drawing Instruments* (1866),
which became the standard authority on the subject and was reprinted in a seventh edition in 1900. Another work, *Experimental Researches into the Properties and Motions of Fluids* (1881), was
commented upon favorably by both Darwin and Tyndall. Among
Stanley's other publications are *Notes on the Nebular Theory*
(1895), *Proposals for a New Reform Bill* (1867), and *Surveying and
Levelling Instruments* (1890). He was a Fellow of the Geological
Society and of the Royal Astronomical Society.

Stanley's versatility included accomplished production as a musician, artist, and architect. His philanthropies followed the pattern
of social philosophy expounded in *The Case of Theodore Fox*. To
the town of Norwood he gave the Stanley Public Hall and Gallery,
for lectures, concerts, and entertainments. Shortly thereafter, he
established a technical school for the education of boys in skilled
scientific mechanics. His utopia is important as a reflection of the
assumption that social problems ought to be amenable to the same
kind of scientific, efficient adjustment and solution that is possible in
mechanics. Of course, the presupposition of this point of view is the
same reliance upon the nature of man as was evidenced by Bellamy.
Just as Bellamy assumes that all men will be good and noble if but
given an opportunity, so Stanley assumes that men will be rational,
accepting the "correct" solution of social problems with the same
eagerness they evidence toward new scientific inventions. To some
extent, Stanley's utopia is an early suggestion of the view that, in
more extreme form, later became known as "Technocracy." Of
primary positive importance in historical perspective is Stanley's
emphasis on the fundamental and primary necessity of political organization to social order.

The Case of The. Fox

I must mention in the first place my regret at the loss of the valuable assistance these pages ought to have received from their author, my fellow boarder, Dr. Aerius Pott, from whose copious notes they are compiled. He was compelled to leave England before their publication from circumstances that were inevitable. Dr. Aerius Pott's special branch of study was hypnotism. Unfortunately for his monetary prospects the doctor was a man of genius, that is to say, a person possessing some ideas of his own. His ideas he assured me he could not hold with sufficient toadyism to others in the field, to ensure success in conjunction with the popular men in his science. With what money he could obtain for his writings for the spiritualistic journals, and from popular lectures, he had prosecuted his hypnotic science as far as he was able. In parting from me he expressed sincere regret for the circumstances which prevented him staying with us until he had completed his great work. He left his most important manuscript in my hands, which was *The Case of Theodore Fox*, with the desire that I should edit it, although it was incomplete by reason of his compulsory departure.

The doctor assures me that in searching history it becomes clear that the most prophetic utterances have emanated from the most poetical minds. The doctor argued that the advanced poetic sentiment went a long way towards explaining the gift of prophecy, and that its most powerful effects would ultimately be obtained by isolation of the prophetic sentiment in the poet through the agency of hypnotism. When Dr. Aerius Potts had determined to prosecute his prophetic investigations, about six months before he left England, he called at the office of "The New Spiritualist." He wrote a note in the office addressed to the editor asking for an audience. After a short conversation with the editor, the doctor described the purpose of his visit, which was to find a sensitive poet imbued with the historical or prophetic instinct, upon whom he thought he might exert his hypnotic influence for the benefit of science, by discovering for mankind some knowledge of the future.

"As regards a poet," the editor replied, "I had an idea that every third man you might meet in the street believed himself to be a poet. As regards the particular kind of poet you require, it is possible that I may help you. I think the author of *Doomsday Glorified* would be the sort of man. His name is Theodore Fox, and he is sure to call within an hour or so, as the poor fellow is quite hard up. You may wait below and see him if you will."

When Theodore Fox entered the office, Dr. Aerius Potts went up to him at once. There was something in his melancholy expression and seedy look which indicated his evident poetic temperament. After the doctor had made his wishes known, the poet soon produced from his pocket a number of semi-prophetic manuscripts which the learned doctor read over with great delight. There were quite a selection of "Millenniums," "Sigh no more, man," "Hungerless," "Thine shall be mine," and other poems, all of which were directed futurewards and to the indefinite. Here was evidently the right man for the prophetic work of the doctor. He offered the poet very moderate terms for his assistance in his hypnotic experiments. The terms were willingly accepted and the seances arranged.

The poet Fox, having the ideas of Dr. Aerius Potts fully impressed upon his mind, fell an easy subject to hypnotic influences. The experiments were made very tentatively at first. The doctor informed us that he led the poet step by step under hypnotism through the historical past into the present, and then beyond far into the future. The last definite period that the poet depicted was A.D. 1950. The doctor found that at A.D. 1950 the poet's ideas were fairly clear and his descriptions often graphic. He therefore decided to neglect all the intermediate stages and make his records, as far as possible, of this period only. The poet's seances with the doctor were twenty in all. The doctor's notes are carried in detail for the latter thirteen seances only, therefore for the sake of sequence we will term the seventh the first.

FIRST SEANCE

"We are now in Paris, my dear Theodore. You promised, when we broke off conversation on Thursday last, you would tell me all about the great changes which led to the glorious sight we have before us in this year of grace 1950!" The doctor always pretended, when the poet was in the hypnotic sleep, to see before him all the poet described. The poet replied to the doctor's question.

"As I told you, Paris has now become the capital of the United States of Europe. This union came about after the great universal European demonstration of the people in 1934, wherein it was decided by the votes of delegates from all States that Europe should hereafter be under one government. With the universal spread of education, every European scholar has been taught English early in life as the most useful and popular language. It was decided that this language should be spoken in the Superior Legislative Assembly as it had become almost universally known all over the world. Our present president of the 'Superior Legislative Assembly' or 'States House of Lords,' as it is now termed, is by birth a German. The council of the United States of Europe is composed of Britons, Germans, Frenchmen, Austrians, Hungarians, Italians, Spaniards, Russians, Turks, Greeks, and other Europeans. We have little jealousy of races now, as the same laws are made for all. Each representative to the European States House of Lords represents the voices of 500,000 voters, who are men and women over twenty-one years of age, throughout all Europe. The whole of Europe is represented by nearly one thousand lords who are elected every three years by postal-ballot."

"This assembly of which you speak, of nearly one thousand lords, must be a rather cumbrous affair," the doctor suggested.

"It is not found to be so," the poet replied. "It works very well in practice. The lords are divided into twenty committees, each of fifty members, with one special minister to each committee, who take up one department of government only, such as education, trade, religion, law, medicine and health, foreign affairs, agriculture, sea-ports and fishing, local government, science, art and so forth. No person can enter a committee without educational knowledge of his special work. A novice on a committee may speak on any subject, but may give no vote for the first year of office. The separate national government of every country advises the persons suitable to be its representative lords of any special department, so that all the various interests may be supported. A man of wealth cannot be a representative unless he has attained the college title of doctor to make him educationally eligible for election. The committees report to the general assembly all their work, which is afterwards legislated upon. Every new law must be accepted by a special committee upon the subject at issue before consideration by the House of Lords."

"How are hitches over local affairs avoided?" the doctor demanded.

"Laws are made and finances administered by national parliaments as before, and every country is responsible for its own duties. Every important law is submitted to the European Legislature (the States Lords) before it is confirmed. This is not a serious matter, as it is sent in the abstract only, and considered by a sub-committee, with the assistance of qualified clerks. The object of this Lords' veto is that no law shall be made that can in any way interfere with practical education, equality of commerce or freedom of trade in Europe."

"You spoke of the European States House of Lords and our parliament being elected by men and women," the doctor said. "I assume by this that men and women have equal rights."

"As electors, women now have equal rights with men," the poet replied. "There is no reason why they should not. As to the elected there may be objections. The States House of Lords is of men only.

A woman who fulfils the function of her being, as a mother of the future race, finds that with maternity there is incapacity for active business life in daily continuity, which is necessary in official work. Where the mother rears the child up to perfect manhood or to virtuous womanhood under her influence, is not her work one of the greatest in the economy of life? But all this should not disfranchise her from the vote her natural talent demands.

"There are women now, as heretofore, who think more of public life than of home, and who have special talent for this life. These are admitted to all governing bodies except the States House of Lords. In our British House of Commons there are at present eighteen ladies, and I have no hesitation in saying that they are of great value to the country. A 'Ladies Popular Government Society' has been formed with the proposed object of taking all government affairs over to their own sex. It really cannot be necessary, as it is evident that the ladies have now advanced in virility in about the same ratio as the men have approached perfect effeminacy, so that there becomes no doubt of the equality of the sexes in physical and governing power."

The doctor felt annoyed with the assertion that manly vigour of mind should diminish in the future. He tried to press for more details without success. The poet appeared to be lost in the subject and became incoherent.

SECOND SEANCE

"Some days ago you spoke of the Republic of the United States of Western Asia," the doctor said. "In the beginning of the century we had only the United States of America as an incorporation of governments. It was thought by men of high political intelligence that the Republican principle of government was not entirely successful. In taking the majority entirely for representation, no selection could be made of the highest intellects; so that the actions of the republican governments, influenced by the lowest grade of humanity, were generally paltry, often unjust, and sometimes bumptious and unfriendly, and never widely humanitarian."

"It has been the constant drift of intelligence in man," the poet replied, "that we should be ruled by fairness. That the individual, *per se*, should stand out as a unit of equal importance in all state affairs. Every privileged class has now broken down. Man can lord it over his fellow man only by superior manhood, that is, by higher intelligence which overrules ignorance. What you speak of in early republics were the first rough mixtures of men poorly educated. Education refines, and veneration comes from this refinement. Look at the advance of our present century to this 1950. There are now only eleven important states in the world. These states are all seeking their own development, without selfish interference with each other. The old United States of North America, which includes Canada, is now perhaps the foremost, from its long establishment. Except the few islands which are colonized, we have no other governments. All these states have quite enough work at present to keep themselves in internal order without interference with other states. The advantages of free trade, a perfect myth to the selfish uneducated man of the past, is now understood from the evidence of experience in Great Britain for nearly a century, so that now there is fully established a mutual friendliness among nations and a cordial interest in each other's general advancement."

To the next question the poet fell into rhyme on generalities, which always indicated that his mind was fatigued with the subject discussed.

> Our progress is evermore
>   That which is great alone lives.
> The past is but the open door
>   That leads to all the present gives.

THIRD SEANCE

"At the end of the last century the Governments of Europe spent a large portion of their incomes in preparations for aggressive and defensive warfare," the doctor said. "Some nations drifted constantly deeper and deeper into debt and ground their peoples down to abject poverty to support the inhuman purposes of war. Did this spirit continue?"

"The thought of bloodshed chills my heart," the poet replied, "and war to me is violence. I have no sympathy with the man—

> Who scars the world and makes it gory
> And dares exult and call this glory.

Now in 1950 in the United States of Europe we have no need of soldiery as we have no international jealousies that violence could satisfy. We have nothing left of the word *military* but drill, as child's play in our schools to keep our bodies healthy—with no thought to destroy them.

"At the last universal convention of the States of the world in 1930 it was decided by unanimous vote, which represented the opinions of the representatives of all nations fully assembled, that humanity must be considered to have advanced beyond the period when *might* could be held as *right*. These decisive votes of the Universal Convention brought about gradually the entire disembodiment of all national troops, when national pride had become a little lowered. The immense income, formerly produced by taxation, when no longer employed for military purposes, appeared to place everybody in a higher position."

"I should like to know a little more of the particulars of the military reform you mention," the doctor replied.

"A factor in the great peace cause was the political force of the working man, who saw, through the influence of the higher education he had now attained, that he was made the tool of the ambitious. That by his earnings the aggressive soldier was supported. That the strongest military powers were the strongest oppressors of his liberty. That a king or president without soldiers must bend directly to the will of the people. He was convinced also that the funds formerly applied to objects of violence were sufficient, if properly used, to offer him peace institutions in the future, wherein he might find rational delight, such as Museums, Libraries, Art and Science Exhibitions and Competitions, Music and intellectual amusements. He could have all these at the cost of preparation for war, and sufficient over and above this to form provident funds for his old age without increase of taxation. The working man realized that war was waste for which he had to pay the loss by his labour, and asserted his electoral powers to the good result which is to be seen in the peace we have now attained."

SIXTH SEANCE
"In speaking of the superior legislative assembly of the States of Europe," the doctor said, "you put education as one of the subjects placed under the direction of a permanent committee. Has not each State power to direct its own internal education?"

"As to direction, if you mean government, certainly, each State administers the laws; but as to the laws themselves in relation to education these are most jealously enforced by the states lords, and are constructed upon scientific methods for the intellectual advancement of the people. Under European unity we have the means of putting a stop to all the former waste of the mental energy of our youth practised by the English. The educated intelligence of the citizen is now recognized as the best source of national wealth. A boy is now taught that which will enable him to raise his position in life. A boy does not now leave school in ignorance of everything he sees around him. He understands perfectly the working of a clock or watch, how gas is made and purified, and all the common principles and effects of electricity. He quite understands the machine which takes him to town in the morning, the press contrivances by which his paper is printed, the telegraph, the telephone and phonograph as it is now made, and all around him. With this knowledge he is happy, as he can make experimental working models of many of these things. In fact he leaves school with more knowledge of general mechanics and science than that attained by the trained mechanic of the early part of the century, so that he is fully qualified to become hereafter a refined workman to the honour of his country. A clever boy is now well advanced in the rudiments of science before he enters the secondary schools at about thirteen, wherein his general studies may be completed up to an advanced line by the time he is fifteen, at which age his intended career is fixed by his parents, who at the same time consult his own inclinations. He then enters the special training colleges for his future life's work. If he intends to become a mechanic in any craft he follows a series of studies devoted to this craft, which embraces both theoretical and practical work. Besides which we have still our polytechnics, which were started late in the last century, wherein young men and women whose occupation requires little mental effort may have their minds trained in interesting knowledge which will be a pleasure to them for life."

"It would be interesting," the doctor said, "to know how far you have carried practical secondary education."

"Education being now not only free in its rudimentary form, but open for the pursuit of all learned professions with every encouragement for advancement, every sufficiently intelligent son or daughter of a citizen of the European States may be what he or she and the parents please. Any one capable of learning may pass under the tuition of the most learned men or women who are our honoured professors. Medicine, law, art and science in all its branches are open, and every one is invited, whose attention to early teaching and general ability qualifies him or her to pass the necessary examination for entry. If a student fails in these higher things he or she may take a humbler walk within his or her capacity. This is not generally less profitable in pecuniary reward, provided one has the necessary tact for the employment, for which every one has attained the rudiments at school."

"It would strike one, from what you have said, that what we termed learning and high art at the commencement of the century has now been entirely shunted. Have we no education for Latin, Greek, Hebrew and Egyptian scholars or for great artists?"

"Oxford and Cambridge are still open to any young man or woman who has means at command, from the parents' savings or otherwise, to pursue learning for itself alone, just as it was in the end of the last century, or a person may, in a competition, take a scholarship which provides means for advanced studies, classical, scientific or artistic, at these colleges. Further, the State now helps in every way in such studies and is as proud as ever of the possession of learned men and women among us."

"I should like now," the doctor said, "to know if intellectual advance (1950) corresponds with the educational advance you have just described?"

"In the sense that the fittest survives it does. But whether the fittest is really the most intellectual in a broad sense I should say that it has not advanced. By the end of the century the machine was superseding the individual constructive quality of the man, thereby providing the only means of competition in the world. With refined machinery, where twenty branches of a business formerly demanded skill and individual cleverness, the boy or girl with training and a little experience could now perform more work, equal in quality, by merely attending to the nearly self-acting machines. By the end of the last century the amusements of the people clearly marked the change of intelligent enjoyment. In the middle of the century (1860) the Polytechnic and the Alhambra in London gave science lectures, always well attended by men and women. Shakespeare and other deeply thought-out dramas were on the stage constantly. At the end of the century the music hall prevailed with other stage frivolities.

"The few constructive brains that are required for the designing of machines and for the limited amount of really technical hand work, now occupy not more than one-tenth of the entire number of persons employed. Of these not more than two per cent. require original talent, so that upon the whole, as less intelligence is required for constructive power, therefore less survives. The above fact does not avoid the necessity of highly trained education; to attain the two per cent. of constructive talent mentioned, the whole mass of the people have to be educated to find the most capable. We have natural talent enough for the average work that is not performed by machinery, but as intelligence increases, higher quality of work is demanded, which we aim at as far as the State will permit."

SEVENTH SEANCE

"Let us now, my Theodore, speak of the advances or refinements made in religion since the beginning of the century (1900), when it formed a much-contested subject of education and politics among the learned. The old churches, I see, remain as they were, which is an evidence of the existence of the old pious spirit which some thought might be reformed off the face of the earth."

"To venerate is human. We may possibly say it is even animal, for no one doubts the abject veneration of the dog for a kind master, whom he worships, and for whom he is ready, at any time, to risk his life. It is part of all natural religion also to venerate a great man, and after his death, when his faults are forgotten, to exalt him by our ever-present faculty of the love of the good and wonderful. The most concrete form of religion in Great Britain that we know of was held by our people in the twelfth and thirteenth centuries, when our great cathedrals, monasteries and abbeys were built as pure god-sake offerings, at the sacrifice by the people of all private luxury. Then nearly every man in this great nation, with his fortune, arms and brains, was ready with all his might and means to help to raise these glorious monuments dedicated to the worship of his God and Christ. The strong religious sentiment, truly god-love, of which we have evidence in the remains of these very buildings, where is it now? We look in vain! It has intellectually slowly passed away, absorbed and generally lost in the cold philosophy of evidences.

"Our European pulpits are now not uncommonly occupied by men and women of high intelligence, endowed with the broad gift of honesty, making no apology for the weak points of their national religion. We have also in the pulpit the glory of science fully acknowledged. The magic lantern has become a common church fixture for graphic demonstration of the facts of science and nature to support our advanced modern religious inspiration. The historical evolution of creeds has now become a matter of general knowledge, and is even taught in some European schools. There are, however, still many sections of religious specialists, who feel they can only venerate and follow the teaching of one master. When this is the inclination, or even, as some assert, the capacity of their minds, it is no doubt for their happiness, and who can object? The number, however, of such special devotees yearly decreases. Every one of more than average intellect forms his own religion from the materials set before him for consideration. Moral and intellectual religion was greatly strengthened early in the century by its separation from State control in European States. A teacher or minister has now generally to depend for his world-position upon his character, merits and ability, instead of upon the patronage or purchase which formerly might set him above a more moral and capable man.

"Seeing there are many creeds, and all of them self-infallible to the believer—to the just mind every faith becomes illogical. Nevertheless, there is no doubt that where the mind is not strong enough to resist evil, any faith may impose a directive influence from the fear of offending a Superintending power. Under this fear men and women may sometimes be made good citizens."

"If our faith in the antique myths which form our religions is gone, we have then nowhere to look for a future state." This was said satirically, as the doctor held quite different opinions from the poet on the subject.

The poet replied, "Immortality is a mental reservation that many of us hold beyond history or myth.

> Spirits, ye beckon me! I come! I come!
> Welcome my yearned-for goal
> To make this living frame a tomb,
> And quickly wing away my soul."

EIGHT SEANCE

"When I was a young man in England (1900)," the doctor said, "civil law, if taken as a standard of justice, was not in a very satisfactory condition. In our courts men of education were licensed and encouraged to misrepresent by every subterfuge the case for plaintiff or defendant."

"With advanced public morals," the poet replied, "the falsehood of a public man becomes worse than that of a private one. Legal untruth was in time acknowledged as being as objectionable as other untruth. The judges early in this century rose in morals above the forms of their courts. Justice now rests in the hands of the States who practically employ their own barristers. If you have a legal plaint to make you lodge it in a public office. If the matter is small, it is decided by the District Public Legal Scrutineer, in the presence of plaintiff and defendant, for a small fee. If the matter is important, or the first decision is unsatisfactory, it is decided by a legal committee or by a jury, to which it is referred by paying slightly higher court fees. If it is necessary to call witnesses, the State calls them at public expense to the extent required by the case. As justice does not now depend in any way upon the loquacious ability of a bantering counsel, there are very few legal matters that cannot be decided in a summary manner with perfect satisfaction to both plaintiff and defendant.

"Crime decreases naturally by the spread of education, a fact well asserted at the end of the last century. If a man has an object in life, the instincts of violence and the craving for ill-gotten gain cease and crime becomes unpopular. Crime is now considered as a mental aberration, and treated as a form of lunacy. It is corrected by personal isolation. The terms of imprisonment gradually increase with the number of convictions, from three months to many years. The isolated districts are constantly becoming less in area as these vices are diminishing. There is no hard (useless) labour as formerly, so the prisoner often gains during confinement a grateful state of mind. Murder is very rare now. The penalty of this crime is isolation for life with other murderers in an open-air prison. There are now only five murderers living who have been convicted throughout the States of Europe. They are all in one prison home in Russia."

"How do you now deal with drunkards?" the doctor asked.

"They have nearly died out," the poet replied. "The States law of A.D. 1925 made drunkenness criminal by infliction of the penalty of isolation, which has produced a marvelous effect.

> Again we mount a higher stage,
> And as we rise we more survey.
> The plain below is murky still,
> But the sun shines brightly over all.
> Anon alone sweet flowers shall bloom,
> And virtue dwell on hill and plain."

TENTH SEANCE

"The arrangements of which you have given some details are for the strong and capable. You must still have among you the blind, deaf, crippled, aged, infirm and diseased, who were maintained through the instrumentality of our Poor Laws and by public or private charity."

"True! " the poet replied. "The great object is to place humanity beyond the need of charity by ceasing to propagate its saddest elements. We have, therefore, separate committees for the blind, deaf, imbecile, crippled, and otherwise defective from birth. The blind have a large area in the country, which is rocky and of little value for agriculture, but otherwise very healthy. After childhood the men have no female society except that of elderly women past maternity, who feel the duty of attending to the blind a pleasure. The women have male society only when they have passed the age of maternity. We have now few cases of congenital blindness. The blind are treated with the greatest care by the State, and their personal enjoyment is considered in every possible way. It is hoped that this human affliction, so far as it is congenital, as it has decreased greatly at the present time, may die out through the attention now devoted to it. Similar institutions to those provided for the blind are now established for the deaf and dumb, but in this case the beauty of the scenery of the country is duly considered by the State.

"Lunacy and idiocy are treated, as the other infirmities of defective humanity mentioned above, by personal isolation. No partial cures in the persons of any lunatics are left to free intercourse, so that now there is no fear of after blood-stain. The great struggle has been in fighting with pious ignorant persons who, under the pretence of charity, have tried all possible means to prevent scientific methods of extermination of this sad disease.

"With regard to old age, this is entirely provided for. Our taxes are sufficient, but personal providence is in no way neglected. We have State provident funds to which a man may subscribe according to scale. These secure to him in his age a position above the State poor grade, as for instance, this may permit him the continuity of occupation at his club after fifty-five years of age, when he is presumed to leave off hard labour, or other privileges his prudence may have secured to him. All provident funds have State assistance, and are investigated for soundness of basis and for perfect security by the Government."

"Late in the last century," the doctor said, "we had a large population of idlers and drunkards who hung about our streets so long as their wives would work, or charity would keep them."

"By State law, charity is now organised so that it cannot do mischief. If a husband does not keep his wife he is isolated by the State, and made to work for her upon State work. If he will not do his work, he runs short of food. If coercion does not succeed with an idler he is isolated on an island where he has to work or perish. The poor remain with us always. If there is a spare loaf wherewith to feed a creature one will surely live to eat it. All we can do by law is to make the creature deserve it."

ELEVENTH SEANCE

"In our last interview," the doctor said, "we discussed contagious diseases, of which we used to say 'flesh is heir to'."

"By following hygienic conditions," the poet replied, "much sickness is preventable, or at least is ameliorated under systematic regulations. At present all cases of sickness are under State control, including hospital cases, which are under the medical branch of the Charity Commissioners. It is now understood that the health of the people is one great source of their usefulness. England has been divided into medical districts, each containing two thousand persons in closely populated parts, and one thousand persons in open districts, these being the 'extreme numbers.' A single doctor superintends each district, with an assistant under him capable of taking his place at any time. In the rare cases of epidemics, the State sends specialists to the infected district.

"Doctors with the highest qualifications and full previous hospital practice are provided by the State. They have good fixed salaries and dwellings, and are not allowed to take any gratuities. In illness medical advice is compulsory to all. In infectious diseases special hospitals or divisions of hospitals are provided. Every one willingly puts himself or herself under this special medical care, as it is the quickest and best possible means of effectual cure. The apothecary, who remains daily in his store, is a qualified practitioner. He dispenses within a prescribed limit drugs for small ailments entirely at State cost, and advises hospital treatment when desirable. Illness is exceptional now; the race has become so much more healthy. There are private doctors, but they are not generally men of mark, as the honour of a high position under the Government, which can only be obtained by examination through merit, is much coveted. Fools still swallow quack medicines as heretofore, and many are lost.

"If you look at the men and women that pass us, trained in intelligence, you see quite an improvement in the healthy appearance of the race in comparison with the accounts we have of society at the beginning of the century. It is anticipated that one hundred years of age will be quite commonly reached by those born at the present time. Many now live some years beyond this."

TWELFTH SEANCE

The doctor asked to have some idea of the advance of science generally. The poet replied that the subject was too large for discussion as there was science in every possible factor of human work. There appeared over the last query to be a little bewilderment in the poet's mind, so the doctor changed the subject.

"You mentioned last Thursday," the doctor said, "that five hours a day for five days a week were the ordinary hours of labour."

"Five hours as a day's work has been fixed by the 'Rights of Labour' Society, for continuous indoor work, and a larger amount cannot be enforced unless under special circumstances. A painter or mason or bricklayer may work in such trades more than the indoor trade-day, or even a double day, in fine summer weather. His work must never exceed in any year his time lost out of the working season, to make it equal five hours a day. Despite all trade rules, social individual freedom is secured by the State for all men. A man may work and join any labour society. Indeed there is nothing so slavish or disadvantageous to the community as uniformity, which is now generally acknowledged."

"Work in my early days was constantly subject to strikes," the doctor said. "Has any remedy been found?"

"Strikes were due to want of a proper understanding between workmen and master. All kinds of work are now recognized at fixed value. A man cannot be idle without paying a penalty for it. The master is satisfied if the workman performs his fair share of work, and the workman with the fixed scale the trade agrees to. This avoids possibility of strikes. There is nothing at present held to be so detestable as Socialism promoted by ignorance, which was active at the commencement of the century, in trying to obtain for the idler the privileges of the active and for the spendthrift those of the prudent and careful. The rule is now one of intelligence. We recognize that some men are fitted to organize the work of others for the general good; that some are more prudent and careful of wealth, and therefore should by right possess it. Intelligent and prudent men rise above the working classes and are recognized by the committees of the 'Rights of Labour' as worthy of being leading men. So that by a general system of equity the folly of strikes and lockouts is avoided. There is work and opportunities for the success of all industrious persons. The great lever of society is wise political organization at home and abroad, which has been the special work of our present century."

THE LAST CHAPTER

While I was editing Dr. Aerius Pott's papers, I had a strong feeling that I ought to see how the poet was getting on after he left the doctor. I could not see how he could make his way, after his mind had experienced so severe a strain under hypnotism.

The following day Constable Nonest, of the A1 division, brought me a note and reported—"I saw an emaciated human form, who appeared almost to fly, in throwing himself over the stone parapet of Waterloo Bridge. This was at the turn of the tide, so that nothing could arrest the shadowy body until it floated into the great ocean to be lost for ever."

When I opened the note I read as follows: "Kindest and most simple hearted of men. The last consolation of my poor faint life was your sympathy. I leave the living as I could not carry the burden of a useless life any longer, to impress sorrow only upon my fellow sojourners. Let me rest in your memory as the dream of one who loved the world much more than he was able to express it. I give you my last words, written weakly, because I am sick at heart, and losing myself in oblivion only to think that—

> "A shadow past as t'were a dream,
>   A poor weak myth has gone;
> 'Twas but a ripple on life's stream,
>   Unfelt and wept by none.
>   "The. Fox."

11

Underground Man

by **Gabriel Tarde (1843-1904)**

Member of the Institute
Professor at the College of France
Translated by Cloudesley Brereton M.A., L. ès L.
With a Preface By H. G. Wells

London
Duckworth & Co.
3 Henrietta Street, Covent Garden, W.C.
1905

Gabriel Tarde   (1843–1904)

was a French criminologist of international reputation. For nearly eighteen years of his early life he was a judge in Sarlat, his birthplace, but after his writings had established his reputation as a criminologist, he was called to Paris in 1894 as head of the Bureau of Statistics of the Ministry of Justice. His publications were manifold, including some poems and plays, but were mainly in the fields of sociology and criminology. He also served in an editorial capacity on several journals and lectured widely. It was only during the last four years of his life that he held a permanent academic position, elected Professor of Modern Philosophy in the Collège de France and member of the Academy of Moral and Political Sciences in the philosophical section. Some of his better known books are: *The Laws of Imitation* (Tr. E. C. Parsons); *La philosophie pénale; Études pénales et sociales; Social Laws* (Tr. H. C. Warren); *Études de psychologie sociale.* (For an analysis of Tarde's sociological theory, see *Gabriel Tarde, An Essay in Sociological Theory*, by M. M. Davis; New York, 1906.)

Tarde's literary ability contributes much to the enjoyment of *Underground Man.* The work was published in France under the title *Fragment d'Histoire Future*, and was published posthumously the year of Tarde's death, 1904. Of the work a friend writes in a dedicatory note: "The whole of Tarde is in this little book. He has put into it . . . his ideas on the influence of art and the importance of love. . . . On reading it we fancy we are again seeing and hearing Tarde." In a preface to the English edition, H. G. Wells regrets the loss of liveliness which is inevitable in translation from French to English, and directs the reader's attention "past the lightness and cheerful superficiality of the opening portions . . . to the tunnels and galleries in which the elusive thought of M. Tarde lurks." There is indeed nothing broad nor obvious about Tarde's satire, and the reader may at times ponder just where Tarde slips over from the indirection of irony into a more positive speculative suggestion of the ideal as it would be in utopia.

There is an inexplicable error in translation in the very first line of *Underground Man*: "It was towards the end of the twentieth century" should read "twenty-fifth century"—but five hundred years is not a matter to quibble about in utopia.

Underground Man

It was towards the end of the twentieth century of the prehistoric era, formerly called the Christian, that took place, as is well known, the unexpected catastrophe with which the present epoch began, that fortunate disaster which compelled the overflowing flood of civilisation to disappear for the benefit of mankind. I have briefly to relate this universal cataclysm and the unhoped-for redemption so rapidly effected within a few centuries of heroic and triumphant efforts. Of course, I shall pass over in silence the particular details which are known to everybody, and shall merely confine myself to the general outlines of the story.

The zenith of human prosperity seemed to have been reached in the superficial and frivolous sense of the word. For the last fifty years, the final establishment of the great Asiatic-American-European confederacy, and its indisputable supremacy over what was still left, here and there, in Oceania and central Africa of barbarous tribes incapable of assimilation, had habituated all the nations, now converted into provinces, to the delights of universal and henceforth inviolable peace. It had required not less than 150 years of warfare to arrive at this wonderful result. But all these horrors were forgotten.

Alongside of the political unity which did away with the enmities of nations, there appeared a linguistic unity which rapidly blotted out the last differences between them. Already since the twentieth century the need of a single common language, similar to Latin in the Middle Ages, had become sufficiently intense among the learned throughout the whole world to induce them to make use of an international idiom in all their writings. At the end of a long struggle for supremacy with English and Spanish, Greek finally established its claims. Gradually, or rather with the rapidity characteristic of all modern progress, its usage descended from strata to strata till it reached the lowest layers of society. All contemporary documents agree in bearing witness to the rapidity, the depth, and the universality of the change which took place in the customs, ideas, and needs, and in all the forms of social life, thus reduced to a common level from one pole to the other, as a result of this unification of language.

The ancient poets who had been dead for centuries, Homer, Sophocles, Euripides, had returned to life, a hundred times more hale and hearty than at the time of Pericles himself. The splendid, untrammelled, and exuberant hexameters of Homer, the stanzas of Sappho, the iambics of Sophocles, furnished unspeakable pleasure, which did the greatest harm to the music of Wagner. Music in general fell to the secondary position to which it really belongs in the hierarchy of the fine arts.

The Universe breathed again. It yawned a little no doubt, but it revelled for the first time in the fulness of peace, in the almost gratuitous abundance of every kind of wealth. It burst into the most brilliant efflorescence, or rather display of poetry and art, but especially of luxury, that the world had as yet seen. It was just at that moment an extraordinary alarm of a novel kind, justly provoked by the astronomical observations made on the tower of Babel, which had been rebuilt as an Eiffel Tower on an enlarged scale, began to spread among the terrified populations.

On several occasions already the sun had given evident signs of weakness. From year to year his spots increased in size and number, and his heat sensibly diminished. People were lost in conjecture. Was his fuel giving out? No one knew. Whatever the reason was, the public concerned itself little with the matter, as in all that is gradual and not sudden. However, the winter of 2489 was so disastrous, it was actually necessary to take the threatening predictions of the alarmists seriously. One reached the point of fearing at any moment a "solar apoplexy." That was the title of a sensational pamphlet which went through twenty thousand editions. The return of the spring was anxiously awaited.

The spring returned at last, and the starry monarch reappeared, but his golden crown was gone, and he himself well-nigh unrecognisable. He was entirely red. The meadows were no longer green, the sky was no longer blue, the Chinese were no longer yellow, all had suddenly changed color as in a transformation scene. Then, by degrees, from the red that he was he became orange. He might then have been compared to a golden apple in the sky, and so during several years he was seen to pass, and all nature with him, through a thousand magnificent or terrible tints—from orange to yellow, from yellow to green, and from green at length to indigo and pale blue.

At the same time disaster succeeded disaster. The entire population of Norway, Northern Russia, and Siberia perished, frozen to death in a single night; the temperate zone was decimated, and what was left of its inhabitants fled before the enormous drifts of snow and ice, and emigrated by hundreds of millions towards the tropics, crowding into the panting trains, several of which, overtaken by tornadoes of snow, disappeared for ever. All that we know for certain is what took place at the time towards the end of the twenty-fifth century in a little district of Arabia Petraea.

Thither had flocked for refuge, in one horde after another, wave after wave, with host upon host frozen one on top of another, as they advanced, the few millions of human creatures who survived of the hundreds of millions that had disappeared. Arabia Petraea had, therefore, along with the Sahara, become the most populous country of the globe. They transported hither by reason of the relative warmth of its climate, I will not say the seat of Government—for alas! Terror alone reigned—but an immense stove which took its place, and whatever remained of Babylon now covered over by a glacier. A new town was constructed in a few months on the plans of an entirely new system of architecture, marvellously adapted for the struggle against the cold. By the most happy of chances some rich and unworked coal mines were discovered on the spot. There was enough fuel there, it seems, to provide warmth for many years to come. And as for food, it was not yet too pressing a problem. The granaries contained several sacks of corn, while waiting for the sun to revive and the corn to sprout again. The sun had certainly revived after the glacial periods; why should it not do so again? asked the optimists.

It was but the hope of a day. A hundred thousand human creatures huddling around the huge government stove, which was no longer equal to restoring their circulation, were turned into icicles in a single night; and the night following, a second hundred thousand perished likewise. Of the beautiful human race, so strong and noble, formed by so many centuries of effort and genius by such an intelligent and extended selection, there would soon have been only left a few thousands, a few hundreds of haggard and trembling specimens, unique trustees of the last ruins of what had once been civilisation.

In this extremity a man arose who did not despair of humanity. His name has been preserved for us. By a singular coincidence he was called Miltiades, like another saviour of Hellenism. In the middle of the central state shelter, a huge vaulted hall with walls ten yards thick, without windows, surrounded with a hundred gigantic furnaces, and perpetually lit up by their hundred flaming maws, Miltiades one day appeared. The remnant of the flower of humanity, of both sexes, splendid even in its misery, was huddled together there. They did not consist of the great men of science with their bald pates, nor even the great actresses, nor the great writers, whose inspiration had deserted them, nor the consequential ones now past their prime, nor of prim old ladies—broncho-pneumonia, alas! had made a clean sweep of them all at the very first frost—but the enthusiastic heirs of their traditions, their secrets, and also of their vacant chairs, that is to say, their pupils, full of talent and promise. Not a single university professor was there, but a crowd of deputies and assistants; not a single minister, but a crowd of young secretaries of state. Not a single mother of a family, but a bevy of artists' models, admirably formed, and inured against the cold by the practice of posing for the nude; above all, a number of fashionable beauties, who had been likewise saved by the excellent hygienic effect of daily wearing low dresses, without taking into account the warmth of their temperament. Youth, beauty, genius, love, infinite treasures of science and art, writers whose pens were of pure gold, artists with marvellous technique, singers one raved about, all that was left of refinement and culture on the earth, was concentrated in this last knot of human beings, which blossomed under the snow like a tuft of rhododendrons, or of Alpine roses at the foot of some mountain summit. But what dejection had fallen on these fair flowers! How sadly drooped these manifold graces!

At the sudden apparition of Miltiades every brow was lifted, every eye was fastened upon him. He requested leave to speak. It was granted him. But let us at this point allow an eye-witness to speak; let us copy an extract of the account that he phono-graphed of this memorable scene. I pass over the part of Miltiades' discourse in which he related the thrilling story of the dangers he had encountered.

"The situation is serious," said he, "nothing like it has been seen since the geological epochs. Is it irretrievable? No! (*Hear! Hear!*) Desperate diseases require desperate remedies. An idea, a glimmer of hope has flashed upon me, but it is so strange, I shall never dare to reveal it to you. (*Speak! Speak!*) The calculation has been made: in two years, three months, and six days, if there still re-mains a morsel of coal there will not remain a morsel of bread! (*Prolonged sensation.*) Therefore if the source of all force, of all motion, and all life is in the sun, and in the sun alone, there is no ground for self-delusion: in two years, three months and six days, the genius of man will be quenched, and through the gloomy heavens the corpse of mankind, like a Siberian mammoth, will roll for everlasting, incapable forever of resurrection. (*Excitement.*)

"But is that the case? No, it is not, it cannot be the case. With all the energy of my heart, which does not come from the sun— the energy which comes from the earth, from our mother earth buried there below, far, far away, for ever hidden from our eyes —I protest against this vain theory, and against so many articles of faith and religion which I have been obliged hitherto to endure in silence. (*Slight murmurs from the centre.*) It is no more by this gesture (*the speaker raises his finger to heaven*) that the hope of salvation should henceforth be expressed, it is by this one. (*He lowers his right hand towards the earth. . . . Signs of aston-*

ishment: a few murmurs of dissent which are immediately repressed by the women.) We must say no more: 'Up there!' but, 'below!' There, below, far below, lies the promised Eden, the abode of deliverance and of bliss: there, and there alone, there are still innumerable conquests and discoveries to be made! (*Bravos to the left.*) Ought I to draw my conclusions? (*Yes! Yes!*) Let us descend into these depths; let us make these abysses our sure retreat."

An objection then came from the right, "With what shall we be fed?"

Miltiades smiled disdainfully and replied: "Nothing is simpler. Is chemistry not capable of manufacturing butter, albumen, and milk? Meanwhile does not disaster itself, by a kind of providential occurrence, place within our reach the best stocked, the most abundant, the most inexhaustible larder that the human race has ever had? Immense stores are lying for us under the ice and snow. Myriads of domestic or wild animals—I dare not add, of men and women (*a general shudder of horror*)—but at least of bullocks, sheep and poultry, frozen instantaneously in a single mass, are lying a few steps away."

From that very day all these exquisite and delicate hands set to work, aided, it is true, by incomparable machines; and before a year was out the galleries of the mines had become sufficiently large and comfortable, sufficiently decorated even and brilliantly lighted, to receive the vast and priceless collections of all kinds, which it was their object to place in safety there, in view of the future.

The day at length arrived on which, all the intellectual inheritance of the past, all the real capital of humanity having been rescued from the general shipwreck, the castaways were able to go down in their turn, henceforth only to think of their own preservation. That day which forms, as everyone knows, the starting point of our new era, called the era of salvation, was a solemn holiday. The sun, however, as if to arouse regret, indulged in a few last bursts of sunshine. On casting a final glance on this brightness, which they were never to behold again, the survivors of mankind could not, we are told, restrain their tears. But that was a short-lived moment of very natural emotion which speedily changed into an outburst of unspeakable delight.

How great in fact was their amazement and their ecstasy! They expected a tomb; they opened their eyes in the most brilliant and interminable galleries of art they could possibly see, in *salons* more beautiful than those of Versailles, in enchanted palaces, in which all extremes of climate, rain, and wind, cold and torrid heat were unknown; where innumerable lamps, veritable suns in brilliancy and moons in softness, shed unceasingly through the blue depths their daylight that knew no night. I am well aware that they had at their disposition a sum of natural forces very superior to all that the preceding ages had been acquainted with. In fact, if they lacked waterfalls, they replaced them very advantageously by the finest falls of temperature that physicists have ever dreamed of. The mining physicists had hardly descended into the bowels of the earth ere they at once perceived that thus placed between the furnaces of the central fires, as it were, and the outer cold, they had at their disposal the most enormous extremes in temperature, and consequently thermic cataracts by the side of which all the cataracts of Abyssinia and Niagara were only toys. At first sight they must have seen that if a few distributing agencies of this prodigious energy were provided, they had power enough there to perform the whole work of mankind—excavation, air supply, water supply, sanitation, locomotion, descent and transport of provisions, etc.

I am well aware of that. I am further aware that ever favoured by fortune, the inseparable friend of daring, the new Troglodytes have never suffered from famine, nor from shortness of supplies. When one of their snow-covered deposits of carcasses threatened to give out, they used to make several trial borings, drive several shafts in an upward direction. They never failed presently to meet with rich finds of food reserves, extensive enough to close the mouths of the alarmists, whereby there resulted on each occasion, according to the law of Malthus, a sudden increase in the population, coupled with the excavation of new underground cities, more flourishing than their older sisters. But in spite of all this, we remain overwhelmed with wonder when we consider the incalculable degree of courage and intelligence lavished on such a work, and solely called into being by an idea which, starting one day from one individual brain, has leavened the whole globe. What giant falls of earth, what murderous explosions, what a death-roll there must have been at the outset of the enterprise! We shall never know what bloodthirsty duels, what rapes, what doleful tragedies, took place in this lawless society, which had not yet been reorganised. The history of the early conquerors and colonists of America, if it could be told in detail, would pale entirely beside it. Let us draw a veil over the proceedings.

From these fruitful though troublous times, and from this beneficial disorder, an advantage has accrued to us which we shall never sufficiently appreciate. Our race, already so beautiful, has been further strengthened and purified by these numerous trials. Shortsightedness itself has disappeared under the prolonged influ-

ence of a light that is pleasing to the eye, and of the habit of reading
books which are written in very large characters. For, from lack
of paper, we are obliged to write on slates, on pillars, obelisks, on
the broad panels of marble, and this necessity, in addition to compelling us to adopt a sober style and contributing to the formation
of taste, prevents the daily newspapers from reappearing, to the
great benefit of the optic nerves and the lobes of the brain. It was,
by the way, an immense misfortune for "pre-salvationist" man to
possess textile plants which allowed him to stereotype without the
slightest trouble on rags of paper without the slightest value, all
his ideas, idle or serious, piled indiscriminately one on the other.
Now, before graving our thoughts on a panel of rock, we take
time to reflect on our subject.

It does not fall within the scope of my rapid sketch to relate
date by date the laborious vicissitudes of humanity since its settlement within the planet from the year 1 of the era of Salvation
to the year 596, in which I write these lines in chalk on slabs of
schist. I should only like to bring out for my contemporaries, who
might very well fail to notice them (for we barely observe what
we have always before our eyes), the distinctive and original features of this modern civilisation of which we are so justly proud.
Now that after many abortive trials and agonizing convulsions it
has succeeded in taking its final shape, we can clearly establish its
essential characteristics. It consists in the complete elimination of
living nature, whether animal or vegetable, man only excepted.
That has produced, so to say, a purification of society.

We are a race of Titans. But, at the same time, whatever ener-
vating element there might have been in the air of our grottoes
has been thereby victoriously combated. Otherwise our air is the
purest that man has ever breathed; all the bad germs with which
the atmosphere was loaded were killed by the cold. Far from being
attacked by anaemia as some predicted, we live in a state of habitual excitement maintained by the multiplicity of our relations and
of our "social tonics" (friendly shakes of the hand, talks, meetings
with charming women, etc.).

If it has been possible for us to realise the most perfect and the
most intense social life that has ever been seen, it is thanks to the
extreme simplicity of our strictly so-called wants. The quota of
absolute necessities being reduced to almost nothing, the quota of
superfluities has been able to be extended to almost everything.
Since we live on so little, there remains abundant time for thought.
A minimum of utilitarian work and a maximum of aesthetic, is
surely civilisation itself in its most essential element. The room left
vacant in the heart by the reduction of our wants is taken up by

the talents—those artistic, poetic, and scientific talents which, as they day by day multiply and take deeper root, become really and truly acquired wants. They really spring, however, from a necessity to produce, and not from a necessity to consume.

We can now comprehend the depth of the truly social revolution which was accomplished from the days when the aesthetic activity, by dint of ever growing, ended by vanquishing utilitarian activity. Henceforth in place of the relation of producer to consumer has been substituted, as preponderating element in human dealings, the relation of the artist to the art-lover. The ancient social ideal was to seek amusement or self-satisfaction apart and to render mutual service. For this we substitute the following: to be one's own servant and mutually to delight one another. Henceforward, to insist once more, society reposes, not on the exchange of services, but on the exchange of admiration or criticism, of favourable or unfavourable judgments. The anarchical regime of greed in all its forms has been succeeded by the autocratic government of enlightened opinion which has become supreme.

Our cities, all in all, are one vast workshop, household and reception hall. And this has happened in the simplest and most inevitable manner in the world. Following the law of separation of the old Herbert Spencer, the selection of heterogeneous talents and vocations was bound to take place of its own accord. In fact, at the end of a century there was already underground in course of development and continuous excavation a city of painters, a city of sculptors, a city of musicians, of poets, of geometricians, of physicists, of chemists, even of naturalists, of psychologists, of scientific or aesthetic specialists of every kind, except, strictly speaking, in philosophy. For we were obliged after several attempts to give up the idea of founding or maintaining a city of philosophers, notably owing to the incessant trouble caused by the tribe of sociologists who are the most unsociable of mankind.

Each of our cities in founding colonies in the region round it, has become the mother of cities similar to itself, in which its own peculiar colour has been multiplied in different tints which reflect and render it more beautiful. It is thus with us that nations are formed whose differences no longer correspond to geographical accidents but to the diversity of the social aptitudes of human nature and of nothing else. Nay, more, in each of them the division of cities is founded on that of schools, the most flourishing of which, at any given moment, raises its particular town to the rank of capital, thanks to the all-powerful favour of the public.

The beginnings and devolution of power, questions which have so deeply agitated humanity of yore, arise with us in the most natural way in the world. There is always among the crowd of our genius, a superior genius who is hailed as such by the almost unanimous acclamation of his pupils at first, and next of his comrades. A man is judged in fact by his peers and according to his productions, not by the incompetent or according to his electoral exploits. In the light of the intimate sense of corporate life which binds and cements us one to another, the elevation of such a dictator to the supreme magistracy has nothing humiliating about it for the pride of the senators who have elected him, and who are the chiefs of all the leading schools they themselves have created. The elector who is a pupil, the elector who is an intelligent and sympathetic admirer identifies himself with the object of his choice. Now it is the particular characteristic of a "Geniocratic" Republic to be based on admiration, not on envy, on sympathy, and not on dislike—on enlightenment, not on illusion.

One would look, by the bye, in vain for a city of lawyers there, or even, for a court of justice. There is no more arable land and therefore no more lawsuits about property or ancient rights. There are no more walls, and therefore no more lawsuits about party walls. As for felonies and misdemeanours, we do not know exactly why, but it is an obvious fact that with the spread of the cult of art they have disappeared as by enchantment, while formerly the progress of industrial life had tripled their numbers in half a century.

Man in becoming a town dweller has become really human. Vulgar wants no longer hinder the progress of the truly human faculties, everyone seems to be born well-bred, just as every one is born a sculptor or musician, philosopher or poet, and speaks the most correct language with the purest accent. An indescribable courtesy, skilled to charm without falsehood, to please without obsequiousness, the most free from fawning one has ever seen, is united to a politeness which has at heart the feeling, not of a social hierarchy to be respected, but of a social harmony to be maintained. It is composed not of more or less degenerate airs of the court, but of more or less faithful reflections of the heart. Its refinement is such as the race who lived on the surface of earth never even dreamed of. It permeates like a fragrant oil all the complicated and delicate machinery of our existence. No unsociableness, no misanthropy can resist it. The charm is too profound. The single threat of ostracism, I do not say of expulsion to the realms above, which would be a death sentence, but of banishment beyond the limits of the usual corporate life, is sufficient to arrest the most criminal natures on the slope of crime.

Patriotism is dead, since there is no longer any native land, but only a native grot. Moreover the guilds which we enter as we please according to our vocations have taken the place of Father-lands. Corporate spirit has exterminated patriotism. In the same fashion the school is on the road not to exterminate but to trans-form the family, which is only right and proper.

But love is left to us. Or rather, be it said without vanity, it is we who discovered and introduced it. Its name has preceded it by a good many centuries. Our ancestors gave it its name, but they spoke of it as the Hebrews spoke of the Messiah. It has revealed itself in our day. In our day it has become incarnate, it has founded the true religion, universal and enduring, that pure and austere moral which is indistinguishable from art. It has been favoured at the outset, beyond all doubt and beyond all expectation, by the charm and beauty of our women, who are all differently yet almost equally accomplished. There is nothing *natural* left in our world below if it be not they.

The inelastic limits of our food supplies have made it a duty for us rigorously to guard against a possible excess in our popu-lation which has reached to-day fifty millions, a figure it can never exceed without danger. We have been obliged to forbid in general under the most severe penalties a practice which apparently was very common and indulged in *ad libitum* by our forefathers. Is it possible that after manufacturing the rubbish heaps of law with which our libraries are lumbered up, they precisely omitted to regulate the only matter considered worthy to-day of regulation? Can we conceive that it could ever have been permissible to the first comer without due authorisation to expose society to the arrival of a new hungry and wailing member—above all at a time when it was not possible to kill a partridge without a game licence, or to import a sack of corn without paying duty? Wiser and more far-sighted, we degrade, and in case of a second offence we con-demn to be thrown into a lake of petroleum, whoever allows him-self to infringe our constitutional law on this point, or rather we should say, should allow himself, for the force of public opinion has got the better of the crime and has rendered our penalties un-necessary. We sometimes, nay very often, see lovers who go mad from love and die in consequence. Others courageously get them-selves hoisted by a lift to the gaping mouth of an extinct volcano and reach the outer air which in a moment freezes them to death. They have scarcely time to regard the azure sky—a magnificent spectacle, so they say—and the twilight hues of the still dying sun or the vast and unstudied disorder of the stars; then locked in each other's arms they fall dead upon the ice! The summit of their fav-orite volcano is completely crowned with their corpses which are admirably preserved always in twos, stark and livid, a living image still of love and agony, of despair and frenzy, but more often of ecstatic repose.

The right to have children is the monopoly and supreme recompense of genius. It is besides a powerful lever for the uplifting and exaltation of the race. Furthermore a man can only exercise it exactly the same number of times as he produces works worthy of a master. But in this respect some indulgence is shown. It even happens pretty frequently that touched by pity for some grand passion that disposes only of a mediocre talent, the affected admiration of the public partly from sympathy and partly from condescension accords a favourable verdict to works of no intrinsic value. Perhaps there are also (in fact there is no doubt about it) for common use other methods of getting round the law.

Ancient society reposed on the fear of punishment, on a penal system which has had its day. Ours, it is clear, is based on the expectation of happiness. The enthusiasm and creative fire aroused by such a perspective are attested by our exhibitions, and borne witness to by the rich luxuriance of our annual art harvests. Such is the moral miracle wrought by our excellence which itself is begotten of love and beauty. But the intellectual marvels which have issued from the same source, merit a still more extended notice. It will be enough for me to indicate them as I go along.

Let us first speak of the sciences. The past has accumulated such undigested masses of astronomical tables, papers and proceedings dealing with measurements, vivisections, and innumerable experiments, that the human mind can live on this capital till the end of time. It was high time that it began at last to arrange and utilize these materials. Now, for the sciences of which I am speaking, the advantage is great from the point of view of their success that they are entirely based on written testimony, and in no way on sense perception, and that they on all occasions invoke the authority of books (for we talk today of whole bibliographies when formerly people spoke of a single Bible—evidently an immense difference). This great and inestimable advantage consists in the extraordinary riches of our libraries in documents of the most diverse kinds which never leave an ingenious theorist in the lurch, and is equal to supporting in a plenary and authoritative fashion the most contradictory opinions at one and the same symposium.

The debates of our *savants* constitute the burning questions which distress us, and which if we had the misfortune to possess a regular press, would not fail to drench our streets in gore. For the questions which are useless and even harmful have always the knack of rousing the passions, provided they are insoluble. These are our religious quarrels. In fact the sum total of the sciences bequeathed to us by the past has become definitely and inevitably a religion. It is perhaps the most profound and fascinating charm of our intellectual leaders. Above all, mathematics, as being the most perfect type of the new sciences, has progressed with giant steps. Descending to fabulous depths, analysis has allowed the astronomers at length to attack and to solve problems whose mere statement would have provoked an incredulous smile in their predecessors. And so they discover every day, chalk in hand, not with the telescope to the eye, I know not how many intramercurial or extra-neptunian planets, and begin to distinguish the planets of the nearer stars. Even the applied sciences have their votaries. Recently one of the latter has at last discovered—such is the irony of destiny—the practical means of steering balloons. These discoveries are useless, I admit, yet are ever beautiful and fertile, fertile in new, if superfluous, beauties. They are welcomed with transports of feverish enthusiasm and win for their originators something better than glory—the happiness that we know so well.

But among the sciences there are two which are still experimental and inductive and in addition pre-eminently useful. It is to this exceptional standing that they perhaps owe, we must admit, the unparalleled rapidity with which they have grown. Their names are chemistry and psychology. Our chemists, inspired perhaps by love and better instructed in the nature of affinities, force their way into the inner life of the molecules and reveal to us their desires, their ideas, and under a fallacious air of conformity, their individual physiognomy. While they thus construct for us the psychology of the atom, our psychologists explain to us the atomic theory of the self. We are indebted to them both for priceless benefits. Our chemists have reassured us against the danger of dying of hunger; our psychologists have claims on our gratitude in freeing us from the fear of death. Permeated by their doctrines we have followed their consequences to their final conclusions with the deductive vigour that is second nature with us. Death appears to us as a dethronement that leads to freedom. That is a well-established doctrine and one on which no discussion would be tolerated. It is, with our devotion to beauty and our faith in the divine omnipotence of love, the foundation of our peace of mind and the starting point of our enthusiasms. Our philosophers themselves avoid touching on it, as on all which is fundamental in our institutions.

There is not, I have already said, a city, but there is a grotto of philosophers, a natural one to which they come, and sit apart from one another or in groups, according to their schools, on chairs formed of granite blocks beside a petrifying well. This spacious grotto contains astounding stalactites, the slow product of continuous droppings which vaguely imitate, in the eyes of those who are not too critical, all kinds of beautiful objects, cups and chandeliers, cathedrals and mirrors—cups which quench no man's thirst, chandeliers which give no light, cathedrals in which no one prays, but mirrors in which one sees oneself more or less faithfully and pleasantly portrayed. There also is to be seen a gloomy and bottomless lake over which hang like so many question-marks, the pendants in the sombre roof and the beards of the thinkers. Such is the ample cave which is exactly identical to the philosophy it shelters, with its crystals sparkling amid its uncertain shadows—full of precipices, it is true. It recalls better than anything else to the new race of men, but with a still greater portion of mirage-like fascination, that diurnal miracle of our forefathers—the starry night. Now the crowd of systematic ideas which slowly form and crystallise there in each brain like mental stalactites is indescribably enormous. While all the former stalactites of thought are for ever ramifying and changing their shape, turning as it were from a table into an altar, or from an eagle into a griffin, new ideas appear here and there still more surprising. There are always, of course, Neo-Aristotelians, Neo-Kantians, Neo-Cartesians, and Neo-Pythagoricians.

But what shall I say of art and poetry? Read our romantic dramas and epics in which all ancient history is magically unrolled. Read also our idylls, our elegies, our epigrams inspired by antiquity, and our poetry of every kind written in a dozen dead languages. You will imagine nothing more fascinating than this renaissance and transfiguration of forgotten idioms, once the glory of antiquity. For our highly refined writers, all that I have praised has no value if their heart is left untouched. They would give for one true and personal note all these feats of skill and sleight of hand. What they adore on bended knee when they have found it, is a short passage, a line, half a line, on which an imperceptible hint of profound passions, or the most fleeting phase, though unexpressed, of love in joy, in suffering or in death has left its impress. Our purest poetry thus joins hands with our most profound psychology. One is the oracle, the other the dogma of one and the same religion.

And yet is it credible? In spite of its beauty, harmony and incomparable charm, our society has also its malcontents. There are here and there certain recusants who declare they are soaked and saturated with the essence, so remarkably pure and so much above proof, of our excessive and compulsory society. They find our realm of beauty too static, our atmosphere of happiness too tranquil. In vain to please them we vary from time to time the intensity and colouring of our illuminations and ventilate our colonnades with a kind of refreshing breeze. They persist in condemning as monotonous our day devoid of clouds and night; our year, devoid of seasons; our towns devoid of country-life. Very curiously when the month of May comes round, this feeling of restlessness which they alone experience at ordinary times, becomes contagious and well-nigh general. And so it is the most melancholy and least busy month of the year.

In reference to this I ought to say that there was recently a false alarm caused by a madman who pretended he had seen the sun coming back to life and melting the ice. At this news which had not been otherwise confirmed, quite a considerable portion of the population became unsettled and gave itself up to the pleasing task of forming plans for an early exodus. Such unhealthy and revolutionary dreams evidently only serve to foment artificial discontent. Luckily a scholar in rummaging in a forgotten corner of the archives put his hand on a big collection of phonographic and cinematographic records which had been amassed by an ancient collector. At this resurrection of another age to the ear and eye, of extinct species and vanished phenomena, an immense astonishment quickly followed by an immense disillusion arose among the most ardent partisans of a return to the ancient regime. We were all angry with it for showing itself so inferior to its reputation. Assuredly the worst of our concerts is more musical than this so-called symphony of nature with full orchestral accompaniment. Thus has been quelled by an ingenious expedient entirely unknown to former governments, this first and only attempt at rebellion. May it be the last.

A certain leaven of discord is beginning, alas, to contaminate our ranks, and our moralists observe not without apprehension sundry symptoms which indicate the relaxation of our morals. The growth in our population is very disquieting, notably since certain chemical discoveries, following upon which we have been too much in a hurry to declare that bread might be made of stones, and that it was no longer worth while to husband our food supplies or to trouble ourselves to maintain at a certain limit the number of mouths to feed.

Simultaneously with the increase in the number of children, there is a diminution in the number of masterpieces. Let us hope that this lamentable movement will soon abate. If the sun once more, as after the different glacial epochs, succeeds in awakening from his lethargy and regains fresh strength, let us pray that only a small part of our population, that which is the most light-headed, the most un-ruly, and the most deeply attacked by incurable "matrimonialitis", will avail itself of the seeming yet deceptive advantages offered by this open air cure and will make a dash upwards for the freedom of those inclement climes! But this is highly improbable if one reflects on the advanced age of the sun and the danger of those relapses common to old age. It is still less desirable.

Let us repeat in the words of Miltiades our august ancestor, blessed are those stars which are extinct, that is to say, the almost entire number of those which people space. We continue firmly to believe that, among the stars as among mankind, the most brilliant are not the best, and that the same causes have brought about elsewhere the same results, compelling other races of men to hide themselves in the bosom of their earth, and there in peace to pursue the happy course of their destiny under unique conditions of absolute inde-pendence and purity, that in short in the heavens as on the earth true happiness lives concealed.

12

Crucible Island

A Romance, an Adventure
and an Experiment

by **Condé B. Pallen**

New York
The Manhattanville Press
23 East Forty-first Street
(1919)

Condé B. Pallen (1858–1929)

was one of the most widely known Catholic journalists and authors of his period. He received his A.B. and A.M. degrees from Georgetown University, and after earning a Ph.D. at St. Louis University, remained at that school for a brief time as Lecturer in Philosophy. The desire for further study took him to Rome, where one of his classmates was the future Pius XI. He was honored by Georgetown University with an honorary LL.D. degree, by Pope Leo XIII with the decoration *Pro Ecclesia et Pontifice*, and by his former colleague, Pope Pius XI, with the Knighthood of St. Gregory.

One of Pallen's major achievements was the conception and initiation of the *Catholic Encyclopedia*, of which he was the managing editor. In spite of a busy career as editor, extensive lecturer, and father of eleven children, Pallen yet found time to produce several scholarly pieces of research, mainly in English literature. Among these publications are the *Philosophy of Literature, What is Liberalism, The Death of Sir Launcelot and other Poems,* and *The Meaning of the Idylls of the King*. Mention of his honorary citations should include the encomium of Tennyson, in a letter to Pallen: "You have seen further into the real meaning of *The Idylls of the King* than any of my commentators."

For all his ability in literary criticism, it is well that Pallen confined his efforts at novel-writing to *Crucible Island*, for his style is awkward, florid, and melodramatic, even by comparison with the standards of the period. His intention is as plain as his satire is broad, an attack upon what he feared in socialist and communist doctrines, the destruction of the values of religion and family. Pallen was distinguished for the vigor of his opposition to the feminist movement, to any restriction of immigration into the United States, and to all forms of "radicalism." He was violently opposed to the recognition of the Soviet government by the United States.

The general position is manifest in the following selection. It is not a particularly interesting work, although there is an intriguing uniqueness in the Irish "brogue" coined by Pallen; but it is a fair sample of the use of the utopian form in the modern period to satirize current schools of socialist thought.

Crucible Island

The prisoner stood facing the Prince.

"So," exclaimed the Prince, "it is to this you have come, Carl Runder!"

"To this," answered the prisoner, "but I glory in it. I am ashamed of nothing. I plotted against you. I would break down your despotism and make this a free land, where there should be no privilege, no rank; all things for all, untrammeled distribution of the goods of life, and none to suffer and none to be exploited."

The Prince smiled. "Men are not angels, and the millenium has not come. But let be argument. You are in my power; you have plotted traitorously against me. Were the conditions reversed, and I in your place, the declared and mortal enemy of the established socialist state, what would you do with me?"

Carl looked steadily at the Prince and said, "Execute you, or incarcerate you for life."

"So be it," said the Prince, "you shall be transported to Schlectland for life. You have pronounced your own sentence."

Schlectland, in Unterwald, was a name of evil odor, an island in the sea from which no man was ever known to return. It was a penal colony. As the prisoner was escorted out of the chamber, an enigmatical smile played over the face of His Highness of Unterwald.

It was a long and bitter voyage for Carl Runder. So this was the end of all his dreams! At last the cessation of the ship's vibration conveyed to him the tidings that they had arrived at the fatal island of Schlectland. As he was rowed ashore with his armed escort, the officer laconically remarked, "Carl Runder, Socialist. To the Spielgarten."

The soldiers, with Carl in their midst, took a road to the right along the shore, then struck off up the mountainside. After two hours' steady climb and another two hours' heavy tramping upward, they reached the summit, proceeded at almost a level for another hour, then descended a steep incline. A halt was called, and the sergeant proceeded to bind Carl's eyes. A sharp command to march he obeyed mechanically, then again he was stopped by an abrupt order to halt. Someone, swiftly unlocking his handcuffs, drew them off. A hand reached to his head and snatched off the bandage, and a voice behind him commanded: "Do not look back or you will be shot down. Go forward; follow the road."

He ran impetuously, as a child would, from some unknown terror, until out of sheer exhaustion he flung himself upon a mossy spot by the roadside. Gradually his breath came back to him and his brain began to clear again. He saw a valley some twenty miles in length and broadening to perhaps ten miles. Great mountains hemmed it in on all sides. Farmhouses were clearly discernible. Some distance down the stream was a town. It was a scene of peace and beauty. Where was he? What did it all mean?

Carl walked on as in a dream. He descended almost to the base of the mountain, when he came on half a dozen men at work, wielding their axes. The man directing the others perceived him first.

"Begorra!" he exclaimed with an unmistakable brogue, "here's another lad for the Spielgarten!"

"Who are you? Where am I?" queried Carl.

"Sure ye're in the Spielgarten and to shtay, at that, too."

"Well, what is the Spielgarten?" impatiently asked Carl.

The other laughed. "The Spielgarten is this blooming valley, and it's a place the man that sent you here has prisinted to the loikes of ye that disagrees with him in the matter o'govermint, an' he says to thim, ye wurrk out ye're own notion of govermint here and let me run mine accordin' to me own ideas."

"Do you mean Socialism?" came from the wondering Carl.

"Bedad, that I do," answered the other. " 'Tis a Socialist colony left to its own devices."

Carl stood for a moment in utter surprise. He was stunned by the news. McCarthy, for so he was called by the others, pulled out a flask, out of which he made Carl drink of a refreshing beverage. McCarthy and his fellow woodsmen with Carl entered the road and followed it into the valley. As they walked, little was said. Carl gave himself up to the strange exaltation which had taken hold of him. He was in a Socialist State! The great dream of his life suddenly rising up before him like a beautiful vision, and yet not a vision, but a practical reality.

•　•　•　•　•

Carl had now been a month in the Spielgarten. He had learned that there existed a secret compact, which had originated in Unterwald, between the governments of Europe, to transport all Socialists to this island, where they might freely work out the socialist scheme. The purpose of the world's rulers was not benevolent, but corrective; it was supposed that the Socialist State would break down. It was, besides, an easy way of getting rid of elements troublesome and dangerous.

The colony had been in existence for fifty years at the time of Carl's advent. The founders were a band of five hundred Socialists who had been transported *en masse* into the valley. What with recruits from without and the natural propagation of the race, which was carefully supervised by the State, the inhabitants of the valley had grown to some ten thousand souls, the majority of whom were native to Spielgarten and had been brought up under the socialist regime. The climate of the island was semi-tropical, the soil fertile; the mountains were profusely timbered and rich in ore. Nothing was materially wanting to supply human needs. At first there were bitter differences of opinion, and it was not until some twenty years after the foundation of the colony that a consistent and logical plan was evolved. The people of the Spielgarten were made up of various nationalities. The largest element was German, and the language spoken was of that nation.

The climate was evidently healthful, and there seemed to be little sickness on the island. The physique of both the men and the women was robust. Indeed, to Carl's eyes, Schlectland seemed a veritable paradise. Oh, that the world might know of the social paradise into which he had been so strangely and happily thrust! The social machinery around him worked so noiselessly and smoothly that it was scarce perceptible. The administration of government seemed remarkably simple, and, as far as he could observe, almost autonomous. Its basis was the popular franchise. All over the age of twenty-one voted, and the suffrage was not restricted to the male sex, but also accorded to women. There was a General Assembly whose members were elected every four years from ten different districts into which the Spielgarten was politically divided. The functions of this body were chiefly legislative, and its enactments became law subject only to the decision of what was called the Council of Welfare, which passed judicially upon the constitutionality of the laws. The Constitution was drawn upon strict Socialist principles and based upon the absolute supremacy of the State. The Common Council of Welfare elected from its own body an executive staff known as the Particular Council of Welfare, whose duty was the administration of the laws, and whose responsibility for the faithful performance of their offices harkened back to the General Assembly, which possessed the constitutional power of impeachment and punishment of any executive officer for malfeasance in the performance of his duties. The Particular Council appointed judges, one for each two districts, who presided over all trials within their respective territories, and from whose decisions appeal could always be made to the Particular Council.

On all sides peace and content reigned. Men went about their various avocations quietly and happily. None questioned, all obeyed. There was no poverty, no inequality, no rank. The State supervised and directed everything. Food, clothing, and shelter were carefully distributed to all alike, and all occasion of envy was inevitably eliminated. While each contributed according to his ability, under State direction, to the common stock, to each was distributed with an even-handed impartiality an equal share. The hours of labor were fixed by law, and so arranged as to fall with little duress upon any. One day of the week was free, and on that day labor was strictly prohibited. Every three months a period of three days was set aside, during which the people might occupy themselves as they pleased;

but if during this time they devoted themselves to labor of a productive nature, the result had to be deposited in the common store.

Carl's wonder grew as he watched and noted the operations of what seemed to him so simple and so perfect a system. Mere living was a bliss, peace and good-will, content and happiness everywhere. He had, indeed, been transported into the golden age.

There were no idlers in the Spielgarten. Each one had his allotted share in the labor of the community. The division of labor was predetermined by the judges of the various districts. If one were discontented with the avocation to which he was assigned, he had the right of an appeal to the Particular Council at the end of six months, and then again at the end of a year, but their decision was final.

At first the colony had experienced difficulty in the division of labor, as there was a tendency to overcrowd the lighter tasks as well as to seek those places which seemed to carry some mark of distinction. But as the native-born element began to preponderate, the leaven of self-seeking brought by the original colonists gradually disappeared, and an appeal was now a rare occurrence. The children were taught from infancy that they were at maturity to be placed at certain assigned tasks, and during youth were trained with a view to the avocation thus predetermined for them. It was inculcated also as a cardinal principle of their ethical code that there was no distinction of merit or reward in the different avocations and conditions of life. The man who dug or ploughed occupied as meritorious and honorable a place in the community as the judge of a district, and no distinction in the distribution of the goods of life was made between them.

When Carl arrived in the colony he was treated as were all recruits from the outside world. As manual labor was always most in demand, he was allotted to that division. This was by no means to his liking, as he was a lawyer by profession. His enthusiasm, however, overcame his repugnance, and he set to work with zeal and energy. At Denis McCarthy's suggestion he was attached to the Irishman's band of woodcutters. McCarthy was a genial companion to whom he had taken a great fancy. The others in the band he soon discovered to be ordinary workmen who chopped away apathetically and exerted themselves at their task as little as possible, and had as little to say. A minimum of performance seemed to be the goal; and it was not long before he learned that a minimum of labor in a given time prevailed throughout the Spielgarten. He was inclined to resent this as a shirking from public duty, and expostulated with Denis over it. They were on their way home after the day's labor, cutting timber a mile east of Marxville.

"But this is simply putting things at the lowest level," urged Carl.

"Surely to get the best out of life is the noblest ambition, and the State with the highest ideal will not stop short of providing the best for the common welfare."

The Irishman interrupted him, as they approached a farmhouse, with the suggestion that they might stop for "a dhrink of wather." As they neared the entrance a young woman emerged from the door. The women Carl had seen in the Spielgarten could lay little claim to beauty, and this apparition of loveliness startled him. He stood for the moment spellbound.

"Indeed, I'm glad to see you, Denis," she said, "and father will be glad, too, I know. Where have you been so long, since we last saw you?"

"Beyont the town there for these two months gone. Here is a recroot I found up there,—Herr Runder, Fraulein Mina."

The young woman held out her hand to Carl, saying with simple sincerity, "Welcome to the Spielgarten, Herr Runder."

Mina's father, John Clausen, welcomed Carl warmly, and began at once to ply him with questions as to the present conditions in the world, showing interest in everything and commenting shrewdly upon Carl's answers. As they were departing, Herr Clausen laid his hand kindly on Carl's shoulder, and bade him come again and frequently, and to her father's invitation, Mina added hers.

John Clausen was an Englishman, who had gone to the University of Heidelberg and had become a member of a Socialist society. In the disorders of 1848 Clausen was apprehended and transported to the Spielgarten. Mina had been educated in the schools of the Spielgarten, but her father had supplemented her studies with all he could remember of the literature and art and history of Europe. Knowledge of this nature was carefully excluded from the schools as unsuited to the purposes of a Socialist community whose end was to form a people on a purely communistic ideal, for the literature and art of Europe had sprung from individualistic sources and breathed the spirit of individualism. From the start Mina's father had impressed upon the child the necessity of reticence and secrecy, for he feared the interference of the State and the transference of the custody of Mina to other hands if it became known that he had instructed her in forbidden things.

As time went on Carl found himself a frequent visitor at the farmhouse. Outside of Clausen and Mina and Denis, Carl had found the people of the Spielgarten in some way alien to him. With Clausen he spoke his mind freely; with others, he found that there was no possibility of discussion, for Socialism in the Spielgarten had settled down into an accepted fact on an immovable basis.

"Some years ago," said Clausen in one of his talks with Carl, "a recruit attempted what he called a reform, and his ideas were in many respects yours, Herr Runder. He gathered a small following amongst other recruits who were then more numerous than they are now. The result was that he was finally apprehended for treason, tried before the Council of Particular Welfare, and condemned to death. You see, the Socialist as well as the Individualistic State takes radical means to defend itself against innovators."

"But is there no freedom of ideas and speech within proper limits in the Socialist State?" expostulated Carl. "Surely this is a tyranny as bad as that against which Socialism is a protest."

"I am afraid that you are right," answered Herr Clausen, "but who is to determine in a Socialist community what ideas are in keeping and what means are fit? Surely not the individual, but the State itself. You may call it despotism, but it is the logical outcome of your own principle."

"But surely," protested Carl, "the conditions which exist here are not the true result of Socialism. This apathy, this indifference to everything except the mere routine of living, this dead level of existence, is simply an arrested phase of Socialism. Its ideal lies beyond. Here is where the leaders fail."

"Leaders!" said Clausen, with a half-smile, "you forget there are no leaders in a Socialist State. Leaders would mean inequality, my dear friend, and that would plunge us at once into individualism."

"But I would make that common aim higher," urged Carl, "I would raise the common level by presenting and inculcating a higher common ideal."

"Yes, *you* would," retorted Clausen. "You cannot rouse the people to an ideal of which they know nothing nor would you be suffered to preach your doctrine."

Carl was impressed, but not convinced, and had started to reply when he was interrupted by the arrival of a stranger. Carl felt an instinctive aversion from the man at once. Herr Clausen welcomed the intruder, with gravity and something of distance in his manner. "This is Herr Runder, Herr Schmidt." A moment after Carl rose and bade the two men adieu.

Mina was standing at the further end of the garden and beckoned him as he came out. "Herr Runder," she said, "I am going to make bold to ask a promise of you. I want to ask you not to talk before others as you speak to father and me. And then be careful to say nothing before Herr Schmidt. He is a dangerous man and a very strict Socialist; it was he who denounced the man of whom father told you, and had him executed."

Mina's voice conveyed a world of solicitude, and Carl felt his heart beat faster. "Mina, Mina," he cried with a sudden impulse, and seizing her hand kissed it fervently, "and do you care, do you care? I love you, I love you, Mina," he went on passionately, "say that you love me."

"I do care for you, Carl," she murmured. "I do love you. I ought not, for it can never be. No, it can never be!" she exclaimed with a poignant emphasis. "They would never allow it in the Spielgarten; they have prohibited it."

"Prohibited what?" asked Carl, perplexed.

"Any free choice between a man and a maid. In the Spielgarten the Particular Council chooses for us."

"But I love you, Mina, and you me, and no man has the right to come between us. What has the Particular Council to do with our loves?"

"I do love you, Carl, but the Particular Council regulates and controls all marriages. It chooses those who are to marry."

"One thing I will never submit to, and that is this infamous rule. To have you taken from me and given to another would be worse than death."

They heard the footsteps of Herr Clausen approaching. He gazed at them a moment and then advanced. In their attitude he read the situation. "Mina, my child," he cried with emotion and held out his arms to her; "I understand; I, too, am fond of Carl, but what can we do, what can we do? It has come at last. I have been fearing it for the past two years. The Particular Council has just been making the quarterly selections and you among others have been chosen. They have chosen you, Mina; God! but the words choke me! They have chosen you, my Mina, for Herr Schmidt!"

Carl was completely taken aback at the suddenness of the blow.

"We will not submit to it," he cried. "Surely there is some way to circumvent it. Can we not appeal to the courts?"

"There is no appeal from the Particular Council. It has absolute control of such matters. It mates and unmates at its will."

"We will appeal to the people."

Herr Clausen looked up at Carl with haggard eye. "No, Carl, it would be useless. The people have long ago become passive instruments in the hands of the State."

"Then we must flee from the Spielgarten," cried Carl.

"See the mountains around you," answered Clausen, "and then the sea beyond; and armed soldiers at every egress to shoot us down. No one has ever succeeded in escaping."

．　．　．　．　．

When Carl returned to Marxville that evening and narrated to Denis McCarthy the events that had occurred at Clausen's, the Irishman's eyes flashed with a dangerous light. Carl continued giving him the details, with many expressions of his own bitter dissent against the way things had shaped themselves in the Spielgarten.

"Denis, I mean it in sober earnest. We must escape from this. We must get away from the Spielgarten, Mina, and her father, you and I. We must explore the way. Do you know anything about the lower end of the valley? The river flows out at that end, perhaps we may find some way out there."

"The river flows into a great gorge there and beyont there's a big cataract, they say."

"Well, can't you arrange to go to that end of the valley to explore for timber? We will set out to-morrow."

It was noon when they arrived at the narrow gorge into which the stream embouched in a swift and foaming rapid. Carl started forward along a narrow ledge jutting out from the constantly increasing precipitousness of the bank. Suddenly he felt the ledge crumbling beneath his precarious footing, and with Denis' startled outcry ringing in his ears, realized that he was falling. Denis could not advance a step farther, as the treacherous ledge on which Carl had just been standing had broken away. After a vain hour spent in the attempt, he turned sadly back, revolving dejectedly in his mind how he was to break the news of the horrible disaster to Mina and her father.

.   .   .   .   .

Carl's loss completely prostrated Mina. She pined and drooped under the grief of his loss with the dreadful prospect of the hated marriage with Herr Schmidt. In the early years of the settlement there had been a sharp conflict over the question of marriage and the family. Some had advocated free choice in marriage and a continuance of the family life. But the more ardent and, indeed, the more consistent Socialists had vigorously opposed it as an institution of the capitalist's world, the very rock and basis of individualism. Family life naturally begot strong and selfish affections. The love of the parent for the child led of necessity to a desire for property. One temporary concession was tolerated, namely, the continuance of the family for those who had entered upon it prior to the adoption of the law. By the new regulation, children, as soon as born, were taken from their mothers and cared for under State supervision. The children were confided to a corps of women called State Mothers, chosen usually from those who had themselves proved childless, or were too old to bear children. When a woman had been mated two years without issue, she was never re-mated, but placed among the State Mothers.

Clausen was thankful that he was allowed to retain Mina and rear her in his own keeping. Now Mina was to be taken from him and mated to Herr Schmidt.

Denis placed his hands on Clausen's shoulders and said with deadly significance, "Herr Clausen, rest aisy for yourself. Mina shall never go to that baste. I'll kill him first."

"What good would that do, Denis?" groaned the anguished father. "The same fate would befall Mina in the end, with someone else selected by the Particular Council, and you would go to the house of Euthanasia."

It was in vain that Clausen expostulated with him.

The Irishman's mind was fixed.

. . . . .

When Carl was precipitated into the turbulent stream below by the breaking of the ledge under his feet, he felt himself seized by the whirling waters and rapidly borne onward. His eyes confusedly caught a low ledge, back of which was an opening into the face of the cliff. As he came to it, with a last effort he threw both arms over it and clung to it with all the tenacity of despair, but his body felt like lead. With his leg as a lever he managed to drag his body up, gasping and fainting, and then rolled over and lost consciousness. When Carl recovered from his swoon, there was yet hope, he thought, seeing how marvelously he had been saved from the cataract. Either river or cliff was impossible. There was but one way, the hazard of the opening in the cliff.

Inch by inch he made his way for what seemed to him an interminable distance. Pushing onward with desperate resolve, he at last saw a faint glimmer of light at a sudden turn of the tunnel. He redoubled his almost spent powers at the prospect of a near release from what had seemed living entombment. He reeled out of the mouth of the cave into the little valley upon which the cavern opened. Back of him rose a lofty range, cutting him off from the Spielgarten. In front of him rose another lofty range, perhaps bordering on the sea. His first thought was to get back into the Spielgarten.

The only alternative was to go up the valley. He had thus gone for about a mile when, to his astonishment, he came upon a rude hut. There were no signs of life about it. Entering, Carl discovered a human body reduced to a mummified state, a man's body. Lying beside the body was a rusted rifle. He perceived on the rough table a belt of cartridges nearly full, and alongside it a notebook with a pencil, as if just laid down by the writer. At a glance, he saw that it was a diary. The first three pages were undecipherable. From this on the writing was perfectly legible and ran as follows:

"I came after a year's sojourn in the Spielgarten to a clear apprehension of the practical working of Socialism in the economic world. The Socialist ideal is completely realized, but the penalty is paid in full. As soon as the child is capable of learning, he is taught the Socialist catechism, whose first questions run as follows:

" 'Q. By whom were you begotten?'

" 'A. By the Sovereign State.'

" 'Q. Why were you begotten?'

" 'A. That I might know, love, and serve the Sovereign State always.'

" 'Q. What is the Sovereign State?'

" 'A. The Sovereign State is Humanity in composite and perfect being.'

" 'Q. Why is the State supreme?'

" 'A. The State is supreme because it is my Creator and Conserver, in which I am and move and have my being and without which I am nothing.'

" 'Q. What is the individual?'

" 'A. The individual is only a part of the whole, and made for the whole, and finds his complete and perfect expression in the Sovereign State. Individuals are made for co-operation only, like feet, like hands, like eyelids, like the rows of the upper and lower teeth.'

"It was at the end of my first year that I received an order from the Particular Council to mate (the word marriage is forbidden in the Spielgarten) with a young woman by the name of Louise. The two great obstacles in the way of the realization of Socialism were the institution of Religion and the institution of the Family. The founders cut out the Family—root and branch. Men and women are mated for two years and their offspring, as soon as born, taken over by the State and reared in the House of Infancy, under the common charge. The mother, when the time comes for the birth of the child, is taken to the House of Maternity for her confinement and never sees her babe. Neither father nor mother know their own children in the Spielgarten. The temporary character of the mating period also conduces to check the growth of any permanent affection between the mothers and the fathers.

"I found, after a time, that I had grown to love Louise, and she in turn reciprocated my love. She was taken to the House of Maternity and when she returned to me she sobbed as if her heart were breaking. 'O Robert, my baby. I begged them to let me hold it, even for a moment, but they would not.' In time a second child was born to her, but Louise died in childbirth. In the Spielgarten are my two children, whom I have never seen and will never know.

"It was not long, just three months after Louise's death, before a second order came to mate again. Then a wild idea flashed upon me—escape! I proceeded to make my preparations. One day after nightfall I set out on my adventure with but one definite thought, to get out of the Spielgarten. At last reaching the bottom of the valley, which I believed to lead out upon the river at the southern end of the island, I soon turned a slight bend, where I came in full view, half a mile below, of a small, concave bay into which the river's flood swept. Beyond lay the sea. I was startled, as my eye caught, in the scene before me, a small square stone structure. The guardians of the Spielgarten had placed a garrison at this point against the possible chance of anyone seeking an exit here. My first thought was one of utter despair, but was this not in furtherance of my design? I drew the conclusion that the garrison's means of communication with the north end of the island, where I had landed before being thrust into the Spielgarten, must be by sea. On the third day of my vigil I was rewarded by discovering in the bay a good-sized tug boat. Did the sailors then come ashore and spend the night in the guardhouse? Seizing the boat while they slept would be an easy matter. God help me—I must make the attempt to escape to-night. . . ." Here the diary abruptly ended. No word or inkling of his fate could be gathered from the faded pages.

The story indicated a way back to the Spielgarten, for return by the way Carl himself had come, through the mountain and the river was an impossibility. Carl began preparations to make his way back over the route described in the diary.

. . . . .

It was the day set for the mating of Mina. So determined and confident seemed Denis that even Clausen began to believe that perhaps the Irishman had hit upon some plan. At the time designated Mina appeared, arrayed in the regulation red robe. She found about fifty other couples assembled. The ceremony was of the simplest:

"Do you, Man, take this Woman for a mate for the period of two years, for the purpose of propagating the race in the service of the Supreme State?"

Schmidt's house was in the suburbs of Marxville. He grabbed her roughly and dragged her in. Mina shrank from his grasp; he caught her to himself suddenly in a fierce embrace. At the same moment Schmidt felt a heavy hand grab him by the collar. Turning with an oath, he beheld Denis McCarthy with eyes aglow with a dangerous fire. Schmidt threw open a drawer of the table and, snatching a revolver from it, thrust it pointblank at the Irishman. Denis stood startled. No weapons were made in the Spielgarten, and it was against the law to possess one. Denis suddenly stooped and threw himself with all his force against the desk, which smashed full against Schmidt's body. The revolver went off with Denis' sudden movebent, the bullet just grazing the top of the Irishman's head. In an instant Denis grabbed Schmidt by the wrist and gripped his throat. The revolver dropped to the floor. Mina tore her red robe into strips, with which Denis promptly bound the hands and feet of Herr Schmidt and secured his mouth with a gag.

Meantime Clausen remained at home in an agony of suspense, waiting to hear from Denis. A figure plodding heavily up the road caught his eye.

"My God, is it you, Carl? We thought you—"

"Yes," said Carl, "I know. You supposed, of course, that I was dead, and it is only by the luckiest chance that I did escape. I have good news for you. We can get out of the Spielgarten. Where is Mina?"

"It was only this evening just after sunset that Mina was mated to Herr Schmidt. Hold yourself, Carl, it's all right—let me tell you. Denis had a plan to save Mina. I firmly believe that he intended to kill Schmidt and I do not doubt that he has done it."

Carl finally yielded reluctantly to Clausen's persuasion, though he was all impatience to seek Mina. "As soon as Mina and Denis come, we must prepare to flee."

They heard the approach of feet on the road. Carl rushed to Mina. "I knew you would come back!"

All immediately set to work to gather what things they might need for their adventure. With hearts beating and with their hopes high, the four fugitives from the Spielgarten started. The ascent was a long and fatiguing climb, then they descended into the valley under Carl's direction. The descent was finally successfully accomplished. Once at the bottom of the cañon in safety, they traversed it to the little hut. There they concluded to remain until they should be able to escape. They agreed that one of them should keep a constant watch for the coming of the tug with provisions for the garrison.

One day Mina was drying her hair, and Clausen noticed little gleaming specks through it. "Where were you washing your hair?" he asked eagerly. "It looks like gold dust, Mina. Show me the spot."

Denis, who was near by, came rushing. "Glory be to God! A bit of this in our pockets when we get out will go a long ways to makin' friends."

They heard Carl's voice calling only a short distance away. "The tug! the tug!" Here was a crisis. To leave now before they could gather enough gold for their advent into the outer world would be folly. It was determined that on her next appearance they would make the attempt to escape.

Ten weeks after the discovery of gold, Denis announced that the tug was approaching. At the noon hour all the soldiers and the sailors proceeded to the shore and plunged in, disporting themselves in great glee in the water. The three men crossed the space between the barracks and the bluff and quietly entered. All three immediately seized rifles and revolvers. They advanced toward the bathers.

"Hands up!" shouted Denis. "Carl, do you and Clausen get in the boat there and go out to the tug and seize it. Is there any of you spalpeens who would like to take the voyage with us? Well, then, I think we'll have to do a little impressin'. I think we will stand in nade of the engineer."

Finally one of the sailors volunteered to go with them. The entire party stepped into the boat, boarded the tug, and weighed anchor. The sailor at the wheel turned to Denis and asked, "Which way?"

Denis looked blank for an instant. "What part of the world are we in, anyhow?"

"Schlectland is in the Atlantic Ocean, about a hundred miles east of the Bahama Islands, and about three hundred miles from the coast of America."

"America, that's it; we'll steer sthraight for America, me lad. That's the land for me, and for all good Irishmen."

They were free at last. Onward the little boat ploughed through the tumbling seas to the land of liberty awaiting them beyond, America.

13

A Modern Utopia

by **H. G. Wells**

London
Chapman & Hall, Ltd.
1905

H. G. Wells (1866–1946)

occupies a unique position in the history of utopian writing. No other person has so extensively explored the numerous literary forms which utopian speculation can utilize; he has contributed to utopian thought one of the classic utopias, he has satirized utopia, and is accountable for a shelf of books of peripheral utopian interest in the areas of fantasy, planning, and prediction. In fact, the utopian interest was dominant in Wells's thought and writing to such an extent that it is difficult to single out one of his numerous works which does not in some way give evidence of that interest. It is amusing that in a prefatory note to *A Modern Utopia*, Wells remarks that this book will in all probability be the last he will write on this theme. His works which are of most direct utopian significance and treatment are: *The Time Machine* (1895), *When the Sleeper Awakes* (1899), *A Modern Utopia* (1905), *In the Days of the Comet* (1912), *The World Set Free* (1914), *Men Like Gods* (1923), *The Open Conspiracy* (1928), and *World Brain* (1937). Some readers may have seen the delightful movie which was made from the short story, *The Man Who Could Work Miracles;* and *The Shape of Things to Come* was also very dramatically presented in this medium.

The family background of Wells was humble; his father was a miserably unsuccessful shopkeeper, his mother a housekeeper, and Wells himself at the age of fifteen was a clerk in a dry-goods shop. This early acquaintance with the economic pressure and drudgery which was the lot of most men of the period unquestionably was the major source of influence which resulted in the utopian interest which dominated the future work of Wells. He escaped by running away from home; by dint of hard work and ability, the latter earning him scholarships, he finally managed to become a student at the University of London at the age of twenty-three, and received a B.S. degree with honors from the Royal College of Science. Shortly afterward, while occupying a position as tutor, a burst blood vessel forced him to turn to the more sedentary vocation of writing.

Wells was perhaps the most aggressively progressive of all utopists. He was not naïvely optimistic about the future of man and society, but he staunchly maintained that any development toward the achievement of the ideal social structure could be brought about only by the employment of scientific methods of social organization. No other utopist evidences less nostalgia for the values of pre-modern decentralized social structure than does Wells. Centralization is for him the keynote of efficiency for the future society, and he recognized from the beginning that nothing less than world centralization would suffice. Thus, he emphasized repeatedly the necessity for one language throughout the world, for a central classification and census bureau, and for the organization of the legislative and judicial functions of the entire world in unified or federated bodies. On the negative side, he seems prepared to concede that this happy state of affairs is not likely to be brought about until the increasing devastation of world war has by attrition left men the alternatives of scientific management or barbarism.

It is regrettable that most of the dramatic passages and almost all of the subtle sallies of the original had to be sacrificed in the following selection for the sake of presenting as much as possible of the substance of Wells's thought. In its literary form, *Modern Utopia* is unusual; while it is definitely in the classic tradition of speculative utopias, the vision of the ideal is always slightly distorted by the inescapable perspective of the real. Wells gives no evidence of that abundant faith which characterized utopists of preceding periods—that man is an essentially noble and rational creature. His reliance is on knowledge and science, on organization and management, not on communitarian brotherly love or the simple satisfactions of artisanship. His companion on the tour of utopia, the botanist, himself no average man but one trained and skilled in science, is the realistic millstone dragging always at Wells's speculative flights. Nor did Wells display the naïveté which anticipated a transformation of man by the mere achievement of economic equality; economic adjustment was but one of the numerous important problems of social organization which must be resolved by scientific control. Wells could hardly then have espoused any simple equalitarian principle; his *samurai* are distinctly a superior class. Yet, to identify the *samurai* with Plato's guardians is as uncritical as to identify a modern battleship with an ancient trireme. Wells is perfectly well aware of the dangers inherent in any stratification of society; the possible disastrous consequences of an extreme division of labor between workers and managers is indeed the theme of *The Time Machine*. Wells tried to portray the *samurai* as an elite characterized only by intelligence and good will, but it is difficult to quiet the suspicion that Wells too indulges in the assumption so common to utopian thought, that men of intelligence and scientific training—or men of dialectical ability or religious persuasion or economic efficiency —will, when vested with the power to control the social order, evidence the good will and benevolence necessary to make the exercise of that power a benefit rather than a debacle. Wells, however, is the most perspicacious of all utopists, and in his later works it will be found that he emphasizes strongly the necessity of world federation, legislation, adjudication, and enforcement of law.

A Modern Utopia

Throughout these papers sounds a note, a distinctive and personal note, a note that tends at times toward stridency; and all that is not, as these words are, in Italics, is in one Voice. The Owner of the Voice you must imagine as sitting at a table reading a manuscript about Utopias. The curtain rises upon him so. But afterwards, if the devices of this declining art of literature prevail, you will go with him through curious and interesting experiences. But over against this writer here presented, there is also another earthly person in the book, who gathers himself together into a distinct personality only after a preliminary complication with the reader. This person is spoken of as a botanist, and he is a leaner, rather taller, graver and much less garrulous man.

• • • • •

TOPOGRAPHICAL

The Utopia of a modern dreamer must needs differ in one fundamental aspect from the Nowheres and Utopias men planned before Darwin quickened the thought of the world. Those were all perfect and static States, a balance of happiness won for ever against the forces of unrest and disorder that inhere in things. But the Modern Utopia must be not static but kinetic, must shape not as a permanent state but as a hopeful stage, leading to a long ascent of stages. That is the first, most generalised difference between a Utopia based upon modern conceptions and all the Utopias that were written in the former time.

There must always be a certain effect of hardness and thinness about Utopian speculations. I doubt if anyone has ever been warmed to desire himself a citizen in the Republic of Plato; I doubt if anyone could stand a month of the relentless publicity of virtue planned by More. No one wants to live in any community of intercourse really, save for the sake of the individualities he would meet there. The fertilising conflict of individualities is the ultimate meaning of the personal life, and all our Utopias no more than schemes for bettering that interplay.

No less than a planet will serve the purpose of a modern Utopia. Time was when a mountain valley or an island seemed to promise sufficient isolation for a polity to maintain itself intact from outward force; but the whole trend of modern thought is against the permanence of any such enclosures. A state powerful enough to keep isolated under modern conditions would be powerful enough to rule the world, would be, indeed, if not actively ruling, yet passively acquiescent in all other human organisations, and so responsible for them altogether. World-state, therefore, it must be.

Suppose now that two of us were upon some high pass in the Alps. We have tramped and botanised and come to a rest, and, sitting among rocks, we have eaten our lunch and finished our bottle of Yvorne, and fallen into a talk of Utopias, and said such things as I have been saying. And behold! in the twinkling of an eye we are in that other world!

We should scarcely note the change. Not a cloud would have gone from the sky. Yet I have an idea that in some obscure manner we should come to feel at once a difference in things. The botanist's glance would, under a subtle attraction, float back to Airolo. "It's queer," he would say quite idly, "but I never noticed that building there to the right before."

"Which building?"

"That to the right—with a queer sort of thing—"

"I see now. Yes. Yes, it's certainly an odd-looking affair. . . . And big, you know! Handsome! I wonder—"

That would interrupt our Utopian speculations. We should both discover that the little towns below had changed—but how, we should not have marked them well enough to know. "It's odd," I should say, for the tenth or eleventh time, with a motion to rise, and we should get up and stretch ourselves, and, still a little puzzled, turn our faces towards the path that clambers down over the tumbled rocks and runs round by the still clear lake and down towards the Hospice of St. Gotthard—if perchance we could still find that path.

Long before we got to that, before even we got to the great high road, we should have hints from the stone cabin in the nape of the pass—it would be gone or wonderfully changed—from the very goats upon the rocks, from the little hut by the rough bridge of stone, that a mighty difference had come to the world of men.

CONCERNING FREEDOMS

Now what sort of question would first occur to two men descending upon the planet of a Modern Utopia? Probably grave solicitude about their personal freedom. Towards the Stranger, the Utopias of the past displayed their least amiable aspect. Would this new sort of Utopian State, spread to the dimensions of a world, be any less forbidding?

What prohibitions should we be under, we two Uitlanders in this Utopian world? We should certainly not be free to kill, assault, or threaten anyone we met, and in that we earth-trained men would not be likely to offend. And until we knew more exactly the Utopian idea of property we should be very chary of touching anything that might conceivably be appropriated. If it was not the property of individuals it might be the property of the State. But beyond that we might have our doubts.

I submit that to the modern-minded man it can be no sort of Utopia worth desiring that does not give the utmost freedom of going to and fro. Free movement is to many people one of the greatest of life's privileges—to go wherever the spirit moves them, to wander and see—and though they have every comfort, every security, every virtuous discipline, they will still be unhappy if that is denied them. Short of damage to things cherished and made, the Utopians will surely have this right, so we may expect no unclimbable walls and fences, nor the discovery of any laws we may transgress in coming down these mountain places.

Glancing back from our Utopian mountain side down which this discourse marches, to the confusions of old earth, we may remark that the need and desire for privacies there is exceptionally great at the present time, that it was less in the past, that in the future it may be less again, and that under the Utopian conditions to which we shall come when presently we strike yonder road, it may be reduced to quite manageable dimensions. Yet, there still remains a considerable claim for privacy in Utopia. The room, or apartments, or home, or mansion, whatever it may be a man or woman maintains, must be private, and under his or her complete dominion. Our Utopia will have, of course, faultless roads and beautifully arranged inter-urban communications, swift trains or motor services or what not, to diffuse its population, and without some anticipatory provisions, the prospect of the residential areas becoming a vast area of defensively walled villa Edens is all too possible. This is a quantitative question, be it remembered, and not to be dismissed by any statement of principle. Our Utopians will meet it, I presume, by detailed regulations, very probably varying locally with local conditions.

Freedom of movement in a Utopia planned under modern conditions must involve something more than unrestricted pedestrian wanderings. In the Modern Utopia travel must be in the common texture of life. The whole Utopian world will be open and accessible and as safe for the wayfarer as France or England is today.

The greater part of the world will be as secure and cheaply and easily accessible to everyone as is Zermatt or Lucerne to a Western European of the middle-class at the present time. The population of Utopia will be a migratory population beyond any earthly precedent, not simply a travelling population, but migratory. The old Utopias were all localised, as localised as a parish councillor; but it is manifest that nowadays even quite ordinary people live over areas that would have made a kingdom in those former days, would have filled the Athenian of the *Laws* with incredulous astonishment; to Sir Thomas More we should seem a breed of nomads. Men may settle down in our Modern Utopia for love and the family at last, but first and most abundantly they will see the world.

So we shall see, as we come down by our little lake in the lap of Lucendro, and even before we reach the road, the first scattered chalets and households in which these migrant people live, the upper summer homes. It is essential to the modern ideal of life that the period of education and growth should be prolonged to as late a period as possible and puberty correspondingly retarded, and by wise regulation the statesmen of Utopia will constantly adjust and readjust regulations and taxation to diminish the proportion of children reared in hot and stimulating conditions. These high mountains will, in the bright sweet summer, be populous with youth.

Were this a story, I should tell at length how much we were helped by the good fortune of picking up a Utopian coin of gold, how at last we adventured into the Utopian inn and found it marvellously easy. You see us the shyest and most watchful of guests; but of the food they put before us and the furnishings of the house, and all our entertainment, it will be better to speak later. We are in a migratory world, we know, one greatly accustomed to foreigners; our mountain clothes are not strange enough to attract acute attention, though ill-made and shabby, no doubt, by Utopian standards; we are dealt with as we might best wish to be dealt with, that is to say as rather untidy, inconspicuous men. We look about us and watch for hints and examples, and indeed, get through with the thing. And after our queer, yet not unpleasant, dinner, in which we remark no meat figures, we go out of the house for a breath of air and for quiet counsel one with another.

Two lovers pass us whispering, and we follow them with our eyes. This Utopia has certainly preserved the fundamental freedom, to love.

Let us come back to Utopia. We were speaking of travel. They will be just beginning to fly in Utopia. The world is immeasurably more disposed to believe this wonder is coming, and coming nearly, than it was five years ago. But unless we are to suppose Utopian scientific knowledge far in advance of ours, they, too, will only be in the same experimental stage as ourselves. In Utopia, however, they will conduct research by the army corps while we conduct it—we don't conduct it! We let it happen. Fools make researches and wise men exploit them—that is our earthly way of dealing with the question, and we thank Heaven for an assumed abundance of financially impotent and sufficiently ingenious fools.

In Utopia, a great multitude of selected men, chosen volunteers, will be collaborating upon this new step in man's struggle with the elements. Bacon's visionary House of Salomon will be a thing realised, and it will be humming with this business. Every university in the world will be urgently working for priority in this aspect of the problem or that. That Utopian research will, I say, go like an eagle's swoop in comparison with the blind-man's fumbling of our terrestrial way. Even before our brief Utopian journey is out, we may get a glimpse of the swift ripening of all this activity, that will be in progress at our coming. Tomorrow, perhaps, or in a day or so, some silent, distant thing will come gliding into view over the mountains, will turn and soar and pass again beyond our astonished sight. . . .

UTOPIAN ECONOMICS

These modern Utopians with the universally diffused good manners, the universal education, the fine freedoms we shall ascribe to them, their world unity, world language, world-wide travellings, world-wide freedom of sale and purchase, will remain mere dream-stuff, incredible even by twilight, until we have shown that at that level the community will still sustain itself. At any rate, the common liberty of the Utopians will not embrace the common liberty to be unserviceable, the most perfect economy of organisation still leaves the fact untouched that all order and security in a State rests on the certainty of getting work done. How will the work of this planet be done? What will be the economics of a modern Utopia?

The older Utopias were all relatively small states; Plato's Republic, for example, was to be smaller than the average English borough, and no distinction was made between the Family, the Local Government, and the State. Plato and Campanella—for all that the latter was a Christian priest—carried communism to its final point and prescribed even a community of husbands and wives, an idea that was brought at last to the test of effectual experiment in the Oneida Community of New York State (1848–1879). This latter body did not long survive its founder, at least as a veritable communism, by reason of the insurgent individualism of its vigorous sons. More, too, denied privacy and ruled an absolute community of goods, at any rate, and so, coming to the Victorian Utopias, did Cabet. But Cabet's communism was one of the "free store" type, and the goods were yours only after you had requisitioned them. That seems the case in the "Nowhere" of Morris also. Compared with the older writers Bellamy and Morris have a vivid sense of individual separation, and their departure from the old homogeneity is sufficiently marked to justify a doubt whether there will be any more thoroughly communistic Utopias for ever.

The State is to be progressive, it is no longer to be static, and this alters the general condition of the Utopian problem profoundly; we have to provide not only for food and clothing, for order and health, but for initiative. The factor that leads the World State on from one phase of development to the next is the interplay of individualities; to speak teleologically, the world exists for the sake of and through initiative, and individuality is the method of initiative.

The World State in this ideal presents itself as the sole land-owner of the earth, with the local municipalities holding, as it were, feudally under it as landlords. The State or these subordinates holds all the sources of energy, and either directly or through its tenants, farmers and agents, develops these sources, and renders the energy available for the work of life. It or its tenants will produce food, and so human energy, and the exploitation of coal and electric power, and the powers of wind and wave and water will be within its right. It will pour out this energy by assignment and lease and acquiescence and what not upon its individual citizens. It will maintain order, maintain roads, maintain a cheap and efficient administration of justice, maintain cheap and rapid locomotion and be the common carrier of the planet, convey and distribute labour, control, let, or administer all natural productions, pay for and secure healthy births and a healthy and vigorous new generation, maintain the public health, coin money and sustain standards of measurement, subsidise research, and reward such commercially unprofitable undertakings as benefit the community as a whole; subsidise when needful chairs of criticism and authors and publications, and collect and distribute information. The State is for Individualities. The State is for Individuals, the law is for freedoms, the world is for experiment, experience, and change: these are the fundamental beliefs upon which a modern Utopia must go.

Within this scheme, which makes the State the source of all energy, and the final legatee, what will be the nature of the property a man may own? Under modern conditions—indeed, under any conditions—a man without some negotiable property is a man without freedom, and the extent of his property is very largely the measure of his freedom. Without any property, without even shelter or food, a man has no choice but to set about getting these things; he is in servitude to his needs until he has secured property to satisfy them. But with a certain small property a man is free to do many things, to take a fortnight's holiday when he chooses, for example, and to try this new departure from his work or that; with so much more, he may take a year of freedom and go to the ends of the earth; with so much more, he may obtain elaborate apparatus and try curious novelties, build himself houses and make gardens, establish businesses and make experiments at large. Very speedily, under terrestrial conditions, the property of a man may reach such proportions that his freedom oppresses the freedom of others. Here, again, is a quantitative question, an adjustment of conflicting freedoms, a quantitative question that too many people insist on making a qualitative one. The object sought in the code of property laws that one would find in operation in Utopia would be the same object that pervades the whole Utopian organisation, namely, a universal maximum of individual freedom.

A modern Utopian most assuredly must have a practically unqualified property in all those things that become, as it were, by possession, extensions and expressions of his personality; his clothing, his jewels, the tools of his employment, his books, the objects of art he may have bought or made, his personal weapons (if Utopia have need of such things), insignia, and so forth. All such things that he has bought with his money or acquired—provided he is not a professional or habitual dealer in such property—will be inalienably his, his to give or lend or keep, free even from taxation. So intimate is this sort of property that I have no doubt Utopia will give a man posthumous rights over it—will permit him to assign it to a successor with at the utmost the payment of a small redemption. A horse, perhaps, in certain districts, or a bicycle, or any such mechanical conveyance personally used, the Utopians might find it well to rank with these possessions. No doubt, too, a house and privacy owned and occupied by a man, and even a man's household furniture, might be held to stand as high or almost as high in the property scale, might be taxed as lightly and transferred under only a slightly heavier redemption, provided he had not let these things on hire, or otherwise alienated them from his intimate self.

For all other property, the Utopians will have a scantier respect; even money unspent by a man, and debts to him that bear no interest, will at his death stand upon a lower level than these things.

What he did not choose to gather and assimilate to himself, or assign for the special education of his children, the State will share in the lion's proportion with heir and legatee. The trend of modern thought is entirely against private property in land or natural objects or products, and in Utopia these things will be the inalienable property of the World State. Subject to the rights of free locomotion, land will be leased out to companies or individuals, but—in view of the unknown necessities of the future—never for a longer period than, let us say, fifty years.

From the conception of mechanical force as coming in from Nature to the service of man arise profound contrasts between the modern and classical Utopias. There appears no limit to the invasion of life by the machine. Now it is only in the last three hundred years that any human being seems to have anticipated this. It stimulates the imagination to remark how entirely it was overlooked as a modifying cause in human development. Plato clearly had no ideas about machines at all as a force affecting social organisation. He never thought of a State that did not rely for its force upon human muscle, just as he never thought of a State that was not primarily organised for warfare hand to hand. An infinitude of nonsense about the Greek mind would never have been written if the distinctive intellectual and artistic quality of Plato's time, its extraordinarily clear definition of certain material conditions as absolutely permanent, coupled with its politico-social instability, had been borne in mind.

By sheer inadvertence, therefore, Plato commenced the tradition of Utopias without machinery, a tradition we find Morris still loyally following, except for certain mechanical barges and such-like toys, in his *News from Nowhere*. There are some foreshadowings of mechanical possibilities in *New Atlantis*, but it is only in the nineteenth century that Utopias appeared in which the fact is clearly recognised that the social fabric rests no longer upon human labour. It was, I believe, Cabet who first in a Utopian work insisted upon the escape of man from irksome labours through the use of machinery. He is the great primitive of modern Utopias, and Bellamy is his American equivalent. Hitherto, either slave labour, or at least class distinctions involving unavoidable labour in the lower class, have been assumed; or there is—as in Morris and the outright Return-to-Nature Utopians—a bold make-believe that all toil may be made a joy. If toil is a blessing, never was blessing so effectually disguised, and the very people who tell us that, hesitate to suggest more than a beautiful ease in the endless day of Heaven. Science stands, a too competent servant, behind her wrangling underbred masters, holding out resources, devices, and remedies they are too stupid to use.

And on its material side a modern Utopia must needs present these gifts as taken, and show a world that is really abolishing the need of labour, abolishing the last base reason for anyone's servitude or inferiority.

FAILURE IN A MODERN UTOPIA

Most Utopias present themselves as going concerns, as happiness in being; all the citizens one is permitted to see are well looking and upright and mentally and morally in tune. But we are under the dominion of a logic that obliges us to take over the actual population of the world with only such moral and mental and physical improvements as lie within their inherent possibilities, and it is our business to ask what Utopia will do with its congenital invalids, its idiots and madmen, its drunkards and men of vicious mind, its cruel and furtive souls, its stupid people, too stupid to be of use to the community, its lumpish, unteachable and unimaginative people? And what will it do with the man who is "poor" all round, the rather spiritless, rather incompetent low-grade man?

The way of Nature in this process is to kill the weaker and the sillier, to crush them, to starve them, to overwhelm them, using the stronger and more cunning as her weapon. But man is the unnatural animal, the rebel child of Nature, and more and more does he turn himself against the harsh and fitful hand that reared him. In the Modern Utopia he will have set himself to change the ancient law. No longer will it be that failures must suffer and perish lest their breed increase, but the breed of failure must not increase, lest they suffer and perish, and the race with them. Now we need not argue here to prove that the resources of the world and the energy of mankind, were they organised sanely, are amply sufficient to supply every material need of every living human being. But there must be a competition in life of some sort to determine who are to be pushed to the edge, and who are to prevail and multiply. Whatever we do, man will remain a competitive creature, and no Utopia will ever save him completely from the emotional drama of struggle, from exultations and humiliations, from pride and prostration and shame. He lives in success and failure just as inevitably as he lives in space and time.

But we may do much to make the margin of failure endurable. Deaths outright from exposure and starvation are now perhaps uncommon, but for the multitude there are only miserable houses, uncomfortable clothes, and bad and insufficient food; fractional starvation and exposure, that is to say. A Utopia planned upon modern lines will certainly have to put an end to that. It will insist upon every citizen being properly housed, well nourished, and in good health, reasonably clean and clothed healthily, and upon that insistence its labour laws will be founded. In a phrasing that will be familiar to everyone interested in social reform, it will maintain a standard of life. The State will stand at the back of the economic struggle as the reserve employer of labour. If it were possible for any citizen in need of money to resort to a place of public employment as a right, and there to work for a week or month without degradation upon certain minimum terms, it seems fairly certain that no one would work, except as the victim of some quite exceptional and temporary accident, for less. The work publicly provided would have to be toilsome, but not cruel nor incapacitating. The State would provide these things for its citizen as though it was his right to require them; he would receive as a shareholder in the common enterprise and not with any insult of charity. But on the other hand it will require that the citizen who renders the minimum of service for these concessions shall not become a parent until he is established in work at a rate above the minimum, and free of any debt he may have incurred. By such obvious devices it will achieve the maximum elimination of its feeble and spiritless folk in every generation with the minimum of suffering and public disorder.

But the mildly incompetent, the spiritless and dull, the poorer sort who are ill, do not exhaust our Utopian problem. There remain idiots and lunatics, there remain perverse and incompetent persons, there are people of weak character who become drunkards, drug takers, and the like. Then there are persons tainted with certain foul and transmissible diseases. All these people spoil the world for others. They may become parents, and with most of them there is manifestly nothing to be done but to seclude them from the great body of the population. You must resort to a kind of social surgery. You cannot have social freedom in your public ways, your children cannot speak to whom they will, your girls and gentlewomen cannot go abroad while some sorts of people go free. So soon as there can be no doubt of the disease or baseness of the individual, so soon must he or she pass out of the common ways of men.

The dreadfulness of all such proposals as this lies in the possibility of their execution falling into the hands of hard, dull, and cruel administrators. But in the case of a Utopia one assumes the best possible government, a government as merciful and deliberate as it is powerful and decisive. No doubt for first offenders, and for all offenders under five-and-twenty, the Modern Utopia will attempt cautionary and remedial treatment. Our world is still vindictive, but the all-reaching State of Utopia will have the strength that begets mercy. Quietly the outcast will go from among his fellow men. The thing must be just public enough to obviate secret tyrannies, and that is all. There will be no killing, no lethal chambers. No doubt Utopia will kill all deformed and monstrous and evilly diseased births, but for the rest, the State will hold itself accountable for their being. There is no justice in Nature perhaps, but the idea of justice must be sacred in any good society. I doubt even if there will be jails. Perhaps islands will be chosen, islands lying apart from the highways of the sea, and to these the State will send its exiles. The State will, of course, secure itself against any children from these people, that is the primary object in their seclusion. This sounds more fantastic than it is. But what else is there to do, unless you kill? You must seclude, but why should you torment? Into such islands of exiles as this a modern Utopia will have to purge itself. There is no alternative that I can contrive.

Will a Utopian be free to be idle?

In a modern Utopia a man will be free to be just as idle or uselessly busy as it pleases him, after he has earned the minimum wage. He must do that, of course, to pay for his keep, to pay his assurance tax against ill-health or old age, and any charge or debt paternity may have brought upon him. The World State of the modern Utopist is no state of moral compulsions. A certain proportion of men at ease is good for the world; work as a moral obligation is the morality of slaves, and so long as no one is overworked there is no need to worry because some few are underworked. Utopia does not exist as a solace for envy. From leisure, in a good moral and intellectual atmosphere, come experiments, come philosophy and the new departures.

In any modern Utopia there must be many leisurely people. We are all too obsessed in the real world by the strenuous ideal, by the idea that the vehement incessant fool is the only righteous man. Nothing done in a hurry, nothing done under strain, is really well done. A State where all are working hard, where none go to and fro, easily and freely, loses touch with the purpose of freedom.

WOMEN IN A MODERN UTOPIA

How would things be "different" in the Modern Utopia? After all it is time we faced the riddle of the problems of marriage and motherhood.

The Modern Utopia is not only to be a sound and happy World State, but it is to be progressing from good to better. But as Malthus demonstrated for all time, a State whose population continues to increase in obedience to unchecked instinct, can progress only from bad to worse. From the view of human comfort and happiness, the increase of population that occurs at each advance in human security is the greatest evil of life.

A mere indiscriminating restriction of the birth-rate—an end practically attained in the homely, old-fashioned civilisation of China by
female infanticide, involves not only the cessation of distresses but
stagnation, and the minor good of a sort of comfort and social
stability is won at too great a sacrifice. Progress depends essentially
on competitive selection, and that we may not escape. Instead of
competing to escape death and wretchedness, we may compete to
give birth and we may heap every sort of consolation prize upon the
losers in that competition.

Let us set aside at once all nonsense of the sort one hears in certain
quarters about the human stud farm. To the modern thinker individuality is the significant fact of life, and the idea of the State,
which is necessarily concerned with the average and general, selecting individualities in order to pair them and improve the race, an
absurdity. But compulsory pairing is one thing, and the maintenance
of general limiting conditions is another, and one well within the
scope of State activity. The State is justified in saying, before you
may add children to the community for the community to educate
and in part to support, you must be above a certain minimum of
personal efficiency, and this you must show by holding a position
of solvency and independence in the world; you must be above a
certain age, and a certain minimum of physical development, and
free of any transmissible disease. You must not be a criminal unless
you have expiated your offence. Failing these simple qualifications,
if you and some person conspire and add to the population of the
State, we will, for the sake of humanity, take over the innocent
victim of your passions, but we shall insist that you are under a debt
to the State of a peculiarly urgent sort, and one you will certainly
pay, even if it is necessary to use restraint to get the payment out
of you: it is a debt that has in the last resort your liberty as a
security, and, moreover, if this thing happens a second time, or if
it is disease or imbecility you have multiplied, we will take an
absolutely effectual guarantee that neither you nor your partner
offend again in this matter.

"Harsh!" you say, and "Poor Humanity!"

You have the gentler alternative to study in your terrestrial slums
and asylums.

The trend of our reasoning has brought us to the conclusion that
the Utopian State will feel justified in intervening between men and
women on two accounts, first on account of paternity, and secondly
on account of the clash of freedoms that may otherwise arise. From
the point of view of a statesman, marriage is the union of a man
and woman in a manner so intimate as to involve the probability of
offspring, and it is of primary importance to the State, first in order

to secure good births, and secondly good home conditions, that these unions should not be free, nor promiscuous, nor practically universal throughout the adult population.

One imagines the parties to a projected marriage first obtaining licenses. From the point of view of the Theoretical Utopian State, these licenses are the feature of primary importance. As a matter of justice, there must be no deception between the two people, and the State will ensure that in certain broad essentials this is so. There would then be a reasonable interval for consideration and withdrawal on the part of either spouse. In the event of the two people persisting in their resolution, they would after this minimum interval signify as much to the local official and the necessary entry would be made in the registers. These formalities would be quite independent of any religious ceremonial the contracting parties might choose, for with religious belief and procedure the modern State has no concern.

This question of marriage is the most complicated and difficult in the whole range of Utopian problems. But it is happily not the most urgent necessity that it should be absolutely solved. There emerges to the modern inquirer certain ideals and desiderata that at least go some way towards completing and expanding the crude primaries of a Utopian marriage law. The sound birth being assured, does there exist any valid reason for the persistence of the Utopian marriage union? Though the Utopian State will pay the mother, and the mother only, for the being and welfare of her legitimate children, there will be a clear advantage in fostering the natural disposition of the father to associate his child's welfare with his individual egotism, and to dispense some of his energies and earnings in supplementing the common provision of the State. It is an absurd disregard of a natural economy to leave the innate philoprogenitiveness of either sex uncultivated. Unless the parents continue in close relationship, if each is passing through a series of marriages, the dangers of a conflict of rights, and of the frittering away of emotions, become very grave. The family will lose homogeneity, and its individuals will have for the mother varied and perhaps incompatible emotional associations. The balance of social advantage is certainly on the side of much more permanent unions, on the side of an arrangement that, subject to ample provisions for a formal divorce without disgrace in cases of incompatibility, would bind, or at least enforce ideals that would tend to bind, a man and woman together for the whole term of her maternal activity, until, that is, the last born of her children was no longer in need of her help.

The second consideration arises out of the artificiality of woman's position. We have laid it down as a general principle that the private morals of an adult citizen are no concern for the State. Whether a man treat his wife in private as a goddess to be propitiated, as a "mystery" to be adored, as an agreeable auxiliary, as a particularly intimate friend, or as the wholesome mother of his children, is entirely a matter for their private intercourse: whether he keep her in Oriental idleness or active co-operation, or leave her to live her independent life, rests with the couple alone, and all the possible friendship and intimacies outside marriage also lie quite beyond the organisation of the modern State. In Utopia, love-making is no concern of the State's beyond the province that the protection of children covers.

It must be reiterated that our reasoning still leaves Utopian marriage an institution with wide possibilities of variation. It must be remembered that a modern Utopia must differ from the Utopias of any preceding age in being world-wide. Into the modern Utopia there must have entered the mental tendencies and origins that gave our own world the polygamy of the Zulus and of Utah, the polyandry of Tibet, the latitudes of experiment permitted in the United States, and the divorceless wedlock of Comte. The tendency of all synthetic processes in matters of law and custom is to reduce and simplify the compulsory canon, to admit alternatives and freedoms; what were laws before become traditions of feeling and style, and in no matter will this be more apparent than in questions affecting the relations of the sexes.

MY UTOPIAN SELF

It falls to few of us to interview our better selves. My Utopian self is, of course, my better self—according to my best endeavors—and I must confess myself fully alive to the difficulties of the situation. When I came to this Utopia I had no thought of any such intimate self-examination.

The whole fabric of that other universe sways for a moment as I come into his room, into his clear and ordered work-room. I am trembling. A figure rather taller than myself stands against the light.

He comes towards me, and I, as I advance to meet him, stumble against a chair. Then, still without a word, we are clasping hands.

I stand now so that the light falls upon him, and I can see his face better. He is a little taller than I, younger looking and sounder looking; he has missed an illness or so, and there is no scar over his eye. His training has been subtly finer than mine; he has made himself a better face than mine. These things I might have counted upon. He wears, I see, that white tunic with the purple band that I have already begun to consider the proper Utopian clothing for grave men, and his face is clean shaven. We forget to speak at first in the intensity of our mutual inspection. When at last I do gain my voice it is to say something quite different from the fine, significant openings of my premeditated dialogues.

"You have a pleasant room," I remark, and look about a little disconcerted because there is no fireplace for me to put my back against, or hearthrug to stand upon. He pushes me a chair, into which I plump, and we hang over an immensity of conversational possibilities.

"I say," I plunge, "what do you think of me? You don't think I'm an impostor?"

"Not now that I have seen you. No."

"Am I so like you?"

"Like me and your story—exactly."

"You haven't any doubt left?" I ask.

"Not in the least, since I saw you enter. You come from the world beyond Sirius, twin to this. Eh?"

"And you don't want to know how I got here?"

"I've ceased even to wonder how *I* got here," he says, with a laugh that echoes mine.

He leans back in his chair, and I in mine, and the absurd parody of our attitudes strikes us both.

"Well?" we say, simultaneously, and laugh together.

I will confess this meeting is more difficult even than I anticipated.

Our conversation at that first encounter would do very little to develop the Modern Utopia in my mind. Inevitably, it would be personal and emotional. He would tell me how he stood in his world, and I how I stood in mine. I should have to tell him things, I should have to explain things—.

No, the conversation would contribute nothing to a modern Utopia.

And so I leave it out.

THE SAMURAI

Neither my Utopian double nor I love emotion sufficiently to cultivate it, and my feelings are in a state of seemly subordination when we meet again. He is now in possession of some clear, general ideas about my own world, and I can broach almost at once the thoughts that have been growing and accumulating since my arrival in this planet of my dreams. We find our interest in humanised statecraft makes us, in spite of our vast difference in training and habits, curiously akin.

To clarify our comparison he tells me something of the history of Utopia. It was several hundred years ago that the great organisation of the *samurai* came into its present form. And it was this organisation's widely sustained activities that had shaped and established the World State in Utopia. The social theorists of Utopia, my double explained, looked for some practical and real classification upon which to base organisation. The assumption that men are unclassifiable, because practically homogeneous, which underlies modern democratic methods and all the fallacies of our equal justice, is alien to the Utopian mind. Throughout Utopia there is no other than provisional classifications, since every being is regarded as finally unique, but for political and social purposes things have long rested upon a classification of temperaments, which attends mainly to differences in the range and quality and character of the individual imagination.

Four main classes of mind were distinguished, called, respectively, the Poietic, the Kinetic, the Dull, and the Base. The Poietic or creative class of mental individuality embraces a wide range of types, but they agree in possessing imaginations that range beyond the known and accepted, and that involve the desire to bring the discoveries made in such excursions, into knowledge and recognition. The Kinetic class consists of types, various, of course, and merging insensibly along the boundary into the less representative constituents of the Poietic group, but distinguished by a more restricted range of imagination. Their imaginations do not range beyond the known, experienced, and accepted. The more vigorous individuals of this class are the most teachable people in the world, and they are generally more moral and most trustworthy than the Poietic types. Below these two classes in the Utopian scheme of things, and merging insensibly into them, come the Dull. The Dull are persons of altogether inadequate imagination, the people who never seem to learn thoroughly, or hear distinctly, or think clearly. Finally, with a bold disregard of the logician's classificatory rules, these Utopian statesmen who devised the World State, hewed out in theory a class of the Base. The Base may, indeed, be either poietic, kinetic, or dull, though most commonly they are the last, and their definition concerns not so much the quality of their imagination as a certain bias in it. The Base have a narrower and more persistent egoistic reference than the common run of humanity. They count as an antagonism to the State organisation.

The problem of combining progress with political stability had never been accomplished in Utopia before that time, any more than it has been accomplished on earth. If, indeed, I am listening to my Utopian self, then they not only decided the problem could be solved, but they solved it.

He tells me how they solved it.

A modern Utopia differs from all the older Utopias in its recognition of the need of poietic activities—but in addition to making poietic activities universally possible, the founders of this modern Utopia sought to supply incentives, which was an altogether more difficult research, a problem in its nature irresolvably complex, and admitting of no systematic solution. But my double told me of a great variety of devices by which poietic men and women were given honour and enlarged freedoms, so soon as they produced an earnest of their quality, and he explained to me how great an ambition they might entertain.

"And finally," said my double, "our Rules ensure a considerable undertsanding of the importance of poietic activities in the majority of the *samurai*, in whose hands as a class all the real power of the world resides."

"Ah!" said I, "and now we come to the thing that interests me most. For it is quite clear, in my mind, that these *samurai* form the real body of the State. All this time that I have spent going to and fro in this planet, it has been growing upon me that this order of men and women, wearing such a uniform as you wear, and with faces strengthened by discipline and touched with devotion, is the Utopian reality. Tell me about these *samurai*, who remind me of Plato's guardians, and whose uniform you yourself are wearing. What are they? Are they an hereditary caste, a specially educated order, an elected class? For, certainly, this world turns upon them as a door upon its hinges."

"I follow the Common Rule, as many men do," said my double, answering my allusion to his uniform almost apologetically. "But my own work is, in its nature, poietic; there is much dissatisfaction with our isolation of criminals upon islands, and I am analysing the psychology of prison officials and criminals in general with a view to some better scheme. I am supposed to be ingenious with expedients in this direction. Typically, the *samurai* are engaged in administrative work. The order is not hereditary—we know just enough of biology and the uncertainties of inheritance to know how silly that would be—and it does not require an early consecration or novitiate or ceremonies and initiations of that sort. The *samurai* are, in fact, volunteers. Any intelligent adult in a reasonably healthy and efficient state may, at any age after five-and-twenty, become one of the *samurai*, and take a hand in the universal control."

"Provided he follows the Rule."

"Precisely—provided he follows the Rule."

"I have heard the phrase, 'voluntary nobility.' "

"That was the idea of our Founders. They made a noble and privileged order—open to the whole world. The Rule was planned to exclude the dull, to be unattractive to the base, and to direct and co-ordinate all sound citizens of good intent.

"The Rule consists of three parts; there is the list of things that qualify, the list of things that must not be done, and the list of things that must be done. There are several different college courses, but one or other must be followed and a satisfactory examination passed at the end—perhaps ten per cent. fail—and the Rule requires that the candidate for the *samurai* must have passed."

"But a very good man is sometimes an idle schoolboy."

"We admit that. And so anyone who has failed to pass the college leaving examination may at any time in later life sit for it again—and again and again. Certain carefully specified things excuse it alto-gether. Next to the intellectual qualification comes the physical, the man must be in sound health, free from certain foul, avoidable, and demoralising diseases, and in good training. We reject men who are fat, or thin and flabby, or whose nerves are shaky—we refer them back to training. And finally the man or woman must be fully adult."

"And now, what is forbidden?"

"We forbid a good deal. Many small pleasures do no great harm, but we think it is well to forbid them, none the less, so that we can weed out the self-indulgent. We think that a constant resistance to little seductions is good for a man's quality. At any rate, it shows that a man is prepared to pay something for his honour and priv-ileges. We prescribe a regimen of food, forbid tobacco, wine, or any alcoholic drink, all narcotic drugs—"

"Meat?"

"In all the round world of Utopia there is no meat. There used to be. But now we cannot stand the thought of slaughter-houses. We never settled the hygienic question of meat-eating at all. This other aspect decided us. I can still remember, as a boy, the rejoicings over the closing of the last slaughter-house."

I reflected. "What else may not the *samurai* do?"

"Acting, singing, or reciting are forbidden them, though they may lecture authoritatively or debate. Nor may the *samurai* do personal services, except in the matter of medicine or surgery; nor may a man under the Rule be any man's servant, pledged to do whatever he is told. He may neither be a servant nor keep one; he must shave and dress and serve himself, carry his own food from the helper's place to the table, redd his sleeping room, and leave it clean—"

"That is all easy enough in a world as ordered as yours. I suppose no *samurai* may bet?"

"Absolutely not. He may insure his life and his old age for the better equipment of his children, or for other specified ends, but that is all his dealings with chance. And he is also forbidden to play games in public or to watch them being played."

"And now," I said, "haven't we got very nearly to the end of your prohibitions? You have forbidden alcohol, drugs, smoking, betting, and usury, games, trade, servants. But isn't there a vow of Chastity?"

"There is a Rule of Chastity here—but not of Celibacy. We know quite clearly that civilisation is an artificial arrangement, and that all the physical and emotional instincts of man are too strong, and his natural instinct of restraint too weak, for him to live easily in the civilised State. Civilisation has developed far more rapidly than man has modified. Our Founders organised motives from all sorts of sources, but I think the chief force to give men self-control is Pride. And, in the matter of love, a straight and clean desire for a clean and straight fellow-creature was our Founders' ideal. They enjoined marriage between equals as the *samurai's* duty to the race. A man under the Rule who loves a woman who does not follow it, must either leave the *samurai* to marry her, or induce her to accept what is called the Woman's Rule, which, while it excepts her from the severer qualifications and disciplines, brings her regimen into a working harmony with his."

Women *samurai* who are married, my double told me, must bear children—if they are to remain married as well as in the order—before the second period for terminating a childless marriage is exhausted. I failed to ask for the precise figures from my double at the time, but I think it is beyond doubt that it is from *samurai* mothers of the Greater or Lesser Rule that a very large proportion of the future population of Utopia will be derived. There can be no doubt that these marriage limitations tend to make the *samurai* something of an hereditary class. Their children, as a rule, become *samurai*. But it is not an exclusive caste; subject to the most reasonable qualifications, anyone who sees fit can enter it at any time, and so, unlike all other privileged castes the world has seen, it increases relatively to the total population, and may indeed at last assimilate almost the whole population of the earth.

So much my double told me readily.

But now he tried to make his religion clear to me. The leading principle of the Utopian religion is the repudiation of the doctrine of original sin; the Utopians hold that man, on the whole, is good. That is their cardinal belief. They accept Religion as they accept Thirst, as something inseparably in the mysterious rhythms of life. Slovenly indulgence in religious inclinations, a failure to think hard and discriminate as fairly as possible in religious matters, is just as alien to the men under the Rule as it would be to drink deeply because they were thirsty, eat until glutted, evade a bath because the day was chilly, or make love to any bright-eyed girl who chanced to look pretty in the dusk. The *samurai* will be forbidden the religion of dramatically lit altars, organ music, and incense; the *samurai* will have emerged above these things.

Clearly the God of the *samurai* is a transcendental and mystical God. So far as the *samurai* have a purpose in common in maintaining the State, and the order and progress of the world, so far, by their discipline and denial, by their public work and effort, they worship God together. But the fount of motives lies in the individual life, it lies in silent and deliberate reflections, and at this, the most striking of all the rules of the *samurai* aims. For seven consecutive days in the year, at least, each man and woman under the Rule must go right out of all the life of man into some wild and solitary place, must speak to no man or woman, and have no sort of intercourse with mankind. They must go bookless and weaponless, without pen or paper, or money. Provisions must be taken for the period of the journey, a rug or sleeping sack—for they must sleep under the open sky—but no means of making a fire. Out they must go, clean out of the world.

I saw more clearly now something I had seen dimly already, in the bearing and the faces of this Utopian chivalry, a faint persistent tinge of detachment from the immediate heats and hurries, the little graces and delights, the tensions and stimulations of the daily world. It pleased me strangely to think of this steadfast yearly pilgrimage of solitude, and how near men might come then to the high distances of God.

After that I remember we fell to talking of the discipline of the Rule, of the Courts that try breaches of it, and interpret doubtful cases. From that we passed to the discussion of the general constitution of this World State. Practically all political power vests in the *samurai*. Not only are they the only administrators, lawyers, practising doctors, and public officials of almost all kinds, but they are the only voters. Yet, by a curious exception, the supreme legislative assembly must have one-tenth, and may have one-half of its members outside the order, because, it is alleged, there is a sort of wisdom that comes of sin and laxness, which is necessary to the perfect ruling of life. Every ruler and official, it is true, is put on his trial every three years before a jury drawn by lot, according to the range of his activities, either from the *samurai* of his municipal area or from the general catalogue of the *samurai*, but the business of this jury is merely to decide whether to continue him in office or to order a new election. In the majority of cases the verdict is continuation.

I remember how, after our third bout of talking, I walked back through the streets of Utopian London to rejoin the botanist at our hotel. No Utopians wear black, and for all the frequency of the *samurai* uniform along the London ways the general effect is of a gaily-coloured population. The Utopians have brought a sounder physiological science than ours to bear upon regimen. They have put off the years of decay. They have extended the level years far into the seventies, and age, when it comes, comes swiftly and easily. The feverish hurry of our earth, the decay that begins before growth has ceased, is replaced by a ripe prolonged maturity. This modern Utopia is an adult world.

Yet youth is here.

For everyone in Utopia who is sane enough to benefit, study and training last until twenty; then comes the travel year, and many are still students until twenty-four or twenty-five. Most are still, in a sense, students throughout life, but it is thought that, unless responsible action is begun in some form in the early twenties, will undergoes a partial atrophy. But the full swing of adult life is hardly attained until thirty is reached. Men marry before the middle thirties, and the women rather earlier, few are mothers before five-and-twenty. The majority of those who become *samurai* do so between twenty-seven and thirty-five. And, between seventeen and thirty, the Utopians have their dealings with love, and the play and excitement of love is a chief interest in life. For the most part they end mated, and love gives place to some special and more enduring interest, though, indeed, there is love between older men and fresh girls, and between youths and maturer women. It is in these most graceful and beautiful years of life that such freedoms of dress as the atmosphere of Utopia permits are to be seen, and the crude bright will and imagination of youth peeps out in ornament and colour.

Figures come into my sight and possess me for a moment and pass, and give place to others. A grave man in a long, fur-trimmed robe, a merchant, maybe, debates some serious matter with a white-tunicked clerk. I turn to mark the straight, blue-black hair. The man must be Chinese.

THE BUBBLE BURSTS

I had already discussed the question of race with the botanist at Lucerne.

"But you would not like," he cried in horror, "your daughter to marry a Chinaman or a negro?"

"I think we shall have all the buff and yellow peoples intermingling pretty freely."

"Chinamen and white women, for example."

"Yes," I said, "you've got to swallow that, anyhow; you *shall* swallow that."

He finds the idea too revolting for comment.

I try and make the thing seem easier for him. "Do try," I said, "to grasp a Modern Utopian's conditions. The Chinaman will speak the same language as his wife—whatever her race may be—he will wear costume of the common civilised fashion, he will have much the same education as his European rival, read the same literature, bow to the same traditions. And you must remember a wife in Utopia is singularly not subject to her husband. . . ."

The botanist proclaims his invincible conclusion: "Everyone would cut her!"

"This is Utopia," I said, and then sought once more to tranquilise his mind. "No doubt among the vulgar, coarse-minded people outside the Rule there may be something of the sort. Every earthly moral blockhead, a little educated, perhaps, is to be found in Utopia. You will, no doubt, find the 'cut' and the 'boycott,' and all those nice little devices by which dull people get a keen edge on life, in their place here, and their place is somewhere—"

I turned a thumb earthward. "There!"

The botanist did not answer for a little while. Then he said, with some temper and great emphasis: "Well, I'm jolly glad anyhow that I'm not to be a permanent resident in this Utopia, *if our daughters are to be married to Hottentots by regulation.* I'm jolly glad."

He turned his back on me.

Now did I say anything of the sort?

I had to bring him, I suppose; there's no getting away from him in this life. But, as I have already observed, the happy ancients went to their Utopias without this sort of company.

"My God!" he says almost forcibly, "what nonsense all this is! All these dreams! All Utopias!"

He does not need to finish his sentence, he waves an unteachable destructive arm.

My Utopia rocks about me.

There is no jerk, no sound, no hint of material shock. We are in London, and clothed in the fashion of the town. The sullen roar of London fills our ears.

I see that I am standing beside an iron seat of poor design in that grey and gawky waste of asphalt—Trafalgar Square, and the botanist, with perplexity in his face, stares from me to a poor, shrivelled, dirt-lined old woman—my God! what a neglected thing she is!—who proffers a box of matches.

He buys almost mechanically, and turns back to me.

"I was saying," he says, "the past rules us absolutely. These dreams—"

His sentence does not complete itself. He looks nervous and irritated.

"You have a trick at times," he says instead, "of making your suggestions so vivid—"

A pinched and dirty little girl, with sores upon her face, stretches out a bunch of wilting violets, in a pitifully thin little fist, and interrupts. "Bunch o' vi'lets—on'y a penny."

"No!" I say curtly, hardening my heart.

A ragged and filthy nursing mother, with her last addition to our Imperial People on her arm, comes out of a drinkshop, and stands a little unsteadily, and wipes mouth and nose comprehensively with the back of a red chapped hand.

"Isn't *that* reality," says the botanist, almost triumphantly, and leaves me aghast at his triumph.

"*That!*" I say belatedly. "It's a thing in a nightmare!"

He shakes his head and smiles—exasperatingly.

I perceive quite abruptly that the botanist and I have reached the limits of our intercourse.

"The world dreams things like that," I say, "because it suffers from an indigestion of such people as you."

But I am back in the world for all that, and my Utopia is done.

It is good discipline for the Utopist to visit this world occasionally.

That is my all about Utopia, and about the desire and need for Utopia, and how that planet lies to this planet that bears the daily lives of men.

14

Classical Utopias 900 B.C.-200 B.C.

At first sight, a leap from H. G. Wells and modern utopianism to the Ancients and their visions of ideal societies may seem startling. But there is method in such an arrangement. The ideas of the older utopists become more significant if more recent examples of imaginary societies are known; the depth, insight, and influence as well as the limitations of both ancient and modern works are thus made more apparent. Moreover, it is far easier to move from familiar and more or less contemporary accounts to antique and strange ones than it would be to plunge immediately into the profundities of Greek thought. Having obtained a familiarity with modern utopias, the reader will recognize similarities and anticipations in the older works and will feel more at home in them.

For example: he will immediately note a resemblance between the Samurai, the superior class in H. G. Wells' *A Modern Utopia* and the Guardians in Plato's *Republic*. This parallel is indicative of the universality of utopian ideas. Indeed, the tendency to utopianize is common to primitive and sophisticated men. Conceptions of Paradise, Arcadia, the Golden Age, the Island of the Blest, Gardens of Eden, and the Land of Cockaigne are reiterant in human thought. They begin as myths and then develop into comprehensive descriptions of ideal societies. But the form in which the latter are written varies greatly. In ancient Greek literature, for example, works utopian or semi-utopian in tendency occur in romances, biographies, voyage accounts, philosophical dialogues, and treatises. Utopianism, explicit or implicit, is discoverable almost everywhere in literature.

According to tradition, Lycurgus, guardian of a king of Sparta who probably lived about the ninth century B.C., drew up an ideal constitution and body of laws for that city. Plutarch, in his life of Lycurgus, states that the latter set up a senate in Sparta to act as a supreme court and to propose legislation to an assembly of all citizens, who had the right to ratify or reject it, without discussion. To root out evils of insolence, envy, avarice, and luxury, he established equality of possessions for all citizens, removed the evils of money by abolishing gold and silver coins, and substituted cumbersome iron ones in their place. He excluded luxuries and superfluous arts and completed his conquest of love of wealth and voluptuousness by forbidding meals at home and obliging all to eat frugal fare at common tables. In his utopia, newborn babies were put to death if weak or deformed; and both sexes were inured to hardship and kept under discipline from an early age. They were given a minimum of learning. The rest of their education was calculated to make them subject to command, to endure labor, to fight, and to conquer. They were encouraged to steal because of the value of such experience for military purposes. The production of strong, healthy offspring was made the prime end of marriage, and the choice of mates was made accordingly. All the men, with the exception of persistent bachelors, were accustomed to watching dances by girls and women in the nude. Beneath this toughened, exclusive, and brutal warrior class were thousands of helots, or serfs, who did the productive work and were denied elementary human rights. In other words, Lycurgus's utopia proved to be an early Fascist state.

Utopias were probably written between the time of Lycurgus and that of Plato (427–347 B.C.). A certain Phaleas, for example, is said to have claimed that the citizens of a state ought to have equal possessions. However, no such work of importance survives.

Athens, after the Peloponnesian War and the rule of the Thirty Tyrants, passed into a period of conspiracies and seditions. Men sought but pleasure and profit. Class divisions became acute: the opulent luxuriated and the poor increasingly suffered. Science, education, and morality all declined. In these circumstances Plato composed his *Republic*, a state ruled by philosophers, protected by warriors, and supported by a class of laborers and artisans. His society was characterized by absolute communism amongst the guardians (including community of women), equality of the sexes, class division, and slavery, by the nationalism of a city-state based on a permanent army, and by the proscription of new ideas from abroad. Plato wrote his utopia in the form of a dialogue concerning the nature of justice. His ideal state is intended to realize that virtue. To that end, necessities, but no needless luxuries, are available to the citizens. His chief interest is in the teaching, ruling class, a small but dominant group: they are philosopher-kings whose supreme virtue is wisdom, and whose purpose is to attain truth and the good of all. The special virtue of the warrior and guardian classes is fortitude, and their function is to protect the state and to maintain order. The class of farmers, artisans, tradesmen and slaves have self-restraint and explicit obedience as their appropriate virtues, and their function is to satisfy the material needs of the community. Justice results from the harmonious coordination of the classes, each doing its duty, so that everyone is doing the job best suited to his capacities. The welfare of the whole and the common good have primacy over selfishness. And the rulers strive to contemplate the Idea of the Good, to be in tune with the Infinite, and to become like that divine principle. As a result, they guide the state justly. Moral virtue in the *Republic* is, therefore, political virtue; and social ethics result from each citizen doing his social duty.

Education is confined to children of the rulers and warriors. Until the second year, the body is cared for. From three to six, religious and moral truths are inculcated by means of carefully selected myths and fables. From seven to ten, gymnastics are stressed in the interest of health, strength, and military prowess. Reading and writing are taught to those from ten to thirteen, and poetry and music for the next two years; but all that is unwholesome, unfavorable to the gods, or conducive to idleness or effeminacy is eliminated, for censorship is rigid in the Republic. From sixteen to eighteen, mathematical sciences are taught. Those who show inferior ability in this connection become warriors, if they are capable of bravery. But those who show a capacity for abstract thought continue their studies until thirty, paying particular attention to the relations of various sciences. The less proficient then are given political posts. For the next five years, the remainder diligently develop their reasoning powers, and then, until the age of fifty, actively engage in various governmental and military capacities. Thereafter, they devote most of their time to philosophic contemplation of the Idea of the Good, taking turns as rulers in the highest offices of the Republic.

In other words, the Platonic educational process is a means of developing and selecting superior men and women to rule the state, although the ultimate goal of these men and women of the dominant class is to make themselves as like divine Goodness as possible. They are denied the right to have private property, are maintained by the state, and eat and live together to such an extent that, for the sake of unity of purpose, wives and children are possessed in common.

Thus Plato provides for a state governed by an artistocracy of philosophers living in communism, and below them a large non-communist body of artisans educated in little but their craft. In his Republic, the individual as such is subordinated to the whole. The harmony and well-being of the state, not of its component parts, is his goal, although the corollary is that in such a state, each person, having found that station of life for which he is best suited, will realize his own well-being. There is much to admire in Plato's advocacy of education in which intellect, body, and morals are harmoniously developed; in his stress on equality of opportunity for both sexes; in his doctrine that the most intelligent and public-spirited should govern their fellow men; and in his denunciation of extreme economic inequalities. His subordination of individual interests to the welfare of the whole, involving as it did the renunciation of private property and family life, is nevertheless generally regarded as going to an extreme. Certainly most men would object to such dictation of their intimate affairs by the state, and condemn a self-lessness, allegedly in the interest of society, which involved them in marital communism. In any case, Plato has not adequately indicated how the masses could be made to accept the beneficent rule of the few. Moreover, one cannot but suspect that in the passage of time, the possession of power might corrupt even philosopher-kings. And finally, the aspect of Plato's Republic which will least appeal to the average, modern, democratic man is the very fact that he is an average man, and that Plato was primarily interested, not in him and his welfare, but in an intellectual aristocracy and an abstract ideal of justice. Nevertheless the influence of the *Republic* has been potent both in subsequent practical political thought and, as will be seen in the works printed below, in utopian speculations.

Contemporary with Plato, almost certainly with his *Republic* as a main target, Aristophanes burlesqued utopias in 393 B.C., with his play *The Ecclesiazusae*. Much of it is devoted to ridiculing the "utopian" sexual relations advocated or described by Plato. Considerable attention is also paid to economic organization. In the drama, women seize power in Athens and plan that all shall be equal in rank and possessions in a communist society, where, it is claimed, all pressure from want will end, and everyone will have what he desires. Crimes will be rare under such circumstances, and those that do occur will be punished by depriving the miscreant of food.

Utopian writing multiplied in the third century B.C., possibly as a result of the interest aroused by Plato and Aristophanes. It was probably during that century that Zeno, the Stoic philosopher, wrote an anarchistic utopia, *The Republic*, which described a society—or lack of society—without marriage, religion, laws, money, or property. Only the worthy were citizens in Zeno's world city, but, unlike the worthy in the political thought of Aristotle, they did not exploit the unworthy, who, though denied citizenship, presumably were the larger group. Apart from this division, Zeno was a universalist, recognizing the brotherhood of all mankind and acknowledging no distinctions of earthly rank and race. He eliminated all apparatus of national groups and particular states, and made his world city a theoretic whole. His was a city of gods and some men. In later Stoic thought, the state became common to the gods and the whole of mankind.

An ideal of fraternal unity also appeared in the best known of the remaining Greek communistic utopias, the Sun State described by Iambulus. It was situated upon the Islands of the Sun in the Indian Ocean. Its people were divided into systems, each ruled by a governor whose powers seem to have been absolute, except that he had to die at a certain age. Wives were held in common, but slavery was unknown. Every citizen filled, in his turn, every office in his system, from servant to governor. These customs and institutions were made possible by the fact that the islands bore crops throughout the year, sometimes without human aid. The people worshiped Heaven and the Sun, and they prized above all things what the

Greeks called *homonoia*, a harmonious concord and unity of minds and hearts, a universalist feeling of full brotherhood. However, Iambulus fails to specify how the separate social systems in his utopia were coordinated.

The idea of a sun state is reiterant in classical thought. Alexander the Great conceived of himself as Alexander Helios, the Sun-King. A similar conception occurs in the Renaissance in Garcilaso de la Vega's account of the civilization of the Incas in Peru, and in Campanella's *City of the Sun;* and it recurs in various subsequent utopias.

The importance of utopian ideas either as a motivation for political action or as propaganda conducive to it is illustrated by the national revolt against Rome raised in 132 B.C. by Aristonius, heir to the throne of Pergamon. Since he called his followers "citizens of the Sun State," and made his appeal to slaves and other men of various nationalities, he seems to have been following Iambulus in promising absence of slavery and racial distinctions. His attempt was unsuccessful.

Iambulus's pretended voyage to the Sun State is written in the form of a philosophic romance in which the utopian theme and love of the marvelous are exploited to serve serious teachings. Hecataeus of Abdera used the romance form in his account of the Hyperboreans, a people who, by profound piety toward Apollo and other gods, arrived at a state of extraordinary felicity, and also in another work, *The Egyptians*, which gave an idealized picture of the ancient monarchy of the Pharaohs and their government—a theme which recurred in one of Fénelon's utopias in the late seventeenth century.

Sometimes classical romances idealized a prince and suggested the utopian society which he would realize. Such were Xenophon's *Cyropaedia* and the *Abaris* of Heraclitus of Pont. In other works pertinent to this survey, the element of fantasy tended to overwhelm the utopianism. Theopompus, for example, described the land of the Meropes, where all was gigantic and where there was a huge gulf full of red air which was neither light nor darkness.

For the most part, Euhemerus avoided pure fantasy of this type. In the third century, probably before 290 B.C., he wrote his *Sacred History*, in which he introduced an account of the utopian Isle of Panchaia. The social disturbances which followed the death of Alexander the Great had made dreams of peace and happiness particularly attractive. Some, like Iambulus, had longed for a communistic republic. Others, impressed by the strength and apparent stability of great empires like that of Egypt, advocated sacerdotal government in a society divided into castes. Euhemerus tried to combine these two systems on Panchaia. He divided the inhabitants into three classes. The first was composed of priests and artisans; the second of laborers; and the third of warriors and herdsmen. The priest-artisan class had complete direction of public affairs. The crops and animals grown by the laborers and herdsmen were handed over to the priests who distributed an equal part of them to each man, reserving a double portion for themselves. No one possessed any private property except a house and garden. However, the communism of Euhemerus was more moderate than that of Iambulus, for the latter extended community to women and children.

The Greeks were not alone in imagining utopias. Amongst the ancient Hebrews Amos, Hosea, Jeremiah, and Ezekiel show incipient utopianism, and similar threads are discoverable in most ancient peoples. But the Greeks seem to have been the first to write comprehensive accounts of functioning imaginary societies, sometimes upholding them as ideals or models towards which men should strive; sometimes proposing them as hypothetical standards by which men could test their own societies; and sometimes inventing them as an exercise of the imagination or as a vehicle of philosophical speculation. Utopias also appear to have been written as escapes from harsh reality, as satisfying dreams. On the other hand, more realistic writers used them as a means of propaganda, or as a disguise behind which they could spread dangerous or tentatively held ideas. Whatever their purpose, these works enabled a comprehensive comparison to be made between existing practices and societies and hypothetical ones. By removing sociological and other problems to a new setting, they gave them perspective, enabled them to be seen more objectively, and gave a clearer idea of their relative magnitude and difficulty—as well as suggesting possible remedies for them. By distortion, simplification, innovation, and fancy, these utopists presented new views of reality, and often helped readers to make more objective judgments on the matters dealt with than they would otherwise have done. Paradoxically, these utopias, by their very distortions and propagandist devices, could be conducive to partiality and prejudice. In any case, they forced the attention of readers to certain specific problems. While in some measure preserving the entirety and interrelatedness of the structure of society, a utopia was a means of simplifying its lines and reducing it to clearer proportions. Thus readers could get a distinct, concrete, and interrelated sense of problems and their possible solutions.

Most of the stock ideas of utopists occur in one or another of the Greek utopias mentioned above: equality of sexes; natural religion; the brotherhood of man; toleration; stress on education; advocacy of eugenics; hatred of tyranny; functionalism of classes; dedication to virtue or to justice; primitivism; anarchism; communism; and statism. In the main, stress on material progress is slight; also lacking is that concentration upon thorough exploitation of available resources, particularly material ones, which is one of the chief marks of utopias since the Renaissance.

Except in the case of Plato's *Republic*, the influence of which is pervasive from Sir Thomas More to H. G. Wells and beyond, it is difficult to discover with any precision how far the thought of later utopists was influenced by their Greek predecessors. Parallels are easy to discover, but in themselves they afford little evidence of borrowing or influence. For ideas about Sun-States, primitive innocence, and the like are rooted in a far wider area of human experience and literature than the relatively small territory included in utopian lands.

Roman and medieval literatures contain no works classifiable as proper utopias. Cicero's *Republic*, St. Augustine's *City of God*, and Dante's *Concerning Monarchy* are on the extreme borderlines of the genre. The peasant revolts of the middle ages were accompanied by some communistic theories and other utopian elements. Medieval accounts of trips to the moon and of various burlesque or allegorical societies have some resemblances to utopias proper. The ideals behind chivalry, feudalism, and the Holy Roman Empire were also somewhat utopian. But the fact remains that from the time of the ancient Greeks till the revival of their influence in the Renaissance, the realms of Utopia, like the glories of Atlantis, disappeared from sight.

BIBLIOGRAPHY: There is need for a comprehensive history of classical utopianism in the English language. The best available treatment is in German: Edgar Salin, *Platon und die Griechische Utopie* (Munich, and Leipzig, 1921). Joyce Oramel Hertzler gives an account of the Prophets as forerunners of the utopians, and of Plato's *Republic* in the *History of Utopian Thought* (New York, 1926). Arthur E. Morgan ranges from China to Peru in examining the origins of utopias in his *Nowhere was Somewhere* (Chapel Hill, 1946). The present editor has borrowed heavily for the above account from the writings of W. W. Tarn, "Alexander the Great and the Unity of Mankind," the Raleigh Lecture to the British Academy, 1933; and "Alexander Helios and the Golden Age," *Journal of Roman Studies*, XXII, Part II (1932), 135 ff. Further material given above is based on R. de Block, *Euhémère, son Livre et sa Doctrine* (Mons, 1876).

Plato's *Republic* is readily available in numerous editions and translations, and the same is true of Xenophon's *Cyropaedia* and Plutarch's

Lives. A translation by B. B. Rogers of Aristophanes' *The Ecclesiazusae* was published in New York by G. P. Putnam's in 1924. Sources for the other Greek utopias mentioned are not readily available to the average reader. Specialists should consult the works of Tarn and Salin cited above for bibliographical details.

15

Utopia

*A Fruitful and Pleasant Work
of the Best State of a Public
Weal, and the New Isle
Called Utopia*

Thomas More

*London
1551
(first published in Latin at Leyden in 1516)*

Published in Latin in 1516, often reprinted, translated into English by Ralph Robinson in 1551, re-translated into English by Gilbert Burnet in 1684, put into almost all European languages and, in the twentieth century, into several Asiatic ones, the *Utopia* of Sir Thomas More is obviously universal in its appeal and ubiquitous in its influence. But great caution is necessary in interpreting it, for it is acclaimed by Protestant and Catholic, by Christian and Communist, by Progressivists and Reactionaries, indeed, by men of all schools of thought, though for widely different reasons. That More himself was recognized as a Saint by the Roman Catholic Church, and, in the same decade, that his *Utopia* was adopted as a textbook in Soviet Russia, indicate the need for caution in assessing both the man and the book.

Some have interpreted the Utopia as a mere literary exercise, as playful speculation intended as amusement for scholars. In evidence is More's failure to use the language of the common man. His writing in Latin and publishing on the Continent would seem to show that the book was intended as a conversation piece, to be read for delectation and after-dinner conversation. Certainly there is little in More's life and other works to justify the view that Hythloday, who describes Utopia, was a spokesman for More. The contrary is certainly made explicit in the last two sentences of the book: "I cannot agree and consent to all things that he said, although he is otherwise, without doubt, a man singularly well learned, and in all worldly matters exactly and profoundly experienced. So I must needs confess and grant that there are many things in the Utopian commonwealth which in our cities I may rather wish for than hope for." Furthermore, it is known that More delighted in irony, that he sometimes exercised his mind in arguments, and that he was not unwilling, for such a purpose, to defend an opinion which he did not accept. For example, his friend Erasmus states that More as a youth attempted a dialogue in which he defended Plato's communism even in the matter of wives. The *Utopia* may well have been a further development of this literary exercise.

On the other hand, many have interpreted the work as a social criticism. Certainly this was the view of Erasmus, who states confidently that More published his *Utopia* "to show the causes of mischief in commonwealths," and that he had the English constitution in mind. This statement seems to imply that the imaginary country is not to be regarded as an ideal or model but as something with which England could be compared in order to discover and analyse the causes of her discontents. The following extract from Book I of *Utopia* illustrates this aspect of the work. Raphael Hythloday, a traveler whom More met in Antwerp, points out various evils in

England before he describes the civilization of Utopia. Hearing that men are put to death for theft in England, he asserts that the punishment passes the limits of justice and harms the commonwealth:

"For simple theft is not so great an offense that it ought to be punished with death. Neither is there any punishment so horrible that it can keep men from stealing who have no other craft whereby to get their living. . . . For great and horrible punishments are appointed for thieves, whereas, much rather, provision should have been made for some means by which they might get their living; so that no man should be driven to this extreme necessity, first to steal, and then to die."

"Yes," quoth he [the cardinal to whom Hythloday was speaking], "this matter is well enough provided for already. There are handicrafts, there is husbandry to get their living by, if they would not willingly be worthless."

"Nay," quoth I, "you shall not 'scape so; for, first of all, I will speak nothing of those that come home from war maimed, . . . and by reason of weakness and lameness are not able to occupy their old crafts and are too aged to learn new; . . . But let us consider those things that chance daily before our eyes. First, there is a great number of gentlemen who cannot be content to live idle themselves, like drones, on that which others have labored for—their tenants, I mean, whom they shave and cut to the quick by raising their rents. . . . These gentlemen, I say, do not only live in idleness themselves, but also carry about with them at their tails a great flock or train of idle and loitering servingmen, who never learned any craft whereby to get their livings. These men, as soon as their master is dead, or they are sick themselves, are straightway thrust out of doors. . . . Then . . . they . . . either starve for hunger or manfully play the thieves. What would you have them do? . . .

"But yet this is not the only necessary cause of stealing. There is another . . . your sheep, that used to be so meek and tame and such small eaters, now, as I hear say, are become so great devourers and so wild that they eat up and swallow down the very men themselves. They consume, destroy, and devour whole fields, houses, and cities. For . . . noblemen and gentlemen, yea, and certain abbots, holy men, God knows, not contenting themselves with their yearly revenues and profits . . . leave no ground for tillage. [In order to engage in the profitable business of sheep-raising], they enclose everything for pastures; they throw down houses; they pluck down towns; and leave nothing standing but only the church, to make it a sheephouse. . . .

Therefore . . . the husbandmen are thrust out of their own
. . . or . . . are compelled to sell all. By one means, therefore,
or another, either by hook or crook, they must needs depart
away, poor, innocent, wretched souls: men, women, husbands,
wives, fatherless children, widows, woeful mothers with their
young babes, and their whole household, small in substance and
much in number, for husbandry requires many hands. Away
they trudge, I say, out of their known and accustomed houses,
finding no places to rest in. All their household stuff, which is
very little worth even if there is time to wait for a good buyer,
they are constrained to sell it for something of no value, being
suddenly thrust out. And when they have soon spent that in
wandering about, what can they else do but steal, and then
justly, God knows, be hanged; or else go about a-begging? And
yet then also they are cast in prison as vagabonds, because they
go about and work not; whom no man will set a-work, though
they ever so willingly offer themselves thereto. For one shepherd or herdman is enough to eat up, with cattle, ground for
which many hands were requisite when it was tilled. And this
is also the cause that victuals are now in many places dearer.
Yea, besides this the price of wool is so risen that poor folks,
who used to work it and make cloth of it, are now able to buy
none at all."

Another interpretation of the *Utopia* is that Hythloday expresses
More's real views, that the latter was advocating a kind of communism, and, accordingly, that his work is to be read as a forerunner of
modern socialism and communism. Further comments by Hythloday will illustrate the basis of this point of view:

". . . wheresoever possessions are private, where money has the
chief influence, it is hard and almost impossible that there the
commonwealth may justly be governed and prosperously flourish—unless you think thus: that justice is executed where all
things come into the hands of evil men; or that prosperity flour-
ishes where all is divided among a few; which few, nevertheless,
do not lead their lives very advantageously, and the residue live
miserably, wretchedly and beggarly.
"Therefore, I consider with myself and weigh in my mind
the wise and godly ordinances of the Utopians, among whom,
with very few laws, all things are so well and advantageously
ordered that virtue is properly rewarded and esteemed; and
yet, all things being held there in common, every man has
abundance of everything. Again, on the other hand, I compare

with them the many nations ever making new laws, yet not one of them all well and sufficiently furnished with laws; where every man calls what he has gotten, his own proper and private goods; where the many new laws daily made are not sufficient for every man to enjoy, defend, and know from another man's that which he calls his own; which fact is plainly shown to be true by the infinite controversies in the law that daily arise, never to be ended. These things, I say, when I consider with myself, I agree well with Plato, and do not marvel that he would make no laws for those who refused the laws by which all men should have and enjoy equal portions of wealth and commodities."

It is possible to give a theological interpretation to the *Utopia*. More describes a people who have been denied the benefits of supernatural revelations: the only truths which they know are those arrived at by the use of their natural reason. Deists have been tempted to see in this an advocacy of natural religion. Certainly the religion of the Utopians was a powerful influence in the rise of deism and in deistic utopias. Nevertheless, since More was a sincere Christian, it is more likely that he was trying to show how far natural man, unaided by divine revelations, could move toward the good life and toward Christian truth. By implication he was saying to the professing Christians of Europe: look at the excellence, virtue and general well-being which man can attain by the use of natural reason alone! Then consider how much more excellent Christians could be if they lived in accordance with reason and the revealed truths of Christianity.

In the opinion of the present editor, More came to the conclusion that the best form of social organization for men who lacked supernatural revelations was the sort of enlightened, humanistic, moderated, disciplined society based on common ownership which he described—a communism very different from that advocated by Marx and professed by Stalin. More's Utopians were ignorant of Christianity before Hythloday's visit to them. It is inconceivable that More, who died a martyr for Christianity as he interpreted it, intended Utopian religion to be adopted by Europeans. A state which was truly ideal in his eyes would have to be a Christian one. Accordingly seems to have been theorizing when he wrote the *Utopia;* he was probably attempting to discover the best possible social organization for *natural* man. His humanistic communism was intended, then, for man in a state of nature. But it is unlikely that he would have advocated it for men who had the supernatural aids of Christianity: what communal life could do for men could be better effected and improved by the practice of Christianity. For those to whom grace and supernatural truths were available, Christian love and brotherhood offered a superior path: Christian communion would supersede natural communism.

Another method of approaching the *Utopia* is to concentrate upon its historical significance. Some critics see More as unprogressive, as applying a combination of the principles of the medieval guild and the medieval monastery to a disciplined, carefully regulated community, which denies itself most luxuries and devotes itself to virtue. Others see in it planned economy, liberal theology, and attention to science (in such things as the use of incubators for hatching eggs), and a marked progressive tendency, which is also noticeable in More's condemnation of war and its alleged glories, his stress upon democratic values and processes, and what amounts to his advocacy of the Four Freedoms.

It is noteworthy that More does not, in effect, attempt to give lessons to God. Other utopists (I.D.M., Foigny, and Cabet, for example), seem to imply that, given the opportunity, they could improve on the work of the Creator. But More gives lessons only to men: for him this is an excellent world if men will make reasonable use of what it offers. As a Christian Humanist he describes a naturalistic society in which human qualities are developed to a maximum, and in which nature and its gifts are so intensively cultivated that they lead natural man logically to the supernatural. It is therefore not surprising that Hythloday found it easy to convert some of the Utopians to Christianity. Nature and reason had brought them to its very threshold.

Russell Ames, who regards the Utopian society as "a protective disguise for the satire and dangerously progressive projects of a humanistic reformer and middle-class citizen," summarizes the most common interpretations of More's account, and finds some truth in all of them:

> The description of Utopia by itself may be considered one or more of a great many different things: 1. A fantastic escape from unpleasant reality. 2. A blueprint for a better society which More thought men might soon establish. 3. A better society which might exist in some far-off time. 4. A better society which More desired but did not believe possible. 5. A reconstruction of medieval social virtues. 6. A revival of primitive Christian communism. 7. A speculative portrait of rumored American societies like that of the Incas. 8. A strictly rational philosophic construction, minus Christianity, for the purposes of moral instruction. 9. A pleasant fable written by a humanist for the amusement of himself and his scholarly friends. 10. A fruit of

classical studies, following Plato's *Republic*. 11. An early plan
for British imperialism. 12. A Christian humanist account of a
scholar's paradise, where philosophers are kings and the church
is purified. 13. A society constructed as the direct opposite to
England for the purpose of disguising social criticism. 14. A description of a desirable and possible organization of city republics.

Professor Ames gives an incisive analysis of these interpretations,
stresses the triumph of More's humanity and intellect over irration-
ality, prejudice, personal convenience, and fear, and discovers, particularly in the first book, evidence that the intention of *Utopia* was
democratic. He concludes that "the humane democracy of the first
book . . . gives us the obvious meaning of the work as a whole, and
also the central meaning of his other writings and of his own life."

The text below is a condensed modernization of Ralph Robinson's
translation (1551). Diction, word order, punctuation, and spelling
have been changed as little as is consistent with brevity and clarity.
Passages merely summarized are placed in brackets.

BIBLIOGRAPHY: A convenient, inexpensive edition of the *Utopia* is
published by Appleton-Crofts in the Crofts Classics series. On More
himself, see R. W. Chambers, *Thomas More* (1936); and the *Life*
by William Roper, More's son-in-law, which occurs in numerous
editions, one of the best being that by E. V. Hitchcock (1935). On
the *Utopia*, see W. E. Campbell, *More's Utopia and his Social Teaching* (1930); Karl Kautsky, *Thomas More and his Utopia* (1890);
Russell Ames, *Citizen Thomas More and his Utopia* (1949).

Utopia

The Island of Utopia contains in breadth two hundred miles, saving
that it comes in towards both the ends, which, forming a circuit of
five hundred miles, fashion the whole island like to the new moon.
Between these two corners the sea runs in, dividing them by eleven
miles, and there spreads into a large sea not much unlike a great
standing pool.

There are in the island fifty-four cities or shire towns all set and
situated alike, and in all points fashioned alike, none of them distant
from the next above one day's journey afoot. There come yearly to
Amaurote out of every city three old men, wise and experienced, to

treat and debate the common matters of the land. For this city in
the midst of the island is taken for the head city. The bounds of
the shires are so appointed for the cities that never a one of them
has less than twenty miles of ground on any side.

They have in all parts of the shire, houses with all tools belonging
to husbandry. These houses are inhabited by citizens who come there
to dwell in turns. No household in the country has fewer than forty
persons, besides two bondmen, all under the rule of the good man
and wife of the house, both very sage and discreet persons. Every
thirty farms have one head ruler called a Philarch. Out of every
one of these come every year into the city thirty persons who have
been two years in the country. In their place, so many fresh are
sent out of the city and are taught by those that have been there a
year already. This yearly changing is to the intent that no man shall
be constrained against his will to continue long in that hard kind of
life. Yet many of them have such a delight in husbandry that they
stay a longer space of years. These husbandmen till the ground,
breed cattle, and make ready wood, which they bring to the city.
They bring up a multitude of poultry; for the hens do not sit upon
the eggs. But by keeping them in an equal heat, the husbandmen
hatch them. The chickens follow men and women instead of the
hens.

Oxen are put to all the labor of plowing and drawing. Corn is
sowed only for bread. For their drink is wine of grapes, apples, or
pears, or else clean water, and many times mead made of honey or
liquorice. Though they know certainly how much victuals the city
(with the shire) uses, yet they sow more corn and breed more cattle
than serves for their own use. And the overplus they divide among
the bordering nations. Whatever necessary things are lacking in
the country, they fetch out of the city: without any exchange they
obtain it from the magistrates. Every month many of them go into
the city on the holy day. When their harvest draws near, what number of harvest men is needful is sent out of the city.

As for their cities, he that knows one of them knows them all:
they are like one to another as far as the nature of the place permits.
Amaurote is the worthiest. The city stands on the side of a low hill,
almost four-square. It begins a little beneath the top of the hill and
continues two miles to the river Anyder. The length of it is somewhat more. There goes a bridge over the river, made of stonework
with gorgeous arches at that part of the city which is farthest from
the sea. Ships may go along all the side of the city. Another river
rises out of the same hill and runs through the city into Anyder. The
Amaurotians have enclosed the head spring of it with strong bul-
warks. Thence the water is brought down in channels of brick into

the city. Where that cannot be done, they gather the rain water in great cisterns.

The city is compassed about with a high and thick wall, a dry ditch overgrown with briars, and, to the fourth side, the river itself. The streets are set forth very handsome both for carriage and against the winds. The houses are of fair building, and on the street side they stand joined together in a long row without any partition. The streets are twenty feet broad. On the back side of the houses lie large gardens, which are closed in with the back part of the streets. Every house has two doors, never locked. Every man that will may go in, for there is nothing within the house that is private or any man's own. And every ten years they change their houses by lot.

They set great store by their gardens. In them they have vineyards, all manner of fruit, herbs, and flowers. It seems that the first founder of this city minded nothing so much as he did these gardens. For King Utopus appointed and drew forth the platform of the city into this fashion that it hath now; but the gallant garnishing he left to his posterity. Their chronicles, containing the history of 1760 years from the first conquest of the island, record that the houses in the beginning were low, with mud walls. But now the houses are built after a gorgeous and gallant sort, with three stories. The outsides are made of hard flint, plaster, or brick, and the inner sides are strengthened with timber. The roofs are flat, covered with a plaster that no fire can hurt. They keep the wind out of their windows with glass; also with fine linen dipped in oil or amber.

Every thirty families or farms choose yearly an officer called the Syphogrant or Philarch. Every ten Syphogrants, with all their three hundred families, are under a Tranibore or chief Philarch.

As concerning the election of the Prince, all the Syphogrants, in number two hundred, are sworn to choose him whom they think most fit and expedient. Then, by a secret election, they name Prince one of those four whom the people before named unto them. For out of the quarters of the city, there are four chosen, out of every quarter one, to stand for election. The Prince's office continues all his lifetime unless he is deposed for suspicion of tyranny. They choose the Tranibores yearly. All other offices are for one year. The Tranibores counsel with the prince concerning the commonwealth. If there are any controversies among the commoners, they end them. They take two Syphogrants to Council, every day a new couple. Nothing touching the commonwealth is ratified unless it has been debated three days in the Council before it is decreed. It is death to have any consultation for the commonwealth outside the Council or the place of the common election. This statute was made that the Prince and Tranibores might not easily conspire to oppress the people by tyranny. Matters of great importance are brought to the election house by the Syphogrants, who open the matter to their families and afterwards report to the Council. Sometimes the matter is brought before the Council of the whole island. This custom the Council also uses: to reason of no matter the same day that it is first proposed.

Husbandry is a science common to all men and women. In this they are instructed from their youth, brought up not only beholding the use of it but practicing it also. Besides husbandry, every one of them learns his own craft, commonly clothworking, masonry, the smith's craft, or the carpenter's science. For there is no other occupation that any number to speak of follows there. Their garments throughout the island are of one fashion (saving that there is a difference between the man's garment and the woman's, between the married and the unmarried), ever more unchanged, comely to the eye, fit for both winter and summer. Every family makes its own. The women, as the weaker sort, are put to the easier crafts. They work wool and flax. For the most part, every man is brought up in his father's craft; but if a man's mind stand to any other, he is by adoption put into a family of that occupation.

The chief and almost the only office of the Syphogrants is to see that no man sits idle, but that everyone applies his own craft with earnest diligence, and yet not toiling like beasts from early morning to late evening. For they assign six hours to work. About eight in the evening they go to bed. All the time between the hours of work, sleep, and eating, they are allowed to bestow every man as he likes best; not to the intent they should misspend this time in riot or slothfulness, but to bestow the time on some other good science, as shall please them. For it is a custom there to have lectures daily. A great multitude of men and women go to hear lectures, as every man's nature is inclined. Yet if any had rather bestow this time upon his own occupation, he is commended.

After supper they bestow one hour in play, in summer in their gardens, in winter in their common halls. There they exercise themselves in music or wholesome communication. Diceplay and such pernicious games they know not; but they use two games not unlike chess.

Seeing they bestow but six hours in work, you may think that the lack of some necessary things may ensue. But that small time is too much; which you shall perceive if you consider how great a part of the people in other countries live idle: almost all women, besides a company of priests and men in religious orders; all rich men, specially all landed men, which commonly are called gentlemen and landed men; also their servants, bragging swashbucklers; also sturdy beggars cloaking their idleness under color of some disease. Truly you shall find them much fewer than you thought, who labor all things that men live by. Now consider how few of these that do work are occupied in necessary works; for many superfluous occupations serve only for riotous and dishonest pleasure. If the multitude that work were divided into the few occupations which the necessary use of nature requires, great plenty of things would ensue. If all these that are now busied about unprofitable occupations, with the whole flock of them that live idly, were set to profitable occupations, little time would be enough and too much to store us with all things requisite for necessity, commodity or pleasure—pleasure true and natural.

In Utopia, in any city with the shire adjoining to it, scarcely five hundred persons of the whole number of men and women who are neither too old or too weak to work are licensed from labor. Among them the Syphogrants are by the laws exempt, yet they exempt not themselves, to the intent they may by their example incite others to work. The same vacation from labor they also enjoy whom the people have given a license from labor for learning. Out of this order of the learned are chosen ambassadors, priests, Tranibores and the Prince. The residue of the people need not work as other nations do; for the building or repairing of houses requires everywhere else men's continual labor, because the unthrifty heir allows the houses that his father built to decay. So his successor is constrained to build anew. Yea, many times one man thinks nothing of the house that cost another much money, and therefore he builds up another in another place. But among the Utopians, where all things are set in a good order, it seldom chances that they choose a new plot to build a house upon. And they not only find quick remedies for present faults but anticipate those that are likely to happen. By this means, their houses last very long with little labor and small reparations.

In their apparel, how few workmen they need! At work they are covered with linen or skins that will last seven years. When they go farther, they cast upon them a cloak which hides the other homely apparel. These cloaks are all of the natural color of the wool. They therefore do not only use much less woolen cloth than is used in other countries, but also the same costs less. But linen cloth is made with less labor and is therefore more used. As for the smallness or fineness of thread, that is passed for a thing of no importance. This is the cause wherefore in other places four or five cloth gowns of diverse colors and as many silk coats are not enough for one man; whereas in Utopia one garment will serve a man most commonly two years. For why should he desire more?

Many times when they have no work to be occupied about, a

proclamation is made that they shall bestow fewer hours in work. For the magistrates do not exercise their citizens in unneedful labors. This end is chiefly minded, that what time may be spared from necessary occupations the citizens should draw to the free liberty of the mind and garnishing of the same. For herein they suppose the felicity of this life to consist.

The city consists of families; the families commonly of kindred. For the women when they are married go into their husband's houses; but the male children continue in their own family, governed by the eldest father unless he dote for age. Then the next in age is put in his place.

To the intent that the prescribed number of citizens should neither decrease nor above measure increase, it is ordained that no family (which in every city are 6,000 altogether, besides those of the country) shall have fewer than ten children about thirteen years of age, or more than sixteen. This number is kept by putting them that are above the number into families of smaller increase. If the whole city increase above the just number, they fill up the lack of other cities. If the multitude throughout the whole island exceed the due number, they choose out of every city certain citizens and build up a town under their own laws in the neighboring land, where the inhabitants have much unoccupied ground. If the inhabitants will not dwell with them, to be ordered by their laws, they drive them out of those bounds; and if they resist, they make war against them. For they count this the most just cause of war, when any people hold a piece of ground to no good use, keeping others from the use of it who, by the law of nature, ought to be nourished by it. If any chance so much diminishes the number of any of their cities that it cannot be filled up without diminishing the just number of the other cities, then they make up the number with citizens fetched out of their own foreign towns; for they had rather allow their own foreign towns to perish than any city of their own island to be diminished.

The eldest, as I said, rules the family. The wives minister to their husbands, the children to their parents, and the younger to their elders. Every city is divided into four equal parts. In every quarter there is a market place full of all manner of things. Thither the works of every family are brought to certain houses and laid up in storehouses. From them every householder fetches whatever he and his have need of, and carries it away without money, exchange, or pledge. For why should anything be denied to him, seeing there is abundance and that it is not to be feared that any man will ask more than he needeth? For a man is sure never to lack. Certainly in all living creatures, either fear of lack causes covetousness and greed, or in man, pride—which vice can have no place among the Utopians.

Next to the market places stand food markets whither are brought all sorts of herbs, fruits, bread, fish, and all manner of four-footed beasts and wild fowl killed and washed by the bondmen, for they permit not their free citizens to accustom themselves to the killing of beasts.

Every street has halls set in equal distance one from another. In these dwell the Syphogrants. And to every hall are appointed thirty families. The stewards of every hall at a certain hour come to the food markets, where they receive food according to the number of their halls. But first respect is had to the sick. For in the circuit of the city, a little without the walls, they have four hospitals, so ample that they seem little towns, with all things necessary furnished, and attendance of cunning physicians.

To these halls at the set hours of dinner and supper comes the whole ward, warned by a brazen trumpet; except such as are sick in the hospitals or in their own houses. No man is forbidden to fetch food of the market to his own house; yet it were folly to dress a bad dinner at home when they may be welcome to good fare at the hall. In this hall, all vile and laborsome toil is done by the bondmen. But the women in turn have charge of cooking and ordering all things thereto belonging. They sit at four tables or more: the men next the wall, the women on the other side of the table, that they may rise without trouble and go into the nursery.

The nurses sit with their young sucklings in a parlor, never without fire, clean water and candles. Every mother is nurse to her own child unless death or sickness prevents it. Also among the nurses sit all the children under the age of five. All the other children under the age of marriage serve at the tables or, if too young, stand by with marvelous silence. That which is given them from the table they eat, and other dinnertime they have none. The old men divide their dainties as they think best, to the younger that sit both sides of them.

They begin every dinner and supper by reading something that pertains to good manners and virtue, but it is short. The elders take occasion for honest communication, but neither sad nor unpleasant; but they gladly hear the young men. No supper is passed without music. They burn sweet gums and spices for perfumes and leave nothing undone that makes for the cheering of the company. For they think no kind of pleasure forbidden whereof comes no harm. In the country they that dwell far from any neighbors dine at home.

If any be desirous to visit another city, they easily obtain license of their Syphogrants or Tranibores unless there is some hindrance. No man goes out alone; but a company is sent with their Prince's letters to testify that they have license to go that journey. Though they carry nothing with them, yet they lack nothing; for wherever they come they are at home. If they tarry in a place longer than one day, then every one of them falls to his own occupation there. If any man without leave walk out of his bounds, he is sharply punished. If he be taken in that fault again, he is punished with bondage.

If any is desirous to walk into the fields that belong to the city he dwells in and obtains the good will of his father and the consent of his wife, he is not prohibited. But he has no food given him until he has wrought out his work. Observing this condition, he may go where he will within the bounds of his own city.

Now you see how little liberty they have to loiter; how they can have no pretense to idleness. There are neither taverns nor stews nor any occasion of vice; so of necessity they must apply their accustomed labors or recreate themselves with honest pastimes.

They have plenty of all things, and seeing they are all partners, no man can be needy. In the Council of Amaurote, as soon as it is known what things are scant in any place, the lack is filled up with the abundance of others. So the whole island is, as it were, one family.

When they have provided for two years, then, of those things whereof they have abundance, they carry into other countries, and the seventh part they give freely to the poor; the residue they sell at a reasonable price. By this trade they bring into their own country not only plenty of gold and silver, but such things as they lack at home, which is almost nothing but iron. And by reason they have long used this trade, now they have abundance of these things. Now therefore they care not whether they sell for ready money or upon trust. If they wish to lend part of that money to another people, they call in their debt; or when they have war. They keep treasure, to be helped by it in sudden dangers, but especially to hire foreign soldiers for unreasonable great wages. For they had rather put strangers in danger than their own countrymen, knowing that for money enough their enemies themselves many times may be bought or through treason set by the ears among themselves.

In the meantime gold and silver they use so that none of them esteem it more than the nature of the thing deserves. And who does not plainly see how far it is inferior to iron? Of gold and silver they make commonly chamber pots and other vessels that serve for most vile uses, and chains wherein they tie their bondmen. Finally, they hang rings of gold about the ears and necks of offenders. Thus they have gold in reproach and infamy. They gather also pearls and diamonds by chance, and therewith they deck their young children. None but children do wear such trifles.

Ambassadors of the Anemolians came to Amaurote while I was there, determined in the gorgeousness of their apparel to dazzle the eyes of the Utopians. There came four ambasadors with gold hanging at their ears, with gold rings and bracelets. How proudly they displayed their peacock feathers! You should have seen children dig their mothers under the sides, saying, "Look, mother, how great a lubber! Yet wears pearls and precious stones, as though he were a little child." But the mother, "Peace, son," says she, "I think he is one of the ambassadors' fools."

They marvel that gold, which of its own nature is so unprofitable, is among all people in so high estimation that man himself is in much less estimation than the gold itself; in so much that a lumpish, block-headed churl with no more wit than an ass shall have wise and good men in subjection because he hath a great heap of gold. This and the like opinions have they conceived partly by education and partly by good literature. For all in their childhood are instructed in learning, and the better part of the people throughout their whole life bestow on learning those spare hours which they have vacant from labors. They are taught in their native tongue.

Of all our famous philosophers, no report had come to them before our coming there; yet in music, logic, arithmetic, and geometry they have found out all that our ancient philosophers taught. They are very cunning in the course of the stars, but all that deceitful divination by the stars, they never as much as dreamed of. Rains, winds, and other courses of tempests they know before by certain tokens.

They discuss the good qualities of the soul, body, and fortune and whether the name of goodness may be applied to all these or only to the gifts of the soul. But the chief question is in what thing the felicity of man consists. They never discuss felicity but they join to philosophy principles taken out of religion: that the soul is immortal and, by the bountiful goodness of God, ordained to felicity; that for our virtues and good deeds rewards are appointed after this life, and for our evil deeds punishments. Though these pertain to religion, they think it fitting that they should be believed and confirmed through reason. But if these principles were annulled, then they would pronounce no man so foolish as not to use all his diligence to obtain pleasure by right or wrong, only avoiding that the lesser pleasure would not hinder the bigger, and that labor for pleasure would bring after it displeasure and sorrow. For they judge it madness to follow painful virtue and to suffer grief without any hope of benefit from it. But they think not felicity to rest in all pleasure, but only in that pleasure that is good and honest; and that our nature is drawn to it by virtue. They define virtue to be a life ordered according to nature, and say that we are ordained to it by God; and that a man follows nature if he is ruled by reason in desiring and refusing things. Furthermore, they think that reason chiefly kindles in men the love and veneration of the Divine Majesty, of whose goodness it is that we are able to attain felicity. They say that reason moves us to lead our life free of care in joy, and to help all others, because of our fellowship in nature, to obtain the same. If it is a point of humanity for man to bring health and comfort to men, and to restore them to joy (that is, pleasure), why may it not be said that nature incites every man to do the same for himself? For a joyful life is either evil—and if it be so you should help no man to it but help all men from it—or else, if you are duty bound to procure it for others, why not chiefly to yourself? For when nature bids you to be good to others, she commands you not to be cruel to yourself. Therefore even nature itself, say they, prescribes to us a joyful life, that is, pleasure, as the end of our operations. And virtue is life ordered according to the law of nature.

Their opinion is that not only covenants among private men should be fulfilled, but also laws which either a good prince has justly published or else the people (being neither oppressed with tyranny nor deceived by fraud), have ratified by common consent, concerning the partition of the comforts of life—that is, the materials of pleasure. If these laws are not broken, it is wisdom that you look to your own wealth. And to do the same for the commonwealth is no less than your duty. But to keep another man from his pleasure while you procure your own is open wrong. Contrariwise, to take something from yourself to give to another, that is humane and gentle and never takes away as much comfort as it brings again. For it is recompensed by the return of benefits and consciousness of the good deed, with remembrance of the thankful love and good will of them to whom you have done it. Finally, God recompenses the gift of a small pleasure with great and everlasting joy. Therefore they think that all our actions and the virtues themselves are referred at last to pleasure and felicity as their end.

Pleasure they call every motion and state of the body or mind in which man naturally delights. Appetite they link with nature, for not only the senses but also right reason desires whatever is naturally pleasant, provided that it may be gotten without injury, and without debarring a greater pleasure or causing painful labor. Likewise, those things are against nature that men by vain imagination feign to be pleasant. For there are many things which of their own nature contain no pleasantness and yet through the malicious enticements of lewd desires are taken for sovereign pleasures. Is it not madness to take pride in vain honors? What natural or true pleasure do you take of another man's bare head or bowed knees? They are of a marvelous madness who rejoice because it was their fortune to come of ancestors whose stock for a long time was counted rich, though their ancestors left them not one foot of land. Yet they think themselves not the less noble. In this number they count them that delight in gems and precious stones. Why should you not take as much pleasure in beholding a counterfeit stone which your eye cannot distinguish from a genuine one? What shall I say of them that take delight only in the beholding or hiding the gold which they will never use? To these foolish pleasures they join dicers, hunters and hawkers. What pleasure is there in casting the dice upon a table, or in hearing the howling of dogs? Or what greater pleasure is there when a dog follows a hare than when a dog follows a dog? You should be moved with pity to see the innocent hare murdered by a dog. Therefore the Utopians have rejected hunting as unworthy of free men; to which craft they appoint their bondmen. For they account hunting the vilest part of butchery.

These and all such like, though the common people take them for pleasures, they, seeing there is no natural pleasantness in them, judge them to have no affinity with true pleasure. For not nature but custom causes men to accept bitter things for sweet. No man's judgment depraved either by sickness or custom can change the nature of pleasure.

They attribute some true pleasures to the soul and some to the body. To the soul they give intelligence and that delectation that comes from the contemplation of truth or the good life past. The pleasures of the body occur when delight is felt by the senses as when we eat and drink, or when itching is eased with scratching, or in the quiet and upright state of the body; for every man's proper health is delectable of itself and is the foundation of all pleasures. They almost all agree that health is a most sovereign pleasure.

They count the pleasures of the mind the chiefest of all. The chief part of them come from the exercise of virtue and conscious-ness of good life. Delight in eating and drinking they hold much to be desired but not otherwise than for health's sake. If any man take this kind of pleasure for his felicity, that man must grant that he will be in most felicity if he lives in continual hunger, thirst, itching, eating, drinking, scratching and rubbing; for these pleasures never come but with their contrary griefs. Wherefore such pleas-ures they think not greatly to be esteemed, but in that they are necessary. However, they delight also in these and acknowledge the love of mother nature, who, with pleasant delight, allures her children to that which of necessity they are driven to use often.

How wretched our life would be if these daily griefs of hunger and thirst could not be driven away except with bitter medicines! But beauty, strength, nimbleness—these, as pleasant gifts of nature, they make much of. But those pleasures received by the ears, eyes, and nose (which nature wills to be peculiar to man, for no other living beasts behold the beauty of the world), these pleasures they accept as pleasant. But in all things they are careful that a lesser pleasure hinder not a greater. They believe that by man's reason no opinion of virtue and pleasure can be found truer than this, unless a better is inspired into man from heaven.

There is in no place of the world a more excellent people nor a more flourishing commonwealth. The people are gentle, quick and fine witted, delighting in quietness and able to abide much bodily labor. They are not greatly desirous of it; but in the exercise of the mind they are never weary.

[I introduced the Greek language and Greek literature to them, also the art of printing and making paper. They make bondmen in continual labor of men guilty of heinous offenses amongst themselves, and of similar men from other countries whom they sometimes buy. They also accept as bondmen of another kind poor laborers who voluntarily come from other countries. These they treat almost as gently as their own citizens except that they put them to a little more labor. Such voluntary bondmen are free to depart at will.

[Those who are incurably ill and in continual pain are urged by the priests and magistrates to kill themselves, but they are not compelled to do so. Suicides under other circumstances are strongly condemned. Women do not marry before their eighteenth, or men before their twenty-second year. Those guilty of sexual offenses are forbidden ever to marry unless pardoned by the Prince. In choosing wives and husbands, the wooer and the woman are shown naked to each other, in the presence of friends, lest there be some deformity. Divorce is allowed for adultery or intolerable wayward habits of either party. The guilty party lives ever after in infamy and out of wedlock, but the innocent spouse is allowed to remarry. Sometimes divorce and remarriage is allowed if a married couple find themselves incompatible. Breakers of wedlock are punished with grievous bondage, and the wronged party is allowed a divorce if desired. Sometimes genuine repentance on the part of the guilty party wins restoration from bondage; but a second offense is punished with death. There are no prescribed punishments for other offenses, such matters being left to the discretion of the Council. Husbands chastise wives, and parents punish children except where a public punishment is in the public interest. Ordinarily, heinous offenses are punished with bondage. If the offenders rebel, they are slain like wild beasts. Those who take their bondage patiently and show genuine repentance are sometimes freed, or their bondage is mitigated. A man who makes a move towards adultery is punished as if he had actually committed it; for in all offenses they count the intention as evil as the deed itself.

[They delight in fools but consider it dishonorable to mock a man for his deformity. They not only deter people from evil with punishments but allure them to virtue with rewards of honor. They live together lovingly. No magistrate is haughty or frightening.

[For such a people, few laws suffice. They think that every man should plead his own cause. They regard a plain, blunt interpretation of the laws as the most just. Indeed, their virtues have caused neighboring free nations to take magistrates from the Utopians. They make no alliances with other nations, for if a man will not respect nature, will he behave for words? Moreover, the Utopians feel that the making of leagues makes men think themselves born enemies to each other and that it is for one country to seek the destruction of another unless there is an alliance. But in their opinion, no man ought to be counted an enemy if he has done no injury. And they believe that fellowship in nature is a strong league, and that men are better knit by love and benevolence than by covenants. They detest war and count nothing so inglorious as glory won in it. Therefore, though they daily practice themselves in the discipline of war, both men and women, they never go into battle except in defense of their own country, or to drive invaders out of their friends' lands, or to deliver from bondage some people oppressed with tyrannny. The Utopians prosecute injuries done to their friends in money matters, but not such injuries to themselves. For if the Utopians are defrauded of goods and no violence is done to their bodies, they simply abstain from trading with that nation until they have received satisfaction. They feel the loss of their friends' money more than their own, because the former is a private loss and harm, whereas they themselves lose nothing but common goods, which were already plentiful at home. They are ashamed to achieve victory with much bloodshed. They rejoice if they vanquish their enemies with craft or deceit, asserting that they have overcome in a way impossible for other living creatures: by power of mind. Their chief purpose in going to war is to obtain something for which they would not have waged battle if it had been previously obtained. But if that is not possible, they take such a cruel vengeance on those that are at fault that the latter are afraid to do the like again. Immediately after war is declared the Utopians have many proclamations set up in the enemy's land. In these they promise great rewards to anyone who will kill the enemy's prince. This produces suspicion and distrust. They also spread dissension by inciting the foreign prince's brother or some of the noblemen to seek the crown; or by stirring up neighboring nations to fight for some old title of right to the enemy country. They provide much money but few or no men to such claimants. Moreover, the Utopians hire foreign soldiers to fight for them, attracting such men by paying greater wages than any other nation will. If necessary the Utopians promise great rewards to these hired soldiers. Most of them never come back, but the rewards are faithfully given to those who do return.

[Next after these mercenaries, the Utopians use the soldiers of the people on whose behalf they entered the war; then the help of other friends; and last of all, volunteers from their own citizens. But if their own country is attacked, they conscript their own citizens to fight, and if any of these prove cowardly, place them in ships with bolder men, or put them on the walls, from which escape is impossible.

[In battles, wives and children are allowed to accompany the men and to help them. As a result they fight bravely and even to the utter destruction of both sides if the enemy continues to resist. For although the Utopians use all possible means to keep themselves from the necessity of fighting, they do so courageously if there is no other remedy. But when they win a battle, they do not pursue their foes with a violent rage of slaughter. They fight with great craft and skill, wearing strong, easily worn armor, and shooting arrows with bows. In close conflict they use not swords but poleaxes. They have invented various secret engines for war.

[If they make a truce, the Utopians observe it. They do not lay waste their enemy's lands but save its crops from harm as far as possible. They hurt no man who is unarmed unless he is a spy. If they win a city by assault, they neither despoil nor sack it. They put to death those who resisted or argued against its surrender, and make bondmen of the other soldiers, leaving the weak multitude untouched. If they know that any citizens advised the surrender of the city, they give them part of the condemned men's goods. The rest is distributed among those who gave their aid. The conquered nation is made to pay the entire expenses of the Utopians.]

There are various kinds of religion in every city. Some worship the sun, some the moon, some a man that was once of excellent virtue. But the wisest believe that there is a Godly Power, unknown, everlasting, incomprehensible, inexplicable, far above the capacity of man, dispersed about the world. Him they call the father of all. To Him alone they attribute the beginnings, the increasings, the proceedings, the changes and the ends of all things. Nor do they give divine honors to any other.

All, though they are of different opinions, agree that there is one principal God, maker and ruler of the whole world. But on this point they disagree: among some He is counted one thing, and among some, another. However, they now begin to agree in that religion which seems, by reason, to excel the rest. After they heard us speak of Christ, you will not believe with what glad minds they found our account agreeable. I think it was no small help that they heard us say that Christ instituted among his followers all things common, and that the same community of ownership remains among the rightest Christian companies [the monasteries]. Many of them consented to our religion and were washed in the water of baptism. But there was no priest. They lack only those sacraments which here none but priests do minister, and they are very desirous of the same. Those who do not agree to Christ's religion do not speak against any man that received it. One of our company was sharply punished: he, as soon as he was baptized, began to condemn all other religions, calling the followers of them devilish and children of everlasting damnation. The Utopians condemned him into exile, not as a despiser of religion but as a seditious person and raiser up of dissension. For King Utopus, as soon as he had gotten the victory, made a decree that it should be lawful for every man to follow what religion he would, and that he might do the best he could to bring others to his opinion if he did it peaceably, quietly, and soberly, without contentious inveighing against others. Utopus thought this decree would make for the furtherance of religion. Therefore he gave every man liberty to believe what he would, saving that no man should think that souls die and perish with the body, or that the world runs by chance, governed by no providence. Such a person they count not of the number of men; for you may be sure that he will mock or break the laws of his country. Therefore he that is thus minded is deprived of all honors, excluded from all offices, and despised. However, they put him to no punishment, because it is in no man's power to believe what he will.

[There are others—and they are allowed to speak their minds, since they ground their opinions on some reason—who believe that the souls of animals are immortal. A man who dies reluctantly is buried with sorrow and prayers; but no one mourns for those who die merrily and full of good hope. They remember the virtues and goodness of such men, for they believe that the dead are personally present among the living as beholders of their words and deeds. They esteem miracles that come outside the regular course of nature, as evidences of the power of God. Some of them are so devoted to religion that they care nothing for learning or any knowledge of secular things. But they shun idleness, thinking felicity after this life is obtained by labor and good deeds. So they take on whatever unpleasant, hard, vile work is to be done, and neither reprove other men's lives nor glory in their own. They are divided into two sects, one that abstains from women, the eating of flesh, and the pleasures of this world; the others embrace matrimony and abstain from no pleasure that does not hinder them from labor. They believe that eating meat makes them stronger to work. The Utopians count this sect the wiser.

[There are thirteen very holy priests in each city. Their office is to give good exhortations and advice, to oversee divine matters and ceremonies, and to be judges of manners. They excommunicate those who live viciously—a punishment which is greatly feared, for, unless such men prove the amendment of their lives to the priests, the Council punishes them as wicked and irreligious. The priests teach the children. Widows and old women may enter the priesthood. The male priests take for their wives the chief women in the country. Religious services in the churches are based upon sacraments and beliefs to which all sects agree. Sacraments peculiar to a sect are performed at home. On the holy day at the end of every month, before they come to church, the wives fall prostrate before their husbands and the children before their parents and confess their sins of omission and commission. In church, men sit on the right and women on the left, and no indecorous behavior is allowed. They sacrifice no animals, but they use incense and candles to encourage devotion, without supposing such things to be any more necessary to the divine nature than are the prayers of men. The people wear white in church, and the priest is clothed in changeable colors. Singing and musical instruments are used to pierce the hearts of the congregation. At the end of the service three set prayers are repeated. The rest of a holy day they pass in play and military exercise.]

I have described the form of that commonwealth which, in my judgment, is not only the best but also that which alone may of good right claim the name of commonwealth or public weal. In other countries, who knows not that he will starve unless he makes some provision for himself? Therefore he is compelled to have regard for himself rather than for the people. Contrariwise, in Utopia, where all things are common to every man, it is not to be feared that any man shall lack anything necessary; and though no man has anything, yet every man is rich. For what can be more rich than for a man to live joyfully and merrily without grief and pensiveness, not concerned for his own living, nor vexed with his wife's importunate complaints, not dreading poverty for his son, nor sorrowing for his daughter's dowry?

Dare any man be so bold as to compare with this equity the justice of other nations? Among them, I forsake God if I can find any sign of equity and justice. For what justice is this, that a rich usurer or any of them that do nothing at all or something not very necessary to the commonwealth, should have a pleasant living, either by idleness or unnecessary business, when, in the meantime, poor laborers, carters, ironsmiths and plowmen are scarcely able to sustain themselves, although without their toil no commonwealth could continue? Yet they get so poor a living that the state of laboring beasts may seem better. These poor wretches are tormented with barren labor at present, and the thought of their beggarly old age kills them. For their daily wage is so little that it will not suffice for the same day.

Is not this an unjust commonwealth which gives great fees to gentlemen, goldsmiths, and such idle persons or devisers of vain pleasures, and makes no provisions for poor laborers without whom the commonwealth cannot continue? But when it has abused the labors of their lusty and flowering age, at last, when they are oppressed with old age, being poor and indigent of all things, it recompenses them with miserable death. Besides this, the rich men, by private fraud and by law, every day snatch away from the poor some part of their daily living.

Therefore, when I consider all these commonwealths which now flourish, I can perceive nothing but a certain conspiracy of rich men procuring their own comforts under the name and title of the commonwealth. They invent all means how to keep safely, without fear of losing, what they have unjustly gathered; and how to hire and abuse the work of the poor for as little money as may be. But these most wicked and vicious men, when they have by their insatiable covetousness divided among themselves all those things which would have sufficed all men, how far are they from the wealth and felicity of the Utopian commonwealth! How great a heap of cares is cut away there because all desire and use of money is banished! How great an occasion of wickedness and mischief is plucked up by the roots! For who knows not that fraud, theft, rapine, brawling, strife, chiding, murder, treason, poisoning die when money dies? And that fear, grief, care, labors, and anxieties perish in the same moment that money perishes? Yea, poverty itself would decrease and vanish away.

Consider some unfruitful year in which many thousands starved. At the end of that penury so much grain might have been found in the rich men's barns that, being divided, no man would have felt that penury. So easily might men get their living if that princess, Lady Money, did not stop up the way between us and our living. All the world would long ago have been brought into the laws of this commonwealth were it not that a lady beast, Pride, the mother of all mischief, prevents it. She measures wealth not by her own comforts but by the miseries and discomforts of others. This hellhound creeps into men's hearts and plucks them back from entering the right path of life, and is so deeply rooted in men's breasts that she cannot be plucked out.

The Utopians have followed those institutions of life by which they have laid foundations of their commonwealth that will last not only wealthily but forever. For seeing that the chief causes of ambition and sedition are plucked up by the roots, there can be no danger of domestic dissension. Since perfect concord remains and wholesome laws are executed at home, the envy of foreign princes is not able to shake the state, though they have many times long ago tried to do it.

When Raphael made an end of his tale, many things came to my mind which, in the manners and laws of that people, seemed to be instituted and founded of no good reason, chiefly in the community of ownership in their lives; by which all nobility, magnificence, worship, honor, and majesty, the true ornaments and honors, as the common opinion is, of commonwealth, are utterly overthrown. Although I cannot agree to all things that he said, yet I must confess that there are many things in the Utopian commonwealth which in our cities I may rather wish than hope for.

16

Utopias from 1500 to 1850

With the rise of humanism and naturalism, and with the general revolution in human thought at the time of the Renaissance, utopianism revived. The medieval ideal of a static, divinely sanctioned order persisted in the writings of Robert Crowley in the sixteenth century, and lingered as the ideal of one aspect of seventeenth-century utopianism, though in national rather than international application. The semiutopian ideal of the Holy Roman universal society persisted through the middle ages and revived in modified form in Tommaso Campanella's *Spanish Monarchy* and in the hopes for a united Christendom which centered about Philip II of Spain. In 1516, Thomas More started a tradition of humanist utopias, the chief of which were probably intended less as models for society than as norms by which to judge it. The revived study of the classics, a movement with which More himself was closely connected, also led to a group of Italian utopias.

These Italian utopias of the sixteenth century are of two types: the "ideal" and the "practical." The first type is universal in basis and application, and presents the *idea* or *ideal* of a state. The other is more specific: it is civic or national in both its nature and its application. The "practical" utopia is thus a model, applicable constitution or plan for society, of the type represented by Harrington's *Oceana* in the following century. An "ideal" utopia like Plato's *Republic* puts forward the philosophical or theoretical end of a state and society, in general, more theoretic terms. During the Renaissance in all countries, the "practical" type predominated, probably because of the prevalence of naturalism. Natural philosophy taught the infallible goodness of natural law as the guide and purifying force of every society. If science was directed to study the laws of nature, and if the laws of nature were utilized to the ends of civil society, conclusions could be drawn which would contribute to the ordering of an ideal society which would be constructed in accordance with the dictates of the new experience. Natural philosophy thus led men to envisage the possibility of a model state governed by few and wise laws deduced from nature and yet dominant over her. Since it was believed that error was absent from nature, it would likewise be absent from this state; nor would anything there contradict the principles of philosophy.

The kind of model state which matured in the humanist, renaissance mind was fixed by the *Utopia* of Sir Thomas More, and by three Italian utopias, "The Imaginary Republic" by Ludovico Agostini, "The Learned World" by Antonio Francesco Doni, and *The Happy City* by Francesco Patrizi. All four, especially the Italian ones, are in the nature of academic exercises devoted to philosophical speculation or the instructive admiration of a utopian people.

An account of one of them will illustrate this. The goal of the citizens in Patrizi's *Happy City* (Venice, 1553) is to get into tune with the Divine Idea and to drink supercelestial waters. The society is divided into six castes or orders. Physical necessities are provided by the three lowest orders, the peasants, artisans, and merchants. Since they are unable to give their souls to civic and contemplative virtues, they cannot attain happiness, and are, accordingly, denied citizenship and its privileges. The superior classes—warriors, governors, and priests—perform civic duties, but their chief aims are the speculative virtues and communion with the highest. However, there is no need to give further details here: the work is essentially a recasting of Plato's *Republic*.

In contrast with such "ideal" works, an example of a "practical" sixteenth-century utopia is to be found in "The Door Opened to the Republic of Evandria," which Ludovico Zuccolo included in his *Dialogues* (Venice, 1625). It is significant because of the light it throws on one origin of utopias. The practice of idealizing an existing city or state is common to all ages, but it was particularly strong in sixteenth-century Italy. Glorifications of Lucca, Florence, and Venice are not far to seek in that period. The transition to an imagined perfect society was an easy one. Zuccolo first described San Marino with admiration for the simple but comfortable life of its citizens. They were poor, but enjoyed a sufficiency of this world's goods; and the result of their poverty was cooperativeness, plain living, freedom from covetousness; a lack of corrupting luxuries and vices; absence of strangers, visitors, and bankers; and consequent freedom from the harms which they might bring. Zuccolo then proceeded to describe a fantastic voyage to the exemplary Republic of Evandria. Its site is remote, and it is further protected by natural barriers. In it wickedness is banished, and a perfect society exists under an annually elected magistracy. Thus Zuccolo's utopia began in glorified reality and was carried to imaginative perfection. In contrast, More started from a consideration of the evils of England and then moved into a speculative dream of an ideal state which he held to be impossible of attainment.

The difference between utopias classified as "ideal" and those grouped as "practical" is one of degree and tendency, but such a difference is quite noticeable if the states of More and Patrizi are compared with those written in the seventeenth century. In general, the latter, influenced no doubt by the Reformation and by developments in natural science, were intended to be practical. Joseph Hall's *Discovery of a New World* is an exception, for it is an academic exercise in burlesque and satire. But the extraordinary utopian efflorescence in the two decades which followed produced in four different countries five accounts of imaginary societies. In varying degrees, all of them may be classified as "practical." Tommaso Campanella not only asserted the practicability of his *City of the Sun*, but participated in a Calabrian revolt to realize his end. I.D.M.'s *Antangil*, though strongly influenced by Plato and More, is obviously intended to be applicable to France in 1616. Bacon's *New Atlantis*, which appeared a decade later, heavily stresses the practical advantages of science and invention; and even Robert Burton's "poetical commonwealth of mine own" proves, on examination, to have realistic reference to the condition of England. Johann Valentin Andreae's Latin utopia, *Christianopolis*, like Campanella's *City of the Sun*, combines metaphysical speculation and immediate applicability.

Sufficient background in the history of utopianism has been given above to make possible a more rapid survey and classification of utopias written before 1850.

One of the main currents was that of communism and socialism. It is traceable back to early accounts of the Golden Age. Developed in the utopias of Plato, Iambulus, and Euhemerus, it recurred in the Middle Ages in such teachings as those of John Ball, which provided an ideological basis for peasant revolts. Thomas More based his *Utopia* on communism but moderated its power by his humanistic stress on education, natural virtues, and the institution of the family. Campanella went to an extreme and provided for community of property and women. After him, for a few decades, communist theory lingered in oral tradition, in poetry about the Golden Age, and in satire. However, in 1652, Gerrard Winstanley published a communist utopia, *The Law of Freedom in a Platform*. Since it is not included in the present anthology, some account of it is necessary. Winstanley was a leader of a tiny group known as the Diggers at the extreme political Left of the Puritan Revolution. As the result of mystical visions and voices he and his fellows attempted to cultivate some rather barren land in Surrey in defiance of those who had property rights over it. Morally their case had some strength, for, having helped to overthrow the despotism of Charles I, they sought to have a small share of England on which they could earn their living. However, when the religious miracle which was expected to fertilize the ground they had chosen failed to materialize, and when landowners and the state interfered with force, they abandoned their attempt. Winstanley's utopia was printed two years later in an effort to persuade Cromwell to set up a somewhat primitivistic communistic system in England.

Winstanley's theme is simple: the earth and its products should belong to all; therefore the land should be returned to its original owners, the people. He decides that the main work of reformation is to reform the clergy, the lawyers, and the law. After reviewing the injustices of economic tyranny, he stresses the favorite seventeenth-century theme of legal and constitutional right, and proves, to his own satisfaction, the laborer's right to the land. He attempts to answer the stock objections to communism, distinguishes between individualism and individuality, and between private and personal property, and halts short of advocating compulsory participation in communism. In his society each man produces for central storehouses from which he draws as his needs demand. The control of this system is under the aegis of clearly expressed laws, strictly enforced. After disposing of freedom to trade, religious freedom, and freedom of inheritance, as bogus types, Winstanley lays down the thesis that true freedom lies where a man receives his nourishment, and that it consists in the free enjoyment of the earth. His description of the governmental function arises out of this conception: "Government," he writes, "is a wise and free ordering of the earth and the manners of mankind by observation of particular laws or rules, so that all the inhabitants may live peaceably in plenty and freedom in the land where they are born and bred." His interpretation of history is a materialistic, economic one. He approaches the doctrine of the dictatorship of the proletariat by confining the vote to men of stern moral character and excluding "kingly" men from the franchise. He describes a pyramided structure of government with an all-powerful "preserver of the peace"—Parliament—at its head. It lacks an executive, but the lack is compensated by the provision of overlapping officials whose only function is to see that the laws are kept. Education is to be severe, comprehensive, and practical. Everyone will follow a trade or profession. Invention and the use of talent will be encouraged. Punishments will take the form of work under a taskmaster. A short civil ceremony will suffice for marriage or divorce. And the institution of the family will be maintained.

Though outwardly "progressive," Winstanley's utopia was retrograde in tendency. It would have resulted in a primitivistic agrarian society inconsistent with the economic development of England and the growth of that country as a great trading nation. But his communism had at least the merit that it was tempered by Christian ethics.

Communism in utopian writing next appeared in *The Australian Land Discovered* by Gabriel de Foigny and *The History of the Sevarites* by Denis Veiras, though it is to be doubted that either of them proposed the abolition of private property with any seriousness. Common ownership of productive goods was more earnestly advocated in the eighteenth century by Morelly in his *Code of Na-*

ture. Francis Babeuf took over his theoretical teachings and attempted to promote them during the French Revolution. Neither of those men wrote a proper utopia, but their teachings probably influenced the author of *Equality or A History of Lithconia*, the first major utopia to be published in America. It was exceptional, for other socialists and communists, Fourier, Saint-Simon, Louis Blanc, Robert Owen, and Proudhon, failed to write proper utopias, but much of their thought is reflected in Étienne Cabet's *A Voyage to Icaria*, one of the most comprehensive communist utopias ever written.

Religious utopias are probably as numerous as communist ones in the period between 1600 and 1850. I.D.M.'s *Antangil*, the first French utopia, is dominated by a type of Puritanism, as are Andreae's *Christianopolis* and Samuel Gott's *Nova Solyma* (London, 1648).

Johann Valentin Andreae's *Christianopolis, the Description of a Christian Commonwealth and Administration* was written in Latin and published at Strassburg in 1619. It has not been included in the present volume because the utopias of I.D.M., Burton, Campanella, and Bacon sufficiently represent the ideal commonwealths of the early seventeenth century. Nevertheless the account merits some consideration.

Andreae (1586–1654) was born at Herrenberg, studied at Tübingen, and traveled widely in Europe. Religious discords in Geneva impressed him unfavorably, but he greatly admired the harmonious unity of customs and morals there. Having entered the Lutheran ministry, he made his congregation at Calw the starting point in an attempt to set up the ideal social system of which he had dreamed ever since his visit to Switzerland. This was the "practical" type of utopianism. His efforts began with the children but soon extended to the working classes at Calw. He organized cloth and dye workers in a mutual protective system supported by free contributions from his friends and parishioners. This association was so successful that it continued into the twentieth century. But Andreae's utopia is "ideal" in type.

Religion, education, morality, and science are the foundation stones of Caphar Salama, "the place of peace" which is the island site of Andreae's utopia. The allegorical content of the work is more considerable than that in Campanella's *City of the Sun*, with which Andreae was familiar. Setting sail in the good ship *Fantasy*, he was shipwrecked on the island which is a miniature of the whole world. Since he was a seeker of truth, he was accepted into the Christian city and well received by its four hundred inhabitants. In it production is carefully planned in advance. Supplies are placed in public storehouses from which the workers receive what they need without the use of money. Life is simple and untainted by luxuries.

Although production and distribution are communistic, houses are inhabited by couples and meals are private. Great attention is paid to education, particularly to the advancement of science and its application to agriculture and industry. Working hours are short, because the laborers are industrious and efficient. Leisure time is devoted primarily to the service of God, the avoidance of temptations, and growth in virtue. Government is by eight men and eight subordinates all full of the spirit of Christianity. "Never have I seen so great an amount of Christian perfection collected into one place." "Their first and highest exertion is to worship God with a pure and faithful soul; the second, to strive towards the highest and chastest morals; and the third, to develop the mental powers." They prize these qualities in men: equality, the desire for peace, and contempt for riches, and, above all, culture of the soul. "The chief point with them is that Christians ought to be different from the world around, in morals as well as religion. . . . They declare that the Gospels require a government different from that of the world."

Thus Christianopolis is the City of God, the communion of practicing Christians throughout the world, symbolized in Andreae's theocratic community.

Samuel Gott's *Nova Solyma, the New Jerusalem* is a livelier work, descriptive of a far less ascetic religious commonwealth. It is couched in the form of a romance of intrigues and adventures. They integrate poorly with his holy community dedicated to God and the bourgeois virtues. Other Puritan works such as Richard Baxter's *A Holy Commonwealth* (1656) and John Eliot's *The Christian Commonwealth* (1659) describe theocracies, but are on the outskirts of Utopia. After 1660, few utopias are classifiable as dedicated primarily to Christianity. Joseph Glanvill's continuation of Bacon's *New Atlantis*, published at the end of his volume of *Essays* in 1676, centers upon religion but is better regarded as an exposition of the doctrines of the Cambridge Latitudinarians than as a proper utopia. However it is interesting to note that Glanvill apparently regarded the utopian genre as the most effective form in which to propound his ideas.

The Christian element in utopias written after 1660 undoubtedly declined, but not the interest in religion. More's Utopians had practiced a naturalistic religion. Following his precedent a series of deistic and libertine utopias appeared in the late seventeenth and eighteenth centuries. The utopias of Foigny and Veiras, Tyssot de Patot's *Voyage of James Massey* (1710), Mercier's *Memoirs of the year 2500* (1770), and G. A. Ellis's *New Britain* (1820), all devote chapters to natural religion and deistic speculations. These are also echoed by Cabet.

Natural science is also important in utopian thought. Bacon's concentration upon it was anticipated slightly by More, largely by Campanella, probably by Andreae, and mildly by Robert Burton (in the utopia which the latter included in the first and second edition of his *Anatomy of Melancholy*). Later editions of the last-mentioned work showed the influence of Baconian science. Likewise under the influence of Bacon, Gott paid some attention to scientific experimentation in his *Nova Solyma,* and Winstanley wrote what is probably his finest prose passage in praise of science. In 1660, *New Atlantis Continued* by R. H. was devoted to adulation of monarchy and glorification of the possibilities of science. Thenceforth nearly all utopias paid some attention to the importance of science in a perfected society. This element is particularly noticeable in the utopias of Mercier and Cabet.

Militarism is also a leading theme in utopias written before 1850. Plato set the precedent of devoting a whole class to the protection of society. Thomas More also paid great attention to the military aspects of his *Utopia,* not that he favored militarism as such, but that realism demanded its inclusion. It is startling to find that his highly moral Utopians, who would have despised bribery at home or any hiring of one free man by another, used both hired soldiers and bribery in wars. The author of *Antangil* may well have been a soldier, for militarism is one of his main preoccupations. The problems of war and peace, defense, military organization, and the like also receive special attention from James Harrington in the various utopias which he wrote in the middle of the seventeenth century; militarism is also stressed by Veiras, and by Foigny (who makes the wars of the Australians against natural and human enemies an integral part of his plot), and, indeed, by almost all the utopias up to 1850. A. G. Ellis, for example, in *New Britain,* is especially concerned with military problems and organization, though he does not allow them to be dominant in his society, as I.D.M. had done in *Antangil.*

The main theme of utopias from 1500 to 1850 was advocacy, explicit or implicit, of the fullest possible, efficient utilization of the available resources of men and materials in a given society. Conservatives found this a means of supporting established ideas, institutions, and ways of life. Radicals, intent upon such total utilization, advocated a revolution in ideas and institutions as necessary to their goal. In general, the conservatives, Bacon, for example, looked to science tempered by morals and religion as the chief means to this full exploitation of resources. Radicals like Cabet, looked less to science than to education and institutional reforms.

However, not all utopists regarded the material basis of society as primary in their utopias. Fénelon and G. A. Ellis, for example, saw the value of the simple life, uncomplicated by luxuries and their accompanying vices. This ascetic, somewhat primitivistic current in utopian thought derived largely from More and was greatly influenced by Rousseau.

Utopias from 1600 to 1850 may be roughly classified in their historical development, as follows. The imaginary states of I.D.M., Campanella, Andreae, Burton, and Bacon constituted what might be called the Utopian Efflorescence of the earlier seventeenth century. Although they vary greatly from each other, all these writers were influenced by Plato and More; all stress the application of modern science in society; all are optimistic in outlook and show the influence of the idea of progress, which previously had not been widespread. These utopias were written between 1600 and 1630. Then a current of utopian fantasy revived—a continuation of the tradition of fantastic voyages which dates back to Iambulus and Euhemerus, and which was frequently echoed in the Middle Ages in such works as *The Anticlaudian* of Alain de Lille and in the voyage of Astolfo to the moon in Ariosto's *Orlando Furioso*. The imaginary societies described by Rabelais and by Joseph Hall in his *Discovery of a New World* were in the same tradition. In 1638 it revived with *The Man in the Moon*, by Francis Godwin, which was rapidly followed by John Wilkins' *Discourse concerning a New World and Another Planet* (1640). Further fantastic celestial voyages and satirical accounts of imaginary commonwealths are contained in D'Ablancourt's translation of Lucian's *True History*, a work of the later period of ancient Greek civilization. Indeed, Lucian may be regarded as the father of this type of superterrestrial "science fiction." D'Ablancourt added a supplement of his own to the *True History* and published both about 1648. The tradition continued in Cyrano de Bergerac's *Comical History* (1656 and 1662), with its satirical accounts of societies on the moon and sun.

Meanwhile Puritan utopianism came to the fore. The tradition established by I.D.M. and Andreae branched into romance literature with Samuel Gott's *Nova Solyma* (1648). The Levellers of the Puritan Revolution had many utopian ideas but failed to write a work in this genre. However, Digger communism produced such a work in Winstanley's *Law of Freedom*. Meanwhile the Fifth Monarchist Puritans propounded semiutopian conceptions of a Kingdom of Christ shortly to be established on earth; and Baxter and Eliot approached the utopian type in *A Holy Commonwealth* and *The Christian Commonwealth*, both of which appeared in 1659. But as secularism began to prevail over Puritanism, less theocratic imaginary states were described: such were Samuel Hartlib's *Macaria* (1641), which was strongly influenced by Bacon; *The Poor Man's Advocate*, by Peter Chamberlen (1649); Robert Norwood's *Pathway unto*

England's Perfect Settlement (1653); Peter Plockhoy's *Way to the Peace and Settlement of these Nations,* and similar works. Few of these completely satisfy the definition of a proper utopia, but all of them propound economic programs intended to realize something approaching a perfect society. Parallel to them were a host of political utopias and related works. These put forth model constitutions. Such were Marchamont Nedham's *Excellency of a Free State* (1656), the anonymous *Chaos* (1659), William Sprigge's *Modest Plea for an Equal Commonwealth* (1659), the various utopias penned by James Harrington, especially his *Oceana* (1656), and a royalist work written in Latin by a Frenchman in England—*Sydromedia* by Antoine Le Grand (1669).

Cyrano de Bergerac's *Comical History* may be classified as the first of a series of French libertine utopias. After England had her Revolution, utopianism declined there, except for semiutopian schemes written largely under the influence of Harrington, of which the anonymous *Free State of Noland* (1696) is representative. But in France the ideological undermining of the *ancien régime* had still to take place, and a potent force in that direction were the libertine utopias by Cyrano, Veiras, Foigny, Claude Gilbert, and Tyssot de Patot. In general, the outlook of these writers was heterodox. Not infrequently blasphemous, they questioned the established orthodoxies of religion, morals, and politics in their period.

German utopianism lagged behind that of the rest of Europe. If Andreae's Latin work is excepted, the first German utopia was the anonymous *State of Ophir (Ophirischer Staat),* a comprehensive, pedestrian, earnest, prodigiously long work published in 1699. It has been largely neglected by scholars, and, like the Latin utopia, *Icaria* (1637), by Joannes Bisselius, deserves further attention. But for reasons of space, both have been omitted from the present anthology.

In the eighteenth century, the fantastic voyage tradition continued and resulted in the semiutopian land of the Houyhnhnms in Swift's *Gulliver's Travels,* and in such works as Simon Berington's *Gaudentio di Lucca.* Ludvig Holberg followed the precedent of Swift in *The Voyages of Niels Klim* (1741); and the constitutional type of utopia, combined with a modified communism, recurred in the accounts of Spensonia by Thomas Spence about 1800. But for the most part, though rich in Rousseauistic and utopian socialist theories, the eighteenth century produced few utopias. *Memoirs of the Year 2500* by Sebastien Mercier, published in French in 1770, is therefore noteworthy. Its intrinsic value is slight, but its historical interest is great, for, in some measure, it forecasts the French Revolution. Moreover, it reflects the sentimentality, the optimism, and, to some extent, the

Rousseauism of the eighteenth century; and it anticipates Romanticism.

The socialist theories of the eighteenth century persisted into the nineteenth in the communism of *Lithconia*, first published in 1802. But the outstanding communist utopia written between 1800 and 1850 was Étienne Cabet's *Voyage to Icaria* (1840). Superficially the picture of a communist society which it presents has some attractiveness, but gradually the reader becomes aware of its monotonous uniformity, the deadening of individual initiative which would result from it, the childishness of its propaganda, and its constant curbs upon personal freedom. Nevertheless, it is significant in the present day for the light it throws on the techniques of modern communist propaganda, and because an analysis of it permits an understanding of the workings of the communist mind, particularly of a certain naïve optimism in it. Readers of *Icaria* who are acquainted with the history of communism and communist experiments in action will discover a wide gap between the theoretical workings of such a society and its actual operation in a real world. They will do well to remember Harrington's observation, that a description of a state functioning in theory should not lead one to regard it as practicable or to prefer it before the lessons of experienced reality and tested success.

In contrast, despite its awkward style, there is a refreshing attractiveness in the simple, democratic, cooperative agrarianism of G. A. Ellis's *New Britain* (1820). The work is far from profound, but it breathes a spirit of genuineness and respect for human individuality which is all too often absent from utopian literature and from attempts to realize utopia in practice.

Note: For the distinction between "ideal" and "practical" utopias, we are indebted to Rodolfo de Mattei, "Contenuto ed Origini dell'Utopia Cittadina nel Seicento," Revista Internazionale di Filosofia de Diritto, *IX (1929), 414-425.*

17

The Discovery of a New World

or, A Description of the South Indies, Hitherto Unknown

By an English Mercury

Joseph Hall

(Translated by John Healey)

London
1609?
(first published in Latin at Frankfort in 1605)

Joseph Hall (1574–1656),

who later became Bishop of Norwich and Exeter, wrote *Mundus Alter et Idem* (A New World, and yet the Same) about 1601–05. The Latin original, published at Frankfort about 1605, was frequently reprinted and translated during the seventeenth century. The world described is a topsy-turvy one, where the vices of Europe become virtues, and ways of living are opposite to the professed morality of his readers. Perhaps it would be more accurate to say that the worst practices of European man are described as the regular modes of life in the Southern World, except that Hall's imaginary peoples have moralities and religions which sanction such practices. His work anticipates Samuel Butler's *Erewhon* and Aldous Huxley's *Brave New World*. The *Mundus Alter et Idem* is *utopia* in the sense of *nowhere;* but it is the opposite of *eutopia*, the ideal society: it is a *dystopia*, if it is permissible to coin a word.

Hall's new world is Europe upside down and, accordingly, is situated in the Antipodes. In the account of it, man, his vices, and the Roman Catholic religion are satirized; the wonderful travel tales of the Middle Ages are burlesqued; the erudite are ridiculed; earnest utopias are mocked; and the corrupt manners of all ages are satirized.

Hall's new world consists of four countries: Crapulia, or Tenterbelly, a land of gluttons, inhabited by gourmands and drunkards; Viraginia, land of viragoes and shrews; Moronia, the country of fools; and Lavernia, peopled by brigands and mountebanks. The main allegory, which binds the work together, is that of a traveler's journey through life. The voyager, Mercurius, a plain but inexperienced Englishman, is a scholar ignorant of many ways of the world. The contrast between his relative innocence and the immorality, folly, and sensuality of the new world brings out the strangeness and enormities of the societies described. Swift used the same device in *Gulliver's Travels*.

The author of a dystopia must have a mental picture of the reality which he is satirizing in the description of an imaginary country; and in the back of his mind, he must have a fairly clear concept of his ideal state. He describes this by antithesis, suggesting how life ought to be by depicting it as it ought not to be. He uses the material which a utopist ordinarily omits, and glorifies vices rather than virtues. By so doing, he reduces the attractiveness of the evil and foolish to absurdity. Indirectly he creates a model of the good and beautiful society in his readers' minds.

In the Crapulian province of Eat-allia, birds fatten so much that they cannot fly away; and fish jump to the hook. Marchpaine, the metropolitan city, is ruled by the fattest citizens. The streets are paved smooth so that the inhabitants do not have to lift their feet.

Eating but one meal a day is a crime. To belch is honorable, and to glut, divine. The inhabitants worship the God Trine (the fork) because he eats up all things.

The soil of Viraginia, or Shee-landt, is fruitful "but badly husbanded." A matriarchal system holds sway. There are no laws. Everything is decided by the number of voices, and parliament is constantly in session.

In populous Moronia or Fooliana, the traveler finds continual talk and a set of Foolosophers. A man is considered wise if he talks to no purpose. In one province, the inhabitants constantly change the plans of cities and wear feathers for clothing: what is good enough for birds is good enough for them. In their university, every man is his own teacher. A College of Gew-gawcasters invent novelties: "He that first devised to blow out bubbles of soap or spittle forth of walnut shell is of as great renown among them as ever was the first printer or gunfounder amongst us of Europe."

In Fooliana the Fat, all claim to be gentlemen: many have pedigrees which go back long before the world was created. Some give banquets once a year and then starve to pay for them. Another group have long names and prolix titles and live chiefly on smoking.

The chief importance of Hall's *Mundus* is as a precursor of utopian literature in the seventeenth century. He propounds no systematic doctrines, and though his dystopias reflect certain interests and tendencies and vices of his period, these are better revealed elsewhere. The figures satirized are universal types, so that Hall gives little information about the problems of his own age and country.

The following brief extracts are from Joseph Healey's translation, which appeared about 1609. His version of Hall's text is quick and boisterous, whereas the original is dignified and ironical. The work exemplifies the satirical possibilities of the utopian genre.

BIBLIOGRAPHY:
Joseph Hall, *The Discovery of a New World*, edited by Huntington Brown (Cambridge, Mass., 1937); Sandford M. Salyer, "Renaissance Influences in Hall's *Mundus Alter et Idem*," *Philological Quarterly*, VI, (Oct., 1927), 324 ff.

The Discovery of a New World

The Discovery of a New World

THE FIRST BOOK. THE DISCOVERY OF THE LAND OF
TENTER-BELLY

CHAPTER IX: THE LAWS OF THE LAND

Gourmands' Hall is a very fair, large house, statefully set forth with arched bay windows, and upon the front of the entrance are these words fairly engraved in letters of gold, TO REVEL, AND TO METHOD, and under it were these verses engraven: *Frolic fatness here doth dwell: keep leanness out and all goes well.* And within, there hung a table chained to a marble pillar, containing these sacred and inviolable laws.

BE IT ENACTED,

1. *That eating but one meal a day, be henceforth held for a capital transgression.*
2. *That he that overthrows a full dish or a cup rashly, or howsoever, be forthwith by virtue of this statute enjoined to stand upright on his feet, and having a dish of broth set between his heels, to eat it all up with a thimble.*
3. *That none eat alone, nor violate the laws of the table by any private suppers; but that every citizen do eat either in the streets or in an open window, upon pain of eating his next meal with his heels upward.*
4. *That whosoever forbeareth to sleep or eat four hours together, do satisfy the state by eating two suppers.*
5. *Yet if the mouth be full, it shall be sufficient to give an answer by holding up the finger.*
6. *That conspirators be forthwith starved to death, and other malefactors punished by the loss of a tooth.*
7. *That all cooks that dress not their meat according to the judicious palate be immediately bound unto stakes, and flesh half roasted hung by them, until some pitiful and hungry spectator take compassion on them, and eat it all up.*
8. *That to belch be held not only lawful, but honorable also: and that the government of the next future feast be assigned unto him that broke wind the strongest at the last.*
9. *That if anyone hold his breath while his belly is a-measuring, he be forthwith made uncapable of all advancement, and condemned to fast one whole day in a grate, where he may behold the rest of the Alderguts at dinner and supper.*

10. *That every man's weekly mangery be brought in a billa vera* [official report] *by his fellow Gourmand . . . to be recorded, and withal that if he have not fulfilled the law in that case enacted, he may be accordingly fined.*

SIGNED: ALL-PAUNCH

Those that are the least offenders are put for four and twenty hours into the Temple of Famine, a prison directly contrary unto our insane asylum. It stands without the city as Aesculap's temple stood without Rome, but not for health's sake (as Plutarch said how that did) but only lest such as are condemned unto that jail should so much as once scent the air of the kitchen. The walls of it are all painted about with all manner of good victuals, only to excite the prisoner's appetite unto his greater plague, and verily one Jesuit or other hath seen these walls, and thereupon devised pictures for their Chambers of Meditation. They use no money. "What have we to do," say they, "with these sapless and unsavory metals?" No, they follow that ancient custom that Aristotle records, and barter goods for goods by way of exchange. Two sparrows is the price of a stare, two stares for a blackbird, two blackbirds for a hen, two hens for a goose, two geese for a lamb, two lambs for a calf; two calves for a goat, and two goats for a cow. And thus they do also in fish and roots, at a set price. The businessmen especially care about this, that neither their stuff be too bad, nor price too great.

THE SECOND BOOK. THE DESCRIPTION OF SHEE-LANDT, OR WOMANDECOIA

CHAPTER III: THE FORMS OF GOVERNMENT AMONG THE GOSSIPPINGOESSES, AND THEIR ELECTIONS OF PERSONS OF STATE

Their state (for aught that I could observe) is popular, each one seeking superiority, and avoiding obedience. They have no laws at all, but do everything by the numbers of voices. But the giving up of their voices struck me into a wonder, being unacquainted therewith, for they set up a cry all together; none gives ear, but each one yells as if she were horn-mad. Is not this able to abash a good man's spirit?

They hold a continual parliament about their more weighty affairs of state, so that Erasmus, were he alive now, would be able to give a strong testimony of women turning suitors. Now this continuance is necessary because of their laws' uncertainty: for the decrees of this day may be all disannulled tomorrow, but the same day they cannot, lest their lawgivers should seem inconstant in their edicts. Everyone's voice is alike in worth the whole city through, but not everyone's dignity; for they have a set number of chosen women (they call them Gravesses), and these have the authority of most honor in each particular city. But they are not born to this dignity, but elected either for their beauty or their eloquence, for by these two are all elections ordered. They had once a custom to elect these Gravesses by voices, but afterwards, everyone giving her voice only for herself, it bred a confusion, and so made them abolish that manner of election; and then they made a decree that only those should have the sway in this envious contention who would profess themselves neither fair nor eloquent. But this brought all to such a pass that in the whole multitude of them you should not find one that would be Electress, the elder sort holding that they had the eloquence, and the younger standing as firm in it that they had the beauty. At length they all agree to pass over these places of Electresses to twelve of the most aged matrons of Old Mumpington (a ruinous village hard by), and so they did, giving them the glorious title of Electresses Gravessiall, to set them the more agog to perform their charges. And besides this honorable style, the honey of age, wealth, and abundance comes continually upon them; for the ambitious young wenches will so bribe and ply them with gifts, to have their voices at the day of election, that I hold there is not a court either more corrupt in giving voices, or more wealthy in given riches. Instead of scepters and swords, the Gravesses have fans and glasses borne before them—huge crystal glasses [mirrors]—and still as they pass through the streets, they prank up their attires by the said glasses, and set all their gewgaws in order as they go along.

THE THIRD BOOK. THE DISCOVERY OF FOOLIANA

CHAPTER IV, SECTION 2: OF THE DUKE AND THE IN-HABITANTS OF SOLITARIA THE SAD

The Duke of Solitaria is generally called by the name of Grumbledoro the Great, a testy and severe man, whose subjects are as like in conditions unto him, as they are unlike to all the rest of the other Foolianders. He hath a huge and spacious palace called Hearts-grief-Court, built all of ebony and jet, in a most magnificent kind of structure. Over the porch are these words enchased in coral: *This is the place where sorrow dwells, and care. Fly far, far hence, all you that mirthful are.*

The people of this nation are generally all hair-begrown, lean, slovenly, swarthy-complexioned, rough-headed, sternly-visaged, and heavy-eyed, fixing their looks as in amazement, and seldom moving their eyeballs: their optic organs stand far into their heads, making them look like so many hollow-eyed skulls. Here it is in vain to look either for city or village: they dwell every man in a place far from other, as hares choose their seats, and profess a kind of life most truly hermitical, partly because they are of too suspicious and fearful a nature to dwell in company, and partly because the Duke hath expressly forbidden all men to build any one house within the sight of another, or within the distance of thus many miles from any habitation whatsoever. They seldom or never stir forth adoors, partly for the continual darkness that covereth all this climate, and partly for their own and their Prince's pleasures. And when they do go abroad they do very seldom salute anyone they meet, for this is one statute in their laws: *Let no man stir abroad but upon necessity, nor salute any man he meets but upon Thursdays.* Go to any of their houses, and knock at the door, you shall stand a good while to cool your toes, and at last be sent away with a snappish answer, for they are the most unsociable creatures under the cope of heaven. But how do they spend their time, think you? Faith, in imagining and framing fictions to themselves of things never done nor never likely to be done, in believing these their fictions, and in following these beliefs. This is the reason why they abhor company, and hate to be interrupted in their airy castle-buildings.

18

An Account fo the Great and Wonderful Kingdom of Antangil

Unknown until the Present Time to All Historians and Cosmographers: Composed of Twenty-Six Highly Beautiful and very Fertile Provinces. With a Description of them and of their Unparalleled Polity, both Civil and Military. Also, an Account of the Education of their Youth, and of their Religion.

I.D.M.

G.T.

Leyden (i.e. Saumur)
1616

The author of this, the earliest utopia in the French language, has not been identified. His chief stress is upon militarism and a Protestantism which resembles that of the Church of England, although the latter is not mentioned. Government is conducted under a constitutional monarch by two chambers elected under a limited suffrage. Great stress is laid upon class distinction, ceremony, uniforms, display, piety, decorum, governmental stability, and armed forces. The real control of the country is in the hands of a carefully educated, privileged, but functional aristocracy. Economic matters receive little attention. The author obviously had read Plato and More, but his own work remained obscure and had little if any influence. A summary follows, with brief extracts translated from the original French edition (Saumur, 1616), by the present editor.

BIBLIOGRAPHY: The utopia is summarized in the Appendix of *Les Successeurs de Cyrano de Bergerac*, ed. Frédéric Lachèvre (Paris, 1922); the full text, prepared by the same editor, was published in Paris in 1933 as *La Première Utopie Française. Le Royaume d'Antangil.*

Antangil

[The author, having arrived in Java in 1598, heard a description of a great kingdom from its ambassador. According to him, Antangil stretches south of Java from the Indian Ocean to Antarctic mountains and is rectangular in shape except that a huge gulf cuts into the north coast. Four navigable rivers cross the country and flow into this gulf. The inhabitants were converted to Christianity by a disciple of St. Thomas named Byrachil, who died a martyr's death in one of the neighboring pagan lands.]

Some two thousand, two hundred years ago, this great expanse of country which we have described was owned by various kings, princes, lords, and republics. Because of the bad order which prevailed in their government and because of the multiplicity of commanders, the rulers were continually involved in unending wars and disputes. They had rendered the land almost desert as a result of the battles and customary massacres which they inflicted on each other because of the ambition and jealousy with which each held his estate. Finally the wisest men, wearying of this continual disorder and perceiving their all too evident ruin, assembled with the kings and princes and the ambassadors of the republics in a neutral, convenient place. They swore to each other by all the gods which they worshiped, to accept and to obey inviolably whatever would be resolved upon and determined in this blessed assembly. After this, each proposed the type of government which he judged the most proper, useful, and suitable for the conservation alike of the nobility, the town-dwellers, and the common people.

Finally when all things had been weighed, debated, and ripely considered, they ordered this flourishing monarchy in the manner described below, in such a way that one must believe that God, enemy of all disorder and confusion, presided over this venerable assembly; for human beings could not possibly have reduced such a deplorable condition into such perfection that for two thousand, two hundred years there has been no need to disturb, change, or alter any of the laws, statutes, and policies which were then set up.

[A hundred and twenty provinces form the kingdom; each contains a hundred towns and villages and a capital city. The households in them are grouped in tens, hundreds, thousands, tens of thousands, and hundreds of thousands. The most able and intelligent father of a family in such a group of ten households commands their inhabitants, supervises their morals, ascertains exactly the value of all goods owned by every household, and prevents disputes among them. If his orders are not obeyed, he appeals to the leaders of the Hundred to which he belongs; they have power to enforce obedience with any punishment short of death.

[Government is exercised by a King, a Viceroy, and two councils: a Senate or Royal Council, and an Estates General or Parliament; but the King's power is only nominal. He presides over the Senate, receives ambassadors, and commands armies if he is present with them—with the assistance of ten senators—but he has no power to inflict punishment. The Senate is elected by the Estates General and is composed of one hundred learned personages who are the greatest in the Kingdom, not in riches, credit, and power, but in excellence and goodness: they are men who love the public more than themselves and are at least forty years old. The Senate is sovereign: it chooses the King and the Viceroy, makes war and peace, and concludes alliances. It also names judges and punishes or deposes them if they attempt to upset or modify anything concerning the state. The only restriction on the Senators' power is that when provincial rights are involved, the Estates General has a deliberative voice to agree, refuse, or modify. Senators are well paid and are provided with magnificent lodgings near the royal palace.

[The Estates General is composed of three representatives from each Province: a noble, a city-dweller, and a villager. These representatives—360 in all—are elected for one year. During that year they reside in Sangil, the national capital, and advise the King and Senate on all matters affecting the public welfare. The Estates General accepts or rejects the decisions of the King and Senate, sends orders to the Provinces to have decisions carried out, and brings official matters and complaints from the Provinces to the attention of the council.

[The expenses of government are met by means of revenues from state-owned mines, the income thus derived being about four million pieces of gold annually, and by means of similar revenues from state-owned agricultural lands, woods, lakes, rivers, ponds, herds and flocks; these bring in an additional six millions. The state does not manage these sources of wealth itself but rents them out annually, choosing by lot, in each instance, between the highest bidder and the holder of the franchise in the previous year. Rents are paid twice a year in the provincial capitals to treasurers, each of whom is assisted by two clerks and by ten sergeants, who are there to enforce payment; they have power to seize and sell property and to imprison those who fail to make their payments. If the funds received are insufficient, everyone is taxed in proportion to the value of his property, that value being known to the head men in the groups of ten households. Resisters are imprisoned. Great attention is paid to militarism, for, "men being more inclined to evil than to good, to ruptures than to friendship, and to war than peace, the Council wished to have always ready a strong force to restrain them and to keep them on the path of duty. Moreover, neighbors are always ready to attack those who are without defense."

[Accordingly military service is compulsory for all able-bodied men from nineteen to fifty-five years old. Military exercises begin at school. Refusal to participate involves loss of civil rights or punishment in the galleys. Deserters are hanged. The higher ranks of the army are recruited almost entirely from the nobility. Nobles who have an annual income of five hundred pounds are required to maintain a serviceable horse for fighting purposes; those who have a greater income maintain proportionately more horses. In time of war, these are made available to the poorer nobles. The soldiers elect the captains, and the captains appoint sergeants and other officers.

[The nation is divided into two categories of citizens, one consisting of the nobles and the rich commoners, and the other, of the mass of the commoners. Those in the first of these groups are educated in arts and sciences by distinguished professors in a national Academy, or in Academies in the provincial capitals. Fees are paid by each student in proportion to the value of his family's possessions, the surplus from the contributions of the wealthy being used for the expenses of the poorer nobles.

[Education at the Academy is divided into three stages, from age six to age twelve, from twelve to eighteen, and from eighteen to twenty-four. In the primary stage, students are first taught to read and write. Grammar, poetry, history, music and some elementary principles of geometry and cosmography are then taught to them.]

At the next stage, the subjects read are rhetoric, mathematics, logic, physics, and metaphysics, along with the study of the finest and most elegant orators and the best parts of medicine. In addition, in spare time such as that after dinner and supper, students are taught designing, painting, architecture, fortification, and perspective; but they always continue with the music and other exercises which began in the primary stage. They also confer with each other and engage in discussions after lessons are finished; thus they confirm what they have learned and render their minds sharp and subtle. . . .

In the third stage, the same exercises are continued, and in addition the pupils learn the laws and ordinances of the Kingdom during two of these years; they also learn how to speak in public for ordinary purposes and they practice speaking for the law courts so as to render themselves experts in judging controversies soundly and in understanding the formalities of the law.

If some are inclined to theology, they may study it and, according to their capacity, be fitted for ecclesiastical honors and duties, as explained above. Indeed, the most religious and accomplished scholars are urged by those in charge of the Academy to enter the ministry, it being the most worthy and most excellent profession of all, for it has God and Religion for its end.

In the remaining four years, they receive practical training and confirm what they have learned. If a war breaks out, they can leave the Academy at the age of twenty and bear arms. Otherwise they must stay until the age of twenty-four, but with liberty to go to the city and to the court and to move about in them: this is not permitted to the others.

[A detailed account of the thorough military training of the youth follows. They engage in realistic mock battles. The following comment is significant:] And the most pleasing of all these combats occurs when the young artisans of the city set themselves to attack or defend the fort against the students of the Academy, for then one sees the notable difference which exists between men who are well fed and exercised and men who are soft, effeminate and lacking enterprise and valor. Such combats greatly encourage these little nurselings of Mars [the students] and give great satisfaction to the King, the Senate and all the nobility of the Kingdom when they see their children well instructed, valiant, and active. For no one [of the nobility] dares to educate his children separately at home, be-

cause they would therefore be forever barred from public positions.
No one is chosen for such positions unless he has been educated in
the Academy, or, if he is a commoner, unless he has done great and
outstanding services which surpass or at least equal the finest deeds
of the nobility. For, in order not to take away from the common
people the desire to do well, it was decided not to cut them off
completely from the road to the honors and dignities of the state.

[Every morning the scholars get up at four o'clock, dress, say
their prayers, read and interpret the catechism and the commandments of God, sing a psalm, listen to a one-hour sermon, and attend
classes until eight o'clock, at which time they eat some bread. Then,
until eleven-thirty, they participate in physical exercises, games,
and contests of all kinds, in order to harden and develop their bodies.
Lunch follows, and after it thanks are given to God through vocal
and instrumental music.

[Education for ordinary commoners is rudimentary. In each
parish, schoolmasters and schoolmistresses teach reading, writing,
arithmetic, the catechism, and the main points of the Christian religion, to both boys and girls. Outstanding pupils are sent to the
Academy and educated without charge if their parents cannot pay
the fees: such pupils become teachers. The other students, upon
graduation, are used to fill public offices. Names are drawn by lot
for them to undertake such duties for one year in the provinces.
Then, after praise or blame for their conduct, lots are again drawn
for another year's service. The same procedure is then repeated, and
thus all state officials are appointed.] Those of the nobility who have
the means accept no public money, for in their opinion it is more
honorable to give and to be generous than to accept when there is
no necessity. . . . As for those who are poor, . . . they are given
three hundred pounds in addition to the hundred which they receive
for the upkeep of their horse. As a result, with this pay and pension
they support themselves quite decently. . . . What also helps them
greatly is the liberality of their rich colleagues and companions:
nothing is dearer to these than their friends, and they have amongst
themselves what is almost a community of all possessions. . . .

[The door of the Academy is not closed to these men when they
wish to go there, although it is closed to all others, whoever they
are, for the Council is unwilling to have so many fine teachings communicated to strangers and to the common people. . . .

[In brief, all the chief offices, honors, and dignities are in the
hands of those who attended the Academy; but the people do not
object, for they are justly and equitably governed by these men,
and the way is left open for anyone who has the capability, so that
he can arrive at dignities like those which we have described. . . .

[The Antangillians observe two sacraments in their form of Christianity: baptism, which, they believe, washes away original sin, giving entrance to the Kingdom of God; and holy communion, which feeds the soul and unites it with Jesus Christ. They believe that without works one cannot be saved, since works are a necessary sign of true faith. They neither pray for the dead, nor seek the intercession of the Saints; and they deny the doctrine that there is a Purgatory. Except for the Cross, which is regarded as a symbol of the death and passion of Jesus, their temples contain no statues, images, or representations. Fasting is enjoined on the day before Easter, Pentecost, Christmas and the Annunciation, but abstinence from meat on Fridays and in Lent is not observed. No ecclesiastic has power superior to other bishops and priests except in matters of order and decorum. Ecclesiastics are expected to lead frugal and sober lives, eating only two meals a day; they are not permitted to be alone with women other than their wives, mothers, and sisters; and chastity is strongly urged upon them. Banquets are permitted to the clergy only under dignified circumstances out of the public eye; games and physical exercises other than discreet walks are forbidden to them. Their houses are plain and provided only with necessities. Their children are well educated and, like their mothers, modestly attired. But public officials are elaborately dressed and attended:] It is very becoming to a great prince and to everyone of authority to be honorably dressed and accompanied when he appears in public. For the luster of clothing and a pompous following inspire inestimable respect and reverence . . . ; people judge that such persons are full of virtue and merit since they bear its marks and signs.

19

The City of the Sun
or, The Idea of a Republic

Tommaso Campanella
Translated specially for this volume by
William J. Gilstrap

(first published in Latin at Frankfort in 1623)

Tommaso Campanella (1568–1639),

born of illiterate parents in Italy, became a most erudite man in a period distinguished for its culture. At the age of fourteen he entered the Dominican Order and six years later fell under the influence of the Jewish astrologist, Abraham, from whom he derived his occult philosophy, and of the rationalist, Telesio, the chief source of his belief in experimental philosophy. Both of these men were opponents of scholastic philosophy, then prevalent throughout Europe. Campanella likewise opposed this philosophy with its stress on logic based on propositions accepted on grounds of authority.

In 1591 Campanella was tried for heresy but was absolved from the charge that communication with spirits was the source of his prodigious knowledge. However, further charges were pressed against him in 1593 and he was imprisoned in Padua. Five years later he returned to Calabria. His interest in astrology was great, and he expected a grand celestial conjunction in 1603, which would bring the universal kingdom of the saints. The year 1600 was one of transition, and Calabria was to give the first example of the true City of God. Accordingly, he supported a plot to liberate the country from the Spaniards with the aid of the Turks. The outbreak was easily suppressed, and Campanella was imprisoned for rebellion and heresy. Despite considerable torture, which was intended to extract a confession from him, he remained firm but was sentenced to perpetual imprisonment. Thereafter, in jail, he was allowed to write in peace. Freed and pensioned in 1629 by Pope Urban VIII, Campanella went to Rome and dreamt of founding, with the aid of the Papacy, a renovated Christianity, a natural religion in which rationalism and mysticism would be combined, a religion which, by force of argument, would reconcile in the bosom of a universal church, Catholics, Protestants, Jews, pagans, and Mahometans. As early as 1599 he had propounded a parallel scheme for the establishment of a universal monarchy under the Spanish crown. In 1635, despairing of the Spaniards, he went to France and proposed to Richelieu that the French should realize the universal monarchy, joining all peoples in an imperial unity of regenerated Christian faith.

Campanella wrote over one hundred works. They cover almost every aspect of human activity and interest, especially philosophy. The utopian genre was admirably suited to his wide range of erudition and experience, for it is a flexible and readily adaptable medium in which almost any ideas and schemes can be synthesized. Certainly *The City of the Sun* is comprehensive. First written in 1602, it was several times revised and rewritten, sometimes in Italian, and sometimes in Latin, the language in which it was first printed, in 1623.

The utopia is Campanella's most characteristic work: it reveals his polemical nature, his grandiose schemes, his paradoxical fusion of rationalism and mysticism, and his indefatigable ingenuity and learning. The description of the *City of the Sun* has been interpreted as variously as More's *Utopia*: different critics see in it an academic speculation, an escapist dream, an idyll, a precise goal for the Calabrian rising to realize, a glorification of the Papacy, a truly Christian society, a highly unorthodox naturalistic state, a return to primitive Christianity, a glorification of paganism, a sensual and somewhat disgusting scheme, a hodgepodge of contradictory notions, an imitation of the utopias of Plato and More, a ruthlessly logical application of philosophical principles, and a forerunner of Marxism, Fascism, scientific materialism, or liberalism. Almost any interpretation and its opposite seem to have been imposed on the work.

The chief cause of these contradictory interpretations is that critics tend to approach utopias with preconceived ideas and to discover and stress only those aspects which are pleasing to them. Marxists, for example, twist the common ownership in More's *Utopia* and in *The City of the Sun* into conformity with their own notions. But Campanella's Solarians do not have equal enjoyment of the common property: a minimum of necessities is accorded to all; but beyond that, goods are given to each man not according to his needs, as Marxist theory teaches, but according to his merits. In clothing and in food, the best goes to those who are apt and zealous in the service of the state.

Another cause of misinterpreting utopias is failure to look at the total work—a danger which readers of the present anthology must guard against. For example, Bacon's attention to science in *New Atlantis* should not be allowed to hide the fact that he also included long sections on the coming of the Christian revelation to Bensalem and on the Feast of the Family. Likewise it should be remembered that a lengthy account of the military side of life in *The City of the Sun* and several paragraphs of complicated astrology have not been included in Campanella's text below, although these aspects are sufficiently indicated in what remains. Such omissions in the past account for the one-sidedness of some of the interpretations of *The City of the Sun*, particularly by readers familiar only with Halliday's expurgated selections from the utopia—selections which hitherto have been the only ones available in the English language. As a result, English-speaking readers have often been unaware of Campanella's emphasis on eugenics and sex relations. Despite the crudity, sensuality, and unorthodoxy of this part of the utopia, his treatment of sex has been retained below, for it reveals more graphically than any other material in his account how logically he worked out the implications of his principles. In an effort to eliminate individualism, selfishness, Machiavellianism, and the irrational from his imaginary society, Campanella subordinated everything to a collective person —the state. As a result he made private confession into a police document and a means of government. Since a man's private conscience and personality were thus to be subordinated to the collective conscience and personality, property and family had also to be sacrificed. For family and property are extensions of self. Property is the outward manifestation and guarantee of human individuality: it is the individual will made visible in things accumulated as a refuge from servitude; and family is an extension of personality. But Campanella repulses the forces of the human personality as sources of corruption, divisions, and crimes. As a result, in the City of the Sun, the state comes first; a man's condition in it depends upon his services to it. His aptitude is judged from his services, and he is classified accordingly. All work is for the state. Men and women, likewise, belong to the state, and as national workers they must produce the best possible future citizens. "Community of wives" is a misleading phrase for their relationships, for no one belongs to anyone either individually or collectively in the Sun State. Marriage is a public function administered by a Ministry of Love. Everyone is classified according to his capacity in this respect as in others, for the alleged good of the country. Under such a system virtue is prized only for its usefulness. Thus courage is valued because it is useful in the defense of the country; and chastity because the preservation of fecundity and strength until maturity results in better children.

Adolph Franck, having made the observations summarized in the last half of the preceding paragraph, concludes as follows: "Campanella offers us what geometricians call 'a refutation by means of an absurdity.' It is a refutation of that old doctrine which subordinates the temporal order and the spiritual order to the same power, or of that other chimaera, no less ancient and no less tyrannical, which seeks to absorb the individual into the state. He teaches us to guard ourselves against excesses of authority as well as against those of liberty. He gives us proof that pantheism is the prime source of all theories which deny liberty and outrage conscience. He shows that those ideas, even when veiled in religious form, are as fatal to religion as they are to reason and the personal dignity of man." This is, of course, Franck's interpretation; Campanella, almost certainly, was *not* trying to teach by means of absurdity: on the contrary, he seems to have believed in the validity of his City. Nevertheless, as Franck has revealed, the utopia has value as a horrible example for those opposed to a society in which the state dominates completely over the individual. The reader must decide for himself how far Campanella favored and how far he was opposing *raison d'état*, the doctrine that the interests of the state justify anything and everything regardless of morals and human rights.

The text below preserves intact and unchanged, except for translation into English, most of Campanella's original as published in Latin at Frankfort in 1623. Several short speeches by the Grand Master have been eliminated as adding nothing to the meaning. In the interests of space and readability complex astrological passages have been removed as well as a section on military matters. Otherwise Mr. Gilstrap's translation is complete.

BIBLIOGRAPHY: General treatments of *The City of the Sun* will be found in the standard histories of utopianism. The detailed criticisms are in foreign languages: Adolph Franck, *Réformateurs et Publicistes de l'Europe* (Paris, 1881); Émile Dermengham, *Thomas Morus et les Utopistes de la Renaissance* (Paris, 1927); Rodolfo de Mattei, *La Politica di Campanella* (Rome, 1927).

The City of the Sun

A Poetic Dialogue between a Grand Master of the Knights Hospitalers and a Genoese Sea Captain, his Guest.

CAPTAIN:

I have already told you how, after traveling around the whole world, I finally came to Taprobana and was forced to go ashore there. As I have already said, I went into a forest from fear of the inhabitants, and when I finally emerged from it, I found myself on an extensive plain directly under the equator. I immediately encountered a large company of armed men and women, many of whom understood our language, and they conducted me forthwith to the City of the Sun.

The greater part of the city lies on an enormous hill which rises out of an extensive plain, but its numerous rings extend far beyond the base of the hill, which is of such size that the diameter of the city is over two miles and the circumference seven miles. Because of the humped shape of the mountain, however, the area is greater than it would be if the city were situated on a plain.

The city is divided into seven huge rings or circles named for the seven planets, and each is connected with the next by four streets passing through four gates facing the four points of the compass. Now the city is so built that if anyone succeeded in storming the first circle he would find it twice as hard to take the second and even harder to take the third, and in each succeeding case he would have to exert twice as much strength and energy as before. Thus anyone wishing to capture the city must storm it seven times. In my opinion, however, not even the first ring can be taken, so thick are its earthworks and so well fortified is it with breastworks, towers, guns, and ditches.

The north gate is covered with iron and is so wrought that it can be raised and lowered and can be easily and securely fastened shut by devices that run in a marvelous fashion into grooves in the thick posts. When I entered the gate I saw a level space seventy paces wide between the first and second walls. From here huge palaces are visible, all joined to the wall of the second ring in such manner that they could all be called one palace. Arches topped by promenading galleries run uninterruptedly around the whole ring on a level with the middle height of the palaces. These arches are supported from beneath by thick, well-formed columns enclosing arcades which resemble peristyles or the cloisters of a monastery.

Now the palaces have no entrances below, except in the inner or concave wall. Through them one enters directly into the lower chambers. The upper chambers are reached by marble stairs which lead to promenading galleries on the inner side similar to those on the outer side. From these one enters the upper rooms, which are very beautiful and have windows in both the concave and the convex walls. The convex or outer wall is eight spans thick, and the concave or inner wall is three, while the walls between are one or perhaps one and a half.

From this ring one steps into the second plain, which is almost three paces narrower than the first. From here he can see the first wall of the next circle, which is adorned with similar promenading galleries above and below. On its inner side is another wall forming the inner wall of the palaces. Here there are more balconies and peristyles and supporting columns below; above there are splendid pictures and the entrances to the upper chambers.

And so one continues to pass through similar circles and double walls enclosing palaces and adorned with promenading galleries extending along their outer side and supported by columns, until he reaches the last circuit, all the while proceeding on a level plain. But after passing through the double gates of the last circle, that is, the one in the outer and the one in the inner wall, one ascends by means of steps, which, however, are so constructed that the ascent is scarcely noticeable, since the path runs in an oblique direction, each step rising almost imperceptibly above the preceding one. On top of the hill is a rather extensive plain, and in the midst of this there rises a temple of marvelous construction.

The temple is built in the form of a perfect circle; it is not surrounded by walls but stands on thick columns, beautifully grouped. Its enormous dome, built with wonderful skill, has in its center or zenith a small dome containing an opening which is right over the altar. There is only one altar. The area within the temple, which is surrounded by columns, has a circumference of more than three hundred and fifty paces.

On the outer side, resting on the capitals of the columns, are arches extending about eight paces outwards. Here rise other columns supporting them, themselves resting on a thick strong wall three paces high. Between the wall and the inner columns there are lower promenades, beautifully paved. On the inner side of the wall, which is interrupted by numerous large doors, there are immovable seats, while among the inner columns supporting the temple there are many handsome portable chairs.

On the altar there is nothing except a large globe with the whole sky depicted on it, and a second globe, on which there is a representation of the earth. On the vault of the large dome can be seen representations of all the stars in the sky from the first to the sixth magnitude, each with its own name and its power to influence earthly affairs indicated in three verses. The poles and the great and small circles are indicated in the temple, at right angles with the horizon, but they are not complete, since there is no wall below. However, they appear to be perfect in their relation to the globes on the altar.

The pavement glitters with precious stones. Seven golden lamps, perpetually lighted, hang suspended, each bearing the name of one of the seven planets.

The small dome at the top of the temple is surrounded by certain beautiful small cells and behind the level space above the enclosures or arches of the inner and outer columns are many large and handsome cells, where about forty-nine priests and men in religious orders live.

A kind of revolving weathervane stands on the very top of the smaller dome, indicating the winds of which they distinguish thirty-six. They know what kind of weather particular winds bring and what changes on land and sea, but only for their own clime. Beneath the weathervane they keep a scroll inscribed with letters of gold.

The great ruler among them is a priest whom they call Sol in their language; we would call him *Metaphysic*. He is head over all in temporal and spiritual matters; and all business matters and lawsuits are settled by him as the final authority. He is assisted by three princes of equal power, Pon, Sin, and Mor, or, in our language, *Power, Wisdom,* and *Love. Power* is concerned with all matters relating to war and peace, and with the military arts. He is supreme after Sol in military affairs. He directs the military magistrates and the soldiery and has the management of munitions, fortifications, the storming of palaces, military machinery, armories, and artisans connected with matters of this sort.

Wisdom is concerned with all the liberal and mechanical arts and the sciences, and their magistrates and teachers, and the schools for instruction. He has under him a magistrate for each science. There is one magistrate called Astrologer, one called Cosmographer, and others called Geometer, Historiographer, Poet, Logician, Rhetorician, Grammarian, Physician, Physicist, Politician, and Moralist. These have only one book, which they call Wisdom, in which all the sciences are written with marvelous conciseness and clearness. This they read to the people after the manner of the Pythagoreans.

Wisdom has had the outer and inner and upper and lower walls of the whole city adorned with the finest paintings and has had all the sciences illustrated in them in a marvelous manner. On the outer walls of the temple and on its curtains (which are lowered when a priest gives an address to prevent his voice from being carried away and eluding his hearers) are depicted the stars, together with their powers and motions, expressed in three verses for each.

On the inner wall of the first ring are shown all the mathematical figures, many more than Archimedes and Euclid discovered. Their size is proportionate to the dimensions of the wall, and they are elegantly drawn, each being accompanied by a concise explanation in verse. There are also definitions, propositions, etc. On the outer, or convex, wall there is, first, a complete and extensive description of the earth as a whole; then, following this, individual tables for each country setting forth briefly in prose the usages, laws, customs, origins, and power of its inhabitants. Also shown, above the alphabet of the City of the Sun, are the alphabets used in all countries.

On the inner side of the second circuit, that is to say, the second ring of buildings, there are paintings of all manner of precious and common stones, minerals, and metals. Accompanying these are actual specimens, together with an explanation of each in two verses. On the outer wall are shown all the seas, rivers, lakes, and springs in the world, also all the wines, oils, and various liquids, together with their sources, qualities, and properties. There are also vessels standing on the arches and composing part of the wall, filled with various liquids from one to three hundred years old, with which they cure various diseases. Hail, snow, thunder, and all atmospheric phenomena are represented with appropriate pictures and verses.

On the inner side of the third ring, all kinds of trees and herbs are depicted, and there are live specimens of some in pots above the arches of the outer wall. These are accompanied by explanations as to where they were first found and what their powers and properties are. Their resemblances to celestial things and to metals, as well as to parts of the human body and things in the sea, are also explained along with their uses in medicine, etc. On the outer wall are all the kinds of fishes found in the rivers, lakes, and seas, together with their habits and peculiarities, their ways of breeding, training, and living, and their uses to the world and to us; also their resemblances to celestial things and to terrestrial objects, whether produced by nature or by art. I was astonished to see fish that looked like a bishop, a chain, a cuirass, a nail, a star, and part of a man's body—all faithful likenesses of things existing among us. Sea urchins also, the purple shellfish, mussels, and whatever the world of water has that is worthy of note, are pictured and described there in a wondrous fashion.

On the fourth inner wall are shown the different kinds of birds, their natures, sizes, habits, colors, manner of living, etc. Included among these is the real phoenix. On the outer wall are shown all the kinds of creeping things: snakes, dragons, worms, and insects such as flies, gnats, horse flies, beetles, and the like, their different states, qualities, venoms, and uses—a great many more than we would imagine.

On the fifth inner wall they have perfect representations of an astonishing number of land animals. We indeed know not the thousandth part of them. Since they are so numerous and since some are of great size, the outer wall of the ring is also devoted to them. Why, of horses alone, how many kinds there are! What beauty of forms is so cleverly displayed there!

On the sixth inner wall are depicted all the mechanical arts, their tools, and the manner in which they are practiced in the various countries. They are placed and described in the order of their importance, and their inventors are named. Then on the outer wall are shown all the inventors in the sciences and in warfare, and all the lawgivers. There I saw Moses, Osiris, Jupiter, Mercury, Lycurgus, Pompilius, Pythagoras, Zamolxis, Solon, and numerous others. They even have Mahomet, although they despise him as a false and base lawgiver. But I saw a representation of Jesus Christ and the Twelve Apostles in a position of high honor, for they consider them very worthy and esteem them highly. I saw Caesar, Alexander, Pyrrhus, Hannibal, and other heroes great in war and peace, especially Romans, depicted in the lower porticoes. And when in my astonishment I asked how it was that they knew our history, they told me that they have among them a knowledge of all languages and that they deliberately send out explorers and ambassadors over the whole earth to become thoroughly acquainted with the customs, strength, government, and history of the various countries, both the good and the bad things about all of them, and then to report their findings to the state. They take great pleasure in this kind of thing. I saw that firearms and printing had been invented before we knew of them, by the Chinese. There are instructors who explain these pictures, and boys customarily learn all the sciences without drudgery and as it were while playing, albeit in a historical manner, until their tenth year.

Love is concerned first of all with reproduction. He sees to it that men and women are so mated as to produce the best offspring. Indeed, they laugh at us for devoting studious care to the breeding of dogs and horses while neglecting human breeding. Likewise, the education of children falls to *Love*, as also medicine, pharmacy, the planting and harvesting of crops and of fruits, agriculture, stock raising, the preparation of the tables, cooking, and everything pertaining to food and clothing and sexual intercourse. He has direction over numerous instructors and instructresses who are concerned with these affairs.

Metaphysic deals with all these matters in cooperation with these three rulers, and nothing is done without him. All the business of the state is transacted among these four, but all readily agree to whatever *Metaphysic* favors.

This race of men came there from India, fleeing from the sword of the Moguls, who were laying waste their country, and from brigands and tyrants. They determined to lead a philosophic life in common. Although community of wives has not been established among the other inhabitants of their country, it is the custom among them. All things among them are held in common, but their distribution is by authority of the magistrates. They have their sciences, and honors, and pleasures in common, so that no one can appropriate anything for himself.

They say that all private property owes its origin and development to each individual's having his own house, wife, and children. From this arises selfishness; for in order to raise a son to riches and honors and leave him as heir to much wealth, each of us becomes either desirous of seizing control of the state (if power of wealth or descent has enabled him to throw off timidity) or greedy, contriving, and hypocritical (if he has little strength, a slender purse, and mean ancestry). But when men have rid themselves of selfishness, there remains only love for the community.

GRAND MASTER:

Well, then, no one would be willing to work, seeing that he expects others to work for his living, as Aristotle argues against Plato on this point.

CAPTAIN:

I do not know how to deal with that argument, but I declare to you that the Solarians burn with an almost unbelievably strong love for their fatherland. The truth is that in proportion to their greater rejection of private ownership, the Solarians' love of their country surpasses that which history tells us prevailed among the Romans, who freely died for their country. Indeed I think that the friars and monks and clergy of our country would be much holier, less fond of property, and more imbued with a feeling of universal charity if they were not weakened by love of relatives or friends or by ambition to rise to higher honors.

GRAND MASTER:

Saint Augustine seems to say that; but I say that among this people friendship is worth nothing, since they have no way of bestowing favors on one another.

CAPTAIN:

Nay, that is certainly not so, for it is worth it all to see no one's being able to receive any gifts from another. They get whatever they need from the community, and the magistrates carefully see to it that no one receives more than he deserves; yet no one is denied anything he needs. Friendship has an opportunity to show itself among them in war, in sickness, in competition in the sciences, wherein they give each other mutual assistance and instruction. Sometimes they help each other with words of praise and advice, with favors, and in other ways as necessary.

All those of the same age call one another brothers; those who are more than twenty-two years old are called fathers; and those who are less than twenty-two are called sons. Moreover, the magistrates take special pains to see to it that no one in the brotherhood inflicts injury on another.

There are magistrates among them corresponding to the name of every virtue among us. There is a magistrate called *Magnanimity*, one called *Fortitude*, and others called *Chastity*, *Liberality*, *Criminal and Civil Justice*, *Sagacity*, *Truth*, *Beneficence*, *Gratitude*, *Cheerfulness*, *Exercise*, *Sobriety*, and so on. The persons selected for duties of this kind are those who have from childhood in the schools been known to be best in the practice of the particular virtue. Thus it is that there are among them no robberies, treacherous murders, rapes, incestuous acts, adulteries, or other crimes of which we accuse one another. They do accuse one another of ingratitude and spite (when one person denies another proper satisfaction), of indolence, surliness, and anger, and of scurrility, gloominess, and lying, which last they abhor more than the plague. And the guilty ones as punishment are deprived of the common table or intercourse with women or other honors for such time as the judge deems suitable for their correction.

GRAND MASTER:
Tell me how the magistrates are chosen.

CAPTAIN:
You will not fully understand that until you learn how they live. Now, first of all, men and women wear practically the same clothing, which is suitable for warfare, with this difference, that the women's toga extends below the knee, while the men's ends above the knee. And both sexes are educated together in all the arts. After the first year, and before three years have passed, the boys learn the language and the alphabet by walking about the walls (on which these are written). The boys are in four groups, and four elders serve as their leaders and teachers.

After a short period they are drilled in gymnastics, running, discus hurling, and games, so that all parts of their bodies will receive equal development. They always go barefooted and bareheaded until the seventh year.

They are all taken at the same time to the workshops of the various trades, such as shoemaking, cooking, metalworking, carpentry, and painting, in order that the direction of each one's talent may be carefully examined. After the seventh year, when they have absorbed the mathematical terms on the walls, they are assembled for lectures in all the natural sciences. There are four lecturers for the same subject, and in the course of four hours all four groups are through with it. While some are taking physical exercise or busying themselves with public services or functions, the others are engaged in attending the lectures. After this, all go into the study of higher mathematics, medicine, and other sciences. They engage in constant and eager disputation and argument with one another, and those who are most proficient in particular sciences, mechanical arts, etc., become magistrates in those fields. They go out into the countryside with their teachers and judges to see and learn how farming and stock raising are carried on. A person who has learned several trades and knows how to practice them well is considered noble and more

outstanding. Accordingly they laugh at us for looking on our tradesmen as ignoble and for considering noble those who learn no trade
but lead idle lives and keep very many servants to cater to their
idleness and wantonness; as a result, so many worthless and wicked
fellows leave a school of vices, as it were, to work the ruin of the
state.

Now, the rest of the officials are chosen by the four principal
officials, Sol, Pon, Sin, and Mor, and by the teachers in the field of
which they are to be put in charge, since these persons know well
who is most adept at the trade or virtue in which a director is to be
appointed. The names are proposed in council by magistrates, but
those who are proposed make no effort in their own behalf as candidates usually do. And anyone who knows anything against the
persons whose names are proposed speaks against them, and anyone
who knows anything in their favor speaks for them.

No one rises to the dignity of Sol without knowing the histories
of all nations, their customs, sacrifices, laws, and forms of government (whether republics or monarchies). In addition, a man who
becomes Sol must know the names of the lawgivers and the inventors
in the arts, as also the natural laws and history of the earth and the
heavens. Likewise, he must also know all the mechanical arts. (He
learns a new one almost every two days, although he does not necessarily become proficient in it in that period of time. However, practice and the study of pictures presently give him proficiency in this
matter). In addition he must know physics, mathematics, and astrology. There is not very much concern about his knowing languages,
since there are numerous interpreters who serve as grammarians in
the state. But above all he must understand metaphysics and theology
and he must know thoroughly the derivations, foundations, and
proofs of all the arts and sciences, the likenesses and differences of
things, the necessity, fate, and harmony of the universe, the power,
wisdom, and love of things and of God, and, as well, the gradations
of being and its symbolic relationship with things in the heavens, on
land, and in the sea, and also its relationship with the ideal things in
God, as far as mortal man can know them. He must also be well read
in the Prophets and in astrology. Thus they know long beforehand
who will be Sol, but no one is raised to so great a dignity until he is
thirty-five years old. He retains the office until someone wiser than
he and more fitted for ruling is found.

GRAND MASTER:

Who indeed can know so much? It seems to me that a man who
devotes himself assiduously to the sciences is unsuited for ruling.

CAPTAIN:

I made that very objection to them. Their answer was: "We are definitely more certain that such a learned man has the knowledge required for ruling than are you who place in authority ignorant men who are thought fitted merely because they are sprung from rulers or have been chosen by the party in power. But our Sol, even supposing that he is most unskilled in government, will never be cruel or wicked or a tyrant, since he possesses so much wisdom. However, let us not fail to state that your objection has validity among you, since you think that the most learned man is the one who has learned the most grammar or Aristotelian logic either in its Aristotelian or some other form. Now, for this sort of knowledge only slavish memory and labor are required. Thus a man is rendered unskillful, since he contemplates not things themselves but only the words in books, and wastes his mind with the dead signs of things. Hence he does not know how God rules things, nor does he know the ways and customs of nature or of the nations. Such a thing cannot happen in the case of our Sol, for, indeed, a man cannot learn so many arts and sciences well who does have a great aptitude for everything and therefore especially for ruling. It is plain to us that a man who has studied only one science does not truly know either it or the others, and he who is fitted for only one science, drawn from books, is unlearned and unskilled. But this is not the case with intellects prepared and expert in every branch of knowledge and suited by their nature for pondering things over, as must necessarily be true of our Sol. Furthermore, in our state the sciences are taught with such facility, as you see, that students learn more here in one year than they do among you in ten or fifteen years. I pray you, test these boys."

When I tested the boys, I was astonished at the truth of what they had said, for they knew my language well. As a matter of fact, three of them must be proficient in our tongue, three in Arabic, three in Polish, and three in each of the other languages, and they are given only such respite from the language as enables them to become the more learned. For that recreation they go out into the plains, one group at one time, another at another time, to run about, shoot arrows and hurl lances, fire arquebuses, hunt wild animals, and become acquainted with plants, rocks, agriculture, and stock raising.

Now the three rulers assisting Sol have to know thoroughly only the arts pertaining to their field of rule. Accordingly, they have only a historical knowledge of the arts which are common to all, but they know their own to perfection, for, of course, they devote themselves to them more than does anybody else. Thus *Power* knows the most about horsemanship, marshaling an army, laying out a camp, manufacturing weapons of every kind and machines of war, devising strategy—in a word, doing everything of a military nature. But in addition to such things these rulers must have been philosophers, historians, politicians, and physicists.

GRAND MASTER:

I wish you would list and define all their public duties and give me more details about the communal education.

CAPTAIN:

They have their dwellings, dormitories, beds, and all else that they need in common. And at the end of every six months their superiors decide who is to sleep in one circle, who in another, and who in the first room, who in a second, the rooms being marked by letters of the alphabet on the lintels of the doors. Men and women alike follow the mechanical and the theoretical occupations, with this difference, that the occupations which require more hard work and those in which one has to go some distance, such as plowing, sowing, gathering produce, working on the threshing floor, and wine making, are practiced by men. But it is customary to select women for milking the cows and making cheese. Likewise, they go to the gardens near the outskirts of the city to gather the vegetables and also to cultivate them. Indeed, the occupations at which one sits or stands, such as weaving, spinning, sewing, cutting the hair and beard, preparing drugs, and making all kinds of clothing, fall to the women. They are excluded, however, from carpentry, smithing, and the manufacture of arms. But if a woman shows an aptitude for painting she is not prevented from following that occupation. Music is given over to the women alone, because they play it more pleasingly, but sometimes also to boys. However, the women do not play drums or trumpets.

The women also prepare the meals and set the tables, but waiting on tables is the special duty of the boys and girls under twenty. Each circle has its own kitchens and storerooms for food and for eating and drinking equipment, and an old man and an old woman preside over each department. These two give orders to those who serve and have the power to chastise, or cause to be chastised, those who are negligent or disobedient; on the other hand, they also observe and single out those individuals who excel in their duties.

All the youth wait on their elders who have passed the age of forty. A master and a mistress see to the time when the youth go to bed in the evening, and also arrange that those whose turn it is take up their duties in the morning, one or two for each room. The young people wait on each other, and woe betide those who are unwilling! They have first and second tables, with seats on either side, and the women are ranged on one side, the men on the other. As in the refectories of the monks, there is no noise, and while they eat, a young man reads a book from a platform, intoning distinctly and loudly, and often the magistrates interrupt at some important part of the reading to make pertinent remarks. Truly it is pleasant to see such splendid-looking young people, neatly clothed, ministering to them so promptly and at the same time to see so many friends, brothers, sons, fathers, and mothers living together with so much decency, grace, and love. Each is given his own napkin, plate, and portion of food. It is the duty of the physicians to tell the cooks what meals are to be prepared on each day and what food is for the old, what for the young, and what for the sick. The magistrates receive a little larger and fatter portion, and they always distribute some of it to the boys at the table who have shown themselves more attentive that day at the lectures and in the debates on wisdom or arms. This is considered to be one of the greatest honors. On holidays they like also to have singing at the table, not by all but by a few or by one voice accompanied by the cithara, etc. Since all alike turn their hands to service, nothing is ever found to be wanting. The elders selected for the purpose preside over the cooking and over those serving in the dining halls. Great stress is placed on cleanliness in the streets, in the living quarters, in utensils, in clothing, in the workshops, and in the warehouses.

They wear a white undergarment next to the body and over this a garment which covers both trunk and legs and has no wrinkles. This has openings on the sides extending from the top down to the ankles and also one passing from the navel between the legs to the buttocks. The edges of these openings are fastened by passing the globular buttons on one side into buttonholes, facing them on the other. The portion covering the legs extends down to the heels. They cover the feet with thick socks, half-buskins as it were, fastened with buckles, and over these they wear shoes. The outermost garment, as we have said, is the toga. So close-fitting are their clothes that when the toga is removed all parts of the body can be clearly seen, no part remaining hidden.

They change their clothes for different ones four times a year, that is, when the sun enters the signs Aries, Cancer, Libra, and Capricorn, and according to circumstances as decided by the physician and the wardrobe keeper in each ring. It is amazing that they have at any given time all the garments they need, whether heavy or light, according to the weather. They all use white clothing, which is washed every month with lye or soap.

The lower rooms are all workshops for trades, kitchens, pantries, storerooms, larders, armories, refectories, and lavatories. Clothes are washed by the pillars of the peristyles, and the water is carried off in canals which drain into sewers. In every street of all the circles there are individual fountains which supply the canals with water brought up almost from the base of the mountain by the simple operation of an ingenious handle. In addition to the water from the fountains there is also water in cisterns, this being rain water which is collected on the roofs and run into the cisterns through sanded ducts.

They wash their bodies often, as the doctor and the master order. All the mechanical occupations are practiced under the peristyles, but the speculative ones are carried on above the galleries and balconies where there are finer paintings, while the more sacred ones are taught in the temple. In the halls and on the battlements of the rings there are solar clocks and bells and pennants indicating the hours and the winds.

GRAND MASTER:
Tell me about their childbearing.

CAPTAIN:
No woman has intercourse with a man until she is nineteen, and a man must be twenty-one, or more if he is pale-complexioned, before he is authorized to participate in procreative activity. However, some are permitted access to barren or pregnant women before this time lest they will be driven to seek some illicit outlet. Elderly mistresses and masters provide facilities for the more passionate and stimulated ones when they receive requests from them secretly or become aware of such need in the gymnasium. Initially, however, they request permission from the First Master of Reproduction, who is the most important doctor of medicine and is subordinate to the triumvir *Love*. Those who are caught committing sodomy are censured and as punishment are forced to wear their shoes around their neck to show that they have perverted the natural order and as it were have put their feet at their head. On each relapse into the practice, the punishment is increased until it reaches the death penalty. Those who abstain from intercourse until their twenty-first year, and more especially those who abstain until their twenty-seventh, receive honors, and their praises are sung at public gatherings. While they are exercising in the gymnasium, all the men and women are naked, as was the custom with the ancient Lacedaemonians; hence the instructors can tell by looking at them which ones are potent in intercourse and which ones are not, and they know which men are physically suited for which women.

They have intercourse every third night, after bathing well. Large and beautiful women are mated only with large and aggressive men, fat ones with lean men, and lean ones with fat men, so as to moderate all the excesses. In the evening after the youths come and make their beds, the men and women go to sleep as the Patron and Matron order them. And those who are undertaking procreation do not have intercourse until they have digested their food and have directed prayers to the Lord in Heaven. In these rooms are beautiful statues of great men, which the women look at; then gazing out of the windows at the sky, they pray God to grant them excellent off-spring. A man and a woman sleep in two separate cells until the hour of intercourse, at which time the Matron rises and opens the door of both cells. This hour is fixed by the astrologer and the physician. [They try to set it at a time when the stars, especially Venus, Mercury, Jupiter, Saturn, Mars, and Sun, and the Moon, are favorable to parents and offspring.]

They consider it wrong for those undertaking procreation not to have abstained from wrong actions and sexual activity for three days before intercourse for this purpose, and for them not to be reconciled with God and devoted to Him. Those who have intercourse with barren or pregnant or low women, whether for pleasure, for therapeutic effect, or for the stimulus derived from it, do not follow this procedure.

The magistrates (who are all priests) and likewise wise teachers engage in procreative activity only after meeting numerous requirements over a period of many days, for from much intellectual activity they have weak animal spirits. They do not pour their energy forth from the brain, since they are always pondering over something; hence, they beget weak offspring. Therefore, much attention is given to this matter, and these wise men are mated with women who are naturally vivacious, vigorous, and shapely. Similarly, keen-minded, quick, lively, and, as it were, passionate men are mated with the fatter and gentler women. They say that purity of the constitution, in which the virtues have their origin, cannot be acquired by practice, and that men who are naturally evil behave well only from fear of the law or of God, and that when that ceases to operate, they destroy the state, either secretly or openly. For this reason procreation must receive undivided and principal attention and natural merits must be examined, not doweries and titles, which betray the race. If a woman does not conceive from one man, she is mated with others, and if at length she is found to be barren, she is made available for communal use, but she is not given the honorable standing of married women in the Council of Procreation in the temple. They do this in order to keep women from making themselves sterile for the sake of a good time.

The women who conceive do not exercise their bodies for fifteen days; after this time they take gentle exercise in order to strengthen their offspring and to open up the channels of nourishment to them; and gradually they strengthen themselves with an ever-increasing amount of exercise. They are permitted to eat only useful foods on the prescription of physicians. After delivery they themselves suckle the newborn children and rear them in communal quarters set apart. They give milk for two years more, as the physician orders. On being weaned, the child is given into the charge of the Matrons if it is a female, or of the Patrons if it is a male. Then the children are pleasantly instructed in the alphabet and in the knowledge of the pictures, in running, walking, and wrestling, also in the historical drawings and in languages, and they are provided with suitable and varied clothing. After the sixth year they take up the natural sciences, then other things as the magistrates consider suitable, and then the mechanical arts. Boys with retarded mentality are sent to farms, and when they have improved, some are brought back to the city. But the majority, since they are conceived under the same constellation, are of the same age and resemble one another in strength, manner, and appearance. This gives rise to much lasting concord in the state, for they treat each other lovingly and helpfully.

Their names are not given to them haphazardly, but are conferred by *Metaphysic* according to their individual qualities, as was the custom among the Romans of old. Thus one is called *Handsome*, another *Big Nose*, another *Thick Legs*, another *Crooked*, another *Lean . . .*

GRAND MASTER:

Pray, tell me, is there any jealousy among them or disappointment on the part of a man who fails to be elected to a magistracy or to attain anything else which he is seeking?

CAPTAIN:

No indeed. For no one lacks necessities or luxuries. Moreover, the begetting of offspring is managed as a religious affair for the good of the state and not of individuals. The magistrates must be obeyed, and, contrary to our opinion, they deny that it is natural for a man to recognize and rear his own offspring, and have his own wife, house, and children. They say, as does St. Thomas, that procreation is for the preservation of the species, not of the individual. Therefore this function has reference to the state and not to individuals, except in so far as they are members of the state. And since individuals generally bring forth children wrongly and rear them wrongly, to the great detriment of the state, this function is scrupulously committed to the magistrates as the main basis of the state, for it is the basis of the commonwealth, not of a portion of it. Thus they distribute the best-endowed male and female breeders in accordance with philosophy. Plato thinks this distribution ought to be made by lot, lest some men see that they are being kept away from the beautiful women and in their jealousy and anger rise against the magistrates, and he thinks that those who do not deserve to be mated with the more beautiful women should be deceived by the magistrates when lots are drawn in such a way that they will always get those who are suited for them, not those that they desire. But deceit of this sort is not necessary among the inhabitants of the City of the Sun in order to make sure that ugly men receive ugly women by lot, since ugliness is unknown among them. Since the women exercise, they acquire good complexions, become strong of limb, tall, and agile; and beauty among them consists of tallness, liveliness, and strength. Therefore, if any woman were to paint her face in order to make herself beautiful, or use high-heeled shoes so as to look tall, or wear lengthened garments to cover her thick legs, she would be subjected to capital punishment. But if any woman did want to do such things, she would have no way to do them, for who would provide her the means? They say that abuses of this sort have their origin among us in the leisure and idleness of the women, whereby they lose their color, grow pale, and become feeble and small. That is why such women require coloring that is applied, and high-heeled shoes, and must be considered beautiful because of a slothful tenderness rather than because of robustness. And so they ruin their own complexion and nature and their offspring at the same time.

Now if any man is seized with a violent love for a woman, he and she are permitted to converse and joke together, bestow garlands of flowers or leaves on each other, and make verses for each other. But if the function of breeding is endangered, under no conditions is intercourse permitted them unless the woman is already pregnant (and the man waits until this is so) or is sterile. But love consisting of eager desire is scarcely known among them; it generally consists only of friendship.

Family affairs and matters of food are of little importance, since each one receives these things according to his needs, except for tokens of honor. It is customary for the state to bestow little gifts or beautiful wreaths or sweets or fine clothes on heroes and heroines at festivals, while they are banqueting.

They all wear white clothing in the city in the daytime, but at night and when they are outside the city, they wear red garments, either of silk or of wool. They detest black as they do dung, and for this reason they dislike the Japanese, who are fond of black.

They consider pride the most execrable vice, and acts of pride are punished with the most severe humiliation. Therefore no one thinks it humiliating to wait on tables or work in the kitchen or tend the sick. . . .

In the City of the Sun, however, since the services and the trades and all kinds of tasks are distributed among all, each one has to work barely four hours a day. The rest of the time is spent in pleasant learning, debating, reading, storytelling, writing, walking, and exercising of mind and body. No game is permitted which is played while sitting, such as dice (whether with one or two dice), chess, and the like. They play with the ball (both the stuffed and the inflated kind), wrestle, hurl poles, and shoot arrows and arquebuses, etc. They claim, moreover, that severe poverty makes men worthless, cunning, deceitful, thievish, contriving, vagabond, mendacious, perjured, etc., and that wealth makes them insolent, proud, ignorant, traitorous, pretentions, deceptive, boastful, wanting in affection, insulting, etc. But communal life makes all at the same time rich and poor; rich since they have everything, poor since they own nothing. At the same time they are not slaves to things; rather, things serve them. In this matter they have great praise for devout Christians and especially for the lives of the Apostles.

GRAND MASTER:

This seems excellent and sacred, but the community of women is too difficult. Saint Clement the Roman says that wives, in accordance with the Apostolic institution, ought to be held in common, and he praises Plato and Socrates, who teach this. But the gloss understands this community of wives to extend to obedience, not to the marriage bed. And Tertullian agrees with the gloss, saying that the first Christians had everything in common except their wives, who, however, were held in common as far as obedience was concerned.

CAPTAIN:

These things I know little of, but I did see that the inhabitants of the City of the Sun had their women in common as regards both obedience and the bed, but not at any and every time as in the case of beasts that mate with whatever female is available; rather they do it only by permission and as a matter of procreation, as I have already stated. However, I think they may be mistaken in this. Yet they defend themselves by giving the opinions of Socrates, Cato, Plato, and St. Clement, but, as you say, improperly understanding them. They say that St. Augustine approves community of every-thing except women as regards the marriage bed, the latter idea being the heresy of the Nicolaitans. They say that our Church has permitted holding things in common in order to avoid a greater evil and not as a measure to promote greater good. It may be that they will abandon this custom some day. Actually, in their subject cities all else is held in common, but not women, except as regards obedience and the occupations. But the inhabitants of the City of the Sun ascribe this to the imperfection of the people of these cities, since the latter have been only partly indoctrinated in their philoso-phy. Nevertheless, they send abroad to explore the customs of various countries, and they always adopt the better ones. . . . They learn to put fear aside completely, and anyone who does show fear is punished severely. They have no dread of death, for they all believe that souls are immortal and that on leaving men's bodies they associate themselves with good or evil spirits according to the deserts of the present life. Although they are Brahmanists and to a degree Pythagoreans, they do not believe in the transmigration of souls, except in some cases, by a degree of God. Nor do they refrain from attacking an enemy of their state and religion who does not deserve humane treatment. Every two months they muster the army, and every day there is practice with arms out in the open country on horseback or inside the walls. There are continual lec-tures on military science, and they have readings of the histories of Moses, Joshua, David, the Maccabees, Caesar, Alexander, Scipio, Hannibal, etc. Then each gives his own opinion as to whether these generals acted well or badly, usefully or honorably, etc., in particular instances, after which the instructor answers and decides the matter. . . . I believe you have heard how their military affairs, agriculture, and stock raising are carried on in common. Anyone who is considered to have learned one of these is honored with the first grade of nobility, but a person who learns several occupations is considered more noble. A man who shows a greater aptitude than usual for a particular art is made a teacher in it. The more toilsome occupations, such as metalwork and building, are considered the praiseworthy, and none refuse to go into these occupations, for the reason that their propensities are evident from their birth star and also that the distribution of labor among them is so arranged that no one does work that is harmful to him, but only that which is good for him. The less laborious occupations fall to the women. All are expected to know how to swim, and for that reason there are pools built outside the walls and also inside, near the fountains.

Commerce is of little use to them, but they know the value of money and they mint some for the use of their ambassadors and spies so that these can maintain themselves abroad. Merchants come to the city from various parts of the world to buy the surplus goods of the city. The people of the City of the Sun decline to take money, but they will accept in exchange goods that they need, and they often buy with money. The young people of the city are much amused when they see these merchants hand over generous amounts of goods in return for a small amount of silver. But the older people do not laugh, for they do not want slaves and foreigners to corrupt the City with their vicious customs. Therefore they do business at the gates and sell the prisoners whom they have captured in war or put them at digging ditches or at other toilsome tasks outside the city.

They always send four bands of soldiers to guard the fields, and these laborers are sent out at the same time. They go out the four gates. From these gates roads with built-up sides extend to the sea so as to facilitate the transportation of goods and the passage of those coming to the city. They are certainly pleasant and generous toward strangers; they maintain them for three days at public expense, after they have first washed their feet. They show them the city and its ways and honor them in the council and at the public table. There are men deputed to take care of and guard the guests. If the latter wish to become citizens of the state they are first tested for a month on a farm and then for another month in the city, after which time a decision is made, and they are accepted with certain ceremonies, oaths, etc.

Agriculture is much followed among them. Not a span of earth goes unused, and they watch the winds and propitious stars. With the exception of a few who are left in the city, all go out into the fields to plow, sow, dig, hoe, reap, pick, and do vineyard work, all this being done to the accompaniment of trumpets, drums, and standards, and they accomplish all the work in a few hours. They use wagons fitted with sails which are borne along even by a contrary wind through a skilful arrangement of wheels against wheels. When there is no wind, one beast draws a large wagon—a goodly sight! Meanwhile the guards take turns at armed patrol.

They do not use dung and filth to fertilize the fields, believing that the plants absorb some of their rottenness and make life short and weak when eaten, just as women who are beautiful from painted applications and from lack of exercise bring forth feeble offspring. Therefore they do not, as it were, paint the earth itself; rather, they exercise it well and use secret remedies so that the fruit is borne quickly and multiplies and is not destroyed. They have for this work a book which they call *The Georgics*. They plow as much land as the need; the rest remains in pasture.

The noble art of breeding and raising horses, cattle, sheep, dogs, and all kinds of domestic and tame animals is held in the highest esteem among them, as it was in the time of Abraham. They bring them together for breeding in such fashion that proper conception will occur. Fine pictures of cattle, horses, sheep, etc., are hung at the scene. Instead of turning the stallions out with the mares to pasture they bring them together at the proper time in enclosures at the country stables when they observe Sagittarius in the horoscope in favorable aspect with Mars and Jupiter. For cattle they observe Taurus, for sheep Aries, and so on. In the same way, domestic fowls are under the Pleiades, including chickens, ducks, and geese, which the women, for whom this is pleasant work, bring to feed near the city. Here there are places where they are penned up and where cheese, butter, and milk products are made. They also raise capons, castrated animals, etc. For all these matters they have a book called *The Bucolics*.

They have an abundance of things, because each wants to be first in his work, because it is slight and rewarding, and because they are all quite obedient. Whoever among them is head of the rest in duties of this kind they call king. They say that this is a proper name for their kings and not for ignorant persons. It is wonderful to see how men and women march together always obedient to their king; they do not regard him with loathing, as we do, since they look on him as a father or an older brother.

They have groves and forests with wild animals, where they often exercise themselves.

The science of navigation has a very high place among them, and they have certain rafts and triremes which sail the sea without oars or the force of the wind but by a wonderful device, and they have also others propelled by winds and oars. They have an excellent knowledge of the stars and of the ebb and flow of the tides. They sail for the sake of becoming acquainted with various peoples and regions and things. They do harm to no one, nor do they permit any injury to themselves. They do not fight except on provocation. They say that the whole earth will in time come to live in accordance with their customs and consequently they are always searching to find out whether there is any country living a more upright and outstanding way of life. They have treaties with the Chinese and with many peoples of the islands and of the continent, Siam, Cochin China, Calicut, etc., to facilitate their exploration. They also have artificial fires for naval and land battles and many secrets of tactics. Thus they almost never fail to be victorious.

GRAND MASTER:

I should like very much to hear what they eat and drink and how, and how long their life is.

CAPTAIN:

They teach that the first concern must be for life of the whole rather than for that of the parts. . . .

Their foods are meat, butter, honey, cheese, dates, and vegetables of various kinds. Originally they were unwilling to slaughter animals, because it seemed cruel. But reflecting later that it was also cruel to kill plants, since they too have feeling, the Solarians saw that they would perish from hunger unless they did ignoble things for the sake of noble ones. Therefore they now eat them all. However, they do not like to kill useful animals, such as cattle and horses. They draw a distinction between useful and harmful foods, using them in accordance with medical science. They keep changing their food three times in a regular rotation: first they eat meat, then fish, then fruits and vegetables and such like, then they go back to meat, so that their nature will become neither too heavy nor too thin. Old people eat more-digestible foods; they eat three times a day and sparingly. The general community eats twice a day, but children eat four times, as the physician directs. They live for the most part to the age of a hundred years, and not a few reach two hundred.

In drinking they are most moderate. Wine is not given to the young until they reach nineteen, unless the state of their health demands it. After this they take it diluted with water, as do the women. Those who are fifty or more put in very little water. They eat the things that are most healthful for the time of year, following faithfully the advice of the chief physician, whose concern this is.

They think nothing harmful when it is brought forth by God, unless when there is abuse by taking too much. Therefore they eat fruits in the summer, since they are moist and juicy and cool, to counteract heat and dryness. In winter they eat dry things, in the autumn grapes, since they were given by God to counteract black bile and sadness.

They also make much use of scents. In the morning when they rise they all comb their hair and wash their face and hands in cold water; then they chew mint or rock parsley or fennel, or they rub these on their hands; the older people may use incense. Then, facing east, they make a short prayer very much like the one which Jesus taught us. Then they go out, some to the work of ministering to the old, some to the dance, some to duties of the state. Later on they assemble for the first lecture, then at the temple, then for physi-

cal exercise. Then they sit down and relax awhile and presently they
go to dinner.

Among them is no gout in the hands or feet, no catarrh, no sci-
atica, no colic ailments, no bloatedness, and no flatulence. . . . For
they dissolve every humor and flatulence by exercise. Therefore
it is considered quite shameful to be seen hawking up or spitting,
for they say that this is a sign of too-little exercise or ignoble slothfulness, or drunkenness or gluttony. . . .

At every new moon and every full moon they call a council after
a sacrifice. All who are twenty years or more are admitted to it.
Each one is asked to tell what is wanting in the state, which magistrates are carrying out their duties well and which badly. Likewise,
after every eight days, the magistrates are assembled, that is, *Sol*,
first and with him *Power, Wisdom,* and *Love,* each of these three
has three magistrates under him, so that there are thirteen of them
in all; these latter have the direction the arts appropriate to them.
Power has military affairs, *Wisdom* the sciences, and *Love* has food,
clothing, breeding, and education. In addition there are the masters of
all groups, who are the captains of ten, fifty, or a hundred women
or men, and they take up state matters. They elect magistrates who
were mentioned in the great council. In like manner, *Sol* and the
three principal rulers assemble every day and they correct, confirm,
and execute matters which were decided at the elections, and they
take other necessary steps. They do not resort to lots unless they
are quite doubtful what decision to make. These magistrates are
changed according to the will of the people, but the first four are
never changed, unless they, taking counsel with themselves, give
up the office to one whom they know to be wiser, more gifted, and
purer than themselves. They are so sensible and honorable that they
gladly yield to a wiser man and learn from him. But this is a rare
occurrence. The heads of the sciences are subordinate to *Wisdom,*
except *Metaphysic,* who is *Sol* himself, who rules over all the sciences, their architect as it were, and he is ashamed not to know
anything that it is possible for men to know. . . .

GRAND MASTER:
    What about their judges?

CAPTAIN:
    I was just coming to that subject. Individuals are judged by
the first master in their trade, and thus all head artisans are judges.
They punish with exile, with flogging, with dishonor, and with
exclusion from the common table, from religious worship, and from
the company of women. Where a case involves great injury, it is

punished with death, and they repay an eye for an eye, a nose for a nose, a tooth for a tooth, etc., according to the law of recompense, if the offense was willful and premeditated. However, when there is a quarrel and the crime is committed without premeditation the sentence is mitigated, not by the judge, however, but by the Triumvirate, by whom it is referred to *Sol*, not for justice but for mercy, for he has the power to pardon. They have no prisons, except one tower used for confining rebels, enemy troops, etc. There is no written statement of a case, which we commonly call a process. The accuser and the witnesses are brought before the judge and *Power*, and the accused makes his defense and is immediately acquitted or condemned by the judge, and if he appeals to the Triumvirate, he is acquitted or condemned the next day. On the third day he is let go free by the indulgence of *Sol* or his sentence is irrevocably confirmed. The accused is reconciled with his accuser and the witnesses as if they were doctors treating his illness, and he embraces and kisses them. No one is put to death or stoned except at the hands of the people, beginning with the accuser and the witnesses, for the Solarians have no executioners or lictors, lest they contaminate the state. Some, given their choice of death, surround themselves with bags of gunpowder, then fire is applied, and they die, while the bystanders urge them to die a good death. At such a time, the whole city laments and beseeches God to desist from His wrath, mourning that it is forced to cut away a rotten limb of the state, as it were. Indeed, they talk and reason with the prisoner himself until he himself accepts and desires the death penalty; otherwise he does not die. But if a crime has been committed against the freedom of the state, against God, or against the supreme magistrates, the punishment is applied without mercy; these crimes are punished with death only. He who is to die is forced scrupulously to state before the people the reasons why he should not die; he must tell the sins of others who ought to die and list the mistakes of the magistrates; and he may assert that they deserve punishment more than he, if that is how it seems to him in good conscience. If his reasoning prevails, he is sent into exile, and he makes amends to the state with prayers, sacrifices, etc. Those named by the accused are not molested but are warned. Sins of frailty and ignorance are punished only by disgracing the person and forcing him to exercise more self-control or to take instruction in those sciences and arts against which he has sinned. And their attitude toward one another is such that they seem to be all members of the same body and of each other.

I should also like you to know that if any transgressor, without waiting to be accused, goes of his own accord to a magistrate and accuses himself and seeks correction, he is freed from the punishment for a secret crime, and the punishment is changed into another, since he has not been accused. They take special care that no one shall slander another; in the event that such a thing does occur, they apply the law of like for like. Since they always move about and work in groups, five witnesses are required to convict a transgressor; otherwise he is let go with a warning after he has sworn an oath. But if he is accused a second or a third time, a doubled punishment is applied on the testimony of two or three witnesses.

Their laws are few, short, and clear, and are written on bronze tablets hanging at the temple doors, that is, on the columns. Indeed on individual columns can be read definitions of things in a metaphysical and very terse style; for example, what God is, what an angel is, what earth, star, man, fate, virtue, etc., are, all done with great wisdom. The definitions of all the virtues are also delineated there; and the judges of all the virtues have their seats, that is, their courts, each under the column where the virtue of which he is judge is defined. When he gives judgment, a judge sits there and says: "My son, thou hast transgressed against the sacred definition of beneficence (or magnanimity, etc.). Read what is written here." And after a discussion, he sentences him to the punishment for the crime of which he is guilty: maleficence, despair, pride, ingratitude, slothfulness, or the like. The sentences, however, are really certain and true medicines, savoring more of pleasantness than of punishment.

GRAND MASTER:

Now you must tell me about the priests, sacrifices, their religion and belief.

CAPTAIN:

The high priest is Sol himself. All the higher magistrates are priests, and it is their duty to purge consciences. Therefore all the people tell their sins to the magistrates in secret confession, as we do, so that the latter may at the same time purge souls and learn which vices are prevalent among the people. Then the sacred magistrates confess their own sins to the supreme rulers and at the same time those of the rest, naming no one, however, but throwing everything together; especially do they confess those sins that are more grievous and that are harmful to the state. Finally, these three men confess the same sins, together with their own, to Sol himself. Thus the latter knows what kinds of transgressions are prevalent in the city and applies timely remedies. Then he offers sacrifice and prayers to God. And before this he confesses the sins of the whole population publicly before God from the altar, as often as amendment is needed, but he does not give the name of any transgressor. Then he absolves the people, warning them to be on their guard against such transgressions. After this he confesses his own sins publicly. Then he offers sacrifice to God, asking Him to pardon the city, to absolve it from its sins, and to instruct and defend it. Also, once a year the rulers of the individual subject cities confess the sins of their people to Sol. Thus he is aware of misdoings in the provinces, and he thereupon applies all human and heavenly remedies.

Sacrifice is conducted as follows: Sol asks the people who among them wishes to give himself as a sacrifice to God for the sake of his fellows, and whoever is more fitted by his holiness offers himself. Ceremonies are held and prayers are offered up. The volunteer is placed on a square table, which is made fast with four buckles to four ropes suspended from four pulley blocks in the small dome. Then they ask the God of mercy to accept this voluntary human sacrifice (not an involuntary animal sacrifice, as among the heathen). Sol orders the ropes to be drawn, and the sacrifice is pulled up to the center of the small dome. There the victim dedicates himself to the most fervent prayers. Food is passed to him by priests who live around the dome, but sparingly, until the sins of the city have been atoned for. With prayer and fasting he beseeches the God of heaven to accept his voluntary sacrifice. After twenty or thirty days, God's anger being appeased, he becomes a priest or sometimes (though very rarely) he returns below, but by way of the outer passage for priests. He is thereafter treated with much honor and good will since he offered his life for his country. But God does not desire death.

Twenty-four priests live in the top of the temple. At midnight, at noon, and in the morning and evening, that is, four times a day, they sing psalms to God. It is their duty to observe the stars and to note with astrolabes their movements and to know all about their effects on human affairs and their powers. Thus they know what change has taken place or will take place in what part of the earth and what time, and they send to find out whether it is actually so or not, and they keep a record of true and false predictions so as to be able from experience to make predictions as correctly as possible. They determine the hours for breeding, for gathering the grapes, etc., and they act as messengers, intercessors, and mediators between God and man. It is generally from among them that Sol is chosen. They write very admirable treatises and investigate the sciences. They do not descend except for dinner and supper, as the spirit descends from the head to the stomach and liver. They have intercourse with women only on rare occasions, and then for the curative effects. Sol goes up to see them every day and consults with them concerning the matters which they have recently investigated for the benefit of the state and of all the countries in the world.

Below in the temple one person from among the people is always standing at the altar praying, and at the end of every hour another relieves him, as we are accustomed to do in the Forty Hours' Devotion. This method of prayer they call perpetual sacrifice. After a meal they return thanks to God with music. Then they sing of the deeds of Christian, Hebrew, and Gentile heroes, and of those of all nations. They take great delight in this because they have ill will toward none. They sing hymns about love, wisdom, and every virtue, under direction of the ruler of that virtue. Each one takes the woman he prefers and they dance nobly and pleasantly under the peristyles. . . .

They honor the sun and the stars as living things and they also honor the statues of God and His temples and altars as live heavenly things, but they do not worship them. They venerate the sun above all. But they honor no created thing with adoration; this they reserve for God alone. They serve Him alone, lest they may fall into tyranny and misery and become slaves to created things as fitting punishment. They contemplate and know God under the image of the sun, which they call the sign of God, His face and living image, and through which light, heat, life, and making of things, indeed all that is good, flow down below. For this reason the altar has been built in the shape of the sun, and the priests adore God in the sun and in the stars, His altars as it were, and in the sky as His temple, and they pray to good angels as intercessors who dwell in the stars, their living abodes. For they believe that God has shown His beauties principally in the heavens and in the sun, His trophy and image. . . .

They claim that there are two physical principles for inferior things, that is, the sun as the father and the earth as the mother. In their opinion the air is an impure portion of sky; all fire is derived from the sun; and the sea is the sweat of the earth, combusted and fused within its bowels. The sea is the bond of union between air and earth, just as blood is the bond of union for spirit and body in living creatures. The universe is an immense living being, and we live in its belly, just as worms live in ours. Therefore we do not belong to the providence of the stars and the sun and earth, but to that of God alone, for in respect to those things which seek nothing but their own aggrandizement, we are born and live by chance; in respect to God, however, whose instruments they are, we are formed by prescience and design, destined for a great end. Therefore we owe gratitude to God as our father and we must recognize that everything is from Him.

The Solarians consider the immortality of souls as beyond doubt, and they think that after death souls are associated with good or bad angels according as they have made themselves like the former or the latter in their deeds in the present life. For all things seek things like themselves. They differ but little from us as regards the places of punishment and rewards. They are in doubt whether there are other worlds beyond ours but count it madness to claim that there is a void, for, they say, there is a void neither inside the world nor outside it, and God, the Infinite Being, does not tolerate a void with Him.

They lay down two metaphysical principles: being, which is **God** supreme, and nonbeing, which is the lack of being and is the condition without which nothing is physically produced. For that which is does not become; therefore that which is becoming was not. Likewise, evil and sin arise from the propensity to nonbeing; sin has its cause, a cause of sufficiency, not of insufficiency. By deficient cause they mean a deficiency in power, wisdom, or will. In this last they put sin, for he who knows and has the power to do good ought also to will to do it, since will arises out of knowledge and power, not they from it. Amazingly, they worship God in trinity, saying that God is the highest power; and that from this proceeds the highest wisdom, which at the same time is the same God; and that from these two proceeds love, which is power and wisdom; for that which proceeds must have the nature of that from which it proceeds. However, they do not know the three persons by name as in our Christian law, since they have not had this revealed to them. But they know that there is this proceeding in God and a relation of Himself, to Himself, in Himself, and from Himself. Therefore, things that are derive their existence metaphysically from power, wisdom, and love in the measure that they have being, and from impotence, unwisdom, and lack of love in the measure that they partake of nonbeing. Through the former they acquire merit; through the latter they sin. They commit sins of nature through lack of power and wisdom, and sins against custom and art through these or through lack of love or through all three. Indeed, an individual sins out of impotence or ignorance by producing a monstrosity. But all these things are foreknown by God, who has no part in any nothingness, and are ordained as by the Most Powerful, the Wisest, and the Best. Therefore, no being can sin in God; it sins away from God. But outside God it does not exist except through us men and in respect to us, not through itself or in respect of itself, since there is deficiency in us, but sufficiency in Him. Therefore, a sin is an act of God to the degree that it has being and sufficiency; but in the measure that it has nonbeing and deficiency, of which the nature of sin consists, it is in us and by us, who through our lack of order incline to sin. . . .

GRAND MASTER:

What do they about Adam's sin?

CAPTAIN:

They simply confess that there is much corruption abroad in the world and that men are not governed by true and higher reasons, that the good are tortured and are not listened to, that the bad have the rule; however, they call the happy lives of such persons unhappiness, for it is a certain nothingness and a show of being what they are not, that is, kings, wise men, strong men, and saints, which they certainly are not. From this they argue that a great disorder has arisen in human affairs as the result of some accident. At first they were inclined to say, with Plato, that in the first ages the heavens revolved from the present west to what we now call the east and that they later on reversed their direction. They say that it is possible that affairs below are controlled by some lower divine power and that it is permitted by the higher divine power; but they consider this assertion a silly one. They think even sillier the statement that Saturn at the beginning ruled well and that then Jupiter ruled less well and then the other planets successively, although they do think that the ages of the world are arranged in accordance with the order of the planets, and they believe that from the changes of the apsides after 1,000 or 1,600 years things can be greatly changed.

This age of ours is apparently to be assigned to Mercury, although it may be varied by great conjunctions and the returns of the anomalies may have fatal force. Finally, they affirm that the Christian who is content to believe that the disorder arose from the sin of Adam is happy. They also think that the ills of punishment more than those of guilt come down to the sons from the fathers.

The guilt returns from the children to the parents in the measure that the latter have been negligent in their procreation and have conceived them at the wrong time or place or with the wrong choice of parents or have neglected their upbringing or have taught and instructed them badly. Therefore they devote careful attention to begetting and upbringing, and they say that the punishment and guilt of both the children and the parents redound to the disadvantage of the state; therefore all countries are now in a wretched condition, and what is worse (they say) is that the evils themselves are called peace and happiness, since people have never known good, and the world seems to them to be ruled by chance. But actually he who observes the construction of the world and the anatomy of

man (which they often study in those condemned to death), of
plants, and of animals, and the uses of the parts and their subparts,
must confess the wisdom and providence of God with loud acclamations. Therefore, man must give himself wholly to religion and
always revere his own Maker. However, only he can do this well
(and still not easily) who inquires earnestly into God's works and
knows them well, who observes His laws and philosophizes correctly
on His works. What you do not wish to be done to you, do not do
to the other person; what you wish others to do for you, do that
for them. It follows from this fact that just as we seek honor and
good things from our children and from men generally, although
we grant but little of these things to them, so do we owe more to
God, from whom we receive everything and through whom we are
all that we are and are where we are. Praise be to Him forever!

GRAND MASTER:

Indeed, since these people, who know only the natural law, so
closely approach Christianity, which adds to the laws of nature
only the sacraments, which give aid in observing those laws, I deduce the valid argument in favor of the Christian religion that it is
the truest of all and that when its abuses have been removed it will
be mistress over the whole world, as the more outstanding theologians teach and hope. They say that this is the reason the Spaniards
discovered the New World (although the first discoverer is our
great Genoese hero Columbus): that the whole world may be
gathered together under one law. Therefore, these philosophers must
be witnesses of the truth, chosen by God. From this I realize that we
do not know what we are doing but are the instruments of God.
Those men seek new regions, led on by their desire for gold and
riches; but God has a higher end in view. The sun attempts to burn
up the earth, not to produce plants, men, etc., but God uses the
struggle between it and them for the production of the latter things.
Praise and glory to Him!

CAPTAIN:

Oh, if you only knew what they say from their astrology and
also from our prophets concerning the coming age and the fact that
our age has more history in it in a hundred years than the whole
world in the preceding 4,000 years, that more books have been published in this century than in the 5,000 years before it, what they say
about the wonderful invention of printing and of arquebuses and the
discovery of the use of the magnet, all of these things being very
clear signs of, and at the same time means for, the gathering together
of all the inhabitants of the earth into one fold. . . .

A new monarchy will arise, and a reformation in laws and arts will come about; there will be prophets and renewment, and they say a great gain is portended for Christianity. But first there will be plucking and rooting out, then building and planting and so on.

Permit me to go, since I have things to do. But you must hear this: they have already discovered the art of flying, the one thing that the world seemed to be lacking. Soon they expect to have optical instruments with which to see more stars, and hearing instruments with which to hear the harmony of the heavens. . . .

They say that what is feminine brings fecundity of things in the heavens and that less robust strength prevails among us. Thus we know that feminine rule has prevailed in this century, for example. . . . Mary in Hungary, Elizabeth in England, Catherine in France, Blanca in Tuscany, Margaret in Belgium, Mary in Scotland, and in Spain, Isabella, the discoveress of the New World. . . .

Heresy, a horrible thing of lust, disposed to bestiality, which re-jects free judgment on the part of man, prevails in Germany, France, England, and almost all of northern Europe through Mars, Venus, and the moon, which are powerful there. However, Spain and Italy, through Sagittarius and Leo, their signs, have held fast to the truth of Christianity, law, and purity. Would that they also had it in their customs! The people of the City of the Sun, through moon and Mercury, with the aid of the apsis of the sun, have new arts. . . . They are adding to human liberty, for they say that if the forty hours that a great philosopher among them was tortured most cruelly by the enemy could not force him to confess even one little word of the things which they sought to find out, since he had determined in his mind to keep silent, then not even the stars, which move slowly and at a distance, can force us to act contrary to our decision. But since they bring about unconscious and gentle change in feeling, he who follows feeling more than reason is subject to them. For the constellation which brought forth foul vapors from the bodies of the heretics, at the same time produced exhalations fragrant with virtue from the founders of the Jesuits, the Minims, and the Capuchins. Under the same constellation, too, Ferdinand Cortez propagated the divine religion of Christ in Mexico.

I shall finish telling you in another conversation the many things that now threaten the world. Heresy is among the works of carnal sense enumerated by St. Paul, and the stars incline sensual people to the thing toward which their own nature inclines them. In the case of rational men, the stars incline men to the rational, true, and holy law of first reason, the word of God, who is ever to be praised. Amen.

GRAND MASTER:

Wait, wait a moment!

CAPTAIN:

I cannot, I cannot.

20

"An Utopia of Mine Own"

Robert Burton

*(extracted from "Democritus to the Reader"
in* The Anatomy of Melancholy, *Oxford, 1651;
London, 1652, as corrected and augmented
from the first edition, Oxford, 1621)*

Robert Burton   (1577–1640)

is a whimsical writer, but his claim that the utopia in "Democritus to the Reader" (the Introductory section of his *Anatomy of Melancholy*) is a mere flight of fancy should not be taken seriously. First printed in Oxford in 1621, the *Anatomy* was reprinted in five more editions, each containing additions by the author. Almost the entire utopia is reprinted below, omissions being indicated by ellipses. The frequent Latin phrases have been Englished.

Primarily a scholar and incidentally a divine, Burton passed most of his life at Christ Church, an Oxford college founded in the previous century. Though reputed a pedant, Burton kept in touch with practical life by assiduously reading pamphlets and books about the economic and social problems of the early seventeenth century, as well as learned works of all kinds. For three years he was Clerk of the Market at Oxford, a fact which accounts for his interest in accurate weights and measures. His utopia is a vehicle for trenchant social comments, for the advocacy of a planned economy which encourages individual enterprise, and for a comprehensive program of social reforms—though he fails to indicate how they are to be attained. The utopia is preceded by an analysis of the evils which beset commonwealths. Having noted the prosperity of the Dutch despite their lack of physical resources, Burton decides that industriousness is the secret of their success, and that England, despite its potential productivity, is relatively unprosperous because of idleness and lack of enterprise. Accordingly, his main theme is to urge efficient utilization of all available resources of land, talent, and manpower. To this end he seeks, in his utopia, to eliminate waste, duplication, and confusion, to encourage the enterprising, to penalize the unenterprising, to provide for the sick and the aged, and to ensure employment for the healthy. The reforms which he advocates are far-reaching, but his purpose is to improve the existing order, not to revolutionize it or overthrow it. His scheme makes due concession to the strength and weakness of human nature. It is timely in advocating a planned economy dedicated to capitalistic productivity and, at the same time, utilizing on a national scale the regulated economy of the medieval city-state. Despite its structure of constant checks and supervision, it is an elastic economy which leaves room for individual enterprise of a reasonable and practical nature. It is dedicated neither to the Kingdom of God, the laboratories of science, the practice of communism, nor the realization of a concept of justice: it is designed primarily to give security and a decent standard of living to all its citizens. Basically, Burton's outlook is materialistic and utilitarian.

BIBLIOGRAPHY: Robert Burton, *The Anatomy of Melancholy*, Everyman's Library, 3 vols., 1932; J. W. Allen, *English Political Thought*, 1938, I, 88 ff.; J. Max Patrick, "Robert Burton's Utopianism," *Philological Quarterly*, XXVII (1948), 345 ff.

"An Utopia of Mine Own"

I will yet, to satisfy and please myself, make an Utopia of mine own, a New Atlantis, a poetical commonwealth, in which I will freely domineer, build cities, make laws, statutes, as I list myself. . . . But I will choose a site, whose latitude shall be forty-five degrees . . . in the midst of the temperate zone, or perhaps under the Equator, that paradise of the world, "where is a perpetual spring"; the longitude for some reasons I will conceal. . . . It shall be divided into twelve or thirteen provinces, and those by hills, rivers, roadways, or some more eminent limits exactly bounded. Each province shall have a metropolis, which shall be so placed as a center almost in a circumference, and the rest at equal distances, some twelve Italian miles asunder, or thereabout, and in them shall be sold all things necessary for the use of man, at stated hours and days; no market towns, markets, or fairs, for they do but beggar cities (no village shall stand six, seven, or eight miles from a city); except those emporiums which are by the seaside, general staples, marts, as Antwerp, Venice, Bergen of old, London, etc. Cities most part shall be situate upon navigable rivers or lakes, creeks, havens; and for their form, regular, round, square, or long square, with fair, broad, and straight streets, houses uniform, built of brick and stone, like Bruges, Brussels, . . . Berne, . . . Cambalu in Tartary, or that Venetian Palma. I will admit very few or no suburbs, and those of baser building, walls only to keep out man and horse, except it be in some frontier towns, or by the seaside, and those fortified after the latest manner of fortification, and situated upon convenient havens, or opportune places. In every so built city, I will have convenient churches, and separate places to bury the dead in, not in churchyards; a fortress in some, not all, to command it, prisons for offenders, opportune marketplaces of all sorts, for corn, meat, cattle, fuel, fish, commodious courts of justice, public halls for all societies, bourses [exchanges], meeting-places, armories in which shall be kept engines for quenching of fire, artillery gardens, public walks, theaters, and spacious fields allotted for all gymnics, sports, and honest recreations, hospitals of all kinds, for children, orphans, old folks, sick men, madmen, soldiers, pest-houses, etc., (not built by begging, or by gouty benefactors, who, when by fraud and rapine they have extorted all their lives, oppressed whole provinces, societies, etc., give some-thing to pious uses, build a satisfactory almshouse, school, or bridge, etc., at their last end, or before perhaps, which is no otherwise than to steal a goose and stick down a feather, rob a thousand to relieve ten); and those hospitals so built and maintained, not by collections, benevolences, donaries, for a set number (as in ours) just so many and no more at such a rate, but for all those that stand in need, be they more or less, and that at public expense, and so always main-tained: "we are not born only for ourselves." I will have conduits of sweet and good water aptly disposed in each town, common granaries, as at Dresden, Stettin, Nuremberg, etc.; colleges of mathe-maticians, musicians, and actors, as of old at Lebedus in Ionia, al-chemists, physicians, artists, and philosophers, that all arts and sciences may sooner be perfected and better learned; and public historiographers, as amongst those ancient Persians, informed and appointed by the State to register all famous acts, and not by each insufficient scribbler, partial or parasitical pedant, as in our times. I will provide public schools of all kinds, singing, dancing, fencing, etc., especially of grammar and languages, not to be taught by those tedious precepts ordinarily used, but by use, example, conversation, as travelers learn abroad, and nurses teach to children.

As I will have all such places, so will I ordain public governors, fit officers to each place, treasurers, aediles, quaestors, overseers of pupils, widows' goods, and all public houses, etc., and those once a year to make strict accounts of all receipts, expenses, to avoid con-fusion, and thus there will be no squandering. . . . They shall be subordinate to those higher officers and governors of each city, which shall not be poor tradesmen and mean artificers, but noble-men, and gentlemen, which shall be tied to residence in those towns they dwell next, at such set times and seasons: for I see no reason . . . that it should be more dishonorable for noblemen to govern the city than the country. . . . I will have no bogs, fens, marshes, vast woods, deserts, heaths, commons, but all enclosed (yet not depopulated, and therefore take heed you mistake me not); for that which is common and every man's, is no man's; the richest countries are still [always] enclosed, as Essex, Kent, with us, etc., Spain, Italy; and where enclosures are least in quantity, they are best husbanded, as about Florence in Italy, Damascus in Syria, etc., which are liker gardens than fields. I will not have a barren acre in all my territories, not so much as the tops of mountains: where nature fails, it shall be supplied by art; lakes and rivers shall not be left desolate. All com-mon highways, bridges, banks, corrivations of waters, aqueducts, channels, public works, building, etc., out of a common stock, curiously [carefully] maintained and kept in repair; no depopulations, engrossings, alterations of wood, arable, but by the consent of some supervisors that shall be appointed for that purpose, to see what reformation ought to be had in all places, what is amiss, how to help it, "what each region will bear, and what it will not produce," what ground is aptest for wood, what for corn, what for cattle, gardens, orchards, fishponds, etc., with a charitable division in every village (not one domineering house greedily to swallow up all, which is too common with us), what for lords, what for tenants; and because they shall be better encouraged to improve such lands they hold, manure, plant trees, drain, fence, etc., they shall have long leases, a known rent, and known fine, to free them from those intolerable exactions of tyrannizing landlords. These supervisors shall likewise appoint what quantity of land in each manor is fit for the lord's desmesnes, what for holding of tenants, how it ought to be husbanded, . . . how to be manured, tilled, rectified, . . . and what proportion is fit for all callings, because private professors [men who claim knowledge and skill—in this instance, in agriculture], are many times idiots, ill husbands, oppressors, covetous, and know not how to improve their own, or else wholly respect their own, and not public good.

Utopian parity is a kind of government to be wished for rather than effected, [Andreae's] Christianopolis, Campanella's City of the Sun, and that New Atlantis [are] witty fictions, but mere chimeras, and Plato's community in many things is impious, absurd, and ridiculous; it takes away all splendor and magnificence. I will have several orders, degrees of nobility, and those hereditary, not rejecting younger brothers in the meantime; for they shall be sufficiently provided for by pensions, or so qualified, brought up in some honest calling, they shall be able to live of themselves. I will have such a [a certain] proportion of ground belonging to every barony; he that buys the land shall buy the barony; he that by riot consumes his patrimony and ancient desmesnes shall forfeit his honors. As some dignities shall be hereditary, so some again by election, or by gift (besides free offices, pensions, annuities), like our bishoprics, prebends, the bassas' palaces in Turkey, the procurators' houses and offices in Venice, which, like the golden apple, shall be given to the worthiest and best deserving both in war and peace, as a reward of their worth and good service, as so many goals for all to aim at (honor is an encouragement to art), and encouragement to others. For I hate these severe, unnatural, harsh, German, French, and Venetian decrees, which exclude plebeians from honors; be they never so wise, rich, virtuous, valiant, and well qualified, they must not be patricians, but keep their own rank; this is to make war on nature, odious to God and men; I abhor it. My form of government shall be monarchical: "Liberty is never more pleasing than under a virtuous prince." Few laws, but those severely kept, plainly put down, and in the mother tongue, that every man may understand. Every city shall have a peculiar trade or privilege, by which it shall be chiefly maintained: and parents shall teach their children (one of three, at least), bring up and instruct them in the mysteries of their own trade. In each town these several tradesmen shall be so aptly disposed [situated], that they shall free the rest from danger or offense: fire-trades, as smiths, forge-men, brewers, bakers, metal-men, etc., shall dwell apart by themselves: dyers, tanners, fellmongers, and such as use water, in convenient places by themselves: noisome or fulsome for bad smells, as butchers' slaughterhouses, chandlers, curriers, in remote places and some back lanes. Fraternities and companies I approve of, as merchants' bourses, colleges of druggers, physicians, musicians, etc., but all trades to be rated in the sale of wares, as our clerks of the market do bakers and brewers; corn itself, what scarcity soever shall come, not to exceed such a price. Of such wares as are transported or brought in, if they be necessary, commodious, and such as nearly concern man's life, as corn, wood, coal, etc., and such provision we cannot want, I will have little or no custom paid, no taxes; but for such things as are for pleasure, delight, or ornament, as wine, spice, tobacco, silk, velvet, cloth of gold, lace, jewels, etc., a greater impost. I will have certain ships sent out for new discoveries every year, and some discreet men appointed to travel into all neighbor kingdoms by land, which shall observe what artificial inventions and good laws are in other countries, customs, alterations, or aught else, concerning war or peace, which may tend to the common good. Ecclesiastical discipline, in the control of bishops, subordinate as the other. No impropriations, no lay patrons of church livings, or one private man, but common societies, corporations, etc., and those rectors of benefices to be chosen out of the universities, examined and approved, as the *literati* [learned governing class] in China. No parish to contain above a thousand auditors [members of a congregation]. If it were possible, I would have such priests as should imitate Christ, charitable lawyers should love their neighbors as themselves, temperate and modest physicians, politicians contemn the world, philosophers should know themselves, noblemen live honestly, tradesmen leave lying and cozening, magistrates corruption, etc.; but this is impossible, I must get such as I may. I will therefore have of lawyers, judges, advocates, physicians, chirurgeons, etc., a set number, and every man, if it be possible, to plead his own cause, to tell that tale to the judge which he doth to his advocate,

as at Fez in Africa, Bantam, Aleppo, Ragusa: "Everyone is expected
to plead his own case." Those advocates, chirurgeons, and physicians
which are allowed, to be maintained out of the common treasure, no
fees to be given or taken upon pain of losing their places; or if they
do, very small fees, and when the cause is fully ended. He that sues
any man shall put in a pledge, which, if it be proved he hath wrong-
fully sued his adversary, rashly or maliciously, he shall forfeit and
lose. Or else, before any suit begin, the plaintiff shall have his com-
plaint approved by a set delegacy to that purpose; if it be of moment, he shall be suffered [allowed] as before to proceed, if otherwise, they shall determine it. All causes shall be pleaded, the parties'
names concealed, if some circumstances do not otherwise require.
Judges and other officers shall be aptly disposed in each province,
villages, cities, as common arbitrators to hear causes and end all
controversies, and those not single, but three at least on the bench
at once to determine or give sentence, and those again to sit by turns
or lots, and not to continue still in the same office. No controversy
to depend [remain unsettled] above a year, but without all delays
and further appeals to be speedily dispatched, and finally concluded
in that time allotted. These and all other inferior magistrates to be
chosen as the *literati* in China, or by those exact suffrages of the
Venetians, and such again not to be eligible, or capable of magistracies, honors, offices, except they be sufficiently qualified for
learning, manners, and that by the strict approbation of deputed
examinators: first scholars to take place, then soldiers; for I am of
Vegetius his opinion, a scholar deserves better than a soldier, because, "A soldier's work lasts for an age, a scholar's for ever." If
they misbehave themselves, they shall be deposed, and accordingly
punished, and whether their offices be annual or otherwise, once a
year they shall be called in question, and give an account; for men
are partial and passionate, merciless, covetous, corrupt, subject to
love, hate, fear, favor, etc.; every authority is under a greater authority: like Solon's Areopagites, or those Roman censors, some shall
visit others, and be visited in turn themselves, they shall oversee that
no prowling officers, under color of authority, shall insult over his
inferiors, as so many wild beasts, oppress, domineer, flay, grind, or
trample on, be partial or corrupt, but that there be justice equally
done, live as friends and brethren together; and which Sesellius
would have and so much desires in his kingdom of France, "a
diapason and sweet harmony of kings, princes, nobles, and plebeians
so mutually tied and involved in love, as well as laws and authority,
as that they never disagree, insult or encroach one upon another."
If any man deserve well in his office he shall be rewarded, "for if
you take away the prize, who embraces virtue for its own sake?"

He that invents anything for public good in any art or science, writes a treatise, or performs any noble exploit at home or abroad, shall be accordingly enriched, honored, and preferred. I say with Hannibal in Ennius, let him be of what condition he will, in all offices, actions, he that deserves best shall have best.

Tilianus in Philonius, out of a charitable mind no doubt, wished all his books were gold and silver, jewels and precious stones, to redeem captives, set free prisoners, and relieve all poor distressed souls that wanted means. Religiously done, I deny not, but to what purpose? Suppose this were so well done, within a little after, though a man had Croesus' wealth to bestow there would be as many more. Wherefore, I will suffer no beggars, rogues, vagabonds, or idle persons at all, that cannot give an account of their lives how they maintain themselves. If they be impotent, lame, blind, and single, they shall be sufficiently maintained in several hospitals, built for that purpose; if married and infirm, past work, or by inevitable loss or some such-like misfortune cast behind, by distribution of corn, house-rest free, annual pensions or money, they shall be relieved, and highly rewarded for their good service they have formerly done; if able, they shall be enforced to work. "For I see no reason" (as he said), "why an epicure or idle drone, a rich glutton, a usurer, should live at ease, and do nothing, live in honor, in all manner of pleasures, and oppress others, whenas in the meantime a poor laborer, a smith, a carpenter, a husbandman that hath spent his time in continual labor, as an ass to carry burdens, to do the commonwealth good, and without whom we cannot live, shall be left in his old age to beg or starve, and lead a miserable life worse than a jument [an old nag]." As all conditions shall be tied to their task, so none shall be overtired, but have their set times of recreations and holidays, to follow their own inclinations, feasts and merry meetings, even to the meanest artificer, or basest servant, once a week to sing or dance, though not all at once, or do whatsoever he shall please. If any be drunk, he shall drink no more wine or strong drink in a twelvemonth after. A bankrupt shall be publicly shamed, and he that cannot pay his debts, if by riot or negligence he have been impoverished, shall be for a twelvemonth imprisoned; if in that space his creditors be not satisfied, he shall be hanged. He that commits sacrilege shall lose his hands; he that bears false witness, or is of perjury convict, shall have his tongue cut out, except he redeem it with his head. Murder, adultery, shall be punished by death, but not theft, except it be some more grievous offense, or notorious offenders: otherwise they shall be condemned to the galleys, mines, be his slaves whom they have offended, during their lives. I hate all hereditary slaves, and that hard law of the Persians . . . that wife and children, friends and allies, should suffer for the father's offense.

No man shall marry until he be twenty-five, no woman till she be twenty, unless permission be given otherwise. If one die, the other party shall not marry till six months after; and because many families are compelled to live niggardly, exhaust and undone by great dowers, none shall be given at all, or very little, and that by supervisors rated. They that are foul shall have a greater portion; if fair, none at all, or very little: howsoever, not to exceed such a rate as those supervisors shall think fit. And when once they come to those years, poverty shall hinder no man from marriage, or any other respect, but all shall be rather enforced than hindered, except they be dismembered, or grievously deformed, infirm, or visited with some enormous hereditary disease in body or mind; in such cases upon a great pain or mulct, man or woman shall not marry, other order shall be taken for them to their content. If people over-abound, they shall be eased by colonies.

No man shall wear weapons in any city. The same attire shall be kept, and that proper to several callings, by which they shall be distinguished. Display at funerals shall be taken away, that intempestive expense moderated, and many others. Brokers, takers of pawns, biting usurers, I will not admit; yet because we converse here with men, not with gods, and for the hardness of men's hearts, I will tolerate some kind of usury. If we were honest, I confess, we should have no use of it, but being as it is, we must necessarily admit it. Howsoever most divines contradict it ("We say that it poisons, but do not mean it"); it must be winked at by politicians. And yet some great doctors approve of it, Calvin, Bucer, Zanchius, P. Martyr, because by so many grand lawyers, decrees of emperors, princes' statutes, customs of commonwealths, churches' approbations, it is permitted, etc., I will therefore allow it. But to no private persons, nor to every man that will, to orphans only, maids, widows, or such as by reason of their age, sex, education, ignorance of trading, know not otherwise how to employ it; and those so approved, not to let it out apart [individually], but to bring their money to a common bank which shall be allowed in every city, as in Genoa, Geneva, Nuremberg, Venice, at 5, 6, 7, not above 8 per centum, as the supervisors, or overseers of finances shall think fit. And as it shall not be lawful for each man to be an usurer that will, so shall it not be lawful for all to take up money at use [interest], not to prodigals and spendthrifts, but to merchants, young tradesmen, such as stand in need or know honestly how to employ it, whose necessity, cause, and condition the said supervisors shall approve of.

I will have no private monopolies to enrich one man and beggar a multitude, multiplicity of offices, or supplying by deputies; weights and measures the same throughout, and those rectified by astronomical observations and the sun's motion, three-score miles to a degree according to observation, 1,000 geometrical paces to a mile, five foot to a pace, twelve inches to a foot, etc.; and from measures known it is an easy matter to rectify weights, etc., to cast up all, and resolve bodies by algebra, stereometry. I hate wars if they be not for the welfare of the people, upon urgent occasion. "We hate the hawk because it is always fighting." Offensive wars, except the cause be very just, I will not allow of. For I do highly magnify that saying of Hannibal of Scipio, in Livy: "It had been a blessed thing for you and us, if God had given that mind to our predecessors, that you had been content with Italy, we with Africa. For neither Sicily nor Sardinia are worth such cost and pains, so many fleets and armies, or so many famous captains' lives." "Fair means shall first be tried"; "peaceful pressure succeeds where violence fails." I will have them proceed with all moderation: "for strategy does more injury to the enemy than unreasoning force." And in such wars to abstain as much as is possible from depopulations, burning of towns, massacring of infants, etc. For defensive wars, I will have forces still ready at a small warning, by land and sea, a prepared navy, soldiers ready for action; and money, which is the sinews of war, in readiness; and a sufficient revenue, a third part as in old Rome and Egypt, reserved for the commonwealth, to avoid those heavy taxes and impositions, as well to defray this charge of wars, as also all other public defalcations, expenses, fees, pensions, reparations, chaste sports, feasts, donaries, rewards, and entertainments. All things in this nature especially I will have maturely done, and with great deliberation: "let it be done without fear, and without remissness or cowardice." "But where am I wandering?" To prosecute the rest would require a volume. Enough! I have been overtedious in this subject; I could have here willingly ranged, but these straits wherein I am included will not permit.

21

New Atlantis

A Work Unfinished

Francis Bacon

London
1627

Francis Bacon (1561–1626),

son of a cultured mother and a father high in the legal profession, was born in London and educated at Cambridge and Gray's Inn. He rose to prominence, partly through his own abilities, partly through the support of such friends as the Earl of Essex, entered Parliament, became Lord Chancellor, was elevated to the peerage as Baron Verulam and Viscount St. Albans. Nevertheless he found time not only to write essays, a treatise on *The Advancement of Learning*, and a *History of Henry VII*, but also to compose his great philosophical and scientific work, *Novum Organum* (The New Method).

The *New Atlantis*, first published in 1627, associates a pretentious scientific program with the Platonic myth of Atlantis, the romantic fascination of a remote island, and the voyage literature of an age of exploration. For the most part, the ideas propounded are not original: scientific academies such as the Royal Society of Physicians, libraries like the Ambrosian at Milan, and botanic gardens like that at Leyden were already known. The new scientific method of experiment, the utilitarian approach to science, and the importance of lecture-demonstrations had already been exemplified in the life of Bernard Palissy in France. Bacon's contribution consists far less in originality than in the effective collection and presentation of significant ideas. He brought home to men's business and bosoms the potentialities of science, helped to separate it alike from the trammels of theology and the obscurities of alchemy, and fired the imagination with a picture of a society based on scientific research and its products. His is a capitalistic utopia based on the unit of the family. Although it is about a distant island, Bacon undoubtedly had the reform of England in mind when he wrote it. However, he carefully preserves existing institutions and, instead of advocating revolution or radical change, superimposes science and advanced knowledge on a society which was essentially that of Jacobean England. His apparent belief that science and knowledge would solve all social problems may seem rather naïve in the light of subsequent human experience. Nevertheless the work is of major importance for demonstrating the potentialities of science, the improvability of mankind, and the possibility of dedicating a state to the welfare of its citizens.

The following text is a cautious modernization of most of the original edition of 1627.

BIBLIOGRAPHY: A useful collection of Bacon's most interesting writings is his *Essays, Advancement of Learning, New Atlantis, and other Pieces*, edited by Richard F. Jones (New York, 1937). Scholars should consult *New Atlantis*, edited by Alfred B. Gough (Oxford,

1915). The biographies by Church, Abbott, and Lovejoy treat Bacon's character harshly; those by James Spedding, Mary Sturt, and Charles Williams are recommended.

New Atlantis

[In 1676, Joseph Glanvill published a continuation of Bacon's *New Atlantis* under the title "Anti-Fanatical Religion and Free Philosophy" in *Essays on Several Important Subjects in Philosophy and Religion*, and prefixed to it a summary of *New Atlantis*. The following extract from Glanvill synopsizes the beginning of Bacon's account.]

"We parted from Peru, with design to pass to China and Japan by the South Sea. And after we had been long driven up and down by contrary winds, and wandered in the greatest wilderness of waters in the world, without the least hopes of making any land in that immense, undiscovered abyss that was beyond the Old World and the New, it pleased God to bring us into the harbor of a most angelical country, that lay hid in the greatest ocean in the universe.

"We found there a people of singular goodness and humanity, who received us with most affectionate kindness, and provided for us with a parentlike care and indulgence. We were lodged in a fair pile of buildings called the Strangers' House, appointed for such occasions; and there we had all things, both for our whole and sick, that belonged to charity and mercy."

[From this point, Bacon's own account continues as follows:]

The next day, about ten of the clock, the Governor came. And when we were set, he began thus: "We of this island of Bensalem" (for so they call it in their language), "have this, that by means of our solitary situation and of the laws of secrecy which we have for our travelers, and our rare admission of strangers, we know well most part of the habitable world, and are ourselves unknown. Therefore because he that knoweth least is fittest to ask questions, it is more reason for the entertainment of the time that ye ask me questions than that I ask you." We answered that we humbly thanked him that he would give us leave so to do, and that we conceived by the taste we had already, that there was no worldly thing on earth more worthy to be known than the state of that happy land. But above all, we said, since that we were met from the several ends of the world, and hoped assuredly that we should meet one day in the kingdom of heaven (for that we were both parts Christians), we desired to know (in respect that land was so remote, and so divided by vast and unknown seas from the land where our Saviour walked on earth) who was the apostle of that nation, and how it was converted to the faith. It appeared in his face that he took great contentment in this our question; he said, "Ye knit my heart to you by asking this question in the first place, for it showeth that you first seek the kingdom of heaven; and I shall gladly and briefly satisfy your demand.

"About twenty years after the ascension of our Saviour, it came to pass that there was seen by the people of Renfusa (a city upon the eastern coast of our island) within night (the night was cloudy and calm), as it might be some mile into the sea, a great pillar of light, not sharp but in form of a column or cylinder, rising from the sea a great way up towards heaven, and on the top of it was seen a large cross of light more bright and resplendent than the body of the pillar. Upon which so strange a spectacle the people of the city gathered apace together upon the sands to wonder; and so after put themselves into a number of small boats to go nearer to this marvelous sight. But when the boats were come within about sixty yards of the pillar, they found themselves all bound, and could go no further; . . . It so fell out that there was in one of the boats one of the wise men of the society of Solomon's House, which house or college (my good brethren) is the very eye of this kingdom, who having awhile attentively and devoutly viewed and contemplated this pillar and cross, fell down upon his face, and then raised himself upon his knees, and lifting up his hands to heaven, made his prayers in this manner:

" 'Lord God of heaven and earth, Thou hast vouchsafed of Thy grace to those of our order to know Thy works of creation and the secrets of them, and to discern (as far as appertaineth to the generations of men) between divine miracles, works of nature, works of art, and impostures and illusions of all sorts. I do here acknowledge and testify before this people that the thing which we now see before our eyes is Thy Finger and a true Miracle; and forasmuch as we learn in our books that Thou never workest miracles but to a divine and excellent end (for the laws of nature are Thine own laws, and Thou exceedest them not but upon great cause), we must humbly beseech Thee to prosper this great sign, and to give us the interpretation and use of it in mercy, which Thou dost in some part secretly promise by sending it unto us.'

"When he had made his prayer, he presently found the boat he was in movable and unbound, whereas all the rest remained still fast, and taking that for an assurance of leave to approach, he caused the boat to be softly and with silence rowed towards the pillar. But ere he came near it, the pillar and cross of light brake up, and cast itself abroad, as it were, into a firmament of many stars, which also vanished soon after, and there was nothing left to be seen but a small ark or chest of cedar, dry and not wet at all with water, though it swam. And in the fore-end of it, which was towards him, grew a small green branch of palm; and when the wise man had taken it with all reverence into his boat, it opened of itself, and there were found in it a Book and a Letter, both written in fine parchment and wrapped in sindons of linen. The Book contained all the canonical books of the Old and New Testament according as you have them (for we know well what the Churches with you receive); and the Apocalypse itself and some other books of the New Testament, which were not at that time written, were nevertheless in the Book. And for the Letter, it was in these words:

"I Bartholomew, a servant of the Highest and Apostle of Jesus Christ, was warned by an angel, that appeared to me in a vision of glory, that I should commit this ark to the floods of the sea. Therefore I do testify and declare unto that people where God shall ordain this ark to come to land, that in the same day is come unto them salvation and peace and good will from the Father and from the Lord Jesus.

"There was also . . . wrought a great miracle, conform to that of the Apostles in the original Gift of Tongues [Acts ii: 1–11]. For there being at that time in this land Hebrews, Persians, and Indians, besides the natives, everyone read upon the Book and Letter as if they had been written in his own language. And thus was this land saved from infidelity (as the remains of the old world was from water) by an ark, through the apostolical and miraculous evangelism of St. Bartholomew." And here he paused, and a messenger came and called him from us. So this was all that passed in that conference.

The next day the same governor came again to us . . . and after we were set again, he said, "Well, the questions are on your part." One of our number said, after a little pause, that . . . we in Europe (notwithstanding all the remote discoveries and navigations of this last age) never heard any of the least inkling or glimpse of this island. This we found wonderful strange, for that all nations have inter-knowledge one of another either by voyage into foreign parts or by strangers that come to them, and though the traveler into a foreign country doth commonly know more by the eye than he that stayeth at home can by relation of the traveler, yet both ways suffice to make a mutual knowledge in some degree on both parts. But for this island, we never heard tell of any ship of theirs that had been

seen to arrive upon any shore of Europe; no, nor of either the East
or West Indies; nor yet of any ship of any other part of the world
that had made return from them. And yet the marvel rested not in
this. For the situation of it (as his lordship said) in the secret conclave of such a vast sea might cause it. But then that they should
have knowledge of the languages, books, affairs of those that lie
such a distance from them, it was a thing we could not tell what to
make of, for that it seemed to us a condition and propriety of divine
powers and beings to be hidden and unseen to others and yet to have
others open and as in a light to them. At this speech the governor
gave a gracious smile, and said, that we did well to ask pardon for
this question we now asked, for that it imported as if we thought
this land a land of magicians, that sent forth spirits of the air into all
parts to bring them news and intelligence of other countries. It was
answered by us all, in all possible humbleness, but yet with a countenance taking knowledge that we knew that he spake it but merrily,
that we were apt enough to think there was somewhat supernatural
in this island, but yet rather as angelical than magical. But to let his
lordship know truly what it was that made us tender and doubtful
to ask this question, it was not any such conceit, but because . . .
this land had laws of secrecy touching strangers. To this he said,
"You remember it aright; and therefore in that I shall say to you
I must reserve some particulars, which it is not lawful for me to
reveal, but there will be enough left to give you satisfaction.

"You shall understand (that which perhaps you will scarce think
credible) that about three thousand years ago, or somewhat more,
the navigation of the world (specially for remote voyages) was
greater than at this day. Do not think with yourselves that I know
not how much it is increased with you within these six-score years:
I know it well; and yet I say greater then than now: whether it was
that the example of the ark, that saved the remnant of men from the
universal deluge, gave men confidence to adventure upon the waters,
or what it was, but such is the truth. The Phoenicians, and especially
the Tyrians, had great fleets. So had the Carthaginians, their colony
which is yet further west. Towards the east, the shipping of Egypt
and of Palestine was likewise great. China also and the great Atlantis
(that you call America), which have now but junks and canoes,
abounded then in tall ships. This island (as appeareth by faithful
registers of those times) had then fifteen hundred strong ships of
great content. Of all this there is with you sparing memory or none,
but we have large knowledge thereof.

"At that time this land was known and frequented by the ships
and vessels of all the nations before named. And (as it cometh to
pass) they had many times men of other countries, that were no

sailors, that came with them, as Persians, Chaldeans, Arabians; so as almost all nations of might and fame resorted hither, of whom we have some stirps and little tribes with us at this day. And for our own ships, they went sundry voyages . . . in the Atlantic and Mediterranean Seas; as to Pekin . . . as far as to the borders of the East Tartary.

"At the same time and an age after, or more, the inhabitants of the great Atlantis did flourish. For though the narration and description which is made by a great man [Plato, in his *Critias*] with you, that the descendants of Neptune planted there; and of the magnificent temple, palace, city, and hill; and the manifold streams of goodly navigable rivers (which, as so many chains, environed the same site and temple); and the several degrees of ascent whereby men did climb up to the same, as if it had been a ladder to heaven [Genesis xxviii: 12], be all poetical and fabulous, yet so much is true, that the said country of Atlantis, as well that of Peru, then called Coya, as that of Mexico, then named Tyrambel, were mighty and proud kingdoms in arms, shipping, and riches, so mighty as at one time (or at least within the space of ten years) they both made two great expeditions: they of Tyrambel through the Atlantic to the Mediterranean Sea; and they of Coya through the South Sea upon this our island. And for the former of these, which was into Europe, the same author amongst you (as it seemeth) had some relation from the Egyptian priest whom he citeth. For assuredly such a thing there was. But whether it were the ancient Athenians that had the glory of the repulse and resistance of those forces, I can say nothing; but certain it is, there never came back either ship or man from that voyage. Neither had the other voyage of those of Coya upon us had better fortune, if they had not met with enemies of greater clemency. For the king of this island (by name Altabin), a wise man and a great warrior, knowing well both his own strength and that of his enemies, handled the matter so, as he cut off their land-forces from their ships, and entoiled both their navy and their camp with a greater power than theirs, both by sea and land, and compelled them to render themselves without striking stroke, and after they were at his mercy, contenting himself only with their oath that they should no more bear arms against him, dismissed them all in safety. But the Divine Revenge overtook not long after those proud enterprises. For within less than the space of one hundred years, the great Atlantis was utterly lost and destroyed, not by a great earthquake, as your man saith (for that whole tract is little subject to earthquakes), but by a particular deluge or inundation. . . . So you see, by this main accident of time we lost our traffic with the Americans, with whom of all others, in regard they lay nearest to us, we had most commerce. As for the other parts of the world, it is most manifest that in the ages following (whether it were in respect of wars or by a natural revolution of time) navigation did everywhere greatly decay, and specially far voyages . . . were altogether left and omitted. So then, that part of intercourse which could be from other nations to sail to us, you see how it hath long since ceased, except it were by some rare accident, as this of yours. But now of the cessation of that other part of intercourse, which might be by our sailing to other nations, I must yield you some other cause. For I cannot say (if I shall say truly)· but our shipping, for number, strength, mariners, pilots, and all things that appertain to navigation, is as great as ever, and therefore why we should sit at home, I shall now give you an account by itself; and it will draw nearer to give you satisfaction to your principal question.

"There reigned in this island, about nineteen hundred years ago, a King, whose memory of all others we most adore, not superstitiously, but as a divine instrument, though a mortal man: his name was Solamona, and we esteem him as the lawgiver of our nation. This king had a large heart, inscrutable for good, and was wholly bent to make his kingdom and people happy. He, therefore, taking into consideration how sufficient and substantive [self-sufficient] this land was to maintain itself without any aid at all of the foreigner, being 5,600 miles in circuit and of rare fertility of soil in the greatest part thereof, and finding also the shipping of this country might be plentifully set on work both by fishing and by transportations from port to port, and likewise by sailing unto some small islands that are not far from us and are under the crown and laws of this state, and recalling into his memory the happy and flourishing estate wherein this land then was, so as it might be a thousand ways altered to the worse, but scarce any one way to the better, thought nothing wanted to his noble and heroical intentions but only (as far as human foresight might reach) to give perpetuity to that which was in his time so happily established. Therefore amongst his other fundamental laws of this kingdom, he did ordain the interdicts and prohibitions which we have touching entrance of strangers, which at that time (though it was after the calamity of America) was frequent, doubting [fearing] novelties and commixture of manners. It is true, the like law against the admission of strangers without license is an ancient law in the kingdom of China, yet continued in use. But there it is a poor thing, and hath made them a curious, ignorant, fearful, foolish nation. But our lawgiver made his law of another temper. For first, he hath preserved all points of humanity in taking order and making provision for the relief of strangers distressed, whereof you have tasted." At which speech (as reason was) we all rose up, and bowed ourselves. He went on. "That king also, still desiring to join humanity and policy together, and thinking it against humanity to detain strangers here against their wills, and against policy that they should return and discover their knowledge of this estate, he took this course: he did ordain that of the strangers that should be permitted to land, as many (at all times) might depart as would; but as many as would stay should have very good conditions and means to live from the state. Wherein he saw so far that now, in so many ages since the prohibition, we have memory not of one ship that ever returned, and but of thirteen persons only at several times that chose to return in our bottoms. What those few that returned may have reported abroad I know not. But you must think, whatsoever they have said could be taken where they came but for a dream. Now for our traveling from hence into parts abroad, our Lawgiver thought fit altogether to restrain it. So is it not in China. For the Chinese sail where they will or can, which showeth that their law of keeping out strangers is a law of pusillanimity and fear. But this restraint of ours hath one only exception, which is admirable, preserving the good which cometh by communicating with strangers, and avoiding the hurt; and I will now open it to you. And here I shall seem a little to digress, but you will by and by find it pertinent. Ye shall understand (my dear friends) that amongst the excellent acts of that king, one above all hath the pre-eminence. It was the erection and institution of an Order or Society which we call *Solomon's House*, the noblest foundation (as we think) that ever was upon the earth, and the lantern of this kingdom. It is dedicated to the study of the Works and Creatures of God. Some think it beareth the founder's name a little corrupted, as if it should be Solamona's House. But the records write it as it is spoken. So as I take it to be denominate of the King of the Hebrews, which is famous with you and no stranger to us. For we have some parts of his works which with you are lost; namely, that Natural History, which he wrote, of all plants from the *cedar of Libanus* to the *moss that groweth out of the wall*, and of all *things that have life and motion*. This maketh me think that our king, finding himself to symbolize [agree] in many things with that king of the Hebrews which lived many years before him, honored him with the title of this foundation. And I am the rather induced to be of this opinion, for that I find in ancient records this Order or Society is sometimes called Solomon's House and sometimes the College of the Six Days Works; whereby I am satisfied that our excellent king had learned from the Hebrews that God had created the world and all that therein is within six days; and therefore he, instituting that House for the finding out of the true nature of all things (whereby God might have the more glory in the workmanship of them, and men the more fruit in the use of them), did give it also that second name. But now to come to our present purpose. When the king had forbidden to all his people navigation into any part that was not under his crown, he made nevertheless this ordinance: that every twelve years there should be set forth out of this kingdom two ships, appointed to several voyages; that in either of these ships there should be a mission of three of the Fellows or Brethren of Solomon's House, whose errand was only to give us knowledge of the affairs and state of those countries to which they were designed, and especially of the sciences, arts, manufactures, and inventions of all the world, and withal to bring unto us books, instruments, and patterns in every kind; that the ships, after they had landed the brethren, should return; and that the brethren should stay abroad till the new mission. These ships are not otherwise fraught [loaded] than with store of victuals and good quantity of treasure to remain with the brethren for the buying of such things and rewarding of such persons as they should think fit. Now for me to tell you how the vulgar sort of mariners are contained [restrained] from being discovered at land; and how they that must be put on shore for any time color [disguise] themselves under the names of other nations; and to what places these voyages have been designed; and what places of *rendezvous* are appointed for the new missions; and the like circumstances of the practices, I may not do it; neither is it much to your desire. But thus, you see, we maintain a trade, not for gold, silver, or jewels, nor for silks, nor for spices, nor any other commodity of matter, but only for God's first creature, which was *Light;* to have *light* [knowledge] (I say) of the growth of all parts of the world." And when he had said this, he was silent; and so were we all. For indeed we were all astonished to hear so strange things so probably told. And he, perceiving that we were willing to say somewhat but had it not ready, in great courtesy took us off, and descended to ask us questions of our voyage and fortunes, and in the end concluded that we might do well to think with ourselves what time of stay we would demand of the state, and bade us not to scant ourselves, for he would procure such time as we desired. Whereupon we all rose up and presented ourselves to kiss the skirt of his tippet, but he would not suffer us and so took his leave. But when it came once amongst our people that the state used [was accustomed] to offer conditions to strangers that would stay, we had work enough to get any of our men to look to our ship, and to keep them from going presently to the governor to crave conditions. But with much ado we refrained them, till we might agree what course to take.

We took ourselves now for free men, seeing there was no danger of our utter perdition, and lived most joyfully, going abroad and seeing what was to be seen in the city and places adjacent within our tether, and obtaining acquaintance with many of the city, not of the meanest quality, at whose hands we found such humanity and such a freedom and desire to take strangers, as it were, into their bosom as was enough to make us forget all that was dear to us in our own countries; and continually we met with many things right worthy of observation and relation, as indeed, if there be a mirror in the world worthy to hold men's eyes, it is that country. One day there were two of our company bidden to a Feast of the Family, as they call it. A most natural, pious, and reverend custom it is, showing that nation to be compounded of all goodness. This is the manner of it. It is granted to any man that shall live to see thirty persons descended of his body alive together, and all above three years old, to make this feast, which is done at the cost of the state. . . .

By that time six or seven days were spent, I was fallen into strait [close] acquaintance with a merchant of that city, whose name was Joabin. He was a Jew, and circumcised, for they have some few stirps of Jews yet remaining among them, whom they leave to their own religion. . . . I desired to know of him what laws and customs they had concerning marriage, and whether they kept marriage well, and whether they were tied to one wife. For that where population is so much affected [desired], and such as with them it seemed to be, there is commonly permission of plurality of wives. To this he said, "You have reason for to commend that excellent institution of the Feast of the Family. And indeed we have experience that those families that are partakers of the blessing of that feast do flourish and prosper ever after in an extraordinary manner. But hear me now, and I will tell you what I know. You shall understand that there is not under the heavens so chaste a nation as this of Bensalem, nor so free from all pollution or foulness. . . . They have also many wise and excellent laws touching marriage. They allow no polygamy. They have ordained that none do intermarry or contract, until a month be passed from their first interview. Marriage without consent of parents they do not make void, but they mulct [penalize] it in the inheritors, for the children of such marriages are not admitted to inherit above a third part of their parents' inheritance. I have read in a book of one of your men [More's *Utopia*], of a Feigned Commonwealth, where the married couple are permitted, before they contract, to see one another naked. This they dislike, for they think it a scorn to give a refusal after so familiar knowledge, but because of many hidden defects in men and women's bodies, they have a more civil way, for they have near every town a couple of pools (which they call *Adam and Eve's pools*) where it is permitted to one of the friends of the man, and another of the friends of the woman, to see them severally bathe naked."

And as we were thus in conference, there came one that seemed to be a messenger, in a rich huke [hooded cloak], that spake with the Jew; whereupon he turned to me and said, "You will pardon me, for I am commanded away in haste." The next morning he came to me again, joyful as it seemed, and said, "There is word come to the governor of the city that one of the Fathers of Solomon's House will be here this day seven-night, . . . When we came in, as we were taught, we bowed low at our first entrance, and when we were come near his chair, he stood up, holding forth his hand ungloved and in posture of blessing; and we everyone of us stooped down and kissed the hem of his tippet. That done, the rest departed and I remained. Then he warned [ordered] the pages forth of the room, and caused me to sit down beside him, and spake to me thus in the Spanish tongue:

"God bless thee, my son; I will give thee the greatest jewel I have. For I will impart unto thee, for the love of God and men, a relation of the true state of Solomon's House. Son, to make you know the true state of Solomon's House, I will keep this order. First, I will set forth unto you the end of our foundation; secondly, the preparations and instruments we have for our works; thirdly, the several employments and functions whereto our fellows are assigned; and fourthly, the ordinances and rites which we observe.

"The end of our Foundation is the knowledge of causes and secret motions of things, and the enlarging of the bounds of human empire, to the effecting of all things possible.

"The preparations and instruments are these. We have large and deep caves of several depths: the deepest are sunk six hundred fathom; and some of them are digged and made under great hills and mountains, so that if you reckon together the depth of the hill and the depth of the cave, they are (some of them) above three miles deep. For we find that the depth of a hill and the depth of a cave from the flat is the same thing, both remote alike from the sun and heaven's beams and from the open air. These caves we call the Lower Region. And we use them for all coagulations, indurations [solidifications], refrigerations, and conservations of bodies. We use them likewise for the imitation of natural mines and the producing also of new artificial metals by compositions and materials which we use, and lay there for many years. We use them also sometimes (which may seem strange) for curing of some diseases and for prolongation of life in some hermits that choose to live there, well accommodated of [provided with] all things necessary; and indeed live very long, by whom also we learn many things.

"We have burials in several earths, where we put divers cements, as the Chinese do their porcelain. But we have them in greater variety, and some of them more fine. We have also great variety of composts [prepared manures] and soils for the making of the earth fruitful.

"We have high towers, the highest about half a mile in height, and some of them likewise set upon high mountains, so that the vantage of the hill with the tower is in the highest of them three miles at least. And these places we call the Upper Region, accounting the air between the high places and the low as a Middle Region. We use these towers, according to their several heights and situations, for insolation [exposure to the sun], refrigeration, conservation, and for the view of divers meteors, as winds, rain, snow, hail, and some of the fiery meteors also. And upon them, in some places, are dwellings of hermits, whom we visit sometimes, and instruct what to observe.

"We have great lakes both salt and fresh, whereof we have use for the fish and fowl. We use them also for burials of some natural bodies, for we find a difference in things buried in earth or in air below the earth and things buried in water. We have also pools, of which some do strain fresh water out of salt, and others by art do turn fresh water into salt. We have also some rocks in the midst of the sea, and some bays upon the shore, for some works wherein is required the air and vapor of the sea. We have likewise violent streams and cataracts, which serve us for many motions, and likewise engines for multiplying and enforcing [intensifying] of winds, to set also on going divers motions.

"We have also a number of artificial wells and fountains, made in imitation of the natural sources and baths, as tincted upon [impregnated with] vitriol, sulphur, steel, brass, lead, niter, and other minerals. And again we have little wells for infusions of many things, where the waters take the virtue [properties of the dissolved materials] quicker and better than in vessels or basins. And amongst them we have a water which we call Water of Paradise, being, by that we do to it, made very sovereign for health and prolongation of life.

"We have also great and spacious houses, where we imitate and demonstrate meteors, as snow, hail, rain, some artificial rains of bodies [solids] and not of water, thunders, lightnings; also generations of bodies in air, as frogs, flies, and divers others.

"We have also fair and large baths of several mixtures for the cure of diseases and the restoring of man's body from arefaction [drying up], and others for the confirming of it in strength of sinews, vital parts, and the very juice and substance of the body.

"We have also large and various orchards and gardens, wherein we do not so much respect beauty as variety of ground and soil, proper for divers trees and herbs, and some very spacious, where trees and berries are set (whereof we make divers kinds of drinks) besides the vineyards. In these we practice likewise all conclusions [experiments] of grafting and inoculating [budding], as well of wild trees as fruit trees, which produceth many effects. And we make (by art) in the same orchards and gardens, trees and flowers to come earlier or later than their seasons, and to come up and bear more speedily than by their natural course they do. We make them also by art greater much than their nature; and their fruit greater and sweeter and of differing taste, smell, color, and figure, from their nature. And many of them we so order as they become of medicinal use.

"We have also means to make divers plants rise by mixtures of earths without seeds, and likewise to make divers new plants differing from the vulgar, and to make one tree or plant turn into another.

"We have also parks and inclosures of all sorts of beasts and birds, which we use not only for view or rareness but likewise for dissections and trials, that thereby we may take light [gain information about] what may be wrought upon the body of man. Wherein we find many strange effects: as continuing life in them, though divers parts, which you account vital, be perished and taken forth; resuscitating of some that seem dead in appearance; and the like. We try also all poisons and other medicines upon them, as well of surgery as physic. By art likewise we make them greater or taller than their kind is, and contrariwise dwarf them, and stay their growth; we make them more fruitful and bearing than their kind [nature] is, and contrariwise barren and not generative. Also we make them differ in color, shape, activity, many ways. We find means to make commixtures and copulations of different kinds, which have produced many new kinds, and them not barren, as the general opinion is. We make a number of kinds of serpents, worms, flies, fishes, of putrefaction, whereof some are advanced (in effect) to be perfect creatures, like beasts or birds, and have sexes, and do propagate. Neither do we this by chance, but we know beforehand of what matter and commixture what kind of those creatures will arise.

"We have also particular pools, where we make trials upon fishes, as we have said before of beasts and birds.

"We have also places for breed and generation of those kinds of worms and flies which are of special use, such as are with you your silkworms and bees.

"I will not hold you long with recounting of our brewhouses, bakehouses, and kitchens, where are made divers drinks, breads, and

meats, rare and of special effects. Wines we have of grapes, and
drinks of other juice of fruits, of grains, and of roots, and of mixtures with honey, sugar, manna, and fruits dried and decocted; also
of the tears of woundings of trees and of the pulp of canes. And
these drinks are of several ages, some to the age or last [duration]
of forty years. We have drinks also brewed with several herbs and
roots and spices; yea with several fleshes and white meats, whereof
some of the drinks are such as they are in effect meat and drink both,
so that divers, especially in age, do desire to live with [on] them,
with little or no meat or bread. And above all, we strive to have
drinks of extreme thin parts to insinuate into the body, and yet without all biting, sharpness, or fretting; insomuch as some of them put
upon the back of your hand will, with a little stay, pass through to
the palm, and yet taste mild to the mouth. We have also waters
which we ripen in that fashion as they become nourishing, so that
they are indeed excellent drink, and many will use no other. Breads
we have of several grains, roots, and kernels; yea and some of flesh
and fish dried, with divers kinds of leavenings and seasonings, so that
some do extremely move appetites; some do nourish so, as divers do
live of them without any other meat, who live very long. So for
meats, we have some of them so beaten and made tender and mor-
tified, yet without all corrupting, as a weak heat of the stomach
will turn them into good chyle, as well as a strong heat would meat
otherwise prepared. We have some meats also and breads and drinks,
which, taken by men, enable them to fast long after, and some other,
that used make the very flesh of men's bodies sensibly more hard
and tough, and their strength far greater than otherwise it would be.

"We have dispensatories or shops of medicines, wherein, you
may easily think, if we have such variety of plants and living creatures more than you have in Europe (for we know what you have),
the simples [herbs], drugs, and ingredients of medicines must likewise be in so much the greater variety. We have them likewise of
divers ages, and long fermentations. And for their preparations, we
have not only all manner of exquisite distillations and separations
[analyses], and especially by gentle heats and percolations through
divers strainers, yea and substances, but also exact forms of composition [compounding them] whereby they incorporate [combine into
new substances] almost, as they were natural simples.

"We have also divers mechanical arts which you have not, and
stuffs made by them, as papers, linen, silks, tissues, dainty works of
feathers of wonderful luster, excellent dyes, and many others; and
shops likewise as well for such as are not brought into vulgar use
amongst us as for those that are. For you must know that of the
things before recited, many of them are grown into use throughout

the kingdom, but yet if they did flow from our invention, we have of them also for patterns and principals [models].

"We have also furnaces of great diversities, and that keep great diversity of heats: fierce and quick; strong and constant; soft and mild; blown, quiet; dry, moist; and the like. But above all, we have heats in imitation of the sun's and heavenly bodies' heats, that pass divers inequalities and (as it were) orbs, progresses, and returns, whereby we produce admirable effects. Besides, we have heats of dungs, and of bellies and maws of living creatures, and of their bloods and bodies, and of hays and herbs laid up moist, of lime unquenched, and such like. Instruments also which generate heat only by motion. And farther, places for strong insolations; and again, places under the earth, which by nature or art yield heat. These divers heats we use, as the nature of the operation which we intend requireth.

"We have also perspective-houses [for the use of optical instruments], where we make demonstrations of all lights and radiations, and of all colors; and out of things uncolored and transparent we can represent unto you all several colors, not in rainbows, as it is in gems and prisms, but of themselves single. We represent [produce] also all multiplications of light, which we carry to great distance, and make so sharp as to discern small points and lines; also all colorations of light, all delusions and deceits of the sight in figures, magnitudes, motions, colors, all demonstrations of shadows. We find also divers means, yet unknown to you, of producing of light originally [originating light] from divers bodies. We procure means of seeing objects afar off, as in the heaven and remote places, and represent things near as afar off and things afar off as near, making feigned distances. We have also helps for the sight, far above spectacles and glasses in use. We have also glasses and means to see small and minute bodies perfectly and distinctly, as the shapes and colors of small flies and worms, grains and flaws in gems, which cannot otherwise be seen, observations in urine and blood, not otherwise to be seen. We make artificial rainbows, halos, and circles about light. We represent also all manner of reflexions, refractions, and multiplications of visual beams of objects.

"We have also precious stones of all kinds, many of them of great beauty and to you unknown; crystals likewise; and glasses of divers kinds; and amongst them some of metals vitrified, and other materials besides those of which you make glass. Also a number of fossils and imperfect minerals, which you have not. Likewise loadstones of prodigious virtue [power], and other rare stones, both natural and artificial.

"We have also sound-houses, where we practice and demonstrate all sounds and their generation. We have harmonies, which you have not, of quarter-sounds and lesser slides of sounds; divers instruments of music likewise to you unknown, some sweeter than any you have, together with bells and rings [chimes] that are dainty and sweet. We represent small sounds as great and deep, likewise great sounds extenuate [thin] and sharp; we make divers tremblings and warblings of sounds, which in their original are entire. We represent and imitate all articulate sounds and letters, and the voices and notes of beasts and birds. We have certain helps which set to the ear do further the hearing greatly. We have also divers strange and artificial echoes, reflecting the voice many times, and as it were tossing it, and some that give back the voice louder than it came, some shriller and some deeper; yea, some rendering the voice differing in the letters or articulate sound from that they receive. We have also means to convey sounds in trunks [tubes] and pipes, in strange lines and distances.

"We have also perfume-houses, wherewith we join also practices of taste. We multiply smells, which may seem strange. We imitate smell, making all smells to breathe out of other mixtures than those that give them. We make divers imitations of taste likewise, so that they will deceive any man's taste. And in this house we contain also a confiture-house, where we make all sweetmeats, dry and moist, and divers pleasant wines, milks, broths, and salads, far in greater variety than you have.

"We have also enginehouses, where are prepared engines and instruments for all sorts of motions. There we imitate and practice to make swifter motions than any you have, either out of your muskets or any engine that you have; and to make them and multiply them more easily and with small force by wheels and other means, and to make them stronger and more violent than yours are, exceeding your greatest cannons and basilisks [a kind of cannon]. We represent also ordnance and instruments of war, and engines of all kinds, and likewise new mixtures and compositions of gunpowder, wildfires burning in water and unquenchable. Also fireworks of all variety both for pleasure and use. We imitate also flights of birds; we have some degrees [partial achievement] of flying in the air; we have ships and boats for going under water, and brooking of seas; also swimming-girdles and supporters. We have divers curious clocks and other like motions of return [oscillation], and some perpetual motions. We imitate also motions of living creatures by images of men, beasts, birds, fishes, and serpents. We have also a great number of other various motions, strange for equality, fineness, and subtilty.

"We have also a mathematical house, where are represented all instruments, as well of geometry as astronomy, exquisitely made.

"We have also houses of deceits of the senses, where we represent all manner of feats of juggling, false apparitions, impostures, and illusions, and their fallacies. And surely you will easily believe that we that have so many things truly natural which induce admiration could in a world of particulars deceive the senses, if we would disguise those things and labor to make them seem more miraculous. But we do hate all impostures and lies; insomuch as we have severely forbidden it to all our fellows, under pain of ignominy and fines, that they do not show any natural work or thing adorned or swelling, but only pure as it is, and without all affectation of strangeness.

"These are (my son) the riches of Solomon's House.

"For the several employments and offices of our fellows, we have twelve that sail into foreign countries, under the names of other nations (for our own we conceal), who bring us the books and abstracts and patterns of experiments of all other parts. These we call Merchants of Light.

"We have three that collect the experiments which are in all books. These we call Depredators.

"We have three that collect the experiments of all mechanical arts, and also of liberal sciences, and also of practices which are not brought into arts. These we call Mystery-men.

"We have three that try new experiments, such as themselves think good. These we call Pioneers or Miners.

"We have three that draw the experiments of the former four into titles and tables, to give the better light for the drawing of observations and axioms out of them. These we call Compilers.

"We have three that bend themselves, looking into the experiments of their fellows, and cast about how to draw out of them things of use and practice for man's life, and knowledge as well for works as for plain demonstration of causes, means of natural divinations, and the easy and clear discovery of the virtues and parts of bodies. These we call Dowry-men or Benefactors.

"Then after divers meetings and consults of our whole number to consider of the former labors and collections, we have three that take care, out of them, to direct new experiments of a higher light, more penetrating into nature than the former. These we call Lamps.

"We have three others that do execute the experiments so directed, and report them. These we call Inoculators.

"Lastly, we have three that raise the former discoveries by experiments into greater observations, axioms, and aphorisms. These we call Interpreters of Nature.

"We have also, as you must think, novices and apprentices, that the succession of the former employed men do not fail, besides a great number of servants and attendants, men and women. And this we do also: we have consultations, which of the inventions and experiences which we have discovered shall be published, and which not; and take all an oath of secrecy for the concealing of those which we think fit to keep secret, though some of those we do reveal sometimes to the state, and some not.

"For our ordinances and rites, we have two very long and fair galleries: in one of these we place patterns and samples of all manner of the more rare and excellent inventions; in the other we place the statues of all principal inventors. There we have the statue of your Columbus, that discovered the West Indies; also the inventor of ships; your monk that was the inventor of ordnance and of gunpowder; the inventor of music; the inventor of letters; the inventor of printing; the inventor of observations of astronomy; the inventor of works in metal; the inventor of glass; the inventor of silk of the worm; the inventor of wine; the inventor of corn and bread; the inventor of sugars; and all these by more certain tradition than you have. Then have we divers inventors of our own, of excellent works, which since you have not seen, it were too long to make descriptions of them; and besides, in the right understanding of those descriptions you might easily err. For upon every invention of value we erect a statue to the inventor and give him a liberal and honorable reward. These statues are some of brass, some of marble and touchstone [jasper], some of cedar and other special woods gilt and adorned, some of iron, some of silver, some of gold.

"We have certain hymns and services, which we say daily, of laud and thanks to God for His marvelous works, and forms of prayers, imploring His aid and blessing for the illumination of our labors and the turning of them into good and holy uses.

"Lastly, we have circuits or visits of divers principal cities of the kingdom, where, as it cometh to pass, we do publish such new profitable inventions as we think good. And we do also declare natural divinations [forecasts] of diseases, plagues, swarms of hurtful creatures, scarcity, tempests, earthquakes, great inundations, comets, temperature of the year, and divers other things; and we give counsel thereupon what the people shall do for the prevention and remedy of them."

And when he had said this, he stood up; and I, as I had been taught, kneeled down; and he laid his right hand upon my head, and said, "God bless thee, my son, and God bless this relation which I have made. I give thee leave to publish it for the good of other nations, for we here are in God's bosom, a land unknown." And so he left me, having assigned a value of about two thousand ducats for a bounty to me and my fellows. For they give great largesses where they come upon all occasions.

[*The rest was not Perfected*]

22

The Rota

*or, A Model of a Free State or
Equal Commonwealth, Once Proposed and
Debated in Brief, and to be again more at large
Proposed to and Debated by a Free and Open
Society of Ingenious Gentlemen*

James Harrington

*London
1660*

James Harrington (1611–1677)

came from a distinguished family of linguists, scholars, and gentlemen. At Trinity College, Oxford, he was probably influenced by the
rational theology of William Chillingworth, although his chief devotion was to ancient and modern languages. In 1631, Harrington
entered the Middle Temple for education in law. He then enlisted
in a volunteer regiment in the Netherlands, visited Denmark, and
moved on through Flanders and France to Italy, learning languages
as he went and making careful observations of political and social
institutions. After being particularly impressed by the constitution
of Venice, which enjoyed a strong oligarchical government famed
for its stability, prosperity, and longevity, he returned to England
through western Germany. He had learned much from his travels.
As H. F. Russell Smith points out, "The Netherlands and Venice
alike captivated his imagination and aroused his enthusiasm, but in a
rather different way. In the Netherlands he had seen what a people
can do. In Venice he was shown what institutions can achieve. The
former turned his interests in the direction of politics; the latter
made him believe in political science. With his faith in the people
and his faith in institutions, his mind was moving in the direction of
republicanism."

Harrington took no part in the English Civil War, but endeavored,
in 1647, to reconcile Puritan and Royalist; for, paradoxically, this
theoretical republican was a warm friend of Charles I. After these
vain efforts, he went into scholarly retirement, translated Virgil,
studied ancient history, and collected political writings. But his central attention was given to the composition of *Oceana*, the best
known of his numerous utopias. It appeared anonymously in 1656,
dedicated to Oliver Cromwell, Lord Protector of England, who, in
the words of Russell Smith, "was given the formidable task of converting England into Oceana and retiring into private life at the
conclusion of his work, to die at the ripe age of one hundred and
sixteen."

Harrington was the author of more than a dozen utopian works.
Throughout them he preserved the same sincerity and consistency:
his basic ideas never changed. *Oceana* is a thinly disguised account
of England and gives an imaginary account of how its dictator set up
a utopian commonwealth. It is no chimerical state which Harrington describes, however, but a social and political organization intended to be immediately applicable to the England of his day. He
divides governments into two kinds: *de jure* governments, which
are founded on reason, justice, and common law: they are "the empire of laws and not of men"; and *de facto* governments, which
subordinate law to force, justice to passion, and general interest to

particular, and put power at the discretion not of laws but of men. According to Harrington, there are two principles in government: the first is empire or power: it depends on force which is based on wealth usually in the form of land; the second is authority: it supposes moral force which is based on virtues such as courage, reason, and wisdom. Power not based on property can only produce violent, short-lived governments: to be durable, property and power must also be just, joining authority to power. In a perfect government, power is in equilibrium with property; and either there are no citizens who have an interest in exciting sedition or those who would be seditious lack the power to act; in such a state there are equal rights and liberties and no oppression; its army is national and popular and is supported at common expense. This kind of government is founded on an Agrarian Law which imposes limits on the amount of property owned by individual men, thus assuring power and independence to the people. The government itself consists of an elective senate chosen for life or a period to propose laws, a popular assembly to vote upon those laws, and an elective assembly to carry them out. The state tolerates all faiths, but, in order to prevent the control of consciences by foreigners, supports a national church in which the priests are popularly elected.

Harrington demonstrates the principles of this ideal government by proofs drawn from the history of the most successful governments of ancient and modern times. Judged by his ideal, the best states were those of the Hebrews, Spartans, Athenians, Carthaginians, Romans, Dutch, and Venetians, though he by no means confines himself to these. Possibly because of the force of Biblical arguments in his period, possibly because he himself had inclinations towards Puritanism, he pays most attention to the Hebrew commonwealth, which he paints as the most perfect of all. He regards it as divinely sanctioned and appeals "to God in the fabric of the commonwealth of Israel, and to the world in the universal series of ancient prudence." He interprets the nature of the Hebrew commonwealth to suit his own principles; though he professes to derive them from it, it is doubtful if his interpretation is very sound. In tracing the history of Oceana, or England, he notes that from the Norman Conquest to the reign of Henry VII, the aristocracy owned four-fifths of the land. However, with the breakdown of feudalism under the Tudors, the preponderance of property passed to the middle class who, having the power which is the consequence of property, revolted in the 1640's. But this revolution was upset by the dictator Cromwell. Accordingly, Harrington asks the dictator to translate his ideal Oceana into fact. (I have used the English equivalents of Oceanic names and history).

The outstanding features of Oceana are as follows. No citizen is allowed to have property worth more than £2,000 a year. As a result, the preponderance of any individual or class is avoided, but the advantages of an aristocracy—its traditions of honor, skill, and and service—are retained. The aristocracy are distinguished from other citizens by merit and fortune alone. The population is classified according to age, fortune, quality, and residence. Men from eighteen to thirty years old perform army service and have no electoral rights in civil affairs; the Ancients (those over thirty) look after political matters. The Knights (those with incomes over £100 a year) control and occupy the most important magisterial positions. For administrative purposes, men are divided and subdivided according to their residence into the following units, starting with the smallest: parishes, hundreds, tribes, ten thousands of parishes, five hundreds of hundreds, and fifties of tribes. Each unit has its appropriate magistrates, officers, and representatives. Citizens vote by ballot to choose between candidates picked out by lot. The governmental executive is named by the senate to hold office for not more than three years.

The chief importance of Harrington's utopias is their clear enunciation of the principle that the economic factor in a state determines its government. This was not an original idea, but Harrington gives it clearer and fuller expression than anyone before him. Moreover, it was a natural idea: whether the principle is universally valid is arguable, but in Harrington's own period changes in political power were being caused by changes in the distribution of wealth.

Oceana and Harrington's other accounts are not utopias in the literary sense of the term. They are magnified constitutions intended as solutions for actual problems. They are graced by little or no story element, few literary devices, and no fantastic suggestions. They have hardly any interest for the general reader and not infrequently bore the scholar.

Harrington is primarily a doctrinaire thinker, although he makes a great show of inductive, historical, and comparative methods. Having fixed upon his main theories, he proceeds to discover them in ancient and modern practice, partly in order to bring out his meaning, partly also, one suspects, in order to persuade his readers with an array of authorities and precedents. He was an ingenious thinker, as is revealed by the skillful fusion of aristocratic and democratic principles in his utopias, by his adroit combination of practical and doctrinaire considerations, and by the careful mixture of materialism and idealism in them.

The influence of Harrington is noticeable in nearly all the utopias written in England during the rest of the seventeenth century: in particular they repeat his advocacy of the balance of property; his separation of the judicial, legislative, and executive functions of government; and his desire for rotation in office and use of the ballot. His influence in America is detectable in the written constitution, the unlimited extension of the elective principle, and the separation of governmental functions; in the equal division of property among children; and in the principles of indirect election. Russell Smith adds, "Short tenure of power, the multiplication of offices, the system of checks and balances, rotation, the ballot, the use of petitions, the popular ratification of constitutional legislation, the special machinery for safeguarding the constitution, religious liberty, popular education—all these things play their part in America. The only important proposal made in *Oceana* which has not survived is the proposal to separate the functions of debate and result. And even this has been more nearly realized in America than in England."

In November, 1659, Harrington formed the Rota Club, which met nightly for political discussions. It was lively, popular, and well attended. Business was conducted in orderly fashion, debates being devoted, for the most part, to such schemes as John Milton's *Ready and Easy Way to Establish a Free Commonwealth*. Among the proposals discussed is that which is printed below. It is an epitome of *Oceana* and was published on January 9, 1660; it had been discussed by the Rota Club on December 20 of the preceding year. The present text is taken from *The Oceana and Other Works of John Harrington*, edited by John Toland (London, 1771).

The Rota

THE PRINCIPLES OF GOVERNMENT

All government is founded upon overbalance in propriety. [I.e., governmental power derives from the possession of wealth or property (propriety); the man or men whose wealth exceeds or overbalances the total wealth of others in the state controls its government.]

If one man hold the overbalance unto [over] the whole people in propriety, his propriety causeth absolute monarchy.

If the few hold the overbalance unto the whole people in propriety, their propriety causes aristocracy or mixed monarchy.

If the whole people be neither overbalanced by the propriety of one, nor of a few, the propriety of the people (or of the many) causeth the democracy or popular government.

The government of one against the balance [the rest] is tyranny.

The government of a few against the balance is oligarchy.

The government of the many, (or attempt of the people to govern) against the balance, is rebellion or anarchy.

Where the balance of propriety is equal, it causeth a state of war.

To hold that government may be founded upon community [common ownership or communism] is to hold that there may be a black swan or a castle in the air; or that what thing soever is as imaginable as what hath been in practice. [In other words, it is ridiculous to believe that something like communism, which may seem to work in theory in some imaginary scheme or fictitious system, is as practical as something which has been practiced in reality. The fact that an idea seems to work out practically in a utopia is no reason for thinking it to be as practicable as an actual working idea.]

If the overbalance of propriety be in one man, it necessitates the form of government to be like that of Turkey [despotism].

If the overbalance of propriety be in the few, it necessitates the form of the government to be like that of king, lords, and commons.

If the people be not overbalanced by one, or a few, they are not capable of any other form of government than that of a senate and a popular assembly; for example, as follows:

FOR THE FORM OR MODEL IN BRIEF OF A FREE STATE OR EQUAL COMMONWEALTH IT HATH BEEN PROPOSED IN THIS MANNER:

1. Let the whole territory of *Oceana* [Harrington's imaginary country; he really has England in mind.] be divided as equally as may be into fifty parts or shires.

2. Let the whole inhabitants (except women, children, and servants) be divided according unto their age into *elders* and *youth;* and according unto their estates into *horse* and *foot* [cavalry and infantry].

3. Let all such as are eighteen years of age or upwards to thirty be accounted *youth;* and all such as are thirty upwards be accounted *elders.*

4. Let all such as have £100 a year or upwards in [from] lands, goods, or money be accounted of the *horse;* and all such as have under be accounted of the *foot* of the commonwealth.

5. Let every parish in a shire elect annually the fifth elder of the same to be for that year a deputy of that parish. If a parish be

to small, let it be laid [added] as to this purpose unto the next. And in this respect, let every part of the territory appertain to some parish.

6. Where there is but one *elder* of the *horse* in a parish, let him be annually eligible, without interval. Where there are more elders of the horse, let no deputy of the parish be re-eligible but after the interval of one year.

7. Where there be four elders of the horse or more, in one and the same parish, let not under two nor above half of them be elected at one and the same election or time.

8. Let the deputies thus elected at the parishes assemble annually at the capital of their shire, and let them then and there elect out of their own number two elders of the horse to be knights or senators, [and] three elders of the horse and four elders of the foot to be of the assembly of the people for the term of three years, enjoining an equal vacation or interval before they can be re-elected in either of these capacities.

9. Let there be elected at the same time in each shire, the first year only, two other knights and seven other deputies, for the term of one year; and two other knights with seven other deputies, for the term of two years; which, in all, constitutes the senate of three hundred knights and the popular assembly of one thousand and fifty deputies, each being upon triennial rotation or annual change in one third part.

10. Let the senate have the whole authority or right of debating and proposing unto the people; let the popular assembly have the whole power of result; and let what shall be proposed by the senate and resolved by the popular assembly be the law of Oceana.

THE CONCLUSION:

Two assemblies thus constituted must necessarily amount unto the understanding and the will, unto the wisdom and the interest of the whole nation; and a commonwealth, where wisdom of the nation proposes and the interest of the people resolves [decides], can never fail in whatever shall be farther necessary for the right constituting of itself.

THE MODEL AT LARGE OF A FREE STATE OR EQUAL COMMONWEALTH, PROPOSED IN FOUR PARTS: FIRST, THE CIVIL; SECONDLY, THE RELIGIOUS PART; THIRDLY, THE MILITARY; FOURTHLY, THE PROVINCIAL.

Part I

FOR THE CIVIL PART, IT IS PROPOSED:

1. That the whole native or proper territory of Oceana (respect had unto the tax-roll, unto the number of people, and to the extent of territory) be cast with as much exactness as can be convenient, into fifty precincts, shires, or tribes.

2. That all citizens, that is, freemen or such as are not servants, be distributed into horse and foot; that such of them as have £100 a year in lands, goods, or money, or above that proportion, be accounted of the horse; and all such as have under that proportion be accounted of the foot.

3. That all elders, or freemen, being thirty years of age or upwards, be capable of civil administration; and that the youth, or such freemen as are between eighteen years of age and thirty, be not capable of civil administration, but of military only, in such manner as shall follow in the military part of this model.

4. That the elders resident in each parish annually assemble in the same, as, for example, upon Monday next ensuing the last of December. That they then and there elect out of their own number every fifth man, or one man out of every five, to be for the term of the year ensuing a deputy of that parish; and that the first and second so elected be overseers or presidents for the regulating of all parochial congregations, whether of the elders or of the youth, during the term for which they were elected.

5. That so many parishes lying nearest together, whose deputies shall amount to one hundred or thereabouts, be cast into one precinct, called a "hundred": and that in each precinct called the hundred, there be a town, village, or place appointed to be the capital of the same.

6. That the parochial deputies elected throughout the hundred assemble annually; for example, upon Monday next ensuing the last of *January*, at the capital of their hundred. That they then and there elect out of the horse of their number one justice of the peace, one juryman, one captain, one ensign; and out of the foot of their number, one other juryman, one high constable, etc.

7. That every twenty hundreds lying nearest and most conveniently together, be cast into one tribe, or shire. That the whole territory being after this manner cast into tribes, or shires, some town, village, or place be appointed unto every tribe, or shire, for the capital of the same: and that these three precincts (that is, the parish, the hundred, and the tribe, or shire), whether the deputies thenceforth annually chosen in the parishes, or hundreds, come to increase or diminish, remain firm and unalterable forever, save only by act of parliament.

8. That the deputies elected in the several parishes, together with their magistrates and other officers, both civil and military, elected in their several hundreds, assemble, or muster, annually; for example, upon Monday next ensuing the last of February, at the capital of their tribe, or shire.

9. That the whole body thus assembled upon the first day of the assembly elect out of the horse of their number one high sheriff, one lieutenant of the tribe, or shire, one *custos rotulorum* [keeper of the rolls], one conductor, and two censors. That the high sheriff be commander-in-chief, the lieutenant-commander in the second place, and the conductor in the third, of this band, or squadron. That the *custos rotulorum* be muster-master and keep the rolls. That the censors be governors of the ballot. And that the term of these magistracies be annual.

10. That the magistrates of the tribe, that is to say, the high sheriff, lieutenant, *custos rotulorum*, the censors, and the conductor, together with the magistrates and officers of the hundred, that is to say, the twenty justices of the peace, the forty jurymen, the twenty high constables, be one troop, and one company apart, called the prerogative troop, or company. That this troop bring in, and assist the justices of assize, hold the quarter sessions in their several capacities, and perform their other functions as formerly.

11. That the magistrates of the tribe or shire, that is to say, the high sheriff, lieutenant, *custos rotulorum*, the censors, and the conductor, together with the twenty justices elected at the hundreds, be a court for the government of the tribe called the *phylarch;* and that this court proceed in all matters of government, as shall from time to time be directed by act of parliament.

12. That the squadron of the tribe upon the second day of their assembly elect two knights and three burgesses out of the horse of their number, and four other burgesses out of the foot of their number. That the knights have session in the senate for the term of three years, and that the burgesses be of the prerogative tribe, or representative of the people, for the like term. That if, in case of death or expulsion, a place become void in the senate or popular assembly, the respective shire or tribe have timely notice from the seigniory and proceed in the manner aforesaid unto extraordinary election of a deputy or senator for the remaining part of the term of the senator or deputy, deceased or expelled.

13. That for the full and perfect institution, at once, of the assemblies mentioned, the squadron of each tribe or shire, in the first year of the commonwealth, elect two knights for the term of one year, two other knights for the term of two years, and lastly, two

knights more for the term of three years; the like for the burgesses, of the horse first, and then for those of the foot.

14. That a magistrate or officer elected at the hundred, be thereby barred from being elected a magistrate of the tribe, or of the first day's election. That no former election whatsoever bar a man of the second day's election at the tribe, or to be chosen a knight or burgess. That a man being chosen a knight or burgess, who before was chosen a magistrate or officer of the hundred or tribe, delegate his former office or magistracy in the hundred or the tribe, to any other deputy, being no magistrate or officer, and being of the same hundred, and of the same order, that is, of the horse, or of the foot respectively. That the whole and every part of the foregoing orders for election in the parishes, the hundreds, and the tribes, be holding and inviolate upon such penalties, in case of failure, as shall hereafter be provided by act of parliament against any parish, hundred, tribe or shire, deputy, or person so offending.

15. That the knights of the annual election in the tribes take their places on Monday next ensuing the last of March in the senate. That the like number of knights, whose session determines [ends] at the same time, recede. That every knight or senator be paid out of the public revenue quarterly £75 during his term of session, and be obliged to sit in purple robes.

16. That annually upon reception of the new knights, the senate proceed unto election of new magistrates and councilors. That for magistrates they elect one archon or general, one orator or speaker, and two censors, each for the term of one year, these promiscuously; and that they elect one commissioner of the great seal and one commissioner of the treasury, each for the term of three years, out of the new knights only.

17. That the archon or general, and the orator or speaker, as consuls of the commonwealth and presidents of the senate, be during the term of their magistracy paid quarterly £500: that the ensigns of these magistracies be a sword borne before the general and a mace before the speaker: that they be obliged to wear ducal robes: and that what is said of the archon or general in this proposition be understood only of the general sitting [in reserve] and not of the general marching [in active service].

18. That the general sitting, in case he be commanded to march, receive field-pay; and that a new general be forthwith elected by the senate to succeed him in the house, with all the rights, ensigns, and emoluments of the general sitting, and this so often as one or more generals are marching.

19. That the three commissioners of the great seal, and the three commissioners of the treasury, using their ensigns and habit and

performing their other functions as formerly, be paid quarterly unto each of them £375.

20. That the censors be each of them chancellor of one university by virtue of their election: that they govern the ballot: that they be presidents of the council for religion: that they have under appeal unto the senate right to note and remove a senator that is scandalous: that each have a silver wand for the ensign of his magistracy: that each be paid quarterly £375 and be obliged to wear scarlet robes.

21. That the general sitting, the speaker, and the six commissioners above said, be the seigniory of this commonwealth.

22. That there be a council of state consisting of fifteen knights, five out of each order or election; and that the same be perpetuated by the annual election of five out of the new knights, or last elected into the senate.

23. That there be a council for religion consisting of twelve knights, four out of each order, and perpetuated by the annual election of four out of the knights last elected into the senate. That there be a council for trade consisting of a like number, elected and perpetuated in the same manner.

24. That there be a council of war, not elected by the senate, but elected by the council of state out of themselves. That this council of war consist of nine knights, three out of each order, and be perpetuated by the annual election of three out of the last knights elected into the council of state.

25. That in case the senate add nine knights more out of their own number into the council of war, the said council be understood by such addition to be dictator of the commonwealth for the term of three months and no longer, except by further order of the senate the said dictatorian power be prolonged for a like term.

26. That the seigniory have sessions and suffrage, with right also, jointly or severally, to propose both in the senate and in all senatorian councils.

27. That each of the three orders or divisions of knights in each senatorian council elect one provost for the term of one week; and that any two provosts of the same council so elected may propose unto the respective council, and not otherwise.

28. That some fair room or rooms well furnished and attended be allowed, at the state's charge, for a free and open academy unto all comers, at some convenient hour or hours, towards the evening. That this academy be governed according to the rules of good breeding or civil conversation, by some or all of the proposers; and that in the same it be lawful for any man, by word of mouth, or by writing, in jest or in earnest, to propose unto the proposers.

29. That for ambassadors-in-ordinary there be four residences, as France, Spain, Venice, and Constantinople. That every resident upon election of a new ambassador-in-ordinary, remove to the next residence in the order nominated, till, having served in them all, he return home. That upon Monday next ensuing the last of November, there be every second year elected by the senate some fit person, being under thirty-five years of age, and not of the senate, nor of the popular assembly. That the party so elected repair upon Monday next ensuing the last of March following, as ambassador-in-ordinary unto the court of France, and there reside for the term of two years, to be computed from the first of April ensuing his election. That every ambassador-in-ordinary be allowed £3,000 a year, during the term of his residencies, and that if a resident come to die, there be an extraordinary election into his residence for his term, and for the remainder of his removes and progress.

30. That all emergent elections be made by scrutiny, that is, by a council or by commissioners proposing, and by the senate resolving in the manner following: that all field officers be proposed by the council of war: that all ambassadors extraordinary be proposed by the council of state: that all judges and sergeants-at-law be proposed by the commissioners of the great seal. That all barons and officers of trust in the exchequer be proposed by the commissioners of the treasury, and that such as are thus proposed and approved by the senate, be held lawfully elected.

31. That the cognizance of all matter of state to be considered or law to be enacted, whether it be provincial or national, domestic or foreign, appertain unto the council of state. That such affairs of either kind as they shall judge to require more secrecy, be remitted by this council, and appertain unto the council of war, being for that end a select part of the same. That the cognizance and protection both of the national religion, and of the liberty of conscience equally established, after the manner to be shown in the religious part of this model, appertain unto the council for religion. That all matter of traffic and regulation of the same appertain unto the council for trade. That in the exercise of these several functions, which naturally are senatorian or authoritative only, no council assume any other power than such only as shall be estated upon the same by act of parliament.

32. That what shall be proposed unto the senate by one or more of the seigniory or proposers-general, or whatever was proposed by any two of the provosts, or particular proposers, unto their respective council, and upon debate at that council shall come to be proposed by the same unto the senate, be necessarily debatable and

debated by the senate. That in all cases wherein power is derived unto the senate by law made or by act of parliament, the result of the senate be ultimate; that in all cases of law to be made, or not already provided for by act of parliament, as war and peace, levy of men or money or the like, the result of the senate be not ultimate. That whatsoever is decreed by the senate upon a case wherein their result is not ultimate, be proposed by the senate unto the prerogative tribe, or representative of the people, except only in cases of such speed or secrecy, wherein the senate shall judge the necessary slowness or openness, in this way of proceeding, to be of detriment or danger unto the commonwealth.

33. That if, upon the motion or proposition of a council or proposer-general, the senate add nine knights promiscuously chosen out of their own number unto the council of war, the same council, as thereby made dictator, have power of life and death, as also to enact laws in all such cases of speed or secrecy for and during the term of three months and no longer, except upon new order from the senate. And that all laws enacted by the dictator be good and valid for the term of one year and no longer, except the same be proposed by the senate and resolved by the people.

34. That the burgesses of the annual election returned by the tribes enter into the prerogative tribe, popular assembly, or representative of the people, upon Monday next ensuing the last of March; and that the like number of burgesses, whose term is expired, recede at the same time. That the burgesses thus entered, elect unto themselves out of their own number, two of the horse, one to be captain, and the other to be cornet of the same; and two of the foot, one to be captain, and the other ensign of the same, each for the term of three years. That these officers being thus elected, the whole tribe or assembly proceed to the election of four annual magistrates, two out of the foot to be tribunes of the foot, and two out of the horse to be tribunes of the horse. That the tribunes be commanders of this tribe-in-chief, so far as it is a military body, and presidents of the same, as it is a civil assembly. And lastly that this whole tribe be paid weekly, as follows: unto each of the tribunes of horse seven pounds. Unto each of the tribunes of foot six pounds. Unto each of the captains of horse five pounds. Unto each of the captains of foot four pounds. Unto each of the cornets three pounds. Unto each of the ensigns two pounds seven shillings. Unto every horseman two pounds; and to every one of the foot one pound ten shillings.

35. That inferior officers, as captains, cornets, ensigns, be only for the military discipline of this squadron or tribe. That the tribunes have session in the senate without suffrage; that they have session of course and with suffrage in the dictatorian council, so often as

it is created by the senate. That they be presidents of the court in all cases, to be judged by the people: and that they have right under an appeal unto popular assembly, to note or remove any deputy or burgess that is scandalous.

36. That peculation or defraudation of the public, all cases tending to the subversion of the government, be triable by this representative; and that there be an appeal unto the same in all cases, and from all magistrates, courts, and councils, whether national or provincial.

37. That the right of debate, as also of proposing to the people, be wholly and only in the senate, without any power at all of result, not derived from the people.

38. That the power of result be wholly and only the popular assembly, without any right at all of debate.

39. That the senate having debated and agreed upon a law to be proposed, cause promulgation of the same to be made for the space of six weeks before proposition, that is, cause the law to be printed and published, so long before it is to be proposed.

40. That promulgation being made, the seigniory demand of the tribunes being present in the senate, an assembly of the people. That the tribunes upon such demand by the seigniory or by the senate, be obliged to assemble the prerogative tribe or representative of the people in arms by sound of trumpet with drums beating, and colors flying, in any town, field, or market-place, being not above six miles distant, upon the day and at the hour appointed, except the meeting through inconvenience of the weather or the like, be prorogued by consent of the seigniory and the tribunes: that the prerogative tribe being assembled accordingly, the senate propose to them by two or more of the senatorian magistrates thereunto appointed, as the first promulgation of the law: that the proposers for the senate open unto the people the occasion, motives, and reasons of the law to be proposed; and the same being done, put it by distinct clauses unto the ballot of the people. That if any material clause or clauses be rejected by the people, they be reviewed by the senate, altered, and proposed, if they think fit, to the third time, but no oftener.

41. That what is thus proposed by the senate and resolved by the people be the law of the land, and no other, except as in the case reserved unto the dictatorian council.

42. That every magistracy, office, or election throughout this whole commonwealth, whether annual or triennial, be understood of consequence to injoin an interval or vacation equal unto the term of the same. That the magistracy of a knight and of a burgess be in this relation understood as one and the same; and that this

order regard only such elections as are national and domestic, and not such as are provincial or foreign.

43. That for an exception to this rule, where there is but one elder of the horse in one and the same parish, that elder be eligible in the same without interval: and where there be four elders of the horse or above in one and the same parish, there be not under nor above half of them eligible at the same election.

44. That throughout all the assemblies and councils of this commonwealth, the quorum consist of one-half in the time of health, and of one-third part in a time of sickness, being so declared by the senate.

Part II

FOR THE RELIGIOUS PART, IT IS PROPOSED:

45. That the universities being prudently reformed, be preserved in their rights and endowments for and towards the education and provision of an able ministry.

46. That the legal and ancient provision for the national ministry be so augmented that the meanest sort of livings or benefices without defalcation from the greater, be each improved to the revenue of one hundred pounds a year, at the least.

47. That a benefice becoming void in any parish, the elders of the same may assemble, and give notice unto the vice-chancellor of either university by certificate, specifying the true value of that benefice: that the vice-chancellor, upon a receipt of such certificate, be obliged to call a congregation of the university: that the congregation of the university to this end assembled, having regard unto the value of the benefice, make choice of a person fitted for the ministerial function, and return him unto the parish so requiring: that the probationer, thus returned unto a parish by either of the universities, exercise the office and receive the benefits as minister of the parish for the term of one year. That the term of one year expired, the elders of the parish assemble, and put the election of the probationer unto the ballot. That if the probationer have three parts in four of the balls or votes in the affirmative, he be thereby ordained and elected minister of that parish; not afterwards to be degraded or removed but by the censors of the tribe, the phylarch of the same, or the council of religion, in such cases as shall be unto them reserved by act of parliament. That in case the probationer come to fail of three parts in four at the ballot, he depart from that parish; and if he return unto the university, it be without diminution of former offices or preferments which he there enjoyed, or any prejudice unto his future preferment; and that it be lawful in this case for any parish to send so often to either university and be the duty of

either vice-chancellor, upon such certificates, to make return of different probationers, till such time as the elders of that parish have fitted themselves with a minister of their own choice and liking.

48. That the national religion be exercised according to a directory in that case, to be made and published by act of parliament. That the national ministry be permitted to have no other public preferment or office in this commonwealth. That a national minister, being convicted of ignorance or scandal, be movable out of his benefice by the censors of the tribe, under an appeal to the phylarch or to the council for religion.

49. That no religion being contrary unto, or destructive of Christianity, nor the public exercise of any religion, being grounded upon or incorporated into a foreign interest, be protected by, or tolerated in this state. That all other religions, with the public exercise of the same, be both tolerated and protected by the council of religion; and that all professors of any such religion, be equally capable of all elections, magistracies, preferments, and offices in this commonwealth, according to the orders of the same.

Part III

FOR THE MILITARY PART IT IS PROPOSED:

50. That annually upon Wednesday next ensuing the last of December, the youth of each parish, under the inspection of two overseers of the same, assemble and elect the fifth man of their number, or one in five of them, to be for the term of that year, deputies of the youth of that parish.

51. That annually, on Wednesday next ensuing the last of January, the said deputies of the respective parishes meet at the capital of the hundred, where there are games and prizes allotted for them, as has been shown elsewhere; that there they elect to themselves out of their own number, one captain, and one ensign. And that of these games and this election, the magistrates and officers of the hundred be presidents and judges for the impartial distribution of the prizes.

52. That annually, upon Wednesday next ensuing the last of February, the youth through the whole tribe thus elected, be received at the capital of the same, by the lieutenant, as commander-in-chief, by the conductor, and by the censors; that under inspection of these magistrates, the said youth be entertained with more splendid games, disciplined in a more military manner, and divided by lot into sundry parts or essays, according to rules elsewhere given.

53. That the whole youth of the tribe thus assembled be the first essay. That out of the first essay there be cast by lot two hundred horse, and six hundred foot; that they whom their friends will, or themselves can mount, be accounted horse; the rest foot. That

these forces amounting in the fifty tribes to ten thousand horse and thirty thousand foot, be always ready to march at a week's warning; and that this be the second essay, or the standing army of the commonwealth.

54. That for the holding of each province, the commonwealth in the first year assign an army of the youth, consisting of seven thousand five hundred foot, and one thousand five hundred horse. That for the perpetuation of these provincial armies, or guards, there be annually at the time and place mentioned, cast out of the first essay of the youth, in each tribe or shire ten horse, and fifty foot; that is, in all the tribes five hundred horse, and two thousand five hundred foot for Marpesia, the like for Pampea, and the like of both orders for the sea-guards, being each obliged to serve for the term of three years upon the state's pay.

55. That the senate and the people, or the dictator, having decreed or declared war, and the field officers being appointed by the council of war, the general, by warrant issued unto the lieutenants of the tribes demand the second essay, or such part of it, as is decreed, whether by way of levy or recruit. That by the same warrant he appoint his time and rendezvous; that the several conductors of the tribes, or shires, deliver him the forces demanded at the time and place appointed. That a general thus marching out with the standing army, a new army be elected out of the first essay as formerly, and a new general be elected by the senate: that so always there be a general sitting, and a standing army, what generals soever be marching. And that in case of invasion, the bands of the elders be obliged unto like duty with those of the youth.

56. That an only son be discharged of these duties without prejudice. That of two brothers, there be but one admitted to foreign service at one time. That of more brothers, not above half. That whoever otherwise refuses his lot, except upon cause shown he be dispensed withal by the phylarch, or upon penitence, he be by them pardoned and restored, by such refusal be incapable of electing or being elected in this commonwealth: as also, that he pay unto the state a fifth of his revenue for protection, besides taxes. That divines, physicians, and lawyers, as also trade not at leisure for the essays, be so far forth exempted from this rule, that they be still capable of all preferments in their respective professions without indemnity.

57. That upon warrants issued forth by the general for recruits or levies, there be an assembly of the phylarch in each tribe: that such volunteers, or men being above thirty years of age, as are desirous of further employment in arms, appear before the phylarch so assembled. That any number of these not exceeding one moiety

of the recruits or levies of that tribe, or shire, may be taken on by the phylarch, so many of the youth being at the discretion of this council disbanded, as are taken on the volunteers. That the levies thus made be conducted by the conductor of the respective tribe, or shire, unto the rendezvous appointed: and that the service of these be without other term or vacation than at the discretion of the senate and the people, or such instructions unto the general as shall by them in that case be provided.

Part IV

FOR THE PROVINCIAL PART IT IS PROPOSED:

58. That upon expiration of magistracy in the senate, or at the annual recess if one-third part of the same, there be elected by the senate out of the part receding into each provincial council four knights for the term of three years, thereby to render each provincial council, presuming it in the beginning to have been constituted of twelve knights, divided after the manner of the senate, by three several lists or elections, of annual, triennial, and perpetual revolution or rotation.

59. That out of the same third part of the senate annually receding, there be unto each province one knight elected for the term of one year. That the knight so elected be the provincial archon, general or governor. That a provincial archon, governor or general, receive annually in April, at his rendezvous appointed, the youth or recruits ejected in the precedent month to that end by the tribes, and by their conductors delivered accordingly. That he repair with the said youth and recruits unto his respective province, and there dismiss that part of the provincial guard or army whose triennial term is expired. That each provincial governor have the conduct of affairs of war and of state in his respective province, with advice of the provincial council; and that he be president of the same.

60. That each provincial council elect three weekly proposers or provosts, after the manner, and to the ends already shown in the constitution of senatorian councils; and that the provost of the senior list during his term, be president of the council in absence of the provincial archon, or general.

61. That each provincial council proceed according unto instructions received from the council of state, and keep intelligence with the same by any two of their provosts, for the government of the province as to matter of war or of state. That upon levies of native or proper arms by the senate and the people, a provincial council, having unto that end received orders, make levies of provincial auxiliaries accordingly. That auxiliary arms upon no occasion whatsoever exceed the proper or native arms in number. That for

the rest, the provincial council maintain the provincials, defraying their peculiar guards and council, by such known proportion of tributes, as on them shall be set by the senate and the people, in their proper rights, laws, liberties, and immunities, so far forth as upon the merits of the cause, whereupon they were subdued, it seemed good unto the senate and the people to confirm them. And that it be lawful for the provincials to appeal from their provincial magistrates, councils, or generals, to the people of *Oceana*.

FINIS

23

A New Discovery of *Terra Australis Incognita* or the Southern World

*by James
Sadeur, a Frenchman, Who, Being
Cast There by a Shipwreck, Lived
Twenty-Five Years in that Country
and Gives a Particular Description
of the Manners, Customs, Religion,
Laws, Studies, and Wars of those
Southern People; and of Some
Animals Peculiar to that Place:
With Several Other Rarities.*

Gabriel de Foigny

*These memoirs were thought so
curious that they were kept secret
in the closet of a late great Minister
of State, and never published till
now since his death.*

*London
1693
(first published in French at Geneva in 1676)*

Gabriel de Foigny   (1630–1692)

was born in France. He became a monk of the Franciscan order but was involved in scandals in 1666 and fled to Switzerland. Calvinist Geneva first befriended and then expelled him. He taught at Morges for several years but was dismissed from his position in 1671 because of alleged drunken vomiting in church and exaction of usury, although friends defended his life as decent, his manners as pious, and his beliefs as orthodox. Their efforts enabled his return to Geneva, but hostility and suspicion continued to be directed toward him. Impelled by his frustrations and by experience of the imperfections of Roman Catholics and Calvinists alike, Foigny envisaged a society in which human nature and institutions are superior. The utopias of More, Bacon, Campanella, Hall, and Cyrano de Bergerac were available to him as models. If the use of this literary form relieved Foigny's troubled soul, his tranquillity was brief. Despite his saucy claim that there could be no indecency in a utopia about people who were strangers to indecency, the Genevan authorities took alarm and condemned his book. Since continuance in Geneva was out of the question, he returned to Roman Catholicism and retired to a monastery in Savoy.

Foigny has been condemned as a plausible but despicable rascal, or pitied as "a poor devil of an adventurer who lived on expedients and was undoubtedly ill treated by men of different churches because he was unable to settle in any of them." Certainly he seems to have been unconventional to a point of amorality, impetuous in action and speech, and inclined to a liberty which amounted almost to license. His ingenuity and audacity enabled him to defend himself for a time, but his mind was too active, too ingenious, too willing to entertain new ideas for a quiet life to be possible.

Foigny's utopia may be interpreted as a projection of his problems upon a wider screen, an attempt to face them and to think his way through them, and an effort to reconcile his desire for liberty with the social need for order and discipline. His account is partly the escape of a maladjusted individual, partly a satire upon the ideas of his persecutors, and partly the expression of a conception of liberty. Beneath his facile use of the voyage type of literature and his impulse toward free thinking for its own sake, a torn and distracted soul is discoverable, a soul seeking in darkness and confusion for some ray of certainty.

Two critics notice Foigny's utopia as a precursor of socialism and communism. A third sees in it an early evidence of the spirit of the eighteenth-century *philosophes* and stresses Foigny's importance as a popularizer of rationalism. Another shows the place of the utopia between exaggerated accounts of actual voyages and the more perfect form of philosophical-social-exotic novel which followed it. A fourth critic relates it to the social and economic background in France, judges it as a reaction against the French governmental system, and finds its chief value in its criticism of institutions and mores. Still another writer shows the place of such fanciful novels of adventure, social satire, and reform in the whole critical era which undermined the French seventeenth century and brought the Age of Enlightenment.

First printed in Geneva as *La Terre Australe Connue* (The Australian Land Discovered) in 1676, the French text was reprinted in 1692 with omissions and revisions which were almost certainly made by Foigny himself. This second edition, translated into English in 1693, is the source of all the extracts below except those from "To the Reader," which were translated from the first edition by the present editor.

BIBLIOGRAPHY: Frédéric Lachèvre, *Les Successeurs de Cyrano de Bergerac* (Paris, 1922). This volume contains a composite of the first two French editions of Foigny's utopia; Geoffroy Atkinson, *The Extraordinary Voyage in French Literature before 1700* (New York, 1920); J. Max Patrick, "A Consideration of *La Terre Australe Connue* by Gabriel de Foigny," *PMLA*, LXI (Sept., 1946), 739–51: this article contains footnote references to writings about Foigny in French and German.

Terra Australis Incognita

TO THE READER

There is no characteristic more natural to Man than his desire to penetrate into what is thought difficult, and to comprehend what seems to be inaccessible. He is born with this passionate desire, and the evidences of it are as plentiful as the new projects which he undertakes. He aspires to mount even into the Heavens, and, not satisfied to reason about the stars and to discuss their qualities, struggles to fathom the mysteries of God. This consideration makes some people marvel when they remember that for four or five hundred years men have talked about an unknown Southern Land although no one, up to the present, has shown the courage and enterprise needed to make it known.

[In 1661, a ship from Madagascar arrived in France. While walking on a plank from the vessel to the mainland, an old man named James Sadeur fell into the water. I rescued him and received him into my home. However, a few days later he died, leaving a manuscript to my care. For fifteen years, I guarded it.] Finally I decided to give it to the public for, while revealing to us infinite traits of the Divine Wisdom, it leads us to marvel at the ways of God, and it confounds those who, calling themselves Christians, live worse than animals, although they are specially favored with grace, while pagans, relying only on the light of nature, manifest more virtues than the Reformed Church claims to uphold. . . .

[Chapters I, II, and III tell how Sadeur was born on the ocean. He brought bad luck to those around him. He was the sole survivor of two shipwrecks, his guardian died of fever, and his rescuers after the third wreck perished in a storm. But Sadeur himself floated on a plank to a new and strange country where fruits of almost magical potency revived him. When monstrous birds and animals attacked, he battled them valiantly, overcame two, and lost consciousness. However two spectators, natives of the utopian land of Australia, rescued him. His hermaphroditic nature, his valor, his nakedness, and his sunburned color combined to make him acceptable to the Australians who would otherwise have killed him as abnormal.]

If there was anything in the world which could persuade me of the inevitable fatality of human things, and the infallible accomplishments of those events, the chain of which composes the destiny of mankind, it would certainly be this history that I am writing; there is not one single accident of my life which has not been serviceable either to direct or support me in this new country, where it was decreed I should one day be driven. My often shipwrecks taught me to bear them; both sexes were necessary for me under pain of being destroyed at my arrival, as I shall show in the sequel of my story. It was my good fortune to be found naked; otherwise I had been known to be a stranger in a land where no one wears any covering; without that terrible combat that I was obliged to maintain against the monstrous fowls I have before mentioned, and which brought me into great reputation amongst those that were witnesses of it, I should have been forced to have submitted to an examination that would have been infallibly followed with my death. In fine, the more all the circumstances of my voyages and perils shall be considered, the more clearly it will appear that there is a certain order of things in the fate of man, and such a chain of effects that nothing can prevent, and which brings us by a thousand imperceptible turnings to the end to which we are destined. . . .

. . . I could not persuade myself that I was in the same country, or with men of the same nature of our Europeans. I was entirely cured [of my wounds] in fifteen days, and in five months learned enough of their language to understand others, and to explain myself to them. [The Australian Territories begin in the 340th Meridian toward the Fifty-second Degree of Southern elevation. They contain twenty-seven countries, which are all very considerable, and are altogether about three thousand leagues in length and four or five hundred in breadth.] But what is most surprising . . . is that there is not one mountain to be seen, the natives having leveled them all. To this prodigy may be added the admirable uniformity of languages, customs, buildings, and other things which are to be met with in this country. It is sufficient to know one quarter to make a certain judgment of the rest; all which without doubt proceeds from the nature of the people, who are all born with an inclination of willing nothing contrary to one another, and if it should happen that any one of them had anything that was not common, 'twould be impossible for him to make use of it.

There are fifteen thousand *Sezains* [provinces] in this prodigious country. Each Sezain contains sixteen Quarters, without counting the *Hab* [public building used for trials, meetings, etc.] and the four *Hebs* [educational institutions]. There are twenty-five houses in each Quarter, and every house has four apartments, which lodge four men each, so that there are four hundred houses in each Sezain, . . . which, being multiplied . . . , will show the number of inhabitants of the whole land to be about four score and sixteen millions, without counting all the youth and masters lodged in the Hebs, in each of which there are at least eight hundred persons; . . . so the young men and the masters . . . amount to near forty-eight millions. . . .

All the Australians are of both sexes, or hermaphrodites, and if it happens that a child is born of but one sex, they strangle him as a monster. They are nimble, and very active. Their flesh is more upon the red than vermilion. They are commonly eight feet high, their face pretty long, forehead large, their eyes in the upper part of their heads, and mouth small. . . . They are so accustomed to go naked that they think they cannot speak of covering themselves without being declared enemies to nature and deprived of reason.

Everyone is obliged to present at least one child to the *Heb*. But they bring them forth in so private a manner, that it is accounted a crime amongst them to speak of the necessary conjunction in the propagation of mankind.

In all the time that I was there, I could never discover how generation work was performed amongst them. I have only observed that they all loved one another with a cordial love, and that they never loved any one more than another. I can affirm that in thirty years that I have been with them, I saw neither quarrel nor animosity amongst them. They know not how to distinguish between mine and thine, they have all things in common amongst them, with so much sincerity and disinterestedness, which charmed me so much the more, because I had never seen the like in Europe.

I always used to speak what I thought, but I was a little too free in declaring what I did not like in their manners, sometimes to a Brother, sometimes to another, even by maintaining with arguments mine own opinions. I spoke of their nakedness with certain terms of aversion, which extremely offended them. One day I stopped a Brother and earnestly demanded of him, with a seeming interest, where were the fathers of these children that were already born, and told him that I thought it ridiculous for them to affect such a silence in that point. This discourse and some others of the like nature gave the Australians a kind of hatred for me, and many of them, having maintained that I was but half a man, had concluded that they ought to destroy me, which would have been, but for the assistance of a venerable old man, Master of the third Order in the *Heb*, called *Suains*, who vindicated my cause several times in the assemblies of the *Hab;* but seeing I still maintained such discourses as offended the brethren, he took me one day by myself, and said in a very cold and grave tone: "It is no longer doubted but thou art a monster: thy evil genius and insolent discourse have made thee detested amongst us. Some have a long time designed to destroy thee, and had it not been for the action which we ourselves saw thee do, thou shouldst have been put to death soon after thou arrivedst here. Tell me freely: who are you, and how came you here?" The fear that those words put in me, together with the obligation that I had to this man, made me ingenuously declare my country, and the adventures that had brought me amongst them.

The old man testified a great deal of pity for me, and assured me that if, for the time to come, I would show myself more reserved in my manners and discourses, what was past should be forgotten. He also told me he should live two years longer to support me, and his lieutenant being but young, he would choose me in his place. "I know well," says he, "that being arrived in a country where you see many things contrary to what is practiced in thine, you have some reasons to be surprised and astonished; but 'tis an inviolable custom with us to suffer no half-man among us, as soon as we discover him, either by his sex or actions. And although both sexes save thee, yet thy manner of acting condemns thee, and therefore thou must correct thyself if thou wilt be suffered amongst us. The best counsel that I can give thee to that end is that thou come without any fear and discover all thy doubts to me, and I will give you all the satisfaction thou canst wish for, provided thou beest discreet." I promised him an inviolable fidelity. . . .

"And to begin the strict commerce that I intend to keep with thee," continued he; ". . . tell me how they live in thy country; if all that inhabit it are men of body and mind like to thee; if avarice and ambition do not reign among them? In fine, explain to me the customs and manners of thy country without any disguise. I demand this one proof of the fidelity and sincerity that thou hast promised me."

I was persuaded in the condition I saw myself reduced to, that to dissemble was to expose my life; . . . I gave him therefore a particular account of my country according to the rules of geography. I made him understand the great continent we dwell in, to which we give the name of Europe and Africa. I extended my discourse at large upon the different kinds of animals which those countries produce, and this good man admired [wondered at] nothing more than what we the most despise: flies, insects, and worms, etc., and could not apprehend how such little animals could enjoy life and arbitrary motion. I made him a particular recital of the several things they were nourished by; from whence he concluded by reasoning which our best physicians have not been ignorant of, that it was impossible that we should be long-lived. In which I agreed with him, and assured him it was very rare to see any person amongst us arrive to a hundred years of age, but that nature had seemed sufficiently to provide for this defect by means of generation, whereby one man and one woman were able to beget ten or twelve children. He slightly passed this matter, pushed on with impatience he had to hear me upon others. I confessed to him that both sexes in one person was so rare among the Europeans that such as happened to be born so passed for monsters amongst them; and as for reasoning, I assured him that almost everyone was taught it, and that there were public lectures made in many places. The old man interrupted me then.

"Thou advancest too much," said he to me. "Take heed thou dost not cut thyself off; mingle not contradictions with thy relations. Thou canst never reconcile the use of reason with the exclusion of both sexes in one person; and what thou addest—that many reason among you, and that they make public lectures in divers places—proves only that reasoning is banished from you.

"The first fruit of reasoning is to know, and this knowledge on necessity carries us to two things: the first, that to be man it is necessary to be entire and complete; the second, that to this end it is necessary to be able to reason upon everything that presents itself to us. Your pretended men have not the first, since they are all imperfect; nor have they the second, since there are so few among them able to reason. . . ."

I answered him that reason taught us a being was perfect when it wanted nothing that constituted its nature, and that therefore to add to it what good things another possessed would not render it more perfect, but rather make it monstrous. "The light of the sun is an admirable thing," added I. "There is nothing more beautiful than this charming creature, by which we see all others, yet it could never be prudent to say that man was imperfect because he possessed not this rich treasure of light. It is necessary, therefore, first, to establish what constitutes the nature and perfection of man; then we must certainly agree, and may judge infallibly of those that are perfect, and such as are defective."

"Thou arguest justly," replied the old man. "I'll convince thee therefore by thy own principles. Thou knowest assuredly that man is made of two things, a body more perfect than that of other animals and a mind more clear and bright. The perfection of the body employs everything that a body may and can contain without deformity; and that of the mind requires a knowledge that extends to whatever can be known, or at least a faculty of reasoning which may conduce to this extent of knowledge. Tell me then, is there not more perfection in possessing solely what composes a human body than in being endowed but with one-half thereof? Now it is certain, that both sexes are necessary for the perfection of an entire man. Wherefore I have reason to say those that have but one are imperfect."

To which I answered that we ought to consider man as other animals in respect to his body, and that, as an animal cannot be called imperfect in its kind because it is but of one sex, so even we cannot reasonably say that man is imperfect because he also is but of one; and that, on the contrary, the confusion of sexes in the same person ought rather to pass for a monstrous thing than for a degree of perfection.

"Thy manner of arguing," answered he, "supposes you to be just as I presume you are: that is, beasts. And if I cannot absolutely say you are such, 'tis because there remain upon you some marks of humanity; and, as you seem to keep a kind of medium between man and beasts, I believe I do you no injury in calling you half-men."

"As to what thou sayest," added he, "that we are like to beasts in respect to our bodies, it is a very great error to distinguish as thou dost between the mind of man and his body. The union of these two parts is after such a manner that one is comprehended in the other; so that all the powers imaginable cannot take anything from man, no, not even from his body, which is so absolutely human that it can never agree with that of a beast; and, by consequence, man in whatsoever belongs to him is perfectly distinct from beasts. . . . Can it be denied that man agrees with the beast in what regards matter, whereof the bodies of each were formed? Is it not equally said of both that they feel, they cry, and perform all the operations of their senses?"

"Yes," said he. "It may be denied, and I formally do it. Man has nothing as man that agrees with the beast. All the chimerical conceptions wherewith thou entertainest thyself are only defects of thy reasoning, which unites what cannot be joined together and disunites what is inseparable; for example, when we say that body in general equally respects man and beast, we mean that the word *body* may be equally applied to both, because of some analogy there is in common between them; yet, however, there is always a most essential difference between them. A beast has perfect conformity only with another beast, and that because their sexes are separate, upon which account it is necessary that they reunite for the propagation of their kind; but this union can never be so perfect to make two animals one perfect being. Neither can they continue long together without being obliged to a separation. Wherefore it is necessary for them to seek again anew for themselves, and they live in a kind of languishment while they are distant one from another. As for us," added he, "we are entire men; wherefore we live without being sensible of any of these animal ardors one for another, and we cannot hear them spoken of without horror. Our love has nothing carnal nor brutal in it; we are sufficiently satisfied in ourselves; we have no need to seek any happiness from without, and live contented, as you see we do."

I could not hear this man speak without reflecting on that great principle of our philosophy, that the more perfect a being is, the less need it has of any assistance from without.

[I explained our European view that the father of a child is the principal cause of it; but he ridiculed this idea and decided that we were half-men, and that in our methods of reproduction we were bestial. But he admitted that I had shown something extraordinary both in courage and in reasoning. I then assured him that my bravery was really the result of despair and pointed out that Europeans sometimes fought among themselves until they had utterly destroyed one another.]

"They are exactly like the Fondins" [a kind of barbarians who bordered upon the Australians], said he, and, as I was going to proceed, "Thou hast," added he, "been with us long enough to know us and to be persuaded of the wisdom of our conduct. This word 'man,' which carries with it so necessary a consequence of reason and humanity, obliges us to a union which is so perfect amongst us that we know not what division and discord is. Wherefore thou must confess either that we are more than men or that we are less than men, since that you are so far from our perfection."

To which I answered, it could not be denied but that the diverse climates contributed much to the different inclinations of their inhabitants; that from thence it happened that some were more eager, others more calm; some dull, others quick; which diversity of temperaments was the ordinary cause of divisions, wars, and all other dissensions which arm men against one another. But he laughed at this reason, maintaining that man as man could never cease to be man, that is, humane, reasonable, affable, without passion, etc., because it is in this that the nature of man consists; and, as the sun cannot be a sun when it does not give light, so a man cannot be a man but he must differ essentially from beasts, in whom madness, gluttony, cruelty, and other vices and passions are a consequence of their imperfect and defective nature; that he who was subject of these defaults was no more than a vain and deceitful image of man, or, rather, a true beast. . . .

"As for us," added he, "we make a profession of being all equal. Our glory consists in being all alike, and to be dignified with the same cares and in the same manner. All the difference that there is is only in the divers exercises to which we apply ourselves so as to find out new inventions that the discoverers may contribute them to the public good."

After this, he spoke to me of habits, which he called superfluities among the Europeans, and I assured him that they had as great a horror among them to see a person naked as the Australians had to see them in clothes; I alleged for reasons of this use modesty, the rigor of the season, and custom.

To this, as I remember, he answered: "Custom so much prevails upon your minds that one would believe everything necessary that you practice from your birth, and that you can't change a custom without as great a violence as changing your own nature."

I replied by insisting upon the reason of divers climate and told him that there were some countries among the Europeans where the cold was insupportable by the body, which was more delicate than that of the Australians, and that there were some that even died upon it, and that it was impossible to subsist without clothes. In fine, I told him that the weakness of the nature of either sex was such that there was no looking upon one that was naked without blushing and shame, and without being sensible of such emotions as modesty obliged me to pass over in silence.

"Is there a consequence in all that you have advanced," said he;

"and from whence can this custom come? Is not this to father upon all the world what is contrary to nature? We are born naked, and we can't be covered without believing that it is shameful to be seen as we are. But as to what you say concerning the rigor of the seasons, I can't, nay, I ought not to give any credit to it; for if this country is so insupportable, what is it that obliges him that knows what reason is, to make it his country? Must not he be more silly than a beast, that will tarry in those places where the air is mortal at certain seasons? When nature makes an animal, it gives him the liberty of motion to seek what is good and avoid that which is evil. How opinionative then is man to stay where he is threatened on all sides, and where he must be in a continual torment to preserve himself! Certainly he must have lost all his senses, if ever he had any. As for the weakness which you call modesty, I have nothing to say to it, since you confess with so much sincerity that it is a fault. It is truly a great weakness which will not permit us to look upon one another without the brutal motions which thou speakest of. Beasts continually see themselves and one another, but this sight causes no alteration in them. How then can you who believe yourselves of a superior order to them be more weak than they? Or else it must be that your sight is weaker than that of animals, since you can't see through a single covering what is under; for there are some of them that can even penetrate through a wall. This is all that I can judge of those of thy country, because thou tellest me they have some sparks of reason, but they are so weak that, instead of enlightening them, they only serve to conduct them more surely in their error. If it is true that their country is inhabitable, at least that they make use of cloth and covering for the ends you have mentioned, they are just like those persons who instead of getting away from an evident danger, reason finely how they may preserve themselves, by covering themselves without avoiding the occasion. But if it be true that clothes render you wise in the eyes of one another, I know not how to compare you better than to little children who no more know an object when once it is veiled.

"As for me I rather believe that it is deformity among you which made you first invent clothing, and that it not only authorizes it now, but also continues it; for there is nothing in a man finer than himself when he is without defects and has all the natural qualities which concur to his entire perfection. . . ."

He said no more on this point, but, without giving me time to answer, he passed to that of covetousness. I early perceived that . . . his idea of it was, "a weakness of mind which consisted in heaping up fine things without any profit."

All the Australians forsake some things that are necessary for their entertainment; but they know not what it is to heap up, nor to keep anything against tomorrow; and their manner of living thus may pass for a perfect image of the state that man at first enjoyed in Paradise.

As for ambition, he had a gross idea of it; but he defined it as a desire of men being elevated above others.

I told him that in Europe they held it for a maxim, that the multitude without any order begat confusion, in which there was no gust of the good things in life, and that order supposed a head to which all others were subject. From hence the old man said that it was the nature of man to be born and live free, and that therefore he could not be subjected without being despoiled of his nature; and that in such a subjection man was made to descend below beasts, because a beast being only made for the service of man, subjection was after some manner natural to it. But one man could not be born for the service of another man. A constraint in this case would be a sort of violence which would even degrade a man after a certain manner from his proper existence. He enlarged much to prove that the subjection of one man to another was a subjection of the humane nature and making a man a sort of slave to himself; which slavery implied such a contradiction and violence as was impossible to conceive. He added that the essence of man consisting in liberty, it could not be taken away without destroying him, and therefore he that would take away another's liberty did tacitly bid him to subsist without his own essence. . . .

It seemed to me that I saw things after another fashion than before. I was for above eight hours, as it were, forced to make continual comparisons between what I was and what I saw. I could not but admire a conduct so opposite to our defective one that I was ashamed to remember how far we were from the perfection of those people. I said to myself, "Can it be true that we are not all made men? . . . If it is not so, what is the difference of those people from us? They are by the ordinary state of life elevated to a pitch of a virtue which we cannot attain but by the greatest efforts of our most noble ideas. Our best morality is not capable of better reasoning, nor more exactness, than what they practice naturally without rules, and without precepts. This union which nothing can alter, this distance from worldly goods, this inviolable purity, in a word, this adherence to strict reason which unites them amongst themselves and carries them to what is good and just, can't be but the fruits of a consummate virtue, than which we can conceive nothing more perfect; but, on the contrary, how many vices and imperfections are we not subject to? This insatiable thirst after riches, those continual dissensions, those black treasons, bloody conspiracies, and cruel butcheries, which we are continually exercising towards one another—don't these things force us to acknowledge that we are guided by passion rather than reason? Is it not to be wished that in this estate, one of these men which we may call barbarians would come to disabuse us, and appear in so much virtue as they practice purely by their natural light, to confound the vanity which we draw from our pretended knowledge, and by the assistance of which we only live like beasts?"

OF THE RELIGION OF THE AUSTRALIANS
There is no subject more curious and secret among the Australians than that of their religion. It is a crime of innovation even to speak of it, either by dispute or a form of explanation. Even the mothers do, with the first principles of knowledge, inspire into the child that of the *Haab*, that is to say, *Incomprehensible*. They believe that this Incomprehensible Being is everywhere, and they have all imaginable veneration for Him; but they recommend carefully to the young men to adore Him always without speaking of Him; and they are persuaded that it was a very great crime to make His divine perfections the subject of their discourses; so that one may in a manner say that their great religion is not to speak of religion. As I had been brought up in maxims very different from theirs, I could have no gust in a worship without ceremonies, nor accommodate myself to a religion where I never heard the name of God mentioned. This caused great disquiet in me for some time, but at length I discovered my troubles to my old philosopher, who, having heard me, took me by the hand, and, conducting me into a walk, he said to me with a very grave air: "Is it possible that you should be more a man in the knowledge of the *Haab* than in your other actions? Open thy heart, and I promise you to conceal nothing from thee." I was ravished to find such a favorable opportunity to learn the particular faith of these people. I then told my old man that we had two sorts of the knowledge of God in Europe, the one natural, the other supernatural. Nature instructed us that there was a Sovereign Being, the Author and Preserver of all things. "I can see this truth," added I, "with my eyes, when I behold the earth, view the heavens, or reflect upon myself: when I see such things as are not made but by a Superior Cause, I am obliged to acknowledge and adore a Being, which cannot be made, and which made all things else. When I consider myself I am assured that I could not be without a beginning. Therefore it follows that a person like me would not give me to be, and, by consequence, this puts me upon seeking out a first Being, who, having had no beginning, must be the original of all other things. When my reason conducted me to this first principle, I concluded evidently

that this Being cannot be limited, because limits suppose a necessity of production and dependence."

The old man, interrupting my discourse in my last words, told me with many fine remarks, that if our Europeans could form this reasoning, they were not altogether deprived of the most solid knowledge.

"I always reasoned thus with myself," added he, "as thou hast done, and although the way of arriving to this truth by these kind of reflections be extremely long, yet I am persuaded that it is feasible. I confess, nevertheless, that the great revolutions of many thousand ages may have caused great alteration in what we see; but my mind permits me not from hence either to contrive an eternity, or apprehend a general production without the conduct of a Sovereign Being who is the Supreme Governor. For this would be an abuse upon Him, and charge Him with error among a thousand revolutions, if we aver that all we see happened by the fortuitous rencounters which have had no other principles but that of local motion and the justing together of little small bodies. This is to perplex one's self in such difficulties as we can never resolve, and to put us in danger of committing an execrable blasphemy. This is to give to the creature what belongs to the Creator, and by consequence to repay Him with an insupportable ingratitude to whom we are obliged for what we are and have. Even at what time we conceive that the eternity of atoms is possible, it is certain the contrary opinion is no less, not to say more probable. This would be as willful a crime as to admit that atoms are capable of sentiment and knowledge. It was these considerations that obliged us about forty-five revolutions since, to suppose a first Being, and to teach it as the foundation of all our principles, without suffering that anyone should teach any doctrine which should oppose this truth." I harkened to the discourse of this man with all the attention that I was capable of. The grace with which he spoke and the weight which he gave to his words persuaded me no less than his reasons; but as I saw he was about to ask me a new question, I prevented [anticipated] him and said that although one should grant the eternity of these little bodies we have spoken of, yet they could never frame this world and diversify it as we now see it, according to this indisputable principle. Things continuing in the same state cannot produce other things different from them. Thus these atoms, having no difference among themselves but number and plurality, could only make formless heaps, and of that same quality with themselves.

"That which is most difficult to certain minds," said he, "is the great obstruction of this Being of Beings, which is no more discoverable than if He was not at all. But I found this reason of little weight, because we have many others which oblige us to believe that He is too far above us to manifest Himself to us otherwise than by His works. If His conduct was particular, I should be at a loss to persuade myself that it was His, since an universal being ought to act after an universal manner."

"But if it be true," replied I, "that you cannot doubt of a first and Sovereign Origin of all things, why have you not established a religion for to adore Him? The Europeans who have such a knowledge of Him as you have have set hours for His worship: they have prayers to call upon Him, and praises to glorify Him with, and His commandments to keep."

"You speak very freely of that *Haab*," said he, interrupting me.

"Yes, without doubt," answered I; " 'tis a subject most agreeable and entertaining to us, for we ought to find nothing more delightful, than to speak of Him on whom we absolutely depend for life and death. Nothing is more just and necessary, since 'tis by this only that we can execute our remembrance of Him, and our reverence toward Him."

"There is nothing more reasonable than that," replied he, "but are your opinions the same touching this *Incomprehensible*? . . ."

I confessed sincerely that our opinions were divided in the conclusions which everyone often drew from the same principles. This causes many sharp contestations, from whence there often arise the most envenomed hatreds, and sometimes even bloody wars, and at other times consequences no less fatal.

This good old man replied very briskly that if I had made any other answer, he would have had no further conference with me, but should have had the greatest contempt for me. "For," said he, " 'tis most certain that men cannot speak of anything that is incomprehensible without having diverse opinions of it; nay, even such as are even contrary one to another. One must be blind," added he, "to be ignorant of a First Principle, but one must be infinite like Him to be able to speak exactly of it; for since we know it is incomprehensible, it naturally follows that we can only speak of it by conjecture, and that all that may be said on the subject may perhaps content the curious but can never satisfy the reasonable man. And we better approve of an absolute silence in the matter than to expose ourselves by putting off many false notions concerning the nature of a Being which is elevated so very much above our understandings. We assemble therefore together in the *Hab* only to acknowledge His Supreme Greatness and to adore His Sovereign Power, and leave each person to the liberty of thinking what he pleases. But we have made an inviolable law never to speak of Him for fear of engaging ourselves by discourse in such errors as might offend Him. I leave it to the learned to judge of a conduct so extraordinary as this is, never to speak in any manner of God. All that I can say of it is, it impresses on the mind an admirable respect for divine things, and produces amongst us such a union of which we meet with no example anywhere else. . . ."

I have only three things to remark upon the sentiments of the Australians concerning the present life. The first is in respect to the beginning; the second, the continuation thereof; and the third, the end: their manner of receiving life, preserving, and ending it. . . .

They have so great an aversion for whatever regards the first beginning of their lives that in a year or thereabouts after my arrival amongst them, two of the brethren, having heard me speak something of it, withdrew from me, with as many signs of horror as if I had committed some great crime. One day when I had discovered myself to my old philosopher, after having censured me a little upon this subject, he entered into a long discourse and brought many proofs and obliged me to believe that children grew within them like fruits upon the trees; but when he saw all his reasons made no impression on my mind and that I could not forbear smiling, he left me without accomplishing it, reproaching me that my incredulity proceeded from the corruption of my manners. . . .

As soon as an Australian has conceived, he quits his apartment and is carried to the *Hab*, where he is received with testimonies of an extraordinary bounty, and is nourished without being obliged to work. They have a certain high place upon which they go to bring forth their child, which is received upon certain balsamic leaves; after which the mother (or person that bore it) takes it and rubs it with those leaves, and gives it suck, without any appearance of having suffered any pain.

They make no use of swaddling clothes or cradles. The milk it receives from the mother gives it so good nourishment that it suffices it without any other food for two years. And the excrements it voids are in so small quantity that it may almost be said, it makes none. They generally speak at eight months; they walk at a year's end; and at two they wean them. They begin to reason at three; and as soon as the mother quits them, the first master of the first company teaches them to read, and at the same time instructs them in the first elements of a more advanced knowledge. They usually are three years under the conduct of the first master, and after, pass under the discipline of the second, who teaches them to write; with whom they continue for four years. And so with the others in proportion, till they are thirty years of age, at which time they are perfect in all sorts of sciences without observing any difference amongst them either for capacity, genius, or learning. When they have thus accomplished the course of all their studies, they may be chosen for lieutenants, that is, to supply the place of those that would leave this life.

I have . . . spoken of their humor [temperament], which is mixed with a certain sweetness full of gravity, that forms the temperament of the most reasonable men, and such as are the fittest for society. They are strong, robust, and vigorous, and their health is never interrupted by the least sickness. This admirable constitution comes without doubt from their birth and excellent nourishment, which they always take with moderation; for our sicknesses are always consequences of the corruption of that blood whereof we are formed, and the excess of the ill food which we are nourished with. In fine, our parents generally communicate to us all the defects that they have contracted by their irregular lives. Their intemperance fills us with such an abundance of superfluous humors which destroy us how strong soever we may be, if we purge not ourselves often. It is the excessive heats that they kindle in their blood by their debauches which cause in us such rising in the flesh and all those scorbutic distempers which spread throughout the whole body. Their choler gives us a disposition to the same vice; their wantonness augments our concupiscence; in a word, they make us just what we are, because they give us what they have.

The Australians are exempted from all these passions; for their parents, never being subject to them, cannot communicate them; and as they have no principle of alteration, so they live in a kind of indifference which they never forsake, except it be to follow the emotions that their reason impresses on them.

We may very near make the same consequences touching the nourishment of the Australians; for if the Europeans have the misfortune only to have such viands for their subsistence as are unhealthful, it commonly happens that they eat more than nature requires. And 'tis these excesses that cause in them such weak stomachs, fevers, and other infirmities which are wholly unknown to the Australians. Their admirable temperance and the goodness of their fruits upon which they live maintains them in such a frame of health, as is never interrupted by any sickness. They are likewise so far from placing any glory in eating or making sumptuous feasts as we do, that they hide themselves, and only eat in secret. They sleep very little because they are persuaded that sleep is too animal in action, from which man ought, if it was possible, wholly to abstain.

They all agree that this life is only a motion full of trouble and agitation. They are persuaded that what we call death is their happiness, and that the greatest good of mankind is to arrive to this term, which puts an end to all his pains; from whence they are indifferent for life, and passionately wish for death. The more I seemed to apprehend death, the more they were confirmed in the thought that I could be no man, since, according to their ideas, I sinned against the first principles of reason. My old man oftentimes spoke to me of it, and these are very near the same reasons he gave me: "We differ from beasts," said he, "in that their understanding penetrates not into the bottom of things; they judge of them only by appearance and color. 'Tis from thence they fly their destruction as the greatest evil, and endeavor to preserve themselves in the greatest good, not considering that, since 'tis an absolute necessity that they perish, all the pains they take to prevent it become vain and useless. Even to argue," continued he, "upon what regards us, it is necessary that we should consider life as an estate of mystery although it consists in the union of a spiritual soul with a material body, whereof the inclinations are perfectly opposite the one to the other. So that to desire to live is to desire to be always enduring the violent shock of these oppositions; and to desire death is but to aspire to that rest which each of those parts enjoys when they are both in their center.

"And, as we have nothing dearer to us than ourselves," added he, "nor can look upon ourselves to be anything else but so many compounds whose dissolution is certain and infallible, we more properly languish than live; and the case being so with us, would it not be better for us not to be at all than to be to no other purpose than to know that shortly we shall be no more? The care we take to preserve ourselves is to no purpose, since, after all, we must die at last. The consideration of our rarest talents and most exquisite improvements in knowledge gives us a second torment, since we can look upon them as no other than transitory enjoyments, whose acquisition has cost us a thousand pains, and yet, whose loss it is no way in our power to prevent. In fine, all that we reflect upon, both within and without us, contributes to render our life so much the more odious and insupportable to us."

I answered to all that that in my opinion these arguments proved too much, and that to give them their full force it would follow that I must needs be sorry for knowing anything that surpasses my understanding, which yet is false because the goodness of judgment consists in being able to rest content with our condition, and to put away those troublesome thoughts that serve only to afflict us, especially when we know not how by any means to remedy them.

"There is something of solidity in thy answer," replied he, "but yet it is weak in two particulars. The one is in supposing we are able to suspend our judgment; and the other, in thinking it possible we should love ourselves without detesting our dissolution. To be able to do the first is to be able with open eyes not to see what is continually before us; and to be able to do the second is to love to be something without hating to be nothing. 'Tis a great weakness to imagine we can possibly live without being affected with the sense of our own destruction; and 'tis still a greater to torment ourselves with the fear of what we know will infallibly come upon us. But it is the utmost degree of folly to seek after preservatives in order to avoid what we know to be absolutely unavoidable. To be able to live without the sense of death is to be able to live without knowing anything of ourselves, since death is inseparable from our nature; and that to consider ourselves in all our several parts is to see we have nothing but what is mortal in us. To be capable of fearing death supposes us able to reconcile two contradictions, since to fear supposes some doubt in us, whether what we fear will happen or not, and that we certainly know that we shall infallibly die, and it is still more absurd to go about to take any preservatives to prevent it, when we know that to be impossible."

I replied that we might justly fear not death itself but its approaches, and that preservatives were useful because they might at least stave it off from us for a while.

"Very good," replied he again. "But dost thou not see that since the necessity of dying is indispensable, the putting it off for a while can be of no other service to us than to keep us the longer under continual pain, grief, and anguish?"

I answered him that these reasons would be of much more weight among our Europeans than among them who know not what it is to suffer, whereas the life of the Europeans was nothing else but a continued chain of miseries and sufferings.

"How!" says he. "Have you any other infirmities than those of being mortal and knowing yourselves to be daily advancing toward death? . . ."

I assured him that our people commonly died in many deaths before they came to die for good and all, and that death came not upon our Europeans but by the violence of those diseases that knocked them down and made them at last faint away under them.

This answer was to him a mystery. And as I was endeavoring to make him comprehend our gouts, our headaches, and our colics, I found he understood me not, and therefore to make him apprehend my meaning, I was forced particularly to explain to him the nature of some of those diseases we suffer; which as soon as he understood, "Is it possible," cried he, "that anyone should be in love with such a life as that?"

I answered that our people did not only love it but used all man-

ner of means to prolong it; from whence he took a fresh occasion
to condemn us either for insensibility or extravagance, not being
able as he said to conceive how a reasonable man that was assured
of his death, and that saw himself daily dying by several sorts of
suffering, and that could not protract his life but in continual languishment, could possibly forbear desiring death as his greatest
happiness. "Our opinions in this matter are vastly different," says
he, "from yours. For we, as soon as we come to understand ourselves, because we think ourselves obliged to love our own selves
and look upon ourselves but as so many victims of a superior cause
that is able every moment to destroy us, we therefore make very
small account of our life, and esteem it but as a happiness which
we can enjoy but as a passenger whilst it is fleeting and passing
from us. The time in which we enjoy it is burdensome to us because it serves for nothing but to raise in us a grief for the loss of
that happiness which it more likely takes from us than at first it
gave to us. In fine, we are weary of living, because we dare not fix
our affection upon ourselves with all that tenderness we might otherwise have, for fear of enduring too great violences of reluctance
when we shall be forced to part from a being we have so much
doted upon."

To that I answered him that reason teaches us that it was always
better to be than not to be, and that 'twas better to live, though
but for a day, than never to live at all. To which he replied that
we were to distinguish two things in our being: one was our general existence that perishes not, and the other our particular existence
or individuality that perishes. The first is indeed better than privation, and that 'tis in that sense it is true that being is preferable
before not being; but that the second—that is the being of our individuality, or particular being—is oftentimes worse than not being,
especially when 'tis accompanied with a knowledge that renders us
unhappy. . . .

And now to proceed with our narration: there never is held any
Assembly at the *Heb* at which there are not twenty or thirty persons that demand the liberty to return to their rest; and they never
refuse any, be they who they will, that produce just reasons for it.
And when anyone has obtained permission to go out of this life,
he presents his lieutenant, who must be at least thirty-six years of
age. The company receives him with joy and gives him the name
of the old man that has a mind to die; which done, they represent
to him the brave actions of his predecessors and tell him they are
confident he will not degenerate from the virtue of him whose place
he is going to supply. When that ceremony is over, the old man
goes merrily to the table furnished for that effect with the fruit of

rest, where he eats to the number of eight of them, . . . which plunge him into an eternal sleep. Then they close up his tomb and return back, beseeching the Sovereign Being to advance those happy moments in which they may have the privilege to enjoy the like rest with their departed brother. In this manner are the Australians born; and thus they live and die.

[Subsequent chapters relate how Sadeur's passions were aroused by the sight of a woman during a military campaign against the barbarous Fondins. Since his ardor was observed by the Australians, they condemned him to death for being irrational and subhuman; however, he contrived to escape on the back of a huge bird which he had tamed. When it fell exhausted into the sea, he was rescued by sailors, who returned him to Europe.]

24

The Adventures of Telemachus
Son of Ulysses

François de Salignac de la Mothe Fénelon

New York
1795
(first published in French at Paris in 1699)

François de Salignac de la Mothe Fénelon (1651–1715)

was born in the province of Périgord, France, of an aristocratic family. Educated at the University of Cahors, he proceeded to Paris and became a priest. Having written a treatise on female education, he was appointed preceptor to the Duke of Burgundy, heir to the French throne. To charm the youth to morality and learning, Fénelon wrote *The Adventures of Telemachus*, basing its plot upon Homer's *Odyssey*. In recognition of six years of effective teaching, the King named Fénelon Archbishop of Cambray, and he was consecrated in 1695. His royal pupil died of a fever in 1712.

The Adventures of Telemachus, first published in French in 1699, is unique in seventeenth-century utopianism because its setting is historical rather than geographic. Other utopists gave remote geographical settings to their lands and placed them in the present or future, but Fénelon put his ideal states in antiquity. His outlook was retrograde: in life he was an aristocratic liberal anxious to create an idealized *ancien régime*, a semifeudal organization; but in his utopias he looked even further back to a dream of a sober, decorous, and self-denying Cretan populace, to an arcadian Boetica, and to a semi-Spartan, semifeudal, agricultural Salentum.

Yet Fénelon does not ignore his contemporary world. He wished it to retreat to paternal utopianism rather than to move to bourgeois-dominated reality. He viewed with alarm the modern societies produced by the Renaissance—societies which were sovereign, independent, and lay, where spiritual power could intervene only through faith or through the conscience of the individual man; and, in reaction, he looked backward and idealized society where complexity was replaced by simplicity, where conscience was unimpeded in its operations, where institutions and surroundings conditioned men to the good life, and where frugal innocence held sway. He was criticizing contemporary society. Disliking the licentiousness of Regency France, he exalted Puritanical morality and Spartan simplicity; in an age of libertinism and increasing skepticism, he sought to restore the sense of the divine. He was prepared to force simplicity of life, and he endeavored to replace the divine right to rule absolutely with the divine right and duty to rule well and soberly. In an era of *fainéant* privileges, he urged a functional aristocracy and monarchy which would be benevolent, patriarchial, and self-denying. In an age of artificiality, he believed in a natural divine order in society and sought to make men realize it. He preached benevolent despotism in reaction to the wicked doctrines of Machiavellian princes and of councilors like Mazarin. He was too much of a man of his own age to neglect the encouragement of trade, although at the same time he advocated the insurance of moral and physical welfare and closeness to God which, in his opinion, were naturally and inevitably produced by the rustic simplicity of agricultural life. It was to cure the ills of the present that he looked back to the old ideals of Tacitus and Livy and the Roman Republic, to the early Christian ideal of universal brotherhood, to a vision of monastical communism among pagans, and to the feudal ideal of mutual responsibility. Although superficially *Telemachus* is the story of the travels and reflections of a young prince in the ancient world, it is actually a romance for Fénelon's own day. In part, it is a satire on Louis XIV's government and contemporary figures.

Telemachus visits Egypt, which is described as utopian in its beautiful order. Tyre is glorified for its trade and the virtues of its people. Boetica is described as a fantasy-utopia, an arcadia of men free from human passions, needs, and vices, a community of innocence. Salentum, a new city being built by Idomeneus, was becoming embroiled in wars when Telemachus and his guardian, Mentor, journeyed to it. Mentor reformed and redirected the state, laying the foundations of a utopia. However, Salentum is a more complex state than Boetica, inasmuch as its population is divided into seven functional classes. The people of Boetica are led by nature, those of Salentum by a philosopher-king who provides the institutions and surroundings needed to mold his peoples anew; for Fénelon, like Foigny, seems to regard men as products of their environments. Accordingly, for Fénelon a good system of economics, education by the state, and, above all, the practice of agriculture are the means to utopia. He ill-reconciles his desire for arcadian simplicity with his advocacy of trade and commerce: he seems to want both innocence and complexity all at once. Moreover, when he dwells on the excellence of following nature, he forgets that nature is not always bland and gentle. His work is largely a reaction from artificiality to simple nature, a jumble of arcadianism, Spartan virtues, Puritanical tendencies, classical austerity, and the practices of "good savages." He was contrasting vicious modernity with the sweetness of natural or well-organized simple life. He was criticizing Louis XIV and quietly denouncing subordination of public welfare to private lusts, and, at the same time, trying to spread generous sentiments and to portray what form true benevolence should take in a benevolent despot.

Fénelon's *Telemachus* influenced later utopian writings, particularly Pierre Lesconvel's *Ideal of a Tranquil and Happy Reign or Account of the Voyage made by the Prince of Montberaud to the Isle of Naudeley*, which was published in French in 1703. This utopia is highly idealistic and gives, more than the seventeenth-

century utopias, a picture of what ought to be done. At the same
time it potently satirizes the defects of European life.

The two extracts given below are from *The Adventures of Telemachus* in John Hawkesworth's translation as revised by G. Gregory.

Telemachus

THE WONDERS OF BOETICA
extracted from BOOK VIII

"The river Boetis flows through a fertile country where the air is
always temperate and the sky serene . . . This region seems to have
preserved all the felicity of the golden age. In the winter, the freez-
ing breath of the north is never felt, and the season is therefore
mild, but in the summer there are always refreshing gales from the
west, which blow about the middle of the day, and in this season,
therefore, the heat is never intense; so that spring and autumn, espoused as it were to each other, walk hand in hand through the
year. The valleys and the plains yield annually a double harvest;
the hedges consist of laurels, pomegranates, jessamines, and other
trees that are not only always green, but in flower; the mountains
are covered with flocks, whose wool, for its superior fineness, is sought
by all nations. This beautiful country contains also many mines of
gold and silver; but the inhabitants, happy in their simplicity, disdain to count silver and gold among their riches, and value that
only which contributes to supply the real and natural wants of mankind.

"When we first traded with these people, we found gold and
silver used for plowshares and, in general, employed promiscuously
with iron. As they carried on no foreign trade, they had no need
of money; they were, almost all, either shepherds or husbandmen;
for, as they suffered no arts to be exercised among them but such
as tended immediately to answer the necessities of life, the number
of artificers was consequently small. Besides, the greater part, even
of those that live by husbandry or keeping of sheep, are skillful in
the exercise of such arts as are necessary to manners so simple and
frugal.

"The women are employed in spinning the wool and manufacturing it into stuffs that are remarkably fine and white; they also make
the bread and dress the victuals, which costs them very little trouble,
for they live chiefly upon fruits and milk, animal food being seldom

eaten among them. Of the skins of their sheep, they make a light sort of covering for their legs and feet, with which they furnish their husbands and children. They also make tents, which are covered either with waxed skins or the bark of trees; they make and wash all the clothes of the family, and keep their houses in great neatness and order. Their clothes, indeed, are easily made, for in that temperate climate they wear only a piece of fine white stuff, which is not formed to the shape of the body, but wrapped round it so as to fall in long plaits and take what figure the wearer thinks fit.

"The men cultivate the ground, and manage their flocks; and the other arts which they practice are those only of forming wood and iron into necessary utensils; and of iron they make little use, except in instruments of tillage. All the arts that relate to architecture are useless to them; for they build no houses. 'It shows too much regard to the earth,' say they, 'to erect a building upon it which will last longer than ourselves; if we are defended from the weather, it is sufficient.' As to the other arts which are so highly esteemed in Greece, in Egypt, and in all other polished nations, they hold them in the greatest detestation as the inventions of vanity and voluptuousness.

"When they are told of nations who have the art of erecting superb buildings and of making splendid furniture of silver and gold, stuffs adorned with embroidery and jewels, exquisite perfumes, delicious meats, and instruments of music, they reply that the people of such nations are extremely unhappy to have employed so much ingenuity and labor to render themselves at once corrupt and wretched. 'These superfluities,' say they, 'effeminate, intoxicate, and torment those who possess them, and tempt those who possess them not, to acquire them by fraud and violence. Can that superfluity be good, which tends only to make men evil? Are the people of these countries more healthy or robust than we are? Do they live longer, or agree better with each other? Do they enjoy more liberty, tranquillity, and cheerfulness? On the contrary, are they not jealous of each other? Are not their hearts corroded with envy and agitated by ambition, avarice, and terror? Are they not incapable of pleasures that are pure and simple, since they are enslaved by artificial wants upon which they make all their happiness to depend?'

"Such," said Adoam, "are the sentiments of this sagacious people, who have acquired wisdom only by the study of nature. They consider our refinements with abhorrence; and it must be confessed that in their simplicity, there is something not only amiable but great. They live in common, without any partition of lands. The head of every family is its king. This patriarchal monarch has a right to punish his children or his grandchildren if they are guilty of a fault; but he first takes the advice of his family. Punishment, indeed, is very rare among them; for innocence of manners, sincerity of heart, and hatred of vice seem to be the natural production of the country. Astrea [justice], who is said to have quitted the earth and ascended to heaven, seems still to be hidden among these happy people. They have no need of judges, for every man submits to the jurisdiction of conscience. They possess all things in common, for the cattle produce milk, and the fields and orchards fruit and grain of every kind, in such abundance that a people so frugal and temperate have no need of property. They have no fixed place of abode, but, when they have consumed the fruits, and exhausted the pasturage of one part of the paradise which they inhabit, they remove their tents to another. They have, therefore, no opposition of interest, but are connected by a fraternal affection which there is nothing to interrupt. This peace, this union, this liberty, they preserve by rejecting the superfluous wealth, and deceitful pleasure. They are all free, and they are all equal.

"Superior wisdom, the result either of long experience or uncommon abilities, is the only mark of distinction among them. The cruel and pestilential cries of fraud, of perjury, of law, or of battle, are never heard in this sacred region so dear to the Gods. This soil has never been distained with human blood; and even that of a lamb has rarely been shed upon it. When the inhabitants are told of bloody battles, rapid conquests, and the subversion of empires, which happen in other countries, they stand aghast with astonishment. 'What,' say they, 'do not men die fast enough, without being destroyed by each other? Can any man be insensible of the brevity of life; and can he who knows it, think life too long? Is it possible to suppose that mankind came into the world merely to propagate misery and to harass and destroy one another?' Neither can the inhabitants of Boetica comprehend how those who, by subjugating great empires, obtain the name of conquerors, came to be so much the object of admiration. 'To place happiness in the government of others,' say they, 'is madness, since to govern well is a painful task; but a desire to govern others against their will is madness in a still greater degree. A wise man cannot, without violence to himself, submit to take upon him the government of a willing people, whom the Gods have committed to his charge, or who apply to him for guidance and protection. To govern people against their will is to become miserable for the false honor of holding others in slavery. A conqueror is one whom the Gods, provoked by the wickedness of mankind, send, in their wrath upon the earth, to ravage kingdoms; to spread round them, in a vast circle, terror, misery, and despair; to destroy the brave, and enslave the free. Has not he who is ambitious of glory sufficient opportunities of acquiring it by managing, with wisdom, what the Gods have entrusted to his care? Can it be imagined that praise is to be merited only by arrogance and injustice, by usurpation and tyranny? War should never be thought of but in the defense of liberty. Happy is he who, not being the slave of another, is free from the frantic ambition of making another a slave to him! These conquerors, who are represented as encircled with glory, resemble rivers that have overflowed their banks, which appear majestic indeed, but which desolate the countries they ought to fertilize.' "

After Adoam had given this description of Boetica, Telemachus, who had listened to it with great delight, asked him several minute questions. "Do the inhabitants of Boetica," said he, "drink wine?"

"They are so far from drinking wine," said Adoam, "that they make none; not because they are without grapes, for no country in the world produces them in greater plenty and perfection, but they content themselves with eating them as they do other fruit and are afraid of wine as the corrupter of mankind. 'Wine,' they say, 'is a species of poison which produces madness, which does not kill men, indeed, but degrades them into brutes. Men may preserve their health and their vigor without wine, but with wine, not their health only, but their virtue is in danger.' "

Telemachus then inquired what laws were established in Boetica relating to marriage.

"No man," said Adoam, "is allowed to have more than one wife; and every man is obliged to keep his wife as long as she lives. In this country, a man's reputation depends as much upon his fidelity to his wife, as a woman's reputation, in other countries, depends upon her fidelity to her husband. No people ever practiced so scrupulous a decorum or were so jealous of their chastity. Their women are beautiful and have that sweet and tender sensibility which is more than beauty; but they borrow no advantages from art: there is all the simplicity of nature both in their manners and their dress, and they take their share of the labor of the day. Their marriages are peaceable, fruitful, and undefiled: the husband and wife seem to be two bodies animated by one soul; the husband manages affairs without, and the wife within; she provides for his refreshment at his return, and seems to live only to please him; she gains his confidence, and, as she charms him yet more by her virtue than her beauty, their happiness is such as death only can destroy. From this temperance, sobriety, and simplicity of manners, they derive longevity and health; and it is common to see among them men of an hundred or an hundred and twenty years old who still preserve their cheerfulness and vigor."

"But how," said Telemachus, "do they escape the calamities of war? Are they never invaded by other nations?"

"Nature," says Adoam, "has separated them from other nations by the sea on one side and by mountains almost inaccessible on the other. Besides, their virtue has impressed foreign powers with reverence and awe. When any contest arises among the neighboring states, they frequently make a common deposit of the territory in question in the hands of the Boeticans, and appoint them arbitrators of the dispute. As these wise people are guilty of no violence, they are never mistrusted; and they laugh when they hear of kings who disagree about the boundaries of their country. 'Are they afraid,' say they, 'that the earth should not have room for its inhabitants? There will always be much more land than can be cultivated; and while any remains unappropriated by cultivation, we should think it folly to defend even our own against those who would invade it.' These people are, indeed, wholly free from pride, fraud, and ambition; they do no injury; they violate no compact; they covet no territory; their neighbors, therefore, having nothing to fear from them, nor any hope of making themselves feared by them, give them no disturbance. They would sooner abandon their country or die upon the spot than submit to a state of slavery; so that the same qualities that render them incapable of subjugating others, render it almost impossible for others to subjugate them. For these reasons there is always a profound peace between them and their neighbors."

Adoam proceeded to give an account of the traffic which the Phoenicians carried on in Boetica. "The inhabitants of that happy country," said he, "were astonished, when they first saw the waves bring strangers from a distant region to their coast: they received us, however, with great benevolence, and gave us part of whatever they had, without asking or expecting a return. They suffered us to establish a colony on the island of Gadira, and offered us whatever should remain of their wool after their own necessities were supplied, sending us, at the same time, a considerable quantity of it as a present; for they have great pleasure in bestowing their superfluities upon strangers.

"As to their mines, they made no use of them; and, therefore, without reluctance, left them entirely to us. Men, they thought, were not overwise, who, with so much labor, searched the bowels of the earth for that which could give no true happiness nor satisfy any natural want. They admonished us not to dig in the earth so deep. 'Content yourselves,' said they, 'with plowing it, and it will yield you real benefits in return; it will yield those things to which gold and silver owe all their value; for gold and silver are valuable only as a means of procuring the necessaries of life.'

"We frequently offered to teach them navigation and carry some of their youth with us into Phoenicia; but they never would consent that their children should live as we do. 'If our children were to go with you,' said they, 'their wants would be soon as numerous as yours: the things which you have made necessary would become necessary to them. They would be restless till these artificial wants were supplied, and they would renounce their virtue, by the practice of dishonest arts, to supply them. They would soon resemble a man of good limbs and a sound constitution, who, having by long inactivity forgotten how to walk, is under the necessity of being carried like a cripple.' As to navigation, they admire it as a curious art, but they believe it to be pernicious: 'If these people,' say they, 'have the necessaries of life in their own country, what do they seek in ours? Will not those things which satisfy the wants of nature satisfy their wants? Surely they who defy the tempest to gratify avarice or luxury, deserve shipwreck!' "

Telemachus listened to this discourse of Adoam with unspeakable delight and rejoiced that there was yet a people in the world, who, by a perfect conformity to the law of nature, were so wise and so happy: "How different," said he, "are the manners of this nation from those which, in nations that have obtained the highest reputation for wisdom, are tainted throughout with vanity and ambition! To us, the follies that have depraved us are so habitual that we can scarcely believe this simplicity, though it is indeed the simplicity of nature, can be real: we consider the manners of this people as a splendid fiction, and they ought to regard ours as a preposterous dream."

THE REFORMATION OF SALENTUM
extracted from BOOK XII

When the army was gone, Idomeneus led Mentor into every quarter of the city. "Let us see," said Mentor, "how many people you have, as well in the city as the country; let us number the whole; and let us also examine how many of them are husbandmen. Let us inquire how much corn, wine, oil, and other necessaries your lands will produce one year with another. We shall then know whether your country will subsist its inhabitants, and whether it will yield a surplus for foreign trade. Let us also see how many vessels you have, and how many sailors to man them, that we may be able to judge of your strength." He then visited the port and went on board every vessel. He informed himself of the several ports to which they traded, what merchandise they carried out, and what they brought back in return; what was the expense of the voyage; what were the loans of the merchants to each other, and what trading societies were established among them, that he might know whether their articles were equitable and faithfully observed. He also inquired what was the risk of the several voyages, and to what losses the trade was exposed, that such restrictions might be made as would prevent the ruin of the merchants, who, sometimes, from too eager a desire of gain, undertake what they are not in a condition to accomplish.

He ordered that bankruptcy should be punished with great severity, because it is generally the effect of rashness and indiscretion if not of fraud: he also formed regulations by which bankruptcies might easily be prevented. He obliged the merchants to give an account of their effects, their profits, their expenses, and their undertakings to magistrates established for that purpose. He ordered that they should never be permitted to risk the property of another, nor more than half their own; that they should undertake by association what they could not undertake singly; and that the observance of the conditions of such association should be enforced by severe penalties. He ordered, also, that trade should be perfectly open and free; and, instead of loading it with imposts, that every merchant who brought the trade of a new nation to the port of Salentum should be entitled to a reward.

These regulations brought people in crowds from all parts, and the trade of Salentum was like the flux and reflux of the sea: riches flowed in upon it with an impetuous abundance, like wave impelling wave. Everything was freely brought in and carried out of the port. Everything that was brought was useful, and everything that was carried out left something of greater advantage in its stead. Justice presided over the port, which was the center of innumerable nations, with inflexible severity; and from the lofty towers that were at once its ornament and defense, freedom, integrity, and honor seemed to call together the merchants of the remotest regions of the earth. And these merchants, whether they came from the shores of the east, where the sun rises from the parting wave to begin the day, or from that boundless ocean, where, wearied with his course, he extinguishes his fires, all lived together in Salentum as in their native country, with security and peace.

Mentor then visited the magazines, warehouses, and manufactories of the interior part of the city. He prohibited the sale of all foreign commodities that might introduce luxury or effeminacy: he regulated the dress and the provisions of the inhabitants of every rank, and the furniture, the size, and ornaments of their houses. He also prohibited all ornaments of silver and gold. "I know but one thing," said he to Idomeneus, "that can render your people modest in their expenses—the example of their prince. It is necessary that there should be a certain dignity in your appearance; but your authority will be sufficiently marked by the guards and the great officers of your court that will always attend you. As to your dress, be content with the finest cloth of a purple color: let the dress of your principal officers be of cloth equally fine; and let your own be distinguished only by the color and a slight embroidery of gold round the edge. Different colors will serve to distinguish different conditions without either gold, or silver, or jewels; and let these conditions be regulated by birth.

"Put the most ancient and illustrious nobility in the first rank. Those who are distinguished by personal merit and the authority of office will be content to stand second to those who have been long in possession of hereditary honor. Men who are not noble by descent will readily yield precedence to those that are, if you take care not to encourage a false opinion of themselves by raising them too suddenly and too high; and never fail to gratify those with praise who are modest in prosperity. No distinction so little excites envy as that which is derived from ancestors by a long descent.

"To stimulate virtue and excite an emulation to serve the state, it will be sufficient to reward public merit with honorary distinctions, a crown or a statue, which may be made the foundation of a new nobility for the children of those to whom they are decreed.

"The habit of persons of the first rank may be white, bordered with a fringe of gold. They may also be distinguished by a gold ring on their finger and a medal of gold impressed with your image, hanging from their neck. Those of the second rank may be dressed in blue, with a silver fringe, and be distinguished by the ring without the medal. The third rank may be dressed in green, and wear the medal without either fringe or ring. The color of the fourth class may be a full yellow; the fifth a pale red; the sixth a mixture of red and white; and the seventh a mixture of white and yellow. Dresses of these different colors will sufficiently distinguish the freemen of your state into seven classes. The habit of slaves should be dark gray. And thus each will be distinguished according to his condition, without expense; and every art which can only gratify pride will be banished from Salentum. All the artificers which are now employed so much to the disadvantage of their country will betake themselves to such arts as are useful, which are few, or to commerce or agriculture. No change must ever be suffered to take place, either in the quality of the stuff or the form of the garment. Men are, by nature, formed for serious and important employments; and it is unworthy of them to invent affected novelties in the clothes that cover them, or to suffer the women, whom such employment would less disgrace, to fall into an extravagance so contemptible and pernicious."

Thus Mentor, like a skillful gardener who lops from his fruit trees the useless wood, endeavored to retrench the parade that insensibly corrupts the manners, and to reduce everything to a frugal and noble simplicity. He regulated even the provisions, not of the slaves only, but those of the highest rank. "What a shame is it," said he, "that men of exalted stations should place their superiority in eating such food as effeminates the mind and subverts the constitution! They ought to value themselves for the regulation of their own desires, for their power of dispensing good to others, and for the reputation which the exercise of private and public virtue will necessarily procure. To the sober and temperate, the simplest food is always pleasant: and the simplest food only can produce the most vigorous health and give, at once, capacity and disposition for the purest and highest enjoyments. Your meal should consist of the best food; but it should always be plainly dressed: the art of cookery is the art of poisoning mankind by rendering appetite still importunate when the wants of nature are supplied . . ."

Mentor suppressed also two kinds of music: the soft and effeminate strains which dissolve the soul into languishment and desire, and the Bacchanalian airs that transport it with causeless, tumultuous, and opprobrious joy. He allowed only that sacred and solemn harmony which, in the temples of the Gods, kindles devotion and celebrates heroic virtue. To the temples also he confined the superb ornaments of architecture: columns, pediments, and porticoes. He gave models in a simple but elegant style of building, for houses that would contain a numerous family on a moderate extent of ground, so designed that they should have a healthful aspect, and apartments sufficiently separated from each other that order and decency might be easily preserved, and that they might be repaired at a small expense. He ordered that every house above the middling class should have a hall and a small peristyle, with separate chambers for all the free persons of the family; but he prohibited, under severe penalties, the superfluous number and magnificence of apartments that ostentation and luxury had introduced. Houses erected upon these models according to the size of the family, served to embellish one part of the city at a small expense and give it a regular appearance; while the other part, which was already finished according to the caprice and vanity of individuals, was, notwithstanding its magnificence, less pleasing and convenient. This city was built in a very short time, because the neighboring coast of Greece furnished very skillful architects, and a great number of masons repaired thither from Epirus and other countries, upon the promise that, after they had finished their work, they should be established in the neighborhood of Salentum, where land should be granted them to clear, and where they would contribute to people the country.

Painting and sculpture were arts which Mentor thought should by no means be proscribed; but he permitted the practice of them to few. He established a school under masters of an exquisite taste, by whom the performances of the pupils were examined. "There should be no mediocrity," said he, "in the arts which are not necessary to life; and, consequently, no youth should be permitted to practice them but such as have a genius to excel. Others were designed, by nature, for less noble occupations and may be very usefully employed in supplying the ordinary wants of the community. Sculptors and painters should be employed only to preserve the memory of great men and great actions; and the representations of whatever has been achieved by heroic virtue, for the service of the public, should be preserved only in public buildings or on the monuments of the dead." But whatever was the moderation or frugality of Mentor, he indulged the taste of magnificence in the great buildings that were intended for public sports, the races of horses and chariots, combats with the census [boxing], wrestling, and all other exercises which render the body more agile and vigorous.

He suppressed a great number of traders that sold wrought stuffs of foreign manufacture; embroidery of an excessive price; vases of silver and gold, embossed with various figures in bas-relief; distilled liquors and perfumes. He ordered, also, that the furniture of every house should be plain and substantial, so as not soon to wear out. The people of Salentum, therefore, who had been used to complain of being poor, began to perceive that they abounded in superfluous riches; but that this superfluity was of a deceitful kind; that they were poor in proportion as they possessed it, and that, in proportion as they relinquished it only, they could be rich. "To become truly rich," said they, "is to despise such riches as exhaust the state, and to lessen the number of our wants by reducing them to the necessities of virtue."

Mentor also took the first opportunity to visit the arsenals and magazines, and examine whether the arms and other necessaries of war were in a good condition. "To be always ready for war," said he, "is the surest way to avoid it." He found many things wanting, and immediately employed artificers in brass and iron to supply the defects. Furnaces were immediately built; and smoke and flame ascended in cloudy volumes, like those that issue from the subterranean fires of Mount Etna. The hammer rang upon the anvil, which groaned under the stroke: the neighboring shores and mountains re-echoed to the sound; and a spectator of these preparatives for war, made by a provident sagacity during a profound peace, might have thought himself in that island where Vulcan animates the Cyclops, by his example, to gorge thunder for the Father of the Gods.

Mentor then went with Idomeneus out of the city, and found a great extent of fertile country wholly uncultivated, besides considerable tracts that were cultivated but in part, through the negligence or poverty of the husbandmen or the want of spirit or the want of hands. "This country," said he to the king, "is ready to enrich its inhabitants, but the inhabitants are not sufficient to cultivate the country; let us, then, remove the superfluous artficers from the city, whose professions serve only to corrupt the manners of the people, and let us employ them in fertilizing these plains and hills. It is a misfortune that these men, having been employed in arts which require a sedentary life, are unused to labor; but we will try to remedy this evil. We will divide these uncultivated lands in lots among them and call in the neighboring people to their assistance, who will gladly undertake the most laborious part of the work upon condition that they shall receive a certain proportion of the produce of the lands they clear. They may afterwards be made proprietors of part of it and be thus incorporated with your people, who are by no means sufficiently numerous. If they prove diligent and obedient to the laws, they will be good subjects and increase your power. The artisans whom you shall transplant from the city to the field will bring up their children to the labors of rural life; and the foreigners, whom you have employed to assist in building your city, have engaged to clear part of your lands and become husbandmen. These men, as soon as they have finished the public buildings, you should incorporate with your people; they will think themselves happy to pass their lives under a government so gentle as that which you have now established; and as they are robust and laborious, their example will animate the transplanted artificers with whom they will be mixed; and, in a short time, your country will abound with a vigorous race wholly devoted to agriculture.

"When this is done, be in no pain about the multiplication of your people; they will, in a short time, become innumerable if you facilitate marriage; and the most simple way of facilitating marriage is the most effectual. All men are naturally inclined to marry, and nothing prevents them from indulging this inclination but the prospect of difficulty and distress. If you do not load them with taxes, their families will never become a burden. The earth is never ungrateful, but always affords sustenance to those who diligently cultivate it. It refuses its bounty only to those who refuse their labor. Husbandmen are always rich in proportion to the number of their children, if their prince does not make them poor; for their children afford them some assistance, even from their infancy: the youngest can drive the flock to pasture, those that are farther advanced can look after the cattle, and those of the third stage can work with their father in the field. In the meantime, the girls assist the mother, who prepares a simple but wholesome repast for those that are abroad, when they return home fatigued with the labor of the day. She milks her cows and her sheep, and the pails overflow with longevity and health; she brings out her little stores, her cheeses and her chestnuts, with fruits that she has preserved from decay; she piles up the social fire, and the family gathers round it; every countenance brightens with the smile of innocence and peace; and some rural ditty diverts them till the night calls them to rest. He that attended the flock returns with his pipe; and, when the family is got together, he sings them some new song that he has learnt at the neighboring village. Those that have been at work in the fields come in with their plow and the weary oxen that hang down their heads and move with a slow and heavy pace notwithstanding the goad, which now urges them in vain. All the sufferings of labor end with the day. The poppies which, at the command of the Gods, are scattered over the earth by the hand of sleep, charm away every care; sweet enchantment lulls all nature into peace; and the weary rest without anticipating the troubles of tomorrow. Happy, indeed, are these unambitious, mistrustless, artless people, if the Gods vouchsafe them a king that disturbs not their blameless joy: and of what horrid inhumanity are they guilty, who, to gratify pride and ambition, wrest from them the sweet product of the field which they owe to the liberality of nature and the sweat of their brow! In the fruitful lap of nature there is inexhaustible plenty for temperance and labor. If none were luxurious and idle, none would be wretched and poor."

"But what shall I do," said Idomeneus, "if the people that I scatter over this fertile country should neglect to cultivate it?"

"You must do," said Mentor, "just contrary to what is commonly done. Rapacious and inconsiderate princes think only of taxing those who are most industrious to improve their lands; because, upon these, they suppose a tax will be more easily levied; and they spare those whom idleness has made indigent. Reverse this mistaken and injurious conduct, which oppresses virtue, rewards vice, and encourages a supineness that is equally fatal to the king and to the state. Let your taxes be heavy upon those who neglect the cultivation of their lands; and add to your taxes fines and other penalties if it is necessary; punish the negligent and the idle as you would a soldier who should desert his post. On the contrary, distinguish those who, in proportion as their families multiply, cultivate their lands with the greater diligence, by special privileges and immunities. Every family will then become numerous; and every one will be animated to labor, not by the desire of gain only, but of honor. The state of husbandry, being no longer wretched, will not longer be contemptible: the plow, once more held in honor, will be guided by the victorious hands that have defended the country: and it will not be less glorious to cultivate a paternal inheritance in the security of peace than to draw the sword in its defense when it is endangered by war. The whole country will bloom around you: the golden ears of ripe corn will again crown the temples of Ceres: Bacchus will tread the grapes in rich clusters under his feet; and wine, more delicious than nectar, will flow from the hills like a river. The valleys will resound to the song of the shepherds, who, dispersed along the banks of a transparent stream, shall join their voices with the pipe; while their flocks shall frolic round them, and feast upon the flowery pasture without fear of the wolf. . . ."

"But," said Idomeneus, "when the people shall be thus blessed with plenty and peace, will not their happiness corrupt their manners; will they not turn against me the very strength I have given them?"

"There is no reason to fear that," said Mentor; "the sycophants of prodigal princes have suggested it as a pretense for oppression; but it may easily be prevented. The laws which we have established with respect to agriculture will render life laborious; and the people, notwithstanding their plenty, will abound only in what is necessary, for we have prohibited the arts that furnish superfluities: and the plenty even of necessaries will be restrained within due bounds by the facility of marriage and the multiplication of families. In proportion as a family becomes numerous, their portion of land being still the same in extent, a more diligent cultivation will become necessary; and this will require incessant labor. Luxury and idleness only render people insolent and rebellious. They will have bread, indeed, and they will have bread enough; but they will have nothing more, except what they can gain from their own ground, by the sweat of their brow.

"That your people may continue in this state of mediocrity, it will be necessary that you should now limit the extent of ground that each family is to possess. We have, you know, divided your people into seven classes, according to their different conditions; and each family, in each class, must be permitted to possess only such an extent of ground as is absolutely necessary to subsist it. This regulation being inviolably observed, the nobles can never get possession of the lands of the poor: every one will have land, but so much only as will make a diligent cultivation necessary. If, in a long course of years, the people should be so much increased that land cannot be found for them at home, they may be sent to form colonies abroad, which will be a new advantage to the mother country.

"I am of opinion that care should be taken, even to prevent wine from being too common in your kingdom. If you find that too many vines are planted, you should cause them to be grubbed up. Some of the most dreadful mischiefs that afflict mankind proceed from wine: it is the cause of disease, quarrels, sedition, idleness, aversion to labor, and every species of domestic disorder. Let wine, then, be considered as a kind of medicine, or as a scarce liquor, to be used only at the sacrifices of the Gods, or in seasons of public festivity. Do not, however, flatter yourself that this regulation can ever take place without the sanction of your own example.

"The laws of Minos, with respect to the education of children, must also be inviolably preserved. Public schools must be established, to teach them the fear of the Gods, the love of their country, a reverence for the laws, and a preference of honor, not only to pleasure, but to life. Magistrates must be appointed to superintend the conduct, not of every family only, but every person. You must keep also your own eye upon them; for you are a king only to be the shepherd of your people and to watch over your flock night and day."

25

The Memoirs of Signior Gaudentio di Lucca:

Taken From His Confession and
Examination Before the Fathers of
the Inquisition at Bologna in Italy,
Making a Discovery of an Unknown
Country in the Midst of the Vast
Deserts of Africa, as Ancient,
Populous, and Civilized, as the
Chinese; With an Account of Their
Antiquity, Origin, Religion, Customs,
Polity, and the Manner How They
Got First Over Those Vast Deserts;
Interspersed With Several Most
Surprising and Curious Incidents

Simon Berington

London
1737

Simon Berington (1680–1755)

was born in England. Being of a Roman Catholic family, he was educated in the English College at Douay, where he received a degree in divinity, was ordained a priest, and for twelve years taught as Professor of Poetry and Philosophy. In 1716, he returned as a missionary to England. There he took charge of a Roman Catholic library at Gray's Inn. Many of his numerous erudite works have never been published.

Gaudentio di Lucca (the short title by which scholars ordinarily refer to the fictitious *Memoirs*), was first published in 1737, but was never acknowledged by its author, despite the fact that some ten editions in English, French, and German appeared during his lifetime. The work gained almost immediate fame and was commonly attributed to Bishop George Berkeley because it seemed to reflect his humanity, wisdom, and gentleness. This attribution enhanced the reputation of *Gaudentio* and led to its being regarded not as a mere romance or account of an imaginary voyage and country, but as "a beautiful Fiction," a "sublime Allegory," rich in philosophical, moral, and religious significance. Why Berington failed to claim it is not clear; perhaps he thought its romanticism inconsistent with priestly gravity; perhaps he feared lest his treatment of the Inquisition would be interpreted as unfavorable to his Church.

Whatever Berington's reasons for silence may have been, *Gaudentio di Lucca* has considerable importance. Lee M. Ellison comments as follows: "Coming at a time when prose fiction was casting about for its appropriate subject-matter and was still in the experimental stages of its art, *Gaudentio* is almost the only specimen of the novel in English between *Crusoe* and *Gulliver* on the one hand, and *Pamela* on the other." Ellison notes further that Berington's utopianism is a product of rationalism and sentimentalism: seventeenth-century rationalists like Bacon and Campanella had seen in Nature "the inexorable order of things as determined by immutable law," law which might be learned by the study of phenomena. They taught that man should find and follow Nature's order. But eighteenth-century sentimentalism changed this conception: "Nature, instead of being merely a rationalistic scheme of things—abstract, impersonal, and coldly indifferent to man as an individual—came to be conceived of as a divine order which included not only the ultimate wisdom but the ultimate good—an active, beneficent influence upon the individual life, a kind of guide, counselor, and friend of man, if he would but hearken to her teachings. It is the lofty, if naïve, idealism engendered by this conception which constitutes the animating principle of Berington's experiment in utopian statecraft. In utter singleness of heart man goes to nature for light and guidance; she gives him a religion of absolute purity, a moral code of elevated simplicity, and a political and social system of excellence superlative."

In this sentimental naturalism Berington was probably influenced by the utopias of Fénelon and by those of Fénelon's disciples: *The Ideal of a Tranquil and Happy Reign,* by Pierre Lesconvel, gives an idealistic picture of the Isle of Naudeley, and *The Life of Sethos* by Jean Terrasson, originally published in French in 1731, deals with ancient Egypt and, being written in the form of memoirs, provides a precedent for Berington in that respect. Fénelon seems to have been familiar with Manetho's utopian report of a paternally governed, pacifistic Egyptian people in remote antiquity, a nation whose lofty natural religion and high natural morality made them excel all others in virtue. This report inspired Fénelon's glorification of Egypt as seen by Telemachus. Terrasson's *Life of Sethos* likewise dealt with a somewhat utopianized Egypt. Berington took over the tradition as a vehicle for his philosophic and social ideas.

Ellison notes that Mezzorania, the utopian African kingdom described by Berington, also shows a close resemblance to more rationally conceived commonwealths of the seventeenth century, especially *The Royal Commentaries of Peru* by Garcilaso de la Vega, *The City of the Sun* by Campanella, and *The History of the Sevarites* by Denis Veiras (or Vairasse).

Berington was a very erudite scholar. Hence it is possible to find many threads of influence in his story. For example, he follows Sir Robert Filmer's *Patriarcha* (1680) in opposing Thomas Hobbes. Indeed, Ellison notes that *Gaudentio* "is the apotheosis of the patriarchal theory of government, along with the corollary principle of strict primogeniture and the proposition that the state is but the family on a vastly greater scale." In this last respect, stress on the importance of the family, Berington was probably influenced by Sir Thomas More's *Utopia,* in which the family is exalted as a sacred and natural institution. However, Ellison suggests that the patriarchal theory may have been primarily intended as a support for the Stuart claimant to the throne of England, and that the real purpose of the work was to serve the cause of Charles Edward, the direct heir of ousted James II, in efforts to regain the English crown for the Stuarts.

At first sight, the naturalism of *Gaudentio* may seem incompatible with a work intended to aid the restoration of a Roman Catholic family to regal power. However, the *Memoirs* should not be interpreted as favoring the deists. Berington's purpose is not to advocate naturalistic religion, but, rather, to refute the deists by showing that natural religion gropes towards the truths of revealed religion and that, instead of a conflict between them, there are analogies and parallels so close as to bring them into complete harmony.

The story takes the form of an account given by Gaudentio to the Holy Inquisition at Bologna. The narrative is repeatedly broken by questions from the Inquisitors and Gaudentio's replies. These have been omitted from the extracts below.

After various adventures, the narrator reaches an immense and beautiful country, Mezzorania, sheltered from the rest of the world by mountains and deserts. Three thousand years before, the ancestors of this nation had lived in happy innocence in what is now Egypt. Their pacifistic religion forbade them to oppose invading shepherd kings from the East. Accordingly, forced to choose between slavery or flight, one patriarch departed into the deserts with his five sons and five daughters. Eventually they discovered an uninhabited but fertile land which they named Mezzorania. Here they lived without contact with the world and its vices for three thousand years, knowing neither war nor invasion, enlightened by the dictates of nature and pure reason.

Gaudentio, who was discovered to be a descendant of a lost daughter of Mezzorania, was welcomed into the national family, married, and lived happily in the African kingdom for years. However, wishing to die in a Christian land, he returned to Italy. There some incautious remarks caused him to be haled before the Inquisition, to whom he related his history.

The following extracts are from *The Adventures of Signior Gaudentio di Lucca*, an edition published at London in 1774.

BIBLIOGRAPHY: Lee Monroe Ellison, "Gaudentio di Lucca: A Forgotten Utopia," *PMLA* L (June, 1935), 494–509; Philip B. Gove, *The Imaginary Voyage in Prose Fiction*, 295–300.

Signior Gaudentio di Lucca

[*In response to the questions addressed to him by his inquisitors, Gaudentio gives an account of the religion of the Mezzoranians and concludes it as follows:*]

The sum, therefore, of the theoretical part of their religion is:

First, that the El is the supreme intellectual, rational, and most noble of all beings; that it is the duty of all intellectual beings to imitate the just laws of reason in him; otherwise they depart from the supreme rule of all their actions, since what is contrary to the most perfect reason in God must be contrary to our own, and by consequence of a deformity highly blameable in his sight; all their prayers, and whatever they ask of this supreme being, is, that they may be just and good as he is.

Secondly, that the sun is the chief, at least instrumental cause of their bodies, and all other physical effects. Your Reverences know better than I can inform you, that this is wrong: to him they address their prayers for the preservation of their lives, the fruits of the earth, etc.

Thirdly, that their parents are the more immediate instrumental cause of their natural being, which they derive partly from the El, and partly from the sun, and they reverence them the more on this account, as being the vicegerents of both, and believe them to be immortal, as to the spiritual or intellectual part, and consequently able and ready to assist them according to the respect they show them by reverencing their tombs and honoring their memories. Though, upon a nicer examination, I found that the superstitious worship they pay to their deceased ancestors was as much a politic as a religious institution, because their government being patriarchal, this inviolable respect they show to their parents makes them obey their elders or governors, not only with the most dutiful observance, but even with a filial love and alacrity.

There are some other points of less consequence, and reducible to these three heads, which your Reverences will observe in the course of my relation. As for the immortality of the soul, rewards and punishments in another life, they believe both, though they have an odd way of explaining them. They suppose, without any hesitation, that the soul is a being independent of matter as to its essence, having faculties of thinking, willing, and choosing, which mere matter, let it be spun ever so fine, and actuated by the quickest and the most subtile motion, can never be capable of; but their notion of their pre-existence with the El, before they were sent into bodies, is very confused. The rewards and punishments in the next life they believe will chiefly consist in this: that in proportion as their actions have been conformable to the just ideas of the supreme being in this life, partaking still more and more of his infinite wisdom, so their souls will approach still nearer to the beautiful intelligence of their divine model in the next. But if their actions in this life have been inconsistent with the supreme reason in God, they shall be permitted to go on forever in that inconsistency and disagreement, till they become so monstrously wicked and enormous, as to become abominable even to themselves.

I found the wisest of them held the metempsychosis, or the transmigration of souls, not as a punishment in the next life, as some of the ancient heathen philosophers did, but as a punishment in this; the chief punishment in the next was explained above. This transmigration of souls is quite different from the received notion of the word. Instead of believing, as the ancients did, that the souls of wicked and voluptuous men, after their deaths, transmigrated into beasts according to the similitude of their vicious inclinations, till, passing through one animal into another, they were permitted to commence men again: I say, these people, instead of believing this, hold a metempsychosis of quite a different nature; not that the souls of men enter into brutes, but that the souls of brutes enter into the bodies of men, even in this life. They say, for example, that the bodies of men and women are such delicate habitations that the souls of brutes are perpetually envying them and contriving to get into them; that, unless the divine light of reason be perpetually attended to, these brutal souls steal in upon them and chain up the rational soul, so that it shall not be able to govern the body, unless it be to carry on the designs of the brutal soul, or at best only make some faint efforts to get out of its slavery. I took it, at first, that this system was merely allegorical, to show the similitude between the passions of men when not directed by reason, and those of brutes. But, upon examination, I found it was their opinion that this transmigration did really happen; insomuch that in my last journey with the Pophar into Egypt, when he saw the Turks, or other strange nations, nay several Armenian and European Christians, he would say to me in his own language, "There goes a hog; there goes a lion, a wolf, a fox, a dog, and the like"; that is, they believe the body of a voluptuous man is possessed by the soul of hog, of a lustful man by that of a goat, a treacherous man by that of a fox, a tyrannical man by that of a wolf, and so of the rest. This belief is instilled into them so early, and with so much care, that it is of very great benefit to keep them within the bounds of reason. If a young man finds himself inclined to any of these passions, he addresses himself immediately to some person whom he thinks of superior wisdom, who assures him that the soul of some certain brute is endeavoring to surprise and captivate his rational soul and take possession of its place. This makes them always watchful and upon their guard against their own passions, not to be surprised by such a merciless enemy. Their immediate remedy is to look steadfastly at the divine light that shines within them, and compare it with its original, till by the force of its rays they drive away those brutal souls, which, as soon as fully discovered in their treacherous attacks (for they come on, say they, by stealth, not daring to attack that divine light directly), are easily repulsed, before they have obtained possession, though it costs a great deal of pains to dislodge them, when once they are got in. The fear of being abandoned to the slavery of these brutal souls is so deeply imprinted in them from their infancy, that they look upon the temperance and regularity of their lives to be in a great measure owing to this doctrine. The same notions hold with their women; into whom their mothers and governesses instill them, as the wise men do to the men; only they believe the brutal souls that enter into women are of a different species from those that enter into men. They say, for instance, that of a chameleon makes them false and inconstant; that of a peacock, coquettish and vain; that of a tigress, cruel and ill-natured; and so of the rest. They add another difference between men and women, that when these brutal souls are entered into them, they are much harder to be driven out from them, than from the men; besides that these brutal souls will lurk undiscovered in women a great while, and are often scarce discernible, till the age of five and twenty or thirty; whereas in most men they discover themselves presently after their entrance.

It was on account of this doctrine, as I found by repeated observations, that they were so addicted to the study of physiognomy, laying down rules to know by the countenance, the lines of the face, and unguarded looks of men, whether the brutal soul has got possession or not, in order to apply proper remedies. This science, however uncertain and doubtful among Christians (who have greater assistance of grace and virtue to resist their passions, those treacherous invaders), is brought to greater perfection and certitude than one would imagine, among such of these people, who, having no such helps, take little care to cultivate and moderate their vicious inclinations, unless they are apprized and forewarned of the danger. Therefore their wise men, whenever they come in company of the younger sort, consider attentively with themselves all the lineaments of the countenance, complexions, motions, habit of body, constitution, tone of the voice, make and turn of the face, nose, ears, etc., but particularly they observe the structure and glances of the eye, with innumerable signs proceeding from it, by which they pretend to discover those passions. I say, they pretend to know by these what brutal soul lays siege to the rational soul, or whether it has already taken possession of its post. If they are strangers, they prudently take care to avoid their company, or at least are on their guard not to have any dealings with them in matters obnoxious to the brutal soul they think them possessed by. But if the person attacked by these brutal souls be of their own nation, they immediately forewarn such to be on his guard, by which, and the dread they have entertained from their youth of these brutal enemies, they are kept in such order, that, as I said, I never saw such moral people in my life. The worst is, they are extremely inclined to be proud and have too great a value for themselves, despising in their hearts all other nations, as if they were nothing but brutes in human shape. However, their wise men take as much care as possible to correct this fault, as far as the ignorance of the law of grace will allow; by putting them often in mind of the miseries and infirmities of human life, which, being real evils, must be in punishment of some fault; that the most perfect are liable to death, which makes no distinction between them and the rest of the world. Besides, humility, and a commiseration for the defects of others, is one of the rays of the divine light that is to guide them. From [as a result of] such documents and instructions of the wiser sort, though they do not care to have any correspondence with other people, seeing them so possessed with those brutal souls, yet they are a most courteous and compassionate people in all their behavior.

Over and above what has been said already of the nature and customs of these people, I shall here observe that their laws are very few in number; but then they are prodigious exact in the observance of them. I have often heard the Pophar, contrary to his custom, make very severe reflections on the lawyers of other countries, who make laws upon laws, and add precepts upon precepts, till the endless number of them makes the fundamental part to be forgotten, leaving nothing but a confused heap of explanations; which may cause ignorant people to doubt whether there is really anything meant by the laws or not. "If I forbid my son," says he, "to do any wrong to anyone, what need is there of reckoning up all the particulars by which a person may be wronged? Show but the fact on both sides, any man of sense and equity can tell if there be any wrong done. For if you multiply an infinity of circumstances, it will be much more difficult to decide what is right, or what is wrong, than if you precisely and absolutely forbid all injury whatsoever." It is almost incredible, with what nicety and equity, and how soon, their judges determine the few disputes they have among them. To weigh the merits of the cause by the weight of the purse would be counted by them one of the greatest enormities. There are no courts for disputes of this nature; all is done by laying the case before their public assemblies, or before any one or two prudent and just men; and the affair is finally decided at once. All the law for *meum* and *tuum* [mine and thine; i.e., private property], among them is, *Thou shalt do no wrong to anyone*, without entering into any further niceties. "Such explanatory suppositions," say they, "oftener show people how they may ingeniously contrive to do an injury, than how to avoid it."

Their laws therefore are nothing but the first principles of natural justice, explained and applied by the elders in the public hearing of all who have a mind to come in when the facts are brought into dispute.

The worship of the Deity, and that excessive and even superstitious reverence they pay to their parents, both alive and dead, is so carefully inculcated to them from their infancy, that there is no need of any written law to enforce it. They look on a man to be possessed with some brutal soul, who should pretend to call in question or neglect this duty.

There is a positive law among them, not to shed human blood voluntarily. They carry this fundamental law of nature to such a height that they never put anyone to death, even for murder, which very rarely happens; that is, once in several ages. If it appears that a person has really murdered another, a thing they think almost impossible, the person convicted is shut up from all commerce of men, with provisions to keep alive as long as nature allows. After his death the fact is proclaimed, as it was when they shut him up, over all the Nomes. His name is blotted out of their genealogies; then his dead body is mangled just in the same manner as he killed the innocent, and afterwards burnt to ashes, which are carried up to the highest part of the deserts, and then tossed up into the air, to be carried away by the winds blowing from their own country: nor is he ever more to be reckoned as one of their race, and there is a general mourning observed throughout the kingdom for nine days.

There is also an express law against adultery and whoredom, which are likewise punished after death. If persons are caught in adultery, they are shut up apart till death; then they are exposed naked as they were surprised, and the body of the woman treated after the most ignominious manner for three days. After which, they are burnt, and their ashes dispersed as before. Whoredom is only punished, in the man, by chaining him to a he-goat, and the woman to a salt bitch, and leading them thus round the Nome. All in the respective Nome, men and women, are to be present at the more signal punishments; and parents are obliged to explain to their children the wickedness and horror of the crime, for a warning for the future. I forgot to tell your Reverences, that if the woman brings forth by adultery, the child is preserved till able to be carried with them when they go into Egypt, and there given to some stranger, with ample provision for its maintenance, but never to be heard of more.

There is also one particular I should have mentioned, relating to injustice. If, for example, the elders find there has been any considerable injustice done, the criminal is obliged to restore nine times the value. If any one be convicted to have imposed upon the judges, he is to be sent out to the skirts of the country, to live by himself for a time proportionable to his guilt, with a mark on his forehead, for all persons to avoid him, lest he should instill his principles into others. All other matters are regulated rather by custom, than by laws, which will be seen when I come to the form of their government, and other particular institutions.

Their form of government, as I had the honor to acquaint your Reverences before, is patriarchal, which they preserve inviolably, being the most tenacious people in the world of their primitive institutions. But the order of the succession is extremely particular, in order to keep up the equality of brotherhood and dignity as exact as they can. Your Reverences, I presume, remember that they all sprung from one family (and lived as such when they were driven out of Egypt), the head of which was priest of the sun. This government they had observed ever since Misrain took possession of that land for his habitation. But when they were secured from all the world in the first vale, as was mentioned before, they established that form of government after a particular manner. The first Pophar, settling in that vale with his five sons, and as many daughters with their husbands, governed them during life, as father or patriarch of them all. Their prodigious veneration for their parents, and separation from all other people, render this form infinitely more practicable than can well be imagined. As they were children of one man, the interest of the whole was the interest of every particular. All the nation of the first transmigration were children, grandchildren, or great grandchildren of the good old man who conducted them thither. Having no wars, or voyages at sea, nor commerce with the distempers as well as vices of other nations, who generally differ in their way of living as well as their climate; having nothing of this, I say, to destroy their people, they not only increased prodigiously, without plurality of wives, but by that and their almost primitive way of living, they preserved their lives to a great old age, most of them living above a hundred years, and some above a hundred and fifty. The first Pophar (say their memoirs) lived till an hundred and fifty-five, and his eldest son, his successor, more robust still, to a hundred and sixty. Presently after his establishment in the first vale, he divided his small dominions into five Nomes, or governments, under his five sons, as was observed before. All were to be subordinate to the eldest; but it was only a patriarchal subordination, relating to the whole. The other governors, and indeed all fathers of families, were entire ministers of the law in their respective families; but these last were liable to the inspection of the more immediate superiors, and all to that of the Grand Pophar, assisted with such a number of counselors as were established afterwards. To give your Reverences a more distinct idea of this wonderful government, it will come much to the same, whether we descend from the chief Pophar to every respective family, or from these upwards. The particularities of the succession I shall consider afterwards. However, it will be easier seen if we take them when their numbers were not so great, at the first beginning of their establishment.

The Pophar, then, having distinguished the bounds of every Nome, I mean in their first transmigration, each son took possession of it for himself and posterity. While each son's children were unmarried, they continued under the government of their father, who made use of as much land as was sufficient for the conveniences and pleasures, as well as the necessaries of life. But as soon as any son was married, or at least when he could be called a father of a family, the father, with consent of the Pophar, allotted him likewise a sufficient quantity for the same end: so they spread and enlarged themselves as it were from the center to a farther extent, much in the same manner as they build their towns, till they had occupied the whole Nome. Here you will say, these people must in process of time increase *ad infinitum,* without lands sufficient to maintain them. This was really the case in the first plantation, which was so entirely occupied by them, that if the famous Pophar, who brought them into the vast continent they now enjoy, had not made that glorious discovery with the danger of his life, they must have returned into Egypt, or ate up one another; but where they are at present, they have room enough, notwithstanding their numbers, for several ages. However, I often represented to the Pophar, that it must come to that at last: the thought made him uneasy at first, and at length put him on a further discovery, as your Reverences will see in the sequel. But such vast numbers of them betaking themselves to arts and manufactures, and the country being so prodigiously fertile, there does not appear any great difficulty in that respect. Of all arts they look upon agriculture as the first in dignity next to the liberal sciences, since that nourishes all the rest; but it comes so easily, and the fruits and legumes are so rich and delicious, that they have little more trouble than to gather them: besides, having two summers, and two springs, each different season produces its peculiar fruits. But to return to the idea of their government, each father of a family governs all his descendants, married or unmarried, as long as he lives. If his sons are fathers, they have a subordinate power under him; if he dies before he comes to such an age, the eldest son, or the eldest uncle, takes care of them, till they are sufficient to set up a family of themselves. The father, on extraordinary occasions, is liable to be inspected by five of the most prudent heads of that district; chosen by common consent; these last, by the heads of the five Nomes, and all the Nomes by the Grand Pophar, assisted with three hundred sixty-five elders, or senators, chosen out of every Nome. What is most particular in this government is that they are all absolute in some manner, and independent, as looking on themselves as all equal in birth; yet in an entire dependency of natural subordination or eldership, which runs through the whole economy, as your Reverences will see when I come to the succession. They are in the same manner lords and proprietors of their own possessions, yet the Pophar and governors can allot and dispose of all for the public emolument, because they look on him to be as much the father of all, as the immediate natural father is of his proper children, and even in some sense their natural father by right of eldership, because they sprung originally from one man, whom the Grand Pophar represents. To this, that natural, or politic, or even superstitious respect they show to their parents contributes so much, that they never dispute, but, on the contrary, revere, the regulations made by their superiors; being satisfied that they are not only just and good, but that it is their own act, since it is done by virtue of a subordination to which they all belong. . . . In a word, the whole country is only one great family governed by the laws of nature, with proper officers, constituted by the whole, for order and common preservation. Every individual looks on himself as a part of that great family. The Grand Pophar is the common father, esteeming all the rest as children and brothers, calling them universally by that name, as they all call one another brothers, bartering and exchanging their commodities as one brother would do with another; and not only so, but they all join in building their towns, public places, schools, etc., laying up all the stores and provisions over and above the present consumption, in public places, for the use of the whole, with overseers and inspectors constituted by common consent, who are to take care chiefly that no disorder be committed. Thus every one contributes to all public expenses, feasts, and the like, which on some occasions are extremely magnificent, affecting external grandeur in all respects. Thus also every man, wherever he goes, enters into what house he pleases, as if it were his own home; this they are doing perpetually throughout the whole country, rather visiting than merchandising; exchanging the rarities of each respective place with those of other parts, just like friends making presents to one another; so that all the roads are like streets of great towns, with people going backward and forward perpetually. They do this the more frequently to keep up a correspondence between the Nomes, lest distances of place should cause any forgetfulness of their being of one family. The plenty of the country affords them everything that nature can call delightful, and that with such ease that infinite numbers are employed in trades and arts, according to their genius, or inclinations; which, by their continual peace and plenty, their long establishment in one country and under one form of government, the natural ingenuity of the people, the so early knowledge of arts, which they brought with them out of Egypt; by the improvements their wise men make in them from time to time; and from what they learn when they pay their visits to their deceased ancestors, they have brought to prodigious perfection. One may say of them, that they are all masters, and all servants; every one has his employment; generally speaking, the younger sort wait on the elders, changing their offices as is thought proper by their superiors, as in a well-regulated community. All their children universally are taught at the public expense, as children of the government, without any distinction but that of personal merit. As the persons deputed for that end judge of their genius or any particular inclination, they are disposed afterwards to those arts and callings for which they seem most proper; the most sublime sciences are the most in respect with them, and are chiefly the employment of their great men and governors, contrary to the custom of other countries; the reason of which is, because these being never chosen till they are fifty years of age, they have had more time to improve themselves, and generally are persons of more extensive capacities. They rightly suppose that persons who excel others in the most rational sciences are not only fittest to govern a rational people, but also most capable of making themselves masters of what they undertake; not but such men, knowing the governors are chosen out of that rank, have an eye in their studies to the rules and arts of governing, which are communicated at a distance by them, according to the talents they remark in the subjects. They do not do this out of any spirit of ambition, employments being rather an honorary trouble than an advantage, but for the real good of the whole. Agriculture, as I said, has the next place of honor after liberal arts; and next to that, those arts are most esteemed which are most necessary; the last of all are those which are of least use, though perhaps the most delightful.

Since every one is employed for the common good more than for themselves, perhaps persons may apprehend that this gives a check to industry, not having that spur of private interest, hoarding up riches, or aggrandizing their families, as is to be found in other nations. I was apprehensive of this myself, when I came to understand their government; but so far from it, that possibly there is not such an industrious race of people in the universe. They place their great ambition in the grandeur of the country, looking on those as narrow and mercenary spirits who can prefer a part to the whole: they pride themselves over other nations on that account; each man having a proportionable share in the public grandeur, the love of glory and praise seems to be their greatest passion. Besides, their wise governors have such ways of stirring up their emulation by public honors, harangues, and panegyrics in their assemblies, with a thousand other ways of show and pageantry, and this for the most minute arts, that were it not for that fraternal love engrafted in them from their infancy, they would be in danger of raising their emulation to too great a height. Those who give indications of greater wisdom and prudence in their conduct than others, are marked out for governors and gradually raised according to their merit. Whoever invents a new art has a statue erected according to the usefulness of it, with his name and family inserted in public records. Whoever distinguishes himself by any particular excellency has suitable marks of distinction paid him on public occasions, as garlands, crowns, acclamations, songs, or hymns in his praise, etc. It is incredible how such rewards as these encourage industry and arts in minds so affected with glory as these people are: on the other hand, their greatest punishments, except for capital crimes, which are punished as above, are by public disgraces.

But now I am speaking of their youth; as they look upon them as seeds of the commonwealth, which if corrupted in the bud will never bring forth fruit; so their particular care is laid out in their education, in which I believe they excel all nations. One cannot say there is one in the whole nation who may be called an idle person, though they indulge their youth very much in proper recreations, endeavoring to keep them as gay as they can, because they are naturally inclined to gravity. Besides daily recreations, they have set times and seasons for public exercises, as riding, vaulting, running, but particularly hunting wild beasts, and fishing for crocodiles and alligators, in their great lakes, which I shall describe to your Reverences on another occasion; yet they are never suffered to go alone, that is, a company of young men together without grave men and persons in authority along with them, who are a guard to them in all their actions: nay, they are never suffered to sleep together, each lying in a single bed, though in a public room, with some grave person in the same room with them. Their women are kept much in the same manner, to prevent inconveniencies which I shall touch upon when I come to the education of their women: and this so universally, that, as there are no idle companions to lead them into extravagancies, so there are no idle and loose women to be found to corrupt their minds. Their whole time, both for men and women, is taken up in employment or public recreations, which, with the early care to instruct them in the fundamental principles of the morality of the country, prevents all those disorders of youth we see elsewhere. Hence too comes that strength of body and mind in their men, and modest blooming beauty in their women; so that among this people nature seems to have kept up to its primitive and original perfection. Besides, that universal likeness in them, proceeding from their conjugal fidelity and exclusion of all foreign mixture in their breed (where all the lineaments of their ancestors, direct and collateral, meet at last in their offspring), gives the parents the comfort of seeing their own bloom and youth renewed in their children; though in my opinion this universal likeness is rather a defect; not but the treasures of nature are so inexhaustible that there are some distinguishing beauties in every face. Their young men and women meet frequently, but then it is in their public assemblies, with grave people mixed along with them. At all public exercises the women are placed in view to see and be seen, in order to inspire the young men with emulation in their performances. They are permitted to be decently familiar on those public occasions, and can choose their lovers respectively, according to their liking, there being no such thing as dowries, or interest, but mere personal merit in the case; but more of this afterwards, when I shall speak more particularly of the education of their women and marriages. This is a short sketch of the government and economy of a people, who are as much distinguished from the customs of others as they are separated by their habitation and country. . . .

As for their women, the Pophar told me it was what gave them the most trouble of anything in their whole government; that by their records their ancestors had held frequent consultations after what manner they were to be managed, there being great difficulties to be feared either from allowing them liberty, or keeping them under restraint. If you allow them liberty, you must depend on their honor, or rather caprice, for your own; if you keep them under confinement, they will be sure to revenge themselves the first opportunity; which they will find in spite of all you can do. "The rules," said he, "by which men are governed, will not hold with women; solid reason, if you can make them sensible of it, will some time or other have an influence on most men; whereas humor [caprice] is what predominates in women. Hit that, you have them; miss it, you do nothing: and yet they are so far from being an indifferent thing in the commonwealth, that much more depends on the right management of them than people imagine. Licentiousness of youth draws innumerable misfortunes on any government, and what greater incentives for licentiousness than lewd women, whether common prostitutes, wanton ladies, or adulteresses? For all loose women belong to one of these classes. Our women," continued he, "are extremely beautiful, as you see; our men strong and vigorous; conjugal fidelity therefore and chastity must be the strongest bonds to keep them in their duty. As for our young men, we keep them in perpetual employment, and animate them to glory by everything that can move generous minds; with our women, we endeavor the same by ways adapted to their genius. But our greatest care of all is to make marriage esteemed by both parties the happiest state that can be wished for in this life. This we believe to depend on making the woman, rather than the man, happy and fixed in her choice; because, if the person be imposed upon her contrary to her own inward inclination, dislike or revenge or perhaps a more shameful passion will make her seek for relief elsewhere; and where women are not virtuous, men will be lewd. We therefore permit the woman to choose entirely for herself, and the men to make their addresses where they please: but the woman is to distinguish her choice by some signal occasion or other, and that too not without great difficulties on both sides, which being surmounted, they esteem themselves arrived at the happy part of all their wishes. The most ardent and tried love determines the choice: this endears the man to her on the one hand, and the difficulty of finding any woman who has not the same inducements to love her husband leaves him no encouragement for his lawless desires among married women; and the single women are either so early engaged with their lovers, or so possessed with the notion that a married man cannot belong to her, that his suit would be entirely vain. In a word, we do not allow the least temporal interest to interfere in the choice, but rather wish our young people should be mutually attracted by esteem and affection. The whole business of courtship is to prove their constancy and to make them so: when we are well assured of this, all obstacles are removed. We found this method to have the least inconveniencies of any, and the best means to preserve conjugal fidelity, on which the good of families so much depends. . . ."

There is one peculiar method allowed by them, in which they differ from all other nations; for whereas these last endeavor to preserve their young people from love, lest they should throw themselves away or make disadvantageous matches; the former, having no interested views in that respect, encourage a generous and honorable love, and make it their care to fix them in the strictest bonds they can, as soon as they judge, by their age and constitution, of their inclinations: this they do sometimes by applauding their choice, but mostly by raising vast difficulties, contrived on purpose, both to try and enhance their constancy. They have histories and stories of heroic examples of fidelity and constancy in both sexes; but particularly for the young women, by which they are taught rather to suffer ten thousand deaths, than violate their plighted faith. One may say they are a nation of faithful lovers; the longer they live together, the more their friendship increases; and infidelity in either sex is looked upon as a capital crime. Add to this, that being all of the same rank and quality, except the regard paid to eldership, and public employments, nothing but personal merit and a liking of each other determines the choice; there must be signal proofs produced that the woman prefers the man before all others, as his services must be distinguished in the same manner. Where this is approved of by the governors or elders, if the woman insists on her demands, it is an inviolable law that that man must be her husband. Their hands are first joined together in public; then they clasp each other in the closest embrace, in which posture the elder of the place, to show that this union is never to be dissolved, takes a circle of the finest tempered steel, woven with flowers, and first lays it over their knees, as they are thus clasping each other, then round their waists, and last of all round their breasts, or hearts, to signify that the ardency of their love must terminate in an indissoluble friendship; which is followed by infinite acclamations and congratulations of the whole assembly. I believe the world cannot furnish such examples of conjugal chastity as are preserved between them by these means. Widowers and widows never marry single persons, and but rarely at all, except left young; when they are to gain each other as before. By such prudent precautions, infinite disorders and misfortunes to the commonwealth are prevented, proceeding not only from disproportionate and forced marriages, but from the licentiousness of idle persons, who either marry for money or live on the spoil of other people till they can get an advantageous match.

26

Niels Klim's
Journey under the Ground

Being a Narrative of His Wonderful
Descent to the Subterranean Lands:
Together With an Account of the
Sensible Animals and Trees Inhabiting   **Ludvig Holberg**
the Planet Nazar and the Firmament

London
1828;
Boston
1845
(first published in Latin at Copenhagen and Leipzig in 1741)

Ludvig (Louis) Holberg   (1684–1754)

was born in Norway but spent most of his life in Denmark, where he was created Baron in 1747 in recognition of his eminence as a satirist, dramatic writer, national historian, and expounder of the principles of public law.

Coming from the pen of such a versatile genius, *Niels Klim's Journey under the Ground* is erudite, amusing, and instructive. Written in Latin about 1730, this imitation of *Gulliver's Travels* was published in 1741. Translations into German, French, Dutch, Danish, English, Swedish, Russian, and Hungarian in the next twenty-two years indicate the extent of its popularity and influence. Altogether, at least sixty editions in eleven different languages have been published. Unfortunately the English translations do not convey the rich humor, subtlety, and satire of the original Latin as effectively as the Germanic and Scandinavian versions. As a result, the Danish classic is less well known to English readers than it deserves.

According to Holberg's *Autobiography*, the object of the whole work is to correct popular errors and to distinguish the semblance of virtue and vice from the reality. Its subordinate design is to expose the monstrous fictions which some authors obtrude upon readers in their descriptions of remote countries. Thus the work combines a complete system of ethics with much light and pleasant matter. But Holberg's imaginary societies are not to be regarded as models. Their purpose is satiric, like the purpose of Hall's *The Discovery of a New World*, and most of the satire is universal in application. For example, Holberg ridicules geniuses who perceive everything at a glance and understand nothing. Such men were common in his day and are still conspicuous. So are loungers who, though always moving, make no progress. The modern reader will easily discover his own follies and prejudices in Niels Klim, and, like Klim, will end by admiring and extolling what at first he condemned.

According to the story, Niels finished his studies of natural philosophy at the University of Copenhagen in 1664 and decided to explore a deep cave not far from his home. The ropes with which he was being lowered into the cave suddenly broke and he found himself precipitated into the abyss "with wonderful velocity." His perturbation was considerable during the first fifteen minutes of the descent, but philosophic speculation gradually prevailed: "I conceived that I must have descended to the subterraneous heavens; and that the opinions of those persons who maintain that the earth is hollow, and that within its shell there is another and a smaller world, with a smaller sun, smaller planets, and smaller stars, all in due proportion, connexion, and systematic arrangement, must be well founded." His speculations were confirmed when his perpendicular movement changed to a circular one, and he found himself converted into a planet twirled round the new earth. When he cast away an unwanted biscuit, it "not only hung dangling in the air, but—O wonderful to relate!—began to describe around me a planetary orbit."

Meanwhile, on the globe below, "philosophers" discovered the new satellite and prognosticated pestilence, famine, or some other dire event. They mistook a piece of rope fastened to Klim for the tail of a comet!

A huge bird seized the stellar hero and descended with him to the planet Nazar below. After escaping from this creature, Niels fell asleep, but was awakened at dawn by the growling of a bull.

The extracts below continue the story. The first of them is from Chapters II to X of John Gierlow's slightly condensed Danish version, published in an English translation in 1845 at Boston. The quotations given above and the account of "Travels round the Planet Nazar" are taken from a translation based directly on the Latin entitled, *Journey to the World Under Ground, Being the Subterranean Travels of Niels Klim* (London, 1828).

BIBLIOGRAPHY: S. C. Hammer, *Ludvig Holberg, the Founder of Norwegian Literature* (Oxford, 1920); Philip B. Gove, *The Imaginary Voyage in Prose Fiction* (New York, 1941), pp. 303–05.

Niels Klim's Journey under the Ground

THE KINGDOM OF POTU

. . . The vicinity of the bull not being pleasing to me, I arose and began to ascend a tree which stood near. As I raised myself by its limbs, it gave a low, yet shrill scream, and I got at the same time a lively slap on my ear, which propelled me headlong to the ground. Here I lay as if struck by lightning, about to give up my spirit, when I heard around me a murmuring noise such as is heard on the Exchange when the merchants are assembled.

I opened my eyes and saw many trees moving about the field. Imagine my agitation, when one of the trees swept towards me, bent one of its branches, and, lifting me from the ground, carried me off, in spite of my woeful cries, followed by an innumerable number of its companions of all kinds and sizes. From their trunks issued certain articulated sounds, which were entirely incomprehensible to me, and of which I retained only the words *"Pikel-Emi,"* on account of their being often repeated. I will here say these words mean *an extraordinary monkey*, which creature they took me to be, from my shape and dress. All this, of course, I learned after being some months among them.

In my present condition, I was far from being able to conceive of the nature of sensible, speaking trees. In truth, so confounded was I that I forgot I could speak myself. As little could I understand the meaning of the slow, solemn procession and the confused murmurs which resounded in the air. I fancied they were reproaching or expressing their contempt of me. I was not far from the truth: for the tree into which I had climbed to escape from the bull was no less than the wife of the sheriff of the neighboring town to which they were now taking me a prisoner. . . .

The sheriff in whose house I was imprisoned had immediately given notice to the King that he had by accident got possession of a somewhat sensible animal of an uncommon figure. The description of my person excited the king's curiosity. Orders were given to the sheriff that I should be taught the language of the country; on which I should be sent to court. A teacher was appointed for me, whose instruction enabled me in a half year to speak very comprehensively. After this preparatory course of private study, I was sent to the seminary, where particular care was taken both of my mental and physical education. Indeed, so enthusiastic were they to naturalize me, that they actually fastened branches to my body to make me look as much as possible like themselves.

During the course of my education, my landlord frequently carried me about the town and pointed out the most remarkable things. *Keba* is the town next in size and importance to the capital of the kingdom of Potu. The inhabitants are distinguished for their sedateness and moderation; old age is more respected by them than by any other community. They are strangely addicted to the pitting of animals against each other; or, as they call it, "play fight." I wondered that so moral a people could enjoy these brutal sports. My landlord noticed my surprise and said that throughout the kingdom it was the custom to vary their lives with a due mixture of earnest duties and amusing pleasures. Theatrical plays are very much in vogue with them. I was vexed, however, to hear that disputations are reckoned suitable for the stage, while with us they are confined to the universities. . . .

My landlord carried me, on a high festival day, to this academy. On this occasion a *Madic*, or teacher in philosophy, was elected. The candidate made a very prosy speech on some philosophical question, after which, without further ceremony, he was entered by the administrators on the list of the public teachers.

On our way home from the academy, we met a criminal led by three watchmen. By sentence of the *Kaki*, he had been bled, and was now on his way to the city hospital. I inquired concerning his crime, and was answered that he had publicly lectured on the being and qualities of God—a subject entirely forbidden in this country. Disputants on these matters are regarded as insane and are always sent to the madhouse, where they are doctored until they recover their sound reason. I exclaimed: "Heaven and Earth! How would such laws operate on our globe, where thousands of priests quarrel every day about the divine attributes, the nature of spirits, and other secrets of the same character? Truly, here they would all be sent straightway to the madhouse." These, among many other singular customs, I observed during my college life. Finally, the time came when, furnished with appropriate testimonies from the teachers, I was ordered to court. Here is my certificate. How angry and confused was I, when I read it!

In accordance with your royal order, we hereby send the animal which sometime since came down to us from the firmament; which animal calls itself *man*. We have, with sedulous care and patient industry, taught this singular creature in our school, and after a very severe examination, pronounce it to be very quick in its perceptions and very docile in its manners. Nevertheless, from its obtuse and miserable judgment—which we believe arises from its too hasty inferences—its ridiculous skepticism on unquestionable points, and its no less ridiculous credulity on doubtful ones, we may scarcely number it among sensible beings. However, as it is far quicker on its legs than any of our race, we humbly suggest that it is very well adapted for the situation of a running-camp-footman. Written at our Seminary at Keba by your Highness' most humble servants.

NEHEK, JOKTAN, RAPASI, KILAK

I returned sorrowfully to my landlord and begged of him, with tears in my eyes, to use his influence to alter the nature of my certificate from the Karatti, and to show them my testimony from the academy of Copenhagen, in which I was represented as a remarkable student. He replied to me that this diploma might be well enough in Copenhagen, where, probably, the shadow was regarded more than the substance, the bark more than the sap; but here, where the kernel was more important than aught else, it was of no use.

He counseled me to bear my fate with patience, and assured me, in the politest manner, of his friendship. Having nothing more to say, I made ready, without delay, for the journey. There traveled in company with me several small trees which had been educated with me in the seminary and were now destined to the capital for preferment.

Our leader was an old Karatti, who rode on an ox because, from his age, he could not walk. Our progress was very slow, so that three days were occupied in our passage. We had a quick and comfortable jaunt, if I except the meeting with some wild monkeys that would spring towards me and pester me now and then. They evidently supposed me to be one of their race. I could not suppress my anger, however, when I observed that the trees seemed to perceive this mistake of the monkeys, which gave the saplings food for laughter at my expense. I must remark that I was carried to court in the same dress which I wore on my descent to the planet, with the boathook in my hand and the rope dragging after me. This was by order of the king, who wished to see me in my own bark.

The kingdom of *Potu* is enclosed within very narrow boundaries and occupies but a small space of the inner globe.

The whole planet *Nazar* is scarcely six hundred miles in circumference and may be traveled over its whole extent without guide or interpreter, for there is but one language throughout. As the Europeans on our globe take the first rank among the nations, so are the Potuans distinguished among the nations of Nazar for their virtue and understanding.

The roads are dotted by stone pillars, which, covered with inscriptions, denote every mile. Affixed to them are hands pointing the road to every city and village—splendid cities and prosperous villages! The country is intersected by greater and lesser canals, on which boats, propelled by oars, skim with wonderful celerity. The oars are driven by self-moving machines, so quietly that very little motion is given to the water. The planet Nazar has the same motion with the earth, and all the peculiarities of the latter planet: night and day; spring, summer, autumn, and winter. The inhabitants consist of oak, lime, poplar, thorn, and pine trees, from which the months—there being six in each subterranean year—take their names. . . .

In Potu is established a very useful law called the Generation Law. This Law varies the liberties and advantages of the people according to the number of children each one possesses. Thus he who is the father of six children is exempted from all common and extraordinary taxes. Therefore generation is quite as useful and desirable in this country as on the earth it is burthensome and dangerous. . . .

No one can hold two offices at once. It is thought that each office, however small, requires the sole attention of its occupant, and that none should be employed in that which they do not understand.

I remember to have heard the philosopher *Rakbasi* speak thus: "Every one should know his own talents, and should impartially judge of his own merits and faults. Otherwise the actor must be considered more sensible than natural men; for he chooses, not the best part, but that which he can execute best. Shall we allow the actor to be wiser on the stage than we in life?"

The inhabitants of this kingdom are not divided into classes, those alone being regarded who are noted for virtue and industry. The highest rank, if rank it may be called, is given to those who possess the greatest number of branches, they being enabled to do the most work.

The system of religion in Potu is very simple. It is forbidden, under pain of banishment to the firmament, to explain the holy books. Whoever dares to dispute the being and nature of the Deity is sent to the madhouse and is bled. "It is foolish," they say, "to attempt to describe that to which our senses are as blind as the eyes of the owl in sunshine." All agree in worshiping a Superior Being, whose omnipotence has created and whose providence maintains all things. Each one is permitted to think and worship as he pleases; they only who publicly attack the prevailing religion are punished as peace-disturbers. The people pray seldom, but with so ardent a devotion that a looker-on would think them enraptured during the continuance of the prayer. . . .

They have many curious notions of religion, which they defend very artfully; for example, when I remarked to some of them whose friendship I had gained, that they could not expect to be blessed after death, since they walked in darkness here, they answered: "He who with severity condemns others is himself in danger of being condemned."

I once advised them to pray every day. They did not deny the importance of prayer, but thought true religion consisted in obeying the will of God. "Suppose," continued they, "that a king has two kinds of subjects: some err every day, violating from ignorance or malice the ruler's commands; they come each day with petitions and deprecations to the palace, beg pardon for their faults, and depart only to recommit them. The others come seldom, and never voluntarily to court, but execute faithfully and diligently every of the king's commands, and thereby evince the respect and loyalty due to him. Will not the king think *these* deserving of his love, as

good subjects and faithful; but, on the contrary, *those* as evil subjects, burthensome as well for their misdeeds as for their frequent
petitions?"

There are five festival days during the year. The first of these,
which takes place at the beginning of the oak month, is solemnized
with great devotion in dark places where not a ray of light is suffered to enter—signifying that the Being they worship is inconceivable. The festival is called the "Inconceivable God's Day." The
whole day, from sunrise to sunset, the people remain immovable,
engaged in earnest and heartfelt prayer. In the four other festivals,
thanks to God for His blessings form the principal ceremonies.

In the kingdom of Potu the crown is inherited, as with us, by
the eldest son of the king, whose power is absolute. The government, however, is rather fatherly than tyrannical. Justice is not
meted and bounded by law alone, but is the result of principle, a
principle of the widest philosophic comprehension. Thus monarchy
and liberty are closely united, which otherwise would be inimical
to each other. The ruler seeks to maintain, as far as possible, an
equality among his subjects. Honors are not limited to any class;
but the poor and more ignorant are called upon to receive their
opinions from, and submit to, the decisions of the richer and more
intelligent. The young are to respect the aged.

The annals of Potu show that some centuries ago certain classes
were highly favored by the laws to the exclusion of the great body
of the people. Frequent disturbances had been the result of this
favoritism, till a citizen of the town Keba proposed an alteration
in the laws by which all distinctions of class were abolished, and,
while the office of king should still remain hereditary, all the other
officers of government should be subject to the will of the people,
all of whom should be allowed to vote who could read and write
at least their names.

According to the custom of the subterraneans in such affairs, this
intelligent and patriotic citizen was led to the market-place with a
rope about his neck: his proposition was considered, and, after grave
deliberation, was adopted as conducive to the general interest. The
mover was then carried in triumph through the city, honored by
the grateful shouts of the people.

He who has most numerous offspring is regarded as the most
deserving citizen: he is honored above all others, without exception.
. . . It is very easy to conceive of the degree in which Alexander
and Julius Caesar would be prized by this people; both of whom
not only had no children themselves but murdered millions of the
offspring of others. . . .

Among the court officers the *Kadori*, or grand chamberlain, is the superior. Next after him comes the *Smizian*, or treasurer. In my time, the seven-branched widow, *Kahagna*, filled the latter place. She was a virtuous and industrious woman. Although her duties were many and important, she nursed the child herself. I remarked once that I thought this to be troublesome and unfit for so great a lady. I was replied to in this wise: "For what purpose has nature given breasts to woman?—for the ornament of the body alone, or for the nourishment of their children?"

The crown prince was a child of six years. His governor was the wisest tree in the kingdom. I have seen an abstract of moral philosophy and policy written by him for the use of the prince, the title of which is *Mahalda Libal Helit*, which in the subterranean language means, "The Country's Rudder." It contains many fundamental and useful precepts, of which I recollect the following:

"1st. Neither praise nor blame should be too hastily credited; judgment should be deferred until accurate knowledge of the matter is obtained.

"2d. When a tree is accused of any crime, and the accusation is supported, then the life of the culprit must be examined, his good and evil actions must be compared, and judgment be given according to the preponderance of either.

"3d. The king must be accurately acquainted with the opinions of his subjects, and must strive to keep union among them.

"4th. Punishment is not less necessary than reward. The former restrains evil; the latter promotes good.

"5th. Sound reason teaches that especial regard should be had to the fitness of candidates to public offices; but, though piety and honesty go to form the greatest merit, yet, as the appearance of these virtues is often imposed on us for the reality, no tree should be severely judged till he gets into office, when he will show himself what he is.

"6th. To make a treasurer of a poor man, or a bankrupt, is to make a hungry wolf purveyor of the kitchen. The case of a rich miser is still stronger; the bankrupt or the penniless may set bounds to their peculation; the miser never has enough.

"7th. When the prevalence of vice renders a reformation necessary, great care and deliberation must be used. To banish at once, and in a mass, old and rooted faults would be like prescribing laxative and restringent medicines at the same time to an invalid.

"8th. They who boldly promise everything and take upon themselves many duties are either fools who know not their own powers or the importance of affairs, or are mean and unjust citizens who regard their own and not their country's welfare."

·　·　·　·　·

In this kingdom are three academies; one in Potu, one in Keba, and one in Nahami.

The sciences taught in them are history, political economy, mathematics, and jurisprudence. Their theological creed is so short that it can be written on two pages. It contains this doctrine simply: that God, the creator of all things, shall be loved and honored; and that He will, in another life, reward us for our virtues and punish us for our vices. Theology forms no part of an academical course, as it is forbidden by law to discuss these matters. Neither is medicine numbered among the studies; for, as the trees live moderately, there is no such thing as internal disease.

The students are employed in solving complicated and difficult questions, and he who most elegantly and clearly explains his question is entitled to a reward. No one studies more than one science, and thus each gets a full knowledge of his peculiar subject.

The teachers themselves are obliged to give, each year, a proof of their learning. The teachers of philosophy are required to solve some problem in morals; the historians, to elaborate some passage in history; the jurists, to elucidate some intricate point of law; these last are the only professors expected to be good orators. I told them that the study of rhetoric was common to all students in our colleges, and that all studies were merged in it. They disapproved of this, saying that, should all mechanics strive to make a masterly shoe, the work of most would be bad, and the shoemakers alone would win the prize.

Besides these academies, there are preparatory gymnasiums, where great pains are taken to discover the bent of the young, that they may be brought up in that science to which they are best fitted. While I was at the seminary of Keba, the bishop had four sons there, preparing for a military course; four others, whose father was a counselor, were learning mechanical arts, and two maidens were studying navigation. The rank and sex of the scholars are entirely overlooked, in their regard to fitness and propriety.

He who challenges another to fight loses forever his right to use weapons and is condemned to live under guardianship as one who cannot curb his passions or temper his judgment. I observed that the names of parties who go to law are kept secret from the judge, he not being an inhabitant of the place where the trial is carried on. The object of this singular law is to prevent all partiality and bribery on the part of the judge, by withholding from him all knowledge of the influence or property of the litigants.

Justice is executed without regard to persons. The king, indeed, is not required to appear in court, but after death, his memory is put to the bar of public opinion, and his life is vindicated or con-

demned through the peoples' advocates. This trial takes place before the Senate, and judgment is freely pronounced according to
the weight of the evidence. A herald proclaims the decision, which
is inscribed on the king's monument. The words used in these trials
are: *Praiseworthy,—good,—not bad,—moderate,—tolerable.* Sentence
must be pronounced by one of these words. . . .

The Potuanic annals show that for centuries only one king has
received the last degree of judgment—*tolerable*—or, in their tongue,
Rip-fac-si. This was King *Mikleta.* Although the Potuans are well
versed in arms, and defend themselves bravely when attacked, they
never make war on others.

But this king, excited by a miserable desire to extend the borders
of his empire, entered into an offensive war with his neighbors and
subdued many of them. The Potuans gained, indeed, in power and
wealth, but they suffered more from the loss of friendship and the
increase of fear and envy in the conquered. The honorable regard
for justice and equity, to which they had hitherto owed their prosperity and supremacy, began from that time to fade. On the death
of Mikleta, however, the people recovered from their folly, and
showed their regret for it, while at the same time they regained
the good will of their neighbors, by putting a blot upon the memory
of their ruler.

But to return to myself: I took but little pleasure in associating
with my companions, a set of absurd trees, who constantly ridiculed
me for my quick perception.

This quality, I have already said, I was blamed for very early in
my career; but by learned trees, with grave and dignified complaisance. These saplings, on the contrary, pestered me with silly
nicknames. For example, they took a malicious delight in calling me
Skabba, which means an untimely or unripe thing.

TRAVELS ROUND THE PLANET NAZAR

. . . In *Quamso,* the first province we arrived in after crossing the
Sound, the inhabitants, who are all oaks, experience no bodily infirmities or sickness, but attain to the greatest age in perfect and
continual health. These people seemed to me, in the beginning, to
be the happiest of all living creatures; but I quickly perceived, in
the slight intercourse I had with them, that I was in considerable
error. I saw correctly enough that no one among them was dejected
or troubled; but, on the other side, neither did I observe anyone
either jovial or glad. In the same manner that the most serene firmament and the softest air make no impression upon us unless we
previously experience snow and rain and sleet and tempests, so have
these trees no conception of their happiness, because it is never

interrupted; and are incapable of perceiving that they are healthy, because they are never sick. They pass away their lives in continual health, but, at the same time, in constant indifference. Every good which is enjoyed without interruption wearies in the long run, and to enjoy fully the sweets and pleasures of life, it is necessary and essential that we sometimes taste its bitters. I can safely say that among no people did I ever find so little civility, politeness, and good nature, so algid, inanimate, and stiff conversation and intercourse as among this. It is a nation without any vice, but which one can neither love nor hate, where no offenses are committed, and where no benevolence or complaisance is to be met with; in short, where nothing is found that can displease, and nothing that is completely agreeable. As, by reason of the continual health which they enjoy, they never have the opportunity of seeing any deceased persons, and as they are never moved to pity or compassion at the sufferings of a fellow creature, they pass away their whole lifetime in a perfectly insensible quiet and repose, and without the least participation in the fate of their brethren; so that not the smallest trace of charity, pity, or beneficence is to be found among them. We, on the contrary, who by means of sickness are reminded of our mortality, and are continually exhorted to hold ourselves in readiness for our last journey, learn by our own sufferings and torments to have pity and compassion upon others. I had, in that country, evident demonstration how far sickness and the danger of death contribute to reciprocal affection, gaiety, and cheerfulness in the intercourse with our fellow creatures; and how unjust we are in murmuring at our Creator because we appear to be born to all these sufferings, which are of such essential service to us and are attended with the happiest consequences.

These oaks are nevertheless subject to sickness, like all other trees, as soon as they arrive in any strange place. I believe, for this reason, that this advantage of health, if it may be called an advantage, ought solely to be attributed to the air and the provisions of the country.

The province *Lalak*, which is called by the surname *Maskatta*, or the Happy, appeared to accord with this appellation. Everything there came forth spontaneously without the least help of art. It was neither necessary to plow nor to sow in that extremely fertile region; in short, I acquired, during my stay here, a thorough knowledge of this land of bliss. . . . But these extraordinary advantages tend not in the least degree to make the inhabitants more happy than anybody else. For, as they have no occasion to work for their support, they sleep away their lives in sloth and indolence and are afflicted with a multitude of disorders. They have worms and corruptions in their bodies, and most of them come to a premature death.

[Klim next visits the kingdom of *Mardak*. The chief tribe there have oval eyes and, consequently, everything appears oval in shape to them. The other tribes have different eyes but are not admitted to public offices unless they will swear that a certain tablet in the Temple of the Sun is oval in shape. Klim saw the tablet, which was square, and became indignant when he found others, who agreed with him, being persecuted for heresy. However, when he returned to *Potu*, a friendly juniper tree observed, "You, my dear Klim, ought not, as it seemeth to me, to be so much astonished that the inequality of vision should be treated here with so much rigor; for, if I remember right, you yourself related that there are in most European states certain ruling stocks and tribes who, because of a peculiar and natural defect in their . . . understanding persecute the others with fire and sword; and yet you extolled these violent measures as very pious regulations, and highly beneficial to the State."

[The principality of *Kimal* was considered the most powerful and richest on the planet, but Klim discovered that riches were not the basis of happiness; for the greatest part of the inhabitants were silver-miners, gold-refiners, or pearl fishers, who spent their lives rummaging for sordid lucre. Other citizens watched over the treasure, but the country was full of robbers. As a result, fear, suspicion, envy, and jealousy raged in every breast, and men wasted their lives in anguish of mind.

[*Quamboja* lies to the east of Kimal. In it, rashness, incontinence, and vices increase with age: the older a man is, the more debauched and dissolute he becomes. No one over forty years old is entrusted with public office. Klim noted how the boys would often reproach impudent old men who were spinning tops or playing hopscotch.

[In *Kokleku*, males are employed in kitchen service and other forms of insignificant drudgery, while females dominate in all important positions. Klim denounced this inversion of ordinary custom as repugnant to common sense, the law of nature, and the common practice of nations, but was told that he was confusing mere customs and regulations with nature, and that the alleged imbecility of females ought to be attributed solely to education. He saw the correctness of this view, for "it is a matter of fact that the Koklekuitish ladies are in general modest, serious, discreet, constant, and reserved; while the men, on the contrary, are sickly, addle-headed, rash, and loquacious."

[Klim had high expectations of the Land of the Philosophers, but found the roads almost impassable and the land uncultivated; for the inhabitants were so busy with sublime and celestial thoughts that they neglected the needs of ordinary living. The visit proved to Klim "that it was much more advisable to study with moderation than to become deranged from too great a store of learning."]

When I had rested myself a little, I proceeded again on my journey, and traveled through several provinces, . . . But when I arrived in *Cabac*, I met with new and very extraordinary things, which to many may appear completely incredible. Among the inhabitants of this State, there are, for example, several who have no heads, and who come entirely headless into the world: they speak with a kind of mouth, which is placed in the middle of their breast. Because of this defect in nature, they are excluded from all arduous occupations in which any brains are required; and there never was an instance of any headless person obtaining an important employment in this country. The posts to which they for the most part are appointed are those that are immediately connected with the Court. From among this headless race, the gentlemen of the bedchamber, stewards of the Prince's household, . . . and suchlike are generally chosen. . . .

Now and then, however, one or the other of them is admitted into the Council, either by particular favor of the authorities or on the ground of family merit, which rarely proves injurious to the state. For experience teaches us that the majority in the Council commonly depends on a very few Senators, and that the rest are merely there to fill up the number and to consent and subscribe to the measures which the few have resolved upon. In this wise there sat in the Council, during the time that I sojourned in the city, two headless benchers whose salaries were just as high as those of the others. For although they, because of this natural defect, were not furnished with very peculiarly bright understandings, nor were their ideas extraordinarily brilliant, yet they gave their votes and assented to the opinions which the others had expressed. In this respect they were more fortunate than their colleagues, for when any affair was amiss in the Senate, no one was ever offended at those who were not possessed of heads, but vented his spleen solely against the rest—a clear proof that it is sometimes a great advantage to be born without a head. In other respects, this city yields to no place upon this globe in pomp and splendor. It can boast of a palace, a university, and a magnificent cathedral.

In the two provinces in which I soon after arrived, namely *Cambara* and *Spelek*, all the inhabitants are lime trees. The distinction among them consists solely in this, that those in the first province never become more than, at the highest, four years old; while those in the second, on the contrary, live to above four hundred years. In *Spelek*, therefore, a person meets with many grand-fathers, great-grandfathers, and great-great-grandfathers and hears numbers of proverbs and old chronicles; so that, on arriving in this country, one might imagine that the time had been retarded for the space of some centuries. As much as I pitied the fate of the former, I, on the other hand, highly extolled the happy state of the latter. But when I had maturely reflected on the real condition of both I noticed that I was completely out in my judgment. In *Cambara*, the inhabitants, in the course of a few months after their birth, arrive at maturity both in body and mind; so that the first year is sufficient for their formation and development, and the other three seemed to be granted to them in order to prepare themselves for death. Under these circumstances, this country appeared to me to be a truly Platonic republic, in which every virtue arrives at the greatest possible perfection. For, as the inhabitants, by reason of their very short lives, are, as it were, continually on the wing, and look upon this life as a gate through which they must shortly pass to enter into the next, their minds are more fixed upon their future than their present state. Everyone, on this account, may there be looked upon as a true philosopher, who, without being at all solicitous about terrestrial affairs, strives, through the fear of God, virtuous actions, and a clear conscience, to prepare himself for an eternal beatitude. In short, this country appeared to be inhabited by none but angels or saints and to be the right school in which all that is virtuous can best be learned. From this may be seen how unreasonably many people murmur at, and even quarrel with, Providence, about the shortness of their lives; for our lives can only be called short, inasmuch as we spend the greatest part of them in idleness, sloth, and voluptuousness; and which would certainly be always long enough, if our time were well employed.

In *Spelek*, on the contrary, where the lives of the inhabitants are prolonged to about four hundred years, every vice which can be found in mankind appears to prevail. The people there have only the present before their eyes, as though they were immortal, and would never decline; and therefore uprightness, integrity, honesty, chastity, and decency, are fled, and have given place to falsehood, deceit, extravagance, luxury, and immortality.

This prolongation of life has still another very lamentable effect. Those persons who, through unfortunate events, lose their property, receive hurts in their limbs, or fall into incurable sickness, are accustomed to curse intolerably their existence, and at last to commit suicide, as they, because of their long lives, see no end to their sufferings. The shortness of life is the most efficacious consolation to all wretched people. Both these countries greatly excited my admiration, and I quitted them with my head filled with philosophical contemplations.

I now traveled over nothing but a barren and rocky tract of country, until at length arrived at *Spalank*, or, as it is generally called, The Land of Innocence. It has obtained this appellation in consequence of the mild dispositions and innocence of its inhabitants. These trees, which are all majestic oaks, are looked upon as the happiest of all mortal beings, because they are free from all vehemence of the passions, and consequently, from every vice. . . .

On my arrival in this province, I experienced that everything which fame had said regarding it, was true; namely, that the inhabitants, solely from their own inclinations, and not from any obligation of the law, really practiced virtue. Every covetousness, wrath, hatred, pride, ambition, discord, and all other human vices, I found were expelled from this country. But at the same time, vices, and many other things which adorn mankind, and exalt the rational above the brute creation, are there wanting. If we except theology, natural philosophy, and astronomy, no other sciences are there cultivated; and jurisprudence, politics, history, morality, the mathematics, elocution, and several others, were sciences which were even not known by name. As envy and ambition do not in the smallest degree exist among this people, there is much need of the gown-mania, which so frequently stimulates people to undertake and achieve the greatest and most laudable enterprises. There was no palace or magnificent building, no senate or sessions-house, and no great wealth; as there were neither magistracy, lawsuits, nor avarice. In a word, there were no vices, or rather there was no taste, art, parade, or suchlike, which are looked upon as accomplishments, that add dignity and greatness to empires, and refine mankind; so that it appears much more like being in a forest of oaks, than in a cultivated state. I remained, therefore, a long time in doubt respecting the judgment I ought to form of this nation, and whether such a natural condition were really desirable to humanity. However, when I at length considered that the want of cultivation can be much better endured than the want of virtue, and that unskillfulness in murder, outrage, theft, and other vices, that are destructive both to soul and body, was nearly allied to unskillfulness in certain sciences, I must acknowledge that this state was happy. . . .

When I quitted this country, I traveled through the province *Kilak*, the inhabitants of which are born with certain marks on their foreheads, which indicate the number of years that each has to live. I looked upon these people in the beginning to be very happy, as death could never surprise them, nor tear them away with all their sins upon their heads. But, as everyone knows on what day he shall die, they all procrastinate their repentance until the very last hour. If, therefore, one were desirous of finding a person among them who led a religious and honest life, one ought to look for such a character among those whose marks on the forehead announced that they were chanting the last verse of their funeral dirge. I observed several walking through the streets with their heads hanging down; these were all persons who must shortly pass on into a future state. They counted the hours and minutes upon their fingers, and looked forward with dread to their momentarily approaching dissolution. This placed conspicuously before my sight the wisdom and goodness of the great Creator towards us in this respect; and I was thoroughly convinced that it was right that God's creatures should be ignorant of the time of the coming of death.

From this place I was ferried over a kind of sound, in a small boat, and landed in the state of *Askarak*. Here I met with wonders entirely new; for, unlike *Cabac*, which produces people without heads, here some of the inhabitants come into the world with no less than seven. These are commonly universal geniuses, of whom the ancients, in time of old, made very much, and worshiped, on account of this gift of nature, with almost a divine adoration; so that they never appointed generals, or elected senators, burgomasters, or lords-lieutenant of counties, of any other lineage than theirs. As they have just as many different schemes, projects, designs, plans, and ways of thinking, as they possess heads, they perform a variety of thing correctly enough, with zeal and alertness; yet while the reins of government were in their hands, there was nothing which they touched or altered, but as they put everything in execution at the same time, and the multiplicity of different ideas in their heads very naturally and very easily made them fall into controversies and disputes with each other, they at length neither knew how to proceed or desist; and their affairs, by degrees, became so involved in disorder, and so embarrassed, that it required whole centuries to bring those things again into order, which the all-knowing authorities had so completely entangled. It was, therefore, once for all, ordained by law, that no seven-headed person, for the future, should ever be appointed to an important situation; and that the state, from that time forward, should be directed solely by plain, simple persons; that is to say, by those who possessed only a single head.

27

Memoirs of the Year 2500

Louis Sébastien Mercier

Translated from the French by
W. Hooper

Philadelphia
1795
(first published in French at Paris in 1770)

Louis Sébastien Mercier   (1740–1814)

was a versatile, somewhat eccentric scholar. After publishing some rather unsatisfactory poetry and teaching as Professor of Rhetoric at Bordeaux, he returned to his native Paris, where he earned his living by writing novels and making translations. He composed several dramas in imitation of English and German plays. His *Essay on Dramatic Art* advocated that plays should deal with modern life and living society, rather than ancient and mythological themes. This interest in drama was reflected in his utopia, *L'An Deux Mille Quatre Cent Quarante, Rêve s'il en Fut Jamais* (The Year 2440, a Dream of What Will Never Be), first published in 1770. When W. Hooper, two years later, prepared an English version, he added another sixty years to the date.

The utopia is a vehicle for Mercier's ideas on a wide range of topics. In fact, few utopias are so comprehensive of human interests. Chapter topics vary from "Funeral Oration of a Peasant" to "Education of a Criminal" and "Emblematical Paintings."

Mercier's other publications covered as wide a range. His many-volumed *Tableau of Paris* aroused such a protest that he found it wise to go for a time to Switzerland and Germany. But he returned to France in time for the Revolution. As a member of the Convention he was a moderate Girondin. Under the Empire, he was a republican. Meanwhile he taught history, attempted to revolutionize the French language, wrote prodigiously on philosophy, morals, politics, history, and drama, added further novels and romances to those already issued from his pen, and edited the works of Rousseau.

Mercier pointed out with reference to his utopia, "I am the true prophet of the Revolution," though he added, "I say this without pride." The *Memoirs of the Year 2500* are significant for a picture of pre-Revolutionary France which is contrasted with its later utopian condition. The work further reveals the influence of eighteenth-century *philosophes*, the sentimentality which marked that century, and the particular influence of Rousseau. The initiation described in Chapter XXI is typical of these aspects, stressing, as it does, God revealed by design in Nature, the design being discovered by means of scientific instruments whose discoveries are interpreted by a priest—one who seems to be at one time a priest of God, Nature, Reason, and Sentiment.

Such views are characteristic of Mercier's period, but other chapters give his own peculiar doctrines. The advocacy of the reduction of human knowledge to a few abridged volumes is paradoxical from the pen of such a voluminous writer, for his own works would surely be among those which would be burned in the bonfires he describes.

The influence of previous utopists on Mercier is easily recognized. Bacon and Campanella seem to have been known to him, for he takes over their advocacy of utilitarian science, though giving a characteristically eighteenth-century emphasis to the doctrine of the scale of nature. Also characteristic of that century, at least in the pre-Revolutionary period, is the revolution in Mercier's story, for it was effected by a benevolent despot who based his work upon the natural goodness of man—a natural goodness which is so great, in Mercier's opinion, that, aided by a somewhat sentimental education, it will produce men who will pay taxes voluntarily!

The text below is a condensation specially prepared for this volume by Herschel M. Sikes. Passages paraphrased are enclosed in brackets. Otherwise the words are Mercier's with most of his repetition and redundancy eliminated. The condensation is based on William Hooper's translation printed by Thomas Dobson of Philadelphia in 1795.

Memoirs of the Year 2500

[I talked to an old Englishman, who condemned the domination of France by Paris and its vices, pointed to the wretches perishing for want, objected to the disproportion of fortunes, and denounced in detail the evils of civilization at that time, 1740. I went to bed and dreamed that ages passed. I awoke an old man in a city of beauty and order, and learned that the date was 2500. One of the natives offered to be my guide, but added: "I cannot be your companion if you are not decently dressed; it is useless, not to say indecent, to wear a murdering weapon by your side." Accordingly, with his help I purchased new clothing.]

When I came out, the crowd still surrounded me; but there was nothing either jeering or insulting in their behavior; merely a buzz from every side: "That's the man who is seven hundred and sixty years old. How unfortunate must he have been in the first part of his life!"

"Things seem to me somewhat to be changed," I said to my guide; "I observe that everyone is dressed in a simple modest manner; and in all our walk, I have not seen either gold clothes or laced ruffles. In my time, a puerile and destructive luxury had turned all their brains; a body without a soul was covered with lace; and the automaton then resembled a man. But, pray, who is that man that passes with a mask on his face? How fast he walks, or rather flies!"

"It is an author that has written a bad book. When I say bad, I speak not of the defects of judgment or style; I mean that he has published dangerous principles inconsistent with that universal morality which speaks to every heart. By way of reparation, he wears a mask to hide his shame till he has effaced it by writing something more rational and beneficial to society. He is daily visited by two worthy citizens, who combat his erroneous opinions, hear his objections, confute them, and engage him to retract when he shall be convinced. Then he will be re-established; he will even acquire from the confession a greater glory; for what is more commendable than to abjure our faults, and to embrace new lights with a noble sincerity?

"Each author answers personally for what he writes, and never conceals his name. It is the public that marks him with disgrace if he oppose those sacred principles which serve as the basis to the conduct and probity of man. Every author, as a public man, is to be judged by the general voice, and not by the caprice of a single critic.

"You may now write against all that offends you. Our government is far above all invective; it fears not the keenest pens; it would accuse itself by fearing them. Its conduct is just and sincere; we can only extol it; and, when the interest of our country requires, every man, in his particular station, becomes an author, without pretending to an exclusive right to that title."

"O heavens! What is it you tell me? A whole nation of authors!"

"Yes; but without ill-nature, pride or disdain. Every man writes the thoughts that occur in his brightest moments. At a certain age, he collects the most judicious reflections that he has made in the course of his days; in his last years, he forms them into a book. On the day of his funeral, it is read aloud; and that is his eulogy. Our children collect with reverence all the reflections of their forefathers, and meditate on them."

"Do you teach your children Greek and Latin?"

"We know better how to employ their time. They formerly taught youth a multiplicity of knowledge that in no degree conduced to the happiness of life. We have selected those objects only that will give them true and useful ideas; they were instructed universally in two dead languages, which were imagined to contain every sort of science, but which could not give them the least idea of those men with whom they were to live. We content ourselves with teaching them the national language, and even permit them to modify it after their own taste; for we do not wish to form grammarians, but men of eloquence. We teach them little history, because history is the disgrace of humanity, every page being crowded with crimes and follies.

"We have a sufficient contempt for metaphysics, those gloomy regions where everyone erects a system of chimeras, and always to no purpose. It is from thence they have drawn imperfect images of the divinity, have disfigured His essence by refining on His attributes, and have confounded human reason by placing it on a slippery point, from whence it is continually ready to fall into doubt. It is by physics, that key to nature, that living and palpable science, we are enabled to run through the labyrinth of this marvelous assemblage of beings, and to perceive the wisdom and power of the Creator. That science, properly investigated, delivers us from an infinity of errors; and the unformed mass of prejudices give place to that pure light which it spreads over all objects. At a certain age we permit a young man to read the poets. Those of the present day know how to unite wisdom with enthusiasm; they do not deceive reason by a cadence and harmony of words. They are the recorders of those great actions that illustrate humanity. Formed by such models, our children acquire just ideas of true greatness; and the plow, the shuttle, and the hammer are become more brilliant objects than the scepter, the diadem, and the imperial robe."

"You have no theologians among you?"

"As our only contemplation on the Supreme Being is to praise and adore Him in silence, without disputing on His divine attributes, which are forever inscrutable, we have determined never more to write on that topic; so much too sublime for our intelligence. It is the soul that communicates with God, and it has no need of foreign aids to raise itself up to Him."

"To live without theology, I can easily enough conceive; but how without law, I can by no means comprehend."

"We have a jurisprudence, but different from yours. You still bear the marks of your ancient servitude; you adopted laws that were made neither for your customs nor your climate."

"But how can cases be decided without the aid of attorneys?"

"Our cases are decided in the best manner imaginable. The bad man can find no advocate among the defenders of equity. Their honor is answerable for the cause they undertake; they oblige the guilty, by refusing to defend them, to appear trembling before a court where they have no advocate. Every man now enjoys the primitive right of pleading his own cause. They never suffer a process to have time sufficient to become perplexed; they are investigated and determined in their origin; the longest time that is allowed for developing any cause, when it is obscure, is that of a year. The judges, moreover, never receive any presents. Justice has spoken by the voice of nature, sovereign legislator, mother of virtue, and of all that is good upon the earth. Founded on reason and humanity, her precepts are wise, clear, concise, and few. All general causes have been foreseen and included in the laws. Particular cases have been derived from them, as the branches that spring from a fertile trunk; and equity, more sagacious than law itself, has applied practical justice to every event.

"The new laws are above all things thrifty of human blood. A criminal, when seized, is exposed in fetters, that he may be a public and striking example of the vigilance of justice. Over the place of his confinement there remains a writing which explains the cause of it. We do not confine men in the darkness of the tomb, a fruitless punishment, and more horrible than death itself! It is in the public eye our prisoners suffer the shame of their chastisement. Every citizen knows why this man is condemned to imprisonment and made to labor at the public works. He whom three chastisements does not reform, is marked, not on the shoulder, but the forehead, and banished forever from his country."

We turned the corner of a street, and I perceived in the midst of a spacious place a circular temple crowned with a magnificent dome. This edifice, supported by a single range of columns, had four grand portals; on the front of each was written, *The Temple of God*. Time had already imprinted a venerable complexion on its walls, from which it received an additional majesty.

The exhortation of the pastor to his flock was simple, natural, and eloquent; but more from the matter than the style. He talked of God only to make Him beloved by men, and to commend humanity, gentleness, and patience; he did not endeavor to display his wit, when it was his business to affect the heart; it was a father that conversed with his children on those matters that were most eligible for them to pursue. These precepts had the greater effect, as they proceeded from the mouth of a man whose character was perfectly amiable. I could never have been tired; for this discourse consisted not of pompous declamation, or vague characters, or far-fetched figures, and still less of scraps of poetry mixed with the prose, by which it commonly becomes yet more insipid.

"It is thus," said my guide, "that every morning we make a public prayer; it lasts an hour, and the rest of the day the doors remain shut. We have scarce any religious feasts; but we have those that are civil, which relax the people without making them licentious. On no day should man remain idle. By the example of nature, which never quits its operations, he ought never to reproach himself with having been quite inactive. Repose, however, is not idleness. Total inaction is a real damage to our country; and cessation from labor is in fact a diminutive of death. The time determined for prayer is sufficient to elevate the mind to God; long services produce inattention and disgust; and all private prayers have less merit than those that excite the public devotion.

"We believe that all souls are equal by their essence, but different by their qualities. The soul of a man and that of a brute are equally immaterial; but one has advanced a step farther than the other toward perfection; and it is that which constitutes its present state, which, however, is at all times liable to change.

"We suppose, moreover, that all the stars and all the planets are inhabited, but that nothing which is contained in one is to be found in another. The human soul ascends to all these worlds, as by a gradual and brilliant ladder that leads, at every step, to the highest degree of perfection. In this journey it forgets nothing it has seen, or has learned; it preserves the magazines of its ideas, which are its most valuable treasure, and by which it is constantly attended. For those groveling souls that are plunged in the filth of vice, or of sloth, they will return to the point from whence they parted, or be yet more degraded. A monarch, at his decease, becomes a mole; a minister [of the crown], a venomous serpent inhabiting some filthy marsh; while the writer he disdained, or rather could not comprehend, hath obtained a glorious rank among intelligent beings, the friends of humanity. What think you of our system?"

"I am charmed with it; it is in no wise inconsistent either with the power or goodness of God. This progressive march, this ascent to different worlds, to the various revolving spheres, all the work of His hands, seems to me perfectly agreeable to the dignity of that Sovereign, who lays open all His dominions to the eye formed to survey them."

"But the wicked," I said, "they who have sinned against the laws of nature, have shut their hearts against the cry of pity, that have murdered the innocent, and reigned for themselves alone, what will become of them?"

"It is not for our weakness, constantly subordinate to so many passions, to say in what manner God will punish them. This, however, is certain; the wicked must feel the weight of justice. Banished far from His sight will be every perfidious and cruel being, and all those that are indifferent to the misfortunes of others. If they humble themselves under the hand that corrects them, if they follow the lights of reason, then their pilgrimage will be greatly abridged. Perhaps too, the most criminal will be deprived of the precious sensation of liberty. They will not be annihilated: persecutors of every kind will yet wretchedly subsist, but in the lowest class of existence; they will be incessantly subject to fresh tortures, that will renew their slavery and their misery; but the duration of their punishment God alone can determine."

. . . . .

"But who is that young man that I see surrounded by a busy crowd? What joy is expressed in all his motions!"

"He comes from being initiated," my guide gravely replied. "Though we have but few ceremonies, yet we have one that answers to what, in your time, they called the *first communion*. We observe the character and most secret actions of a young man. When we perceive that he searches out solitary places for reflection; when we surprise him with melting eye, gazing earnestly on the vaulted roof of heaven, contemplating, in a sweet ecstasy, the azure curtain that seems ready to be drawn from before him, then there is no time to lose; then reason appears to have attained its full maturity, and he is become capable of receiving to advantage a display of the wonders of creation.

"We make choice of a serene night, when the starry host shine forth in their fullest luster. Accompanied by his friends and relations, the young man is conducted to our observatory; his eye is instantly applied to a telescope; we cause Saturn, Jupiter, Mars, all the mighty bodies that float in order amidst the ethereal space, to pass before him. We open to him the infinite abyss; those radiant globes press in crowds upon his astonished sight; then a venerable pastor says to him, with an awful, majestic voice, 'Young man, behold the God of the universe, who reveals himself to thee in the midst of His works, whose extensive power exceeds not only the sight of man, but even his imagination; adore that Creator, whose resplendent majesty is impressed on these stars that obey His laws. When thou beholdest these prodigies, the works of His hand, think with what bounty He is able to reward the heart that is devoted to Him. Remember, that among His stupendous works, man, endowed with the faculty of discerning them, holds the first rank; and that, as the child of God, he ought to venerate that respectable title.'

"The scene is then changed; a microscope is brought, and a new universe, more wonderful than the former, is displayed before him. Those animated points that his eye for the first time beholds, that move in their inconceivable exility and are endowed with the same organs as the giants of the earth, present to him a new attribute of the intelligence of the Creator.

"The pastor then proceeds in the same tone: 'Feeble beings as we are, placed between two infinities, let us adore in silence the same hand that has illumined so many suns, and impressed with life these imperceptible atoms. That sight, doubtless, which has composed the delicate structure of the heart, the nerves, can easily penetrate the inmost recesses of our hearts. Let us render our thoughts all worthy to be known by God.'

"The young man remains agitated and astonished; he weeps with joy; he cannot satisfy his ardent curiosity; he is transported; his words are nothing but a long hymn of admiration; his heart pants with surprise and awe. How is he filled with the divine presence! How does the telescope render him worthy to be an inhabitant of this wonderful universe! He is cured of his terrestrial ambition and of the little hatreds that it engenders; he respects all men as animated with the same breath of life. His glory, from that hour, is to reap in the heaven, store of wonders; he appears to himself of more consequence since he has been endowed with the capacity of understanding these great truths; he says to himself, 'God is manifest to me; my eye has visited Saturn. I find that my being is more noble than I imagined, since the Supreme has vouchsafed to establish a relation between my nihility and his greatness. O! how happy am I to have received life and intelligence! I begin to see what will be the lot of the virtuous man. O most bountiful God, grant that I may eternally love and adore Thee!'

"He returns many times to feast on these sublime objects. From that day he is initiated to the rank of thinking beings; but he religiously keeps the secret, that others, who have not yet attained the age to enjoy such prodigies, may feel the same degree of pleasure and surprise.

"Three things are held in peculiar honor among us; to be the father of a child, to cultivate a field, and to build a house. The culture of the land is also moderate; the husbandman does not toil from early dawn till after sunset, and, exhausted, sink, imploring in vain a small portion of what springs from the labor of his hands. Our fertile plains resound with songs of joy; the father of each family sets the example: the task is easy; and when it is done, joy begins; the intervals of repose render their labor more vigorous; and it is constantly attended by sports or rural dances. Formerly, they went to the towns in search of pleasure; now they find it in the villages, where each one bears a smiling visage.

"You will easily conceive, therefore, that having no monks, nor priests, nor numerous domestics, nor useless valets, nor workmen employed in childish luxuries, a few hours of labor are sufficient for the public wants. Our lands produce plenteous crops of every kind; what is superfluous we send to foreigners, and receive in return other commodities. You will find our markets abundant in all things necessary to life; pulse, fruits, fowls, fish, etc. The rich do not, by their extravagance, oppress the poor; far from us is the fear of not having a sufficiency; we never practice the insatiable avidity of procuring three times more than we can consume; we regard dissipation with horror. If nature, during one year, treats us with rigor, the scarcity does not cost the lives of thousands; the granaries are opened, and the wise precautions of man soften the inclemency of the air and the wrath of heaven.

"We have four theaters, in the middle of the four quarters of the city. They are supported by the government; for they are made public schools of taste and morality. We have discovered all that influence which the ascendency of genius has over sensible minds. Genius has produced the most wonderful effects, without labor and without violence. It is in the hands of the great poets that are deposited, so to say, the hearts of their fellow citizens, and which they modify after their own pleasure. How criminal are they, when they produce dangerous principles! Our dramatic authors have no other view than the improvement of human nature; they all strive to elevate and strengthen the mind, and to render it independent and virtuous."

We arrived at a spacious place, in the midst of which was situated an edifice of a majestic composition. The inside of the theater formed an advanced semicircle; so that the spectators were all commodiously distributed. Every one was seated; the company was brilliant; the ladies were elegantly dressed, and decently disposed.

The performance opened with a symphony adapted to the piece that was to be represented.

"Are we at the opera?" I exclaimed; "this music is sublime."

"We have found the means of uniting, without confusion, the two exhibitions in one, or rather of reviving the alliance of poetry and music that was formed by the ancients. During the interacts of our dramas, they entertain the audience with animated songs that paint the sentiments and dispose the mind for the enjoyment of what is going to be offered. Far from us is banished all effeminate, capricious, or noisy music, that speaks not to the heart. Your opera was a grotesque, monstrous composition. We have preserved all of it that was good."

As he said these words, the curtain rose. What most affected me was the truth that ran through this drama. They had been very cautious not to disfigure this pathetic subject by improbabilities, or by the monotony of our rhyming verses; the poet, in following the steps of this cruel event, had attached himself to those incidents only which the deplorable situation of each victim produced, or rather he had borrowed their language; for all the art consists in faithfully repeating the voice of nature.

We came out of the theater without trouble or confusion; the passages were numerous and convenient. I beheld the streets perfectly light. I saw not at any corner those prostitutes, who invited the passenger in a brutal style to an entertainment as insipid as gross. All those places of debauchery, where men went to degrade their nature, were no longer tolerated. I observed that there were guards who preserved the public security and prevented any one from disturbing the hours of repose. "You there see," said my guide, "the only sort of soldiers for which we have any occasion; we have no devouring army to maintain in time of peace. The sovereigns of the earth have deigned to hear the voice of philosophy. Connected by the strongest bands, by those of interest, which they have discovered after so many ages of error, kings, by common consent, have fixed bounds to their dominions, such as nature itself seems to have assigned in separating them by seas, by forests, or mountains. They have learned that a kingdom of but small extent is susceptible of the best form of government. Those ancient prejudices, not less dangerous, that divided men on account of their belief, are also abolished. We regard all men as our friends and brethren. The Indian and the Chinese are our countrymen, when they once set foot on our land. We teach our children to regard all mankind as composing one and the same family, assembled under the eye of one common father. It is printing that, by enlightening mankind, has produced this grand revolution."

The Librarian, who was a man of real learning, presented himself to me; and well considering all the objections, as well as reproaches that I made, he gave me the following account. "Convinced by the most strict observation that the mind is embarrassed by a thousand extrinsic difficulties, we were sensible that a numerous library was the seat of the greatest extravagancies and the most idle chimeras. In your time, to the disgrace of reason, men first wrote and then thought. We follow the opposite course; and have therefore destroyed all those authors who buried their thoughts under a monstrous heap of words or phrases."

"What have you done? Proceed if you please."

"By a unanimous consent, we brought together books which we judged either frivolous, useless, or dangerous. Of these we formed a pyramid that resembled, in height and bulk, an enormous tower. Journals crowned this strange edifice; and it was covered with ordinances of bishops, remonstrances of parliaments, petitions, and funeral orations; it was composed of five or six hundred thousand commentators, of eight hundred thousand volumes of law, of fifty thousand dictionaries, of a hundred thousand poems, of sixteen hundred thousand voyages and travels, and of a billion of romances. This tremendous mass was set on fire, and offered as an expiatory sacrifice to veracity, to good sense, and true taste. We have therefore done from an enlightened zeal what the barbarians once did from one that was blind: however, those of the greatest judgment among us extracted the substance of thousands of volumes, which they have included in a small duodecimo. We have abridged what seemed of most importance; the best have been reprinted; and the whole corrected according to the true principles of morality. At the beginning, each science is treated in parts; everyone applies his attention to that portion which has fallen to his lot. By this method nothing can escape. It was necessary for you to make an innumerable quantity of books; it is our business to collect the scattered parts. This closet, that you see, contains those books that have escaped the flames. Their number is small; but by their merit they have obtained the approbation of our age."

I approached with curiosity: and on examining the first division, I found that of the Greeks they had preserved Homer, Sophocles, Euripides, Demosthenes, Plato, and particularly our friend Plutarch; but they had burned Herodotus, Sappho, Anacreon, and the vile Aristophanes. In the second division appropriated to the Latin authors I found Virgil, Pliny, and Titus Livy entire; but they had burned Lucretius, except some poetic passages, because his physics they found false, and his morals dangerous. They had destroyed the tedious pleadings of Cicero, an able rhetor rather than a man of eloquence; but they had preserved his philosophic works. The third division contained the English authors, and here I found the greatest number of volumes. Milton, Shakespeare, Pope, Young, and Richardson, here still enjoyed their full renown. That futile reproach we make them, of their want of taste, was disregarded by men, who, charmed with just and strong ideas knew how to meditate on what they had read. At last, I came to the French writers. I hastily seized the first three volumes: they were Descartes, Montaigne, and Charron. Montaigne had suffered from retrenchment; but as he is the philosopher, who of all others was the best acquainted with human nature, his writings were preserved, though all his ideas are not absolutely irreproachable. The visionary Malebranche, the gloomy Nicole, the unpitying Arnauld, and the cruel Bourdaloue, they had burned.

I inquired for the historians, and the librarian said, "We assign that province in part to our painters. Facts have a philosophical certainty, which is to be expressed by the pencil. However, we have made a slight extract, painting each age in strong characters, and describing those persons only who have had a real influence on the destiny of empires. We have omitted those reigns where there were nothing to be seen but wars and cruelties. They ought to be concealed; for nothing should be presented that will not do honor to humanity. We have treated human nature like that son who revered his father, and covered with a veil the disorders of inebriety."

Not far from this spot, I beheld a vast temple that struck me with awe and admiration. On its frontispiece was written, *An Abridgement of the Universe.* In different parts were placed marble statues, with these inscriptions: *To the inventor of the saw; To the inventor of the plane, the screw, the pulley*, etc. All the different sorts of animals, vegetables, and minerals were placed under the four wings, and were visible by one glance of the eye. What an immense and astonishing assemblage! Under the first wing were seen all from the cedar to the hyssop. Under the second, from the eagle to the fly. Under the third, from the elephant to the ant. Under the fourth, from the whale to the gudgeon.

That scale of beings, so contested in our day, which many philosophers had judiciously supposed, was here confirmed by the clearest evidence. We saw distinctly that the several species run, so to speak, into each other; that by the delicate and sensible connections between the stone and the plant, the plant and the animal, the animal and man, there remained interstices; that their growth, duration, and destruction were determined by the same causes. It was moreover remarked that nature in all her operations tended to the formation of man; and that laboring that important work, she endeavored, by various essays, to arrive at the gradual term of his perfection, which seemed to be the utmost effort of her power.

I found myself oppressed by the weight of so many miracles. My eyes embraced all the luxury of nature. How at that moment did I reverence its Author! What homage did I render to His power, His wisdom, and what is even still more precious, His goodness! How important a being does man appear when ranging among these wonders collected by His hands; and which seem created for Him, as He alone has the power of discerning their various properties!

"By what wonderful perseverance," I said, "have you been able to perform so great a work?"

They replied: "We leave nothing to chance. Chance is a synonymous word with ignorance. Sagacity, labor, and patience are the instruments by which nature is compelled to discover her most hidden treasures. Men have learned to derive every possible advantage from the gifts they have received. By perceiving the degree to which they could ascend, they have been stimulated by glory to pursue the boundless career that is set before them. The life of a single man is too short; and what have we done? We have united the force of each individual; they have acquired an immense empire; the one finished what the other began. The chain was never interrupted, but each link closely connected with that which went before; thus it has been extended through several centuries, and this chain of ideas and of successive labor may one day surround and embrace the universe. It is not merely a personal glory, but the interest of the human race, scarce thought of in your days, that supports the most difficult enterprises.

"We no longer amuse ourselves with vain systems. The torch of experience alone directs our steps. Our end is to know the secret causes of each appearance, and to extend the dominion of man, by providing him with the means of executing all those labors that can aggrandize his existence.

"Walk into these gardens, where botany has received all the perfection of which it was susceptible. Your blind philosophers complained that the earth was replete with poisons. We have discovered, that they are the most efficacious remedies that can be employed. Providence has here been justified. We now no longer hear complaints upon the earth; no mournful voice cries out, "All is evil!" We say that in the sight of God, "All is good!" We have extracted from plants certain penetrating and benign juices, which, by insinuating themselves into the pores of the skin, mix with our fluids, establish the temperament, and render the body more healthful, more supple and robust. We have discovered the secret of dissolving the stone without burning the entrails. We now cure the phthisis, and every other disorder formerly deemed incurable."

What related to acoustics was not less miraculous. They had acquired the art of imitating all the articulations of the human voice and the various notes of birds. By touching certain springs we seemed to be instantly transported to some wild forest, where we heard the roarings of the lion, the tiger, and the bear, who seemed to be in conflict with each other. The noise rent the ear. You would have said that the echo, still more terrible, repeated at a distance those horrid and barbarous cries. But soon the songs of nightingales succeeded to those discordant sounds. By their harmonious organs each particle of the air became melodious; the ear discerned even the tremblings of their amorous wings, and those tender and enchanting sounds which the voice of man can never perfectly imitate. To the intoxication of pleasure was joined voluptuous sensation.

This people, who had constantly a moral aim even in the prodigies of art, had happily deduced an advantage from this surprising invention. When a young prince talked of combats, they conducted him to a room which they properly named *Hell*. The artist immediately put the springs in motion, and saluted his ear with all the horrors of a battle, the cries of rage and of grief, the lamentations of the dying, the sounds of terror, the bellowing of that hideous thunder which is the signal of destruction and bears the execrable sound of death. If nature did not then prevail on his mind, if he did not send forth a cry of horror, if his countenance remained unmoved and placid, he was confined to that room the remainder of his days. Every morning, however, they repeated a piece of this music, that he might be satisfied without the destruction of the human race.

The director of this cabinet, to my great surprise, exhibited all his infernal opera, without acquainting me of his intention. "O heavens! mercy! mercy!" I cried with all my strength, stopping my ears. "O spare me, spare me!"

He stopped the exhibition. "How!" he said, "does not this please you?"

"None but a demon," I replied, "can be pleased with such an horrid uproar."

"This, however, was in your time a very common diversion, which the kings and princes of Europe all enjoyed, as they did the chase, which, as has been very justly remarked, is the true picture of war. Your poets moreover extolled them for having frightened all the birds from the sky for ten leagues round, and for sagaciously providing provender for the raven; but, above all things, those poets were extremely fond of describing a battle."

They conducted me to the cabinet of the mathematics. It appeared richly stored, and in the most perfect order. In a word, I here found the greatest variety of the most accurate instruments for the use of geometry, astronomy, and the other sciences. They whispered, moreover, that many remarkable, and even wonderful secrets were confided to the care of a small number of their sages, for there are matters, good in themselves, that may be abused in their application. The human mind, in their opinion, was not yet sufficiently strong to make use of the most rare or most powerful discoveries without danger.

"May I ask what is the present form of government? Is it monarchical, democratic, or aristocratic?"

"It is neither of them; it is rational, and made for man. Monarchy is no more. Monarchical governments, as you know, lose themselves in depotism, as the rivers are lost in the bosom of the ocean; and despotism soon sinks under its own weight. This has been all literally accomplished, and never was there a more certain prophecy. Freed from oppression, we have taken care not to place all the strength and springs of government, all the rights and attributes of power, in the hands of one man. Instructed by the misfortunes of past ages, we are become less imprudent. If Socrates or Marcus Aurelius should again visit the earth, we should not confide to them an arbitrary power; not from a mistrust, but from a fear of depreciating the sacred character of a free citizen.

"Can you believe it? The revolution was effected without trouble, and by the heroism of one great man. A philosophic prince, worthy of a throne because he regarded it with indifference, put the estates of the nation in possession of their ancient prerogatives; hence each province is the guardian of its own security and its own happiness; its principle of life is not too far distant from it; it is within itself, always ready to assist the whole, and to remedy evils that may arise. The absolute sovereignty is now abolished; the chief magistrate preserves the name of king; but he does not foolishly attempt to bear all that burden which oppressed his ancestors. The legislative power of the kingdom is lodged in the states assembled. The administration of affairs, as well political as civil, is assigned to the senate; and the monarch, armed with the sword of justice, watches over the execution of the laws. He proposes every useful establishment. The senate is responsible to the king, and the king and senate are responsible to the states, which are assembled every two years. All is there decided by the majority of voices. The enacting of new laws, the filling of vacant posts, and the redressing of grievances appertain to them. Particular or unforeseen cases are left to the wisdom of the monarch. The laws reign, and no man is above them; which was a horrid evil in your Gothic government. The general good of the nation is founded on the security of each individual. One fears but the laws. The sovereign himself is sensible that they hang over his head. We have conciliated what seemed almost incompatible, the good of the nation with that of individuals. They even pretended that the general happiness of a state was necessarily distinct from that of some of its members. We have not espoused that barbarous policy.

"There are censors who have the right of expelling from about the prince all who are inclined to irreligion, to licentiousness, to falsehood, and to that baneful art of covering virtue with ridicule. Our citizens are all equal; the only distinctions we know are those which naturally arise among men from their virtue, their genius, and industry.

"Besides those precautions used to prevent the monarch from forgetting, in time of public calamities, what he owes to the poor, he observes every year a solemn fast, which continues for three days, during which time he suffers continual hunger and thirst, and sleeps upon the ground. This severe and salutary fast imprints on his heart the most tender commiseration towards the necessitous."

"But," I said, "these changes must have been long, laborious, and difficult. What efforts you must have made!"

The philosopher with a pleasing smile, replied, "Good is not more difficult than evil. The human passions are frightful obstacles; but when the mind is once convinced of its true interest, the man becomes just and faithful. It seems to me that a single person might govern the world, if the hearts of men were disposed to toleration and equity. Notwithstanding the common inconsequence of those of your age, it was foreseen that reason would one day make a great progress; its effects have become visible, and the happy principles of a wise government have been the first fruits of its reformation."

My affable and polite instructor continued in the same free manner. "You should know that our women have no other portion than their virtue and their charms; they are, therefore, interested in improving their moral faculties. Every citizen, though he should be of the lowest class, may claim a daughter of the highest, provided she consent, and there be no seduction or disproportion of age. Everyone resumes the primitive equality of nature in forming a contract so pure, so free, and so necessary to our happiness as is that of matrimony. There end the bounds of paternal power, and that of civil authority. Our marriages are fortunate, because interest does not soil their amiable bands. You cannot easily imagine how many vices and foibles, such as slander, jealousy, idleness, the pride of excelling a rival, crimes of every kind, have been banished by this simple law. Women, instead of exercising their vanity, have cultivated their minds; and in lieu of riches, have furnished themselves with gentleness, modesty, and patience. Music and dancing no longer form their principal accomplishments; they have vouchsafed to learn the arts of economy, of pleasing their husbands, and educating their children. That extreme inequality of rank and fortune, the most destructive vice in every political society, is here no longer seen; the meanest citizen has no reason to blush at his condition; he associates with the highest, who disdains not his connection. The law has equaled mankind to the greatest degree in its power."

"But," I said, "notwithstanding all your improvements, man is still man, liable to weakness, humor, and disgust. If Discord, with her torch, should take the place of Hymen, what do you then? Are divorces permitted?"

"Doubtless, when they are founded on legitimate reasons. When both parties, for example, solicit a divorce at the same time, an incompatibility of humors is sufficient to dissolve the band. People marry only to be happy. It is a contract of which peace and mutual regard should be the end. We are not so senseless as to force two people to live together, whose hearts are estranged from each other, and thereby to renew the punishment of the cruel Mezentius, who fastened a living body to a loathsome carcass. A divorce is the only eligible remedy, as it at least renders to society two persons that are lost by their connection with each other. But (would you believe it?) the greater the facility is, the more averse they are to profit by it, as there is a sort of dishonor in not being able to bear together the troubles of a transient life. Our women, virtuous by principle, are delighted with domestic pleasures. They suckle their own children without thinking it a labor; and as it is done with affection, their milk is pure and plentiful. The body of the child is early invigorated; he is taught to swim, to hurl, and to carry burdens. The bodily education appears to us of importance. We form his constitution before we exercise his mind, which should not be that of a parrot, but that of a man.

"His mother watches over the morning of his rising thoughts; she reflects on the method to be pursued in forming his mind to virtue, how she shall turn his sensibility into humanity, his pride into greatness of soul, and his curiosity into a knowledge of sublime truths. She meditates on those engaging fables she shall use, not to conceal the truth, but to render it more amiable. She carefully weighs her words and actions, that no one of them may make a bad impression on his heart. Thus she preserves him from that breath of vice, by which the flower of innocence is so suddenly withered.

"In the more advanced age, when his mind is able to distinguish those connections by which he is united to society, then, instead of that futile knowledge with which the minds of youth are indiscriminately loaded, his mother, with that natural and tender eloquence peculiar to women, teaches him what are manners, decency, virtue. She makes choice of that season, when nature, dressed in all her splendor, speaks to the most insensible heart, when the genial breath of spring has decorated the groves, the fields, and forests, with all their ornaments. 'My Son', she says, pressing him to her maternal bosom, 'behold these verdant fields, these trees adorned with spreading branches; it is not long since, deprived of all their ornaments, they were congealed by that cold which pierces the inward parts of the earth, but there is a gracious Being, who is our common Parent, and who never abandons His children. He dwells in heaven, and from thence beholds, with the kindness of a father, all His creatures. At the moment that He smiles, the sun darts its rays, the trees flourish, the earth is crowned with flowers, and with herbs for the nourishment of those beasts whose milk we drink. And why do we so love the Lord? Hear, O my child! It is because He is powerful and good; all that you see is the work of His hands, and all this is nothing to what is concealed from you. Eternity, for which every immortal soul was created, will afford thee an endless procession of joy and wonder. His power and goodness know no bounds. He loves us, because we are His children. From day to day He will show us greater kindness if we are virtuous, that is if we obey His laws. O! my son, how can we but adore and bless his name!' At these words the mother and the child fall prostrate, and their united prayers ascend together to the throne of heaven.

"It is thus that she possesses him with the idea of a God, that she nourishes his soul with the milk of truth, and that she says to herself, 'I will fulfill the will of the Creator who has committed him to my care. I will be severe to those baneful passions that may injure his happiness; to the tenderness of a mother I will unite the unwearied vigilance of a friend.'

"You have seen at what age he is initiated to the communion of the two infinities. Such is our education. It is, as you see, altogether sentimental. We detest that jeering wit which was the most terrible scourge of your age. It dried up, it burned all it touched, and its buffooneries were the source of all your vices. But, if a frivolous disposition be so dangerous, what is reason itself without sentiment? A meagre frame, without color, without grace, and almost without life. What are new, and even profound ideas, if they have nothing animating and affecting? What need have I of a cold truth that chills my blood? It loses its force and its effect. It is in the heart that truth displays its charms and its power. We cherish that eloquence which abounds in lively and striking pictures. It gives wings of fire to our thoughts, and the pleasure of being affected is joined to that of being enlightened.

"Our philosophy is not severe, and why should it be? Why not crown it with flowers? Are disgustful or mournful ideas more honorable to virtue than those that are pleasing and salutary? We think that pleasure proceeding from a beneficent hand is not sent upon earth to make us shun its approach. Pleasure is not a monster, it is as Young says [in his poem *Night Thoughts*], virtue under a gayer title. Far from endeavoring to destroy the passions, the invisible movers of our being, we regard them as precious gifts that we should carefully economize. Happy is the man endowed with strong passions; they form his glory, his grandeur, and his opulence. A wise man among us cultivates his mind, discards his prejudices, and acquires useful and agreeable sciences. All the arts that can extend his judgment and render it more discerning are exercised and improved by his mind. That done, he attends to the voice of nature only, subject to the law of reason, and reason directs him to happiness.

"Tell me, I beseech you, how are your public taxes levied?"

As a full answer, the worthy man led me to a strong chest. On this chest was written, "Tribute Due to the King Representing the State." Hard by was another chest, with these words, "Free Gifts." I saw several people, with easy, cheerful, contented looks, throw sealed packets into the chest, as in our days they threw letters into the post office. I was so astonished at this easy manner of paying taxes, that I made a thousand ridiculous inquiries.

"That large coffer you see," they said, "is our receiver-general of the finances. It is there that every citizen deposits his contribution for the support of the state. We are there obliged to deposit the fiftieth part of our annual income. He that has no property, or what is only just sufficient for his maintenance, is exempt. For why should we take bread from him whose daily labor is but sufficient for his maintenance? In the other coffer are the voluntary offerings intended for the execution of such projects as have been approved by the public. This sometimes is richer than the other. For we love liberality in our gifts, and no other motive is necessary to excite it than equity and a love for the state. Whenever our king sends forth an useful edict, that merits the public approbation, we run in crowds to the chest with our marks of acknowledgment. There is a similar trunk in every quarter of the city, and in every city in the provinces, which receives the contributions of the country.

"How!" I said. "Do you leave it to the good will of the people to pay their taxes? There must be then a great number that pay nothing without your knowing it."

"Not at all. We give with a free will. Our tribute is not by compulsion, but founded on reason and equity. There is scarce a man among us who does not esteem it a point of honor to discharge the most sacred and most legitimate of all debts. Besides, if a man in condition to pay should dare to neglect it, you there see the table on which the name of the head of every family is engraved, by which we should soon see who had not thrown in his packet, on which should be his seal. In that case he covers himself with an eternal infamy, and we regard him as you regard a thief."

· · · · ·

"It seems, by what you have told me, that France has no longer any colonies in the new world, that each part of America forms a separate kingdom though united under one spirit of legislation."

"We should be highly ridiculous to send our dear fellow citizens two thousand leagues from us. Our climate is at least as good as that of America. Every necessary production is here common, and by nature excellent. The colonies were to France what a country house is to a private person; the house in the country, sooner' or later, ruins that in town.

"We have a commerce, but it consists merely in the exchange of superfluities among ourselves. We have prudently banished three natural poisons, of which you made perpetual use: snuff, coffee, and tea. You stuffed your heads with a villainous powder that deprived you of what little memory you had. You burned your stomach with liquors that destroyed it. Those nervous disorders so common among you were owing to the effeminate liquor which carried off the nourishing juice of the animal life. We cultivate an interior commerce only, of which we find the good effects; founded principally on agriculture, it distributes the most necessary aliments. It satisfies the wants of man, but not his pride. Foreign traffic was the real father of that destructive luxury, which produced in its turn that horrid inequality of fortunes, which caused all the wealth of the nation to pass into a few hands. Because a woman could carry in her ears the patrimony of ten families, the peasant was forced to sell the land of his ancestors, and to fly with tears from that soil where he found nought but misery and disgrace, for those insatiable monsters, who had accumulated the gold, even derided the misfortunes of those they had plundered. We began by destroying those great companies that absorbed all the fortunes of individuals, annihilated the generous boldness of a nation and gave as deadly a blow to morality as to the state.

"It may be very agreeable to sip chocolate, to breathe the odor of spices, to eat sugar and bananas, to drink Barbados water, and to be clothed in the gaudy stuffs of India. But are these sensations sufficiently voluptuous to close our eyes against the crowd of unheard-of evils that your luxury engendered in the two hemispheres? Blind barbarians! You have been but too well convinced by a fatal experience. A thirst for gold extolled by every heart, amiable moderation banished by avidity, justice and virtue regarded as chimeras, avarice pale, and restless, plowing the waves, and peopling with carcasses the depths of the ocean! A whole race of men bought and sold, treated as the vilest animals! Kings become merchants, covering the seas with blood for the flag of a frigate! Gold, to conclude, flowing from the mines of Peru like a flaming river, and running into Europe, burned up the roots of happiness and was then forever lost on the eastern world, where superstition buried in the earth, on one side, what avarice had painfully drawn from it, on the other. Behold a faithful picture of the advantages that foreign commerce produced to the world!

"Our vessels do not make the tour of the globe, to bring back cochineal and indigo. Know you where are our mines? Where is our Peru? In labor and assiduity. All that promotes ease and convenience, that directly tends to assist nature, is cultivated with the greatest care. All that belongs to pomp, to ostentation and vanity, to a puerile desire of an exclusive profession of what is merely the work of fancy, is severely prohibited. We have cast into the sea those deceitful diamonds, those dangerous pearls, and all those whimsical stones that rendered the heart like them, impenetrable. You thought yourselves highly ingenious in the refinements of luxury, but your pursuits were merely after superfluities, after the shadow of greatness. You were not even voluptuous. Your futile and miserable inventions were confined to a day. You were nothing more than children fond of glaring objects, incapable of satisfying your real wants. Ignorant of the art of happiness, you fatigued yourselves, far from the object of your pursuits, and mistook, at every step, the image for the reality."

28

The Constitution of Spensonia

A Country in Fairyland Situated
Between Utopia and Oceana,
Brought from Thence by Captain Swallow

Thomas Spence

London
1803

Thomas Spence (1750–1814),

born at Newcastle-on-Tyne in England, enjoyed little formal education and less money and became a teacher of elementary English. Throughout his life he was oppressed by a sense of the injustice of a society in which people like his father toiled hard but remained miserably poor. In his studies, he "found every art and science a perfect whole. Nothing was in anarchy but language and politics." Accordingly he worked out a scientific system of phonetic spelling, in which he published several of his works. Politics he also "reduced to order, . . . by a new Constitution." He read a paper on this new constitution to the Newcastle Philosophical Society in 1775. In it, he assumed that property in land and liberty among men were both equal in a state of nature, and he taught that society is a mutual agreement among the citizens of a country to maintain each other's rights and privileges; that is, to maintain the right to live and the right to a means of subsistence. Accordingly, he asserted that the land in any neighborhood belongs at all times to its living inhabitants in an equal manner. Since these "rights" were no longer enjoyed by all men, Spence urged a Plan. The inhabitants of each parish should meet to take possession of their rights and to form a corporation which would be sovereign lord of its own territories. Parish land would then be rented in small lots to tenants, the rent to be used to maintain the poor of the parish, pay a share of governmental expenses, and provide money for local works. Government would be conducted by ballot votes in parish meetings, in committees, and a House of Representatives.

Spence published this lecture and was forthwith expelled from the Philosophical Society for his indecorum. Though distressed by this action, he continued to develop and spread his doctrines. An anecdote reveals his typical doctrines. A forester once challenged him for gathering nuts on private property. "Why not?" asked Spence. "Would you question a monkey or a squirrel about such a business? Am I to be treated as inferior to one of those creatures? or have I a less right? But who are you that thus take it upon you to interrupt me?" The forester replied that he would seize Spence for trespassing. "Indeed," returned the latter, "but how can I trespass here where no man ever planted or cultivated? For these nuts are the spontaneous gifts of Nature ordained alike for the sustenance of man and beast that choose to gather them, and therefore they are common."

"I tell you," replied the forester, "this wood is not common. It belongs to the Duke of Portland."

"Oh! my service to the Duke of Portland," came the rejoinder. "Nature knows no more of him than of me. Therefore as in Nature's storehouse the rule is 'First come, first served,' so the Duke of Portland must look sharp if he wants any nuts."

The good-humored forester allowed Spence to continue gathering the nuts. Had he been less amused, he might well have answered Spence by treating him as if he were not inferior to a squirrel—namely, by shooting him. Or he could have applied Spence's own argument of "First come, first served," by thus forcibly demonstrating that the Dukes of Portland had already gained possession.

In 1792 Spence left Newcastle for London, where he kept a bookstall. He sold reform literature such as Tom Paine's *Rights of Man*, but devoted his chief industry to advertising his Plan. In this connection he successively issued cheap periodicals. The first and most famous of these, *Pig's Meat*, was a penny weekly directed to what Burke had called "the swinish multitude." It was succeeded by similar publications and pamphlets. However, Spence was prosecuted for selling Paine's literature and his own, being four times indicted and three times imprisoned before 1795. In 1798 and 1801, he was again arrested. On the last of these occasions he was tried for "seditious libel" and gloried in the opportunity to preach his doctrines. Being found guilty, he was sentenced to twelve months in jail, fined £20, and required to give security in £500 for his good behavior during the next five years. A Spencean Society was formed but, during Spence's lifetime, was no more than a poor workmen's club for improving the world in general and the lot of the workers in particular. The reformer himself spent the years from 1801 to 1814 in obscurity, publishing little, though continuing to sell pamphlets. However, the Luddite Riots and general unrest in 1814 seemed to provide a fresh opportunity to advertise his Plan. Accordingly, his followers, now increased in numbers, were reorganized as the Society of Spencean Philanthropists, and he began to publish a periodical, *Giant-Killer, or Anti-Landlord*. But only three numbers had appeared when Spence died in September, 1814. The Spencean Philanthropists continued till they were effectually suppressed by the British government in 1820.

Basically Spence's Plan is to nationalize the land, which is to be administered for the nation by parish councils controlled by the central government. These parochial and central representative bodies are to be elected by ballot under an extended franchise. Universal military training will be set up. Nationalization of land would, Spence believed, secure the means of subsistence to every man, whereupon the evils of society would vanish.

Spence was largely influenced by More's *Utopia*, Harrington's *Oceana*, and the theories of the Physiocrats. His own thought had considerable influence on Robert Owen and, through him, on later socialists. His basic Plan developed in a series of ephemeral publications, most of which do not survive, from about 1783. The *Constitution of Spensonia* appeared in three editions in 1803. It was a revision of a pamphlet published by Spence in 1798 entitled, *The Constitution of a Perfect Commonwealth, being the French Constitution of 1794 Amended and Rendered Entirely Conformable to the Rights of Man.* But accounts of Spensonia had been printed as early as 1794 in his newspaper, *Pig's Meat.* In the following reprint, the division of the Constitution into separate, numbered clauses grouped under headings has been abandoned.

BIBLIOGRAPHY: Olive D. Rudkin, *Thomas Spence and his Connections* (London, 1927); Arthur W. Waters, *Trial of Thomas Spence* (Leamington Spa, 1917).

The Constitution of Spensonia

DECLARATION

The Spensonian people, convinced that forgetfulness and contempt for the natural Rights of Man are the only cause of the crimes and misfortunes of the world, have resolved to expose in a declaration their sacred and inalienable rights, in order that all citizens, being always able to compare the acts of the government with the ends of every social institution, may never suffer themselves to be oppressed and degraded by tyranny; and that the people may always have before their eyes the basis of their liberty and happiness; the magistrates, the rule of their conduct and duty; and legislators, the object of their mission.

They acknowledge therefore and proclaim in the presence of the Supreme Being, the following declarations of the Rights of Man and Citizens:

The end of society is common happiness. Government is instituted to secure to man the enjoyment of his natural and imprescriptible rights. These rights are Equality, Liberty, Safety, and Property, natural and acquired.

All men are equal by nature and before the law and have a continual and inalienable property in the earth and its natural productions. The law is the free and solemn expression of the general will. It ought to be the same for all, whether it protects or punishes. It cannot order but what is just and useful to society. It cannot forbid but what is hurtful. Social laws, therefore, can never proscribe natural rights. And every man, woman, and child still retain from the day of their birth to the day of their death, their primigenial right to the soil of their respective parishes. Thus, after a Parish, out of its rents has remitted to the State and County its legal quota towards their expenses, and provided for defraying its own proper contingencies, the remainder of the rents is the indisputable joint property of all the men, women, and children having settlement in the Parish, and ought to be equally divided among them.

All male citizens are equally admissible to public employments. Free people know no other motives of preference in their elections than virtue and talents. Liberty is that power which belongs to a man of doing everything that does not hurt the right of another. Its principle is nature; its rule, justice; its protection, the law; and its moral limits are defined by this maxim: "Do not to another what you would not wish done unto yourself." The right of manifesting one's thoughts and opinions either by the press or in any other manner, the right of assembling peaceably, and the free exercise of religious worship cannot be forbidden. Whatever is not forbidden by the law cannot be prevented. No one can be forced to do that which the law does not order.

Safety consists in the protection granted by society to each citizen for the preservation of his person, his rights, and his property. The law avenges public and individual liberty of the abuses committed against them by power. No person can be accused, arrested, or confined, but in cases determined by the law and according to the form which it prescribes. Every citizen summoned or seized by the authority of the law ought immediately to obey. He renders himself culpable by resistance. Every act exercised against a man to which the cases in the law do not apply, and in which its forms are not observed, is arbitrary and tyrannical. Respect for the laws forbids him to submit to such acts; and if attempts are made to execute them by violence, he has a right to repel force by force. Those who shall solicit, dispatch, sign, execute, or cause to be executed arbitrary acts are culpable and ought to be punished. Every man being supposed innocent until he has been declared guilty, if it is judged indispensable to arrest him, all severity not necessary to secure his person ought to be strictly repressed by the law. No one ought to be tried and punished until he has been legally summoned, and in virtue of a law published previous to the commission of the crime. A law which should punish crimes committed before it existed would be tyrannical. The retroactive effect given to a law would be a crime. The law ought not to decree any punishments but such as are strictly and evidently necessary. Punishments ought to be proportioned to the crime, and useful to society.

The right of property is that which belongs to every citizen to enjoy and dispose of according to his pleasure, property, revenues, labor, and industry. Here his property in land is excepted, which, being inseparably incorporated with that of his fellow parishioners, is inalienable.

No kind of labor, culture, or commerce can be forbidden to the industrious citizen. Every man may engage his services and his time, but he cannot sell himself; his person is not alienable property. The law does not acknowledge servitude. There can exist only an engagement of care and gratitude between the man who labors and the man who employs him. No one can be deprived of the smallest portion of his property without his consent except when the public necessity, legally ascertained, evidently requires it, and on condition of a just and previous indemnification.

No public revenue can be established but for general utility and to relieve the public wants. Every citizen has a right to concur in the establishment of such revenue, to watch over the use made of it, and to call for a statement of expenditure. Public aids are a sacred debt. The society is obliged to provide for the subsistence of the unfortunate, either by procuring them work, or by procuring the means of existence to those who are unable to labor.

Instruction is the want of all, and the society ought to favor with all its power the progress of the public reason, and to place instruction within the reach of every citizen.

The social guarantee consists in the actions of all to secure to each the enjoyment and preservation of his rights. This guarantee rests on the national sovereignty. The social guarantee cannot exist if the limits of public functions are not clearly determined by the law, and if the responsibility of all public functionaries is not secured. The sovereignty resides in the people; it is one and indivisible, imprescriptible and inalienable. No proportion of the people can exercise the power of the whole; but each section of the sovereign assembled ought to enjoy the right of expressing its will in the perfect liberty. Every individual who arrogates to himself the sovereignty, or who usurps the exercise of it, ought to be put to death by freemen. A people have always the right of revising, amending, and changing their Constitution. One generation cannot subject to its law future generations. Every citizen has an equal right of concurring in the formation of the law and in the nomination of his mandatories or agents. The public functions cannot be considered as distinctions or rewards, but as duties. Crimes committed by the mandatories of the people and their agents ought never to remain unpunished. No one has a right to pretend to be more inviolable than other citizens.

The right of presenting petitions to the depositories of public authority belongs to every individual. The exercise of this right cannot in any case be forbidden, suspended, or limited.

Resistance to oppression is the consequence of the other rights of man. Oppression is exercised against a social body, when even one of its members is oppressed. Oppression is exercised against each member when the social body is oppressed. When the government violates the rights of the people, insurrection becomes to the people and to every portion of the people the most sacred and the most indispensable of duties.

THE COMMONWEALTH

The Spensonian Commonwealth is one and indivisible. The Spensonian people is distributed for the exercise of its sovereignty and for the management of its landed property into Parishes. It is distributed for administration and for justice into Counties and Parishes.

Every man or woman born or otherwise having acquired a settlement in a Parish of Spensonia and of the age of twenty-one years complete is admitted to the exercise of the rights of a Spensonian Citizen as far as their sex will allow. Female citizens have the same right of suffrage in their respective Parishes as the men, because they have equal property in the country and are equally subject to the laws; and, indeed, they are in every respect, as well on their account as on account of their children, as deeply interested in every public transaction; but in consideration of the delicacy of their sex, they are exempted from, and are ineligible to, all public employments.

Every man, woman, and child, whether born in wedlock or not (for nature and justice know nothing of illegitimacy), is entitled quarterly to an equal share of the rents [revenues] of the Parish where they have settlement. But the public aids to the State and the County must first be deducted, and the expenses of the Parish provided for. The settlement of every man whether native or foreigner is in that Parish wherein he last dwelt a full year. . . . No person can receive dividends or have a vote in two Parishes at the same time. A child, though born in the last hour of the quarter, and a person dying in the first hour of the quarter, shall nevertheless each of them be entitled to their quarterly dividends, because such occasions are expensive and the Parish must lean to the generous side.

The exercise of the rights of a citizen with respect to voting or public employments is suspended by the state of accusation and by condemnation to punishments infamous or afflictive till recapitation [restoration of citizenship]; but his right to a share of the Parish revenues as a human being can never be annulled but by death or banishment.

The sovereign people is the universality of Spensonian Citizens. It nominates directly its Deputies. It delegates to electors the choice of administrators, of Public Arbitrators, or Criminal Judges, and Judges of Appeal.

The land with its natural appurtenances (according to the law of nature) is the common estate of the inhabitants. A Parish is therefore a compact portion of the country designedly not too large, that it may the more easily be managed by the inhabitants with respect to its revenues and police. A Parish can levy no tolls nor assessments but the rents of its territory. Its police appertains to it. It nominates its own officers. It supports a public school.

Farmers and such as are able to build and repair their own houses must have leases of twenty-one years but no longer, that the most desirable situations may not be always engrossed in the same hands, and that farms and other tenements may now and then find their value in order that the Parish revenue receive no damage by places leased for less than they will bring. For the more effectual preservation of justice in this business, all considerable farms and tenements must at the expiration of a lease be let by public auction after due advertisement in the public prints. Every leaseholder must build according to the regulations laid down by the Parish for the sake of order and duration. They must also leave their buildings, fixtures, fences, etc., at the end of their leases, in good tenantable repair and condition, and their lands in good tilth, becoming the public spirit of Spensonia.

No deputy landlords are allowed. Therefore no leaseholder can parcel out his houses or lands to subtenants. All unfurnished lodgings or parcels of land can only be let by the Parish. Nevertheless an innkeeper or private person may occasionally accommodate strangers or others with lodgings in their own furnished apartments, and their cattle with pasturage, etc. And a settlement may be gained by thus residing a great part or even the whole of the year in the Parish in such furnished lodgings.

Strangers from abroad or Spensonians from other Parishes who may become necessitous through sickness or otherwise before they have gained a settlement, must be supported by the Parish in which they then sojourn. But, such poor being accounted the poor of the nation at large, the Parishes, before they send off their quarterly poundage to the State, shall deduct therefrom the expenses they have been at in supporting such poor strangers. Parishes in towns must always keep a sufficiency of small and convenient apartments in good repair for the accommodations of laborers, journeymen, mechanics, widows, and others who desire and require but little room. These shall be let by the porter at equitable rents. Country Parishes shall have a sufficiency of cottages or small and convenient dwellings with little parcels of land adjoining for gardens, etc., to accommodate laborers in husbandry, smiths, cartwrights, and other tradesmen and people wishing to live in the country; these to be let by the year at equitable rents. If a competition arise about one of these small tenements in town or country on account of its more than common desirable situation, etc., it shall be let by auction and a lease granted. This will prevent murmuring, and also the tenements from being let under value to the detriment of the Parish. If any Parish in town or country should become so full of inhabitants as to have all its small tenements occupied, and yet more should be wanted, then it shall divide the first large sort of tenement that becomes vacant by the expiration of its lease into such small tenements that the free course of population be not impeded. It shall not be deemed unconstitutional to hold more tenements or leases than one, and even in sundry Parishes, because a person's health or business may require him to occupy tenements in different situations at the same time; as, for instance, in both town and country; or he may wish to secure the possession of some desirable tenement that is to be let, before the lease of the place he holds at present expires.

Such persons shall vote and receive dividends in but one Parish. A leaseholder may give up his lease to the Parish or sell the remainder of the term it has to run. The Parishes shall receive rent quarterly from the State and County for lands used for official buildings. Each Parish shall keep a supply of corn as a reserve in case of famine or scarcity. The law will regulate the grain business. Instead of thorns, briars, and brambles, hedges will be made of useful fruit trees. Hunting is forbidden. Game may be killed only by an occupier on his own property. Rents will be paid quarterly. An accounting of the rents and dividends will be published.

The Parishes are the sole basis of the National Representation. There is one deputy for each Parish if the number of Parishes in the nation do not exceed one thousand. If above one thousand, then the Parishes in each county shall be classed in pairs . . . And so in like manner with any number of Parishes, [grouping them together so] that the National Representation may never exceed one thousand.

The election proceeds in every Parish of a class on the same day, and after casting up the votes, a Commissioner is sent, for the general casting-up, to the place pointed out by the Parish. The nomination is made by the absolute majority of individual suffrages. If the casting-up does not give an absolute majority, a second vote is proceeded to, and the votes are taken for the two citizens who had the most voices. In the case of equality of voices, the eldest has the preference, either to be on the ballot or elected. In case of equality of age, lot decides. Every male citizen exercising the rights of citizens is eligible through the extent of the Commonwealth. . . . The Spensonian people assemble every year in their Parishes on the first of May for the elections. They proceed, whatever be the number of citizens present having a right to vote.

The citizens meet in their Parishes [and] nominate two electives for the County. The Electoral Assemblies proceed in their elections as the parishes.

The Legislative Body is one and indivisible and permanent. Its session is for a year. It meets the first of July. The National Assembly cannot be constituted if it does not consist of one more than half the Deputies. The Deputies cannot be examined, accused, or tried at any time for the opinions they have delivered in the Legislative Body. They may for a criminal act be seized, but a warrant of arrest or a warrant summoning to appear cannot be granted against them unless authorized by the Legislative Body.

The sittings of the National Assembly are public. The minutes of the sittings are printed. It cannot deliberate if it be not composed of——members at least. It cannot refuse to hear its members speak in the order which they have demanded to be heard. It deliberates by a majority of the members present. Fifty members have a right to require the appeal nominal. It has the right of censure on the conduct of its members in its bosom. The police appertains to it in the place of its sittings and in the external circuit which it has determined.

The Legislative Body proposes laws and passes decrees. Under the general name of laws are comprehended the acts of the Legislative Body concerning the legislation, civil and criminal; the general administration of the national revenues, and the ordinary expenses of the Commonwealth; the title, the weight and impression, and the denomination of money; the declaration of war; the public instruction; the public honors to the memory of great men. Under the particular name of decrees are included the acts of the Legislative Body concerning the annual establishment of the land and sea forces; the permission or the prohibition of the passage of foreign troops through the Spensonian territory; the introduction of foreign naval forces into the ports of the Commonwealth; the measures of general safety and tranquillity; the annual and momentary distribution of public succors and works; the orders for the fabrication of money of every kind; the unforeseen and extraordinary expenses; the measures local and particular to an administration or any kind of public works; the defense of the territory; the ratification of treaties; the nomination and the removal of commanders-in-chief of armies; the prosecution of the responsibility of members of the council and the public functionaries; the accusation of persons charged with plots against the general safety of the commonwealth . . . ; national recompenses.

The plans of laws are preceded by reports. The discussion cannot be opened and the law cannot be provisionally resolved upon till fifteen days after the report. The plan is printed and sent to all the Parishes of the commonwealth under this title, "Law Proposed." Forty days after the sending of the Law Proposed, if, in more than one-half of the counties, the tenth of the Parishes have not objected to it, the plan is accepted and becomes law. If there be an objection, the Legislative Body convokes the Parishes.

Laws, decrees, judgments, and all public acts are entitled, "In the Name of the Spensonian People, the year of the Spensonian Commonwealth."

There is one Executive Council composed of twenty-four members. The Electoral Assembly of each County nominates one candidate if the number of Counties in the nation exceeds twenty-four; but, if under, then each County nominates two. The Legislative Body chooses the members of the Council from the general list. One-half of it is renewed by each Legislature in the last month of the session. The Council is charged with the direction and superintendence of the general administration. It cannot act but in execution of the laws and decrees of the Legislative Body. It nominates, not of its own body, the Agents-in-Chief of the general administration of the Commonwealth. The Legislative Body determines the number and functions of these Agents. These Agents do not form a council. They are separated without intermediate correspondence between them; they exercise no personal authority. The Council nominates, not of its own body, the External Agents of the Commonwealth. It negotiates treaties. The members of the Council, in case of malversation, are accused by the Legislative Body. The Council is responsible for the nonexecution of laws and decrees, and for abuses which it does not denounce. It recalls and replaces the Agents in its nomination. It is bound to denounce them, if there be occasion, before the judicial authorities.

The Executive Council resides near the Legislative Body. It has admittance and a separate seat in the place of sittings. It is heard as often as it has an account to give. The Legislative Body calls it into the place of its sittings in whole or in part when it thinks fit.

There is a central administration in each County. The officers and administrators are nominated by the Electoral Assemblies of the County. The administrations are renewed one-half every year. The administrators and county officers have no character of representation; they cannot in any case modify the acts of the Legislative Body or suspend the execution of them. The Legislative Body determines the functions of the County officers and administrators, the rules of their subordinations and the penalties they may incur. The sittings of administrations are public. The Electoral Assemblies assess their Parishes by a pound rate, quarterly, towards defraying the public expenses of the County, as in building and repairing county edifices, . . . The accounts of the County are settled annually and, being as minutely printed as to give satisfaction, are sent to the Parishes.

The code of civil and criminal laws is uniform for all the commonwealth. No infringement can be made of the right which citizens have to cause their differences to be pronounced upon by arbitrators of their choice. The decision of these arbitrators is final if the citizens have not reserved the right of objecting to them. There are Justices of the Peace elected by the citizens in the Parishes. They conciliate and judge without expense. There are Public Arbitrators elected by the Electoral Assemblies. Their number and their circuits are fixed by the Legislative Body. They take cognizance of disputes which have not been finally determined by the private arbitrations of the Justices of the Peace. They deliberate in public; they give their opinions aloud; they pronounce in the last resort on verbal defenses or simple memorials without procedures and without expense; they assign the reasons of their decisions. The Justices of the Peace and the Public Arbitrators are elected every year.

In criminal cases no citizen can be tried but by an examination received by a Jury or decreed by the Legislative Body. The accused have counsel chosen by themselves or nominated officially. The process is public. The fact and the intention are declared by a Jury of Judgment. The punishment is applied by a Criminal Tribunal. Criminal Judges are elected every year by the Electoral Assembly.

There is one Tribunal of Appeal for the whole Commonwealth. This Tribunal does not take cognizance of the merits of the case; it pronounces on the violation of forms and an express contravention of the law. The members of the Tribunal are nominated every year by the Electoral Assembly.

The National Treasury is the central point of the receipts and expenses of the Commonwealth. It is supplied by an assessment, raised quarterly, of —— in pound on the rents of the Parishes by the Legislative Body. This assessment being sufficient for all national purposes, and being sent up by the Parishes every quarter without expenses, renders revenues, laws, and officers unnecessary. The affairs of the Treasury are administered by accountable Agents nominated by the Executive Council. These Agents are superintended by Commissioners nominated by the Legislative Body, not of its own members, and responsible for abuses which they do not denounce.

The accounts of the Agents of the National Treasure and of the Administrators of the Public Money are given in annually to responsible Commissioners nominated by the Executive Council. These verifications are superintended by Commissioners in the nomination of the Legislative Body, not of its own members, and responsible for errors and abuses which they do not denounce. The Legislative Body passes the accounts. The national accounts are printed yearly, sufficiently minute to give satisfaction, and sent to the Parishes.

The general forces of the Commonwealth are composed of the whole people. The Commonwealth maintains in its pay, even in times of peace, an armed force by sea and land. All the Spensonians are soldiers; they are all exercised in the use of arms. There is no Generalissimo. Difference of ranks, their distinctive marks, and subordination subsist only with relation to service and during its continuance. The public force employed for maintaining order and peace in the interior does not act but on the requisition in writing of the constituted authorities. The public force employed against enemies from without acts under the orders of the Executive Council. No armed bodies can deliberate.

If in more than half the Counties, the tenth of the Parishes of each, regularly assembled, demand the revision of the Constitutional Act or the change of some of its articles, the Legislative Body is bound to convoke all the Parishes of the Commonwealth to know if there be ground for a revision of the Constitution. The Assembly of Revision is formed by two members from each County. The Assembly of Revision exercises no functions of legislation or of government; it confines itself to the revision of the constitutional laws. All the authorities continue the exercise of their functions till the change proposed in the Assembly of Revision shall have been accepted by the people, and till the new authorities shall have been put in motion. The Assembly of Revision addresses immediately to the Parishes the plan of reform which it has agreed upon. It is dissolved as soon as its plan has been addressed.

The Spensonian People is the friend and natural ally of every free people. It does not interfere in the government of other nations. It does not suffer other nations to interfere in its own. It gives an asylum to foreigners banished from their countries for the cause of liberty; it refuses it to tyrants. It does not make peace with an enemy that occupies its territory.

The Constitution guarantees to all Spensonians Equality, Liberty, Safety, Property, parochial and private, the free exercise of worship, a common instruction, public succors; the indefinite liberty of the press, the right of petition, the right of meeting in popular societies, the enjoyment of all the Rights of Man. The Spensonian Commonwealth honors loyalty, courage, filial piety, misfortune. It puts the deposit of its Constitution under the guard of all virtues. The Declaration of Rights and the Constitutional Act are engraven on tables in the bosom of the Legislative Body and the public places.

Spensonia disclaims all financial benefits from foreign provinces, dominions, or colonies. Yet because the unparalleled encouragement to marriage, and of the influx of foreigners must inevitably so increase the number of inhabitants under this Constitution that colonies enjoying the same blessings must be established as inviting offings for the redundance of population in the mother country to flow to: all the colonies, therefore, that now belong to Spensonia or shall be hereafter established by her are declared independent states as soon as they adopt and put in practice similar constitutions. They shall then be considered as in the most intimate state of alliance, and entitled to all the protection the mother country can afford.

To promote cleanliness and refresh the spirit of men and laboring animals, the weeks in Spensonia are but five days each; each fifth day being a day or Sabbath of Rest. Thus will the fourth day of the week be always a market day and pay day for laborers.

FINIS

EPILOGUE

What pity, friends, that we should be
So much deprived of liberty!
Indictments one upon another
Continually do us bother. . . .
And though my book's in queer lingo,
I will send it to St. Domingo . . .
For who can tell but the Millennium
May take its rise from my poor Cranium? . . .

29

Equality

or, A History of Lithconia

Boston
1863
(first published serially at Philadelphia in 1802;
first book edition, Philadelphia, 1837)

Equality—A Political Romance first appeared in eight serial install-
ments in 1802 in *The Temple of Reason*, a weekly edited in Philadelphia by D. Driscol for the spread of deism. The editors claimed
that a ship's captain had given them the manuscript, which was found
among the papers of a gentleman who died at sea. The work was
reissued in 1837 by the Liberal Union of Philadelphia with the addition of an editor's preface and two footnotes, mention of the first
editor as *John* Driscol, and a change of title to *Equality, or A History
of Lithconia*. In pamphlet form, the work was republished in Boston
by J. P. Mendum in 1863. There is some reason for believing that
the author may have been Dr. James Reynolds of Philadelphia. In
1947, a new edition with a bibliographical note was published by the
Prime Press in Philadelphia. The extracts below are based on this
text.

Equality

AUTHOR'S PREFACE

It has been said that the man who could find out the means of making two blades of grass or ears of corn grow where there was only
one would deserve the gratitude and thanks of mankind: so it may
with equal truth be asserted that he who should be able to show the
manner of multiplying human enjoyments would deserve well of
the human race. The *summum bonum* [greatest good], like the philosopher's stone, has been long sought for without being found.
The only approach that has been made towards the discovery has
been in the form of governments. A few are happy or at least have
sufficient enjoyment under every possible form; but that is the most
desirable and what we should seek after with assiduity which would
diffuse enjoyments, rational and substantial enjoyments, among the
greatest number of citizens. Men have some enjoyments which are
founded in nature, and others that are factitious or imaginary. If we
take up those only which nature holds out, endeavor to multiply
them, and make them common to the human race, we are then doing
the greatest possible good. . . . Is it living, to exist without friendship? Is life worth the possessing without love? Do men enjoy themselves either in idleness or slavery? No: Happiness is what we are
always seeking after, but on finding that it eludes our grasp, we lay
the fault on the construction of the universe and the God of nature,
when it is only in the folly of human institutions. Whatever is within
the power of man, either as an individual or associated, it would be

folly to expect from the gods. Man must seek for resources in his own mind; when that fails, it is sufficient time to apply to heaven for assistance. . . . Next to the utility of multiplying the means of human enjoyment is the endeavor to root out the malevolent passions or remove their causes. Hatred, jealousy, pride, revenge have their origin also in the imperfection of the social compact. We are all subject to these passions when placed in certain circumstances, and if, by the constitution of society, these circumstances are often recurring, we begin to think these passions are so implanted in our nature that it is impossible to avoid them. The doctrine of waging an eternal warfare against the passions has not been successful; we should rather remove their causes than enter into such a conflict. One nation has obtained the character of being proud, another of being jealous, a third of cherishing a spirit of revenge. It is the same with individuals. What has given them this character, but the circumstances in which they have been respectively placed, and the nature of their institutions? In order to make an essential difference in the character of a nation, it must be accomplished by an alteration in the laws of descent, in religion, in the nature of the contract between the sexes, or in the distribution of the political powers of the state. Where the laws of descent divide the estates among the children, there can be no family pride, and where there is no established religion, the cause of hatred and animosity, which always reigns between those who hold opposite opinions, is totally removed. With respect to marriage, or a contract between the sexes: sometimes it has been a political and at other times a religious institution. . . . It would certainly be a pleasing reflection if the necessity for prostitution could be cut off. It is a blot on the character of civilization and on republicanism, and shows, though much has been gained to human enjoyment, yet, in this respect, that is, in the pleasure of love, we are yet Goths and Vandals.

If the laws of Lithconia will throw any light upon this subject, it will be a sufficient recompense for all my trouble in writing an account of their customs and manners. . . .

CHAPTER I

In those regions lately discovered by political philosophers, there is an island, the singularity of whose government and manners deserves the attention of the curious, and the particular notice of those who would wish to make discoveries in those latitudes in time coming.

Having been engaged in exploring those seas where lie the countries of Utopia, Brobdingnag, Lilliput, etc., and touching to take in fresh water at an island, which I afterwards found to be called Lithconia, I was so struck with the order and regularity with which everything was conducted, that I was resolved to stay some time amongst them, to observe whether there was anything in their constitution or form of government worthy of being recorded for the instruction of our modern politicians. . . .

. . . I was conducted to a man, who seemed to be past the prime of life, but active, healthy and robust. His first enquiry was, how I intended to employ myself during my residence on the island? I informed him that I wished to travel and visit the principal towns and villages in order to make such observations on the manners, customs and laws of the people, as my time and abilities would permit. When the elder understood this, he let me know the impracticability of my scheme, by reason of my not being furnished with those marks or signs, by which alone I could obtain provisions on my journey. These signs I immediately supposed to be money; upon which I drew out my purse and showed him a hundred guineas, which I imagined would be a sufficient passport to every town in the island, at least for the short time I had to stay. He smiled at my simplicity; and, at the same time, gave me to understand that such pieces of metal would be of no service to me in the country of Lithconia. But the good man, when he saw my disappointment and embarrassment, bid me have comfort, for that I surely would be willing, as he saw I was able, to perform some labor, at the appointed times, which alone could obtain for me the privilege of traveling. By making further inquiries I found that there was no money in the country, that the lands are in common, and that labor is a duty required of every citizen till a certain age, and, that duty being performed, the remainder of his time is his own. I therefore agreed to take my share of labor, being convinced I should have sufficient time to spare both for excursion and observation.

Four hours each day is set aside for work; this I could easily accomplish, and walk a moderate day's journey afterwards; . . .

Having obtained my certificate and dined, I would walk sixteen or twenty miles along the best roads in the world, before supper, to obtain which I had nothing to do, but present my certificate to the *Menardon,* or director of labor, who immediately showed me where I might sup, sleep, and what I should employ myself in next day. . . .

There is the same regulation for the natives. No man is permitted to do another's work, though he may anticipate his own. The practice of suffering the work allotted to one man to be performed by his neighbor, was formerly, say the Lithconians, the beginning of barter, and barter introduced money, which was the root of all evil. Therefore, if a man were to perform three days labor in one, he cannot bestow it upon any individual, supposing it a thing which might be separated from other labor; for industry is a duty which every man owes the state, and which he is not required to perform unless he be able. There is, therefore, no occasion to perform it by proxy.

Nothing but fame or love of country can induce a Lithconian to extra labor, but these two passions frequently produce great exertions. All the ornamental part of the country, whether it be the decorations of buildings, or statues and paintings, are all produced by these principles; for the regulations of the state require only the useful.

A clock-maker made a curious clock at leisure hours: the metal, the wood and tools were all the property of the community; he could not purchase them. By making the materials into a clock, he had only improved the goods of the community, and, as he could not, in justice, bestow the clock upon any person, it became the property of the state, and no people being more fond of public ornament than the Lithconians, was put up in the great workshop for workers in metal, adorned with some elegant mason work, and a handsome copy of verses engraved underneath, celebrating the genius of the artists and transmitting their names to posterity together with that of the poet. The whole was the extra labor of young men stimulated by no other motives than the passions above mentioned.

There are no towns or markets in all the island of Lithconia: the whole is only one large city upon a grand scale; for the roads, from one end of the island to the other, have houses (with a small opening betwixt each house), on both sides all the way, and there are fifty such roads from north to south, the length of the island, and upwards of two hundred from east to west.

The houses are all built upon one plan, two stories high, which contain nine sleeping apartments, a kitchen and public hall, with offices behind: no houses are built on the back ground, except for cattle; so that there is no such thing as a cluster of houses that may be called a town. At the crossings a square of one hundred yards is left vacant, without any houses, adjoining to which the public buildings, such as granaries, workshops, etc., are regularly erected.

I found in the history of the country, that there were formerly large towns, as in Europe; but the evils, natural and moral, which are the concomitant of great cities, made them think of abandoning them and building in the manner above described. But what finally determined them was an earthquake, which destroyed 1000 houses, a fire which burned 3000 in the principal city, and the plague which swept away 500,000 inhabitants from the different cities of the empire. But since the people have spread themselves over the country, no such calamities have afflicted them.

As to markets, there are three large stores in each district, one for provisions of every kind, one for clothing, and a third for household utensils and furniture. The keepers of provisions, whose stores are supplied from the field, send round, twice a week, in covered carts, to each house, every necessary for the consumption of a family. Clothing is distributed once a year, and household utensils as they are wanted; so that no idle people are seen lounging behind the counters, anxiously expecting customers, whom they may impose upon. Two men will distribute as much provisions as half the hucksters, grocers, bakers, and butchers in Philadelphia: and two more can distribute as much clothing in one month as all the Quakers in Pennsylvania will sell in a year. Hence that host of shopkeepers, which seem so necessary in barbarous countries, is here unknown.

The agriculturist and manufacturer has only to deposit his commodities in the public stores; he has nothing to do with the knavery of merchandise, and the words, "a good market," if such a term were in use here, could only have one idea, viz. *a plentiful supply;* whereas it is well known that what is a good market for the seller is a bad one to the buyer in all the disjointed countries in Europe and America.

Every person above the age of fifteen has a separate apartment. From five to fifteen, two sleep together; and children under five sleep in the mother's chamber. They are distributed in the houses as chance, passion, or accident direct, male and female promiscuously.

CHAPTER II

Marriage, formerly, I understand, was held as sacred here as in other countries; but when things were put on a rational footing, it fell gradually into disuse; for children being the property of the state, educated and brought up at the public expense, and as women could live as well single as united, young people were seldom at the trouble to make such a contract. Children were born, and no man thought it his business or interest to inquire who was the father. But a thousand inconveniences arose out of this legislative negligence, which, for the sake of order, and to make love a blessing to society, it was necessary to correct. The great evil that called for legislative interference was the frequent quarrels that took place between rival lovers.

Weak women were too often unable to determine, between two admirers, which should have the preference, and it was necessary, for the good of society, that she should decide. To accomplish this, it was decreed that every young woman of each district, who had arrived at a certain age, should, on the first day of the year after, inscribe the name of her lover in the matrimonial register of the district. Next day, all the young men, unengaged, go to examine this register, and as many as are satisfied with the girls who have chosen them, signify their assent to the recorder. After which it would be regarded as a high misdemeanor if either of the parties should be found to admit or give encouragement to another lover.

This kind of marriage, however, occasions no separation of property from the stock of the community, nor any of the property of the parties. They continue to live in separate apartments, and never sleep together only every seventh night. Whether this last regulation is a positive law or only a political custom, I could never learn; but it certainly has the happiest effects. It seems to be an institution or custom calculated to make the most of love, the only solace of mankind, and to make it last to the longest possible period of our existence. Nevertheless, it sometimes happens that lovers thus united become dissatisfied with each other, and that for the happiness of one or both of the parties, a separation is necessary. In that case the party aggrieved announces his or her intention of erasing the opposite party's name from the matrimonial register. Four weeks is then given for further deliberation, and if at the end of that time the same resolution is persisted in, the process of separation is recorded, and the parties are at liberty to inscribe other names on the register.

When a young woman is within three months of her time, she announces the same to the senior who has the immediate direction of her work, who exempts her from attendance, and a nurse is allowed, if necessary, and everything else convenient to accommodate her; and if she have a safe delivery, there are always rejoicings, entertainments and mirth among the neighbors.

Here are no parents repining at the increase of a family, from the fear of being unable to support them.

Here the laws do not make the trembling female swear to the father of her child; for no man can have any reason to deny or confess his offspring; and child-murder, a crime so frequent in barbarous nations—a crime which the happier females of Lithconia would shudder at the idea of—is totally unknown.

Here there is no occasion for asylums for the wretched and outcast female, because none are wretched or outcast. . . .

Friendship I found to be more frequent and durable here than in any other country. For, if we consider that it is the equality of men's conditions and the similarity of their pursuits that unite men in the bonds of friendship, we shall not be surprised to find attachments more lasting in this country, where all men are equal. What is it that produces false and inconstant friends in barbarous nations, but the fickleness of fortune (occasioned by a want of government), which is forever altering men's conditions and changing their pursuits? . . .

And so much are their institutions favorable to friendship that if two persons of congenial spirits meet and find a pleasure in the company and conversation of each other, they have the liberty of dwelling in the same house if they please; for a person may remove to any part of the island, or to any house where there is a vacancy: nothing can hinder him but the want of a certificate that he has performed the accustomed labor; having done that, he is at perfect liberty; nor has the senior the power . . . to refuse a certificate. Hence the houses are in general occupied by nine or ten persons whom love or friendship has drawn together. If any difference arises (which is but seldom), one of the parties retires to another house, where he thinks of meeting with people more congenial to his temper and disposition.

Every year at the end of harvest, all the men and women above fifty years assemble together in their respective districts; the oldest presides and the youngest is the secretary; those above sixty may attend or not as they please.

Those who have the superintendence of the workshops, the care of the warehouses and granaries, and the distribution of every necessary, being all above fifty years and necessarily present in the assembly, give in their accounts of the produce of the fields, of the workshops, of the consumption, and of what remains in stock; likewise what has been received from and delivered to other districts; all which is laid before the meeting. The secretary makes out a general return, which is carried, with other matters, to the grand assembly of the ancients, in the center of the island, by the oldest man of each district who chooses to go, above sixty; and if all above sixty decline, which they have the privilege of doing, then he or she that is nearest that age is obliged to go. It therefore happens that all the public business of every kind generally falls upon those between fifty and sixty.

Here is no election, and consequently no intriguing for places. Every man or woman, if they live long enough, will succeed in their turn to the duties of administration. None can be excepted but those who are suffering the punishments due to crimes.

Elections for the purpose of choosing men of great abilities or men best acquainted with the interests of nations or who are most conversant in the constitution and laws of the state or those who have much at stake in the country and are supposed on that account to have the greatest interest in its prosperity and welfare are unnecessary here. Every man's stake in the country is equal. The laws are not contained in huge volumes; they are written in the hearts of the Lithconians. Every child of five years can repeat, without book, the whole code: and the abilities required of those whose duty it is to attend the grand assembly are not so great as the ordinary duties of superintending workshops, instructing youth, adjusting differences, etc., require. Besides, those who have a right to attend the grand assembly never think of making new laws: they assemble to fulfill the laws already made, which say, "Let thy neighbors partake of thy abundance, that thou mayest partake of theirs."

In this meeting the accounts from every district are read over, and the wants of one directed to be supplied out of the abundance of another. It is also settled, what quantity of each article of necessity should be produced or manufactured in the districts for the ensuing year, and likewise, what quantity may be exported or imported.

These matters being arranged, every one retires to his home and communicates the result to a meeting of the seniors in his district, who make the necessary regulations for the reception of such articles as they may want, and for the conveyance of the superfluities to the districts requiring them.

This whole country has the appearance of one vast manufactory conducted by one mind; and although it was some time before I could understand the motions of this immense machine, it being so new, and what I had no previous conception of; yet after I had got a perfect comprehension of all its parts, it appeared much more simple than any other form of government in the world.

Labor is performed by every citizen equally. The exceptions are:

    1st. Infants under five years.

    2d. Women in the last three months of their time, and nine months afterward, if they have a happy delivery.

    3d. All sick persons whatever.

    4th. Every man and woman above fifty years, who have, in right of their age, the direction of labor, the instruction of youth, the distribution of goods, and the exercise of the judicial powers.

As to what in other countries is called the legislature, there is no such thing, unless we call the district meetings, which have been already noticed, a legislative body, or the grand assembly of ancients. But both these bodies have more the appearance of an executive deliberating upon the best mode of carrying the principles of justice into execution, than a legislature.

By the fundamental laws or constitution of Lithconia, crimes are divided into two classes—personal and public—personal comprehending everything which may be done to injure the person of another, such as murder, maiming, striking, abusive language, and want of respect or attention. Public crimes are such things as injure the community, as idleness, waste, and negligence, or disobedience to the command of the seniors.

In personal crimes (except murder), he who receives the offense must be the accuser; but for murder or public crimes, any of the elders may—and it is their duty to—accuse. The punishment for murder is death. Every other crime is punished at the discretion of the jurors. For personal crimes the party offended may forgive; but for crimes against the society or public, there is no pardon.

In every district there is a person who is called the *serastedor* or recorder, whose business it is to keep a list of the jurors, and the record of the trials.

Every man and woman in the district, above fifty, is ranged alphabetically in the list of jurors; on each trial fifteen are taken as they stand on the list. Every succeeding trial has five struck off and five added, which makes every juryman stand three trials. In pronouncing a man guilty they must be unanimous; but in affixing the punishment, the majority is sufficient. There is no other judge. The recorder has no further business but to record minutely the proceedings and receive the verdict. The oldest man of the jury pronounces the sentence.

As there is no such thing as debtor and creditor, so there is no property to contend for; consequently no lawyers.

As every trial commences immediately after the accusation, and as no person can possibly escape from justice, so there are no jails, which are the nurseries of vice in barbarous nations. To give instruction and advice being the duty of the seniors, there is no occasion for priests or physicians, and, it being every man's duty to defend his country, there can be no soldiers by profession.

CHAPTER III

The period of life of one man is employed in nearly the same manner as any other. To give the history, then, of one Lithconian, is to describe the manners of the nation.

Children, as has been already observed, until five years old remain with the mother. From their earliest age they are instructed in the principles of equal rights. No such words as *mine* and *thine* are ever heard. *Ours* and *yours* are words which are made use of, when speaking of districts, and even that phraseology is discouraged, and, consequently, not reckoned so polite as to mention the name of the district.

Children are also taught to repeat by memory the short sentences which are the principles of their government—their politics and morals—upon which the verdicts of juries are founded, and which serve them for a constitution and laws. For the Lithconians are not a people that are progressing from a state of nature to what is vulgarly called, civilization; on the contrary, they are progressing from civil society to a state of nature, if they have not already arrived at that state: for in the history of the country, many and surprising revolutions are recorded.

But previous to the revolution which settled the present system of things, there was a wonderful propensity or desire in the men of those times to form constitutions or fundamental laws, which should, like the laws of the Medes and Persians, be unalterable and eternal.

History records no less than ten infallible constitutions, all declared to be founded on the rights of man, in the short period of forty years; each of which, in its turn, gave way to its successor, and was buried in oblivion. After the failure of the first ten, the idea of infallibility was abandoned and the period of their existence was then limited to a certain number of years, when a revisal was to take place. This scheme also failing, it was at last discovered that the will of the people was paramount to every system of laws; and the only good thing produced by this fermentation of opinion and changes of government was that of getting the people into the habit of peaceably expressing their will, and of having it accurately known. This was indeed one great point gained, as it was the first step to every subsequent improvement.

But quitting this digression, let us proceed in showing how the life of a Lithconian is spent. At five he begins to be under the direction of one of the seniors, who instructs him gradually in all the duties of a citizen. His first task is to work at some easy employment one hour a day, and one hour more is employed in learning to read; the rest of his time is spent in play in the open air. These are the duties of the sixth year.

The seventh year, half an hour per day is added to the time required for work; and so on, half an hour every year, till it comes to four per day, which has been found, upon experience, to be sufficient for all the labor of the state.

All labor is performed either in the public workshops or in the fields. At my different stages I made a point of going through as many of the workshops as my time would allow, there being in them always something curious to be seen, if it were nothing but the order and regularity with which everything was conducted; here was always industry, without bustle, hurry, or confusion.

Instead of workshops being mean, cold, and inconvenient, as in other countries, I found them elegant, well finished, and furnished with every convenience.

The first I entered was the joiners' shop of the district. One hundred benches were ranged on each side of the lower apartment. On the second story were as many lathes and benches for turning. Adjoining was a large hall for placing the work when finished, and previous to its distribution. The company of so many young active men at work together makes labor rather a recreation than otherwise, and the senior who has the superintendence of the shop feels delighted at the alacrity and promptness with which his orders are obeyed. No bad debts sour his mind. He rejoices in the ease, independence, and superiority which crown his old age.

But the spinning and weaving far surpassed my conception, both which are performed by the power of water. Cotton, woollen and linen are all spun by machinery, but in different districts. In the fourth part of the island, where cotton grows, there it is spun and wove. In the middle of the country, where there are the best sheep, there wool is manufactured into cloth; and towards the north, where the land is suitable for flax, linen is the staple commodity.

The looms are also moved by the force of water, in which cloth is wove ten yards wide. A great deal of time, attention, and labor is saved in all their manufactories by not having any necessity for weighing the materials upon delivery to the workmen, and entering the same in books. Hence there are no clerks employed, as in other countries, merely to keep men honest: indeed the temptation to steal or embezzle the materials or finished work of the manufactories, is reduced to nothing, since no man can appropriate anything to his own use, or conceal it from the public eye.

From the age of fifteen, he begins to be taught the nicer branches of the arts: at eighteen he is generally considered a finished adept in his profession: he amuses himself with the use of arms; is fond of all kinds of exercise and diversion; attachments take place with some favorite female; and in this manner his life is spent between love, friendship, amusements, and the arts, till he arrives at fifty years, when he undertakes the direction and management of some portion of the national industry, or assists in the instruction of youth and the distribution of justice. At sixty, no social duties are any longer required, though they are not forbidden him; and peace, serenity, and independence accompany him through the remainder of his days.

Such is the life of the Lithconians.

Poverty and riches, as may be easily conceived, are words not to be found in the language. There are no distinctions, but what are founded in nature; no artificial inequalities. When a person's rank in society is mentioned, it is only by the natural distinctions of infancy, youth, manhood, and seniority. Hence the sources of the malevolent passions are dried up. No man looks upon his neighbor's riches with envy, nor with contempt upon another's poverty. The only pride or ambition is in that of excelling in the mechanic arts, or handling with dexterity the tools of a man's profession.

Family pride has long been extinct in this island, there being only one great family which comprehends all the Lithconians. Even national pride is unknown, as they have never been at war for many ages. So their seniors have not had occasion to deceive them by a false estimation of themselves, or degradation of their neighbors. They have no *natural enemies*, as is frequent with barbarous nations. The people of the neighboring islands, or the more remote inhabitants of the continent, are all naturally friends (without being allies) of Lithconia, however they may disagree and quarrel among themselves.

Variety of dress and equipage is also unknown. Every citizen having a certain quantity of clothes distributed to him at stated periods, the whole country appears almost in uniform. The only difference that I could perceive was that some people, better economists than others, had their clothes fresh and clean; consequently had a better appearance. But the women, without exception, are remarkable for economy and neatness in dress. In their headdress I remarked a fanciful variety, which I found to be decorations of their own invention, this being the only part of their dress which is subject to fashion or fancy.

The whole island may be compared to a city spread over a large garden: not a spot can be seen but what is in a high state of cultivation. Every district is divided into as many fields as is thought convenient and advantageous for culture, and numbered from one upwards: each field is entered into a book—on one page the crops and management, and on the other the produce. The management for each succeeding year is determined at the annual meeting of each district; a matter which is easily settled, as the approved routine of crops is always preferred, except in a limited number of fields, reserved for experiments.

The old men who have the superintendence of those fields may, if necessary, demand from the workshops as many hands over and above the ordinary agriculturists, as will execute the intended labor.

Any man who finds out a method of making the soil produce more abundantly may, if he pleases, be exempt from work. He who invents a machine to facilitate or expedite labor has the same reward. Here are no idle disputes about the propriety of introducing machines into practice, no vain fears of depriving the poor of work and of the means of subsistence. Every man is convinced that he who can make useful labor more easy and expeditious, or who makes three grains of wheat to grow where there were only two, augments the number of the enjoyments of every Lithconian, and deserves the applause of his country. Therefore, no country in the world has such excellent tools or perfect machinery as are to be found here. Nothing excites ridicule so much as a man laboring with a bad instrument, or machine out of repair. On the other hand, nothing seems to give a Lithconian so much pleasure as the sight of a dextrous workman using an excellent machine.

The genius of this people has been displayed in nothing so much as in their aqueducts, public baths, canals, and roads, which excel everything of the kind I ever saw: besides, they have a kind of road, peculiar to this country, for the transportation of heavy commodities in those places where a level may be without much difficulty obtained, yet not sufficient water for the supply of a canal. These are first made upon a perfect level, by means of bridges, mounds of earth, or cutting a little from the tops of hills; then a track of cast iron is laid for each wheel, which is concave, and rises above the road about a foot, the carriages having their wheels made convex to fit the track, so that the carriage runs upon a smooth surface, on level ground; and by this means one horse can draw as much as four on the ordinary roads. One-horse carriages are in most use here; but one man will conduct five or six along these roads at those seasons of the year when the interchange of commodities takes place between the districts. At other times the roads are not much occupied, except in leading to and from the fields, or on the seventh day, which, as in other countries, is a day of cessation from labor and, consequently, devoted to pleasure and recreation. It is on those days that they mount their wicker coach, which is impelled forward, not by the power of horses, but by the force of the persons within, who, turning a crank, give motion to the axle-tree and wheels fixed thereon. Along the roads above described, these carriages move with incredible swiftness and are turned at pleasure by the action of a set of reins upon the fore-wheels, which are made as in other four-wheeled carriages.

These roads, though they require a great industry to perfect them at first, are easily kept in repair. I have been told that one of them extends above five hundred miles, besides the smaller branches which run into it.

Here are no idle people employed to collect tolls, nor annuitants living in splendid idleness upon the profits of these tolls; indeed it would be endless to recount the many institutions which are found necessary to barbarous countries to patch up a bad government; but which are not wanting, because unnecessary, in the perfect government of Lithconia. For example: of what use would an infirmary be here, where not only the sick, but those in health, are all maintained, from the public stock—or an insurance company from fire, where no loss can fall upon an individual—or banks, where there are no bills to discount—or hospitals for the poor, where there are no poor—or for orphans, where there are no orphans—or Magdalens, where there are no prostitutes to reform? In a word, there is no charitable institution of any kind. In this country charity remains where nature placed it—in the heart.

Although they are not destitute of religion, I could perceive neither an order of men, nor a place, dedicated to divine worship. That part of the duty of the priesthood which consists in teaching morality is chiefly practiced by the old men, who have made eloquence their favorite pursuit.

The principal theme of their declamation is the evil of idleness and waste of the public stores—from whence (say they) proceeds the judgment of famine, upon the whole land. Indeed their morality is so intimately interwoven with their constitution and laws that a stranger would find it a hard matter to distinguish whether their discourses belonged properly to law or religion—whether it was a priest, or lawyer, that spoke—when it was neither one nor the other. Their religion is the love of order and harmony; their constitution and laws is that order and harmony systemized.

As to the mysterious rites of their religion, which I did not understand, I shall say nothing, only that they appeared to consist chiefly of vocal and instrumental music and dancing, in which every person joined, and was always performed in the open air. Every instrument was also equally sacred. The organ has no peculiar privileges here. Stringed instruments have the preference of wind instruments, in general, because the performer can play and sing at the same time; for without a vocal accompaniment, instrumental, in the opinion of the Lithconians, is only half music. When they play in concert, which they sometimes do, with a thousand voices and instruments, it is always some studied piece adapted to the occasion —the grandeur and harmony of which would astonish an inhabitant of the barbarous nations of Europe, unaccustomed as they are to such concerts. But when an individual performs, it is always an extempore piece, except when they are either learning to play, or practicing for the public festivals; for it would be deemed puerile to amuse themselves with the lessons even of the greatest masters. The subject of these extempore pieces is always love, or religion, or more properly devotion; for they seem to have no idea of any other subject being adapted for music; and therefore they have no hunting, historical, drinking or war songs; nevertheless beautiful descriptions of nature are not wanting in their songs of love. Music may be considered here as a principal branch of liberal education;

if the word *liberal* be a proper expression where a thing is rather taken than bestowed.

Education, or instruction, is bestowed or held out to every member of the community alike; but some, as in every other country, not having so great a genius, talent or capacity for knowledge as others, will not imbibe so great a quantity.

Painting and the lovers of that sublime art are held in high estimation. . . .

There are also few young men or women of bright parts but who are taught the art of printing, there being one printing-press to each district, with a sufficient number of types of various founts. Every person is at liberty to use them under the direction of a senior, and to throw off a limited number of sheets, at spare hours, of any piece of his own production; but if the work be judged of sufficient importance by the grand assembly, and time can be spared from the necessary labors of the state, it is then ordered that a certain number of copies be printed in the ordinary time of labor, and distributed to the districts.

It has been already observed, that there are in Lithconia no soldiers by profession; but it must also be observed, that every man is a defender of his country, and obliged to learn the art of acting in the field together, as soldiers in other countries. . . .

CHAPTER VIII

We shall now hasten to that part of the history which gives an account of the revolutions which led them to the genuine system of property. It appears, as has been already observed, that for many thousands of years there had been always men of superior talents, who considered all the evils with which they saw themselves surrounded had certainly their origin in the folly of human institutions; and that the remedy was within the powers of human reason, if it could only be exerted to that end. But these men were continually watched and persecuted by the privileged classes above mentioned; and particularly, by the class of deceivers, who were urged on by the robbers and abetted by the swindlers, etc.

Notwithstanding the intelligent class saw the pernicious tendency of the others, their artillery was directed only against the deceivers. By this means the other classes, not seeing themselves attacked, either stood neutral or joined the intelligent class. The deceivers, thus abandoned, soon lost their influence, and the lies by which they had imposed upon mankind were every day detected. No sooner was the power of the deceivers abridged and investigation laid open in some measure to the people, than they began to suspect the class of public robbers; and the men of intelligence, seeing the people on their side, took courage, called in question their right of plunder; and, what was fortunate for them was that the murderers took part against the robbers, and their power was also very much curtailed, though the class still had an existence, and continued to commit great depredations on the community. . . .

. . . It was soon discovered that a great portion of the evils of which mankind complain lurked under the laws, unperceived and unquestioned by reason of the sacred character they had assumed. Reason would have nothing sacred; she now entered boldly into the sanctuary of the law, as she had before done into the sanctuary of the deceivers. Every law which militated against the eternal principles of justice and reason was proscribed, and it was thought better to have no rule of conduct than one which admitted uncertainty or doubt; and it was founded upon this principle, that where there is no law there is no transgression. Jurors began to give in their verdict in these words, "The law is silent"; or, when the first lawyers of the country discovered a diversity of opinion by long harangues and numerous quotations, the jury was sure to bring in a verdict of, "The law is obscure," from which verdict no judge could pass a sentence of punishment. Such conduct frequently occurring among rational jurors had two good effects: first, to make legislators more attentive and correct; and second, to banish from the bar that host of swindlers who had been so long fanning the flames of discord and living on the contentions of their fellow citizens. It was not long after the class of swindlers had been swept from the courts of justice and the legislators had simplified the laws, before the inutility of the judges themselves was apparent, and jurors, as has been mentioned in the first part of this work, were found adequate to all the purposes of distributive justice.

In those days it seemed to be the first object in the attention of intelligent men to endeavor, with all their might, to bring law and justice into union; and the genuine system of property began to be spoken of, as no visionary phantom, but as a good, which might be realized. Philosophers mentioned it in terms of approbation, and the people listened with attention: but the class of idlers, which was the only formidable class that remained, was its bitter and avowed enemies.

Every man of reflection saw that a revolution in the system of property of such magnitude could not be accomplished without great difficulty and hazarding the peace of society, and the wisest were puzzled to find an opening that would admit an entering wedge. But when men are zealous in a cause and never lose sight of the darling object, occasions will present themselves which would otherwise be overlooked, and which the attentive and intelligent observer seizes with avidity. When, by the force of the elective principle, the people had placed men of intelligence, their steady friends, into the legislature, it became a maxim that as long as moral evil existed, a government could not be called the best possible; it was presumable that there was still occasion for the exertion of his faculties, and that it was folly to look beyond the moon for remedies which, if infinite wisdom rules on high, must be placed within his grasp.

The evil which called forth the attention of the men of those times, and produced considerable agitation, was the care society as such ought to take of the aged, the lunatic, the widow, orphan, illegitimate children and their mothers, and finally, to put an end to prostitution, and the diseases which accompany it. It was proposed that an adequate provision should be made, by law, for people reduced to the above circumstances; and the idlers, fearing that the burden should principally fall on this class, wished to have no alteration or innovations upon the ancient practice, or, if anything was done, it should be by a tax that should operate equally upon the citizens; and as for the mothers of illegitimate children and their offspring, and the whole host of prostitutes and their encouragers, nothing but the severest punishment, said they, could put a stop to the growing evil, which, it is true, had increased to an alarming degree, ever since the threatenings of eternal punishment had ceased with the class of deceivers.

On the contrary, it was insisted on, by the intelligent, that society were bound to relieve every kind of distress brought on by the operations of nature; that getting children was an irresistible dictate of nature and ought not to be held as a crime or subject to punishment; that prostitution was an excrescence from a bad law, which would perish when the law which gave it being ceased to exist: and in order to find a steppingstone by which the river might be crossed, it was proposed, instead of a tax, that the laws of descent should be altered, and the benefits arising therefrom extended to those objects of what was then called "charity." In a word, the law of descent was confined to the descendant in a right line, and those of a collateral branch were cut off from the succession.

It was therefore enacted that all real and personal estates which had no heirs in a right line should be vested in the nation for the benefit of that description of people above enumerated, whom the ancient institutions had abandoned to chance, to infamy, or at best, to a miserable and scanty subsistence.

The natural operation of this law, in a short time, made an ample provision for those who had before been the outcasts of society.

It had also that effect which was foreseen by the promoters of it, namely, to prevent young women of no fortune from entering into the state of matrimony. They saw that themselves and their off-spring would be treated with more care and attention from that fund than they possibly could be by the industry of the best man that ever existed. From that moment there were few marriages, except among the rich; so that while the funds were increasing, the objects which it was destined to support were increasing also.

At the commencement of this institution, these bastards were put apprentices to mechanical arts, at the age of fifteen; at twenty-one a handsome sum was bestowed on them to begin the world; but, as it frequently happened that these young people saw their children educated under the same institution, and whatever fortunes they might gain in life naturally, or rather lawfully, descended to the same fund, they procured a law by which they were permitted to remain attached to the institution: from this period that part of the community who possessed separate property were every year diminishing in number, and they saw themselves subjected to a thousand cares and anxieties from which those who lived in common were totally exempt; while at the same time all the riches and property of the nation were running with a rapid current into the aggregate fund.

This state of society is described by the historians as being very stormy and factious; when the two parties became nearly balanced, the separate-property men, who still had the government in their hands, and being pressed for money, as all such governments are, proposed to seize upon the aggregate property, and sell it, as they said, for the benefit of the nation. But the equal-right men, who had labored indefatigably to render the aggregate fund beneficial to those whom the law had placed under its protection, were convinced that it would be better for mankind, and produce a greater sum of happiness, if all the property in the community were under like regulations; and many men of intelligence, though possessed of great fortunes, thought it to their advantage to sink it in the aggregate fund rather than expose their children to the caprice of fortune.

These contentions continued for many years. In the meanwhile the families possessing separate property were growing fewer in number: they saw themselves loaded with a thousand anxieties, from which those who lived under the genuine system of property were totally exempt. Pride, however, for a long time, prevented them from joining the institution, and the same pride pushed on the society to take every step which should render the members of it comfortable and happy.

To give retirement and peace to the aged, every person after the age of sixty was exempted from duty: and to give wisdom and experience to their councils, the principle of election was laid aside for that of seniority, which had an affect not at first foreseen, that of producing almost perfect unanimity.

30

New Britain

*A Narrative of a Journey by Mr. Ellis to a Country So Called
by Its Inhabitants, Discovered in the Vast Plain of the
Missouri in North America and Inhabited by a People of
British Origin Who Lived Under an Equitable System
of Society Productive of Peculiar Independence and
Happiness: Also, Some Account of Their
Constitution, Customs, and Philosophical
Opinions; Together With a Brief Sketch of
Their History From the Time of Their Departure
From Great Britain "Through the distorting glass of
Prejudice All nature seems awry; and but its own
Wide-warp'd creations straight: but Reason's eye
Beholds in every line of nature—truth, Immortal truth;
and sees a God in all."*

G. A. Ellis

—NEW BRITISH POEM

*London
1820*

The author of this unique utopia, apparently an Englishman, states in his "Preface" that he is not "a literary man," and apologizes for his style. Furthermore, he excuses the "many marks of haste in the preparation of it for the press" on the ground of his "want of adequate leisure." Apart from these statements, nothing has been discovered about him by the present editor.

The only edition of *New Britain,* a volume of 340 pages, was published in London in 1820 by W. Simpkin and R. Marshall. It shows the influence of the Romantic attitude toward Nature, for the author upholds the simple, natural life of virtue, though not as primitivistic a one as that of the "good savage." Ellis adheres to the Wordsworthian doctrine that to obey Nature is to obey God. Admittedly Nature has its cruel side, its storms, wild beasts, and volcanoes; but these are exceptional. Basically Nature is good, well-ordered, and divinely planned. It is expressive of the Reason, and Reason, likewise, is to be found in the nature of man.

Nevertheless Ellis recognizes that the nature of man has its faults: there is in man a dangerous selfish principle, which is the source of most human evils. The utopia is, in essence, a scheme for controlling that selfishness through brotherly cooperation, through laws which forbid a man to own more land or other resources than he can use, and through practice of a clean, simple life. Though in an American setting, the life of the New Britons is not radically different from that of More's Utopians. It could almost be called Utopian life modernized in terms of 1820, except that a degree of private property remains, and voluntary cooperativeness rather than communism is given the chief stress. The society described is like a huge, democratic, hospitable, lower-middle-class family. The units in it resemble a medieval village of yeomen without overlords or a hierarchical church: each man has his own farm and his own trade. As far as possible, each unit, whether family, county, or some other division, is self-sustaining.

Limitation on ownership is not the only means used to curb the selfish principle in man; education and the practice of a greatly decentralized democracy also conduce to the restraint of human selfishness. The absence of money, servants, and undue luxury; the rigid control of population, and the refusal to engage in commerce, all militate further against any tendency to personal aggrandizement. Ellis's view is that "as the only rational beings on earth, men ought to be the happiest; at least they ought to be the freest from corporeal evils, and still more so from those that are mutually inflicted." The intention of the institutions and regulations of New Britain is, therefore, "to bring mankind as near as we possibly can to that state in which they would be if they were sufficiently virtuous to live in so-

ciety without laws." As one of his characters, Sir George, observes
to a group of New Britons, "In other words, you are philosophers and
will not be kings: you are wise and do not need them." The New
Britons avoid that "prolific and inexhaustible source of uneasiness, the
perpetual striving to surpass our neighbors in the accumulation of
wealth and to possess many times more of the goods of life than
we can possibly enjoy. . . . Instead of striving for an unjust share
of what God hath given to all, and in place of continual anxiety
about possessions and pecuniary matters, we have a perfect certainty
of our full share of all that is needful to happiness, to the end of
life, and to . . . all generations while they have the wisdom and
virtue to live according to the dictates of reason and the rules of
justice."

The extracts given below give a fairly full picture of Ellis's utopia
and its constitution. In the other chapters of his book he gives lengthy
accounts of the military establishment and the religious opinions
of the New Britons. The military organization is, of course, a popular, nonaggressive one. Religious toleration prevails, the population
being about equally divided between Christians and deists. Free,
orderly discussion of religion is permitted in the interests of truth,
but the Christians believe it their duty to follow the rules of Jesus
simply, without comment, and without disputation. However, Ellis
includes a long explanation of the deists' belief in God and immortality, the variant views on immateriality and materiality, and the
different doctrines on the nature of the soul. These are followed by
an account of New British opinions on the means of sensation, the
nature of the will, and the attributes of the Deity, and by some indication of progress in mechanical improvements and a discussion of
teachings concerning the effect of atmospheric pressure upon evapo-
ration. The work concludes with an abstract of New British history
from the original migration in the time of Henry VIII, and a collection of miscellaneous observations.

New Britain

[We set sail from England in the company of Mr. and Mrs. Herbert-
son and their little daughter, and arrived in New York. There Sir
George and I and the Herbertsons hired a light wagon and commenced our journey west on April 7, 1818. "It would be tedious to
those who have read accounts of the abundant fare, the inconveniences, and the indelicacy of manners of most of the American inns,

to repeat such particulars." We continued west for eight days to the Ouisconsing river, passed it, and went north. For some days we were forced to halt on the banks of a swollen river where we were joined by an old Indian and a young one who was "an Apollo in symmetry" and "a Mercury in agility." In due time two sisters of the latter appeared, one of them being more beautiful "than any of the representations of Venus I ever saw." We successfully forded this and other streams and continued on through the plain of the Missouri. On the far side of it, we climbed a mound and discovered houses and cultivated country. We had arrived at New Britain.]

. . . Sir George, like me, had been surprised at not seeing or coming to any large towns; but now that we could see a considerable distance all round us, without observing one, Sir George said to Mr. T—— "Pray how far are we to travel before we come to one of your large towns?" Mr. T——, replying as follows, astonished us both. "We have not a single large town, of the description you inquire for, in the whole nation. It is composed entirely of villages in the manner you have seen; a number of these form a division; an uncertain number of these divisions, forming as nearly as possible a large square, compose a county; a number of counties classed so as to be most compact, form a district; and these districts, which are now increased to seven, compose our country. We consider it wise to live upon the spot where our necessaries of life are produced; and not to congregate in great cities, and thus have to fetch them from a distance. We by this, prevent a few from rising into improper consequence, and the many from sinking into servility; the inevitable result of their different employments in such large collections of men, which appear to us to be large masses of human corruption. We also thus prevent that degradation of moral character, which would be alike despicable in those who would be so unjust as to grasp at more than what is needful of property or power, and in those who would be mean enough to submit to servility, or to the privation of any part of their just and equal rights. We read attentively the histories of other nations; and we consider that we have discovered the true source of all their misfortunes, collectively and individually, to be the love of unreasonable wealth and power. Be not then surprised that we most determinedly avoid in ourselves, and prevent in others, these, as the greatest evils, which the people of other countries eagerly pursue as their greatest good."

There was a simplicity of eloquence in his recital of this account, which evidently showed it to be the general sentiment, not Mr. T——'s particular view of a proper state of society. Sir George observed, "There is in this plan of society, so widely different from every other which I have known or read of, a principle productive of general happiness beyond any of them. It must certainly," said he, "prevent that poverty, vice, and misery, so prevalent in other countries; but it cannot lead individuals to those possessions which give the relative superiority attainable in them."

Our companion replied, "We are educated to despise every thing which can, in the remotest manner, injure another. Where a man succeeds in this way, were he to think justly, he could not be happy in the possession of that which degraded, or injured his brethren: nor is he happy: he has only heaped up cares and anxieties to himself, and injustice upon his neighbor. We have none of those corroding cases, which wear down, alike, the pursuers and the possessors of wealth and power."

Sir George said, "Do all your countrymen hold opinions like these? Do they all despise wealth and power?"

Mr. T—— replied, "We all with one accord, from the knowledge that it is for the good of all, despise what you call wealth. You have seen the source from whence I draw the comforts and conveniences of life; in this respect the greatest man in the country and I are equals. As to power, we think it honorable to be able to advise or guide others in difficulties or dangers which may possibly occur; but to endeavor to attain it by sinister means, or by biasing the free suffrages of our neighbors, or when attained, to hold, or strain it beyond the law, or justice, would be attended with inexpiable disgrace; a disgrace which no wise man would put himself in danger of incurring for any consideration."

Sir George, after a pause of astonishment, said, "Indeed you are an extraordinary people! In our country, which ranks with the first in Europe for talents and justice, our greatest men pursue with avidity both power and wealth."

Our companion replied, "Such men may be, and no doubt are, men of great knowledge and talents; but they permit the love of wealth and power to impede their view; they thus become shortsighted, and are not wise; real wisdom would prefer justice, which is true honor, freedom from care, and the general welfare, to this unreal good."

Our intelligent friend now left us awhile to speak to a person in the village through which we were passing. Mr. H—— looked round upon us all and said, "Now have I deceived you?" "Deceived us," said I, repeating his words, and turning to Sir George, and addressing myself to him, "You are now I hope convinced that Europeans have not attained the summit of possible civilization." He replied, "I am astonished at what I see and hear; yet my judgment tells me that it is but the result to be reasonably expected from their customs and manners. We have found a people where everyone is an agriculturist, and also a useful mechanic or professional man; yet as careless of accumulation as the savages. We see them, on the borders of unappropriated forests and savannahs, inclosing only the small necessary portion of land, where others would have appropriated large domains. I am now almost convinced there may have been a golden age; I am fully persuaded there may be one; it rests with man; let reason reign, and the work is done: there is no need to go through the intermediate ones of brass and silver. But these people despise gold in the light in which Europeans value it; yet, to Europeans, to whom it gives so many ideas of comparison, it is a good mean for description of the content and happiness of this people; while iron, of which fetters are made, accords well with the cares and miseries of the states we have left behind us. . . ."

Sir George inquired why they did not appropriate, to each, larger portions of land than those attached to their houses, having so extensive a country before them?

Our host replied, "From serious and attentive investigation of what contributes to happiness, we have determined not to possess more land than the quantity requisite for comfortable subsistence; and with our sense of what is productive of happiness, no individual will be troubled with more than the small portions which you see attached to our dwellings. Neither with our ideas of good policy, will we allow of any innovation upon this principle of moderation and equity; as such innovation would most certainly induce a state of society which would render uncertain the means of support to some of its members. We do not consider it just for a man to acquire all he can: such conduct would tend to deprive his neighbors of their rights, and to enslave his equals. Prevailing luxury and general happiness are the opposing scales of human life."

We asked our host how it was, that in a country where we had not seen a single shop for the sale of anything, we saw him surrounded with every convenience of life, and numerous elegancies?

He said, "It is thus: we assign about four hours every weekday to labor; less than half of this, upon an average, suffices for our agriculture and gardening; the remainder of this time, everyone, without exception, applies to some trade or useful employment, which is the source of what you see; and also of one of the greatest pleasures of life, that of reciprocal presents, and marks of attachment. Every village contains almost every useful business among its inhabitants; and villages, divisions, counties, and even districts, as well as individuals, are continually giving and receiving the various surplus of their industry, arising from both their labor and possessions. Having no money, we cannot hoard large possessions in a small compass; and everyone finds, that to be beloved and esteemed, or to have many conveniences, he must perform his part in this commerce of kindness; idleness justly tends to privation."

"To give you an idea of the manner in which these things are done, I will detail an instance; my neighbor on the left is a tanner, and his son, who continues with him, adds to tanning the business of a currier; all the hides and skins which the village produces are taken to his tanyard by himself or others; also, all the bark which we can strip from our trees is preserved and taken there; all these he receives without any conditions, except those of public utility. He tans or dresses this stock. His son, and another person, who is a harness maker, as well as a currier, prepare it for the use of the shoemakers and others. Shoes being a necessary of great consumption, we have four shoemakers in this village, besides the assistance of their youth, or others who are learning the business. All this way, you perceive, there is neither barter, nor money passing between the parties; the shoes are as much a common stock as the skins, hides, and bark, and are distributed to those who want them. In return, the tanner, the currier, and the shoemakers receive unconditionally the aid of the smith, the carpenter, and the mason; have their wool woven, their hats made, their domestic utensils of every description provided; their watches made or repaired by the watchmakers; muskets, etc., by the gunmaker; books, by the printers; and, in this manner, every other thing needful or desirable, in the same proportion as they produce theirs. It has become proverbial here, that a man has fewest of the things produced by his own business; and scarcely anyone reserves the best for himself."

Sir George inquired if they made no distinction in employments. "Are there," said he, "none that are considered more respectable than others?"

Our entertainer answered: "Whatever it is necessary for men to do for the general good is accounted equally honorable, or is rather not accounted of at all, as we have no distinction. There is no disgrace in any man doing what someone must do. . . ."

We spent the evening in making and answering inquiries. In the morning, when we were about to proceed, we recollected it was Sunday, and therefore stayed where we were. We passed the day as they did, in reading, having the Bible and other books provided for us; but no remarks were made, or questions asked us. There was, in the conduct of all whom we saw, a silent reverential awe of the Great Author of all, in which each seemed to say to his fellow men— "Approach unmolested in thy own way. . . ."

[Sir George asked how and why the New Britains kept up to date in military matters. Our guide replied that groups of one or two hundred men frequently visited the United States.] They have thus full opportunity to obtain all the new information on every subject; to purchase all the new books on the military, and every other science, whether English or American; and also any production worth the carriage, in general literature. For these purposes they are provided with plenty of silver from that which our lead mines yield, which they dispose of for dollars to be more convenient. They also examine every new discovery in mechanism, observe the state of military discipline, and every other improvement, with a view to improvement at home. They also purchase series of English and American newspapers; which are here publicly read and commented upon, and which form the most powerful and persuasive negative lessons for contentment with our own state that could possibly be devised. "No man," say those travelers, "would wish to exchange his state of life, when he sees the ignorance of the greater part, or the care and anxiety which pervade the whole of the Americans; their happiest circumstances of life, when viewed in all their bearings, are far beneath the level of ours." To the second part of the question he answered, "We in some measure may be considered to play at soldiers; it is an amusement, and we perform it in the best way we are able; yet we consider it an important duty, for when we read of the mad freaks of ambition which disgrace mankind, both as performers and spectators of the sanguinary scenes, they convince us that we know not how soon we may be attacked; and we, therefore, do not think it prudent to have to learn the art of self-defense when we should be defending ourselves. We shall never be the aggressors, but we fear no power that can be brought against us. . . ."

. . . We found the chief president to be a man of extraordinary mind.

Sir George asked him if it was usual with all their presidents to cultivate their own land, or that attached to the house of the presidency. He replied, "All our people consider health as one of the first blessings of life, and that nothing contributes so much to its preservation as moderate field labor, which to each man is not more than two hours a day. The seven district presidents and the chief president are exempt during the year of their presidency from their other employments, on account of their leaving their homes for the year. On this account also, those who have not a son able to cultivate their land at home have it cultivated by their neighbors."

We expressed a desire to understand their form of government, which appeared to be carried on so completely without state, and almost without trouble.

The president said . . . , "You will find it merely the framework of a government, ready to be put together at an hour's notice, in case of necessity, not one of those ponderous machines which disgrace most of the countries of the world and wear down their people in supplying the moving power."

. . . The village (for it is only a village where the seat of government is) is built and arranged in the same way as those already described. The Stranger's House is much larger than that of the other villages; as it is expected that more strangers will come here, than to most other places; and it is thought merely hospitable to provide them with an independent residence during their stay, in case they should prefer it to residing with any of the villagers. There is in the traveler's house of this village separate accommodation for seven families.

The next peculiarity we noticed was, a large range of storehouses of immense capacity, which are filled with all kinds of public stores, including arms, provisions, corn, and all sorts of useful articles. These are mostly kept filled from the surplus of districts and counties, and are drawn upon by the neighborhood only when required by the extra consumption caused by large or general meetings of the presidents of counties and divisions. We understood it had been once proposed to build suitable houses of accommodation for the representatives, on those occasions, but it was overruled on a general petition of all the inhabitants of the villages in the neighborhood, praying not to be deprived of the opportunity of exercising their hospitality, and stating that it must be more comfortable for the representatives to accept of their attentions at their own houses than to have to accommodate themselves, even with all the assistance they could give them by the plan proposed.

The house of government is a beautiful building of white marble. The external appearance is plain, but noble, something like the body of St. Paul's, London, but wider, and not so high. It is an oblong square, with three principal entrances, which lead to the three houses of assembly. One is for the chief president and the presidents of the districts, another for the representatives of counties, and the other, the central one, and which is much the largest, for the representatives of divisions: the presidents of counties or divisions are also their representatives. It contains also several subordinate offices, and repositories for records and other valuable writings belonging to the state. Copies of all writings of importance are also kept in the government houses of each of the districts.

This village has also its town-house, in which are the schools, the libraries, the hall for the village business, etc., like all the others. I have been the more particular in describing this village, as its variations from other villages are only its public buildings, and these are upon the same plan, on a larger scale, as the public buildings of districts, counties, and divisions; each of which has them, for the particular business or stores of each district, county or division; but with only one house of assembly for the district or county, as all meet together for the consideration of local business; and the divisions have only the town-house of the village for their house of assembly.

A little after one we returned to dinner. . . . Sir George, soon after the ladies had retired, reminded the president of his promise. . . .

"Our government," said he, "emanates from the whole people. They are the solid rock, upon which all power is founded; and in which its chief, and inferior fountains, have their source. We do not say, like the political writers of many countries, that when the fountain is polluted, the streams which flow from it must also be impure; but, that while this primary rock retains its strong adhesive powers of reason and justice, the fountains and the streams must be pure; or, if rendered turbid by incidental obstructions, they would soon run themselves clear in the channels of a sound country; and that nothing less than the loss of firmness in the rock itself can destroy or materially affect this purity. If this rock continues firm, all other evils are partial; a failure in this only would be irremediable; it would be of no use to alter the course of the stream, if the whole country were to become unsound. To prevent this greatest of all political evils, we educate with the greatest care every inhabitant of the country; we ingraft upon all, without the least distinction, all the knowledge we can communicate, or they receive; concluding, from the fullest persuasion, that a thorough understanding of what is just and right is the true and best method of maintaining just and free institutions. We consider ignorance as the prolific parent of evil in human life, and that from it arise all the ills which men are continually heaping upon each other: among the chief of which is, the unjust and inordinate desire of property and power. We firmly believe that all our happiness depends upon preventing the entrance into our country of both the parent and the offspring. As a free people we formed a constitution for ourselves, and thereby gave ourselves a government; when a governor gives a constitution to a people, it is making an ostentatious display of generosity in giving back only a part of their own. I have, as well as I am able, described to you, what we judge to be the true source of all just power; and I will now endeavor to explain how we guide it to a point, or rather direct it in one stream, in cases of necessity. This leads me to give you a brief account of our constitution.

"A decree of the people, as a principle and part of the constitution, commands our executive government to consist of a chief president of the country, a president of each district, a president of each county, a president of each division, and a magistrate for each village; who are every one elected annually, by a simple majority of votes, and their election takes place a year in advance; none of whom can be elected to fill the same situation till after an interval of two years. As to subordinate officers, all who are capable of the duty required may be called upon for their assistance in time of need. The members of the executive have no power, separately or collectively, to increase or diminish their own authority or that of any part of them. They are perfectly subordinate to the principles of the constitution, by which their offices were created, and to the primary laws. The presidents assemble twice every year at the government house for public business: the chief president and the district presidents in one house of assembly, the county presidents in the second, and the division presidents in the third. I believe that it has before been mentioned to you that the presidents of counties and divisions are also the representatives of their respective counties and divisions. These members of the executive have, when collected in assemblies, the power of legislation, as it respects laws explanatory or declaratory of the primary laws; and in all other matters which do not interfere with, or infringe upon, the principles of the constitution, or the primary laws. There is a district house of assembly in every one of the seven districts, in which the president of the district and the presidents of the counties of the district meet quarterly in assembly upon district business; there is a house of assembly in every county, in which the president of the county and the presidents of the divisions of the county assemble quarterly on county business; and the hall of the village, in which the division president resides, or any other of the village halls in the division, which may be thought more convenient, is the house of assembly for the meeting quarterly, or oftener, of the division president and the village magistrates, for the business of the division. Every village magistrate, president of a division, president of a county, or president of a district, must be respectively inhabitants of the village, division, county, or district, for which they are elected.

"Every house has a vote; the right of voting belongs to the father, or to the head of the family; where there is no father, and the mother survives, the right devolves upon her; and where both the parents are dead, and the house is still occupied by the family, the eldest son has the right, if he be above the age of twenty-one years: it is only on the failure of all these, that any family is without a vote. The votes of every village, whether for their own magistrate, the president of the division, of the county, the district, or the chief president, are given in the village hall. In elections for divisions, the magistrate of each village, in their respective divisions, takes up the votes of the village to the division-house, and adds them to the poll, with the name of the village and the number of each candidate. In elections for counties, the presidents of divisions receive the votes from the several village magistrates, and take them up to the county-house, and add them to the poll. In elections for districts, the presidents of counties receive the votes from the presidents of divisions, who have received them from the village magistrates, and add them to the poll at the district-house. And, in like manner, at the election of the chief president, the magistrates of villages give in the votes of their respective villages, to the presidents of the divisions, who give those of their divisions to the presidents of the counties; who give those of the counties to the presidents of the districts; who also take those of the districts to the government-house. The result of the election is declared in all these elections by the presidents who last receive the votes. The presidents of divisions and counties are also the representatives of divisions and counties, in their respective assemblies.

"We thus prevent the bustle and inconvenience of numerous meetings, and the trouble of voters going from home. To prevent the possibility of fraud, the result of every election above that of a village magistrate is published. . . .

"The three houses of assembly enact laws for all which may be required between man and man; for all internal regulations between districts, divisions, and villages, for all concerns which are local, and for all which are termed moral laws. They also regulate the detail of those laws which are primary or constitutional; such being enactments by the whole people, and which cannot be altered but by the people, in the manner I shall describe. I shall only first observe, that any enactment may have its origin with any one in any of the three houses of assembly, by motion; or by memorial from any individual or number of individuals not in office. These memorials or proposals become laws after passing the three legislative powers and the president in three readings (the chief president attends the readings and debates, but does not join them, in the house of the district presidents); and they may become part of the constitution by passing the legislative assemblies, as I have just mentioned, and being afterwards approved by the people, demonstrated by four-fifths of the votes of the whole.

"I hope I have made myself understood, that the plan of our constitution is that the members of the three houses of representatives, and the chief president, as already detailed (who are annually elected by the people), cannot add to, or diminish their own power, or the power of each other, either jointly or separately. That any act of the whole respecting each other, or the whole of them, would be null and void, and of no effect. And that any alteration in their power, separately or together, must arise from a majority of four-fifths of the votes of the whole people; as this law of the constitution was first enacted.

"It is also a part of the constitution, that every officer of the public, from the chief president to the village magistrate, is elected a year in advance; that is, we who are now in office, through every gradation, had all our successors for the ensuing year elected before we came into office; and before we leave it, each must preside at the election of a successor for his successor. We consider this to have many very important advantages beside that of preventing confusion. No man can succeed to the same office again, till two years have elapsed from the time of his going out of it. In cases of improper or suspicious conduct, the people can remove any officer in the country: the power that makes can abrogate.

"It is necessary to remark, that any alteration in the constitution, or in the primary laws, which are equally sacred, and in fact, are part of the constitution, as they cannot be altered or annulled but by the same power which can alter or abolish it, must be by the suffrages of four-fifths of the whole people entitled to vote: in these cases, none who are entitled, as before described, to a vote are allowed to stand neuter. So tenacious are we of keeping entire a constitution and laws which are very generally esteemed by us, the best and happiest we can devise. All other, or what may be called common elections, are decided by simple majority.

"In addition to the principles of the constitution, of which I have recited some of the leading ones, the laws which we call primary or constitutional are—

"1st. It is enacted that all land taken into cultivation, or occupied, by the people of New Britain, shall be divided into lots or portions, each of dimensions which must be decided by its quality, equal to the production of the necessaries and the comforts of life for a family. That on each portion, there shall be a house erected, of the usual size of those built throughout the country, of the materials which the neighborhood affords, by common effort and mutual assistance. That the surplus produce from the portions, where the family is small and does not consume it, be stored for the public use, to form a general store throughout the country of a full year's stock beforehand, to meet incidental wants and to guard against the possibility of famine. This arrangement is just and necessary, as the wants of all families will vary; almost everyone will at one time have to spare and will at another time have need of all their produce; and what is for the security and good of the whole, all must support. It is therefore unjust and unlawful for anyone to neglect making his portion productive to the utmost of his power because he may not want the whole produce for his own use. That system which brings a portion of the labor of youth to the assistance of age, or the surplus of all to the relief of the necessities of others, is the securest of all riches; it forms an unfailing resource for all.

"2nd. Justice is the foundation virtue upon which every other virtue must be erected. It is not just for individuals to acquire by power or address all that may be thus acquired (though the common practice of almost all nations), as it leads inevitably to tyranny and slavery, which are alike inconsistent with justice. It is therefore enacted that every man, having attained the age or time at which the commonweal permits his settling in life, that of marrying, shall have one house with its portion of land in his own right; but on no account or consideration whatever, more than one.

"3rd. It is enacted that every man shall cultivate his own portion and shall bring up his children to the practice of cultivation; and that every one shall also learn and practice some useful business for the general comfort and convenience, and shall bring up his children in the same practice. That no one shall have or possess a slave or slaves; or shall have a servant or servants, hired or otherwise, male, or female; or shall permit himself or herself to be hired as a servant; but that all shall labor for, and assist each other, in cases of need, as equals and brethren: as God created all mankind.

"4th. It is enacted that no money of any kind, or note for money, be coined or made current in New Britain; that no metal in bars, pieces, or otherwise, or any gems or precious stones be used as a medium of exchange or of valuing any commodity or product of industry; such marks of value being convenient for accumulation, which produces tyranny and slavery; but that all the produce of the time usually allotted to labor be given and received as a common stock. That time being the real and only valuable brought by man to the social stock, where all give an equal portion of it, all are equally entitled, whatever be their particular production. If any should refuse to give the usual portion of their time for the comfort and convenience of all, they are not entitled to receive from the common stock as a right, but may have their wants supplied by individuals in the way of charity, if any should be inclined thus to encourage the breakers of the law and the idle.

"5th. That, as it is neither good for the mental nor bodily health of man, to live in continual labor; and as no acquisition of decoration in dress or furniture can be an adequate compensation for so great a sacrifice, it is enacted that the labor of man be confined within two hours a day, for the cultivation of his land and the management of his stock, as absolutely necessary; and that it be confined within two hours more a day, for the production of needful comforts and conveniences, by means of the business or businesses he may understand: that this be considered as an average, as in cases of absolute need the time may be extended to meet the necessity. And it is understood that as knowledge is requisite to understand what is just in society before we can effectually support it, that no consideration shall allow the spirit of this enactment to be departed from; but that the remaining part of the six days allotted to labor, after the four hours of each before specified, be at the disposal of everyone, for the attainment and communication of knowledge, the performance of domestic duties, and for healthful exercises.

"6th. It is enacted that every village throughout the country, that is or may be erected, shall have a village-house, containing four schoolrooms; three libraries, for morality, science, and amusement; a room, or rooms, for philosophical instruments; rooms for depositing machinery useful for building, models, and the village stores; and a hall for the transaction of its public business. That every village is entitled for its library to a copy of every work produced or reprinted in the country, as soon as copies can be sufficiently multiplied by those who make printing their business. That these libraries be, and are, the equal right of everyone. That thus, all the knowledge of the country may be equally and generally diffused throughout it; all its genius and talent educed for the common good; and that those who have only the usual share of talent may have it cultivated and thereby expanded to its utmost capability: that ignorance, the parent of injustice, and its attendant evils, may be banished the land.

"7th. It is enacted that every child, both male and female, be educated publicly. That there be in every village two schools for the males and two for the females; the first schools for each sex to be appropriated to those from five to eleven years of age, and the second to those from eleven to the completion of sixteen. From sixteen to the completion of eighteen years of age, the youth of each sex to be assistant teachers; at once to benefit others and themselves and to fix upon their minds what they have learned. That it is the duty of every adult, male and female, to assist in this most important of all duties; and that they do it alternately; and in such numbers, and to those classes, as may best render their attention efficient. And it is further enacted that the three assemblies of the country and the chief president do make a declaratory law or laws for the particular regulations in this matter, which may be now or hereafter required.

"8th. It is enacted, to prevent the introduction of want and distress and their attendant evils into the country, that none shall marry till they have in possession in their own right, by age and rotation, a house and portion for their occupation. That as, in the old settled parts of the country, this will always lay a restraint and be a cause of delay for some years to all, it is binding equally upon all and everyone; and that no deviation from this law, which is strictly necessary to the general welfare, can, on any account or unforeseen circumstance, be allowed, but on four-fifths of the voters of the division approving of it, and on its being also approved of by the county and district courts; equal restraint being necessary for the general good. Any person having been once married, and having a family equal or nearly approaching to what his or her portion will support, cannot marry again, unless such family are of age to manage the portion, and the man or woman marrying such person is in possession of, or entitled to a portion so free, either in his or her division, or on the borders, as to be equal to their support, and that of their probable family: this to be judged of, and decided as aforesaid. That those who prefer marrying early to waiting their rotation for the sake of settling in their native division or in that of the person they have chosen (they having the choice of either division when they live in separate ones), may, on providing a habitation upon any portion unoccupied in any of the villages on the borders of the country, marry when they please, after both the parties have attained the age of twenty-one years. Earlier marriages are on no account permitted, as they tend to induce a weak state of health in the females of the country, and to the production of a weak and sickly progeny. No marriage is valid which takes place contrary to these regulations. To prevent errors, the birth of every child is to be registered in a book kept in the village-house by the magistrate; and a copy of each village register is to be kept in the division-house under the care of the president of division. Both the parents of any child, the fruit of connection before marriage, shall be put back upon the marriage rotation list, seven years; and they shall not be of age to occupy a new portion upon the borders till they have attained the age of twenty-eight years. When the country becomes bounded by our neighbors so as to admit of no more occupation of new portions, then, the whole of the people to be subject to the law of regulation of marriages, as by this enacted for the old settled parts of the country; each couple waiting their seniority to occupy the vacancies continually occurring. Laws declaratory of the foregoing, or regulating the plan of seniority for couples where there is considerable disproportion of age; or for the occupation of portions where families, altered in their relations or dependence by age or death, wish to live unitedly may be passed by the three assemblies of the country, and the chief president; but it is to be understood that they have no power to enact any law which shall in any wise infringe upon the true intent, spirit, and meaning of this primary law. This, though apparently too restrictive and rigorous, is, in truth, vitally important and essential to the continuance of the happiness of the community and to the permanent welfare of the state.

"9th. That commerce is, too generally, a system of injustice, thriving upon, or using particular information to take advantage of the want of it in others; and that all manufactures for commerce contribute to the vices of avarice and unjust accumulation. That its obvious tendency is to an improper state of labor and danger to many, for the advantage of a few, dividing society into slaves and tyrants, though the odious fact be attempted to be softened down by other appellations. It sacrifices, to furnish a few with contemptible luxuries (which add nothing to real comfort, but most of which generate disease and shorten life), the liberty, the certainty of competence, and consequently, the happiness of all. Commerce and the manufactures which support it, when successful, increase population, by causing early marriages (where there is no restraint) and by other means, so that the consumption of the necessaries of life cannot be supplied by the country. It still increases while this deceitful appearance of good continues, and supplies itself with the necessaries of life from other countries. When those countries manufacture for themselves, the demand fails; the means of importing the necessaries of life fail with it; the produce of the country is insufficient for its inhabitants; and the dreadful consequences are famine and misery, and not infrequently anarchy and bloodshed. It is therefore enacted that no commerce, or manufactures for commerce, be allowed on any pretense. It is understood that this law does not prevent the intercourse of our people with others to give the surplus of the necessaries of life, of our country, to supply the occasional deficiencies of theirs; but not so as to encourage their deficiencies of system; and that this surplus, on those occasions, must be given, and received, in the spirit of universal citizenship, without the contemptible restrictions of a bargain. And that this law does not interfere with, but encourages, the diffusion and reception of knowledge and useful discoveries, in a spirit despising avarice.

"10th. Fully convinced that all wars for conquest and aggrandizement are unjust, in which governments use the lives and property of the people as mere engines of power and weights in the balance in opposition to rival governments; and that the people of New Britain may never become instruments of such injustice and murder, it is enacted that no war is or can be permitted but in defense.

That to prevent this principle of humanity and justice from inviting the attacks of other people, and also to prevent designing, wicked, and ambitious men from attempting to raise themselves over the people of this nation, supposing them to be weak and unprepared to resist any attempt upon their liberty, and thereby altering and enslaving the state; it is further enacted that every man of able body shall be, and is, a soldier; and is hereby bound to render himself an efficient defender of the country, constitution, and laws, against every enemy, internal and external, that may arise. The detail of this primary law to be regulated by an act of the three assemblies of the state, and the president.

"11th. It is enacted, that in the worship of God, the Great Author of All, there shall be no establishment; but that everyone shall approach, and worship Him, in the manner in which, in his or her judgment and conscience, he or she may consider the most acceptable. That it is unlawful for any person, or number of persons, in the confidence of the truth of their own opinions, to dictate to others, or to accuse them of error, as every person is equally fallible and liable to err, and everyone has equally his future happiness at stake, and consequently has an equal inducement to be sincere; that standing alone, in opinion, does not constitute error, neither do numbers set up truth. It is enjoined that no person, for the sake of conformity, shall follow any profession of faith which they do not judge to be the best, as it would be an offense to the Deity, and would introduce hypocrisy into the land; and, that all do examine for themselves; for to be indifferent in this most important matter is highly reprehensible, irrational, and impious. And that it be impressed upon the minds of all, that it is the most egregious vanity in man, to think that anything he can do, or any form of worship he may follow, can augment the honor of the Great Author of Life; but that it is the duty of man, amidst every diversity of opinion, to be honestly and sincerely guided by reason, and to make justice and humanity the chief rule and measure of his conduct. That no religion can be wrong, which induces attention and submission to that which ennobles our nature, reason; and that none can be right which teaches or permits the violation of it. That this life is the vestibule of existence, that virtue and wisdom will accompany mankind to other states of being, while all other acquisitions, which have not these for their stamina and foundation, will fail and depart from them; that, therefore it is of the very first importance, how time, life's true riches, be spent; and that no plan of life can be right, no system of religion true, that is not founded on reason, the distinguishing nature of man, the true use and exercise of which includes every virtue, and thus comprises true wisdom.

"12th. That the three assemblies of the country, and the president, have power to enact laws, declaratory and explanatory of these primary laws; but that they have no power to alter or infringe upon them in any case or manner whatever."

The president now observed, "I have related to you these primary laws, in their true spirit, though for want of a better memory, not in every case, in their express words; but as they are in the possession of everyone, you can have a copy, and correct my deviations. I have also given some of the reasons for the enactment of them, perhaps a little improperly, with the laws themselves.

"To these primary laws, we prefix this great rule of permission and restraint, as our moral sun to light us to just enactments, and to regulate our decisions in all cases. "Thou mayest do all things, which all may do without injury to anyone; thou mayest not do anything, but what all may do, without injury to anyone. . . ."

31

A Voyage to Icaria

Étienne Cabet

FRATERNITY

All for each		*Each for all*
	Love	
	Justice	
Solidarity	*Mutual Aid*	*Education*
Equality—Liberty	*Universal Assurance*	*Intelligence—Reason*
Eligibility	*Organization of Work*	*Morality*
Unity	*Machines for the Profit of All*	*Order*
Peace.	*Increase of Production*	*Union.*
	Equitable Distribution of Products	
	Suppression of Misery	
The First Right:	*Increasing Ameliorations*	*The First Duty:*
To Live.	*Marriage and Family*	*To Work*
	Continual Progress	
	Abundance	
To each	*Arts*	*From each*
according to his need.		*according to his capacity.*

COMMON HAPPINESS

Paris
1845
(first published in French at Paris in 1840)

Étienne Cabet   (1788–1856)

was born in Dijon, France. Educated in law, he practiced at the bar till 1820, but turned to politics and writing. He became a leader in the Carbonari, served as Attorney-General of Corsica, was dismissed for attacking the government in his *History of the Revolution of 1830*, was elected to the French legislature, was prosecuted for his political criticisms, and went into exile to England in 1834. There he became a disciple of the socialist and successful factory-owner, Robert Owen. In 1838, inspired by a reading of More's *Utopia*, Cabet wrote *A Voyage to Icaria* (in French) and published it in 1840, a year after returning to France. He also wrote numerous newspaper articles and a history of the French Revolution.

Like Robert Owen, who had attempted in 1825 to realize his theories in a utopian community at New Harmony, Indiana, Cabet decided to put his Icarian scheme into practice. Encouraged by Owen, he purchased land on the Red River in Texas, drew up a plan for a colony based on community of property, and sent out sixty-nine of his disciples to found utopia there in 1848. When Cabet himself arrived at New Orleans in the next year with a second band of enthusiasts, he discovered that the first group had suffered from yellow fever and were already disorganized. Undismayed, he bought or rented houses and farms at Nauvoo in Illinois, from which the Mormons had recently been driven, and at one time had more than fifteen hundred Icarians there. Except for a trip to Paris, Cabet remained at Nauvoo as dictator of his little community. But dissensions arose and Cabet was voted out of the presidency in 1856; whereupon he left for St. Louis with 180 loyal followers. There he died in the same year. Hard work in St. Louis enabled the disciples to save money, which they pooled, and to settle in Cheltenham about twenty miles away. Largely owing to the guidance of an intellectual named Mercadier, the colony operated with some success for a few years. But inability to keep up payments for their lands and difficulties provoked by the Civil War wrecked the community. In 1864, it was dissolved.

A few of the Cheltenham Icarians returned to join the Nauvoo colonists who, by this time, had left the urban complications of Nauvoo and had settled at Corning in Iowa. From 1860 to 1878, the community was fairly happy. The inhabitants enjoyed a simple life but one with little comfort. In 1874, according to Nordhoff: "The children look remarkably healthy, and on Sunday were dressed with great taste. The living is still of the plainest. In the common dining-hall they assemble in groups at the tables, which were without a cloth, and they drink out of tin cups, and pour their water from tin cans. 'It is very plain,' said one to me; 'but we are independent—no man's servants—and we are content.'

"They sell about two thousand five hundred pounds of wool each year, and a certain number of cattle and hogs; and these, with the earnings of their mills, are the sources of their income.

"Their number does not increase, though four or five years ago they were reduced to thirty members; but since then, seven who went off have returned. I should say that they had passed over the hardest times, and that a moderate degree of prosperity is possible to them now; but they have waited long for it. I judge that they had but poor skill in management and no business talent; but certainly they had abundant courage and determination."

Four years later, in 1878, the society again split into two camps, and the police had to interfere to maintain order. As a result of a lawsuit, the older colonists took one thousand dollars and began a new settlement next door to the old one on Icarian land which had not yet been cultivated. The younger group remained for a few years in the old settlement but most of its members left in 1883 to found Icaria Speranza eighteen miles from San Francisco. This daughter community died of prosperity; for its lands grew greatly in value, and in 1886 the members divided it, abandoned communism, and decided that they preferred competitive capitalistic democracy to Cabet's old dream of "rational, democratic communism." The mother community was likewise dissolved. However, New Icaria, the community founded by the old colonists at Corning, persisted with increasing prosperity but decreasing numbers. This group should be regarded as a family in a capitalist society rather than as Cabetian communists. For toward the end of the nineteenth century, only nine men were left, and six of them were over sixty. The end came in 1898 when the old members, conscious of the increased value of their lands and desirous of enjoying the pleasures of private ownership, voted unanimously for a dissolution. In effect, the Icarian experiment had become a joint stock company whose profits were divided among the shareholders in proportion to their shares. What success the communities enjoyed was chiefly consequent upon subsidies from enthusiasts, contributions from new members, unrepaid loans, and increases in land values in a predominantly capitalistic society. Failure was due to the colonists' individualist instincts; to poor work and insufficient work; to dislike of regimentation; to inadequate leadership; to the growth in the younger generation of a preference for the ways of the free capitalism which they saw around them; and to the multitudes of petty clashes which are inevitably involved in a regulated communal existence.

Cabet's *Icaria* is included here as an example of Utopian Socialism of particular interest because of the attempts made to realize it in America, and because of the failure of those attempts. His brand of communism is based on the doctrines that social inequalities are survivals of man's savage state when, all being ignorant, might was right; that brotherly love and altruism are natural instincts which need development; that all men, by nature, are brethren; that social and political inequality is a breach of the law of nature; and that community cannot be established by conspiracy and violence, as Babeuf taught, but is to be achieved by means of discussion, propaganda, persuasion, and force of public opinion. Cabet's benevolent interpretation of human nature is closer to Rousseauism than to the actual human beings of his day. His supposition that nature teaches perfect equality is belied by obvious inequalities of climate, geography, and heredity. His communism has a respect for bourgeois morality which is absent from that of Marx. Nevertheless, his utopian society, with its extreme regimentation and standardization, with its ridiculous adulation of its founder, Icar, and with its denial of distinction, uniqueness, and significant variation is unlikely to appeal to modern Americans. To refuse to anyone the use or experience of anything which cannot be made available to all is to deprive men of some of their most precious possessions.

The text below is based on *Voyage en Icarie* published in Paris in 1845, five years after the original edition. Cabet's style is dull and repetitive, and the work is inordinately long. Accordingly the somewhat insipid love story, which is far from integral to the main story, is omitted, as well as a mass of trivia. Condensed and paraphrased passages are enclosed in brackets. Ellipses indicate omissions. The remaining portions are freely translated into English by the present editor.

BIBLIOGRAPHY: Albert Shaw, *Icaria, A Chapter in Communistic History* (New York, 1884); Charles Nordhoff, *The Communistic Societies of the United States* (New York, 1875); Jules J. Prudhonneaux, *Icarie et son Fondateur* (Paris, 1907); Sylvester A. Pietrowski, *Étienne Cabet and the Voyage en Icarie* (Washington, 1935); Charles Gide, *Communist and Co-operative Colonies* (New York, n.d., translated from the French edition of 1928), pp. 132–154; Joyce O. Hertzler, *The History of Utopian Thought* (New York, 1926), pp. 204–208; M. Kaufmann, *Utopias* (London, 1879), pp. 123–142.

Étienne Cabet

A Voyage to Icaria

[The author and Lord Carisdall travel to Icaria in 1836 and are hospitably received. Gradually they learn the details of Icarian organization.]

PRINCIPLES OF SOCIAL ORGANIZATION IN ICARIA

"Essentially," said Dinaros, "man is distinguished from all other living beings by his *reason*, his *perfectibility*, and his *sociability*. Being profoundly convinced by experience that happiness cannot exist without association and equality, the Icarians constitute a SOCIETY founded on a basis of perfect EQUALITY. All are *partners, citizens, equal in rights and duties;* all share equally the *burdens* and the *benefits* of association; likewise, all form a single FAMILY whose members are united by the bonds of FRATERNITY. Thus we form a *People* or a *Nation* of brothers, and the purpose of all our laws is to establish among us absolute equality in all cases where such equality is not materially impossible."

"Nevertheless," said Lord Carisdall to him, "has not Nature herself established inequality by giving men physical and intellectual qualities which are almost always unequal?"

"That is true," he replied; "but has not Nature given all men the same desire to be happy, the same right to *existence* and *happiness*, the same love of equality, the intelligence and the REASON necessary for organizing happiness, society, and equality? Moreover, my lord, do not stop with this objection, for we have solved the problem, and you are going to see complete *social equality*. Just as we form one society, one people, and one family, so our territory, with its mines below and its buildings above, forms a single domain, which is our social domain. All personal goods of the partners, with all products of land and industry, form a single social capital. This social domain and this social capital belong indivisibly to the People, who cultivate and work them in common, who administer them by themselves or by their agents, and who then partake equally of all the products."

"But that is COMMUNITY OF GOODS," he cried.

"Quite so," replied Valmor's grandfather, "are you frightened by communalism?"

"No; but—but people have always called it impossible."

"Impossible! Why, you're going to see for yourself."

"All the Icarians are associated and equal," continued Dinaros; "all must have a trade and work the same number of hours; but they all use their intelligence to find every possible means of rendering the labor brief, varied, agreeable, and safe. All the equipment and materials used in work are furnished out of the social capital, for all products of earth and industry are deposited in public storehouses. We are all fed, dressed, lodged, and furnished from the social capital, and we are all *the same,* according to sex, age, and some other circumstances provided for by law. Thus the Republic or the Community is the sole owner of everything; it organizes the workers and looks after the construction of workshops and stores; it causes the land to be cultivated, houses to be built, and all things to be produced which are needed for food, clothing, lodging, and pleasure; in other words, the community feeds, lodges and provides for every family and every citizen.

"Since EDUCATION is regarded by us as the basis and foundation of society, the Republic furnishes it for all children, and furnishes it equally for them, just as it gives nourishment equally to all. All receive the same elementary education and special instruction suitable for a particular profession; and the purpose of this education is to make good workers, good parents, good citizens, and true men.

"Such, essentially, is our social organization, and these few words enable you to discover all the rest of it. You should now understand that we have neither *poor people* nor *servants.* You should also understand how it is that the Republic is the sole owner of all the horses, carriages, and hotels which you have seen, and why it is that the state feeds travelers and transports them without charge. Moreover, you should understand that because each of us receives everything that we need, *money, buying* and *selling* are completely useless to us."

"Yes," Carisdall replied, "I understand quite well, but . . ."

"Come now, my lord," said the old man, smiling; "you see Communalism spread out before your very eyes, and nevertheless you refuse to believe it! Go on, Dinaros, explain our political organization to him."

"Since we are all partners, citizens, equal in rights, we are all voters eligible for public office, all members of the People and of the popular militia. United together we compose the NATION or rather the PEOPLE, for with us the People is the total of all Icarians, without exception. I do not need to tell you that the People is SOVEREIGN, and that to them alone belongs, along with SOVEREIGNTY, the power to draw up their social contract, their constitution, and their laws; we cannot even imagine an individual, family or class making the absurd pretension of being our master.

"The People, being sovereign, have the right to govern through their constitution and laws everything pertaining to themselves, their actions, their nourishment, their clothing, their housing, their education, their work, and even their pleasures. If the entire Icarian People could easily and frequently gather together in a hall or on a plain, they would exercise their sovereignty by writing their own constitution and laws. Because of the physical impossibility of gathering in this way, they DELEGATE all the powers which they cannot exercise directly and reserve the rest to themselves. They delegate to a Popular ASSEMBLY the power to prepare their constitution and laws, and to an EXECUTORY or executive body the power to effect them; but the People reserve the right to elect its representatives and all the members of the Executive, to approve or reject their proposals and their acts, to render justice, to maintain order and public peace.

"All public officials are thus the agents of the People; all are *elective, temporary, responsible*, and *revocable;* and to prevent ambitious encroachments, the legislative and executive powers are always kept separate.

"Our POPULAR ASSEMBLY is composed of 2,000 deputies who deliberate together in a single chamber. It is permanent in the sense that it is always or almost always in session; and it is renewed each half-year. Its most important laws, as in the case of the constitution, are submitted for acceptance by the people.

"The EXECUTIVE, composed of a President and fifteen other members, renewable every half-year, is necessarily subordinated to the POPULAR ASSEMBLY.

"All the reserved powers, elections, deliberations, and judgments of the People are exercised in these *assemblies*. And to facilitate the exercise of these rights, the territory is divided into 100 little *Provinces*, subdivided into 1,000 *Communes* which are approximately equal in size and population. Each Provincial city is in the center of its Province, and each Communal city in the center of its Commune; and things are so arranged that all the citizens actually attend the popular assemblies.

"So that no interest will be neglected, each Commune and each Province devotes itself to its communal and provincial affairs at the same time as all the other Communes and Provinces—in other words, the whole People and its Assembly are devoting themselves to general or national interests. Being thus divided into 1,000 communal assemblies, the People participate in the discussion of its laws, sometimes after, sometimes before, the deliberation of its Representatives.

"So that the People can discuss with perfect knowledge of affairs, all proceedings are carried on openly and PUBLICLY, all facts are verified by *Statistics*, and everything is published in the popular *Journal* distributed to all citizens. And to ensure that each discussion is complete and exhaustive, the popular Representative Assem-

bly and each communal assembly—in other words, the entire People
—is divided into fifteen grand primary COMMITTEES, for *constitutional* matters, *education, agriculture, industry, food, clothing,
housing, furniture, statistics*, etc. Thus each grand committee takes
in a fifteenth part of the mass of the citizens; and all the intelligence
of a populace composed of persons well brought up and well educated is continually active to discover and to apply all possible improvements and perfecting. Thus our political organization is a
democratic REPUBLIC, even an almost pure DEMOCRACY."

"Yes, my lord," added Valmor's father, "in this country the entire People makes the laws, and makes them only in their own interest—that is, in the common interest—and always carries them out
with pleasure, since they are their own work and the expression of
their sovereign will. And as we have already stated, this unanimous
will is dedicated to the creation of social and political equality,
equality of happiness and rights, universal and absolute equality.
Education, food, clothing, housing, furniture, work, pleasures, the
right to vote, the right of eligibility for office, and the right of deliberating upon proposals, all are equal for each of us. Our provinces, our communes, our cities, our villages, our farms, and our
homes are, as far as possible, alike. In brief, you will find equality
and happiness everywhere here. . . .

"I shall not tell you how Icaria, like almost all other countries,
was conquered and laid waste by wicked conquerors, then oppressed
and tyrannized over by wicked kings and wicked aristocrats who
made the workers and their poor wives very unhappy and miserable: that is the unhappy lot of humanity throughout the world.
For centuries, history saw only frightful combats between the *rich*
and the *poor*, and revolutions and horrible massacres. . . . However, in 1782, a tyrant was overthrown. Happily, the good and
courageous *Icar*, whom the people elected as Dictator, proved to be
the best of men. It is to him and our high-minded ancestors, his
companions, that we owe the happiness which we enjoy. He and
they organized the Republic and the Communality, having braved
death and having performed immense labors to ensure the happiness
of their wives and children. . . ."

"Icar electrified us!" cried the grandfather. . . . "To him alone be
glory and honor! Let us sing, my children! Let us sing Icar and fatherland!" Together we sang their hymn of praise to Icar and their
national song. . . .

EDUCATION
". . . . in the age of our regeneration a large committee planned
our organization for public education after examining all the ancient

and modern systems and after gathering all the theories about it.

"The LAW then regulated the different *kinds of education* (physical, intellectual, moral, industrial, and civic), and, for each kind, made regulations governing the *materials* for education, the *times* and *order* of studies, and the *methods* of teaching.

"All Icarians, without distinction of sex and profession, receive the same *general* or *elementary* education embracing the elements of all human knowledge. All those who practice the same industrial or scientific profession receive in addition the same *special* or *professional* education, a training which includes the whole theory and practice of that profession.

"Education is *domestic* on the part which is entrusted to parents and carried on at home, and *public* or *common* in the part entrusted to the popular instructors in the national schools. You will easily realize that the Republic easily finds the necessary Teachers, both male and female, however numerous they may be; for the teaching profession is the most highly honored here, since it is probably the one which contributes most to the Community and which has the most influence on common happiness. You will also appreciate the fact that these teachers easily acquire in the *normal* schools all the knowledge and practical skill which is desirable; above all, they acquire habits of patience, gentleness, and fatherly goodness. But what you cannot guess is that since education has been exactly the same for all during the past fifty years, and since everyone is accustomed to teach others what he knows, there is not a father today who cannot educate his sons, not a mother who is not capable of educating her daughters, not a brother or sister who lacks sufficient education to give instruction to younger brothers and sisters, and, indeed, not a single man or woman who is unable in case of need to teach fellow citizens below his age.

"Now I shall begin with *physical* education, for we regard it as the foundation of all the other kinds.

"The Committee examined and discussed everything; the People or the *Law* laid down regulations for everything.

"First, you need to know that the Republic guards its children not only from their birth but even during their mothers' pregnancy. Immediately after marriage, young couples are taught everything that they need to know for the welfare of the mother and children; the Republic has taken care to have *books* composed on anatomy, hygiene, etc., and to make available courses of lectures needed for this purpose. New instructions are given for pregnancy, pointing out all the precautions which the mother must take for herself and for the child which is to be born. Members of the family and almost always several midwives attend the birth. In this connection further instructions are provided: they are always drawn up by doctors and set forth in fullest detail everything necessary for the health of the mother and the physical well-being of the child. And do not think that there is one woman in the country who is ignorant of what she ought to know: to provide the Republic with children who are as perfect and as happy as possible is considered the most important of public services, accordingly, the constitution neglects no educational means which will make mothers capable of fulfilling this function perfectly.

[Besides being provided with useful treatises, wives are obliged to attend special courses in *maternity* and to hear discussions not only concerning nursing and weaning the child, teething problems, and the feeding, clothing and bathing of babies, but also lectures on the development of all his organs so that they may be brought to perfection. Questions concerning intellectual and moral education are also dealt with, for the mothers are in charge of the training of their children for the first five years. So great is the importance attached to rearing of children that a *Mothers' Journal* full of useful observations is printed. In brief, our parents truly deserve the names *father* and *mother*.

[If a child is born weak or malformed, every care is taken to correct these defects at home or in special hospitals, full use being made of various ingenious instruments provided for such purposes by the Republic. Mothers always suckle their own children if possible. Nor are mothers separated from their children after weaning them, for the mothers continue to provide protection and love for their offspring. And during pregnancy, women are respected and honored and kept free from worry. Many great discoveries have been made about the rearing of children as a result of forty years of such great care for them. As the result, Icarian children are the most perfect in the world.

[As soon as a child is quite strong, gymnastic exercises at home and then at school are enforced for him by the state, so that all parts of his body may be perfectly developed. All their games are directed toward development of grace, agility, strength, and health: to these ends the children march, run, jump, climb, ride horseback, dance, skate, participate in military drill, and perform simple tasks. Such exercises are, as a general rule, the same for both sexes.

[In accordance with the *Law*, every care is taken to develop intelligence. Until the age of five, such education is domestic: during these years, mothers and fathers teach children to speak, read, and write, as well as giving them a prodigious quantity of practical knowledge. Public education combined with continued training at home is provided from the fifth to the seventeenth or eighteenth years. Children go to school at nine in the morning and stay there until six. They rise at five and busy themselves until nine with housework, dressing, studies and breakfast. After returning from school, they devote themselves to walks, games, conversation and study; and everything is made edifying.

[At an early stage, a child learns to read aloud; later he takes a course in declamation. As a result, everyone learns to read and speak well. From the time that he first learns to write he is made to write legibly; as a result, all Icarian handwriting is clear and well-formed.]

"Our language is so regular and so easy that we learn it without noticing; after that, less than a month is needed to learn perfectly the rules and theory of the language under the direction of a teacher who leads his students to compose a grammar rather than limiting himself to explaining it to them. The study of literature and the art of oratory is put off until later, but as soon as the child learns to write, his mother accustoms him to the composition of little letters and recitations for absent relatives and friends. She also trains him to narrate orally, to make replies, to ask questions, and even to discuss."

[We do not let our children waste time on dead languages or foreign ones. Copies of all foreign books, ancient and modern, are available for scholars in our public libraries, as well as excellent translations of the most useful of these. Since our own language is almost perfect, we prefer to devote ourselves to more useful knowledge than foreign tongues. However, a certain number of young people study languages in preparation for careers as translators, professors, interpreters, and official travelers sent forth by the Republic. Since such linguistic studies are professional training, they do not begin before the age of eighteen is reached.

[Linear drawing is studied from early childhood, so that all Icarians are proficient in it. But painting, engraving, sculpture, and the like are regarded as special training for professions and therefore are taught only to students over eighteen. The elements of geology, geography, mineralogy, biology, botany, chemistry, physics, and astronomy are taught to children from an early age. Only after all these studies are they exposed to religion and divinity. Elementary arithmetic and geometry are likewise taught to all, so that every Icarian knows how to count, to measure, and even to draw a plan. The study of vocal and instrumental music is carried on for all from early childhood. The elements of agriculture, mechanics, and industry are also part of our general education. And all this elementary education is the same for boys and girls though it is often conducted in separate buildings. Moreover, women have shown themselves to be as intelligent as men. Indeed, many of our women are leaders in medicine, fine arts, teaching, and even astronomy. Special or professional education begins at age seventeen for girls and a year later for boys. But general education does not cease then, for at this stage, elementary courses in literature, universal history, anatomy, hygiene, and maternity begin. These courses are compulsory for all young people until they are twenty or twenty-one and are given after the morning work. Even then, education does not cease, for the Republic offers courses for the people of all ages; for example, a course in the History of Mankind. Journals and books provide other means of continued education.]

"We wish to teach a child as much as possible, and as a consequence, to make use of all imaginable means of rendering each study easy, rapid, and agreeable: our great principle is that every lesson should be a game, and every game a lesson.

"All the inventive powers of the members of the *Committee* were exhausted in the effort to find and to multiply such means; and whenever experience leads to the discovery of a new one, it is quickly adopted. The beauty and convenience of schools, the patience and gentleness of the instructors as well as their competence, the simplicity of methods, the clarity of demonstrations, the mixture of study and games, all combine to achieve this goal.

"Since we have the good fortune to have a perfectly regular language, and since everyone speaks equally well, a child learns naturally and effortlessly. Nevertheless we follow a definite system, whose efficacy has been demonstrated by experience, for the choice and order of words and ideas to be communicated to the student, care being taken in each instance to show him the *thing* which is being named. From that moment or even earlier, the father and mother make a special effort to avoid giving their beloved child any *false ideas, errors*, or *prejudices* such as those which formerly were suggested by servants or even by ignorant, ill-bred parents.

"You will scarcely believe how many precautions the *committee* for education took to teach children the most rapid and agreeable manner of reading. It deliberated for a long time over the choice of the best method; the one chosen is applied by the mother: it makes this early stage of learning a pleasant experience for which the child is so eager that it is he who wants to have the lesson; and they are so clever about encouraging his interest that he cannot help but retain what he is taught. Add to that that our language is much easier to learn since it is written exactly as it is pronounced and since it contains no equivocal or useless letters. Moreover, this first great step in education was formerly costly to the child in the woes it caused and the time it took up, for which the instructor had to pay with boredom, but today it is no more than a few months' amusement for the child and its mother."

[The choice of books for such young children is important. We have only one for children of the same age. It is called *The Children's Friend*. Notice its pretty binding, colored pictures, fine paper, and magnificent printing. You will find only simplicity, clarity, charm, interest, and information contained in this little book, without a single word, thing, or idea out of the reach of a child's mind. The work is constantly revised and has no equal.]

"The mother explains everything to the child, and interrogates him to make sure that he understands and knows everything that he has read. Then, at school, when all the children of the same age are assembled, the schoolmistress (for she is a woman) has them read and questions them in a way which captures the attention of each one. If one of them hesitates, another gives the answer, but the mistress gives an explanation herself only when no one else can give it. And when, after six months, the child has read, or rather, devoured, this little book, you would be astonished at the prodigious amount of knowledge that he has already acquired!

"I need not tell you that the teacher is almost a second mother. . . .

"We have similar books for each age; but the *Children's Library* is not very extensive, for we think that a small number of excellent books which the child knows well is infinitely more valuable than a confusion of good ones, or, above all, a mixture of mediocre and bad ones. In addition we have introduced a tremendous innovation in the composition of textbooks for the primary grades: texts in the previously dry fields of geography and arithmetic, for example, are written in the form of charming stories.

"The child learns *writing* in accordance with the same principles, by playing joyfully under the direction of his mother. She explains to him the reason for everything that she is doing and everything that she causes him to do; for there always is a reason why one acts in one manner rather than in another, and one of our great principles is to exercise successively the intelligence and the judgment of the child by accustoming him to reason about everything, always demanding the cause, and always explaining the motive. So the mother explains to her child how he should hold a pen, and why; how he should place his paper, and why; and when the children are gathered at school, the master asks them all the *why* and *wherefore*, what sort of writing a certain position will produce, and what position must have resulted in certain writing. It is the *theory* of writing; and in all parts of education, even in gymnastics and games, we always combine theory and practice. Now you will understand how it is that all those who know how to write are capable of teaching others.

"This method of exercising reason is applied to everything and is used continually by all those who come into contact with the child. Far from repressing his *curiosity* when a desire for instruction prompts it, people indicate their approval by answering all his questions; and they even arouse curiosity constantly by always asking the motive and cause for everything that he sees. . . .

"Elementary arithmetic and geometry are taught in school with devices and procedures which make this study attractive for the students, especially since theory and practice are combined. The greater part of the conduct of the studies takes place in the national workshops and stores, so that the child learns to count, to weigh, and to measure all kinds of material and products. Or he is taken into the fields to be taught to measure surfaces and to solve problems of trigonometry on the land. . . .

"Each child learns the entire Constitution by heart; and it is impossible to find an Icarian who does not know perfectly everything which concerns the electors, the National Assembly and its members, the Popular Assemblies, and the National Guard; there is no one who is not familiar with what a magistrate may and may not do, and with everything that the law permits or forbids. Anyone who neglected his civic education would be deprived of the right to exercise his citizenship; but no one would expose himself to such shame and misfortune. The women also learn the elements of this civic education so that they will not be strangers to anything which concerns them, and so that they will completely understand matters which busy their husbands to such an extent.

"Finally, although we hope for lasting peace, both internal and external, all citizens are members of the national guard and are drilled in the use of arms and military maneuvers from their eighteenth to their twentieth years: . . . At twenty-one a youth becomes a citizen; and, as you see, the young Icarians are brought up to be good patriots as well as good sons, good husbands, good fathers, good neighbors, and finally, true men. I may add that they are men of peace and order; for the fundamental maxim of civic education is a maxim which they are taught from infancy and which they are made to put into practice continually: it is, that after a full and free discussion in which each has had an opportunity to explain his opinion, the *minority* must submit without regret to the *majority;* for otherwise there would be no other method of deciding other than brute force and war, victory and conquest, which would lead to tyranny and oppression."

"With your Community and your Education," said I, "you do not have many crimes, do you?"

"What crimes do you think we could have today?" replied Valmor, who overheard our conversation. "Can we know theft of any kind when we have no money and each man possesses everything he can desire? One would have to be a fool to be a robber! How could there be assassinations, incendiary acts, and poisonings if robbery is impossible? How could there even be *suicides* when everyone is happy?"

"But," I replied, "is it not possible to have murders, duels, and suicides for other causes; for example, because of love or jealousy?"

"Our education," replied Valmor, "makes *men* out of us, and we learn both to respect the rights and the will of others, and to follow the dictates of reason and justice in all things: the Icarians are nearly all philosophers who, from their infancy, know how to master their passions."

"You see, then," said Dinaros, "that with a single stroke, Communalism suppresses and prevents thefts and thieves, crimes and criminals, so that we no longer need courts or prisons or punishments. . . ."

WORK AND INDUSTRY

". . . First, you must recall the chief facts, facts which are a key to all the others. I have already told them to you, but I am going to repeat them in a few words: we live in community of goods and work, of rights and duties, of benefits and expenses. We have neither private property nor money, nor buying, nor selling. We are equal in all respects except those which are absolutely impossible to achieve. We all work equally for the Republic or the Community. It is the Community which gathers all products from the soil and from industry, and which distributes them equally among us; it is the Community which nourishes us, clothes us, lodges us, instructs us, and furnishes us, equally for all, with whatever we need.

"Remember also that the purpose of all our laws is to render the People as happy as possible, beginning with the necessary, then adding the useful, and finishing with the agreeable without fixing any limit. For example, if we could give everyone a carriage, each would receive such a carriage; but since this is impossible, no one has one, although everyone may use the common carriages which are made as commodious and agreeable as possible.

"You will see the application of these principles in the *organization of work.*

"Each year the Republic or Community decides all the objects which need to be produced or manufactured for feeding, clothing, lodging and furnishing the People. It is the Community and only the Community which sees that they are manufactured by its workers, in its own establishments; for all industries and factories are national; all the workers are national; it is the Community which looks after the construction of its workshops, always choosing the most appropriate sites and the most perfect plans, organizing immense factories, grouping all those whose union is advantageous, and never hesitating to make necessary expenditures to obtain a useful result. It is the Republic which decides upon the processes of manufacture, always choosing the best, ever making haste to publish all discoveries, all inventions, and all improvements. It is again the state which instructs its numerous workers, supplies them with raw materials and tools, and distributes the work to them, dividing it up among them in the most productive manner, paying them in kind rather than in money. It is the state which then receives all the manufactured goods and deposits them in its immense storehouses so that eventually it can divide the goods among all its workers or, rather, its children.

"And this Republic which imposes its will and disposes of things in this way is the Committee of Industry, the National Representative, the People itself.

"You can see immediately the incalculable *economy* in every respect and the incalculable advantages of all kinds which must necessarily result from this basic general arrangement!

"Everyone is a national laborer working for the Republic. All persons, male and female, without exception are employed in one of the arts, crafts or professions set up by the law.

"Minors do not begin work until the age of eighteen for boys and seventeen for girls, the earlier years being dedicated to education and the development of their powers. Old people are exempted from work, starting at sixty-five for men and fifty for women: however, the work tires so little and is even so agreeable that few take the exemption, but continue in their usual occupation or make themselves useful in some other way.

"There is no need to tell you that invalids are exempted from work; however, lest the privilege be abused, invalids must go to a hospital, a hospital which in other respects is more like a palace. And I need not tell you that any worker can have a holiday in cases determined by the law, if he has the consent of his fellow workers.

"I have just told you that the work is agreeable and is not tiring: indeed, our laws spare nothing to make it such, so that you cannot find a manufacturer as benevolent to his employees as the Republic is to its workers. Machines are multiplied without limit, to such an extent that they replace two hundred million horses or three billion workers; and these machines perform all the dangerous, fatiguing, unhealthy, dirty and repulsive work . . . Everything concurs to render work agreeable: education which from infancy teaches the love and high evaluation of labor; the cleanliness and convenience of the factories; the singing which enspirits and cheers the workers; the equality of work for all; its moderate duration; and the honor with which all kinds of work are held in public opinion, all kinds being esteemed equally."

"What!" I cried, "all trades are esteemed equally, the shoemaker as much as the doctor?"

"Undoubtedly so. You will stop being astonished at that, for it is the law which determines all trades and professions which may be carried on, and all the goods to be manufactured: no other occupations are taught or allowed, and no other manufacturing is permitted. For example, we have no such occupation as tavern-keeper, and no manufacturer of daggers in our cutlery-works. All our manufactures and professions are, then, equal *in the eyes of the law*, and, if judged in one particular respect, equally *necessary*: from the time when the law decrees that there will be shoemakers and doctors it necessarily follows that there must be both of them. Since everyone cannot become a doctor, it is necessary for shoemakers to be as happy and contented as doctors so that some people will want to be shoemakers; consequently, perfect equality, as far as that is possible, must be established between them. As a result, all of them are equally esteemed if they devote the same amount of time for the Republic."

"And you make no distinction for sense, intelligence, and genius?"

"No: in reality, are not all of these gifts of nature? Would it be just to punish in some way a man less endowed with these? Should not reason and society make up for the inequality which is produced by blind chance? If a man's genius makes him more useful than another, is he not rewarded by the satisfaction which he experiences? If we wish to make a distinction, should it not be in favor of the more laborious kinds of work and professions, so as to compensate for them in some way, and to encourage them? To sum up: our laws make a doctor as honored and as happy as possible. Why, then, should he complain if a shoemaker is equal to him in these respects?

"Nevertheless, although by our system of education a desire has already been aroused almost sufficiently in each person to make himself ever more useful to the Community, we have a means of exciting useful *emulation*. Any worker who as a result of patriotism performs more than his duty or who makes a discovery which is useful for his profession wins particular esteem or public *distinctions*, or even national *honors*."

"And what about the lazy?"

"The lazy! We do not have any of them. Why do you think that there would be any when work is so agreeable and when idleness and laziness are as much despised in our country as robbery is elsewhere? . . .

"The working day, which at first was from ten to eighteen hours long, and which was successively shortened, is today fixed at seven hours in summer and six hours in winter, from six or seven o'clock in the morning until one in the afternoon. We shall shorten it again as often as it is possible to do so, if new machines take the place of workers, or if there is a lessened need for making things (constructing buildings, for example) which makes a great number of workers unnecessary. But it is probable that shortening of working time is now at its *minimum*, for if some industries grow smaller, other new industries replace them, it being understood that we continually endeavor to increase our pleasures. Last year, for example, when a new piece of furniture was added to the furniture which we then had in each household, a hundred thousand workers were needed to produce it; accordingly we took the hundred thousand workers from the mass of the laboring population and increased the daily period of general work by five minutes.

"In each household, the wives and daughters perform all the domestic tasks together from five to six o'clock in the morning to half-past eight; and from nine to one they devote themselves to the work of their profession in the factories."

"Pregnant women and those who are nursing their children are no doubt exempted from work?"

"That's right. Moreover, the chief woman in each family is exempted from factory toil, because looking after the family and the home is also an occupation useful to the Republic.

"All laborers in each occupation work together in immense common factories. . . . Mobile, portable workshops for labors which are performed in the open air likewise provide all possible conveniences. . . ."

"Have you noticed the *order* which prevails in the midst of this universal movement? Here as in all our factories, each person has his post, his job, and what might be called his grade, for some direct the others; this group supplies the materials for that one; and all carry out their tasks with accuracy and pleasure. Wouldn't you say that this whole group constitutes a single vast machine in which each wheel faithfully performs its function?"

"Yes indeed; this discipline amazes me."

"But why should you be surprised? In each factory the rules are decided upon and the officials are *elected* by the workers themselves, except that the regulations common to all the factories are laid down by the elected representatives of the entire People, or, in other words, by those who represent the workers in all the factories. Citizens are required to fulfill only regulations and laws which they make themselves, and as a consequence each citizen always carries them out without hesitation or repugnance. . . ."

DISTRIBUTION OF PROFESSIONS

". . . . Every year, in the ten days preceding the anniversary of our Revolution, the Republic, having statistically determined the number of workers necessary for each profession, publishes the list for each commune and invites the young men who are eighteen years old to *make a choice*. If there is competition, the positions are assigned in accordance with competitive examinations which are judged by a Jury composed of the competitors themselves." [The positions are then divided up, but before beginning actual work the youths are given special professional education for periods varying with the demands of their respective professions. Each is taught the theory and history of his profession and receives practical training in a period of apprenticeship. Similar opportunities are open to girls to enter professions, or industries appropriate for women, or household work.] . . .

"Have you noticed the regular movement of our population? At five o'clock, everyone gets up; as six approaches, all our public vehicles and the streets are full of men going to their factories; at nine, the women and the children appear; from nine to one the population is in the factories or the schools; at one-thirty the whole mass of workers leave the factories to join their families and neighbors in the people's restaurants; from two to three, everyone eats; from three to nine, the entire population goes out into the gardens, terraces, streets, promenades, popular assemblies, lecture halls, theaters and all other public places; at ten, everyone goes to bed; and during the night, from ten to five o'clock, the streets are deserted."

"Then you have a curfew? Isn't that a tyrannical law?"

"Imposed by a tyrant it certainly would be an intolerable vexation; but adopted by an entire People in the interest of its health and of good order in work, it is the most reasonable and useful of our laws, and it is the one which is best carried out. . . ."

WRITERS, LEARNED MEN, LAWYERS, JUDGES

[No book may be published without approval of the Republic. The education of writers is careful. At the age of seventeen or eighteen, a youth who wishes to be a writer must pass an examination which is intended to test his talents. Then for five or six years he is given a special education. No opportunity is given to publish bad books; every opportunity is given for the publication of good ones. The Republic asks its trained writers for whatever compositions it deems useful, independently of those voluntarily produced by them. Special committees decide upon the worth of writings. The system is applied to all branches of letters, sciences, and arts.

[Since the boys and girls learn the elements of every form of knowledge, including literature, all Icarians have the ability to express themselves in words. The perfection of the Icarian language and the habit of concise expression, which is taught from infancy, also increase writing ability. As a result, any workman is able to send to the newspapers well-composed articles containing useful observations.

[Members of learned professions, such as chemists, engineers, and astronomers, are generally ready at the age of twenty-five to concentrate the rest of their existences on their chosen fields. From this source come the experimenters, professors, etc.

[Huge workshops are provided for writers (historians, poets, etc.), for learned men (chemists, astronomers, etc.), and for artists (painters, sculptors, etc.), all built according to model plans. The Republic spares no expense to facilitate these activities and to make their results known. The works are approved or rejected by a vote of learned men in conference, and are published, if approved, by the Republic for free distribution. Moreover, the Republic arranges for necessary revisions of published works and arranges to have dangerous or useless books burned, although some copies of ancient works are preserved in the national libraries as examples of the ignorance and folly of the past and the progress of the present.

[Those who wish careers in jurisprudence devote five or six years, after they reach the ages of seventeen and eighteen, to special study tested by examinations. They learn the jurisprudence and legislative history not only of Icaria but of other nations as well, and practice is stressed equally with theory. But criminal lawyers and judges are unnecessary, for in Icaria there can be neither crimes nor trials, since there is neither money nor property. What use would there be for a penal code, a code for criminal procedure, a code for civil cases? However, some crimes such as calumny are recognized, although the force of education and the fraternal spirit are so strong that there has been no calumny trial for twenty years. Punishment for such crimes is public condemnation, deprivation of certain rights, and exclusion from public places and even from private homes for varying periods. There are no prisons, for there is no need for them. Asked if there are not crimes of passion, the Icarians reply that there are not, but if there were, the guilty party would be regarded as insane. There are no policemen, for in Icaria there is no need to lock doors; in any case, all citizens are obliged to see that the laws are carried out and to take action if they see any breaches of them.

[The Popular Assembly judges some offenses, but each school is a tribunal to judge offenses against it; each factory judges offenses committed by its workmen; each family judges faults within it. Everywhere judgment is by one's equals. Feminine offenses in factories are judged by female workers. The little offenses committed in the dining halls are judged by those who eat there. Moreover, any citizen has a right to interpose in the name of the law between two disputing citizens, whereupon a priest or any other citizen acts as arbitrator. We even have a tribunal of historians to pass historical judgment on men who are dead, and a historical museum to glorify heroes of the past and to expose the infamy of the enemies of humanity.]

A WOMEN'S FACTORY. ROMANCE. MARRIAGE
[The strangers visit a factory run entirely by women for the designing and manufacturing of women's apparel. The account tells in ecstatic language of the beauty of the workers and their surroundings. Mass production of hats is described; each piece is made separately, the parts being sewn together in separate stages. The strangers arrived during the hour of silence, which was followed by the workers' singing a hymn to the glory of Icar, and other songs.

[I read a novel which was devoted to the theme of marriage, and learned that in Icaria there are no dowries. Since all have the same education, all are equally satisfactory as spouses. But young Icarians, knowing that marriage can mean either hell or heaven, accept a life partner only when they know him or her perfectly. To enable this, young people are given unrestricted liberty to converse or walk with each other, provided that their mothers or fathers are present. Education, public opinion, and the watchfulness of parents and other citizens prevent secret liaisons. The advice of parents on the matter of choosing a mate is always highly regarded, for parents never have a merely personal interest in opposing a marriage. Full instructions in the duties and obligations of marriage are provided by parents and books. But admonitions are scarcely needed as a basis for a happy marriage, for the common education, the freedom from idleness, and other aspects of Icarian life almost guarantee successful marriage.

Indeed, the finest feature of the social organization set up by Icar was to arrange things so that husbands and wives would be virtuous without special effort. And if by some chance a marriage should not be happy, parents and duty would make the partners see that their true interest would be to accept the situation and to put up generously with each other's faults. The priest would also exhort them to seek happiness or at least peace in virtue.

[However, if a marriage proves to be unhappy and the families concerned judge that a divorce is indispensable, it is possible; and the right of remarriage is acknowledged in such cases. Since marriage is regarded as the basis of the family and the nation, voluntary celibacy is regarded with suspicion and held to be an act of ingratitude. Concubinage and adultery are regarded as unpardonable crimes and viewed with such horror that they do not occur. In any case, the Republic so orders things that adultery would simply not be possible: the would-be criminals could find no place for the deed. Only one woman succeeded in breaking this law during the past twenty years. Rape is unknown; seduction is almost impossible, for what could the seducer offer? There are no wife-beatings, abortions, infanticides, poisonings of wives by husbands, deceitful gallantries, duels, or dangerous jealousies.]

AGRICULTURE
[The strangers visit a farm and find it run by a patriarchal household composed of the farmer and his wife, and his sons and their wives and children, about forty in all. During dinner the grandfather questions the grandchildren, eliciting from them lists of animals, birds, and insects which do harm to crops, a history of useful animals, and the like. The house in which they all live resembles those in the city except that it is larger. The walls bear plans and pictures which teach useful precepts for agriculture. Because of ample means of rapid transportation, farmers are not cut off from the schools, lectures, and public spectacles of the cities.

[A visit to the kitchen garden (which is looked after by the farmer's wife and her niece) reveals vegetables of all kinds. In forty years, the production of such crops has doubled and tripled, thanks to improvements in agriculture. The flower-garden proves to be redolent with roses. The apiary and orchards are visited. An elaborate irrigation system, fed by penetration into subterranean lakes and streams, serves for beauty, for fish, and for washing and refreshment. Fruit trees are cared for scientifically and improved by careful selection, grafting, pruning, and similar means.

[Agricultural education is thorough. All citizens learn the elements of agriculture, both practical and theoretical. At the age of seventeen or eighteen, children of farm laborers are free to choose some other profession than agriculture if some family in the city will agree to adopt them; likewise, city youth may become farmers by being accepted into some rural household. Those who wish to be farmers are given a year's intensive education in agriculture, after which they return to the paternal farm to complete their training.

[Agriculturists learn the elements and quality of all kinds of metals, stones, and earths; everything pertaining to winds, seasons, temperatures; everything concerning crops and how to use them to make wine, cider, etc.; and everything necessary concerning animals and plants, both useful and harmful. Farmers' daughters receive essentially the same education, but concentrate on dairying, poultry, vegetables, flowers, and fruits.

[Different areas specialize in crops for which they are specifically suited. Each farm has its *territorial statistics,* that is, scientific data about its characteristics and potentialities, and instructions for its particular farmer. The education of farmers continues after they leave school, being provided by experienced parents and by governmental publications.

[The strangers witness the usual magnificent buildings, this time devoted to housing animals, smoking meat, sheltering wagons and machinery, etc. The whole was, of course, constructed according to the model plans: as a result, cleanliness, order, convenience, and even elegance prevailed. Mechanization was highly advanced. And the clothing of the farmers and workers combined utility and attractiveness.

[The nature of agriculture is such that farmers must work more than a daily six or seven hours as in the cities. But they work at will or in accordance with the seasons and find their labors highly agreeable. Not an inch of land is neglected, but all of it is put to use. No space is wasted on useless walls and fences. And there is no cause to worry about anyone's touching or spoiling anything, for the Icarian educational system teaches everyone to be careful about such matters; moreover, no farmer would refuse to provide flowers or fruit if they were asked for.]

"The Republic requires from each Commune the agricultural and industrial production most suitable for the nature of its terrain and its situation; and the Republic takes the surplus from each Commune and brings to it the products needed there."

[Such is the distribution of products; no one else would accomplish it as well, for no commercial company could have such unity and power or could inspire such support from the entire people, nor have such transportation facilities at its command. The government likewise carries on foreign commerce, conducting negotiations directly with foreign governments.]

RELIGION

". . . In the first place, we have replaced the words *God*, *Divinity*, *Religion*, and *Church* with new expressions so perfectly defined that they can give no occasion for ambiguity.

"Secondly, here, as in all matters, *education* is the basis of the entire system. Until they reach the age of sixteen or seventeen, children never hear religion spoken of, and are not enrolled under any religious banner. The law forbids parents and strangers alike to influence them before they reach the age of reason. Only when that age (sixteen or seventeen) is reached, when their general education is almost finished, does a professor of philosophy and not a priest, expose them, during the course of a year, to accounts of all religious systems and opinions, omitting none.

". . . At the age of sixteen or seventeen each adopts the opinion which seems to him to be the best, being fully aware of his reasons, and freely chooses the religion which suits him. Whatever his belief may be, it is respected; whatever cult he adopts, it is permitted him; and whenever a sect is large enough to have a temple and a priest, the Republic provides both.

"To tell the truth, our universal or popular religion is only a system of *morals* and *philosophy*, and its only use is to bring men to love each other like brothers, giving them as a rule for conduct three precepts which include all rules. 'Love your neighbor as yourself. Do no evil to another which you would not want him to do to you. And do for others everything good that you desire for yourself.'

"Our worship is extremely simple: each person admires God, thanks Him, prays to Him and adores Him as he pleases in his own home. We do have some temples in which to receive religious instruction and to worship in common. But we think that justice, fraternity, and, as a consequence, submission to the general will and to love of our country and of humanity, constitute the religion which is most pleasing to the Deity. In our opinion, the man who adores and pleases Him best is the one who is the best father, the best son, the best citizen, and, especially, the man who best loves and honors his wife as his creator's masterpiece. We consider that the privations and sufferings imposed by fanaticism are contrary to divine goodness; and we also believe that the whole of nature is the finest temple in which one can do homage to the Supreme Being. . . .

"To end this account briefly, I shall add that our *priests* have no power, not even in spiritual matters; that they can neither punish nor absolve; that they are only preachers on morals, religious instructors, counselors, guides, and sympathetic friends, happy when they themselves have no need of consolations and counsel! . . ."

[We have priestesses for women, just as we have priests for men. Their training is the same. Priesthood, like the practice of medicine, is a profession. When the period of general education is completed, a person who wishes to be a priest must first pass a qualifying examination. If he is successful, he studies eloquence, ethics, philosophy, and religion until he is twenty-five. During this period he also devotes himself to teaching young people. He must marry before he is twenty-five so as to free himself from passions and so as to be an example to others. After this period of study and teaching, he is again examined to prove that he is worthy and capable of advising or comforting those who need advice or comfort, although usually parents and friends are adequate in these respects. If the examination is successful, the youth is enrolled among the candidates from whom the citizens of each area elect their priest. They are elected for five-year periods only.]

NEWSPAPERS

[Liberty of the press is necessary as a means of opposing aristocracies and kings, but is intolerable in a well-ordered community if it involves the publication of lies, contradictions, calumnies, and the like.

[The Icarians avoid this danger (1) by establishing a social and political order which would render useless the hostility of the press; (2) by permitting only one communal newspaper in each Commune, only one provincial paper in each Province, and only one national newspaper; (3) by entrusting the writing of these journals to public officials elected by the People or their representatives—officials who are disinterested, temporary, and subject to recall. Moreover, newspapers are allowed to publish only objective accounts and facts, without discussion or editorial comment. Like any other citizen, a journalist can submit his schemes to his Communal Assembly for discussion and acceptance or refusal. He needs no other means of publication. In other words, the Icarian version of *liberty of the press* is the right to make proposals to the popular Assemblies. And the views of these Assemblies constitute our *public opinion*. Since the press publishes full accounts of the deliberations of those bodies, full expression is given to public opinion.

[The journalists elected are the most able writers: they take pride in presenting facts and analyzing discussions with clarity, order and brevity, without dramatics, and without omission of anything important.]

THE EXECUTIVE

"Our first fundamental rule is that the Executive Power is essentially subordinated to the Legislative Power and is uniquely responsible for carrying out its decisions, its orders, and its will; but it always acts *in the name of the People and the National Assembly*.

"As a result it is, of course, *accountable, responsible*, and *removable*. You also need to know that it is *elective* and *temporary* in nature.

"Another radical principle is that this power is never entrusted to one man but to a body headed by a President and known as the *Executory*. Thus we have no *President of the Republic* but only a President of the executive body, the Executory of the Republic.

"Each legislative body has its Executive, so that we have a *National* Executive, a hundred *Provincial* Executives, and a thousand *Communal* Executives. The National Executive is composed of sixteen members called *Executors General* (which is also regarded as one of the chief Committees of the National Assembly.) Each of these Executors General is a kind of Minister, for each has his own Department, and their President is literally President of a Council of Ministers. Attached to the National Executive in the Capital, in the chief provincial cities, and in each communal town are all the necessary subordinate officials. The sixteen Executors General are elected for two years; half of the National Executive is renewed yearly, like the National Assembly. The people do the electing from a triple list of candidates named by the National Assembly. All the subordinate officials are elected, some by the Executive, some by the National Assembly, but in most cases by the People. But the responsibility of the Executive for the acts of its subordinates is limited to matters where the blame may properly be attributed to it.

"The Executors General and their President are lodged in the National Palace next to the National Assembly; and all their ministries or offices are also there or in the vicinity, so that correspondence between the National Assembly and its Executive is extremely simple.

"There is no need to point out that the Executive has no guards, no civil list, and no rewards different from those of any other official; an Executor is no better fed or lodged than any other citizen; for in Icaria all public offices are only professions, and all professions are public offices. All magisterial positions are burdens from which no one can be excused without good reason, and which often do not even entitle one to be freed from factory work.

"As a result, the Executive has no means of misleading or corrupting, or of intimidation or usurpation.

". . . Like all our Representatives, officeholders, and citizens, our President at this time . . . is a worker, a stonemason who returns to his profession in the intervals between sessions; and all his children work in the factories. . . ."

[The Provincial Executives are organized on lines similar to the national one. Communal Executives are also composed of sixteen members, one of whom is President. They are elected by the People of the Commune, and each of them is put in charge of a specialty and is responsible for the direction of numerous subordinate officials —numerous so that each of these officials can carry out his task without adding too great a burden to his ordinary work, and also so that as many citizens as possible may become accustomed to managing public affairs. So the schools, hospitals, factories, stores, monuments, theaters, streets, walks, and open places are full of special officials. Nevertheless there is no army, no active national guard, and no police force. Similarly there are no jailers, no prisons, no taxes, no money, no customs, and no fiscal agents. However, there are officials in charge of the collection and distribution of industrial and agricultural products, directors of factories, and officials of all kinds to protect the citizens and to watch over their interests and their pleasures. All these officials are annually elected by the People. They are present at all the Assemblies and are always ready to account for their acts to these bodies. These public servants and the citizens treat each other with the respect due to a sovereign people and its agents. Theoretically you would expect that a citizen would be permitted to resist an official who was abusing his authority, but in practice Icarians are obliged to obey any official who speaks in the name of the People and the Law. However, it is then possible to bring the official before the People for judgment and punishment. No one is allowed impunity. An infraction of a law is a crime, above all, if it is committed by those who make the law or are entrusted with carrying it out.

[A ball is described. Everyone dances amid superb surroundings in glorious attire but with decorum. Men dance with men, and women with women, except that a husband and wife are permitted to dance together. Balls, both indoor and outdoor ones, are frequent, the music being artificially produced.

(Omitted: The History of Icar; an account of Icarian Theaters with selections from some of their plays; annual Icarian festivals.)]

COLONIES

". . . For a long time we had no need of colonies. But foreseeing that we would in time have an excessive population, we prepared to promote a colonial establishment in a fertile, almost desert area which was inhabited by a slight population of savage people; we wished to begin a vast plan for civilizing them.

"Thus when we judged it to be convenient to begin the Colony, there was no need for any kind of violence. Once established among them, we multiplied our missionaries among them and their voyagers to our shores. We gave them an example of work without demanding it from them; we led them insensibly to desire it by making them witnesses of its marvelous results; and today, after less than thirty years, we have created a magnificent colony which is as flourishing as Icaria; we have civilized seven or eight small populations which now emulate us; and we have spread civilization in such a way that it will never stop growing."

RELIGION (*continued*)

[Two years after the Revolution, Icar called a Grand Council composed of priests, professors, philosophers, moralists, learned men and writers, all elected by their fellows, to discuss questions concerning religion and divinity. This Council of wise, judicious men gathered all opinions which individual citizens chose to address to them. All of these were examined and discussed during a four-year period, and all questions were decided by a large majority, often unanimously. It was unanimously decided that there is a *God* who is the *First Cause*, and that everything which we see in this universe is the *effect* of this cause; that this God is not known and likewise, that His form is not known. The Councilmen decided that they would like to believe that man was made in the image of God, but that they had no knowledge on this matter. They unanimously decided that the revelation claimed by Moses was not made by a God with a human shape, that the Bible is a man-made book, and that it contains much that is false, that Jesus Christ was not a God but a man, a man who deserves a place in the highest rank of humanity because of his devotion to human welfare and his proclamation of the principles of EQUALITY, FRATERNITY, and COMMUNITY. The Icarians do not claim to know how the world and man in particular were formed; nor why man is exposed to physical and moral suffering. They believe that the Bible was once useful but is now out of date and that there is no longer any need to believe in Paradise as a compensation for the miseries of this world. Likewise, the victims of tyranny used to find it needful to believe in a hell where tyrants would be punished, but such a belief is useless to the Icarians. For the Icarian population the solace and comfort of revealed religion is unnecessary: reason suffices for them. Their real religion is that of communalism and happiness. (An extensive attack on orthodox Christianity follows.)]

FOREIGN RELATIONS

[Having proclaimed the principle of fraternity between Icaria and all other peoples, Icar and the Republic fully accepted the consequences of this principle; they never did anything harmful to a foreign People and never refused a service which was sought from them, if its performance were possible. But Icar's chief principle was to interfere as little as possible in the affairs of his neighbors, to leave them to themselves, and to do nothing to accelerate the establishment of Communalism in them, for he was convinced that Icaria was the country in which the attempt was most likely to succeed and that, accordingly, all nations would profit by it, whereas poor attempts elsewhere might discredit the Icarian experiment. As a result, Icaria used her influence to moderate the zeal of foreign leaders for such attempts. Only after its own system was successfully established did Icaria admit a small nation on our frontiers which had asked to be merged into our country, and we then declared that we would not consent to any other additions. We were content with close alliances, with fraternal relations, commerce, and good offices of all kinds.

[But now we are strong enough to apply our principle of fraternity more widely and to facilitate the establishment of communalism everywhere, to encourage associations for its promotion abroad, and to welcome visitors who may be won over by our example.

(Part II is devoted to a history of Icaria and its revolution, an attempt to answer objections to communalism, and two chapters entitled, "The Progress of Democracy and Equality." These are followed by citations of the opinions of philosophers on equality and communism from the early Greeks to Sismondi, a chapter on the future of humanity, and one on associations and propaganda for the promotion of communalism.

Part III is devoted to a résumé of the doctrines and principles of communalism.)]

32

Contemporary Utopian Thought

Cabet's *Icaria* represents the epitome of the communitarian ideal in utopian literature. Henceforth, as we have already noted, it was to become rapidly and increasingly apparent that the utopian community was so unrealistic that it could provide no more than a setting for fantasy or satire. Modern utopia must be a state, and indeed it was already beginning to be evident that modern utopia must be the world. If we could believe that this enlarged perspective presents problems of organization so baffling and complicated as to discourage the idealization of the utopist, we might anticipate in the future a decline of utopian speculation to the production of an occasional fantasy or satire. The will to utopia is made of sterner stuff. The noblest part of man has ever been his dissatisfaction with anything less than the ideal. Wherever there have been men worthy of the name, there has persisted the utopian dream.

It is true that the past thirty-five years have not provided an ideal climate for speculation about ideal societies. Amid the ruins of protracted world conflict are to be found the remains of that ivory tower from which the future looked bright, and men, while small, from that perspective threw shadows of lengthening stature. Contemporary utopists stand forlornly or angrily in the midst of the devastation, contemplating the wisdom of converting the remnants of that shining tower into an underground shelter. Fear rather than hope is in the atmosphere, or, if not actual fear, at least lack of confidence in the progress of the future. Constructive utopian speculation cannot but be inhibited by the weight of such a prevailing atmosphere, and the paucity of speculative constructions of the ideal social organization in the contemporary period is quite understandable. Only in satire and fantasy can the utopist find escape from his frustration; but the satirical is not necessarily an entirely negative enterprise, for it may prove to have been the essential task of clearing away the debris of bombed-out structures in preparation for the construction of new and more substantial edifices. It is to the utopists of the future that we shall look for the design and detail of the new ideal.

Much has already been cleared away by the utopists. The development of utopian thought during the modern period has been amazingly rapid, and there is a marked difference between the works covering roughly the first half of the modern period and those of the recent and contemporary years. The utopist has kept pace with the increasing tempo of the past century. It was only a scant hundred years ago, as we have seen, that utopists realized the inadequacy of the communitarian ideal as the principle of future social organization. The utopists of the latter half of the nineteenth century turned almost uniformly to efficiency in economic organization as the principle of the ideal society. Then, before this new plan for utopia could be completely exploited in speculation, the self-critical analysis of utopian thought had disclosed the inadequacies and dangers of elevating the material criterion of the economic to a position of value determination in social organization. Even as early as 1890, William Morris responded with shocked disgust to the "cockney dream" in which all values were subordinated to economic efficiency, and in 1903 William Stanley asserted the priority of political order in the ideal society and the subordination of the economic to the political principle. There were two developments in utopian speculation which brought about this quick and cursory rejection of the newly acclaimed principle of economic efficiency as satisfactory for the organization of utopia. The first was exemplified by Morris: a refusal to consider as ideal a hierarchy in which all other values were determined in respect to their relation to the economic. The other development began with the recognition that the community ideal was unrealistic. However, the utopists of this period, in their enthusiastic optimism over the anticipated consequences of achieving ideal order in economic production and distribution, assumed that the achievement of the economic ideal would resolve all other problems of social organization as well. One problem which they assumed would thus be resolved was that concerning the geographical or political boundaries of utopia and its involved relations with other states. It was already beginning to be clear to utopists that anything less than world organization would be so far short of ideal that it could not be utopian. Therefore, it must be assumed that the economic ideal of utopia would shortly, through a kind of economic necessity, become the ideal of the world. Such was the assumption made, for instance, by Bellamy, with the accompanying conviction that the realization of the economic ideal would resolve all political conflicts between states and nations as it had theoretically resolved all conflicts between individuals within the previous capitalistic society. In fact, Bellamy considered that the occasional eruption of international conflicts into war was trivial compared to the economic struggle for existence. To the suggestion of the visitor, in *Equality*, that people must consider the guarantee of international peace the most signal achievement of the new social order, Bellamy's Dr. Leete replies:

> Of course, it is a great thing in itself, but so incomparably less important than the abolition of the economic war between man and man that we regard it as merely incidental to the latter. . . . From our point of view, your wars, while of course

very foolish, were comparatively humane and altogether petty exhibitions as contrasted with the fratricidal economic struggle.

Of course, Bellamy was referring to wars which were "very rare," in which "only men took part," which were "out of sight and sound of the masses," wherein "the rules of war forbade unnecessary cruelty," and which appealed to "sentiments" of "courage and devotion." Within a few years, utopists were to see in their speculation on the future the possibility of war so destructive and diabolical as to lay waste the earth, to reduce men and women and children to barbarians, to destroy all values, including economic efficiency. The prospects of peace within one nation or country became, in fifty years, as unrealistic to the utopist as had been the communitarian ideal in the middle of the nineteenth century. It is interesting to note how very briefly utopian speculation paused over the possibility of the national entity as a potential form of utopia. The quick stride from the communitarian ideal to the idealization of a world organization changed the pattern of utopian thought so completely and so quickly that the historical tradition seemed momentarily broken.

As utopists recognized the inability of economic efficiency to accomplish alone the ideal of social structure, it was natural that they should turn to other methods in their construction. Throughout the history of utopian speculation, practically all conceivable principles of social organization have been resorted to as holding promise of ideal achievement. Intellectual guardianship, religious faith, economic equality, the brotherhood of man, aesthetic sublimation—all these have served in varying degrees of determinism as the guiding principle of utopia. The one remaining principle of social organization which has suffered the greatest neglect by utopists is the *political*, which one might think *is* the principle of social organization. It is somewhat difficult to explain this apparent suspicion of the political on the part of utopists. Perhaps it is because the political is difficult to idealize into perfection, even in speculation; in utopian idealization, the political as a principle of control has a tendency to take the form of rather obvious dictatorship. Utopists of the recent and contemporary period who base their construction on the political evidence this tendency. Colonel Edward House's *Philip Dru: Administrator* (1912), for example, describes a military dictator who brought about a successful revolution in the United States. He was a very utopian dictator, however, for, after establishing an ideal administration in the country, he voluntarily relinquished his power and retired to Europe. Pataud and Pauget tell "How We Shall Bring About the Revolution," the subtitle of their *Syndicalism and the*

Cooperative Commonwealth (1913). This latter work is on the periphery of utopian literature, as is Berens and Singer, *The Story of My Dictatorship* (1910). A utopian dictator as mild as Philip Dru is the hero of Frederick Palmer's *So A Leader Came* (1932). It is significant to note that in the contemporary period the military has almost universally been permitted a place only in the stage of transition toward utopia. In other words, the military function has come to occupy a completely negative place in utopian speculation. Very rarely are military discipline and drill even suggested as an essential part of the training of youth.

The utopists of the modern and contemporary period did not, of course, leave entirely out of account the political aspect of social organization, but historically it has never been given the precedence in utopia that has successively been accorded to science and education, religion, communal brotherly cooperation, or economics. With the necessity in the present day for the utopist to speculate in terms of nothing less than world organization, it seems likely that the future history of utopian thought will manifest a new pattern, with emphasis on the political as the principle upon which utopia is to be organized. The political principle has already been made the subject of a satire as scathing as those directed against the economic principle (Orwell, *Nineteen Eighty-four*). Anticipatory of this attention to constitution, law, and politics are Spence, Donnelly, Thirion (*Neustria*, 1901), Stanley, House, and, to some extent, Wells. In the meantime, recent and contemporary utopian works are of a variety which is representative of the entire range of historical utopian speculation.

There have even appeared examples of a regression to the theocratic principle for the achievement of utopia. This is interesting in view of the steady decline throughout the modern period of the importance attached to religion in utopia; there is an almost unanimous opinion that religion in the ideal society will be non-institutional. However, Robert Hugh Benson wrote a satire, *Lord of the World* (1907), prophesying the dire catastrophe of a triumph of Protestant humanism. In 1911, he offset this gloomy foreboding with his own picture of utopia, *The Dawn of All*. This ideal society, which is world-wide, comes about by the conversion of the entire population to the Catholic religion; the world is now ruled from Rome, with all the trappings and ritual of medieval tradition, including heresy trials. No less fanatical, but somewhat more fantastic, is Norman Watts, who, in *The Man Who Could Not Sin* (1938), looks for the millennium in a literal return to earth of Jesus Christ. Brotherly love is thence established by fiat (rule in this case being from Jerusalem), and any persons or groups who object or revolt are simply extinguished by a blinding flash of light directed upon them by the Savior. Politics and economics appear to be not the only principles subject to transformation into dictatorship.

Brown's *Limanora* (1903) is an outstanding example of the use of the classic utopian community, with emphasis on the family unit, as a rhetorical device for the reassertion of individual values and their necessary priority in the organization of ideal society—although Brown's dissociation of the biological and community aspects of family is unique. This appreciation of individual values was also the theme of William Dean Howells in *Through the Eye of the Needle* (1907). However, most of the recent concern for the loss of values through mechanization, centralization, and industrialized economy has been evidenced in the form of satire. By reason of the emphasis of the immediately preceding period, and because it is mainly industrialization that is seen as the cause of this value debacle, these satires have been directed toward the economic interpretation of man, society, and value. Best known, perhaps, of these works is Huxley's *Brave New World* (1932), in which, if one is to presume from Mr. Huxley's subsequent flight from reality, he scared himself worse than most of his readers. The book is, indeed, one of the classics of utopian literature, although by the time it was written, the depreciation of the economic through satire had been pretty thoroughly exploited. *Brave New World*, however, stands as the finest single satire of the economic because of its literary merit, the fine irony, and the clear recognition of what it is that is non-utopian about the society described. Stephen Leacock, in *Afternoons in Utopia* (1932) is primarily concerned with the future of education, but the orientation is again economic. In 1950, the universities have stopped having classes and have concentrated on club-life and commercialized athletics. By 2050, the university has become a holding corporation and is beginning to dispose of its property because it is so valuable as real estate. Leacock foresees the failure of capitalism because it spends all its energy on machinery and production, and the subsequent failure of communism in a revolt of the people to regain the values of family, religion, private property, and, paradoxically, efficiency in production.

There were many earlier works which delightfully satirized economic determinism. Archibald Marshall describes life in *Upsidonia* (1917), where the economic is still the principle of evaluation, but in reverse. The rich are so despised that it is felt necessary to establish for them special schools where they learn how to use up their money in luxurious living. There is such a surplus of wealth that it is considered charity to accept worldly goods from another, and only the poor are held in high esteem. What to do with aristocrats after the world has become socialist is the concern of Pezet, who puts them in *Aristokia* (1919). This spot becomes a European tourist attraction, delighting the workers on their "workers'-holidays" with a view of bygone splendor and leisure. Pezet sees socialism simply as the substitution of one ruling class for another, and he seems not at all sure that the socialist end of "work" is any more praiseworthy than the aristocrat's end of leisure. The peace and stabilization of central Europe are ingeniously contrived by Ronald Knox in his *Memories of the Future* (1923) by making inkeepers rulers, on the assumption that innkeepers will avoid all conflict in the interest of good business. Government is still a matter of party representation, but elections are openly determined by the amount of money paid to the voters. Attendance at church and school is rewarded by cash payments, and England has launched a program of selling peerages to the United States in order to pay off her war debt. In Anatole France's *Penguin Island* (1908), law is determined by property, and the army is devoted to the defense of capital; when he comes to the positive construction of *The White Stone* (1905), a total elimination of private property is advocated. The late Don Marquis, in a collection of subtly witty comments from his newspaper writings, *The Almost Perfect State* (1927), argues that all programs which are directed against the idle rich are futile because everybody wants to be idle and rich. The way to solve economic problems, he suggests, is to get rid of them. This is by no means as trivial a suggestion as it might at first appear. As early as 1871, Edward Bulwer Lytton eliminated economic problems in his *Coming Race* with the discovery of *vril*, a portable source of energy having some suggestion of atomic power; and Tarde reduces the economic to insignificance in his underground world. Gilbert and Sullivan's *Utopia, Ltd.*, the project of a promoter, is despotism tempered with dynamite; it is so successfully utopian in its "dull prosperity" that party politics have to be introduced to relieve the monotony. Certainly no other principle of organization utilized by utopists has been so satirized as the economic, and in one sense this is indicative of a stage of technological disillusionment. The great promise of science, invention, and industry, while it is the stuff of which utopian dreams are made, yet has to be fashioned through speculation into the ideal. Modern utopia differs from Eden in that it must be made, not found.

There have also been works of peripheral utopian satire directed against a particular state. *Meccania* (1918), by Owen Gregory, is the ironic construction of a state in which German *Kultur* prevails; and Jaffe's *Abdera and the Revolt of the Asses* (1937) continues the satire of German development to Hitler. It was to be expected that the Russian experiment would produce satirical reaction; three of the most interesting examples are Zamiatin's *We* (1924), Fialko's *The New City* (Tr. 1937), and Orwell's *Nineteen Eighty-four* (1949). Orwell's work is a utopian horror-story and deserves a place beside Huxley's in the line of classic satires. It is a revolting picture of the possible police-state of the future, most progressive in its utilization of scientific techniques for the maintenance of the absolute dictatorship of "Big Brother." In this most un-utopian society of the future, every room is equipped with two-way television by means of which the secret police may at any time not only tune in on conversations, but observe one's expression as well. An individual can not only be purged from this society, but, through an elaborate system of newspaper and reference corrections, his very existence and identity can be erased from history.

The once diverting and often suggestive field of utopian fantasy has been exploited, perhaps under the comic-book influence, into a bastard literary device known as "science fiction." This product bears about the same resemblance to utopian speculation that the tales of Horatio Alger bore to the economic theories of Adam Smith. There have been in the modern period, however, several works in the tradition of utopian fantasy. Contemporary utopian fantasies are more likely to reflect literary skill than profound social or political significance. In fact, utopia has today become a device or vehicle available for purely literary purposes, and will probably be exploited as was the murder-mystery idea. Utopias of the period indicate the development of a pattern in dramatic exposition and the frequent employment of that pattern by writers of literary note and ability. Representative contemporary figures who have thus used the utopian literary form are Hilton, Hauptmann, Maurois, and Graves. James Hilton's *Lost Horizon* (1933) is a trivial effort in this direction, popularized through the medium of the movies. *The Island of the Great Mother* (1924), by Gerhart Hauptmann, is the scene of an experiment in gynocracy; sex is surrounded with mystic rites, but as children grow up, the men soon prove more ingenious and resourceful than the women and take over authority. Another island, described by André Maurois, *A Voyage to the Island of the Articoles* (Tr. 1929), was purchased outright in 1861 by an English novelist with the proceeds from a "bad book," and established as a utopian aesthetic retreat. The Articoles are the class of artists and writers who are preserved from economic and other worries by the class of Beos. By substantial artistic production, it is just possible for a Beos to become a member of the Articoles. There is an interesting parallel with Lytton's *Coming Race* in the admission of a decided absence of artistic stimulation and creativity under utopian circumstances. New Crete is the setting for *Watch the North Wind Rise* (1949), by Robert Graves. This civilization is the end-product of devastating world war, scientific madness, and a series of experiments suggested by a "Sophocrat" in a "Critique of Utopias"! His practical conclusion was that "we must retrace our steps or perish." It is difficult to determine from the obtuse allegory of this work the precise meaning intended, if any. The social framework is communal under a kind of theocratic hierarchy; custom is law, interpreted by the poets and enforced by fear of the Goddess. The "Goddess" is a sexy creature, and the rites which she inspires are indeed fantastic. Other examples of the obtuse allegory are C. S. Lewis's *Out of the Silent Planet* (1938) and *Perelandra* (1944), descriptions of "trans-sensuous" flights to other planets, replete with cosmic characters and pseudometaphysical innuendo. *Islandia* (1942), by Austin Tappan Wright, has certain similarities to Brown's island of Limanora. The economy is agricultural, and the proposal by one party to open the country for trade with the world and exploitation of natural resources is decisively defeated. As in *Limanora*, the unit of society is the family, structured according to a careful distinction of four phases of love: *alia*, the generalized love of family and place of residence; *amia*, nonsexual love for a friend; *apia*, sexual desire; and *ania*, the desire for proper married life. There appears to be no necessary connection between *apia* and *ania;* in a relation of *apia*, the woman remains with her own family, but when she marries she must go to the place of her husband's family and become one of them. An interesting contemporary fantasy concerns the discovery of the lost island of Atlantis, described in *The Sunken World* (1948), by Stanton A. Coblentz. Thirty-one hundred years ago, so runs the tale, the residents of Atlantis decided to leave the world of war and strife; by a fantastically ingenious method, part of their island was enclosed in thick glass and lowered to the floor of the ocean. Here they continued a stable and happy existence, taking full advantage of the most mechanized resources, until the chance collision of a submarine with the protecting glass enclosure started a fracture which, despite their most heroic efforts, finally let in the ocean to flood the sunken world.

It has been noted that there has been almost no constructive utopian speculation in the contemporary period, but in conclusion we must remark one recent work: *Walden Two* (1948), by B. F. Skinner. This utopist is a psychologist, inventor of a "mechanical baby-tender," presently engaged, according to latest reports, on experiments testing the habit-learning capacities of pigeons. Halfway through this contemporary utopia, the reader may feel sure, as we did, that this is a beautifully ironic satire on what has been called "behavioral engineering." The longer one stays in this better world of the psychologist, however, the plainer it becomes that the inspiration is not satiric, but messianic. This is indeed the behaviorally engineered society, and while it was to be expected that sooner or later the principle of psychological conditioning would be made the basis of a serious construction of utopia—Brown anticipated it in *Limanora* —yet not even the effective satire of Huxley is adequate preparation for the shocking horror of the idea when positively presented. Of all the dictatorships espoused by utopists, this is the most profound, and incipient dictators might well find in this utopia a guidebook of political practice. The citizen of this ideal society is placed during his first year in a sterile cubicle, wherein his conditioning begins. During the carefree days of childhood, Spartan control is taught by giving each child a sugar-coated lollipop in the morning. If that evening the sugar shows no sign of a surreptitious lick, the little guinea-pig-citizen is rewarded with the privilege of eating the lollipop. Since brighter children quickly learn to minimize temptation by putting the lollipop out of sight, "in a later experiment the children wear their lollipops like crucifixes for a few hours."

"Instead of the cross, the lollipop
   About my neck was hung."

In nauseating conclusion, the perpetrator of this "modern" utopia looks down from a nearby hill on the community which is his handiwork and proclaims: "I like to play God! Who wouldn't, under the circumstances? After all, even Jesus Christ thought he was God."

It is ironic to conclude our survey of utopian speculation in the pessimistic mood engendered by *Walden Two*. We have descended from the heights of confidence in man's capacities and noble aspiration for his progressive betterment to a nadir of ignominy in which he is placed on a par with pigeons. Out of respect for the true utopian spirit, we feel constrained to add one current work which, while it is not a "classic," yet demonstrates that utopia has survived the pressures and frustrations of the contemporary period.

33

Worlds to Watch and Ward

Anonymous

1947

The author of *Worlds to Watch and Ward* has preferred to remain anonymous, and while the editors consider this an excess of modesty in consideration of the quality of the work, we must respect his wish.

Worlds to Watch and Ward was written in 1947 as the final assignment in a course in utopian thought when the author, a pilot in the U.S. Marine Corps during World War II, was an undergraduate student. In the meantime, he has received a degree in law and has been admitted to the bar.

There are apparent in this utopian fragment numerous points of continuity with the utopists whose works have been presented in this volume, as well as one or two unique and ingenious suggestions by the present author. The most interesting feature of this selection, however, is the subtlety with which the traditional utopian pattern is examined and used. In this respect, the work is reminiscent of Tarde, arousing in the reader a suspicion that satire and suggestion are here so blended that it is utopia itself, not a particular state or condition, that is being satirized.

The following selection is presented in its entirety; no changes in the text have been made other than two or three corrections of typographical errors. It seems particularly fitting to conclude our survey of utopian visions of future states with these speculations of a representative student and veteran of today.

The following is an account of the Prime Minister's speech of Jenna 4th 17795:

MY FELLOW CITIZENS: On the 16th of Gurno, 17695, our scientists observed and recorded what turned out to be the first indication that life existed on Earth. Before that date the planet had been considered uninhabitable because of its nearness to the Sun. It was thought that no form of life could exist there for temperatures had been predicted in the neighborhood of seventy-five givors! This first sign of inhabitants on the distant world was a radio-active explosion in the southwestern part of what was afterward learned was a country called the "United States." Dr. Raal Gudok recorded the disturbance at Murov University, and immediately published his findings in our leading scientific journals. Many prominent Trimor physicists attacked Dr. Gudok's findings, but all critics were silenced when two similar disturbances were recorded soon afterward, apparently centered in an island of the western edge of the Earth's largest ocean. The recording of two more explosions of identical nature on that ocean completely substantiated the hypothesis that some form of life existed there, for in the latter explosions, Dr. Daar Gatkat of Stuba Institute obtained irrefutable data that the disturbances were similar to that induced by our ancient "lakkar bomb" in the Medieval War. Some manner of intelligence had fashioned that bomb!

Plans had been underway for the exploration of Earth for some time and these marvelous discoveries provided the impetus for their final realization. Controller Haad Preed selected a crew from among the men he had taken on his first expedition to Mars, assembled all manner of the latest machines of science, and left Venus with a flight of seven small rockets on the fifth of Geza of that same year —a remarkable achievement!

The Preed expedition landed safely on the South Pole of Earth on Mara 20 the following year. It had been predicted that this spot was the only location on the Earth's surface suitable to sustain our form of life. These predictions were borne out, for the climate was the equivalent of a normal summer day on Venus. Argon masks were essential for every member of the party while they remained on Earth, for that planet has an atmosphere radically different from ours. Exposure to it for more than two or three minnors is fatal.

Our expedition established an operating base immediately on a stretch of high plateau ringed with ice and snow. Work proceeded well into the following year until the supply of argon ran dangerously low. With the marvelous ray machines at their disposal, our explorers were able to learn much about the planet without leaving their base of operations. Visual remote recordings were made of activities on the various continents—all without actually coming in contact with the inhabitants.

One of the explorers, while surveying a site for the installation of a sweep screen recorder, accidentally stumbled on some relics apparently fashioned by the Earth Creatures. These particular findings were crude parts of some type of primitive vehicle designed to provide surface transportation. Further search revealed other signs that this area had either been inhabited recently or at least explored by Earthmen. The latter suspicion turned out to be the true one.

In the second maata of their stay on the polar cap, our party was disturbed by the approach of ships manned by Earthmen. Our warning devices picked them up long before they reached the pole, so Controller Preed and his lieutenants had ample time to decide on a course of action. At first, it appeared that the Earth Creatures had discovered the presence of the explorers, but even if this were the case, Preed was confident that the Earthmen would be no match for our superior weapons and intelligence. Preed resolved to stay on the polar cap, concealing his elaborate installations and rockets in ice caves, hoping that he would be able to observe these strange creatures at close range and perhaps capture one or two of them alive to take back to Venus for examination.

Controller Preed's daring plan worked. Our explorers were never discovered, and by a timely coincidence one of the unique flying machines used by these creatures smashed into a mountain immediately above the camp. Its occupants were carefully removed from the wreckage, given medical aid by our doctors, and preserved in danka for the trip to Venus. There were five Earth Creatures embalmed like this, but only three survived the return trip.

Much valuable information was learned from these captured Earthmen when they were subjected to the thought machine. I shall not dwell on a description of either the men or their planet as it existed at that time; those aspects have been covered thoroughly by writers, lecturers and educators, so that there is not one among you who is not familiar with both the creatures and their world.

What I shall attempt to do is to present a comprehensive picture of my recent observations on Earth, pointing out what has happened since our first visit there ten leadas or one hundred Earth years ago.

The most striking fact that I observed on my visit was the phenomenal progress made in the realm of law and government. One country has come to the fore and assumed leadership of the individual nations of the world. That country is the United States. It is positively amazing how these peoples have awakened to their responsibilities on Earth. Of course, I do not mean to infer that they have even approached the splendid social organization we enjoy here on Venus, but the improvement that has come on Earth through the influence of the United States has been truly remarkable. From a planet of heterogeneous warring nations, the Earth has been transformed into a world of well-regulated peaceful social units.

To deduce specific reasons for the change is an impossible task, for in any such transformation, no one reason or even several reasons can ever be named as the cause. It is only possible to examine what has happened and hope to draw some lesson from the facts as they exist. On that basis I submit one observation as being, in my opinion as a neutral observer, the primary doctrine behind the whole movement. That doctrine was a new conception of what actually constitutes the matrix of social order.

If you remember, Controller Preed's expedition reported, and the captive Earthmen confirmed, that the leading elements of the Earth's civilization were still actively supporting the perpetuation of a superstitious cult. This particular belief had been a carry-over from the primitive days of man's existence on Earth. So important was this doctrine to the majority of people in the more civilized societies that its tenets had been spread to nearly all parts of the world. Yet, in spite of the open acknowledgement of the cult, most of the members of it failed to live up to its basic dispensations. This peculiar situation is difficult for any of us to understand, because our civilization went through this stage so many years ago that only our best historians can give us any insight into the matter. Suffice to say, that in the course of time, the cult had perpetuated itself until it existed for its own existence, and no longer served more than a parasitic purpose. True, it had contributed much to the early organization of Earthman's society and had been especially effective in establishing standards of morality, but while Earthman had benefited by its influence on his morals, he could derive nothing more from it. The failure of the officers of this cult to become aware of their extension of influence into unwarranted areas of Earthman's activity resulted in successively widening breaches between Earthman and the cult. The actual removal of the cult from Earthman's life has been, for all practical purposes, accomplished. A few token representations still exist, but they serve no purpose except to speed their own death.

This repudiation of a force that was almost synonymous with Earthman's awareness of his world was not altogether due to its failure to perform within the area of Earthman's activity. While this would have been sufficient reason to cause the complete breakdown of the cult over a period of time, another factor, necessarily less effective, was operating to hasten the realization that the cult had outlived its usefulness. This factor was intelligence. The experience of living itself had demonstrated certain undeniable facts of experience to Earthman. Possessing a limited amount of intelligence (considerably less than ours), he was slow to become aware of their importance. Eventually, these facts of experience became evident to him in concrete situations which he could perceive and to which he could apply what little intelligence he had. Thus, he became a legislator and learned how to formulate law and direct the activities of society.

Proceeding with haphazard tread upon the stage of society, Earthman promulgated restrictive and abortive regulations, only occasionally hitting upon a good law. Over the centuries, by this hit and miss effort, certain vaguely defined channels became evident and Earthman perceived that he could provide some direction, however inadequate, to the course of history. Although the great majority of the Earth Creatures were content to drift along with the stream of what had been established, there remained enough dissatisfied, intelligent men in every generation to stir the lazy atti-

tudes of at least a part of these intellectual loafers who sought
refuge in such establishments as the superstitious cult. Time was
the ultimate master. The movement away from the blind faith and
complacency was evident at the period of our first exploration; it
has progressed by leaps and bounds since then.

The transition was swift when it came. Oddly enough, it was a
peaceful change. It would appear that the abolition for all practical purposes of a force so deeply rooted in Earthman's life would
meet with violent opposition, if only from the inertia of the force
itself. But when the time came for the change, the world was prepared with another doctrine to replace the void left by the removal
of the cult, and the cult found that the harangues of its officers for
the perpetuation of its form fell on deaf ears. Powerless to combat
the spread of science and education and unwilling to move within
the new streams of experience that were being established, the cult
died an inglorious death, its officers threatening mankind with superstitious curses.

Law was the new doctrine that replaced the cult. If Earthman
had learned any lesson in the history of life, it was that society was
based, not on faith or blind belief, but on the order that intelligence
had introduced—on what of rationality Earthman had introduced
into society. Earthman accepted Law as the primary consideration
in social organization, and bent himself to the improvement of it,
knowing from experience that here was the only fruitful avenue for
the direction of the one attribute he possessed—intelligence.

The example of the United States when it accepted the doctrine
of Law is illuminating. You recall how that country had been born
from an assertion of what Earthman ought to be in society. Documents such as the Declaration of Independence, the Bill of Rights
and the Constitution were proclaimed as objectifying the "inalienable rights of man." Those documents served useful purposes in the
establishment of that country, but the people were not naive enough
to retain them for long. Within fifty years after the conflict in
which the lakkar bomb was used, the people of the United States
had been forced to assume so much responsibility for the world's
peaceful organization that the more intelligent thinkers among them
proved to the now politically mature citizens that rights exist only
under law. Today the documents are observed as curious historical
relics of an expedient moment in history.

Acceptance of the new doctrine of society based upon Law co-
incided with the period of greatest scientific development. This
happy coincidence provided the new doctrine with a powerful
weapon. When the Earthman learned to apply science to law and
to experiment in law as he had done in the physical fields of re-

search, tremendous strides were made in social progress. In applying the new principles the United States again took the lead and reorganized its government. Previously, the functions of that government had been divided into three main departments: the executive, the legislative, and the judicial. With the removal of the Constitution limiting the powers of government, the people of the United States had shown that they were no longer afraid of government. Ancient fears, occasioned by the arbitrary power wielded by autonomous sovereigns, had made necessary the limiting of governmental powers; but the new dependence of the people on the doctrine of Law had meant a new conception of government, not as the commander of society, but as the director of society.

Now, there are only two divisions of government: the "legistrative" and the "speculative." The legistrative branch, as the name implies, combines the functions of the legislative and the administrative divisions into one homogeneous department boasting the ability to comprehend both the enactment and enforceability of a law in one economical consideration, thereby eliminating much of the hit and miss method of legislation and ineffectiveness of administration. Of course, the caliber of Earthmen entering this department has been improved by the attractive compensation and honor attached to service. These inducements, together with the realization of its importance by the intelligent young men of the country, assures that the department will only draw the best of recruits for its offices.

Relegation of the written constitution to the status of a museum piece, signaled the end of the judicial function as it had existed under the old government. No longer was it necessary to check government action against the provisions of a rigid document. Instead, a new function was assumed by the department previously dominated by the Supreme Court. This function is "speculation." It is now the practice for the most learned men in the country to be asked by the President to serve on the Speculative Board. Here, they are given a free hand in speculating. Nothing more is asked of them. They may proceed in any way they please, examining society, discussing its problems, and seeking solutions. When they have arrived at a conclusion or have formulated a policy, they appear before the legistrative body and submit their recommendations. The legistrative body is under no compulsion to act on the advice of the Speculative Board; it may use it or not as it sees fit. The only function of the Speculative Board is to THINK.

Economics and government have become closely related in the organization. No one could follow the conscience and thought of Earthmen from the beginning of time and treat socialism as an unimportant matter. Too many converging lines lead to it. It seems that every positive impulse of constructive action and thought, no matter where or how it started, or in what direction it moved, has moved unconsciously toward this goal. The impulse of the artist wishing to beautify the visible world through the united efforts of a free race alive to beauty; the impulse of the philanthropist, longing for the relief of the material distress produced by "modern" living; the impulse of the practical man, noting the waste of a free competitive system, and the economy of centralization—all these move into the strong, comprehensive growing intention to affect the course of social development by the action of resolute human will.

Earthpeople of three great classes, those who cared most for the graces, those who cared most for the comforts, and those who cared most for the virtues of life, were drawn toward socialism with a force which all felt and many, an increasing number, did not even seek to resist. The extension of the authority of the democratic state over industrial matters seemed to all these different temperaments to offer at least the first and most hopeful experiment in the direction of social betterment.

Experience with large corporations dictated the transformation to a corporate democratic form of government for the United States. This fact is important, since it marks a vital difference between the emergence of the corporate form of government in the United States as against the earlier existence of more rigid socialistic forms in other countries. England had assumed the socialistic form because she had become a relatively poor country, and socialism provided the most efficient means of organizing what wealth she had. The United States, on the other hand, turned to the corporate democratic form because it offered the most effective and efficient means of directing its own national affairs and assuming the responsibilities of world guidance. Far from being a poor country when it turned to corporate democracy, the United States had reached the greatest wave of prosperity the world had ever known. It continues to set the standard of living and pattern of life for the rest of Earth. Experience with industrial corporations had taught the Americans one basic lesson, that although corporations were blind, stumbling, autonomous institutions that were almost insensitive to the application of Earthman's intelligence, they still remained the only effective means available with which society could cope with its problems.

Turning to considerations of social importance, we find that in the interim since our first expedition, that primitive manifestation of barbarism, the family, has almost entirely disappeared. This organization of the parents and their offspring into a social unit was on its way to extinction for some time. The only force that perpetuated it was that unlovely superstitious cult. When the cult broke down, the family went with it. Now, the extremely important influence of environment on the growing child is handled scientifically by the state. His hereditary characteristics are given full opportunity to develop themselves and are directed by scientific means into channels that will bear fruit for society. Education has become a primary factor in filling the gap left by the family group. The state has seen to it that no effort is spared to allow every individual the maximum opportunity to become the best that he can be, both for himself and for his society.

Militarily, the planet Earth is impotent. The great portion of its effort is concerned with the regulation of world affairs and to this end the United States has contributed what there is of organized force. This force consists of a vast network of small mobile task units, equipped to rocket to any spot on the planet's surface and effect a remedy for the disturbance of the peace.

We have previously abstained from relations with the planet Earth, for we have feared repercussions similar to those that occurred when we extended the hand of friendship to the planet Mars. That bitter experience taught us, by years of fighting, the folly of attempting to deal with a disorganized assemblage of warlike nations. My recent visit to the Earth has convinced me that if we are ever to have relations with that planet, we should do it immediately. Earth is ready to assume her part of the responsibility. I am sure of that. Under the able leadership of the United States, Earth has established a stable well-articulated society. We should find little difficulty in coming to a reasonable understanding.

And so, Citizens of Venus, I solicit your support in behalf of my proposed interplanetary policy to open up the planet Earth to the universe. Citizens of Venus, we must go forward! Show by your voting tomorrow that you are aware of the place Venus must take in the universe. Ratify my interplanetary policy and I assure you that within a leada we will have added a new planet to our empire. All the untold wealth of that distant world shall be ours to command as we please. Vote for it, Citizens of Venus, and as you go to the polls tomorrow, remember the stirring words of our own great Karto:

"They call you proud and hard,
    Venus, my Venus;
You with worlds to watch and ward,
    Venus, my own!
You whose mailed hand keeps the keys
    Of such teeming destinies!"